U.S. Department of
Homeland Security

United States
Coast Guard

Commandant
United States

MW00562558

COMDTNOTE 16114
14 MAY 2009

CANCELLED:
13 MAY 2010

COMMANDANT NOTICE 16114

Subj: CH-2 TO BOAT CREW SEAMANSHIP MANUAL, COMDTINST M16114.5C

1. PURPOSE. This Notice publishes change two to the Boat Crew Seamanship Manual, COMDTINST M16114.5C.

2. ACTION. Area, district, and sector commanders, commanders of maintenance and logistics commands, Commander Deployable Operations Group, commanding officers of integrated support commands, commanding officers of headquarters units, assistant commandants for directorates, Judge Advocate General and special staff elements at headquarters shall ensure compliance with the provisions of this Manual. Internet Release Authorized.

3. DIRECTIVES AFFECTED. None.

4. SUMMARY. This notice changes the Action Paragraph from; Internet Release is Not Authorized to read Internet Release Authorized.

5. PROCEDURES. No paper distribution of this change will be made. An electronic version will be located on the Information and Technology CG-612 intranet at http://cgweb2.comdt.uscg.mil/CGDirectives/Welcome.htm and CG Central at http://cgcentralweb.uscg.mil/cLink/00000118.

6. ENVIRONMENTAL ASPECT AND IMPACT CONSIDERATIONS. Environmental considerations were examined in developing this Notice and were determined to be not applicable.

DISTRIBUTION – SDL 152

	a	b	c	d	e	f	g	h	i	j	k	l	m	n	o	p	q	r	s	t	u	v	w	x	y	z
A	1	1		1	1	1	1	1	1	1		1	1	1	1	1	1		1		1					
B	1	1	1		1	1		1	1	1				1	1	1		1				1				
C				1	1				1		1			1		1							1		1	1
D		1		1				1					1													
E	1									1	1	1							1	1						
F																										
G			1	1	1																					
H																										

7. FORMS/REPORT. None.

WAYNE E. JUSTICE/s/
Rear Admiral, U.S. Coast Guard
Assistant Commandant for Capability

U.S. Department of Homeland Security

United States Coast Guard

Commandant
United States Coast Guard

2100 2nd S.W.
Washington, DC 20593-0001
Staff Symbol: CG-731
Phone: (202) 372-2200
Fax: (202) 372-2909

COMDTNOTE 16114
25 JULY 2008

CANCELLED:
24 JULY 2009

COMMANDANT NOTICE 16114

Subj: CH-1 TO BOAT CREW SEAMANSHIP MANUAL, COMDTINST M16114.5C

1. PURPOSE. This Notice publishes change one to the Boat Crew Seamanship Manual, COMDTINST M16114.5C.

2. ACTION. Area, district, and sector commanders, commanders of maintenance and logistics commands, Commander Deployable Operations Group, commanding officers of integrated support commands, commanding officers of headquarters units, assistant commandants for directorates, Judge Advocate General and special staff elements at headquarters shall ensure compliance with the provisions of this manual. Internet release is not authorized.

3. DIRECTIVES AFFECTED. None.

4. SUMMARY. Enclosure (1) summarizes the substantial changes throughout the Manual.

5. PROCEDURES. No paper distribution will be made of this Manual. Official distribution will be via the Coast Guard Directive System CD-ROM. An electronic version will be located on the Information and Technology CG-612 CGWEB and WWW website at http://cgcentral.uscg.mil/ (Once in CG-Central click on the "RESOURCES" Tab and then "Directives".) and http://cgweb2.comdt.uscg.mil/cgdirectives/welcome.htm. For personnel who keep a paper copy of the Manual remove and replace the following pages:

Remove	Insert
Table of Contents Pages i-xxxviii	Table of Contents CH-1 Pages i-xliv
Pages 1-5 through 1-16	Pages 1-5 through 1-18
Pages 2-17 through 2-18	Pages 2-17 through 2-18
Pages 3-13 through 3-14	Pages 3-13 through 3-14
Pages 5-9 through 5-48	Pages 5-9 through 5-50

DISTRIBUTION – SDL No. 149

	a	b	c	d	e	f	g	h	i	j	k	l	m	n	o	p	q	r	s	t	u	v	w	x	y	z
A	5	2	5		5	4	1	1	1	1		1	2	2	1	1	1	1	1		2					
B		8	20		5			5		1				20												
C	1	1		1	1				5					1		1							3			4
D	1	1		2				10					1													
E	1		5							1	1	1		1					4	1						
F																										
G			1																							
H																										

NON-STANDARD DISTRIBUTION: 6 EXTRA COPIES TO MLC'S

Pages 6-9 through 6-10	Pages 6-9 through 6-10
Pages 6-19 through 6-20	Pages 6-19 through 6-20
Pages 6-29 through 6-30	Pages 6-29 through 6-30
Pages 6-35 through 6-36	Pages 6-35 through 6-36
Pages 6-39 through 6-40	Pages 6-39 through 6-40
Pages 10-19 through 10-20	Pages 10-19 through 10-20
Pages 11-11 through 11-24	Pages 11-11 through 11-24
Pages 14-9 through 14-10	Pages 14-9 through 14-10
Pages 14-17 through 14-18	Pages 14-17 through 14-18
Pages 14-23 through 14-24	Pages 14-23 through 14-24
Pages 15-15 through 15-34	Pages 15-15 through 15-34
Pages 16-3 through 16-8	Pages 16-3 through 16-8
Pages 16-11 through 16-12	Pages 16-11 through 16-12
Pages 16-19 through 16-28	Pages 16-19 through 16-28
Pages 18-17 through 18-18	Pages 18-17 through 18-18
Pages 18-21 through 18-60	Pages 18-21 through 18-54
Pages 19-9 through 19-12	Pages 19-9 through 19-12
Pages 20-3 through 20-4	Pages 20-3 through 20-4
Pages 20-19 through 20-20	Pages 20-19 through 20-20
Pages 20-23 through 20-36	Pages 20-23 through 20-36
Pages A-3 through A-30	Pages A-3 through A-30
Pages B-3 through B-22	Pages B-3 through B-22
Pages Index -1 through Index -12	Pages Index -1 through Index - 9

6. ENVIRONMENTAL ASPECT AND IMPACT CONSIDERATIONS. Environmental considerations were examined in developing this Manual and were determined to be not applicable.

7. FORMS/REPORT. None.

WAYNE E. JUSTICE/s/
Assistant Commandant for Capability

Encl: (1) Summary of changes to the Boat Crew Seamanship Manual

SUMMARY OF CHANGES

CHAPTER 1

Article 1.B.8.	Included content regarding protection of marine protected species.
Article 1.C.2.	Added marine protected species to list of lookout requirements.
Article 1.C.4.	Item 6 directs minimal duties for lookouts when operating in area of whales and turtles.
Article 1.C.6.	Added note listing clues for detecting marine mammals and sea turtles.

Chapter 2

Article 2.G.1.a.	Deleted typo from previous edition.

Chapter 3

Article 3.G.12.	Removed mention of brand name synthetic fibers "Thermax" and "Capilene".

Chapter 5

Article 5.C.4.	Rewrote CPR section and added figure 5-2: "EMT Basic Protocol Decision to Withold or Stop CPR in Adults" and 5-3: "EMT Basic Protocol for Hypothermia."

Chapter 6

Article 6.A.30.c.	Changed effective temperatures for use of PML's from 0 deg C and 32 deg F to 10 deg C and 50 deg F.
Article 6.D.1.	Changed contents of Crew Survival Vest from "Personal Emergency Position Indicating Radio Beacon (PEPIRB)" to "Personal Locator Beacon (PLB)".
Article 6.D.26.	Changed section to Operation for Personal Locator Beacon (PLB).
Article 6.F.2.	Added note directing crew to place life raft on windward side of vessel in case of fire to avoid smoke and fumes.
Article 6.G.3.	Added bullet directing activation of PML

	to assist in locating other survivors after boat egress.

Chapter 10

Article 10.B.6.	Updated Figure 10-12.

Chapter 11

Article 11.E.	Added section on cell phone communications.

Chapter 14

Figure 14-8	Updated figure.
Article 14.B.32.	Added section on electronic charts.

Chapter 15

Article 15.E.6. through 15.E.8.	Added sections for Self Locating Datum Marker Buoy (SLDMB)

Chapter 16

Article 16.A.3.	Changed steps 2 and 3 in Procedures table.
Article 16.A.8.	Reworded section and added caution warning against throwing flotation directly at PIW.
Article 16.A.9.	Changed wording of section and added note.
Article 16.A.14.	Step 1: deleted bullet concerning crewmember throwing ring buoy. Step 2: added condition "if PIW is no longer visible" to final bullet.
Article 16.A.23.	Changed verbiage of section to ensure coxswain directs action of the crew member.
Article 16.A.30.	Added note directing use of life like dummy.
Article 16.A.33.	Added caution concerning use of boat hook to recover PIW.
Article 16.A.33.a.	Added note concerning surface swimmer qualification.

Chapter 18

Article 18.E.18.	Made minor changes to verbiage of this section.
Article 18.E.21. - 18.E.25.	Deleted Fire Monitor and In-Line Proportioner sections.

Chapter 19

Article 19.B.3.c.	Updated protective gear.
Article 19.B.3.g.	Added warning about static electricity discharge from a helicopter.
Article 19.B.4.	Added information regarding the dangers of static electricity and proper safety precautions.
Article 19.B.6.	Updated figure 19-9.

Chapter 20

Article 20.A.3.	Added note defining the term "Knockdown".
Article 20.B.11.c.	Deleted "knockdown" from section as its use was inconsistent with the definition of "knockdown" in 20.A.3.
Article 20.C.10.	Changed section to "Knockdown and Rollover Causes" from just "Rollover Causes".

Appendix A

Appendix A	Updated glossary.

Appendix B

Appendix B	Updated list of Acronyms.

This page intentionally left blank.

RECORD OF CHANGES

Change Number	Date of Change	Date Entered	Entered by
1	Included	Included	CG-731
2	Included	Included	CG-731

This page intentionally left blank.

U.S. Department of
Homeland Security

United States
Coast Guard

Commandant
United States Coast Guard

2100 Second Street, S.W.
Washington, DC 20593 0001
Staff Symbol: G OCS
Phone: (202) 267 2868

COMDTINST M16114.5C
SEP 16 2003

COMMANDANT INSTRUCTION M16114.5C

Subj: BOAT CREW SEAMANSHIP MANUAL

1. PURPOSE. The Boat Crew Seamanship Manual presents the approved methods and procedures for the conduct of Coast Guard boat operations. The Coast Guard Auxiliary, for the conduct of vessel facility operations, also uses this Manual.

2. ACTION. Area and district commanders, commanders of maintenance and logistics commands, commanding officers of headquarters units, and assistant commandants for directorates, Chief Counsel, special staff offices at Headquarters, group commanders, boat unit commanding officers and officers-in-charge shall ensure the contents of this Manual are utilized in all boat operations where applicable. Internet release authorized.

3. DIRECTIVES AFFECTED. The Boat Crew Seamanship Manual, COMDTINST M16114.5B is canceled.

4. DISCUSSION.

   a. This update incorporates and standardizes the current best practices employed within the Coast Guard boat operations community. It is intended to be the primary reference for the Boat Crew Training Program and shore based boat operations and seamanship training.

   b. This text represents a major revision of the previous Boat Crew Seamanship Manual last released in February 1998. The format has been changed to present information in a more readable style while at the same time reducing the overall size of the Manual.

5. PROCEDURES. The standard methods and procedures presented in this Manual apply to all boat operations, crew training and certification.

   a. Commanding Officers/Officers-in-Charge shall ensure that personnel tasked with boat crew responsibilities are trained in all methods and procedures in this Manual.

DISTRIBUTION SDL No.140

	a	b	c	d	e	f	g	h	i	j	k	l	m	n	o	p	q	r	s	t	u	v	w	x	y	z
A	5	2	5		5	4	1	1	1	1		1	2	2	1	1	1	1	1		2					
B		8	20		5			5		1				20												
C	1	1		1	1				5					1									3			4
D	1	1		2				10					1													
E	1		5							1	1	1		1					4	1						
F																										
G			1																							
H																										

NON STANDARD DISTRIBUTION: 6 EXTRA COPIES TO MLC'S

b. Units that conduct boat operations or provide oversight of the operations shall use the information, processes and procedures set forth in this Manual as a standard when conducting evaluations of boat crew performance.

c. Training facilities and traveling training teams conducting boat operations training shall use this Manual as the primary reference text for all training objectives and lesson plans.

6. CHANGES. This Manual is under continual review and will be updated as necessary. Recommendations for improvement or corrections are eagerly sought from all users. It is of critical importance that the most current and safest procedures be reflected within this text. All recommendations should be forwarded to the Office of Boat Forces (G-OCS), Coast Guard Headquarters.

7. ENVIRONMENTAL ASPECT and IMPACT CONSIDERATIONS. Environmental considerations were examined in the development of this Manual and have been determined to be not applicable.

8. FORMS/REPORTS. None.

D. S. BELZ /s/
Assistant Commandant for Operations

Table of Contents

List of Figures

CH-1

List of Tables

This page intentionally left blank.

Introduction

Seamanship plays an important role in safe and efficient operations for personnel assigned to boat forces. While local directives will govern which methods of achieving certain operations are the best, there are certain basic principles and subject matter areas that form a firm background of good seamanship. The purpose of this Manual is to explain good seamanship principles and subject matter areas and how they apply to boat-force operations. The subjects and principles include boat crew duties and responsibilities, first aid, boat handling, communications, weather and oceanography, boat characteristics and other subjects, theories, and techniques learned over time by skilled mariners. Above all, it is the goal of this Manual to provide the safest, most efficient methods, techniques and informational guidance possible for boat-force personnel executing some of the most challenging and dangerous missions in the Coast Guard.

References

References listed throughout this Manual may be obtained from the CG Directives System on CG Web at http://cgweb2.comdt.uscg mil/cgdirectives/welcome htm.

Warnings, Cautions, Notes, and Memory Aids

The following definitions apply to Warnings, Cautions, Notes and Memory Aids found throughout the Manual.

Warning

WARNING — Operating procedures or techniques that must be carefully followed to avoid personal injury or loss of life.

Caution

CAUTION! — Operating procedures or techniques that must be carefully followed to avoid equipment damage.

Note

NOTE — An operating procedure or technique essential to emphasize.

Memory Aid

MEMORY AID — A phrase or pneumonic device used to assist in memorization of a concept.

Generalization

Because of the need to generalize, wording such as “normally,” “etc.,” “usually,” and “such as” is employed throughout this Manual.

Words or clauses of this nature shall not be used as loopholes, nor shall they be expanded to include a manoeuvres, situation, or circumstances that should not be performed or encountered.

This page intentionally left blank.

Chapter 1
Boat Crew Duties and Responsibilities

Introduction

Coast Guard and Auxiliary boat crews perform duties requiring both skill and knowledge. This chapter discusses general crew duties and related procedures for watchstanding necessary for the successful completion of Coast Guard missions. The general duties for crewmembers are outlined in this chapter. Assignments and procedures for specific tasks, such as towing or retrieving people from the water, are found in other chapters.

NOTE

More specific information for Auxiliary boat crews may be found in the *Auxiliary Operations Policy Manual*, COMDTINST M16798.3 (series).

In this chapter

This chapter contains the following sections:

Section A. The Boat Crew

Introduction

There are three basic boat crew positions on Coast Guard boats:

- Coxswain.
- Engineer (the Auxiliary program does not have a boat engineer position).
- Crew member.

A.1. Determining Crew Size

There are several factors in determining crew size:

- Boat type.
- Operational need.
- Minimum crew size prescribed by higher authority.

A.2. Minimum Crew Size

Commandant sets minimum crew sizes for standard boats. For example, the 47' motor life boat (MLB) carries a minimum crew of four -- a coxswain, an engineer, and two crew members. Area and District Commanders set minimum crew sizes for non-standard boats assigned to their units. Coast Guard boats and Auxiliary facilities may carry two to six people as crew. Many times, only a coxswain and a crew member comprise the crew for a non-standard boat, Auxiliary facility, or for a cutter's boat.

A.3. Qualification and Certification

Boat crew members, engineers, and coxswains are qualified and certified in accordance with the *U.S. Coast Guard Boat Operations and Training (BOAT) Manual, Volume I*, COMDTINST M16114.32 (series) and the *U.S. Coast Guard Boat Operations and Training (BOAT) Manual, Volume II*, COMDTINST M16114.33 (series). Qualification as a boat crew member is a prerequisite to qualification as a boat engineer or a coxswain. Auxiliarists are not permitted to be certified as a coxswain on Coast Guard boats, but they may qualify as a crew member or boat engineer. Auxiliarists' qualifications for crewing Auxiliary facilities are covered in the *Auxiliary Boat Crew Training and Qualification Guide - Crewman and Coxswain*, COMDTINST M16798.28 (series).

A.4. The Auxiliary

An auxiliarist on official orders may perform many Coast Guard duties, including boat crew member and boat engineer, but is not a military member of the Coast Guard. Although trained and qualified to an equivalent level, the Auxiliary member may not be assigned any authority or responsibility specifically reserved by regulation for military or law enforcement personnel.

The mission of Auxiliary operations is to provide operational, logistic, and training support to appropriate Coast Guard programs. 14 USC 826 and 831 authorize the Coast Guard to use suitably trained auxiliarists and Auxiliary facilities. The operational use of auxiliarists and their boats, aircraft, and radio stations is encouraged. Unit Commanders may use Auxiliary resources for missions already authorized by Commandant Policy and as outlined in *Chapter 1* of the *Auxiliary Operations Policy Manual*, COMDTINST M16798.3 (series).

A.4.a. Auxiliary Surface Facilities

There are several ownership categories as defined in the *Auxiliary Operations Policy Manual*, COMDTINST M16798.3 (series) for Auxiliary facilities:

- Privately owned boats (owned by auxiliarists).
- Corporate owned boats.
- Coast Guard owned boats designated as a facility authorized by G-OCS.
- Coast Guard surveyed boats given to the Auxiliary for official purposes as authorized by Commandant (G-CFM).

A.4.b. Auxiliary Crew

An auxiliarist does not have to accept orders. Auxiliarists should apply risk management principles to make the determination to accept or decline orders. If an auxiliarist accepts orders, they must promptly notify:

- Order-issuing authority and/or the Unit Commander if they cannot carry out the mission.
- Unit by land line or other method immediately before the facility's departure to be sure an accurate accounting is on record.

A.4.c. Auxiliary Coxswain/Operator

An Auxiliary coxswain (operator) assigned to any surface facility under orders is the person responsible for the boat, the safety and conduct of the crew and passengers, and completion of the assigned mission. Since the coxswain is responsible for assigning (and often selecting) their crew for each patrol, the Unit Commander may not know the identity of all crew members. Therefore, the names of all of the crew (including trainees/passengers) must be passed to the Unit Commander prior to the facility departing on any sortie. A designated coxswain of a facility under orders may abort any mission due to weather, engine, equipment failure, crew fatigue, injury, or other reasons. Likewise, an owner of a facility (coxswain or not), if aboard, may abort the mission if, in the opinion of the owner, the facility or crew is being placed in jeopardy. In either case, the coxswain/operator shall immediately notify the order-issuing authority and/or Unit Commander.

For further guidance, refer to *Auxiliary Operations Policy Manual*, COMDTINST M16798.3 (series) and directives issued by the District Director of Auxiliary.

Section B. Boat Crew Duties

Introduction

The Coast Guard and Auxiliary boat crew training programs are based on the concept that sailors receive the best training while underway. This Manual, and specifically this chapter, is designed to provide an outline of the duties typically performed by various members of boat crews and the skills and knowledge required to perform tasks assigned. For people seeking to be members of a boat crew, it is fundamental that they understand these duties and the importance of crewmembers working together as a team.

In this section

This section contains the following information:

Trainee

B.1. Description

A trainee can be either a Coast Guard active duty, Auxiliary (referred to as candidate), or reservist who seeks to qualify as a boat crew member. The trainee rides onboard to observe actual operational missions and to gain "hands on" experience under the close tutelage of a qualified crew member. The trainee cannot be counted as a member of the crew towards a platform's minimum crew requirements unless so stated in that Specific Boat Type Operator's Handbook, COMDTINST M16114 (series).

B.2. Knowledge and Performance Skills

The duties of a trainee are to learn and safely perform the practical tasks prescribed for crew members. These duties are described in the *Boat Operations and Training (BOAT) Manual, Volume II*, COMDTINST M16114.33 (series) and are performed under the supervision of a qualified crew member assigned to the boat.

Boat Crew Member

B.3. Description

Crew members safely perform their duties under the supervision of a coxswain. They stand:

- Helm.
- Lookout.
- Towing watches.
- Anchor watch.

They also:

- Rig towing and mooring lines.
- Act as the surface swimmer.
- Administer first aid.
- Operate damage control equipment.

This position provides valuable training for future duties and responsibilities.

NOTE

> Refer to the *U.S. Coast Guard Addendum to the United States National Search and Rescue Supplement (NSS) to the International Aeronautical and Maritime Search and Rescue Manual*, COMDTINST M16130.2 (series) for policy on swimmers. The auxiliary does not have surface swimmers.

B.4. Knowledge and Performance Skills

To be effective, boat crew members must execute orders quickly and must have the following knowledge and performance skills:

- Marlinespike seamanship and line handling.
- Basic navigation (including radar) and boat handling.
- Survival, safety, and damage control equipment.
- Emergency and casualty control.
- Watchstanding and communications.
- First aid.

B.4.a. Risk Management

A keen knowledge of the boat's characteristics and limitations as well as the boat's equipment outfit and stowage plan will be invaluable in times of crisis. Frequent drills practicing the procedures for different emergency circumstances will teach crew members how to react correctly to each situation. All crew members must continuously think about emergency situations and answer the hypothetical question, "What should I do if...?" so that it can be instantly put into action when the question becomes, "What do I do now?"

B.4.b. Knowing the Operating Area

Boat crew members must have knowledge of their local operating area (OPAREA), also called area of responsibility (AOR).

Engineer

B.5. Description

In addition to all of the duties and responsibilities of a boat crew member, boat engineers are responsible for propulsion and auxiliary machinery while underway. Other responsibilities include the preventive and corrective maintenance performed on the boat in port.

NOTE There is no engineer position in the Auxiliary program.

B.6. Knowledge and Performance Skills

The knowledge and performance skills required for boat engineers are as extensive as those for coxswains. They must be able to take quick and proper action when faced with any boat engineering casualty. In addition to basic crew member skills, engineers must have the following knowledge and performance skills:

- Demonstrating complete knowledge of general engineering specifications and functional performance characteristics.
- Performing pre-start, light off, and securing functions for propulsion machinery.
- Monitoring, detecting, and responding to machinery and electrical system casualties or failures.
- Operating auxiliary machinery and systems, e.g., pumps, eductors, tillers, etc.
- Using onboard damage control equipment to minimize damage from fire, grounding, or collision.

Coxswain

B.7. Description

Coast Guard boats underway must have a coxswain onboard who is certified by the Unit Commander to operate that particular type of boat. The district director of Auxiliary certifies Auxiliary coxswains to operate an Auxiliary facility. Coxswains are in charge of the boat and crew. The coxswain's duty is unique. The coxswain's range and degree of responsibility are comparable to that of a cutter's deck watch officer. The Coast Guard places great trust in the coxswain's ability to provide effective boat crew leadership, *Chapter 4, Team Coordination And Risk Management*.

The extent of the coxswain's responsibility and authority are specified in *United States Coast Guard Regulations 1992*, COMDTINST M5000.3 (series). Coxswains shall be responsible, in order of priority, for the following:

- Safety and conduct of passengers and crew.
- Safe operation and navigation of the boat.
- Completion of the sortie(s) or mission(s).

Coxswains will respond to the following:

- Hazards to life or property.
- Violations of laws or regulations, except for auxiliarists.
- Discrepancies in aids to navigation.

B.8. Knowledge and Performance Skills

The knowledge and performance skills required for coxswains are extensive. Coxswains must apply good judgment, intelligence, and initiative. They must make decisions with the safety of their crew and boat in mind. In addition to basic crew member skills, a coxswain must have the following knowledge and performance skills:

- Demonstrating leadership that effectively coordinates, directs, and guides the performance of the boat crew during watches and tasks (e.g., towing, fog navigation, and man overboard).
- Demonstrating correct application of regulations, policy, and guidance delineated by the Unit Commander or higher authority to the circumstances at hand (e.g., safe navigation, safe speed, law enforcement, and rendering assistance).
- Knowing the boat's limitations:
  - maximum sea conditions in which a boat can operate,
  - maximum wind conditions in which boat can operate, and
  - maximum size of boat that can be towed by your boat (facility).
- Navigating and piloting a boat.
- Knowing the local OPAREA with minimal reference to charts and publications.
  - including the locations of whale high-use areas,
  - critical habitats,
  - National Marine Sanctuaries, and
  - other marine protected areas within the OPAREA.
- Demonstrating boat handling skills to safely and prudently control the movement of a boat while underway.
- Understanding the principles of risk management and incorporating them into the decision-making process. These principles include detection, identification, evaluation, and mitigation or control risk as part of making decisions (e.g., slow to safe speed in restricted visibility, cast off a tow because the assisted vessel is losing stability, speed and how to maneuver to avoid a whale strike).
- Demonstrating correct application of regulations, policy and guidance surrounding marine protected species issues (i.e., speed and approach guidance around whales, whale strike reporting protocols, procedures when you encounter an entangled marine mammal, etc).

NOTE ✍

> More information on USCG policy and guidance applicable to marine mammals, sea turtles and marine protected areas can be found on the CG-5314 website: http://cgweb.comdt.uscg.mil/G-OPL/LMR-MPS/LMR-MPS.htm.

Surfman

B.9. Description

The surfman is a highly motivated, experienced boat handler capable of operating a Motor Lifeboat (MLB) or Special Purpose Craft (SPC) in surf. The surfman also leads, motivates and trains boat crews to operate in these extreme types of conditions.

NOTE ✍

> There is no surfman position in the Auxiliary program.

A surfman is expected to have additional responsibilities at an MLB/SPC Station that include:

- Boat crew management in high risk, high stress situations.
- Monitor all levels of training. They must train and pass their skills and experience on to new coxswains.
- Make important risk assessment decisions during heavy weather and surf conditions.
- Oversee readiness of equipment and personnel.
- Stand watch during heavy weather and surf conditions.

B.10. Knowledge and Performance Skills

A surfman must be previously qualified and certified as an MLB or SPC coxswain. In addition to basic coxswain skills, surfmen must have the following knowledge and performance skills:

- Thorough understanding of ocean currents, weather, and hydrodynamics. How they pertain to the local bar/inlet conditions.
- Boat handling skills and procedures while operating in surf.
- Boat crew safety and emergency procedures.

Section C. Watchstanding Responsibilities

Introduction

Under the direction of the coxswain, crew members are assigned various watches which are described in this section.

In this section

This section contains the following information:

Lookout Watch

C.1. Description

The *Navigation Rules, International - Inland,* COMDTINST M16672.2 (series) states that "Every vessel shall at all times maintain a proper lookout by sight and hearing as well as by all available means appropriate in the prevailing circumstances and conditions, so as to make a full appraisal of the situation and of the risk of collision."

NOTE

> Although not specifically assigned the duty of lookout, the entire crew must perform lookout duties unless directed otherwise.

C.2. Assign and Station

Coxswains must assign and station lookouts properly in order to comply with the requirement noted above. Lookouts must report to the coxswain everything seen, smelled, or heard as well as everything they think they see, smell, or hear. If in doubt, report it! A sharp lookout is often the first means of protection for the boat to avoid trouble, not to mention locating situations to investigate (e.g., vessels/people in distress, law enforcement, or pollution). Some examples are:

- Ships.
- Land.
- Obstructions.
- Lights.
- Buoys.
- Beacons.
- Discolored water.
- Reefs.
- Fog signals.
- Whales.
- Sea Turtles.

NOTE It is most important for the coxswain to consider the experience level and abilities of individual crewmembers when making assignments. In the past, the inappropriate assignment of crew duties has contributed to mishaps resulting in fatalities.

NOTE More in-depth information on lookout duties and responsibilities can be found in the *Shipboard Lookout Manual*, CG-414 and *Navy's Lookout Training Handbook*, NAVEDTRA 12968-A.

C.3. Guidelines

The following guidelines must be used to stand a proper lookout watch:

- Remain alert and give full attention to the assigned duty.
- Remain at Station until relieved.
- Do not distract others with excessive conversation. (However, some conversation among crewmembers may be beneficial in reducing fatigue and maintaining alertness.)
- Speak loudly and distinctly when making a report.
- If the object sighted, smelled or heard cannot be positively identified, report what is believed at that moment.
- Repeat report until it is acknowledged by the coxswain.
- When conditions impair ability to see, smell, or hear; report the condition so the coxswain can take corrective action.
- Report everything seen including floating material, even if it has to be reported several times.
- Make certain duties are understood. If duties are not understand, ask for more information.

C.4. Lookout Positioning

Lookouts must be posted by the coxswain so they have the best possible chance of seeing and hearing an approaching vessel or searching for an object in the water. The coxswain should perform the following procedures when positioning lookouts:

Step	Procedure
1	Choose a boat speed that enables lookouts to effectively and safely perform their duties.
2	Position lookouts so they can effectively and safely perform their duties under the operating conditions (e.g., restricted visibility, boat speed, sea state, weather).
3	During periods of rain, sleet, and snow or when taking spray over the bow, select lookout positions that minimize impairment of vision.
4	During a search, post two lookouts when able. Lookouts should be positioned on each side of the vessel so that each can scan a sector from dead ahead to directly aft.
5	Select a stable location that will not place the lookouts in danger of being blown or swept overboard.
6	When whales are spotted in the area or the boat is within 3 NM of shore, lookout duties should be kept to a minimum to allow for early detection and decrease the likelihood of whale and turtle strikes.

C.5. Lookout Equipment

Standing a proper lookout watch means using all available equipment to improve chance of early detection. These items include binoculars, sunglasses, and night vision equipment.

Binoculars are the lookout's best tool to increase their distance vision capabilities. They are very good for identifying contacts far off and obtaining detailed information when they get closer. While they do increase the distance the eye can see, they also reduce a person's field of vision or how much the eye can see. It is important to remember to switch between using binoculars and just eyes to make sure nothing goes unnoticed.

On a sunny day, a large portion of the horizon might be difficult to observe due to the sun's reflection on the surface of the water. A good pair of sunglasses will reduce eyestrain and glare allowing vision where normally it would be difficult.

The use of night vision equipment increases the chance of detecting objects in the dark. This equipment easily detects even the faintest source of light. They can also be very useful when looking for an unlit object if there is sufficient background lighting. Care should be taken when using this equipment, since pointing it at a bright light might diminish night vision and damage the equipment.

C.6. Object Identification

Lookouts must report what they see, smell, or hear with as much detail as possible. Object type is immediately important (vessel, buoy, breaking waves), but additional details may help the coxswain in decision-making. The following are some obvious characteristics of objects:

- Color.
- Shape.
- Size.

At night, lookouts must identify the color of all lights. This is the specific reason why all boat crew members must have normal color vision.

NOTE

> Marine mammals and sea turtles can be tricky to detect. Look for these clues: blows, spouts, dorsal fins, heads, splashes, turtle shells, and flukes. For more information, refer to your whale wheel.

C.7. Relative Bearing

Lookouts make reports using relative bearings only. The relative bearing of another object depends on its location in relation to the vessel's hull. They start off with 000°, which is straight off the bow or dead ahead. The bearings increase moving clockwise around the vessel all the way to 359°. Straight out from the starboard beam of the vessel would be 090°, dead astern would be 180°, and straight out from the port beam of the vessel would be 270°. (see **Figure 1-1**)

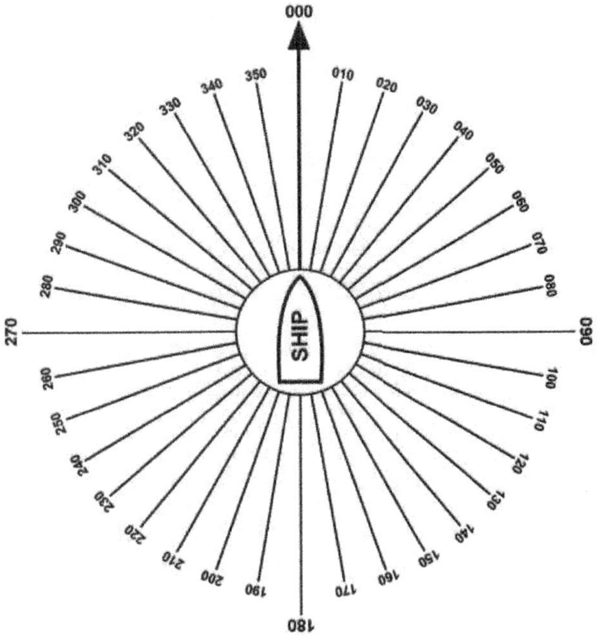

Figure 1-1
Relative Bearings

The following procedures are important in reporting relative bearings:

<table>
<tr><th>Step</th><th>Procedure</th></tr>
<tr><td>1</td><td>Study the diagram on major reference points of relative bearings. Picture in your mind the complete circle of relative bearings around the boat in 10° increments.</td></tr>
<tr><td>2</td><td>Bearings are always reported in three digits and distinctly spoken digit by digit. To ensure one number is not mistaken for another, the following pronunciation is required:
<table>
<tr><th colspan="2">Numeral spoken as</th><th colspan="2">Numeral spoken as</th></tr>
<tr><td>0</td><td>ZERO</td><td>5</td><td>FI-YIV</td></tr>
<tr><td>1</td><td>WUN</td><td>6</td><td>SIX</td></tr>
<tr><td>2</td><td>TOO</td><td>7</td><td>SEVEN</td></tr>
<tr><td>3</td><td>THUH-REE</td><td>8</td><td>ATE</td></tr>
<tr><td>4</td><td>FO-WER</td><td>9</td><td>NINER</td></tr>
</table>
</td></tr>
</table>

Step	Procedure
3	The following procedures are important in reporting relative bearings:

Bearing	Reported as
000°	ZERO ZERO ZERO
010°	ZERO WUN ZERO
045°	ZERO FO-WER FI-YIV
090°	ZERO NINER ZERO
135°	WUN THUH-REE FI-YIV
180°	WUN ATE ZERO
225°	TOO TOO FI-YIV
260°	TOO SIX ZERO
270°	TOO SEVEN ZERO
315°	THUH-REE ONE FI-YIV

C.8. Position Angle

Objects in the sky are located by their relative bearing and position angle. The position angle of an aircraft is its height in degrees above the horizon as seen from the boat. The horizon is 0° and directly overhead is 90° or "Zenith." The position angle can never be more than 90°. Position angles are reported in one or two digits and the word "Position Angle" is always spoken before the numerals. (see **Figure 1-2**)

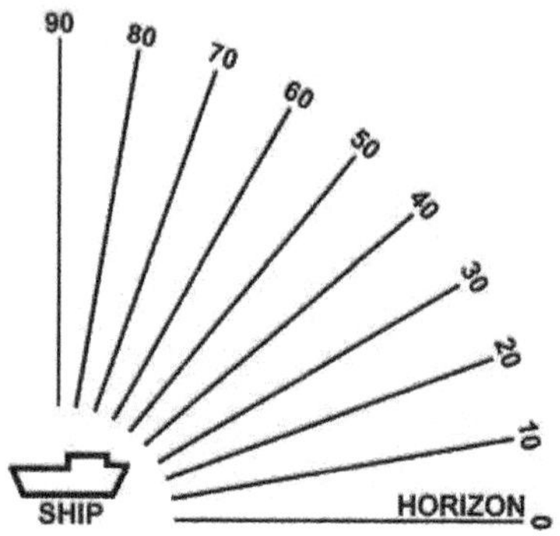

Figure 1-2
Position Angles

CH-1

C.9. Distance

Report distances in yards. Knowing the distance to the horizon, land, or other reference point, will help estimate distance. Dividing the distance from the starting point to the point of reference, provides an estimate of the distance to another object. Ranges in yards are reported digit by digit, except when reporting yards in hundreds or thousands, which are spoken as listed below:

Number of Yards	Spoken as
50	FI-YIV ZERO
500	FI-YIV HUNDRED
5000	FI-YIV THOUSAND

C.10. Making Reports

When making reports, the lookout names or provides a description of the object sighted, the direction (in relative degrees), the position angle (if an air contact), and the range to the object (in yards) are required and must be reported in the following format:

- Object name or description.
- Bearing.
- Position Angle (air contact only).
- Range.

For example:

Discolored water on a bearing of 340° relative to the bow of the boat and at a distance of 2,000 yards.

Reported as: "Discolored water Bearing THUH-REE FO-WER ZERO, Range TOO THOUSAND".

An aircraft bearing 280° relative to the bow of the ship, 30° above the horizon, and at a distance of 9,000 yards.

Reported as: "Aircraft Bearing TOO ATE ZERO, Position Angle THUH-REE ZERO, Range NINER THOUSAND".

C.11. Scanning

The lookout's method of eye search is called scanning. Scanning is a step-by-step method of visually searching for objects. Good scanning techniques will ensure that objects are not missed. Scanning also reduces eye fatigue. Development of a systematic scanning technique is important. There are two common scanning methods:

- Left to right and back again.
- Top to bottom and bottom to top.

In either case, move eyes in increments. This creates overlaps in field of vision and fewer objects will be missed.

Step	Procedure
1	When looking for an object, scan the sky, sea, and horizon slowly and regularly. Scan from left-to-right and back again or from top-to-bottom and bottom-to-top.
2	When scanning, do not look directly at the horizon; look above it. Move head from side to side and keep eyes fixed. This will give any stationary objects in the field of vision the appearance of moving and make them easier to see. One technique is to scan in small steps of about 10° and have them slightly overlap while moving across the field of view.
3	Fatigue, boredom, and environmental conditions affect scanning. For example, after prolonged scanning, with little or no contrast, the eyes develop a tendency to focus short of where the person is looking. To prevent this, periodically focus on a close object such as whitecaps or the bow of the boat.

NOTE

For more details on scanning, refer to the *U.S. Coast Guard Addendum to the United States National Search and Rescue Supplement (NSS) to the International Aeronautical and Maritime Search and Rescue Manual*, COMDTINST M16130.2 (series).

C.11.a. Fog Scanning

In the fog, a contact might be heard long before it's seen. Early detection is vital. Since the fog reduces visual distance, binoculars are not recommended. It is better to have a wide field of vision than a narrow magnified one. It is also important to position the lookout where they will not be hindered by background noise and other distractions. Usually the bow is best, if conditions allow. In severe fog, a second designated lookout should be stationed to cover the aft portion of the vessel.

Night Lookout Watch

C.12. Description

Although the duties for day and night lookout are the same, safety and caution during night watches are especially important. Though it might be easier to acquire a contact on the horizon at night because of its navigation lights, it's obviously more difficult to pick up unlighted objects such as rocks, shoals, and buoys. Eyes respond slower at night and pick up moving objects more readily than a fixed object.

C.13. Guidelines

The guidelines for lookout watches also apply for night lookout watches.

NOTE

Night vision is based on the eyes receiving and interpreting a different type of light than exists during daylight.

C.14. Dark Adaptation

Going from a brightly lit room to a very dark room initially decreases vision. As time in the darkness increases, vision improves and things that were not visible on the initial point of entry are now clear. As eyes adjust to the weak light, vision gradually improves. This is called dark adaptation. Before operating in dark conditions, it is recommended to prepare by moving into a dark environment or wearing goggles equipped with red lenses for 30 minutes prior to getting underway. Care should be taken not to expose eyes to bright lights once they are adjusted. Even a quick flash of light can destroy night vision. Chart and cabin lights, as well as flashlights, should be equipped with red filters to ensure night vision is maintained while underway.

NOTE Avoid looking at bright lights during nighttime operations. When a light must be used, use a red light.

C.15. Night Scanning

As a night lookout, scan the horizon in a series of small sectors allowing eyes to adjust to each. When looking at an object, look all around it, not directly at it. This "off-center vision" allows the object to be seen clearer than trying to stare directly at it. Once located, use binoculars to assist with identification. The use of electronic night vision equipment is highly recommended for early detection.

C.16. Night Fog

In nighttime fog conditions, any source of light (navigation lights) will reflect back off the fog and reduce night vision. This effect will reduce the lookout's ability to detect contacts in various sectors surrounding the boat. Extra care should be used when operating at night in the fog. The use of spotlights is not recommended unless identifying objects that are within close range.

Helm Watch

C.17. Description

The helm watch or helmsman is responsible for the following:

- Safely steering the boat.
- Maintaining a course.
- Carrying out all helm commands given by the coxswain.

The helm watch can be carried out by the coxswain or by any designated crew member. Every crew member should learn to steer and control the boat. They must be able to maneuver the boat using both the primary and emergency steering systems (if equipped) as well as the engine(s).

C.18. Guidelines

When a boat uses a helmsman, there are several guidelines for the helm watch:

- Check with the coxswain for any special instructions and for the course to be steered.
- Repeat all commands given by the coxswain.
- Execute all commands given by the coxswain.
- Maintain a given course within 5°.
- Remain at the helm until properly relieved.
- Execute maneuvers only when expressly ordered, however, minor changes in heading to avoid debris, which could damage propeller or rudders, are essential.
- Operate the emergency tiller (if equipped) during loss of steering.
- Properly inform relief of all pertinent information.

Towing Watch

C.19. Description

A towing watch is normally performed aft on the boat. The primary duty of the towing watch is to keep the towline and the boat being towed under constant observation. For more information on towing procedures, see *Chapter 17, Towing.*

C.20. Guidelines

The guidelines for standing this watch are as follows:

- Report any unusual conditions, equipment failure, or problems to the coxswain immediately.
- Observe how the tow is riding (e.g., in step, listing, or yawing).
- Ensure chafing gear is riding in place.
- Adjust the scope of the towline upon command of the coxswain.
- Keep deck space area clear of unnecessary gear and people.
- Stay clear of the immediate area around the towline due to possible line snap back.
- Know when and how to do an emergency breakaway.

C.21. Observed Danger

The towing watch must be aware of and report any signs of danger. Many of the signs of danger include:

- Yawing - disabled boat veers from one side to the other which may cause one or both boats to capsize.
- List increasing on towed boat.
- In step - the proper distance between the towed boat and the towing boat to maintain control and prevent breaking the tow line.
- Towed boat taking on water.
- Deck hardware failure due to stress, no backing plates, etc.
- Towline about to part due to stress, chafing, or other damage.
- Towed boat overtaking boat due to sudden reduction in speed.
- Positioning of towed boat's crew.
- Slack tow line in the water that may foul propeller or rudder.

C.22. Maintaining Watch

A tow watch should be maintained until the disabled boat is moored or until relieved. When relieved, all important information should be passed to the relief (i.e., problems with chafing gear, towed boat yaws, etc.).

Anchor Watch

C.23. Description

When the boat is anchored, an anchor watch is set. The person on watch must ensure that the anchor line does not chafe and that the anchor does not drag. The individual on watch also looks for other vessels in the area. Even when the boat is anchored, there is the possibility that it can be hit by another boat. For more information on anchoring procedures, see *Chapter 10, Section H.*

C.24. Guidelines

The following guidelines should be used when standing anchor watch:

- Check the strain on the anchor line frequently.
- Check that the anchor line is not chafing.
- Confirm the position of the boat at least every 15 minutes, or at shorter intervals as directed by the coxswain.
- Report bearing or range (distance) changes to the coxswain immediately.
- Report approaching vessels to the coxswain immediately.
- Report major changes in wind velocity or direction.
- Check for current or tidal changes.
- Report any unusual conditions.

C.25. Checking for Chafing

Once the anchor is set, chafing gear should be applied to the anchor line. It is the job of the anchor watch to ensure chafing gear stays in place and the anchor line does not chafe through.

C.26. Checking for Dragging

There are two methods to determine if the anchor is dragging:

- Check for tension on the anchor line.
- Check the boat's position.

If the anchor is dragging over the bottom, sometimes vibration can be felt in the line. The boat's position should be periodically checked by taking a navigational fix. Both methods above should always be used.

C.27. Checking Position

It is important to routinely check the boat's position to ensure it is not drifting or dragging anchor:

- Take compass bearings to three separate objects spread at least 45° apart. Any bearing changes may indicate that the boat is beginning to drift.
- On a boat equipped with radar, determine the distance (range) to three points of land on the radar screen. Any change in the ranges may indicate anchor drag.
- On a LORAN or GPS equipped boat, mark the boat's position with the necessary equipment. Periodically check the LAT/LONG readout. Any change would show the boat's position is changing.
- Make a note of each time the bearings or ranges are checked. Also note the boat's position and the depth of water regularly. A small note pad is acceptable for this purpose. If the water depth or position changes, the anchor may be dragging.

As the wind or water current changes direction, the boat will swing about its anchor. This swing circle is centered on the position of the anchor. The swing circle's radius is equal to the boat's length plus the length of anchor line/chain that has veered (Example: 40-foot boat + 150 feet of anchor line out = 190-foot swing circle). The swing circle must be clear of other vessels and underwater obstructions. When checking the boat's position, it should fall inside the swing circle.

This page intentionally left blank.

Chapter 2
Auxiliary Operational Missions/Patrols

Introduction

Shore units will get their boats underway to conduct a variety of patrols. The intent of this chapter is to discuss types of boat patrols and their respective procedures. Patrols may have different titles for the same type of task or one general title to cover many tasks. The Coast Guard encourages the Auxiliary to conduct multi-mission patrols when practical. Examples include safety, familiarization, training, harbor, and regatta patrols. In all cases, the crew is underway at the direction of the Operational Commander. The patrol may be in response to a known problem or meant as a method of prevention or early detection.

In this chapter

This chapter contains the following sections:

Section A. Safety Patrols

Introduction

Safety patrols directly support the Coast Guard's maritime safety responsibilities. For the Auxiliary, the safety patrol supports the search and rescue (SAR) mission specifically to locate and help persons and boats in distress. While a routine safety, non-distress patrol is being conducted, it is common practice to perform other missions, such as checking aids to navigation (AtoN), pollution levels, and reporting any unusual events or scenarios to their Operational Commander.

In this section

This section contains the following information:

Benefits of Safety Patrols

A.1. Description

Safety patrols provide important benefits for the boat crew, Coast Guard, and the public. These benefits include:

- Practice for the crew and familiarization with their AOR.
- Public seeing the Coast Guard in action.
- Public awareness that distress assistance is available.
- Increased opportunity for the boating public to obtain boating safety information or navigation hazard notices.
- Information for the federal, state, and local agencies responsible for updating navigation aids and charts.
- Detection of unreported events, including SAR and pollution.
- Detection and reporting of any unusual, suspicious, or abnormal events.

NOTE

> Patrols scheduled before sundown, or on receipt of a severe storm warning are to help boaters to get to a secure harbor. This is considered "preventive SAR".

Auxiliary Safety Patrol Boat Duties

A.2. Description

A boat on patrol should always be ready to answer distress or assistance calls expediently, even when ordered to stand by at a pier. To help boaters, many boat crews carry additional equipment, perhaps an extra battery and a good array of tools onboard. The District Commander may require boats to carry equipment to meet the unique needs of the district.

A.3. Coxswain's Responsibility

Coxswains should know and follow the local guidance and all Coast Guard directives outlining policy and procedures. This information comes from the Coast Guard Group Commander, Director of Auxiliary, or order-issuing authority in response to the local needs or changing conditions. Before getting underway, the coxswain should:

- Know the patrol area and review factors such as tidal action, weather patterns, fishing areas, and navigational aids.
- Verify that fuel tanks are full and all equipment is checked and operating properly.
- Ensure that the crew is outfitted in the correct uniform and appropriate personal protective equipment (PPE). (All crew members must be properly trained and certified on all PPE.)
- Verify that at least one other crew member is qualified to operate the boat in case the coxswain needs to seek relief.
- Ensure all crew members are physically capable of performing the mission.
- Provide a thorough briefing on the boat, its equipment, and its operation. Specifically address possible hazards, risk awareness, and situation awareness.
- Once satisfied, go to the assigned patrol sector and notify the Operational Commander of your arrival or departure, the number and names of persons onboard, and verify that conditions are within the facility's operational standards.

A.4. Reporting Responsibility

Proper reports keep boaters and the Coast Guard informed about boat patrols and local boating conditions. Whether it is a routine position report, a sea condition report, or a log entry, all reports should be accurate.

A.4.a. Operational Status Reports

While on patrol, a facility must have two-way communications with their Unit Commander. If the facility is unable to contact their Unit Commander, every attempt should be made to use another Coast Guard unit, Auxiliary unit, or federal/state agency to relay their information to their Unit Commander. Facility operators must follow Coast Guard reporting requirements during a patrol. If communications are lost for more than the designated reporting period, the mission must be aborted, the facility moved to a safe haven, and the order issuing authority advised as soon as possible.

A.4.b. Patrol Logs

A log of significant patrol activities should be kept. The narrative of each event should be a brief accurate description of situations, procedures, actions, and activities. The log will help backup reports sent to the Coast Guard and answer any inquiries.

A.4.c. Sea Condition/Weather Reports

Auxiliarists on patrol may report on-scene weather and sea conditions to their Unit Commander. Auxiliary radio stations and communication watchstanders may respond to public weather information requests as per Coast Guard policy, and guidelines established for local Coast Guard units, or Coast Guard unit communication watchstanders.

A.5. Patrolling

A preliminary sweep of the area is made to establish familiarity with the prevailing conditions, potential trouble areas, and to announce to local boaters that patrolling is underway. The coxswain should keep the boat's speed down while patrolling to enable the crew to keep a sharp lookout in all directions and to conserve fuel.

A.6. Patrolling During Heavy Weather

In the event of a sudden storm, pleasure boaters may need assistance. While a coxswain should never jeopardize the safety of their crew, it is important to render assistance if it is safe to do so. Prudence shall be used to prevent damage to the facility or injury to the crew. Operational limitations established by the order issuing authority shall not be exceeded.

A.7. Assistance

While on patrol, boat crews will encounter many types of assistance situations. They should always approach them with caution, considering the different policies and procedures concerning assistance, including:

- *U.S. Coast Guard Addendum to the United States National Search and Rescue Supplement (NSS) to the International Aeronautical and Maritime Search and Rescue Manual*, COMDTINST M16130.2 (series).
- Maritime SAR Assistance Policy.
- *Auxiliary Operations Policy Manual*, COMDTINST M16798.3 (series), *Chapter 4*.
- General salvage policy.
- Risk assessment processes.
- Proper operations to help the boat.
- Other concerns, such as the need for additional boats to help.

NOTE Do not hesitate to call for additional help as necessary when providing assistance.

A.8. Assisting Other Patrols

When a safety patrol boat, in an adjoining area, is assigned an assistance mission, boats in the surrounding areas should move to the line between the two sectors. This allows them to answer a call in either of the sectors. Precise direction should be obtained from the Operational Commander.

A.9. Permission to Secure

When it is time to end the patrol, the appropriate Coast Guard unit is notified and permission to secure is requested. A final sweep normally will be made through the patrol area before securing.

NOTE A patrol boat that is damaged or has a crewmember injured while on official patrol must contact the Coast Guard Operational Commander as soon as possible, and follow the prescribed procedures for the situation.

Section B. Regatta Patrols and Marine Parades

Introduction

A regatta or marine parade is an organized water event of limited duration that is conducted according to a prearranged schedule. Regattas involve both participant and spectator boats in activities such as, racing, water skiing, demonstrations, and similar grouped or classed marine skills and equipment. The safety of the participant boats is the responsibility of the sponsoring organization, unless they ask for Coast Guard assistance. The safety of the spectator boats is a Coast Guard responsibility, but should be verified with the event sponsors. The sponsor of the marine event is responsible for applying for approval of the event. The application must be submitted to the proper Coast Guard or civil authority at least 30 days prior to the event. For new or major marine events, the application should be submitted well in advance (90-120 days).

In this section

This section contains the following information:

Patrolling Regattas

B.1. Functions of a Regatta Patrol

Regattas usually take place over a closed course where patrol sectors are established alongside and at each end of the course. The primary functions of a regatta patrol are to control the spectator boats and transient craft for their protection, and to ensure safety hazards do not enter into the event area.

NOTE

> The primary responsibility to protect participants from the hazards of the event, including other participants, rests with the sponsoring organization.

B.2. Selecting the Patrol Commander

The Coast Guard District Commander, captain-of-the-port (COTP), or Group Commander will designate the patrol commander (PATCOM) for a regatta or marine event. The PATCOM is normally a Coast Guard commissioned officer, warrant officer, or an appropriate auxiliarist assigned as AUXPATCOM (in the absence of active duty PATCOM).

NOTE

> Written instructions will describe the authority of the Auxiliarist to act as PATCOM. These instructions include: patrol requirements; pre-brief to all participants - duties and responsibilities; establish communication frequencies and networks; and instructions for completing after patrol reports. The Auxiliary must coordinate and cooperate with any law enforcement agency that might be on scene.

B.3. Designating an Auxiliary Boat Commander

When a regatta or marine event is under the control of a Coast Guard PATCOM and the Auxiliary is also assisting, an Auxiliary Boat Commander (AUXCOM) will be designated. AUXCOM will work closely with the PATCOM to coordinate the Auxiliary boats and personnel and, act as liaison to prepare for, conduct, and secure the event. (AUXCOM is also that person's radio call sign during the event.)

B.4. Establishing Sectors

The length, size, and shape of the course depend upon the type of regatta. To maintain operational control, regatta event courses are usually divided into sectors. (see **Figure 2-1**) All sectors should be as small as is reasonable to allow patrols to regulate traffic and keep obstructions or boats from the course. Small sectors may limit mobility. Large sectors are too difficult for patrol boats to cover effectively, and spectator boats might get too close to the course before a patrol boat can issue a warning. Patrol boats should move only within their assigned sectors. The following procedures should help the PATCOM/AUXPATCOM to establish and assign sectors:

Step	Procedure
1	Divide large patrol areas into at least five sectors, one to three sectors along each outer side, and at least two at each end.
2	Operate all boats from the same charts.
3	Mark the charts with the patrol sectors.
4	Assign each patrol boat to a patrol sector.
5	Ensure that each boat reports its location and movements.
6	Establish more sectors as needed (e.g., change in course size or more spectator boats than expected).

B.5. Grid System

The grid system is an effective method of organizing patrol area operations. When using the grid system, transparent grid overlays are essential. All grids must be identical in size and identification. (see **Figure 2-1**) The benefits of using grids are:

- PATCOM/AUXPATCOM and the patrol boat captains can read grid coordinates exactly.
- Coxswains can request assistance, by giving a location, using the grid on the chart.
- PATCOM/AUXPATCOM can also assign additional patrol boats to the position.
- Location of a distress can be easily shown.

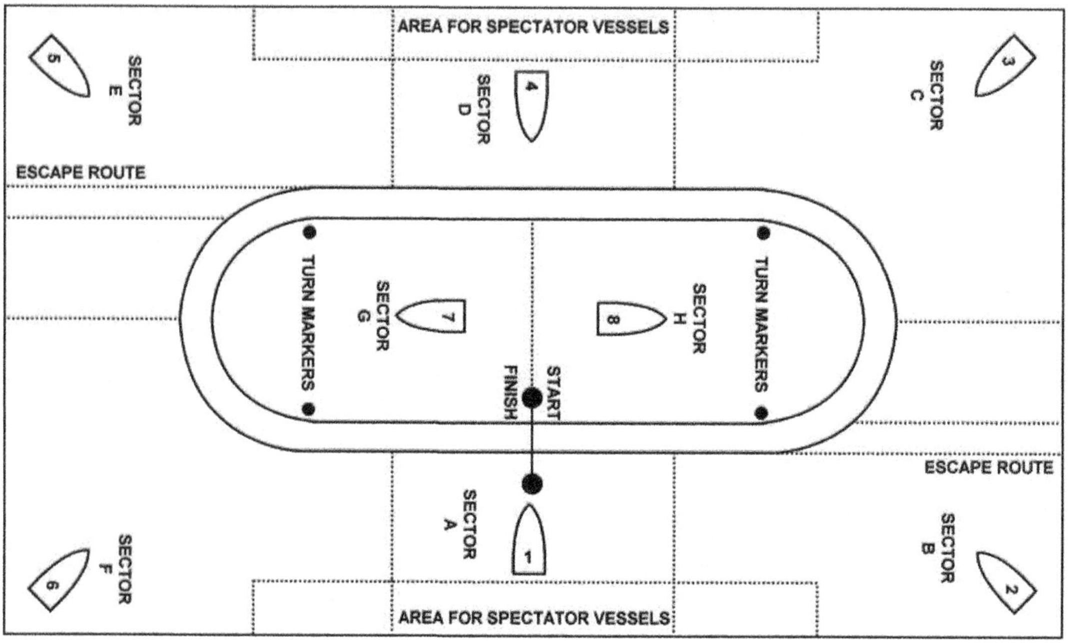

Figure 2-1
Typical Patrol Assignments and Sectors

B.6. Patrolling Various Regattas

Knowing the sponsor rules, the boats involved, and patrol responsibilities is vital to ensuring the safety of the crew, participant boats, and spectators. **Table 2-1** introduces the responsibilities of the sponsor and patrol boats during powerboat, sailing, rowing, and other various regattas.

Table 2-1
Patrolling Various Regattas

Sponsor Organization Responsibility	Any type of regatta is usually sponsored by an organization. Powerboats may have a corporate sponsor; sailboats, are sponsored by yachting clubs or associations; and rowing regattas are usually sanctioned by a prep school or collegiate organization. The sponsors have rules that the participants of a race must follow. At times, the sponsors provide especially trained crews to assist during emergencies.
Patrol Boat Responsibility	Only assist a participant or spectator boat if agreed upon or requested by the sponsor and approved by the Patrol Commander. Know the sponsor's rules. Be aware of the construction, use, and particulars of the boats used in the regatta. During an emergency with either the participant or spectator boats, an abrupt action by an inexperienced boat crew may cause a participant's disqualification.
NOTE	PATCOM/AUXPATCOM should keep close liaison with regatta sponsor officials before, during, and after the regatta event.

Regattas	Powerboat	Sailing	Rowing (crew racing)
Course Layout	Large rectangle or long oval course involving the escape valve idea, diagonally opposite at each end, enabling race boats to leave the course. (see **Figure 2-1**)	Nearly all courses are triangular, allowing for use of the basic sailing positions. Course must be laid out to conform to the prevailing wind direction. (see **Figure 2-2**)	The races are held on a straight course with marker craft on either side and a moving screen behind to prevent spectator boats from interfering.
Operation Sectors	Use boats as moving or stationary screens along sides of the course. Maintain a line, behind which spectator boats stay. The ends of the course require moving screens if it is longer than it is wide, to keep spectators from entering the course.	Course type and maneuvering calls for a combination of marker, stationary boats, and moving screen boats to stop passing boats from entering the course. Moving screen patrol move with the regatta. (see **Figure 2-3**)	Use stationary positions and do not leave these positions unless assistance is required. (see **Figure 2-4**)
Participant Boat Particulars	Fragile construction. Sensitive to wakes.	Possibility of capsizing. Identifying capsized boats difficult because of lack of noise and sailboats closely grouped.	The craft are very light, have a very low freeboard, and require quiet water.
Handling Participant Boat Emergencies	Emergencies on the course should be left to the sponsor rescue craft, unless asked.	Ask the skipper if assistance is wanted, then allow him to direct the operation.	Check with event sponsors, assume it is okay to assist participants; they usually do not wear life preservers.

Table 2-1 (continued)
Patrolling Various Regattas

Regattas	Powerboat	Sailing	Rowing (crew racing)
Spectator Boats	Sponsors and patrols share responsibility for the safety of spectator boats. Keep spectator boat wakes small.	Sponsors and patrols share responsibility for the safety of spectator boats. Tactfully attempt to keep spectator boats from entering the course or going between the sailboats. This happens when a spectator or transient boat is unaware of an ongoing race, or they presume they may proceed following navigation rules.	Sponsors and patrols share responsibility for the safety of spectator boats. Ensure that all spectator boats are in place well before the start of the race so that wake-driven wave action will subside. Prevent spectator boats from entering the course.
Other Responsibilities	Move about looking out for debris that may endanger participant or spectator boats.	Be alert to course legs being moved or rotated, and advise patrol boats.	Keep wakes down.
In Addition	Special communication problems may arise when operating near loud engines, and may require traffic control signs, headphones, etc.	Racing sailboats take advantage of wind conditions and are tacking back and forth along the course. Try not to place patrol boats in the infield because they could be in the way. Instead, set patrol boats downwind and astern of the participating boats. Discuss assisting, sailboat righting, and towing at the pre-race briefing.	Patrol boats should minimize the use of hailing equipment whenever the rowers are nearby to eliminate interference with their cadence. Other types of rowing regattas feature dories, lifeboats, whaleboats, canoes, and even bathtubs. Patrol these regattas in the same manner as crew races.

Patrol Boat Assignments

B.7. Examining the Course After completing all pre-race activities, the PATCOM/AUXPATCOM dispatches the boats to their patrol positions. En route and within its sector, each patrol boat should examine the course for objects or debris that could affect participant, spectator, or patrol boat safety. This is especially important in events involving high-speed racing craft. Items such as a partially submerged soft drink container can cause a disaster if struck by a race boat at high speeds.

B.8. Using Patrol Boats Patrol boats on regatta patrol may be used two ways, either as marker boats or screen boats.

B.8.a. Marker Boats Marker boats are positioned at designated places, either stationary or mobile, to mark limits of restricted areas. The event sponsor must provide marker boats to locate turning points for the regatta participants.

B.8.b. Screen Boats Screen vessels should be used as either moving or stationary screens. These boats maneuver in formation around the perimeter of the racecourse to be between the participants and the spectators. A stationary screen boat acts in the same manner as the marker boat.

NOTE Wakes could create hazards to boats in events. Patrol and spectator boats' speed must be kept to a minimum. In an emergency, patrol boats can increase their speed.

B.9. Displaying Boat Ensigns Boats on regatta patrol must display the proper identification signs, and all crewmembers must be in proper uniform. If an active duty Coast Guard PATCOM rides on an Auxiliary boat, the Auxiliary ensign shall be temporarily removed, and the Coast Guard ensign displayed along with the special Coast Guard patrol signs.

B.10. Patrol Boat Each patrol crew has the responsibility to maintain a sharp lookout. Patrol observers should not become so engrossed in a racing event that they ignore the movement of the participants and the spectators within their sector.

B.11. Closing a Section Under certain conditions, it is necessary for the Coast Guard to close a section of the course or the area in which the event is being held. It is a responsibility of the patrol boats to constantly be present in these areas. If there are not enough patrol boats, floats or log booms should be used. Spectators should be warned so that they will not strike these objects.

B.12. Anchoring Spectator Boats All spectator boats should be anchored only in designated areas. All boats must anchor so that they do not swing into restricted zones. It is necessary to be alert for weather changes, a wind shift, or a current condition that might cause anchored boats to swing into the restricted zones.

B.13. Spectator Boats Spectator boat areas should be patrolled to ensure all boats are safely clear of the course or safety zone. Each spectator boat that is not in a proper position should be advised in a courteous manner to move to a safe position. In case of failure to comply with a request, all facts regarding the circumstances should be reported to the PATCOM/AUXPATCOM for action.

NOTE The auxiliary does not have any law enforcement authority. The words "please" and "thank you" should be used and all message should be conveyed in a courteous tone of voice.

B.14. Assisting in a Casualty

Patrol boats must advise the PATCOM/AUXPATCOM of all problems in case the event needs to be stopped or the course closed temporarily. No patrol boat will leave its sector unless ordered to do so by the PATCOM/AUXPATCOM. Action is taken only on direction from the PATCOM/AUXPATCOM, so as to maintain order and efficiency of the operation. The following table summarizes possible emergency situations and the initial actions to take:

If...	Then...
You observe a casualty	Advise the PATCOM/AUXPATCOM of all details, who will direct the proper patrol boat to the scene. If a participant boat is the casualty, the event's sponsor may be the only boat to respond.
An accident occurs within the patrol boat's sector	Assist immediately. If no arrangement has been made with the event sponsors, "stand by, observe" but defer all action to the (sponsor) committee boats designated for that purpose.
A boat is assigned to help outside its sector	Report to the PATCOM/AUXPATCOM upon completion of the assistance.
There is an emergency	Rescue the people first before any attempt is made to salvage a boat. The protection of lives and personal safety are more important than the saving of property

B.15. Securing a Regatta Patrol

A regatta patrol operation should not be secured until the course area is clear. The PATCOM/AUXPATCOM will designate one patrol boat or more, if required, to make a final sweep of the area. This will ensure that the course is in the condition it was in before the regatta. Any debris or markers that have not been picked up should be reported to the PATCOM/AUXPATCOM. They will relay this information to the sponsoring organization that has the responsibility for policing the area.

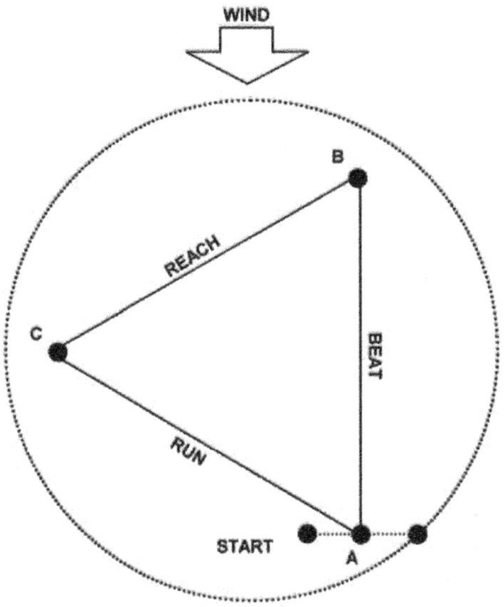

Figure 2-2
Typical Sailboat Regatta Course

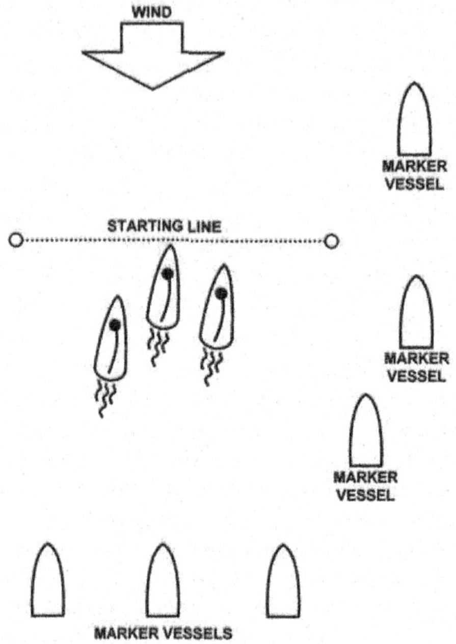

Figure 2-3
Typical Sailboat Regatta Patrol

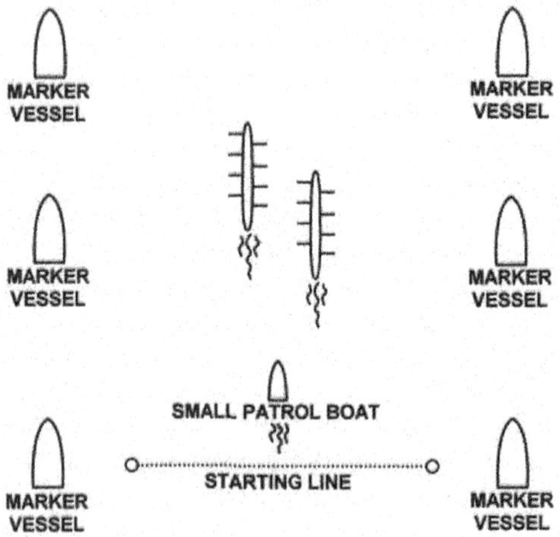

Figure 2-4
Typical Rowing Regatta Patrol

Marine Parades

B.16. Description

The term "marine parade" denotes a boat or a group of boats participating in a parade. Depending upon the nature of the event, a patrol boat will maintain the grouping or allow it to vary. The event is usually moving, and does not ordinarily retrace its path, although the parade may end at its starting point.

A PATCOM/AUXPATCOM will normally be assigned. PATCOM/AUXPATCOM and patrol boat duties typically include:

- Selecting a vantage point for the PATCOM/AUXPATCOM with maximum visibility of the event; usually a moving facility.
- Maintaining communications between the PATCOM/AUXPATCOM and the marine parade marshal or committee.
- Maintaining parade configuration per established routes and times.
- Assigning patrol boats to:
  - Stationary sectors along the parade course containing spectator boats that are to remain within a prescribed limit.
  - Move sectors of patrol boats ahead, behind, and alongside the participating boats.
  - Sectors between the welcomed boat and the moving welcoming fleet, for such events.
  - Prevent transient boats from disrupting the parade.
  - Render assistance to life threatening situations and endangered property.

Section C. Aids to Navigation Patrols

Introduction

Coast Guard Regulations state that coxswains shall make every effort to observe and report any aid to navigation (AtoN) that is out of order or off Station. (The boat crew assists by keeping a sharp eye out for discrepancies.) This is usually accomplished underway while on routine operations. However, Coast Guard resources may be directed to get underway specifically to check for AtoN discrepancies. In addition to patrolling, local boat resources may be used to assist the AtoN units that maintain and service these aids as per *Coast Guard Auxiliary Aids To Navigation Program*, COMDTINST 16500.16 (series).

C.1. Reporting AtoN Discrepancies

Any aids that are damaged, off Station, or otherwise not serving their intended purpose (i.e., not watching properly) should be reported to the Coast Guard unit. The aid, its location, and the discrepancy should be clearly identified. The chart, *Light List*, or Local Notice to Mariners should be used to verify the correct AtoN information.

The Auxiliary has established procedures for their reporting of AtoN discrepancies. The following criteria is used to select the method of reporting a discrepancy:

Criticality	Report by	Criteria
Critical	Radio	Failure to report by the most expeditious means may result in loss of life and/or damage to a boat. *Examples*: • Aid iced and light obscured. • Light signal failure. • Light signal showing improper characteristic. • Buoy sinking or submerged. • Aid off Station/adrift/missing. • Radiobeacon off the air (improper characteristic).
Urgent	Telephone	Failure to report will result in no danger of loss of life or boat damage. However, the discrepancy may contribute to the stranding of a boat. *Examples*: • Daymarks missing. • Sound signal failure. • Radiobeacon timing sequence incorrect.
Routine	U.S. Mail E-mail Telephone	Failure to report will result in a very low likelihood of a grounding or stranding, but corrective maintenance is necessary. *Examples*: • Signal obscured (by foliage or other objects). • Daymark faded. • Structure leaning. • Bird's nest present. • Daymarks improper • Retroreflective material missing or inadequate. • Numbers missing.

Section D. Chart Updating Patrols

Introduction

The Auxiliary has a formal agreement with the National Oceanic and Atmospheric Administration-National Ocean Service (NOAA-NOS), an agency under the Department of Commerce. The agreement provides for liaison and cooperation to provide accurate and up-to-date chart information to the boating public.

The agreement between NOAA-NOS and the Auxiliary authorizes and encourages the scheduling of safety patrols to verify the accuracy of published navigation charts. These patrols, called Chart Updating Patrols, are not restricted solely to areas covered by NOAA-NOS charts. Other federal and state agencies also publish charts or maps used by the boater. Chart updating patrols on local, state, and federal waters covered by these charts are also authorized.

D.1. Discrepancies

Any discrepancies found should be reported on the appropriate chart updating form.

Members of the Auxiliary need not be performing on a scheduled patrol to notice and report discrepancies. Alert coxswains should always compare chart information with the actual conditions and report differences. Chart updating patrols should always be alert to the actions and activities of other boaters and be ready to render assistance.

Section E. Disaster Patrols

Introduction

District or unit standard operating procedures (SOPs) typically provide for patrolling in the event of a natural or manmade disaster. This type of patrol, sometimes called a disaster patrol, deals with emergencies either imminent, in progress, or the result of events such as hurricanes, storms, waterfront explosions, fires, or floods. Coast Guard Unit Commanders should coordinate with local Auxiliary Flotilla/Division Officers to pre-establish in writing (and practice) a response disaster plan delineating the duties of Auxiliary members and their facilities for specific assistance or integrating into unit duties.

E.1. Role of Boat Crew

The boat crew may be used to transmit warnings to waterfront and isolated areas. They can also transport supplies and personnel, evacuate stricken areas, and coordinate boat traffic. This includes acting as guides to safe moorings, to secure small craft, or to perform any other tasks necessary to speed preparations for, or relief from, emergency conditions.

E.2. Role of Coast Guard

The Coast Guard is typically part of any local emergency management plan. In this role, Coast Guard boats may be called upon to assist in evacuations of the civilian population. As seen in many disasters, there often are people who do not want to evacuate ahead of time. The Coast Guard has federal law enforcement powers (the Auxiliary does not), but the local officials are the proper people to handle these civil situations and to provide guidance. However, politely explaining the situation may convince a reluctant person to take the right action.

Section F. Port Security and Maritime Pollution

Introduction

Port security and maritime pollution issues fall under the Coast Guard Directorate of Marine Safety and Maritime Environmental Protection. Typically, the COTP is the field unit responsible for implementing these programs. The COTP may have the resources or may have to call upon local Coast Guard facilities to provide boats. Port security is concerned with waterside security measures, typically within a security zone. Maritime pollution patrols focus on detecting, reporting, and monitoring oil spills and hazardous material discharges into U.S. navigable waters.

F.1. Security Zone Patrol

There is no federal, state, or local military service or civilian agency with the waterside resources, expertise, and lawful maritime authority comparable to that of the Coast Guard. The COTP has developed tactics and countermeasures to deal with waterborne threats. Assets likely to be at risk include:

- Ships.
- Pier or port complexes.
- Waterfront facilities.
- People.

F.1.a. Operations

The COTP will provide specialized equipment and training, if needed. A command center should be established with direct control by the COTP over all Coast Guard deployed resources. Most security zone enforcement requires simple patrolling or "policing" of the zone boundaries. One or two boats patrolling the perimeter usually do this. The security zone may be established around a fixed site such as a pier, or it may be a moving security zone for a vessel underway. The moving security zone usually requires at least two boats.

NOTE No security operation is routine. Crewmembers should stay alert and aware of surroundings at all times.

F.2. Pollution Patrol

There are usually two types of pollution patrol:

- A patrol to detect or prevent spills.
- A patrol in response to a spill.

The boat may be given specific areas to visually inspect or given general direction to cruise along the waterfront and shoreline to look for any discharges.

F.2.a. Detection or Prevention

The COTP may coordinate with the local Operational Commander to have a boat patrol to detect any unreported spills or discharges. Early detection this way may keep the incident from growing into a major spill. Also, the source of the spill may be identified. This may stop someone from intentionally discharging pollution and also identify the person or company who will pay the costs for cleanup.

F.2.b. Response to a Spill

Response to a pollution incident will often involve boats in some type of patrol duty, such as monitoring the situation. The person coordinating the response to the incident, the On-Scene Commander (OSC), will have an incident command structure to provide tasking and guidance for boat operations.

F.3. Safety and Security Patrol

The Coast Guard may deploy Auxiliary facilities to patrol safety and security zones established by the COTP. The Auxiliary may conduct these patrols with or without Coast Guard boarding officers (officers or petty officers authorized to conduct law enforcement) onboard. Auxiliarists operating facilities without Coast Guard boarding officers onboard may function in an advisory or informational mode (which includes directing the movement of boats in the vicinity of the zone), but may not exercise law enforcement authority.

Section G. Law Enforcement (Prohibitions/Assistance) Policy

Introduction

Auxiliarists cannot execute direct law enforcement missions, but may support certain Coast Guard law enforcement activities. The key restriction is that no command can vest auxiliarists with general police powers (e.g., power to search, seize, or arrest) or give auxiliarists any direct role in law enforcement action. However, a Unit Commander may request an auxiliarist employ an operational facility to provide transportation of logistics support to Coast Guard personnel enforcing general vessel safety laws (e.g., to conduct CG-4100 boardings) where there is a low chance of detecting criminal activities. Unit Commanders should review current policy concerning operational guidelines as per *Auxiliary Operations Policy Manual, COMDINST M16798.3 (series), Chapter 4* prior to requesting Auxiliary support regarding any law enforcement.

CAUTION ! In the event any problem occurs on the vessel being boarded, the only option available to the auxiliary crew is to back off and request assistance from the Coast Guard Unit Commander.

G.1. Coast Guard Boarding from Auxiliary Facility

Coast Guard officers and petty officers may conduct boardings from an Auxiliary vessel facility which is crewed by auxiliarists (as a boarding platform) but only under the condition that there is a low chance of detecting unlawful activity or conduct during the boarding. The Coast Guard may not request or require auxiliarists to take any direct law enforcement actions.

G.1.a. Directing Movement of Auxiliary Facility

Coast Guard officers and petty officers utilizing an Auxiliary vessel facility and crew as a boarding platform may request the operator to take certain actions in the movement of the facility, but should not violate navigational rules nor create a situation that places any vessel in navigational extremis. With such requests, the Auxiliary operator has sole responsibility for the safety of the facility and crew. If the requested movement(s) are not within the capability of the facility or Auxiliary operator, or if in the auxiliarist's judgment, would hazard the facility or crew, the auxiliarist must decline the request.

G.2. Auxiliarist Translators

Auxiliarists are authorized to assist the Coast Guard (federal, state, when approved by Unit Commander) law enforcement officials as translators providing there is a low chance of criminal activity, or via radio/telephone/electronic communication.

G.3. Prohibitions

Auxiliarists are prohibited from the following:

- Actual boarding of a boat or vessel for law enforcement purposes.
- Carrying firearms (by hand or holster) or any related law enforcement equipment (e.g., handcuffs, pepper spray, etc.) on their person.
- Investigating complaints of negligent operations or serving subpoenas.

This page intentionally left blank.

Chapter 3
Crew Efficiency Factors

Introduction

This chapter specifies the physical fitness standards that all crewmembers are required to meet. It also describes some of the hazards and unique discomforts boat crews cope with when operating boats in the marine environment. The combination of many factors such as extreme hot or cold weather, fatigue, and seasickness are all factors that can impair crew performance. Understanding these factors will help crewmembers remain at the highest level of efficiency while underway.

NOTE

Specific treatment procedures for the conditions described in this chapter are covered in *Chapter 5, First Aid* of this Manual.

In this chapter

This chapter contains the following sections:

Section A. Physical Fitness Standards

Introduction

All Coast Guard crewmembers are required to meet the following standards of physical fitness. Physical fitness standards are required to ensure crewmembers have sufficient strength, flexibility, and endurance to safely perform duties during normal and adverse conditions. Knowing these standards will ensure that personnel are able to accurately gauge their level of fitness and make improvements where necessary. **Table 3-1** lists the minimum required fitness standards.

NOTE Auxiliary physical standards are found in the *Auxiliary Operations Policy Manual,* COMDTINST M16798.3 (series) for being a crewmember on an Auxiliary facility.

Table 3-1
Physical Fitness Standards

Males	Push-Ups	Sit-Ups	Sit and Reach	1.5-Mile Run	12-Minute Swim
Under 30	29	38	16.5"	12:51	500 yds.
30 to 39	24	35	15.5"	13:36	450 yds.
40 to 49	18	29	14.25"	14:29	400 yds.
50 to 59	15	25	12.5"	15:26	350 yds.
60+	13	22	11.5"	16:43	300 yds.
Females	**Push-Ups**	**Sit-Ups**	**Sit and Reach**	**1.5-Mile Run**	**12-Minute Swim**
Under 30	23	32	19.25"	15:26	400 yds.
30 to 39	19	25	18.25"	15:57	350 yds.
40 to 49	13	20	17.25"	16:58	300 yds.
50 to 59	11	16	16.25"	17:55	250 yds.
60+	9	15	16.25"	18:44	200 yds.

Notes:

- 12-minute swim test chart is based on Dr. Kenneth Cooper's research.
- Push-ups and sit-ups must be performed within a one-minute time period.
- Either the 1.5-mile run or the 12-minute swim may be performed to meet the standard.

The following physical fitness standards are provided with specific procedures:

- Arm and Shoulder Strength
- Abdominal and Trunk Strength
- Flexibility
- Endurance

A.1. Arm and Shoulder Strength

The requirements for arm and shoulder strength are to perform as many correct push-ups as possible in one minute.

One-Minute Push-Ups	Step	Procedure
Perform as many correct push-ups as possible in one minute.	1	Start with hands shoulder-width apart.
	2	Males will be on hands and toes only; females may place knees on the deck and position hands slightly forward of shoulders.
	3	In the up position, the elbows must be fully extended.
	4	For a proper push-up to be completed, lower the body until the chest is within one fist distance of the deck, and then return to the up position.
NOTE		The back must be kept straight the entire time.

A.2. Abdominal and Trunk Strength

The requirements for abdominal and trunk strength are to perform as many correct sit-ups as possible in one minute.

One-Minute Sit-Ups	Step	Procedure
Perform as many correct sit-ups as possible in one minute.	1	Lie on back, bend knees, place heels flat on floor about 18 inches away from buttocks, and keep fingers loosely on side of head. Hands may not come off of side of head for sit-up to count.
NOTE		Feet may be anchored.
	2	In the up position, elbows will touch the knees, then return so that both shoulder blades are touching the deck.
	3	The buttocks should never leave the deck.
NOTE		Any resting should be done in the up position.

A.3. Flexibility

To meet the flexibility standard, the trainee must be able to reach to at least a specified measurement sitting with feet against a box that has a yardstick on top of the box, with the 15-inch mark even with the edge of the box.

Sit and Reach	Step	Procedure
Place a yardstick on top of a box with the 15-inch mark even with the edge of the box.	1	Warm up and stretch sufficiently.
	2	Remove shoes and sit with feet flat against the box.
NOTE		The 15-inch mark is between the individual's feet with the end of the yardstick, 0 inches through 15 inches, extending forward towards the subject's knees.
	3	Keep feet no more than 8 inches apart.
	4	Place the hands exactly together, one on top of the other, with the fingers extended.
	5	Keep the knees extended and the hands together.
	6	Lean forward without lunging and reach as far down the yardstick as possible.
	7	Record the reach to the nearest ½ inch.
	8	Three trials are allowed to pass the minimum standard.

A.4. Endurance

The requirement to meet the endurance standard is to run/walk 1.5 miles within a prescribed time period or swim a designated length within twelve minutes.

1.5-Mile Run/Walk	Step	Procedure
For the endurance qualification, an individual will be required to run/walk 1.5 miles or perform a 12-minute swim.	1	Refrain from smoking or eating for 2 hours prior to this test.
	2	Warm up and stretch sufficiently.
	3	Run or walk 1.5 miles in the required amount of time for the appropriate age bracket.
	4	If possible, receive pacing assistance, either by having a trained pacer run alongside or by calling out lap times during the test.
	5	Be forewarned not to start out too fast and not to run to complete exhaustion during the test.
	6	At the end of the test, walk for an additional 5 minutes to aid in recovery.
12-Minute Swim	**Step**	**Procedure**
The 12-minute swim is an alternative method to fulfill the endurance qualification.	1	Warm up and stretch sufficiently.
	2	Swim the required distance for the appropriate age bracket in 12 minutes.
	3	Use whichever stroke desired and rest as necessary.

A.5. Annual Assessment

Annual assessment should be performed by a unit wellness representative (WR), unit fitness leader (FL), or independent support command wellness coordinator (WC) who has been trained to perform the same fitness assessments. These personnel not only perform the annual test, but also create unit or individual fitness routines to maintain or increase physical fitness.

Section B. Crew Fatigue

Introduction

The crew's physiological well-being plays an important role in the safe and successful accomplishment of each Coast Guard mission. A crewmember will assist people during the worst conditions. At times, they may feel like they have reached the limits of their physical and mental endurance.

B.1. Fatigue

Mental and physical fatigues are among the greatest dangers during rough weather operations. The hazard of fatigue dramatically reduces the powers of observation, concentration, and judgment. This reduces the ability to exert the effort necessary, and increases the probability that chances will be taken and prescribed safety precautions may be disregarded. The following are examples of situations that may cause fatigue:

- Operating in extreme hot or cold weather conditions.
- Eye strain from hours of looking through sea-spray blurred windshields.
- The effort of holding on and maintaining balance.
- Stress.
- Exposure to noise.
- Exposure to the sun.
- Poor physical conditioning.
- Lack of sleep.
- Boredom.

The safety of the crew and other passengers should always be the foremost concern.

B.2. Crew Responsibility

The crew's safety and welfare are the coxswain's primary responsibility. Coxswains must be constantly aware of stress signs evident in their crews, learn to recognize fatigue, and take corrective action. Crewmembers must watch each other's condition to prevent excessive fatigue from taking its toll. The ability of each member to respond to normal conversation and to complete routine tasks should be observed.

B.3. Symptoms

The primary symptoms of fatigue are:

- Inability to focus or concentrate/narrowed attention span.
- Mental confusion or judgment error.
- Decreased coordination of motor skills and sensory ability (hearing, seeing).
- Increased irritability.
- Decreased performance.
- Decreased concern for safety.

Any one of these symptoms can cause mistakes in judgment or cause taking shortcuts that could threaten the safety of the mission and crew. It is important to ward off the effects of fatigue before it gets too great. Fatigue can lead to faulty decisions and a "don't care" type of attitude.

B.4. Prevention

Coxswains must be aware of the dangers that exist when crewmembers push themselves beyond reasonable limits of performance. They should help eliminate mistakes caused by fatigue. Coxswains must not hesitate to call for assistance when fatigue begins to impair the efficiency of their crew.

Some preventive measures are:

- Adequate rest.
- Appropriate dress for weather conditions.
- Rotate crew duties.
- Provide food and refreshments suitable for conditions.
- Observe other crewmembers for signs of fatigue.

B.4.a. Environmental Conditions

Despite the normal operating climate in a particular area, all crewmembers must dress (or have clothing available) for unexpected weather. Keeping warm in cold weather and cool in hot weather helps prevent fatigue. Some other environmental conditions that also promote fatigue are:

- Motion sickness.
- Glare from the sun.
- Wind and rough sea conditions.
- Rain or snow.
- Vibration (boat engine).

NOTE

> Information on Boat Crew Fatigue Standards may be found in the *U.S. Coast Guard Boat Operations and Training (BOAT) Manual, Volume I,* COMDTINST M16114.32 (series).

Section C. Motion Sickness

Introduction

Motion sickness, or seasickness, is nausea and/or vomiting caused by an imbalance between visual images and the portion of the middle ear that senses motion. This section discusses the causes and symptoms of motion sickness, as well as the methods of prevention.

C.1. Causes of Motion Sickness

Mental and physical stress, as well as the rolling or pitching motion of a boat, contributes to motion sickness. Reading chart work, or other tasks that require close attention, will aggravate motion sickness.

C.2. Symptoms

The motion of the boat, especially when the boat's heading produces a wallowing or rolling motion, can cause the typical symptoms of nausea and vomiting. The primary symptoms of seasickness are:

- Nausea and vomiting.
- Increased salivation.
- Unusual paleness.
- Sweating.
- Drowsiness.
- Overall weakness.
- Stomach discomfort.

CAUTION !

Some anti-motion sickness medications may cause drowsiness. Consult a medical professional to determine if other alternatives are available.

C.3. Prevention / Medication

Besides taking medication, there are other things that can be done to help prevent seasickness:

- Stay out of confined spaces.
- Stay above deck in the fresh air.
- Avoid concentrating on the movement of the boat by looking out over the water toward the horizon or shoreline.
- Avoid smoking.

Motion sickness can often be prevented or made less severe with different kinds of anti-motion medication, including the use of Scopolamine patches. Crewmembers who are especially susceptible to motion discomfort should take anti-motion medication throughout their watch since they never know when they will be dispatched on a mission. Medication taken just before getting underway may not have its maximum effect during the mission.

CAUTION !

Do not take anti-motion medication if any of these restrictions apply.

C.4. Medication Restrictions

Antimotion Sickness Medications, COMDTINST 6710.15 (series) restricts medication use. Specifically, it must not be given under the following circumstances:

- Without medical supervision.
- Within 12 hours of alcohol consumption.
- To pregnant crewmembers.

Section D. Lethal Fumes

Introduction

Crewmembers are constantly at risk of injury or death from exposure to lethal fumes both on and off duty. Carbon monoxide (CO) is a colorless and odorless gas. It is the most common lethal gas encountered during boat operations.

D.1. Conditions Where CO may be Present

The following conditions are associated with CO poisoning:

- Fuel-burning devices.
- Enclosed areas.
- Underway.
- Fires.

D.1.a. Fuel-Burning Devices

Operating any of the following fuel-burning devices produces CO fumes:

- Gasoline or diesel engines.
- Portable dewatering pumps.
- Propane or alcohol stoves.
- Acetylene torches.
- Kerosene heaters.

D.1.b. Enclosed Areas

Personnel can be quickly affected by CO fumes in areas such as closed cockpits or unventilated spaces below decks and under the following conditions:

- Sleeping in a closed cabin while using certain types of catalytic and/or flame producing heaters.
- Working in an engine compartment with the engines operating.
- Working a defective exhaust system has allowed fumes to accumulate in a confined space.

NOTE

When located in a compartment that may be affected by lethal fumes, breathable air may be found near the deck. Crouch or crawl on the deck to reach an exit.

D.1.c. Underway

The boat does not need to be stationary for a problem with CO fumes to occur. For example, a following wind can circulate exhaust gases throughout the cockpit of a slow-moving boat.

The construction of some cockpits or cabins can cause eddies from a wind current to draw fumes back aboard.

D.1.d. Fires

Breathing the by-products of a fire is another source of dangerous fumes. Even a recently extinguished fire is still dangerous. Fires can also create other highly lethal fumes such as cyanide gases. This happens when different types of plastics, upholstery, cushions, or electronics insulation burn.

D.2. Symptoms

Symptoms of lethal fume poisoning can include one or more of the following:

- Throbbing temples.
- Dizziness.
- Ears ringing.
- Watering and itching eyes.
- Headache.
- Cherry-pink skin color.

D.3. Prevention

Crewmembers should always ensure adequate circulation of fresh air throughout the vessel. Minimizing the effect of exhaust fumes on the vessel is key and may be as simple as:

- Making a minor course change.
- Increasing speed.
- Opening a window.
- Cracking open a door, etc.

D.4. Response to Victims

The first senses affected by poisonous gases are those that control a person's judgment and decision-making ability. Once dangerous fumes affect a person, they may not be able to help themselves. The following responses should be conducted as appropriate:

- If CO or any other type of poisoning is suspected, remove the conscious victim to fresh air and get medical help immediately.
- If the victim is unconscious, do not try to assist them alone. Needless casualties occur from people trying to help someone overcome by lethal fumes, only to become victims themselves. See if the victim is responsive by calling out to them. If there is no response, immediately call for assistance and wait in a clean atmosphere until help arrives.

Section E. Noise

Introduction

Any continual noise at the same pitch can distract, lull, or aggravate to the point where it adversely affects temperament and the ability to perform properly.

E.1. Noise as a Fatigue Factor

Loud noise can cause hearing loss and contribute to excessive fatigue. Coxswains should be aware of the effect noise may be having on the crew.

E.2. Noise Management

The following are a few measures to help manage noise:

- Make minor changes to engine speed.
- Adjust radio controls so they produce a minimum amount of static.
- Use single hearing protection whenever noise levels exceed 85 decibels and double hearing protection for noise levels over 104 decibels. (see **Figure 3-1** for decibel scale)

Guidelines for preserving hearing are contained in *Safety and Environmental Health Manual,* COMDTINST M5100.47 (series), and *Medical Manual,* COMDTINST M6000.1 (series).

NOTE Ear protection is required when working in, or making rounds in, an enclosed engineering space.

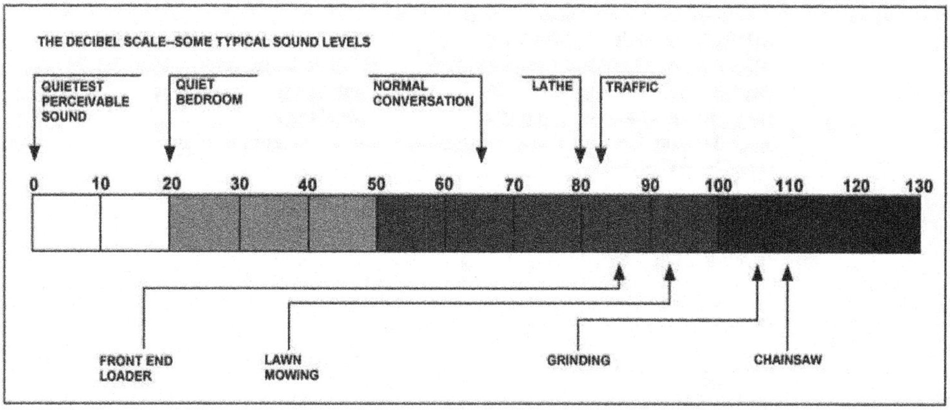

Figure 3-1
Decibel Scale

Section F. Drugs and Alcohol

Introduction

Alcohol and drug use causes slower reaction time, lack of coordination, slurred speech, drowsiness, or an overconfident attitude. Hangovers also cause irritability, drowsiness, sea-sickness, and a lack of concentration. Crewmembers who knowingly get underway for a Coast Guard mission while under the influence are violating Coast Guard policy and put themselves and others at risk.

F.1. Prescription Drugs

Prescription drugs have the ability to adversely affect or incapacitate crewmembers. Certain medications can be as incapacitating as alcohol. In addition, many medications, if taken with alcohol, accentuate the action of both. Crewmembers must always notify the command while taking prescription drugs which may affect performance or prevent performance of duties.

F.2. Alcohol

Alcohol is a well recognized central nervous system depressant. It is one of the most frequently used and abused drugs in our society. Even small amounts of alcohol in the blood can seriously impair judgment, reflexes, muscular control and reduce the restorative effects of sleep.

The level of alcohol in the body varies with the frequency and amount of alcohol intake, the length of time following cessation of drinking and an individual's body weight. A zero alcohol level is essential for boat crew personnel to meet the rigorous demands of boat operations.

Detectable blood alcohol or symptomatic hangovers are causes for restricting boat crew personnel from operations. Although some personnel metabolize alcohol quicker than others, at least eight hours is required for up to two drinks and twelve hours after three or more. This time span allows an adequate margin of safety before resuming operations.

F.3. Tobacco

The nicotine contained in tobacco is a quick-acting poison. Excessive smoking causes depression of the nervous system and impairment of vision. The carbon monoxide resulting from the combustion of tobacco is absorbed by the bloodstream in preference to oxygen, resulting in a lowering of altitude tolerance. Tobacco smoke also irritates the respiratory system.

F.4. Caffeine

The drug caffeine, contained in coffee, tea and many soft drinks, can produce an adverse effect on the body. The amount of caffeine contained in just two cups of coffee appreciably affects the rates of blood-flow and respiration. In small amounts, coffee can be considered a nervous system stimulant. Excessive amounts may produce nervousness, inability to concentrate, headaches, and dizziness. Individuals accustomed to daily intake of caffeine may develop headaches and experience a loss of sharpness if daily intake is stopped or significantly curtailed.

Section G. Cold-Related Factors

Introduction

The purpose of this section is to briefly describe the precautions to take while operating in cold weather. Cold rain, snow, ice storms, and high winds can develop with very little warning in certain parts of the country. Preparation before encountering these kinds of conditions and understanding the effects of cold on personnel safety is vital.

In this section

This section contains the following information:

Effects of Cold Weather

WARNING

> Excessive loss of body heat, which can occur even in mild weather conditions, may lead to hypothermia.

G.1. Operating in a Cold Climate

Operating in a cold climate presents the challenge of keeping warm while effectively carrying out the mission. As the temperature drops or clothing becomes wet, more insulation is required to keep the body from losing its heat.

WARNING

> Prolonged exposure to the wind may lead to hypothermia and/or frostbite.

G.2. Wind

Wind affects body temperature. Those parts of the body exposed directly to the wind will lose heat quickly, a condition commonly referred to as "wind chill." On bare skin, wind will significantly reduce skin temperature, through evaporation, to below the actual air temperature.

G.3. Crew Fatigue

The combination of rough seas, cold temperatures, and wet conditions can quickly cause the crew to become less effective. Crew fatigue will occur more quickly when these conditions are present. Many accidents occur when cold induced fatigue sets in because the mind loses attentiveness and physical coordination diminishes. Even a crew that is moderately cold and damp will exhibit a decrease in reaction time which is also a symptom of the onset of hypothermia.

Hypothermia

G.4. Body Temperature

Hypothermia is the loss of internal body temperature. Normal internal body temperature is 98.6° F (39° C) and is automatically regulated by our bodies to remain very close to this temperature at all times. A minor deviation either up or down interferes with the bodily processes. Being too cold will adversely affect the body. Even a minor loss of internal body temperature may cause incapacitation.

WARNING Never give hypothermia victims anything by mouth, especially alcohol.

G.5. Symptoms

Signs that a person may be suffering from hypothermia include:

- Pale appearance.
- Skin cold to the touch.
- Pupils are dilated and will not adjust properly when exposed to light.
- Poor coordination.
- Slurred speech / appears to be intoxicated.
- Incoherent thinking.
- Unconsciousness.
- Muscle rigidity.
- Weak pulse.
- Very slow and labored breathing.
- Irregular heart beat.

A hypothermic person will tremble and shiver, however, these symptoms may not always be present. When a person stops shivering, their hypothermia may have advanced beyond the initial stages.

G.6. Prevention

Cold and hypothermia affect crew safety and mission performance, and prevention must be a top priority. The Coast Guard outfits its boat crews with hypothermia protective clothing which is designed to prolong their exposure to the elements making them more effective. The clothing must be worn properly and maintained in accordance with its maintenance schedule in order for it to maintain its effectiveness.

G.7. Waivers for Wearing PPE

The Commanding Officer (CO) or Officer-in-Charge (OIC) may waive the requirement for wearing a hypothermia protective device on a case-by-case basis if the degree of risk to hypothermia is minimal, such as in nonhazardous daylight operations in calm water. However, proper PPE must be carried onboard. More detailed information concerning hypothermia protective clothing, requirements for when it should be worn and CO/OIC waiver requirements can be found in the *Rescue and Survival Systems Manual*, COMDTINST M10470.10 (series).

NOTE Units shall carry hypothermia protective devices onboard under waiver conditions (except for ship's boats operating within sight of the ship). Coxswains shall make sure crewmembers don a hypothermia protective device when waiver conditions no longer apply (for example, when they encounter or anticipate heavy weather or hazardous operating conditions).

NOTE Auxiliary boat crews must gain approval and direction from their Operational Commander for waivers.

G.8. Treatment

Treatment for hypothermia is covered in *Chapter 5, First Aid.*

Frostbite

G.9. Development Factors

Frostbite is the development of ice crystals within body tissues. Frostbite is most likely to develop in air temperatures less than 20° F (-6.6° C). The following factors contribute to frostbite development:

- Cold stressors (wind, air temperature, and exposure to water).
- Any restriction of blood-flow.
- Lack of appropriate protection.
- Skin exposure.

G.10. Symptoms

A frostbite victim will complain of painful cold and numbness in the affected area. Waxy white or yellow-white, hard, cold, and insensitive areas will develop. As the area begins to thaw, it will be extremely painful and swelling (reddish-purple) or blisters may appear. Areas prone to frostbite include all extremities where the blood has traveled farthest from the heart, such as the hands, feet, face, and ear lobes. A patient suffering from frostbite should also be treated for hypothermia.

WARNING

Any person who has had frostbite previously is at an increased risk for cold exposure injury in that same area of the body.

G.11. Prevention

Cold weather clothing and equipment is essential to preventing cold-related injuries and fatigue. Such items include thermal boots, woolen socks, watch caps, gloves, and thermal undergarments (polypropylene) made of fleece or pile. During cold conditions, coxswains should discuss the possibilities of frostbite with the crew before getting underway.

Layering Clothing

G.12. First Layer - Wicking

Staying dry is an essential factor to maintaining body temperature. Clothing worn next to the skin must carry or "wick" moisture away from the body. Cotton clothing can pose particular problems. They absorb and retain moisture, which will rob body heat through evaporation. Wool has good insulating properties even when wet, but it is less than ideal because it stays wet. Modern synthetic wicking fibers such as polypropylene do not retain moisture. They will actually draw moisture from the skin and transport it to an absorbent outer layer. This clothing works well by itself, or it can be combined with a second layer for extreme cold.

G.13. Second Layer - Insulation

The insulating effect of a fabric is related to how much air it can trap. This is why a loose-knit or fuzzy material is better than one that is tightly knit. It is also why two thin layers of a given material are better than one thick one. The second layer traps air, which retains body heat, while absorbing excess moisture from the first layer. Wool or cotton thermals are an acceptable second layer if worn over a wicking layer, but a number of synthetic fleece or pile garments do a much better job. An example of this is the fleece coverall.

G.14. Third Layer - Moisture Barrier

The outer layer should stop wind and water, so the inner layers can work as designed. Choices include the anti-exposure coverall, dry suit, or rain gear. The dry suits and rain gear have no insulating properties and will require extra insulation for cold weather. Also, as most dry suits do not "breathe," an absorbent second layer is needed so that perspiration has a place to go.

CH-1

G.15. Extremities

Most heat loss occurs through the extremities, especially the head. It is particularly important to cover these areas well. It is still important to layer properly, but thinner, or all-in-one materials must be used to reduce bulk. For the head, a wool cap may work, but a heavy wicking hood or cap worn alone or under a wool cap will keep you drier and warmer. A rain hat/hood/sou'wester should be considered for wet weather. Gloves should be waterproof, and a wicking liner glove will work better than wool. High top rubber boots are the only option for wet weather. A wicking liner sock under a wool, cotton, or fleece outer sock will provide the best warmth. Insoles should be non-absorbent. A perforated foam insole also works well.

Section H. Sun and Heat-Related Factors

Introduction

Crewmembers must be aware of the dangers of too much exposure to the sun and take preventive measures to guard against a decrease in performance. Intense sunlight and extreme heat can increase crew fatigue and reduce effectiveness. This section discusses the various sun and heat-related factors that crewmembers may encounter during their activities.

NOTE

Detailed treatment information on all heat related injuries can be found in *Chapter 5, First Aid.*

In this Section

This section contains the following information:

Sunburn

H.1. Description

Continuous exposure to the sun can cause sunburn and other complications such as heat stroke, dehydration, etc. Unprotected exposed skin will suffer from premature aging and an increased chance of skin cancer.

H.2. Symptoms

Sunburn appears as redness, swelling, or blistering of the skin. Other effects of overexposure to the sun are fever, gastrointestinal symptoms, malaise, and pigment changes in the skin.

H.3. Prevention

If exposed to the sun for prolonged periods of time, crewmembers must take precautions. Staying in the shade when possible is a start. However, just getting out of direct sunlight is not always enough since sun can be just as harmful when reflected off a bright surface, such as sand or water. Sun-screen lotion with a sun protection factor (SPF) of 15 or higher should be used. Protective clothing such as a hat with a brim and sunglasses with UV protection for eyes should be worn.

NOTE

For additional information on heat related injuries, refer to *Preventive Heat Casualties,* COMDTPUB P6200.12 (series).

H.4. Treatment

Most sunburns do not appear fully until exposure to the sun for several hours. Treatment consists of applying cool wet towels to the affected area. Cooling the skin temperature is very important. Keeping the skin moist but being wary of what product is applied is also essential. Many lotions contain perfumes, alcohol, or wax that will only aggravate the burn. Several types of first aid sprays give fast but short-lived relief.

Dehydration

WARNING

Do not use salt tablets unless prescribed by a physician. The use of salt tablets does not improve well-being despite the amount of perspiration or salt/electrolyte loss.

H.5. Description

An adequate fluid intake is essential to remain hydrated while underway. Fluids are lost from the body in several ways. The most obvious loss is through the kidneys. The less obvious loss of body fluid occurs through perspiration from the skin and respiration through the lungs. As a result, an average, healthy adult requires two or three liters of fluid a day to replace these losses. Extremely warm weather significantly increases the loss of fluids. Staying away from liquids such as tea, alcohol, coffee, and soft drinks is advisable as these liquids speed up fluid loss.

One vital element of body fluids that must be maintained is electrolytes. "Electrolyte" is a medical/scientific term for salts, specifically ions. Electrolytes are important because the body uses them to maintain voltage across cell membranes and to carry electrical impulses for moving the muscles. The body loses electrolytes mostly through perspiration. In most cases, a normal diet and drinking plenty of fluids will maintain an adequate electrolyte level.

H.6. Symptoms

Healthy adults must satisfy their water and electrolyte requirements. When water and electrolytes are not replaced, the body experiences dehydration. Drinking alcohol and caffeine increases dehydration. At first there is thirst and general discomfort, followed by an inclination to slow physical movement, and a loss of appetite. As more water is lost, an individual becomes sleepy and experiences a rise in body temperature. By the time the body loses 5% of body weight in fluids, the individual begins to feel nauseated. When 6 to 10% of body fluids are lost, symptoms increase in this order:

- Dry mouth.
- Dizziness.
- Headache.
- Difficulty in breathing.
- Tingling in the arms and legs.
- Skin color turns bluish.
- Indistinct speech.
- Inability to walk.
- Cramping legs and stomach.

H.7. Prevention

Drinking fresh clean water is the best and easiest method to replace fluid loss and prevent dehydration. Almost all fluids are suitable including fruit juices, soups, and water. Drinks that do not contain sodium (salt) are recommended. Crewmembers should drink plenty of fluids throughout the day, especially in warm, dry climates. Taking along an ample supply of water is a must during prolonged periods away from a water source.

WARNING

Never force fluid by mouth to a person who is unconscious or semiconscious.

H.8. Treatment

The signs of dehydration can be subtle and therefore, crewmembers should be particularly watchful of each other under extreme conditions of sun and heat. The crew should be encouraged to drink fluids throughout the mission. Rotating crews between tasks where they are exposed to the sun and shade will help prevent dehydration. If a crewmember becomes dehydrated, the person should be immediately removed from further exposure to heat and/or sun and should receive prompt medical attention. Mild dehydration cases will become serious if the level of activity and environmental conditions do not change.

Heat Rash (Prickly Heat)

H.9. Description

Heat rash is prevalent among those living and working in warm, humid climates or in hot spaces ashore or aboard boats. It may occur in cool weather if a person overdresses.

H.10. Symptoms

Heat rash is caused by:

- Breakdown of the body's ability to perspire.
- Decreased evaporative cooling of the skin.

Heat rash interferes with sleep, resulting in decreased efficiency and increased cumulative fatigue, making the individual susceptible to more serious heat disorders. Heat rash also accelerates the onset of heat stroke. Symptoms are:

- Pink or red minute lesions.
- Skin irritation (prickling).
- Frequent, severe itching.

H.11. Prevention

Coxswains and crewmembers must be aware of negative effects brought on by heat rash, and be alert for symptoms when operating in a hot environment. Rotating crews between heat-related tasks and those jobs in a cooler environment would help prevent heat rash from occurring.

H.12. Treatment

If heat rash occurs, the crewmember should be removed from further exposure to excessive heat immediately. Positive action should be taken to prevent the onset of more serious disorders. Cool, wet towels should be applied to the affected areas.

Heat Cramps

H.13. Description

Heat cramps are painful contractions caused by excessive salt and water depletion. Heat cramps may occur as an isolated occurrence with normal body temperature or during heat exhaustion. Recently stressed muscles are prone to heat cramps, particularly those muscles in the extremities and abdomen.

H.14. Symptoms

The victim's legs will be drawn up into the fetal position and excessive sweating will occur. The victim may grimace and cry out in pain.

H.15. Prevention The guidelines discussed previously for other heat-related illnesses should be followed.

H.16. Treatment Heat cramps can be treated by placing the victim in a cool place and encouraging the victim to lie down in a comfortable position. Cool drinks should be offered to replace fluid loss. Solutions containing electrolytes, like a sports drink, are also useful, however, the ingestion of excessive salt should not be allowed. Cramped muscles must not be treated with heat packs or massage. Prompt medical assistance is recommended for severe or persistent conditions.

Heat Exhaustion

H.17. Description Heat exhaustion typically occurs when people exercise heavily or work in a warm, humid environment where body fluids are lost through heavy sweating. Fluid loss can result in a decrease of blood-flow to vital organs. In heat exhaustion, sweat does not evaporate as it should, possibly because of high humidity or too many layers of clothing. As a result, the body is not cooled effectively.

H.18. Symptoms When suffering from heat exhaustion, a person collapses and sweats profusely. The victim has pale skin, a pounding heart, nausea, headache, and acts restless.

H.19. Prevention The guidelines discussed previously for other heat-related illnesses should be followed.

H.20. Treatment First aid treatment should be provided immediately followed by rapid removal (in a litter, if possible) of the patient to a location that can provide proper medical care.

Heat Stroke

H.21. Description Heat stroke is a major medical emergency and results from the complete breakdown of the body's sweating and heat regulatory mechanisms. Heat stroke or "sun stroke" is caused by operating in bright sun or working in a hot environment, such as an engine compartment. The onset of heat stroke is very rapid.

H.22. Symptoms The major symptoms of heat stroke are:

- Red skin, hot and dry to the touch (cessation of sweating).
- Characteristic body temperature above 105° F (40.5° C).
- Headache.
- Weak and rapid pulse.
- Confusion, violence, lack of coordination, delirium, and/or unconsciousness.
- Brain damage (if immediate medical treatment is not given).

H.23. Prevention The guidelines discussed previously for other heat-related illnesses should be followed.

WARNING No matter which type of operation or assigned mission is being conducted, all incidents of heat stroke must be considered as medical emergencies.

H.24. Treatment Heat stroke is the most serious of all heat disorders and is an immediate threat to life. There is a high mortality rate associated with heat stroke. It is important to remember that heat exhaustion is the result of overloaded heat balance mechanisms that are still functioning. Heat stroke strikes the victim when the thermo-regulatory mechanisms are not functioning, and the main avenue of heat loss, evaporation of sweat, is blocked. The patient must be treated immediately, or death may occur. It is best to carefully remove the victim to a cooler environment and seek medical assistance.

Susceptibility to Heat Problems

H.25. Description Personnel who are not accustomed to strenuous physical activity in hot and humid environments are particularly susceptible to heat injuries. Excess body weight contributes to this susceptibility.

H.26. Clothing and Equipment Impermeable clothing does not "breath" and thus greatly increases an individual's susceptibility to heat-related illnesses. Clothing acts as a barrier that prevents evaporative cooling. Many synthetic fabrics reduce the absorption and dispersal of sweat needed to achieve optimum heat loss by evaporation.

Clothing and equipment should be worn so that there is free circulation of air between the uniform and the body surface. Wearing shirt collars, shirt cuffs, and trouser bottoms open will aid in ventilation. However, this practice may not be permissible in those areas where loose fitting or open style clothing would present a safety hazard (e.g., around machinery with moving parts).

In full sunlight or a high radiant heat source (e.g., machinery spaces), keeping the body covered with permeable clothing reduces the radiant heat load upon the body. When not working in these areas, removal of the outer layer of clothing will help reduce body temperature. Impermeable clothing must be avoided. If impermeable clothing must be worn, precautions should be taken to avoid the rapid buildup of body heat. Heat illnesses may be manifested in minutes if impermeable clothing is worn.

H.27. Fever Febrile illnesses (fever) increase the chance of rapid heat buildup within the body. The presence of fever before heat stress exposure reduces the allowable exposure times.

H.28. Fatigue Cumulative fatigue may develop slowly. Failure to recognize this slow development increases an individual's susceptibility to heat-related problems.

H.29. Prior Heat Illnesses Prior heat illnesses lead to heat illnesses of greater severity with each incidence. There are two major preventive measures:

- Water.
- Salt.

H.29.a. Water The body needs water only in quantities sufficient to prevent dehydration and electrolyte imbalances that result from losses in sweat, urine, etc. Under conditions of profuse sweating, each person will require one pint (0.5 liters) or more of fluid intake per hour. Water should be taken in small quantities at frequent intervals, such as every 20 or 30 minutes.

H.29.b. Salt

The average diet provides from 15 - 20 grams of salt daily. This amount of salt is adequate for the prevention of most heat-related illnesses.

This page intentionally left blank.

Chapter 4
Team Coordination and Risk Management

Introduction

This chapter addresses human error and risk based decision-making. Both greatly affect the safety of boat operations. Human error has been and continues to be a significant cause of boat mishaps. Ineffective risk management has placed many boats and crews at greater risk than necessary. Technical knowledge and skill alone cannot prevent mishaps. It also takes teamwork that recognizes, minimizes, and corrects human errors and a systematic process to continuously assess and manage safety risks.

Prudent seamen have exhibited and human factors researchers have described seven critical skills that reduce the potential for human error-induced mishaps (see *Section A* of this chapter). Within these skills are important processes that serve to control safety risks and improve team performance. These critical skills are collectively titled "Team Coordination". The processes are risk management, crew briefing, and crew debriefing.

This chapter mandates the use of team coordination, risk management, crew briefing, and crew debriefing as part of standard boat operations. It describes the skills, performance standards, coxswain responsibilities and training requirements for each. It also describes the risk management, crew briefing and crew debriefing processes. To promote these skills and processes, performance in team coordination shall be assessed as part of crew debriefings, ready for operations (RFO) inspections, and Standardization Team visits.

NOTE

Additional information concerning team coordination and risk management can be found within *Team Coordination Training*, COMDTINST 1541.1 (series), *Operational Risk Management*, COMDTINST 3500.3, and *Risk-Based Decision-Making*, COMDTINST 16010.3.

In this chapter

This chapter contains the following sections:

Section A. Team Coordination

Introduction

A team is a collection of people that uses the technical abilities of its members to achieve a common mission. This section discusses how team coordination can:

- Control human error.
- Manage safety risks.
- Provide directions for continuous improvement in team performance.

A.1. Members of the Team

The boat crew consisting of the coxswain and crewmembers is a team. But it also is a part of a larger team. Boat crews seldom perform missions without interacting with other people. Members of this larger team are:

- The mission coordinator (the OIC or duty officer).
- Other assigned Coast Guard assets (aircraft, boats, and cutters).
- Other government, commercial and private parties (federal, state, and local officials).
- Commercial salvagers and Good Samaritans.
- The "customer".

In this case, the customer is the person or vessel which is the focus of the mission. The mission is the reason for getting the boat underway.

A.2. Coxswain

The coxswain wears two hats as:

- The person in charge of the boat team.
- A member of the larger team.

Because the majority of boat missions have inherent safety risks, effective coordination of the boat team and the larger team is a cornerstone for mishap prevention.

A.3. Team Coordination Skills

Proper use of team coordination tools requires team members, coxswain, and boat crew to routinely use all seven team coordination skills all the time. The skills are the good habits of exemplary leaders. They have been tested within complex missions, under ever changing conditions, and when crew stress and safety risks were high. Like the navigational rules of the road, when team coordination and risk management is properly used, an adequate safety margin for mission operations can be maintained.

The seven team coordination skills are:

Skill	Description
Leadership	• Directing and guiding the activities on the boat. • Stimulating the crew to work together as a team. • Providing feedback to the crew regarding their performance.
Mission Analysis	• Making plans. • Managing risks. • Organizing and briefing the crew. • Assigning tasks. • Monitoring mission effectiveness, including debriefing the crew.
Adaptability and Flexibility	• Altering a course or action to meet changing demands. • Managing stress, workload and fatigue to maintain an optimal performance level. • Working effectively with others.
Situation Awareness	Knowing at all times what is happening to: • the boat, • the coxswain and crew, and • the mission.
Decision-Making	Applying logical and sound judgment based on the available information.
Communication	Clearly and accurately sending and acknowledging information, instructions and commands, as well as providing useful feedback.
Assertiveness	• Actively participating in problem-solving, by stating and maintaining a position until convinced by the facts that this position is wrong. • Speaking up and/or taking action when appropriate

Section B. Team Coordination Standards

Introduction

Team coordination standards identify expected behaviors among the mission coordinator, coxswain, and crew necessary to affect safe mission performance. These standards represent the expected performance in all missions.

Coxswain responsibilities represent the minimum required actions of a coxswain to achieve team coordination and risk management. These standards and responsibilities shall be evaluated as part of crew debriefings, RFO inspections, and Standardization Team visits.

In this section

This section contains the following information:

Leadership Standard

B.1. Boat Crew Responsibilities

The following points outline the standards of leadership for a boat crew team:

- The boat crew respects each other. The climate is an open one, where the crew is free to talk and ask questions about the mission.
- Regardless of assigned duties, the individual with the most information about the situation-at-hand is allowed to participate in mission decisions.
- When disagreements arise, the coxswain and crew directly confront the issues over which the disagreements began.
- The primary focus is on solutions to problems. The solutions are generally seen as reasonable. Problem resolution ends on a positive note with very little grumbling among the coxswain and crew.

B.2. Coxswain Responsibilities

The coxswain shall:

- Be in charge and give clear and understandable direction to the boat crew.
- Monitor crew safety and progress. If unable to monitor safety, shall designate a safety observer.
- Balance and monitor crew workload and manage crew stress.
- Remain approachable and open to ideas and suggestions.
- Update the crew on significant mission changes.
- Provide to the crew timely, constructive feedback on performance.
- Provide to the mission coordinator timely updates on boat status.

Mission Analysis Standard

B.3. Boat Crew Responsibilities

The following procedures outline the standards of mission analysis:

Step	Procedure
1	The mission coordinator, coxswain, and crew know the mission objective.
2	The mission coordinator and coxswain discuss a plan for the mission.
3	Potential problems are briefly discussed.
4	Time is taken to: • Assess risks. • Eliminate unnecessary risks. • Reduce unacceptable risks.
5	The crew is briefed on the plan and may provide suggestions.
6	Mission tasks are assigned to specific individuals.
7	Contingency planning is accomplished by the mission coordinator and coxswain.
8	As additional information becomes available, the plan is updated.
9	Some discussion takes place to clarify actions in the event of unexpected problems.
10	The coxswain reviews crew actions and conducts a debriefing of the mission.
11	Strengths and weaknesses are identified; remedial actions are assigned to improve future performance.

B.4. Coxswain Responsibilities

The coxswain shall:

- Discuss mission objectives and hazards with the mission coordinator as part of planning before getting underway. Understand level of risk that the mission has and how much risk the coxswain is authorized to take.
- Take no unnecessary risks and have contingencies to deal with unacceptable risks.
- Brief the crew on mission objectives and the plan. Permit open discussion to ensure that tasks are understood and crew ideas are considered.
- Update plans based on changes in the situation and/or mission objectives.
- Debrief the crew on mission performance; identify areas for improvement.

Adaptability and Flexibility Standard

B.5. Boat Crew Responsibilities

The following points outline the standards of adaptability and flexibility for a boat crew team:

- Most distractions are avoided. The crew polices each other for fixation; takes positive action to regain situation awareness.
- The coxswain can decide what information and activities are mission essential. Most nonessential information is set aside.
- Crew tasks are prioritized to ensure safe performance. The boat crew is aware of each other's workload. When a crewmember appears overloaded, the workload is redistributed.
- The mission coordinator and coxswain are alert to possible crew fatigue, complacency, or high stress.

B.6. Coxswain Responsibilities

The coxswain shall:

- Remain aware of own stress and own hazardous thought patterns. Take positive action to counter subconscious tendencies to react to the excitement of the moment or arbitrarily discard information that conflicts with own perceptions.
- Implement cross-checks of coxswain and crew actions to combat the affects of fatigue for night missions or those that extend time awake beyond 18 hours.
- Remain alert to the effects of complacency and high stress on the crew. Take positive action to manage crew stress.
- Remain alert to work overload within the crew, and redistribute work as necessary.
- Notify the mission coordinator if the physiological condition of the crew becomes a safety concern.

Situation Awareness Standard

B.7. Boat Crew Responsibilities

The following procedures outline the standards of situation awareness for a boat crew team:

Step	Procedure
1	The coxswain provides the mission coordinator and the crew with mission status (e.g., current operations and/or perceived location).
2	Changes to situation awareness are verbalized.
3	The crew or mission coordinator recognizes that a risk decision or action must be made and offers suggestions or information to the coxswain. The mission coordinator serves as a check of the coxswain's risk decisions.
4	If the mission coordinator perceives the boat or crew is taking unacceptable risks, positive action is taken to control the situation (e.g., stopping or slowing boat activities and/or providing additional assets).
5	The boat crew checks each other's task performance for errors. Anyone who makes a mistake is informed and makes needed corrections.
6	The coxswain maintains an effective lookout.

B.8. Coxswain Responsibilities

The coxswain shall:

- Not get underway without an understanding of the mission objective, the known risks, and a plan of action.
- Ensure that the crew understands the mission plan and assigned tasks.
- Remain alert to mistakes in planning and crew errors. Likewise, empower the crew to double-check the coxswain's decisions and actions.
- Remain vigilant to changes in the situation. Remain alert to conflicting or ambiguous information that may indicate that the perceived situation is different than the actual one.
- Periodically update the mission coordinator and the crew as to the perceived situation.

Decision-Making Standard

B.9. Boat Crew Responsibilities

The following points outline the standards of decision-making for a boat crew team:

- Coxswain decisions reflect a willingness to use available information from all sources.
- Most decisions are timely, but may be affected by stress.
- Most decisions are appropriate for the situation; however, the crew may overlook options or discount risk.
- The boat crew does not exhibit hazardous thought patterns (e.g., anti-authority, invincibility, impulsiveness, machismo, or resignation).
- Before the coxswain decides and implements a change in objective, the situation may worsen; however, mission accomplishment is not affected and no loss occurs.

B.10. Coxswain Responsibilities

The coxswain shall:

- Assess current situation and available information to determine ability to meet mission objectives.
- Make use of available time to develop contingencies or alternative courses of actions.
- Consciously weigh the risks versus the gains. Implement the best contingency or action to address the situation.
- Monitor the situation to ensure the decision produces the desired outcome.

Communication Standard

B.11. Boat Crew Responsibilities

The following points outline the standards of communication for a boat crew team:

- The boat crew and mission coordinator communicate about the mission as required. Standard terminology is used.
- Receivers acknowledge messages. Receivers ask questions when they do not understand.
- Senders usually pursue confirmation when no response is forthcoming and the message is important.
- When changes to crew tasks occur, all hands are aware. The coxswain states risk decisions to the mission coordinator and crew and, as time permits, informs the crew of the reasons and any adjustments they have to make.
- The mission coordinator and crew acknowledges their awareness of the risk decisions. Anyone may ask mission-related questions to clarify information.

B.12. Coxswain Responsibilities

The coxswain shall:

- Use standard terminology in giving commands to the crew and in conducting external communications.
- Ensure that information and orders conveyed to the crew are acknowledged by the intended receiver.
- Communicate intentions associated with risks to the mission coordinator and the crew.

Assertiveness Standard

B.13. Boat Crew Responsibilities

The following points outline the standards of assertiveness for a boat crew team:

- The mission coordinator, coxswain and/or crew occasionally raise questions about the plan or actions when they are either in doubt, or when they believe the boat is standing in danger. Most of these questions are relevant to risk decision-making.
- The coxswain alerts the crew or mission coordinator when input is needed to make risk decisions.
- The crew or mission coordinator responds to the coxswain's request with pertinent, brief, and timely information. Everyone remains open to questions about the mission.
- Suggestions are listened to without criticism.
- Requests for task assistance are made when overloaded.

B.14. Coxswain Responsibilities

The coxswain shall:

- Speak up when an error or poor judgment is perceived.
- Notify the mission coordinator when the coxswain perceives
  - Level of risk has changed.
  - Mission is beyond the capabilities of the boat.
  - Crew has become overloaded or overly fatigued.
- Encourage input and feedback from the crew.
- Treat questions and concerns of the crew with respect.

Section C. Risk Management Process

Introduction

Risk management shall be performed during the planning and execution of missions. Risk management is an element of the mission analysis skill and is a process to identify and control unacceptable safety risks. Every mission event (getting underway, transit, on-scene operations, and mooring) has some level of risk and not all of the risks are known. Every event requires that risks are kept within controls (safeguards) that have been designed to handle them.

Examples of these controls include the proper use of installed communications and navigation systems and proper execution of operating procedures. Effective risk management is highly dependent upon technical knowledge and experience.

C.1. Four Rules of Risk Management

To use the risk management process correctly, the team must follow four rules.

C.1.a. Rule #1

Integrate risk management into mission planning and execution.

- Risk management is a repetitive and continuous process.
- Risk management is most effective when it is proactive. It requires that when new information on risks is received, the ability to control those risks is reviewed. It requires the coxswain and crew to remain vigilant and think safely until the boat is secured and the mission is over.

C.1.b. Rule #2

Accept no unnecessary risks.

- Unnecessary risk does not contribute to the safe accomplishment of the mission. It is operating beyond the known capabilities of the crew and/or boat without considering other alternatives.
- Unnecessary risks are often taken when decision-makers rationalize that the boat is the only alternative or that urgency is more important than safety.
- Unnecessary risk taking constitutes gambling with lives and government/private property.

C.1.c. Rule #3

Make risk decisions at the appropriate level. Many times mishaps occur because the level of risk is not perceived by an individual.

- Understanding of risk is highly dependent upon technical knowledge and expertise. Therefore, risk decisions must be made by clear-thinking, technically competent people with an understanding of the situation.
- The mission coordinator and coxswain should work as a team in making risk decisions.

C.1.d. Rule #4

Accept risks if benefits outweigh costs. Eliminating unnecessary risk leaves risk that is either acceptable or unacceptable for mission accomplishment.

- He/she who owns the mission owns the risk.
- In some cases, mission directives outline what is acceptable (like sustaining personnel injury and equipment damage to save lives). However, in high stress situations, the line between acceptable and unacceptable may become fuzzy.
- Again, clear-thinking, technically competent people with an understanding of the situation must be involved in the risk decision.
- Again, the mission coordinator and coxswain should work as a team in making risk versus gain decisions.

C.2. Risk Management Process

Continuous risk management during the course of boat operations requires cycling through the following seven steps.

C.2.a. Step 1

Define the mission objective and tasks.

C.2.b. Step 2

Identify possible hazards to the boat and the crew. Hazards include anything that could go wrong with the equipment, the environment, or the team.

- Equipment: Is the equipment functioning properly and can it be expected to function properly throughout the mission?
- Environment: How will the weather, sea conditions, proximity to shoals, vessel traffic, and available light affect the mission?
- People: Is the team properly trained and capable of handling the demands of the mission? Are they fatigued, complacent, or suffering from physical or mental stress?

To ensure that few hazards are missed, they must be discussed within the crew and between the coxswain and mission coordinator. The following risk categories should be used to facilitate discussion:

Risk Category	Description
Planning	Is there adequate time and information to develop a good plan? As the planning time increases and more information becomes available, the risk is reduced. As mission complexity increases, the time for planning should also increase.
Event Complexity	The mission is made up of a chain of events. How complex are these events? Do they require significant know-how to perform? Many routine events are complex. As the event requires more know-how and attention to perform correctly, the possibility that something could go wrong increases. Event complexity can be greatly increased by darkness, which in turn increases risk.
Asset Selection	Is the boat and this coxswain and crew best suited to perform this mission? Is the ready boat the right boat? The capability and readiness condition of the boat along with the qualifications, experience, and physiological condition (health and alertness) of the coxswain and crew must be compared to the event complexity and environmental conditions

Risk Category	Description
Communications and Supervision	• External c3ommunications and supervision - Will the boat be able to maintain good communications with the mission coordinator and other on-scene units? Will the mission coordinator be able to provide real-time oversight of boat activities as a double-check for safety? The less capable the communications, the higher the possibility that relevant information will not reach decision-makers. Risk control may be less effective, double-checks will be more difficult. • Communications within the boat - Can the crew hear orders over the ambient noise? Are they assertively communicating through accurate, bold, and concise statements? • Supervision of the boat crew - Even if the boat crew is qualified to perform tasks, supervision by the coxswain can act as a control to further minimize risk. The higher the safety risk, the more the coxswain needs to be focused on observing and checking. When coxswains are actively involved in doing tasks, they can be easily distracted and should not be considered effective safety observers in moderate to high risk conditions.
Environmental Conditions	• Are the current and forecasted conditions, in transit and on-scene, within the capability of the boat and the crew? As the environment changes, risk controls need to be updated.

C.2.c. Step 3

Risk is a function of severity, probability and exposure.

- Severity describes the potential loss. Should something go wrong, what would be the injury to personnel or damage to equipment.
- Probability is the likelihood that the consequences described above will happen.
- Exposure is the amount of time people or equipment will be exposed to the hazard.

Each risk category must be examined in terms of severity, probability, and exposure to arrive at a subjective rating of risk. Again, it is useful to discuss individual perceptions of risk among the crew and between the coxswain and mission coordinator.

Risk Category	Description
High Risk	• Risks cannot be managed with constant control. • Loss in terms of personnel injury or equipment damage is expected. • The boat and/or crew is operating beyond their capability. • Whether this risk is acceptable or not is dependent upon the mission objective. • High risk must be communicated to the mission coordinator. • An example is entering the surf zone with a utility boat.
Medium Risk	• Risks are manageable with constant control. • Loss is not expected if the situation remains stable, the crew adheres to all standard operating procedures, and boat systems respond as designed. • The boat and/or crew are operating at their capability.
Low Risk	• Risks are manageable with control as required. • Loss is not expected because the mission has established margins of safety in place and the objective will be modified if the margins are reduced. • The boat and/or crew are operating within their capability. • An example is transit of a familiar area at a safe speed, during the day, in good visibility, with a full, qualified crew aboard.

C.2.d. Step 4

Unnecessary risk has to be eliminated. What changes can be made to reduce risks to an acceptable level without changing the mission objective? This can be done by examining:

- Changes to the planned optempo (ex. slowing).
- Command and control (ex. more guidance and/or supervision).
- Mission tasks (ex. simplifying).
- Timing of tasks (ex. sequential vice concurrent or daylight vice nighttime).
- Boat requirements (ex. more capable) or crew qualifications (ex. more experienced).
- Number of assigned boats (ex. standby) and/or crew (ex. additional members).
- Required equipment and/or protective equipment.

If the discussion of options is limited to those that can be provided by the boat, few are available. This step needs to evaluate the options the larger team can recommend to reduce risk. The larger team may have additional resources. The larger team may be able to spread out the risk among responders or transfer the risk to more capable assets.

C.2.e. Step 5

Did the mission coordinator validate that the risk assumed by the coxswain is worth the mission objective? If risks seem unacceptable, can the mission objective be modified to reduce risk to an acceptable level?

C.2.f. Step 6

This decision implements the best option given the risks and gains. In executing the decision, the crew is made aware of what the expected outcome should be.

C.2.g. Step 7

Did the action achieve the desired outcome? Are the risks within the mission changing? If so, repeat the steps to manage those risks.

Section D. Informal Crew Briefing and Debriefing

Introduction

Informal crew briefings are required before the boat gets underway. Briefings for the coxswain and the crew help create a shared mental picture of what is expected to happen and strives to set rules for the mission.

Informal crew debriefings should be performed after most missions. The debriefing is the best opportunity to evaluate performance and recognize individual and team accomplishment. When correctly performed, the debriefing can serve as a valuable tool for continuous improvement. It can show the way from just 'doing things right' to knowing how to do "right things right".

WARNING

The wearing of jewelry, including rings, wristwatches, necklaces or other items not consisting of organizational clothing, PPE, or uniform articles by boat crew members engaged in hoisting, towing, or other deck evolutions where the potential for snagging exists **is prohibited**. OICs and coxswains will address this during all pre-underway briefs and coxswains shall ensure jewelry is removed prior to beginning all deck evolutions.

D.1. Informal Crew Briefing

The informal crew briefing shall be comprised of the following topics:

- Mission objective.
- Duties and responsibilities.
- Positive climate for teamwork.
- Improvement goals.

D.1.a. Mission Objective

Include the mission objective, known information and risks regarding the mission, and the planned course of action.

D.1.b. Duties and Responsibilities

Be specific in assigning duties and responsibilities. Mission coordinator expectations should be understood by the coxswain and conveyed to the crew. Do not let the crew have to second guess what needs to be done, or in special situations, how it should be done.

D.1.c. Positive Climate for Teamwork

Establish a positive climate for teamwork. The crew is encouraged to double-check each other, point out errors, speak up when they have relevant information, and ask questions when they do not understand.

D.1.d. Improvement Goals

Restate the goal for improving one or two weak areas in crew coordination. This goal was generated from a previous crew debriefing. Try to be as specific as possible in describing what is considered an improvement.

D.2. Informal Crew Debriefing

The informal crew debriefing shall cover the following topics:

- Major events.
- Level of performance.
- Outcome of events.
- Evaluation of goals.
- Establishment of goals.

D.2.a. Major Events

Recap major events of the mission (e.g., preparations, transit, on-scene operations).

D.2.b. Level of Performance

Determine level of performance within key events. Key events include the following:

- Crew briefing.
- Critical navigation segments of the transit.
- Bar crossings.
- Approaches to vessels.
- Personnel transfers.
- Other hazardous parts of the assigned mission.

D.2.c. Outcome of Events

Have the coxswain and crew, and when possible the command, discuss what human behavior or risk decisions affected the outcome in these events. This discussion is for professional growth and learning.

D.2.d. Evaluation of Goals

Determine if the goal to improve one or two weak coordination areas has been met.

D.2.e. Establishment of Goals

Set, change, or affirm a specific goal for improving one or two weak areas in crew coordination. Goals are set or changed with the knowledge and guidance of the command.

Chapter 5
First Aid

Introduction

This chapter provides basic first aid and transporting information for injuries encountered in the marine environment. First aid is doing what must be done before expert help is available. It may include:

- Providing immediate temporary assistance.
- Saving life.
- Preventing further injury or unfavorable progression.
- Preserving vitality and resistance to infection.
- Delivering the victim if necessary.

In this chapter

This chapter contains the following sections:

Section A. Crewmembers' Roles

Introduction

Proper knowledge and skill in first aid are essential for boat crewmembers. A well-trained crew that responds effectively and professionally to an emergency situation may be the difference between life and death or temporary injury and disability of the victim.

A.1. Responsibilities

The Coast Guard authorizes crewmembers to render first aid, consistent with their training, in their role as emergency assistants regardless of their first aid qualifications. A Unit Commander should always be advised of emergency medical situations. In addition, crewmembers must contact the Station or Group watchstander and request immediate medical assistance for serious injury cases so that appropriate medical resources can be contacted. The Station or Group will activate an established Emergency Medical Services (EMS) system such as 911, or local fire/rescue squad. Crewmembers providing first aid must do the following:

- Evaluate the scene.
- Consider whether or not the rescuers are trained and equipped to safely render assistance.
- Protect themselves from injury or infection.
- Keep calm.
- Act quickly.
- Call Station or Group as appropriate to activate EMS if necessary.

A.1.a. Scene Assessment

When responding, a quick survey of the scene is performed. An unsafe scene should not be entered until the crew is fully prepared and protected against hazards such as exposed live electrical wires, toxic vapors, fire, blood, or body fluids. As rescuers, it's important for the area around the injured to be safe before attempting first aid. Rescuer injury while administering first aid will only complicate an already difficult situation.

A.1.b. Initial Patient Assessment

Crewmembers should stop and assess the overall condition of the victim, and determine whether or not assisting the patient with the resources at hand is possible or if it requires further help. When more definitive care is required for more serious injury cases, assistance should be sought immediately by calling for help and activating the local EMS system. The following information is important to notice during an initial assessment:

- Number of patients.
- General condition of patient(s).
- Mechanism (type) of injury.
- Patient(s) level of consciousness.
- Causes or symptoms of shock:
  - Mechanisms consistent with a serious injury such as a gun shot wound, fall from a great height, major burn, crushing accident, etc.
  - If the patient's state-of-health has been compromised, for example, prolonged exposure to the elements, dehydration, malnourishment, etc.

NOTE

In this section, serious injury cases are considered those that need attention from a medical professional. A serious case also may be one in which the crew decides the injury is beyond its medical capabilities.

WARNING

Unprotected crewmembers, who come in direct contact with human blood, should immediately report each incident to their Operational Commander's servicing medical facility and follow professional medical advice. Refer to *Prevention of Bloodborne Pathogen Transmission*, COMDTINST M6220.8 (series) for more information.

A.1.c. Protective Devices

Human blood may contain bloodborne pathogens such as Hepatitis B virus and HIV which causes Hepatitis B and AIDS, respectively. Crewmembers should take all reasonable precautions to prevent direct contact with human blood by wearing PPE such as clean disposable gloves or more complete equipment depending on the degree of contamination before making contact with the patient. Coast Guard boats and Stations are equipped with biohazardous bodily fluid PPE mass casualty response kits. If available, masks and eye protection should be worn in any instance of known or suspected respiratory infection (i.e., TB). Blood-soaked gloves and other material should be disposed of with great care. A medical clinic or emergency room can be contacted for disposal advice. Coast Guard units should maintain information on medical waste disposal.

A.2. Handling and Transporting of Injured

Transporting injured persons aboard boats to medical treatment facilities is a serious problem regularly encountered by boat crewmembers. In many situations, it is difficult, if not impossible, for medical help to reach victims. Therefore, the boat crew must possess a basic knowledge of how to transport injured persons safely and quickly to a location where appropriate medical treatment is available.

A.2.a. Coxswain Duty

The sooner a victim arrives at a place where medical attention is available, the better. It is the responsibility of the coxswain and crew to safely transport the victim as rapidly as possible, while preventing further injury, shock, or unnecessary pain.

A.2.b. Moving a Patient

Moving a patient is precise work and any carelessness is unacceptable. It requires close teamwork and great care. Even procedures that may seem simple and obvious, such as placing a patient on a stretcher, demand training, coordination, and skill.

These are important rules to remember when transporting an injured person:

- Notify Station so that appropriate medical resources can be activated.
- If possible, avoid moving the patient until that person is examined and all injuries are protected by properly applied splints, dressing, etc.
- If head or neck injury is suspected, immobilize prior to movement.
- Seek assistance before moving a patient.
- For conscious patients, always explain the move procedure in advance.
- Patient movements should be careful, deliberate, and the minimum required.
- Almost all patients are transported laying down.

Section B. Treatment for Shock

Introduction

Shock can be effectively reduced or eliminated if proper steps are taken. It is important that crewmembers understand how to identify and treat shock. It may accompany injury and can reduce a victim's ability to deal with and survive serious injuries. Shock by itself, even when no injuries are involved, can be very serious and life threatening. Crewmembers must be aware of the events and symptoms that cause shock.

In this section

This section contains the following information:

Shock Syndrome

B.1. Description

Shock is a depressed physiological or mental state. Shock syndrome, a set of symptoms which occur together, can change throughout treating an injury and are unique for every casualty. Signs and symptoms may develop rapidly or be delayed for up to several hours after the apparent cause. The symptoms usually precede the signs. Several types of shock exist, therefore, recognizing and treating shock immediately is important. Some syndromes do not appear in every casualty nor are they equally noticeable.

NOTE

Shock can occur at anytime during first aid and should be assessed first and monitored throughout treatment.

B.2. Causes

Some events that typically cause shock are:

- Trauma (bleeding, blunt (e.g., a fall, being struck by a blunt object, etc.), fractures, and burns).
- Allergic reactions.
- Hypothermia.
- Drugs.
- Toxins.
- Heart attack.
- Illnesses such as diabetes.
- Emotional.

B.3. Symptoms

Symptoms include:

- Restlessness.
- Fainting.
- Thirst.
- Nausea.
- Weakness.
- Anxiousness.
- Fright.
- Dizziness.

Signs include:

- Pulse - weak and rapid.
- Breathing - shallow, rapid, and irregular.
- Skin - cold, clammy (sweating).
- Pupils – dilated.
- State of consciousness - alert (may be deceiving) to unconscious.

B.4. Assessment

Strong signs and symptoms of shock can be identified by skin color, pulse rate, monitoring respiration, and a victim's level of consciousness. The following table describes the strong signs of shock.

Area	Normal	Signs of Shock
Skin color	Adult skin is normally dry, not excessively pale or wet to the touch.	A person in shock may have pale looking skin that is cold and clammy to the touch.
Eyes	Responsive to movement and light conditions.	Pupils appear to be dilated.
Pulse	Normal pulse for an adult is regular, strong, and between 60-100 beats per minute.	A shock patient will appear restless, and has a pulse that feels weak and is more rapid than normal, usually greater than 100 beats per minute.
Respiration	Normal adult respiration is between 16-24 breaths per minute.	A strong indicator of respiratory distress would be less than 16 breaths per minute, rapid and irregular, or greater than 24 breaths per minute. Immediate assistance is required in these instances to avoid respiratory arrest.
Consciousness	Any time a patient's level of consciousness is other than fully alert, it is a serious indication to seek medical assistance immediately.	Person can appear anywhere from alert (may be deceiving) to unconscious.

B.5. Treatment

To properly treat shock once it has been identified, boat crewmembers must administer initial treatment, followed by executing steps to ensure the effects of shock are kept at a minimum.

B.5.a. Initial Treatment

Initial treatment for shock includes limiting a patient's activity, ideally having the person lie down and remain alert for the signs and symptoms of shock. If unconscious, appropriate treatment is to activate EMS and institute resuscitation procedures.

If CPR is not necessary, the victim should remain lying down, should be kept warm, if not already overheated, and should be checked for other injuries.

B.5.b. Continuing Treatment

Additional procedures must be followed and completed in order to control the effects of shock upon the victim:

- Check for "medic alert" or other information tags.
- Obtain history for medical problems (heart disease, diabetes, allergies, medications).
- Notify Station or Group to obtain help and transport as advised.
- Provide specific treatment if advised and trained to do so.
- If there is not a head injury or breathing trouble, place victim flat on back and elevate the lower extremities about 8 to 10 inches. Be careful of any other injuries (see **Figure 5-1**).

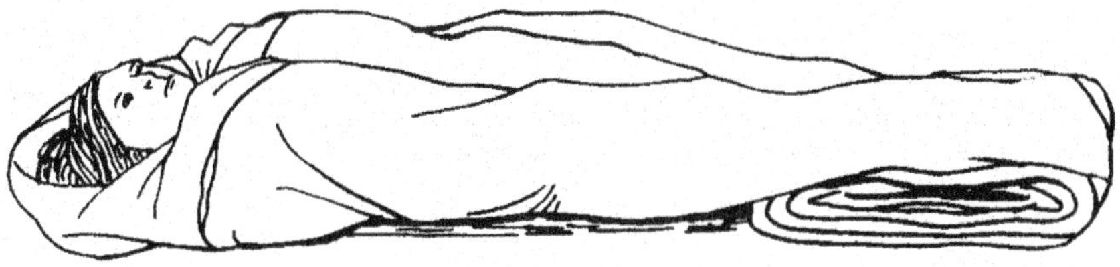

Figure 5-1
Elevating Lower Extremities

- Perform cardiopulmonary resuscitation (CPR), if indicated and trained to provide.
- Warm with blankets. If hot, do not warm.
- If conscious, moisten lips, if requested.
- Do not allow patient to eat or drink.
- Never give alcohol.
- Handle gently.

Anaphylactic Shock

B.6. Description

Anaphylactic shock is a rapid, extreme allergic reaction. People who are subject to this type of shock should carry medical identification at all times. Sensitivity reactions can occur within seconds of contact and can result in death within minutes of contact. It is imperative to be able to recognize the signs and symptoms of anaphylactic shock in order to relay the gravity of the situation to qualified medical personnel.

B.7. Causes

Anaphylactic shock can be caused by eating fish or shellfish, ingesting particular types of berries or oral drugs such as penicillin. Insect stings from yellow jackets, hornets, wasps, etc., injected drugs, exercise, cold, and inhaled substances such as pollen or dust may also cause sensitivity reactions.

B.8. Symptoms

Symptoms of anaphylactic shock include:

- Skin: itching, hives (raised rash), flushing (redness).
- Swelling of lips, tongue, feet, throat, hands.
- Respiratory tract: wheezing, shortness of breath, coughing.
- Gastrointestinal: nausea and vomiting, abdominal cramps, diarrhea.
- Headache.
- Altered mental status.
- Loss of consciousness.

Onset of symptoms may be rapid, within seconds, or delayed (up to two hours). The signs for anaphylaxis are the same as those of shock.

B.9. Assessment

Anaphylactic shock is a severe, sometimes life-threatening, allergic reaction that can occur within minutes of exposure to an offending substance. The substance may enter the body orally or through contact. Anaphylactic shock can be identified by visual changes to the subject's normal appearance and by changes in vital signs. The following table provides indications that a person may be encountering anaphylactic shock.

Area	Normal	Signs of Shock
Skin color	Adult skin is normally dry, not excessively pale or wet to the touch.	Sudden appearance of hives. Widespread blotchy swelling of the skin. Paleness, bluish skin color. Tingling in lips, mouth and tongue are also common.
Eyes	Responsive to movement and light conditions.	Pupils may be dilated.
Pulse	Normal pulse for an adult is regular, strong, and between 60-100 beats per minute.	Increased pulse rate, or weak and thin pulse accompanied by a drop in blood pressure (shock). Blood pressure remains low even when lying down.
Respiration	Normal adult respiration is between 16-24 breaths per minute.	Wheezing or difficulty in breathing. Chest tightness. Coughing. Throat swelling, with a feeling of throat tightness, a lump in throat, hoarseness or obstructed air flow.
Consciousness	Any time a patient's level of consciousness is other than fully alert, it is a serious indication to seek medical assistance immediately.	Light-headedness or fainting.
Internal		Nausea, vomiting, abdominal cramps, diarrhea.

B.10. Treatment

Anaphylactic shock requires medication to counteract the allergic reaction to the substance. If the victim carries an epinephrine kit, crewmembers may assist them in administration, if trained. The victim should be treated for shock and, if necessary, administered CPR. All that is observed or performed should be recorded while keeping Station appraised of the situation so that appropriate medical resources can be activated. Medical attention should be obtained regardless of patient's response. Anaphylactic shock can be very serious resulting in death within a few minutes.

Section C. Resuscitation Methods and Emergencies

Introduction

When a person stops breathing, seconds count. Death can occur within four to six minutes after respiratory failure. It is imperative to start resuscitation immediately. Boat crewmembers are required to attend training annually to learn and maintain effective resuscitation methods and skills. Auxiliary crewmembers, although not required, are encouraged to maintain their skills through training by qualified, certified instructors and maintain their record of certification.

Events that may cause people to stop breathing include:

- Near drowning.
- Suffocation.
- Electrocution.
- Poison gas.
- Heart attack.
- Drug overdose.
- Choking.

In this section

This section contains the following information:

Resuscitation Procedures

C.1. Description

Resuscitation is a general term that covers all measures taken to restore life or consciousness to an individual. Measures taken to restore life include artificial respiration, cardiac compression, and CPR.

C.2. Artificial Respiration

Artificial respiration, starting normal respiratory function, includes rescue breathing maneuvers such as mouth-to-mouth, mouth-to-nose, and mouth-to-stoma. A stoma is the opening in the lower neck through which individuals breathe when they have had their voice box removed.

C.3. Cardiac Compression

Cardiac compression is a method used to restore normal blood-flow to the brain.

C.4. CPR

CPR uses both artificial respirations and chest compressions to revive a victim in respiratory and cardiac arrest. The standard protocols of shore-based civilian EMS systems usually require starting CPR in the field and rapidly transporting these patients to a hospital for continued resuscitation efforts. However, Coast Guard's maritime SAR operations usually involve prolonged response intervals, which exceed the accepted response intervals for successful resuscitation. In addition, the Coast Guard has increased operational risks for boat and aircrew SAR responders, which must also be weighed with the probability of patient benefit when making operational risk management decisions. Risks include aircraft and vessel mishaps, personal injury, and blood borne pathogen exposures. There are also the emotional risks to rescuers and families associated with futile resuscitation efforts.

A Coast Guard Emergency Medical Services basic protocol with criteria for not starting and or not continuing CPR in adults has been developed (see **Figure 5-2**). If the patient is believed to be hypothermic, follow the protocol for hypothermia (see **Figure 5-3**).

Step	Procedure
1	Make sure the area around the victim is safe to be in.
2	Ensure there are universal precautions: gloves, pocket mask, etc.
3	Check the level of responsiveness of the victim by tapping and shouting, "Are you OK?"
4	If no response, notify EMS.
5	Position the victim on their back.
6	Open the airway with a head-tilt, chin-lift, or jaw thrust maneuver.
7	LOOK, LISTEN and FEEL for 5-10 seconds. • LOOK to see if the chest rises and falls. • LISTEN for air exhalation through the nose or mouth. • FEEL for breath coming from the nose or mouth. If there is no sign of breathing, check the victim's airway to ensure there is nothing blocking it and try opening the airway again.
8	If there is still no sign of breathing, administer two rescue breaths with a duration of two seconds each.
9	LOOK, LISTEN and FEEL for sign of breathing again as well as check for signs of circulation (movement, pink warm skin).
10	If there is no sign of breathing or circulation, start CPR procedure prescribed by the American Heart Association or American Red Cross for basic life support.
11	If victim recovers, treat for shock and monitor conditions.
12	If victim's heart stops or respiratory failure reoccurs after initial resuscitation, start again at step 3.

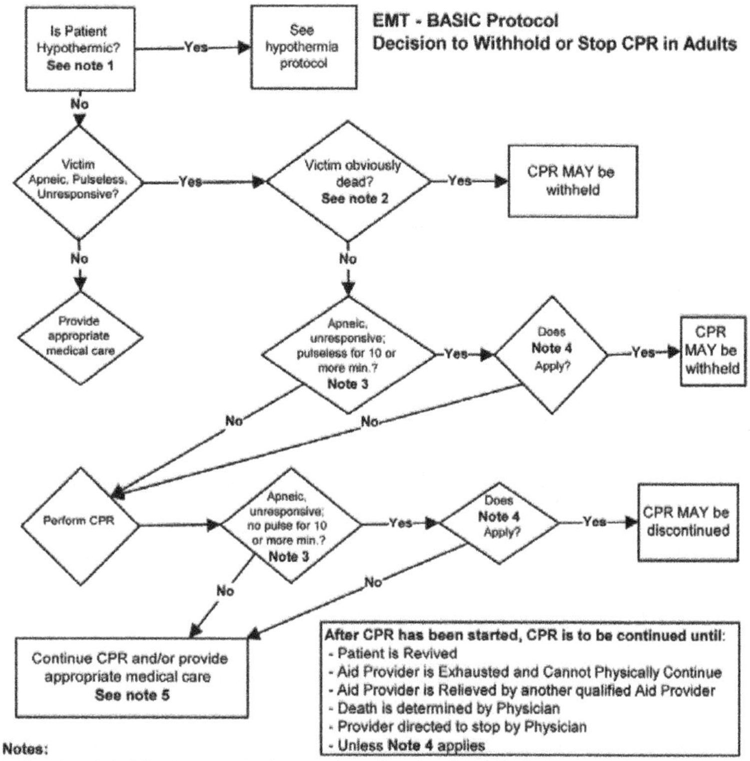

Notes:

1. Hypothermia is defined as a core body temperature of less than 35oC (95oF). For suspected Hypothermic patients, follow the Hypothermia protocol.
2. Obviously dead patients include those that are decapitated, incinerated, have major organs (heart, lungs, brain or liver) separated, or for whom rigor mortis or lividity is present.
3. The following must be observed and recorded by CG EMS provider: No pulse in carotid artery or cardiac apex for 60 seconds (if available, a cardiac monitor must be used); No respiratory effort for 60 seconds despite open airway (if available, a stethoscope must be used for confirmation); Unresponsive to painful stimulus such as a sternal rub and no tendon reflexes; No pupillary reflexes (i.e. pupils non-responsive to light and remain fixed and dilated) and no corneal reflexes; No evidence of drug overdose as the cause of unresponsivenenss.
4. This is a SAR or MedEvac Mission, where higher level medical care is more than 30 minutes away, contact with a physician is impossible and the patient is 18 years of age or older.
5. When patient is not obviously dead, CG EMS providers will start and continue CPR until: Patient revives, EMS provider becomes physically exhausted and cannot continue, EMS provider is relieved by another qualified aid provider, death is determined by a physician, or aid provider directed to stop by a physician.

Figure 5-2
EMT- Basic Protocol Decision to Withhold or Stop CPR in Adults

CH-1

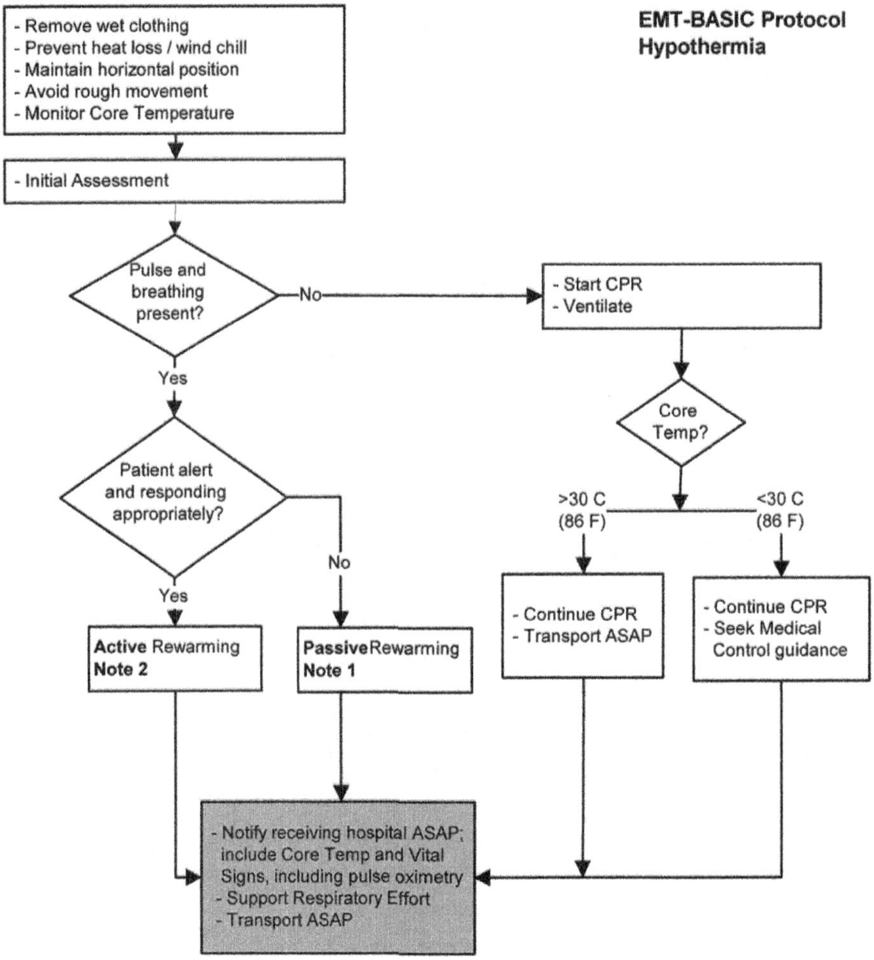
EMT-BASIC Protocol
Hypothermia
- Remove wet clothing
- Prevent heat loss / wind chill
- Maintain horizontal position
- Avoid rough movement
- Monitor Core Temperature
- Initial Assessment
Pulse and breathing present?
No
- Start CPR
- Ventilate
Yes
Core Temp?
>30 C (86 F)
<30 C (86 F)
Patient alert and responding appropriately?
Yes
No
Active Rewarming Note 2
Passive Rewarming Note 1
- Continue CPR
- Transport ASAP
- Continue CPR
- Seek Medical Control guidance
- Notify receiving hospital ASAP; include Core Temp and Vital Signs, including pulse oximetry
- Support Respiratory Effort
- Transport ASAP

Document:
- Signs and Symptoms
- Vital Signs
- Pulse oximetry % (SpO2)
- Core Temp
- Mechanism of Injury
- Treatment
- Response to Treatment
- Submersion time
- Wind Speed
- Water Temperature

Note 1. Active methods include: electrical or charcoal warming devices, hot water baths, heating pads, radiant heat sources and warming beds.

Note 2. Passive methods include: use of insulating blankets and Thermal Recovery Capsules (TRCs).

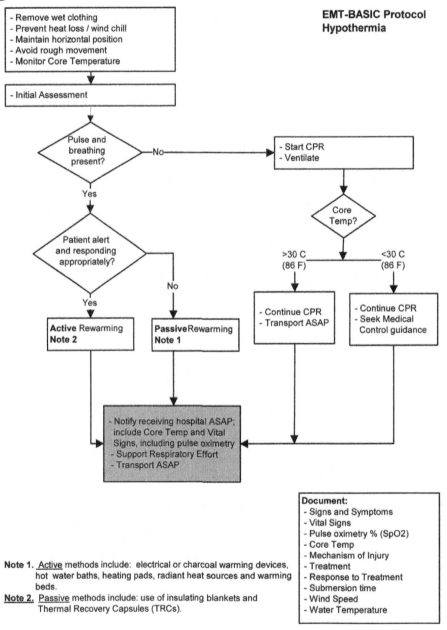

Figure 5-3
EMT - Basic Protocol Hypothermia

CH-1

C.4.a. Obstructed Airway Procedures

An obstruction to the airway such as choking on an object can cause a victim to stop breathing or inability to provide rescue breathing. The following procedures should be performed if the victim begins choking:

Step	Procedure
1	If victim is still able to breath or cough, monitor the situation until either the victim frees the article from their throat, or they can no longer breath on their own.
2	If they are no longer able to breath, notify EMS.
3	Attempt to free the article from their throat by the following methods: • Back blows for infants. • Chest thrusts for obese or pregnant persons. • Abdominal thrusts (Heimlich maneuver). • Continue back blows, chest thrusts or abdominal thrusts until the object is removed, or until the patient goes unresponsive.
4	If the object is still not cleared, lay the victim of their back and open the airway using the head-tilt, chin-lift method and check for breathing using the LOOK, LISTEN and FEEL techniques.
5	If no signs of breathing, attempt one rescue breath. If unsuccessful, reposition the head and try one more rescue breath.
6	If second ventilation is unsuccessful, begin CPR looking in the mouth before each attempted rescue breath.
7	A finger sweep of the mouth can be performed (ADULTS ONLY), but be careful not to force the object deeper into the throat.
8	If object is removed, check airway, breathing, and circulation. If no signs of breathing, but signs of circulation, administer rescue breaths. If no sign of breathing or circulation, begin CPR.

Heart Attack

C.5. Description

A heart attack is always considered a medical emergency since the victim is in significant danger of going into cardiopulmonary arrest and dying. Medical assistance should be contacted immediately.

C.6. Symptoms

There are many symptoms of a heart attack, some of which may not be noticed or recognized by a victim. Though heart attacks can occur without displaying all of these symptoms, the following are all symptoms of a heart attack:

- Severe, crushing type of pain under the breastbone, arms, neck, and jaw.
- Profuse sweating.
- Shortness of breath.
- Extreme anxiety.
- Nausea and vomiting.
- Bluish discoloration of lips, fingernails, and skin.

C.7. Treatment

The following is the treatment for a heart attack:

- Keep the victim quiet and at rest.
- Administer oxygen (if available and trained to do so).
- Place the victim in the position of most comfort. Sometimes the victim may want to sit up, especially if the person is short of breath.
- Seek immediate medical assistance, activate local EMS.
- Determine if the victim is on any type of medication for a heart condition such as nitroglycerin. If so, determine if the victim has taken the medication as prescribed.
- Reassure the patient that assistance is on the way or that transport to a hospital is imminent.
- Transport as quickly, but as safely, as possible.

Stroke

C.8. Description

A stroke is any bleeding or clotting affecting the blood vessels of the brain. Strokes can be mild or extremely serious and care must be taken to treat and transport stroke victims so that additional injury does not occur. Seek medical attention immediately.

C.9. Symptoms

The symptoms of a major stroke are:

- Unconsciousness.
- Shock.
- Confusion.
- Dizziness.
- Numbness/weakness to one side of the body.
- Seizures.
- Impaired vision.

However, if brain damage is slight, the only symptoms may be:

- Headache.
- Facial droop.
- Difficulty speaking, or limited usage of or difficulty in using a limb.

C.10. Treatment

The following is the treatment for stroke:

- Activate EMS.
- Obtain medical assistance immediately.
- Treat as for shock.
- If the victim has difficulty breathing, help the person maintain an open airway and provide rescue breathing if needed.

Scuba Incidents

C.11. Description

The Coast Guard has no statutory responsibility for providing recompression treatment equipment or for managing decompression sickness cases in SAR situations involving self-contained underwater breathing apparatus (SCUBA) diving accidents. However, individuals may request Coast Guard assistance in locating appropriate treatment facilities and for transport to such facilities.

C.12. Coast Guard Action

The Coast Guard shall limit assistance to arranging or providing transportation for victims and advising interested parties of the location for the nearest recompression facility. The Coast Guard boat crew should treat for shock (do not elevate the legs), while arranging for evacuations.

C.13. Types of Scuba Incidents

Scuba diving accidents include all types of body injuries and near drowning. Commonly, a scuba diving accident occurs due to an existing medical problem. There are two special problems usually seen in scuba diving accidents:

- Air emboli.
- The "bends".

C.13.a. Air Emboli

Air emboli, or air bubbles in a diver's blood, are most often found in divers who hold their breath during ascent. This typically happens following an equipment failure, or some other underwater emergency. Divers can develop an air embolism in very shallow waters. The onset of symptoms is often rapid and a victim's senses may become distorted. Victims may have convulsions and can quickly lose consciousness.

C.13.b. The "Bends"

"Bends" is decompression sickness, which may occur as the result of coming up too quickly from a deep, prolonged dive. Rapid ascent defeats the body's ability to filter escaping gases through the lungs resulting in nitrogen gas bubbles in the blood stream. The onset of the "bends" is usually slow for scuba divers, taking from one to 48 hours to appear. Divers increase the risk of decompression sickness if they fly within 12 hours after a dive. The symptoms and signs of decompression sickness include deep pain to the muscles and joints, choking, coughing, labored breathing, chest pains, and blotches on the skin (mottling).

NOTE

Immediately transport or evacuate all patients with possible air emboli or decompression sickness ("bends") to the nearest medical facility.

C.13.c. Associated Medical Problems

Major medical problems associated with the escape of air into the chest cavity or tissues may occur in asthmatics who participate in scuba activities. The symptoms may be acute shortness of breath and the signs may be similar to shock. Immediate advance medical attention is required. EMS should be activated. The victim should be transported as quickly as possible and treated for shock.

C.14. Treating Scuba Incidents

If a diver experiences either mild or severe symptoms on surfacing:

- Immediately notify EMS and start transport to nearest recompression facility.
- Place the diver on his/her left side with head down, and provide oxygen if available.
- Treat for shock.
- Get dive profile.
- Secure dive gear for transport with patient.

C.15. Equipment Availability

Each District Rescue Coordination Center (RCC) and Group Operations Center (OPCEN) has information on all recompression chambers located within its area of operations. In addition, Diver's Alert Network (DAN) can be contacted by telephone for further assistance at (919) 684-8111. The RCC or OPCEN will need the following medical information to arrange the correct response for a scuba incident:

- Depth of the victim's diving activities.
- Number of dives that day.
- Victim's overall medical condition including current level of consciousness.
- First occurrence of victim's symptoms (i.e., during ascent, immediately after reaching the surface, etc.).
- Problems which may have occurred during the dive, such as a panic ascent, loss of air at depth, or equipment failure.

Section D. Treatment for Wounds, Fractures, and Burns

Introduction

In emergency situations, boat crewmembers must be able to temporarily treat severe hemorrhaging wounds, broken bones, and burn victims. As first responder, boat crewmembers must try to keep a victim calm, immobile, and alive until professional medical assistance can be provided.

In this section

This section contains the following information:

Bandages

D.1. Types of Bandages

A bandage is a strip of woven material that holds a wound, dressing, or splint in place, helping to immobilize, support, and protect an injured part of the body. Preferably, sterile bandage material in standard first aid or EMT kits should be used. Otherwise, any large piece of clean cloth can be used as a bandage, binder, or sling.

Various types of bandages come in first aid kits. They are designed to be adaptable to many different situations. For example, some are for covering large areas but may be used as slings, and others are useful as a thick pad for applying pressure over a wound to control hemorrhaging. The following table describes the different types of bandages and their uses:

Bandage Type	Use
Binder	A binder of muslin is used for injuries to the chest or abdomen. Use a large towel or part of a sheet as a substitute for a binder. Hold the binder in place with pins, multiple ties, or other bandages e.g., cravat bandages. Do not apply a binder so tightly that it interferes with breathing.
Gauze Bandages	Gauze is useful as a bandage for almost any part of the body. Most common uses of gauze bandages are as circular bandages and spiral bandages.
Band-Aids®	Band-Aids® or substitutes are useful for small wounds that are clean.
Triangular Bandages	Triangular bandages are useful as an emergency cover for an entire scalp, hand, foot, or other large area. Also, use these bandages as a sling for a fracture or other injury to an arm or hand. A triangular bandage can be rolled into a cravat bandage (a long, narrow strip). It is also useful as a Figure eight bandage, tie for a splint, constricting band, or tourniquet. A folded cravat bandage can serve as an emergency dressing for control of bleeding, or over another dressing, to provide protection and pressure.

D.2. Bandage Application

There are two general principles for bandage application:

- A bandage should be snug, but not so tight as to interfere with circulation either at the time of application or later if swelling occurs.
- A bandage is useless if tied too loose.

D.3. Circulation

Interfering with circulation is prevented by:

- Leaving the person's fingertips or toes exposed when applying a splint or bandage to arms or legs.
- Loosening bandages immediately if a victim complains of numbness or a tingling sensation.
- Watching for swelling, color changes, and cold or cool tips of fingers or toes.

Bleeding

D.4. Types of Bleeding

Hemorrhage, or bleeding, is the escape of blood from arteries, veins, or even capillaries because of a break in their walls. There are several different types of bleeding. Boat crewmembers must learn to recognize the basic types in order to know how to stop the hemorrhaging as quickly as possible. Types of bleeding include:

- Arterial.
- Venous.
- Capillary.

D.4.a. Arterial Bleeding

Arterial bleeding is characterized by blood that is coming from an artery, is bright red, and gushes forth in jets or spurts that are synchronized with the victim's pulse.

D.4.b. Venous Bleeding

Venous bleeding is characterized by blood that is coming from a vein, is dark red, and comes in a steady flow.

D.4.c. Capillary Bleeding

Capillary bleeding is characterized by blood that is coming from damaged capillaries (smaller veins), is bright red, and oozes from the wound.

D.5. Prevention of Bloodborne Pathogens

The risk of acquiring a bloodborne pathogen such as Hepatitis B or HIV should be evaluated. Risk may be managed by the use of appropriate PPE. At least latex or vinyl gloves must be used. More extensive equipment may be required depending on the situation. If the crewmember is not trained or equipped to handle the situation, he/she should notify the Group or Station so that appropriately trained and equipped personnel can be mobilized. The crewmember should not become involved if not adequately protected.

D.6. Universal Medical Precaution

In those instances where crewmembers may be exposed to human tissues (e.g., blood, seepage from burns, saliva, urine or feces), members should take appropriate precautions to prevent contamination by using protective gloves and goggles. Additional precautionary measures include the wearing of masks and protective gowns or aprons. Under all circumstances, thorough washing of hands and any contaminated area should be done with soap and water. Even if gloves have been used, the crewmember should thoroughly wash hands with soap and water.

D.7. Control of Bleeding

Control of a severe hemorrhage is always urgent. With only 10 pints of blood in the human body, arterial bleeding can cause death in a short time.

WARNING

To avoid any contact with infectious fluids, including blood, always wear clean, disposable gloves when performing first aid.

D.7.a. Direct Pressure

The best method to control hemorrhaging is by applying direct pressure to the wound. To apply direct pressure, the palm of a gloved hand should be placed over the wound. Sterile, disposable gloves should be used. An ungloved hand should never be placed onto an exposed wound. To reduce the flow of bleeding, the injury should be raised so that it is at a level higher than the heart. This should only be done if a change in position will not cause additional harm to a victim. If immediately available, or if direct pressure does not control the bleeding, a thick pad of cloth held between the gloved hand and the wound may be used. **(see Figure 5-4)**

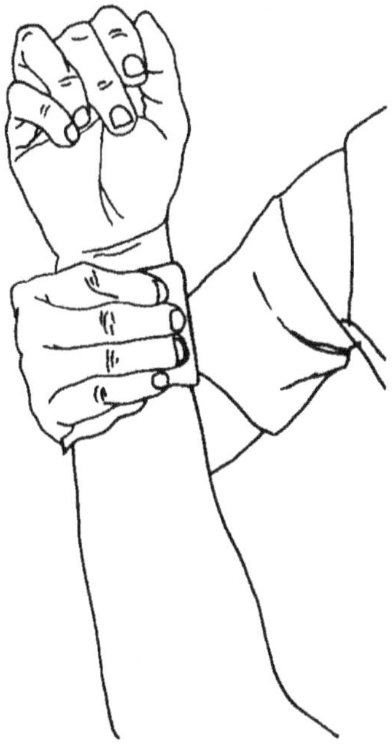

Figure 5-4
Applying Direct Pressure

D.7.b. Pressure Points

If bleeding persists after applying direct pressure or if there is severe arterial bleeding, digital pressure can be applied at pressure points. Pressure points are areas in the body where a major artery flows over a bony prominence. By applying pressure to these areas of the body, blood-flow to the area of the wound is further reduced. (see **Figure 5-5**)

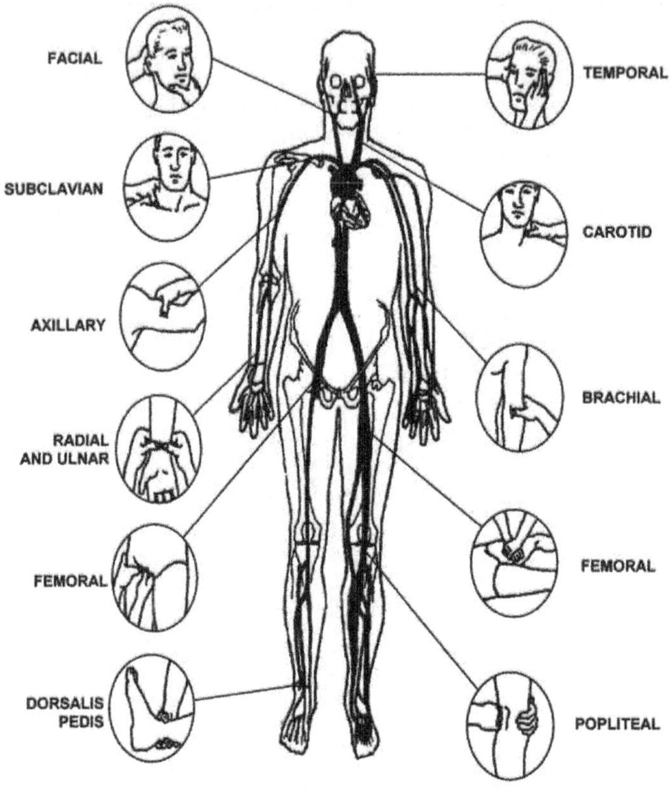

Figure 5-5
Pressure Points

CAUTION ! Always be extremely careful when applying indirect pressure (pressure points) as it may cause damage to the limb due to inadequate blood flow. Do not substitute indirect pressure for direct pressure, use both simultaneously.

Refer to the following for location of pressure points and related areas, and the appropriate procedures to apply pressure to each area:

Pressure Point	Location	Procedure
Temporal	Scalp or head.	Use this pressure point for no longer than 30 seconds as it may cut off blood to the brain.
Facial	In the "ridge" along the lower edge of the bony structure of the jaw.	Use only for a minute or two to help slow blood-flow from a cut on the face.
Carotid	Begin at the trachea at the midline of the neck.	Slide your fingers to the sight of the bleeding and feel for the pulsations of the carotid artery. Place fingers over the artery and thumb behind the neck. Apply pressure by squeezing fingers toward the thumb. Never apply pressure to both sides of the neck at the same time. Apply pressure for only a few seconds as this procedure cuts off blood circulation to the brain.
Subclavian	Deep behind the collar bone in the "sink" of the shoulder.	Push thumb through the thick layer of muscle at the top of the shoulder and press the artery against the collarbone.
Auxillary	Under the upper arm.	Press the artery just under the upper arm against the bone from underneath.
Brachial	Groove on the inside of the arm and elbow; two locations, near the elbow joint.	Apply pressure to the point, grasp the victim's arm with the thumb on the outside of the arm and fingers on the inside. Press fingers towards the thumb. (see **Figure 5-6**)
Radial and Ulnar	Radial point located on forearm close to the wrist on the thumb side of the hand; ulnar point located on little finger side of the hand.	Apply pressure to both points to control bleeding of the hand. Use the radial point to control bleeding of the wrist.
Femoral	Front center part of the crease in the groin area, pelvic basin; two locations.	Used to control severe bleeding on the lower extremity and any bleeding caused by leg amputation. Place heel of the hand directly on the point and apply a small amount of pressure to the artery across the pelvic basin.

Pressure Point	Location	Procedure
Popliteal	Back of the knee.	Apply pressure to the point to control bleeding from a leg wound.
Dorsalis Pedis	Top of foot.	Apply pressure to control bleeding from the foot and toes.

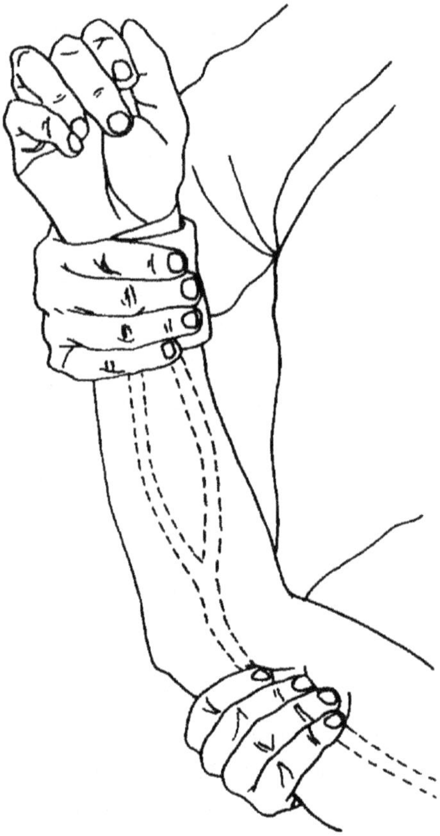

Figure 5-6
Brachial Artery

D.8. Treatment

Refer to the following procedures for treating hemorrhages:

Step	Procedure
Bandage Application	Apply a sterile bandage, if available, or clean piece of gauze or cloth to the wound. Do not remove this dressing if it becomes blood soaked. Reinforce the dressing with a second or third bandage on top of the original one. Elevating the extremity after applying direct pressure should control most bleeding.
Pressure Bandage	A pressure bandage can replace direct hand pressure on most parts of the body. Apply the pressure bandage by placing the center of the bandage or strip of cloth directly over the pad. Hold the pad in place by circling the bandage ends around the body part and tie it off with a knot directly over the pad. (see **Figure 5-7**)
Elevating Injured Area	If direct pressure does not control the bleeding, then elevate the injured area, but only if no bone injury is involved.
Pressure Points	Apply pressure by placing the heel of the gloved hand directly over the spot. Lean forward with the arm straight to apply direct and constant pressure.
Tourniquet	If severe bleeding cannot be controlled after trying all other means and the victim is in danger of bleeding to death, use a tourniquet. Remember that a tourniquet is useful only on arms and legs. A tourniquet is a constricting band placed around an extremity, then tightened until bleeding from an artery has stopped. When a tourniquet is required, use the tourniquets available in a standard Coast Guard first aid kit. Otherwise, use any wide gauge material such as a webbed belt strap with a buckle.

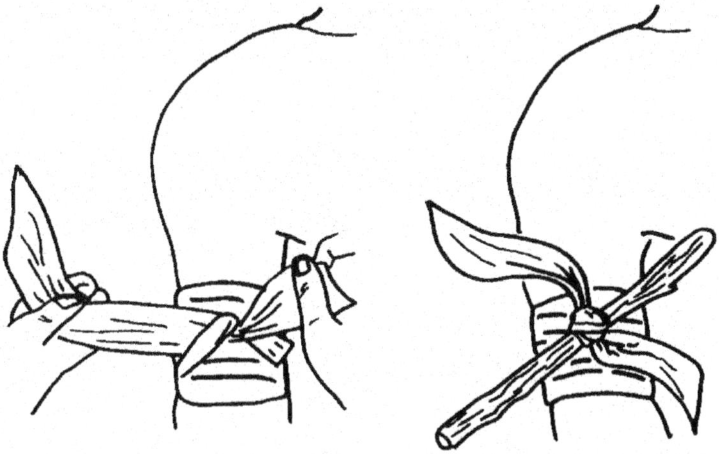

Figure 5-7
Pressure Bandage

WARNING

Tourniquets can be extremely dangerous! Tourniquets should only be used when a victim is in danger of bleeding to death! A tourniquet should only be tight enough to stop the bleeding! Never hide a tourniquet with a splint or bandage.

D.8.a. Applying Tourniquets

Refer to the following procedures when applying a tourniquet:

Step	Procedure
1	Place the tourniquet two to three inches above the wound, but not touching the wound edges. If the wound is in a joint area or just below a joint, place the tourniquet directly above the joint.
2	Wrap the tourniquet band tightly around the limb twice and secure it in place.
3	Attach a note to the victim giving the location of the tourniquet and the time that it was applied. Always leave the tourniquet exposed to view. If it is not possible to attach a note, write the letter "T" on the patient's forehead with a grease pen, lipstick, or other suitable marker, and show the time it was applied.
4	After making the decision, and applying a tourniquet, DO NOT LOOSEN IT.
5	Continue to treat for shock and obtain medical attention IMMEDIATELY.

Fractures (Broken Bones)

CAUTION !

Broken bones are frequently encountered by boat crews in the course of many rescue situations. It is important to develop the ability to identify fractures immediately and treat them properly. Failure to do so can seriously complicate a fracture as well as cause other injuries.

D.9. Types of Fractures

A fracture is a broken or cracked bone. For performing first aid, boat crewmembers should be aware that there are two types of fractures:

- Compound (open) fracture: The bone has broken and an open wound is present. The bone may protrude from the wound, leaving little doubt that there is a fracture.
- Simple (closed) fracture: No open wound is present, but the bone may be broken or cracked. Care must be taken when handling a closed fracture; careless treatment may cause an open fracture, lacerate a blood vessel, or cause other injuries.

D.10. Symptoms

Indications that a fracture has occurred may include:

- Pain, swelling, and discoloration at the injury site.
- Misalignment (deformity) and/or disability of the injured part.
- Victim's indication (may have heard a "crack" or "snap").

D.11. Handling a Fracture

Every suspected fracture should be treated as if it were a fracture until it is proven otherwise. The following procedures outline the proper treatment for a fracture:

Step	Procedure
1	Do not attempt to straighten broken limbs. Eliminate all unnecessary handling of the injured part. Be gentle and use great care when handling any broken limb.
2	Protect and immobilize all injured areas. Check for the possibility of more than one fracture. Do not be deceived by the absence of deformity and/or disability. (In many fracture cases, the victim may still have some ability to use the limb). Keep the broken bone ends and the joints immobilized above and below the injury.
3	Check pulse in the area of the fracture before and after splint application.
	WARNING Never hide a tourniquet with a splint or bandage.
4	Use a splint to immobilize the fracture. Selecting exactly the proper splint is less important than achieving immobilization. Whenever possible, splint a fractured arm to the patient's chest and a fractured leg to the other (unbroken) leg. Apply splints before moving the victim, while avoiding manipulating the injured areas. Apply the splint snugly, but do not cut off circulation. Splints should be well padded. Leave tips of fingers and toes exposed and check them often for circulation adequacy.
5	Treat the injured person for shock. (Refer to *Section B* of this chapter.) Be alert for the development of shock during treatment. Shock may develop as a result of the fracture, pain from the treatment or other injuries not evident on initial assessment.

D.12. Treatment of Specific Bones

There are 206 bones in the human body. Several of these bones, if broken or injured, require very specific treatment based on the sensitive nature of their functions or their proximity to delicate organs or arteries.

D.12.a. Spine

Any actual or suspected damage to the spine requires definitive care and careful management. Permanent disability, paralysis, or death can result from a spine injury. The following are procedures to treat spine injuries:

Step	Procedure
1	Treat all suspected spinal injuries by maintaining alignment and immobilizing the spine as quickly and completely as possible.
2	Seek further medical assistance immediately.
3	Move a patient only as a last resort.
4	Keep a patient flat and do not move the person's head.
5	When transporting a patient, immobilize on a rigid stretcher and carry the patient face up.
6	Do not splint neck and spine fractures unless properly trained.

D.12.b. Skull

The primary aim is to prevent further injury to the head. Time should not be spent figuring out whether there is a fracture or penetration to the skull. The following precautions should be utilized when dealing with head injuries:

Step	Procedure
1	Keep the patient as still as possible.
2	Keep the patient warm and do not give the person anything to drink or any pain medication.
3	Control bleeding using absorbent dressings without applying direct pressure.
4	Seek immediate medical assistance.

D.12.c. Extremities

When encountering actual or suspected fractures to any of a victim's extremities, the following general procedures must be followed:

Step	Procedure
1	Check for a pulse and sensation of touch in fingers or toes before and after a splint has been applied. If either of these is absent, it increases the likelihood of permanent damage. Make certain a splint is not applied over a bony prominence or tied too tightly. Loosen, if necessary, to reestablish feeling and pulse.
2	If possible, splint the injured part in proper alignment. If this is not possible, splint to immobilize the limb in the position found.
3	If bone ends protrude from the skin, cover the exposed bone with a sterile dressing and handle with great care when splinting.

D.12.d. Forearm

For forearm fractures, the following procedures must be performed:

Step	Procedure
1	Place two well padded splints, top and bottom, from elbow to wrist.
2	Bandage in place.
3	Hold the forearm across the chest with a sling. (see **Figure 5-8**)

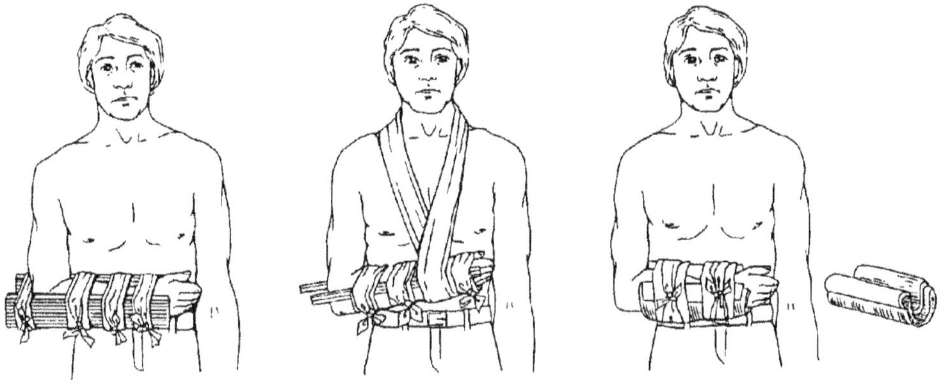

Figure 5-8
Broken Forearm

D.12.e. Upper Arm

For upper arm fractures, the following procedures must be performed:

Step	Procedure
1	For fracture near the shoulder, put a towel or pad in the armpit, bandage the arm to the body, and support the forearm in a sling.
2	For fracture of the middle upper arm, use one splint on the outside of the arm, shoulder to elbow. Fasten the arm to the body and support the forearm in a sling.
3	For a fracture near the elbow, do not move the arm at all. Splint it as it is found. (see **Figure 5-9**)

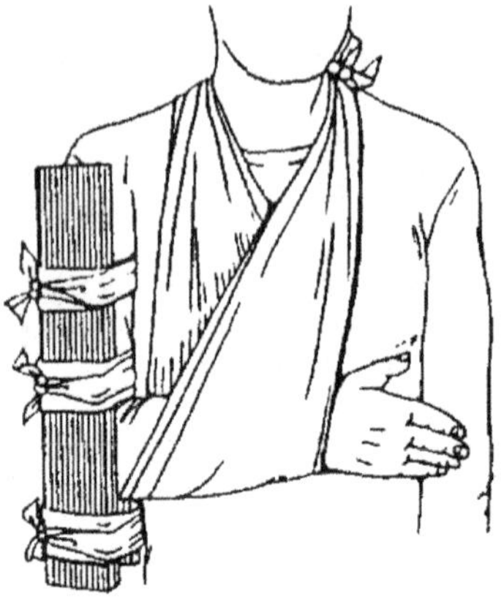

Splinting fracture of middle upper arm.

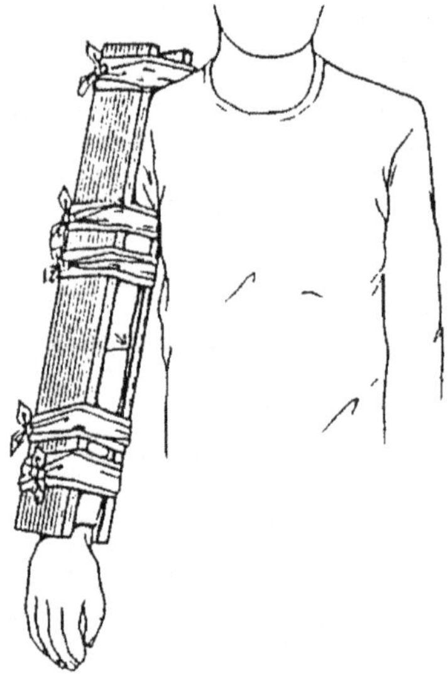

Splinting fracture of arm near elbow.

Figure 5-9
Broken Upper Arm

D.12 f. Thigh

Due to the large artery and muscle mass, a thigh injury is often a major injury and a traction splint may be required. Medical assistance must be sought immediately. This treatment management requires an emergency medical technician (EMT) or person with more detailed training.

If an EMT or other qualified person is unavailable, perform the following procedures:

Step	Procedure
1	Use two splints, an outside one from armpit to foot and an inside one from crotch to foot.
2	Fasten the splints around the ankle, over the knee, below the hip, around the pelvis, and below the armpit.
3	Tie both legs together. Do not move a patient until this has been done. (see **Figure 5-10**) This injury is often associated with major trauma, and bleeding may occur if the thigh bone severs the adjacent femoral artery. The patient should be monitored closely for signs of shock and the leg should not be manipulated.

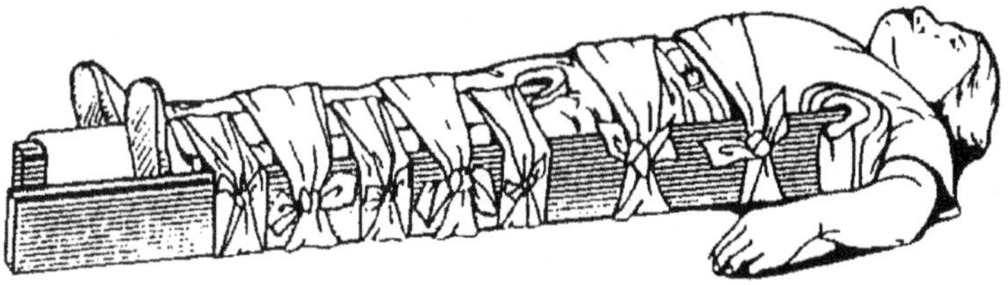

Figure 5-10
Broken Thigh

D.12.g. Lower Leg

To treat a broken lower leg, perform the following procedures:

Step	Procedure
1	Use three splints, one on each side and one underneath.
2	Always pad the splints well, especially under the knee and at the ankle bones.
3	Use a pillow under the leg with the edges brought around in front and pinned; then add two side splints. (see **Figure 5-11**)

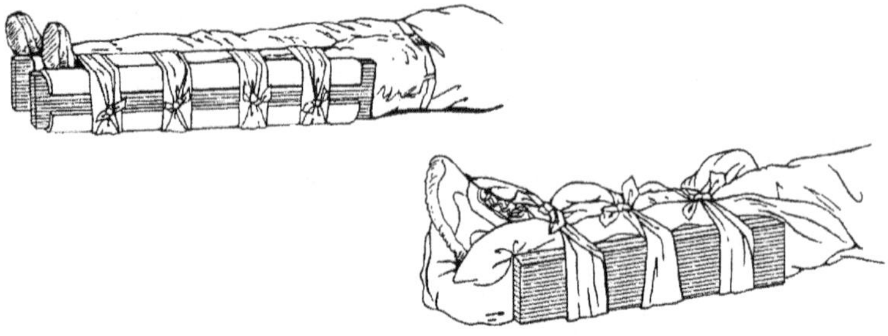

Figure 5-11
Broken Lower Leg

D.12 h. Collarbone

Use the following procedures to immobilize the collarbone:

Step	Procedure
1	On the injured side, place the forearm across the chest, palm turned in, thumb up, with hand four inches above the elbow.
2	Support the arm in this position with a sling.
3	Fasten the arm to the body with several turns of bandages around the body and over the hand to keep the arm close against the body. (see **Figure 5-12**)

Figure 5-12
Broken Collarbone

D.12.i. Rib

A broken rib can be very painful and very dangerous because of the opportunity for a broken rib to puncture a lung. A patient coughing up frothy bright red blood may have a punctured lung. Immediate assistance should be sought and EMS should be activated.

If the crewmember believes that a rib is broken, but the victim indicates that there is no pain, then nothing should be done to try to ease pain. (see **Figure 5-13**)

If oxygen is available and the crewmember is properly trained to do so, he/she may administer oxygen with the patient at rest in a sitting position. This eases the effort required to breathe. Patients with known or suspected fractured ribs should be given a high priority for transport to a medical facility.

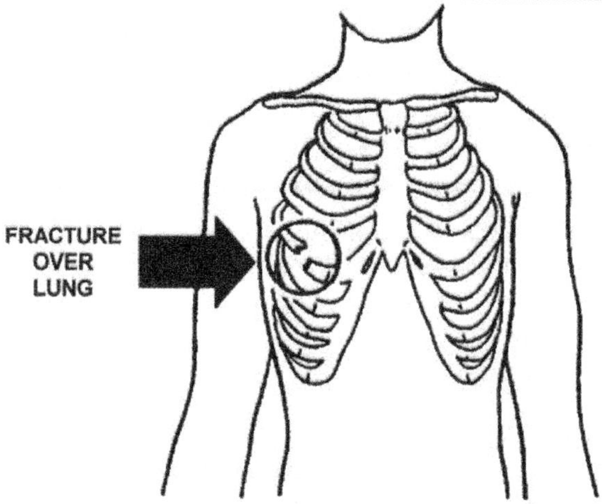

Figure 5-13
Broken Rib

D.12.j. Nose

If an injury to the nose occurs, utilize the following procedures:

Step	Procedure
1	Stop the bleeding.
2	If conscious, have the patient sit and lean forward applying gentle pressure to the sides of the nose.
3	Apply a cold compress or an ice bag over the nose to ease pain, reduce swelling, and assist in stopping the bleeding.
4	Place unconscious victim on his or her side to keep airway open.

D.12 k. Jaw

If an injury to the jaw area interferes with a victim's breathing, utilize the following procedures:

Step	Procedure
1	Pull the lower jaw and tongue forward and keep them forward.
2	Apply a four-tailed bandage under the jaw, with two ends tied on top of the front of the head.
3	Tie the other two tails on top of the head, and at the back, so that the bandage pulls the jaw up and to the rear.

A bandage must support and immobilize the jaw, but not press on the throat. An unconscious victim should be placed on his or her side, while a conscious victim should sit up.

WARNING Never "log-roll" a victim with a pelvic fracture.

D.12.l. Pelvis

A patient with a pelvis injury should be treated for shock, but should not be moved unless absolutely necessary. When moving a patient, the person should be treated the same as a victim with a fractured spine.

- Bandage the legs together at the ankles and knees and place a pillow at each hip and secure them.
- Fasten the patient securely to the stretcher.

A pelvis injury is often associated with major trauma and frequently involves bleeding that is undetectable. The patient should be closely monitored for signs of shock which may be caused by heavy internal bleeding.

Burns

D.13. Causes of Burns

Causes of burns include:

- Thermal.
- Chemical.
- Sunburn.
- Electric shock.
- Radiation.

NOTE Burns, regardless of the cause, may cause a person to go into shock.

D.14. Burn Classification

Burns can range from minor irritations to life threatening and disabling. Proper first aid, administered quickly, can minimize damage resulting from burns and can make the difference between life and death in serious situations. For these reasons, it is very important that boat crewmembers be able to quickly determine the type and seriousness of burns in order to treat them quickly and properly. In general, the size of the burn is more important than the degree of the burn. Burns are classified by depth or degree of skin damage. The following are the three general classifications of burns:

- First-degree.
- Second-degree.
- Third-degree.

D.14.a. First-Degree

First-degree burns are the mildest form of burns. These burns involve only the outer layer of skin and produce redness, increased warmth, tenderness, and mild pain.

D.14.b. Second-Degree

Second-degree burns extend through the outer layers of the skin. These burns involve the inner layers of the skin, but not enough to prevent rapid regeneration. They produce blisters and are characterized by severe pain, redness, and warmth.

D.14.c. Third-Degree

Third-degree burns are those that penetrate the full thickness of the skin, destroying both the outer and inner layers. Severe pain, characteristic of second-degree burns, may be absent because nerve endings have been destroyed. Color may range from white and lifeless to black (charred). Healing requires many months, and usually results in scarring of the skin tissue. Skin grafts are generally required to achieve full healing.

NOTE

> Burns of the respiratory tract are very serious and may be diagnosed by singed eyelashes, hoarseness, sore throat, or coughing of blood.

D.15. Burn First Aid

In order to determine roughly what percentage of a victim's body surface area has suffered some type of damage (burns, etc.), the following estimates for adult patients should be used:

- Chest = 8%
- Back = 8%
- Each arm = 9%
- Each leg = 18%
- Head = 9%
- Genitals = 1%

General first aid procedures for all burns include the following:

- Eliminate the source of the burn. Extinguish and remove smoldering clothing. Do not remove charred clothing that may be sticking to the burn.
- For burns resulting from electrical shock, ensure the patient is no longer receiving electrical shock.
- Treat to prevent or reduce shock.
- Try to prevent infection.
- Do not apply any type of ointment on burns.

In addition to these general steps, the following are first aid procedures for burns that apply specifically to particular classes of burns:

Burn Type	First Aid Procedure
First-Degree	• Immerse in cool water until pain is relieved. • Flush chemical burns for at least 20 minutes. • Cover with clean or sterile dressing.
Second-Degree	• Use the same treatment as for first-degree burns. • Do not break open any blisters. • Cover with a dry, sterile, non-adhesive dressing. • For deep second-degree burns, follow the procedures for third-degree burns.
Third-Degree	• For third-degree, or deep, second-degree burns: • Cover the burn to reduce exposure to air. • Cool the burn. • Do not remove clothing unless smoldering. • Treat for shock even if not apparent. • Always obtain medical care. • Monitor the patient's airway. • Assess vital signs every 5 minutes. • Give nothing to eat or drink. • Do not place ice on the burn. • Do not apply ointments to the burn. Burns of the respiratory tract are always a medical emergency.

D.16. Chemical Burns

Chemical burns of the skin or eyes produce the same type of burn as flash fires, flames, steam, or hot liquids. The following procedures should be performed:

Step	Procedure
1	Wash the chemical away completely, as quickly as possible, using large quantities of water.
2	Continue flushing the burn for at least 20 minutes.
3	When the burn involves an eye, flush the eye with water for up to 20 minutes.
4	Cover both eyes with a clean, dry, protective dressing and seek medical attention as quickly as possible.
5	Give first aid for shock.
6	If the chemical is a powder, brush off as much as possible before flushing with water.

Section E. Environmental Injuries

Introduction

Environmental injuries occur when an individual suffers from over-exposure to extreme environmental elements or when taking poor precautions for activities in environmental elements. In severe cases, environmental injuries can cause permanent damage or loss of life. These types of injuries include emergencies caused by heat or cold such as heat stroke or hypothermia.

Additionally, these injuries are not only limited to environmental conditions, but include other environmental factors such as injuries inflicted by non-human predators of the habitat. In the marine habitat, environmental injuries include those inflicted by aquatic life.

In this section

This section contains the following information:

Emergencies Caused by Heat

E.1. Exposure to Heat

Excessive heat or prolonged exposure to heat can cause at least three types of emergencies:

- Heat cramps.
- Heat exhaustion.
- Heat stroke.

E.2. Heat Cramps

Heat cramps are painful contractions of various skeletal muscles. They are caused by depletion of salts from body fluids, normally due to excessive sweating.

E.2.a. Symptoms

Heat cramps affect the muscles of the extremities and abdominal wall. Pain may be severe. Body temperature may be normal or elevated.

E.2.b. Treatment

The treatment for heat cramps is drinking cool fluids which afford both relief and continued protection. "Sport" drinks may speed up recovery. Re-exposure to heat should be avoided for at least 12 hours.

NOTE

The use of hot packs on cramped muscles will only make the situation worse. DO NOT administer salt tablets for heat cramps!

E.3. Heat Exhaustion

Heat exhaustion results from too much fluid lost by perspiration. Even the most physically fit person can fall victim to heat exhaustion while working in a hot environment. With proper treatment, heat exhaustion is seldom fatal.

E.3.a. Symptoms

The signs and symptoms of heat exhaustion are similar to those of shock. An individual that collapses in the heat and continues to perspire freely almost surely has heat exhaustion. The presence of sweating usually rules out heat stroke.

E.3.b. Treatment

To treat a person with heat exhaustion, utilize the following procedures:

Step	Procedure
1	Remove the patient from the hot environment to a cool location.
2	Place a patient on his or her back, with legs elevated.
3	Cool a patient but DO NOT chill. Be aware of shivering.
4	If the victim is conscious, administer cool sips of water or sports drink.
5	Treat for shock.
6	If equipped and trained, administer oxygen.

With general supportive treatment, a victim of heat exhaustion will usually recover consciousness promptly, although the person may not feel well for some time. Re-exposure to heat should be avoided for at least 24 hours.

E.4. Heat Stroke

Heat stroke is a serious medical emergency. The most important sign of heat stroke is an extreme elevation of body temperature, indicating failure of the body's sweating mechanism. Heat stroke calls for immediate measures to reduce body temperatures in order to prevent brain damage and/or death.

E.4.a. Symptoms

The symptoms of heat stroke are:

- Headache.
- Dizziness.
- Irritability.
- Disturbed vision.

A person will suddenly become unconscious and have hot, dry skin, and contracted pupils. A heat stroke victim will also have a strong pulse, may have convulsions, and will have a body temperature that ranges from 105° F to 109° F.

E.4.b. Treatment

To treat a person with heat stroke, utilize the following procedures:

Step	Procedure
1	Seek help and activate the local EMS.
2	Place the patient in the shade or a cool place. Assess breathing and circulation, loosen clothing, and lay the victim down with the head and shoulders slightly elevated.
3	Begin the movement of air by fanning with a shirt, electric fan or other means.
4	Reduce the body temperature as rapidly as possible to prevent brain damage. Total immersion in a cool water bath is probably the most efficient method. If this is not possible, decrease the patient's body temperature by pouring cool or cold water over the body and apply ice packs to "hot spots" (neck, groin, armpits). Avoid direct ice to skin contact if possible. Cover the patient with sheets soaked in ice water and continue to re-apply cold water as needed.
5	DO NOT give anything by mouth.
6	Treat for shock.

NOTE Carry out these procedures while seeking additional medical assistance.

Emergencies Caused by Cold

E.5. Exposure to Cold

The type and severity of cold injuries depends on the temperature and amount of exposure an individual has endured. Refer to the following for a description of various cold injury causes and symptoms:

Injury	Cause	Signs/Symptoms
Chilblains	Repeated exposure for several hours to temperatures between 32° F and 60° F, generally associated with high humidity.	Redness and swelling, itching dermatitis, tingling, and deep aches in later stages.
Immersion Foot	Exposure to cold water, 50° F and below, for 12 hours or more, or exposure to water of approximately 70° F for several days.	Swelling of the legs and feet, cyanosis (a bluish discoloration, especially of the skin due to a lack of properly oxygenated blood), numbness, tingling, itching, blisters, intense burning, and neuromuscular changes.
Trench Foot	Exposure to cold between 32° F and 50° F, damp weather for periods ranging from several hours to 14 days. The average length of exposure to produce symptoms is three days.	Swelling of the legs and feet, cyanosis, blisters, intense burning, and neuromuscular changes. The body part affected blanches, tingles, then becomes numb.
Frostbite	Generally, brief exposure to extreme cold, -20° F and below, or exposure to approximately 0° F weather for several hours will cause frostbite.	First burning and stinging then numbness. Ice crystals in the skin which cause white or gray waxy color, skin moves over bony prominences, edema (excessive accumulation of fluids within portions of the body), blisters, pain, loss of motion, gangrene, and loss of tissue in later stages.
Freezing	Exposure of skin to temperatures of –20° F and below. May happen rapidly to exposed toes and fingers with other extremities involved as exposure is prolonged.	Ice crystals in entire thickness of the body part, including the bone, which is indicated by pallid, yellow waxy color; skin will not move over bony prominences. After thawing, patient may experience edema, large blisters, intense pain, loss of motion, gangrene, and possibly the loss of the body part.

E.6. Treatment

When treating cold injuries:

DOs	DON'Ts
• Take care when removing clothing or gear so as not to injure the numbed skin. Remove only if blankets or dry clothing are available. • Cover the area with a dry dressing and warm with a blanket. • Exercise care to prevent infection if open sores are present. • Under the supervision of a medical professional, rapidly warm a frostbitten body part in a controlled temperature water bath (105° F to 110° F). Attempt this only where there is a certainty of the water temperature. • Transport the patient to an appropriate medical facility as soon as possible. • Monitor for shock.	• Do not place anything constricting on the affected area. • Do not give the victim alcohol or tobacco. • Do not massage or rub the affected parts. • Do not break blisters. • Do not thaw an affected part if the transport time is short or if there is a possibility that the body part may refreeze after warming.

NOTE Never underestimate cold injuries! Tissue loss and nerve damage are caused by these types of injuries.

Hypothermia

E.7. Loss of Body Heat

Hypothermia is a lowering of a person's core temperature. It occurs when a person suffers a loss of body heat. General body hypothermia is the leading cause of death among shipwrecked crews and other disasters at sea. If not recognized and treated promptly, hypothermia can rapidly turn survivors into fatalities. Survivors in critical hypothermia conditions may suffer a fatal loss of body temperature from physical exertion, or as a result of any delay in taking immediate and positive measures to restore body heat. Struggling survivors, trying to aid in their own rescue, may drive their body temperature down to the point where unconsciousness and/or death results. Survivors removed from the water and left untreated may suffer further critical loss in body temperature, bringing on death after being rescued. Survivors in "warm" water can also suffer from hypothermia if exposed for long enough periods of time. Also, cold air temperatures can bring on hypothermia if adequate protective clothing is not worn.

E.8. Survivability

Survival times in water vary considerably. Survival depends on the type of clothing worn, the amount of physical exertion, the blood alcohol levels, and other factors. Some survivors, when taken aboard during a SAR case, may appear to be under the influence of drugs or alcohol. A person moderately hypothermic will manifest symptoms of an intoxicated person.

E.9. Symptoms

When a victim is suffering from hypothermia, some symptoms are visible and some must be measured to establish a diagnosis. Symptoms include:

- Low body temperature.
- Low blood pressure.
- Slow, weak pulse.
- Unconsciousness.
- General appearance.
- Cold skin.
- May simulate or accompany shock.

Signs may include:

- Shivering.
- Clouded mental capacity (may seem disoriented).
- Slow and labored breathing.
- Weak and slow pulse (may be irregular or absent).
- Dilated pupils.
- Slurred speech (may seem intoxicated).

Visible symptoms are outwardly visible symptoms that can help to identify hypothermia victims:

- Level of consciousness becomes clouded as their body temperature approaches 90° F and they generally lose consciousness at 85° F.
- Pale in appearance, with constricted pupils, and slow and labored respiration. Violent shivering or muscular rigidity may be present. Victims may appear to be intoxicated.
- Begin treatment if a victim's skin feels cold to the touch.

CAUTION ! Do not attempt to take rectal temperatures in the field.

E.9.a. Body Temperature

Body temperature is the most useful yardstick for identifying hypothermia. Hypothermia victims will have a rectal temperature below normal (normal is 98° F to 99° F). Only rectal temperatures are of value, since it is the body's core temperature that determines the severity of hypothermia. Neither oral or auxiliary temperatures, nor the temperatures of the extremities, reflect core temperature. The patient should be treated as visible signs and symptoms suggest.

Temperature	Visible Signs and Symptoms
96° F - 99° F	• Intense uncontrollable shivering. • Impaired ability to perform complex tasks.
91° F - 95° F	• Violent shivering. • Difficulty speaking. • Luggish movements. • Amnesia begins.
86° F - 90° F	• Shivering is replaced by muscular rigidity. • Muscle coordination impaired. • Erratic movements.
81° F - 85° F	• Irrational. • Stupor. • Lost contact with surroundings. • Pulse and respiration slow.
78° F - 80° F	• No response to words. • Reflexes stop working. • Heartbeat is erratic. • Victim loses consciousness.
Below 78° F	• Failure of heart and lungs. • Internal bleeding; death.

NOTE The leading cause of death in cold water maritime accidents is hypothermia.

E.9.b. Blood Pressure

Hypothermia victims may have a lower than normal blood pressure (normal is about 120/80).

CAUTION ! Do not allow a person to perform any physical activity other than what is absolutely necessary. Exertion can use up large amounts of body heat which is necessary to raise the survivor's internal body temperature.

E.10. Rescue Precautions

When it is suspected a survivor has critical hypothermia, rescue attempts should be made that avoid rough handling and minimize the amount of exertion by a victim. This can be accomplished by sending a surface swimmer into the water to assist the survivor into the rescue craft. Care should be taken to handle the victim gently. Excessive movement may cause heart beat irregularities which can be fatal. During the rescue and afterwards, the patient should be kept calm and quiet.

E.11. Basic Treatment

Treatment for hypothermia will depend on both the condition of the patient and treatment facilities available. Survivors who are rational and capable of recounting their experiences, although shivering dramatically, will generally only require that wet clothes be removed and replaced with dry clothes or blankets and a warm environment to rest.

E.12. Advanced Treatment

In more serious cases, where victims are semiconscious or near death, a medical facility should be contacted as soon as possible for detailed instructions for proper care and handling. While awaiting medical instructions, immediately administer first aid to survivors using the following procedures:

Step	Procedure
1	After recovering a victim from the cold, avoid rough handling of the victim as this can cause further harm. Check for the presence of breathing and heartbeat. If the victim is not breathing and has no heartbeat, begin CPR immediately. If the victim is breathing, and has a pulse, gently transfer the person to a warm environment. Be sure to check the person's breathing and heart beat frequently. Always remain prepared to immediately begin CPR if breathing and heart beat stop. Activate EMS and obtain medical help.
2	Lay an unconsciousness or semiconscious victim face up with the head slightly lower than the rest of the body. If vomiting occurs, turn the patient's head to one side. Observe respiration closely and remove any secretions from the victim's nose and mouth.
3	Remove the victim's clothes with minimum movement of the body. Cut the clothes away with scissors or a knife if necessary. If a patient cannot be removed to a compartment to be warmed with blankets, dry clothing, or other warming methods, then DO NOT remove wet clothing. Under these circumstances, the wet clothing is better than no clothing.
Step	Procedure
CAUTION !	Semiconscious or unconscious persons should not be given anything to eat or drink.
4	Do not give anything orally, especially alcohol.
5	Insulate a victim from further heat loss by wrapping the person in a blanket. Do not attempt to aggressively rewarm an unconscious or semiconscious victim, as rapid warming can cause dangerous complications. Do not rub frozen body areas. A victim will be very sensitive to rough handling. The primary objective after a person has been removed from the water is to prevent the person from getting colder.
6	If properly trained and equipped, administer warm, humidified oxygen by face mask. The oxygen will not only assist victims if they are having difficulty breathing or have a low respiratory rate, it will also provide rewarming of the internal body core.

Step	Procedure
WARNING	Hypothermia patients are very prone to burns. Hot packs, heating pads, and hot water bottles may cause third degree burns and must be administered with extreme care.
7	When there will be a delay getting a victim to a hospital, begin gentle rewarming techniques. Rewarming techniques include: • Wrapping the victim in a blanket. Under the blanket, apply heating pads or hot water bottles (if available) to the victim's head, neck and groin. • Applying your body warmth by direct body-to-body contact with a victim. A blanket should be wrapped around you and the victim to preserve the heat.
8	Treat for shock. Be alert to the basics of shock treatment discussed in *Section B* of this chapter.
9	Evacuate a victim to a medical facility soon after or during emergency treatment. A medical phone patch can be set up through the Coast Guard Station if needed. A helicopter with an EMT can be sent to provide help and to evacuate a victim.

Near-Drowning

E.13. Mammalian Diving Reflex

Victims who inhale water or who are found floating face-down in the water may be suffering from near-drowning. Medical researchers have only recently discovered the phenomena of the "mammalian diving reflex." In this condition, a person immersed in water (particularly a child), even under ice, could still be alive. Even after extended periods of time, the body delivers a tiny trickle of oxygen to the brain. A victim also exhibits an almost complete constriction of all peripheral blood vessels. Their respiration and circulation almost stop. Properly administered CPR may successfully revive a near-drowning victim without serious complications, even after being underwater for an hour or longer.

E.14. Treatment

To treat a person in a near-drowning situation, perform the following procedures:

Step	Procedure
1	Evaluate ABC's
2	Identify any other injuries.
3	Activate EMS.
4	Initiate CPR if indicated and if trained.
5	Treat for shock.
6	Inform Station of status of victim.
7	Transport as soon as possible.
8	Remove wet clothing (if dry clothes or blankets available).
9	Treat for hypothermia as appropriate.
10	Constantly monitor the victim's airway.
11	Reevaluate victim's vital signs every 5 minutes.
12	Document: • Length of submersion. • Water temperature. • Fresh or salt water. • Drug or alcohol use. • Any treatment rendered.

Fish Bites and Stings

E.15. Types of Bites and Stings

Fish bites and stings are another common problem encountered by boat crews during rescues. They can range from innocuous to deadly, and boat crewmembers must be constantly alert to identify bites and stings as quickly as possible.

Victims may suffer many different types of fish bites and stings. The types encountered will depend in large part on the area of operations and the sea life that exists there. It is important to become familiar with the most common types of fish bites and stings that are encountered and the proper treatments for them.

E.16. Effects and Treatment

The following describes the effects and proper treatment for various fish bites/stings encountered:

Bite/Sting	Effects	Treatment
Shark & Barracuda Bites	Generally loss of large amounts of tissue.	Prompt and vigorous action to control hemorrhage and shock are required to save a victim's life. Control bleeding with pressure dressings, if possible. If not, use pressure points or tourniquets. Seek medical help immediately.
Fish Stings	Symptoms include: • Burning. • Stinging. • Redness. • Swelling. • Rash. • Blisters. • Abdominal cramps. • Numbness. • Dizziness. • Shock.	Individuals extremely sensitive to fish stings may rapidly go into shock and require immediate evacuation to save their life.

Portuguese Man-of-War & Jellyfish	• Burning. • Stinging. • Redness. • Jelly-like matter from tentacles stuck on the body.	• Remove any remaining tentacles to prevent further damage. • Rinse the area with clean fresh or salt water and apply an ice pack to reduce pain. • Check with local medical facilities to learn advanced treatment for local species. • If the sting is serious, treat for shock and seek medical attention.
Stingray Injuries	Typically a small open wound with swelling.	• Immediately irrigate the wound from a stingray with cold salt water. Most of the toxins will wash out and the cold water will reduce the pain. • Immerse the wounded area in hot water for 30 to 60 minutes. Keep the water as hot as a patient can tolerate without injury. • Apply hot compresses to wounds in areas not lending themselves to complete immersion. • Apply a sterile dressing after the soaking.

Section F. Miscellaneous Emergencies

Introduction

Boat crewmembers will face a variety of emergencies that will require performing first aid. This section discusses miscellaneous emergencies that boat crewmembers will encounter aboard their own vessel or when dealing with marine casualties.

In this section

This section contains the following information:

Carbon Monoxide Poisoning

F.1. Description

Carbon monoxide (CO) is a colorless, odorless toxic gas that is the product of incomplete combustion. Motor vehicles, heaters, and appliances that use carbon based fuels are the main sources of this poison.

F.2. Signs and Symptoms

Signs and symptoms of carbon monoxide poisoning can include the following:

- Headache.
- Dizziness.
- Fatigue.
- Weakness.
- Drowsiness.
- Nausea.
- Vomiting.
- Loss of consciousness.
- Skin pallor.
- Shortness of breath on exertion.
- Palpitation.
- Confusion.
- Irritability.
- Irrational behavior.

F.3. Treatment

Utilize the following procedures when treating for carbon monoxide poisoning:

Step	Procedure
1	Remove patient from the carbon monoxide containing atmosphere.
2	Treat the patient for shock.
3	Administer oxygen if available and trained to do so.
4	Start CPR as appropriate.

Poisoning by Mouth

F.4. Description

When poisoning occurs, it is vital that proper first aid be given immediately.

F.5. Seeking Advice

The product container will often include specific treatment instructions. If poisoning has occurred, medical assistance should be sought immediately. The boat crew should contact its unit, provide information about substance taken, an estimate of the quantity taken, and have the unit immediately contact the local poison control center. The container and any samples of vomit should be taken with the victim when transporting to a medical facility.

F.6. Medical Assistance Not Available

If medical advice is not immediately available and the patient is conscious, an attempt should be made to determine if the poison is a strong acid, alkali, or petroleum product. If this is the case, no attempt should be made to induce vomiting.

CAUTION !

> Determine if the victim shows signs of a sensitivity reaction to the substance. This will indicate a victim in anaphylactic shock. In this case, treat the victim accordingly (Refer to *Section B* of this chapter.)

F.7. Treatment

Closely observe the basics for shock treatment during transport described in *Section B* of this chapter.

Eye Injuries

F.8. Description

Eye injuries are potentially serious, and may be permanent, unless handled promptly and properly. Eyes should be moist. Any dressing applied to eyes should also be moist to prevent excessive drying.

Eye movement is conjugal, that is if one eye moves, the other also moves in the same manner. When dealing with a penetrating injury to an eye, or a foreign object in an eye, the objective is to limit eye movement. Because of conjugal movement, this is best accomplished by covering both eyes. In most cases, a patient with an eye injury is transported sitting up.

F.9. Blindness

Patients who have experienced a blinding injury become totally dependent upon their rescuer. These patients should never be left alone. Constant contact and continuous conversation with them should be maintained to reduce anxiety.

F.10. Types of Eye Injuries

There are many injuries that may occur to a victim's eyes. Any eye injury is normally the cause of great anxiety for a victim, many times causing more concern than more serious injuries to other parts of the body. As a boat crewmember, this should be kept in mind while rescuing or treating victims with eye injuries.

F.11. Symptoms and Treatments

The following table describes the symptoms and appropriate treatments for the various eye injuries:

Eye Injury	Symptom	Treatment
Blunt Eye Trauma	Blows to a victim's head and eye area may result in a fracture to the orbit (the bony socket encircling the eye), entrapping vessels and nerves to the eye.	Managing such injuries requires covering both eyes with a moist dressing. This is important since movement by an uninjured eye is mimicked by the injured eye. Refer the patient to medical care for follow-up. Since this injury may involve a head injury, closely observe the patient for signs of further damage.
Penetrating Objects and Foreign Bodies	Common objects include fish hooks, wood splinters, or pieces of glass.	Any object that has penetrated the eye must not be removed as first aid treatment. Cover both eyes with a moist dressing, and support the object if it protrudes to prevent movement. A protective cup for the eye can be made from a plastic or styrofoam cup taped over the eye, with a moist dressing inside. Immediately refer the patient for further medical care.
Caustics, Acids, or Burns	May include remains of the substance itself, pain, swelling, discoloration of the skin, peeling of skin, and blisters.	Immediately flush both eyes with large quantities of gently flowing water. Each eye should be flushed with water for a minimum of 10-15 minutes away from the unaffected eye. Never use a neutralizing agent for flushing, use only plain tap water. A moist dressing may be helpful. After flushing, refer the patient for further medical care.

This page intentionally left blank.

Chapter 6
Survival Equipment and Pyrotechnics

Introduction

The danger of falling overboard, capsizing, or sinking is always present while underway. Few people can stay alive for long in the water without some type of survival equipment. Fear, fatigue, and exposure are the enemies of water survival. The desire to live, and the ability to think clearly and proficiently use available equipment can make the difference between life and death. The boat coxswain has overall responsibility for the safety of the boat and crew including ensuring that all required safety equipment is onboard, readily accessible, in working condition, and its use and operation understood by all. However, each boat crewmember has the personal responsibility to stay alert and knowledgeable in these matters. This chapter addresses the characteristics and use of survival gear and signaling devices, including pyrotechnics.

NOTE

For specific policies, guidance, and technical information concerning configuration, application, stowage, and maintenance of survival equipment discussed in this chapter, refer to the *Rescue and Survival Systems Manual*, COMDTINST M10470.10 (series).

In this chapter

This chapter contains the following sections:

Section A. Personal Flotation Device (PFD)

Introduction

The term personal flotation device (PFD) is a general name for the various types of devices designed to keep a person afloat in water. PFDs include life preservers, vests, cushions, rings, and other throwable items. They are available in five different types: Type I, II, III, IV and V. Each type of PFD provides a certain amount of flotation.

Regardless of the type, all PFDs must be Coast Guard-approved, meaning they comply with Coast Guard specifications and regulations relating to performance, construction, and materials. A usable PFD is labeled Coast Guard-approved, in good serviceable condition, and of appropriate size for the intended user. Each boat crewmember must wear a usable PFD appropriate for the weather conditions and operations in which he/she will be performing.

NOTE A wearable PFD can save a life, but only if it is worn.

In this Section

This section contains the following information:

Type I PFD

A.1. Description

The Type I PFD, or "offshore life jacket," is a one-piece, reversible PFD intended primarily for use by survivors, passengers on towed vessels, or prisoners aboard vessels. A Type I PFD provides an unconscious person the greatest chance of survival in the water. The Type I PFD is the only wearable device required to be reversible. It comes in two sizes, an adult size (90 pounds and over) which provides at least 20 pounds of buoyancy and a child size (less than 90 pounds) which provides at least 11 pounds of buoyancy. The PFD must be international orange in color.

A.2. Advantages

A Type I PFD is effective for all waters, especially open, rough, or remote waters where rescue may be delayed. It is designed to turn most unconscious wearers in the water from a face-down position to a vertical or slightly backward position, allowing the wearer to maintain that position. It provides at least 11-20 pounds of buoyancy. This buoyancy will allow the wearer to relax and save energy while in the water, thus extending survival time.

A.3. Disadvantages

There are three major disadvantages to this type of PFD:

- It is bulky and restricts movement.
- Its buoyancy restricts the underwater swimming ability needed to escape from a capsized boat or to avoid burning oil or other hazards on the surface of the water.
- It provides minimal protection against hypothermia.

NOTE This type of PFD is not recommended for use by boat crews because it restricts mobility.

A.4. Donning

Before entering the water, don and adjust a Type I PFD using the following procedures:

WARNING For safety, always tuck all loose straps into your pockets, shirt, or belt. Adjust straps on injured people before they are lowered into the water.

Step	Procedure
1	Grasp the PFD at the lower part of head opening and pull outward to expand opening.
2	Slip your head through opening.
3	Pass the body strap around the back and fasten at the front of the PFD, then adjust the strap for a snug fit.

A.5. Entering the Water

Use the following procedures to enter the water:

NOTE Follow these steps before entering the water wearing any type of PFD or combination of cold weather protective device (e.g., dry suit) and PFD.

Step	Procedure
1	Ensure all straps on the PFD are securely fastened, tightened to a snug fit, and tucked in to prevent them from snagging.
2	Stand on the boat's gunwale, on the windward side, at a point closest to the water.
3	Check surrounding area for hazards and verify depth of water.
4	Fold arms across chest and grip the PFD with fingers. This will prevent the PFD from riding-up and striking the chin or neck.
5	Keep the body erect and legs held together and crossed when entering the water. It is better to gently slip in, if possible, rather than jumping.
6	If jumping into water is necessary with chemicals, oil, or burning oil on the surface, place one hand over mouth with palm under chin and split fingers tightly squeezing nostrils shut. Place other hand on the PFD collar to keep it in place.

Type II PFD

A.6. Description

The Type II PFD, also known as a "near-shore buoyant vest," is a wearable device that will turn some unconscious wearers to a face-up position in the water. It comes in different colors and in three categories:

- Adult (more than 90 pounds) which provides at least 15.5 pounds of buoyancy.
- Child, medium (50 to 90 pounds) which provides at least 11 pounds of buoyancy.
- Infant (available in two sizes, less than 50 pounds and less than 30 pounds), which provides at least 7 pounds of buoyancy.

A.7. Advantages

This type is usually more comfortable to wear than the Type I. It is usually the preferred PFD if there is a chance of a quick rescue, such as when other boats or people are nearby.

A.8. Disadvantages

The turning characteristic of the Type II is not as strong as with a Type I because of a lesser amount of flotation material, and therefore, under similar conditions, will not be as effective in turning a person to a face-up position.

A.9. Donning

Before entering the water, don and adjust a Type II PFD using the following procedures:

Step	Procedure
1	Grasp the PFD at the lower part of head opening and pull outward to expand opening.
2	Slip head through opening.
3	Pass the body strap around the back and fasten at the front of the PFD, then adjust the strap for a snug fit.
4	Secure the chest ties with a bow knot for a snug fit.

A.10. Entering the Water

To enter the water while wearing a Type II PFD, follow the instructions in paragraph A.5 above.

Type III PFD

A.11. Description

The Type III PFD, also known as a "flotation aid," is routinely worn aboard boats when freedom of movement is required and the risk of falling over the side is minimal. It is not designed to turn an unconscious wearer to a face-up position; the design is such that conscious wearers can place themselves in a vertical or slightly backward position. It has a minimum of 15.5 pounds of buoyancy and comes in many sizes and colors. **Figure 6-1** shows the Type III PFD vest that boat crews are authorized to wear. Most approved flotation coats ("float coats") are also Type III PFDs.

Figure 6-1
Type III PFD Vest

A.12. Dynamic Strength-Tested Type III PFDs

With the Coast Guard's inventory of high-speed boats increasing, the need for PFDs that provide proper protection for entering the water at high speed has increased. Dynamic strength-tested Type III PFDs are available to boat crews that operate at these high speeds (i.e. greater than 30 knots). Additional securing methods have been added to the Type III style of vest to ensure a secure fit. More information on these PFDs can be found in the *Rescue and Survival Systems Manual*, COMDTINST M10470.10 (series).

A.13. Advantages

Type III PFDs offer boat crewmembers greater comfort and freedom of movement. It is designed so wearers can place themselves in a face-up position in the water. The Type III PFD allows greater wearing comfort and is particularly useful when water-skiing, sailing, hunting from a boat, or other water activities.

WARNING

The Type III PFD will not provide an adequate level of buoyancy when worn with a full complement of law enforcement gear. If unable to remain afloat, jettison easily accessible equipment.

A.14. Disadvantages

The following are some disadvantages to the Type III PFD:

- Flotation characteristics are marginal and not suitable for wear in heavy seas.
- Tendency to ride-up on the wearer in the water.
- Wearer may have to tilt head back to avoid a face-down posture in the water.
- While the Type III has the same amount of buoyancy material as the Type II PFD, the distribution of the flotation material in a Type III reduces or eliminates the turning ability.

A.15. Donning

Before entering the water, don and adjust a Type III PFD using the following procedures:

Step	Procedure
1	Place your arms through the openings in the vest.
2	Close zipper, if provided. Close front slide fasteners.
3	Adjust waist straps for a snug fit.
4	Secure any additional belts, zippers, and straps the PFD provides for high-speed operation.

Type IV PFD

A.16. Description

The Type IV PFD is a Coast Guard-approved device that is thrown to a person-in-the-water and is grasped by the user until rescued. The most common Type IV devices are buoyant cushions and ring buoys. Buoyant cushions come in many different colors. Ring buoys (see **Figure 6-2**) must be white or orange in color.

Figure 6-2
Ring Buoy

A.17. Advantages

An advantage of the Type IV PFD is that since it is not worn like other PFDs, there are no size restrictions. This type of PFD is designed to be stored on deck for easy deployment should someone fall overboard. If quickly deployed following a man overboard, the Type IV PFD also acts as a marker assisting in returning to the area where the person originally fell overboard. (See *Chapter 16* for more information on Person-in-the-Water Recovery).

A.18. Disadvantages

A disadvantage of the Type IV PFD is that it is not worn, although some can be secured to the body once reached in the water.

Type V PFD

A.19. Description

Type V PFDs are also known as "special-use devices." They are intended for specific activities and may be carried instead of another PFD only if used according to the approval condition on the label. For example, a Type V PFD designed for use during commercial white-water rafting will only be acceptable during commercial rafting. It is not acceptable for other activities unless specified on the label. Examples of Type V PFDs are

- Coast Guard work vest with unicellular foam pads.
- Thermal protective PFDs (anti-exposure coveralls/immersion suits).
- CG authorized hybrid automatic/manual inflatable PFDs.

A.20. Hypothermia Protection

Some Type V devices provide significant hypothermia protection. Refer to *Section B* of this chapter for more information on the anti-exposure coverall and immersion suit.

A.21. Inflatable PFDs

Automatic/manual inflatable PFDs have been added to the list of allowable survival equipment for boat crews. As with other Type V PFDs, the inflatable is designed for specific operating conditions that give it certain advantages and disadvantages.

A.22. Advantages

The Type V inflatable PFD offers boat crewmembers greater comfort and maneuverability compared to the typical Type III vest. Lightweight and not as bulky, the Type V inflatable is especially beneficial to units in warmer climates. When inflated, the Type V provides more buoyancy as well as the positive righting feature found in a Type II PFD. Some Type V inflatables provide storage pockets/pouches which, when properly outfitted, eliminate the need for wearing the Boat Crew Survival Vest mentioned later in this chapter.

A.23. Disadvantages

The initial purchase price and preventive maintenance costs of the Type V inflatable are greater than that of the typical Type III vest. It also requires more frequent and complicated preventive maintenance. As with any other automated feature, if the auto-inflate mechanism were inoperative, the PFD would have to be manually inflated. This could be a problem if the crewmember was knocked unconscious while falling overboard. Also, current inflatable PFDs are not dynamic strength-tested for high-speed boat operations.

A.24. Donning

There are several different styles of Type V inflatable PFDs approved for Coast Guard use. Each has a specific method of donning, equipment storage, and activation. Prior to use, each crewmember must complete the performance qualification standards for that specific style of inflatable PFD. These can be found in *Chapter 4* of the *Rescue and Survival Systems Manual*, COMDTINST M10470.10 (series).

PFD Storage and Care

A.25. Description

Despite the mildew inhibitor treatment that is required by manufacturers for PFDs, stowing them in moist locations will increase deterioration of the fabric. Heat, moisture, and sunlight will increase the deterioration of the parts of PFDs.

A.26. Storage

PFDs should be stored in a cool, dry place out of direct sunlight. A "dry" area is considered any suitable area where water will not condense on a PFD. All PFDs should be kept away from oil, paint, and greasy substances. The Coast Guard does not consider any PFD "readily accessible" if it is kept in its original wrapper. Persons under stress may be unable to get them out promptly. Also, the wrapper can trap moisture leading to mildew and rot.

NOTE Remember, more important than their storage condition is that they are readily accessible.

A.27. Care

If a PFD requires cleaning, it should be washed in fresh, warm water with a mild detergent, then rinsed in clean, fresh water. Additional maintenance requirements for all styles of PFDs used in the Coast Guard can be found in the *Rescue and Survival Systems Manual*, COMDTINST M10470.10 (series).

PFD Survival Equipment

A.28. Description

PFD survival equipment is attached to a PFD to provide a means of signaling a position from the surface of the water using sight and sound signals.

A.29. Standard Outfitting

All PFDs in service shall be outfitted with two accessories:

- Whistle secured to the PFD with a lanyard.
- Distress signal light (battery-operated strobe light or the personnel marker light (PML) chemical light) secured to the PFD.

The requirement for a whistle and a distress signal light may be waived if the PFD is worn in conjunction with a properly outfitted boat crew survival vest or survival equipment pocket/pouch (both discussed later in this chapter) found on Type V inflatables. Only trained personnel should be outfitted with the survival vest. For passengers not familiar with the contents of the survival vest, their PFD should be outfitted with the required whistle and distress signal light.

NOTE Auxiliary PFD survival equipment requirements are in the *Auxiliary Operations Policy Manual*, COMDTINST M16798.3 (series).

CAUTION ! The PML replaces only the distress signal light that is required to be attached to all PFDs in service. It does not replace the distress signal light (SDU-5/E or CG-1 strobe) that boat crewmembers are required to carry in their boat crew signal kit.

CAUTION ! There is a seal at one end of the PML that holds the protective sleeve in place. If this seal is broken, replace the PML immediately.

A.30. Personnel Marker Light (PML)

A PML is a device that uses either battery or chemical action to provide light for the wearer to be seen during darkness. The yellow-green light of a PML is visible for a distance of approximately one mile on a clear night, and lasts as long as eight hours. It is the only chemical light approved for use as a distress signal light on a PFD. A certified PML complies with regulation 46 CFR 161.012 (Coast Guard-approved). (see **Figure 6-3**)

A.30.a. Design

Large marine supply houses carry Coast Guard-approved PMLs. PMLs are specifically designed to be attached to a PFD without damaging or interfering with the PFD's performance. The PML's hard plastic sleeve protects the glass ampules inside the tube from breakage and deterioration from the effects of light.

A.30.b. Activation

There are three procedures needed to activate the PML:

Step	Procedure
1	Squeeze the handle to break the glass vials of activating chemical compounds suspended inside the tube.
2	Remove the black sleeve.
3	Squeeze the handle again if the PML does not light.

A.30.c. Effects of Temperature

The intensity of the PML's light signal in cold weather (below 10° C/50° F) is reduced. In colder temperatures, the light will last longer, but will not have the same brilliance as in warmer conditions. Units that consistently operate in temperatures below 10° C/50° F shall use distress signal lights in place of PMLs.

NOTE

> Most batteries or chemicals have a useful shelf-life of about two years. Therefore, check PMLs for the expiration date (located somewhere on the device) to find out when replacement is in order.

NOTE

> The time period a chemical light provides effective illumination depends upon its age and the temperature. A recently purchased light stick used in 21-27° C (70-80° F) temperatures (ideal conditions) will provide 8 to 12 hours of light. As the device gets older, its effective period is considerably less.

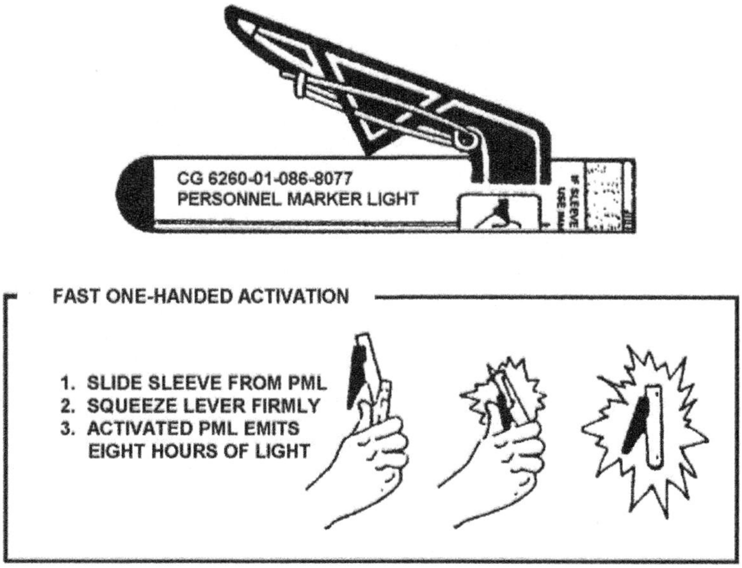
CG 6260-01-086-8077
PERSONNEL MARKER LIGHT
FAST ONE-HANDED ACTIVATION
1. SLIDE SLEEVE FROM PML
2. SQUEEZE LEVER FIRMLY
3. ACTIVATED PML EMITS EIGHT HOURS OF LIGHT

Figure 6-3
Personnel Marker Light (PML)

CH-1

A.31. Retroreflective Material

Most styles of PFDs used today have retroreflective material already attached. When this material is illuminated by a light source, it is reflected back, making it much easier to locate the PFD in the dark. However, some PFDs (Navy standard with collar & ring buoys) do not come with retroreflective material attached. Coast Guard-approved reflective material must be applied to the PFD in accordance with the *Rescue and Survival Systems Manual*, COMDTINST M10470.10 (series).

Standard Navy Preserver

A.32. Description

The Standard Navy Preserver, although not Coast Guard-approved, is a common PFD used by the naval services. This preserver is one of the best devices for keeping a person afloat; however, its major drawback is that it requires training to become familiar with the many straps and fastenings used to don this device quickly and properly. Consequently, the Standard Navy Preserver is not Coast Guard-approved for civilian use. Any auxiliarist who plans to go aboard a Coast Guard boat or cutter as crew (or passenger) should request instructions in donning this PFD.

Section B. Hypothermia Protective Clothing

Introduction

Accidentally falling into cold water has two potentially lethal consequences: drowning and hypothermia. Previously, the protection provided by PFDs against drowning was discussed. The Coast Guard requires active duty Coast Guard and Auxiliary crews to wear hypothermia protective clothing in heavy weather or hazardous operating conditions. However, the Operational Commander may waive this requirement. For further information on waivers, refer to the *Rescue and Survival Systems Manual*, COMDTINST M10470.10 (series).

Hypothermia protective clothing is designed to permit functioning in cold weather and water conditions. There are four primary types used by the Coast Guard:

- Anti-exposure coverall.
- Dry suit (or approved replacement).
- Wet suit (cutter swimmers only).
- Immersion suit.

NOTE

> A special type float coat, with a Type V-approval label, meets the same flotation requirements as the anti-exposure coverall, but provides only partial covering and less thermal protection.

In this section

This section contains the following information:

Requirements

B.1. Description

The Unit Commander may waive the requirement for hypothermia protective clothing for boat crewmembers on a case-by-case basis when the degree of risk to exposure and hypothermia is minimal (e.g., non-hazardous daylight operations in calm water). When a waiver is granted, hypothermia protective clothing must be carried on the boat. Coxswains shall require boat crewmembers to don proper hypothermia protective clothing during heavy weather or hazardous operations (e.g., recovery of a person from the water or helicopter operations). Unit Commanders are responsible for the enforcement of this policy for Auxiliary facilities under their operational control. If an Auxiliary facility is granted a waiver, it is not required to carry protective clothing aboard.

NOTE

Timely rescue is a high priority when victims are in the water. When the boat has prior knowledge of a victim in the water, the surface swimmer, if available, will don a dry or wet suit and swimmer's safety harness before entering the water. Coxswains of boats operating in water temperatures that dictate the use of a dry or wet suit shall ensure that the surface swimmer is correctly outfitted.

B.2. Temperature Requirements

Coxswains, crewmembers, boarding officers and boarding team members operating in or being carried by shore- or cutter-based boats shall wear the hypothermia protection and survival equipment indicated in **Figure 6-4**. The figure reflects the minimum required equipment. Additional protection may be worn at the crewmember's discretion. Use **Figure 6-4** as follows:

- Draw a horizontal line across the graph that is equal to the water temperature for the mission.
- Draw a vertical line up the graph that is equal to the air temperature for the mission.
- Don the equipment identified in the shaded area where the lines intersect.

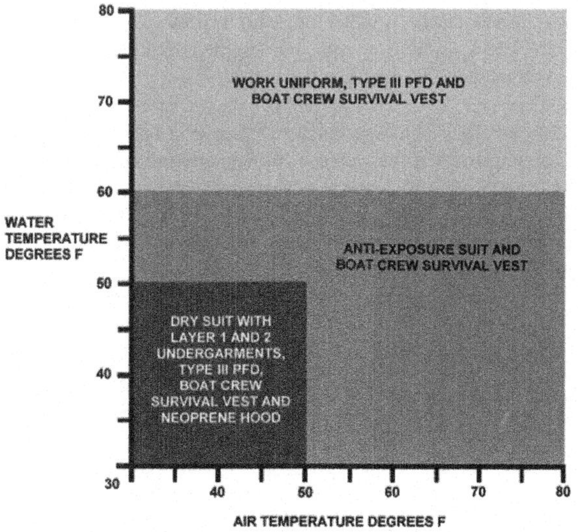

Figure 6-4
Air and Water Temperature - Required Survival Equipment

WARNING

> More layers of clothing reduce maneuverability that can be dangerous for boat crewmembers. Also, remember to wear insulated socks and boots (with reinforced toe), hoods, face masks, goggles and gloves as required to protect against the elements. (see *Chapter 3, Crew Efficiency Factors*)

B.3. Layered Clothing

The best way to avoid cold-related injuries is to wear proper clothing. When choosing clothing combinations, the best advice is to layer clothing. As the work effort changes or when an article of clothing becomes damp, the number of layers can be adjusted for comfort.

B.4. Maintaining Body Heat

Wet clothing robs the body of heat by breaking down the thermal protection of insulated clothing. It is extremely important to replace wet clothing as soon as possible to prevent cold-related injuries, particularly if the person is idle after a period of heavy perspiring. Many cold weather medical problems involve wet hands, feet and head. These areas should receive special care.

B.5. Wearing a PFD

Boat crewmembers shall wear a PFD at all times when wearing the dry suit. Crewmembers should not wear a PFD over an anti-exposure coverall.

NOTE

> A wet suit is not authorized for use by boat crewmembers - it may be worn by a cutter surface swimmer.

B.6. Distress Signal Devices

Boat crewmembers shall wear the boat crew survival vest over the PFD. If wearing the Type V inflatable PFD, the distress signaling equipment found in the survival vest will be stored in the inflatable's storage pocket/pouch. Surface swimmers wearing a dry or wet suit may carry a distress signal light and a signal whistle in lieu of the contents of the boat crew survival vest. Wearing a PML is recommended for boat crewmembers and the surface swimmer.

Anti-Exposure Coverall

B.7. Description

Anti-exposure coveralls are Type V PFDs. The anti-exposure coverall is the standard garment for moderate weather operations with closed cockpit boats. (see **Figure 6-5**) It provides good durability and out-of-water protection from the elements, but limited protection from hypothermia in the water.

B.8. Characteristics

Anti-exposure coveralls are constructed with a fabric cover and a closed cell foam lining. These suits provide a full range of movement and come in a variety of sizes. They provide adequate mobility and protection from limited exposure to outside elements such as wind and spray. The flotation characteristics of the coverall are similar to those of the Type III PFD. The approved coveralls feature an orally inflated pillow for a better flotation angle for extended periods of exposure.

WARNING

Wearing a type I or III PFD over an anti-exposure coverall may be dangerous in certain situations. The additional buoyancy may restrict the wearer's ability to swim out from under a capsized boat. In extreme situations, where buoyancy is a limitation instead of an advantage, it may be necessary to remove the PFD.

CAUTION !

When wearing this type of suit, it is important to tighten all closures and adjustments before entering the water. A loose-fitting suit may allow too much water in and greatly reduce the thermal effectiveness of the suit, leading to hypothermia.

B.9. Use

Anti-exposure coveralls provide hypothermia protection when the wearer is only periodically exposed to conditions which cause hypothermia. When more than periodic exposure is anticipated, even on boats with closed cockpits, a dry suit should be worn.

B.10. Donning

Anti-exposure coveralls are designed to be worn over the uniform in the same manner as standard coveralls. For added protection, polypropylene thermal underwear should be worn as a moisture wicking layer next to the skin. Also, insulated socks and boots (with reinforced toe), hoods, face masks, goggles and gloves should be used to protect against the elements.

B.11. Entering the Water

Before entering the water with anti-exposure coveralls, perform the following procedures:

Step	Procedure
1	Ensure the zipper is completely closed.
2	Tighten straps at the neck, waist, thigh, and ankle to reduce transfer of cold water inside the suit. This increases the degree of hypothermia protection.
3	Orally inflate the pillow behind the collar. This will provide support for the head.

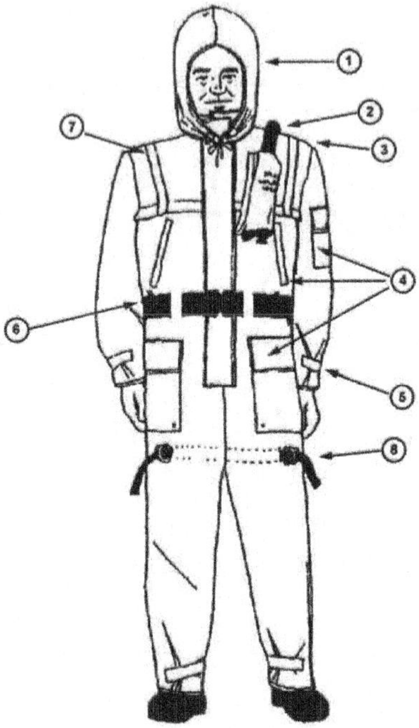

1. LINED HOOD
2. ORAL INFLATION TUBE
3. INFLATABLE HOOD
4. POCKETS
5. WRIST CLOSURES
6. ADJUSTABLE BELT
7. RETROREFLECTIVE TAPE
8. LEG STRAPS

Figure 6-5
Anti-Exposure Coverall

Dry Suit

WARNING

> Dry suits provide no inherent buoyancy. A PFD must be worn over a dry suit at all times while underway.

B.12. Description

The dry suit provides protection in areas where exposure to wind, spray, cold water, and hypothermia is likely. (see **Figure 6-6**) The dry suit, with proper undergarments, provides the best protection for crewmembers in adverse weather and cold-water immersion.

When the mission performed by the member is more likely to cause excess damage to a dry suit (AtoN maintenance, fisheries boardings), other Coast Guard authorized hypothermia protective clothing may be worn. Details on all authorized PFDs can be found in the *Rescue and Survival Systems Manual*, COMDTINST M10470.10 (series).

B.13. Characteristics

Dry suits are constructed of a trilaminate, breathable fabric. They have watertight seals at the neck, wrist, and ankles to keep the wearer dry and are designed so that one common size will fit most adults.

WARNING

Dry suits alone provide inadequate insulation or hypothermic protection. Wear thermal underwear layered underneath the dry suit. Fully close the zipper prior to entering the water. Consult the *Rescue and Survival Systems Manual*, COMDTINST M10470.10 (series) for a complete list of undergarments.

B.14. Use

When worn with a PFD and proper undergarments, a dry suit offers mobility and superior protection against the effects of wind, spray and cold-water immersion.

B.15. Donning

Don a dry suit as described in the *Rescue and Survival Systems Manual*, COMDTINST M10470.10 (series). Multifilament polypropylene thermal underwear must be worn under the suit for proper protection against cold. By layering underwear, crewmembers achieve maximum protection from hypothermia. Consequently, this suit is more bulky and loose fitting than a diver's wet suit. PFDs must also be worn because a dry suit has no inherent buoyancy. A dry suit is not a PFD.

B.16. Entering the Water

Before entering the water, perform the following procedures:

Step	Procedure
1	Slip on a wet suit hood.
2	Close all zippers and tighten all wrist and ankle straps.
3	Put on gloves.

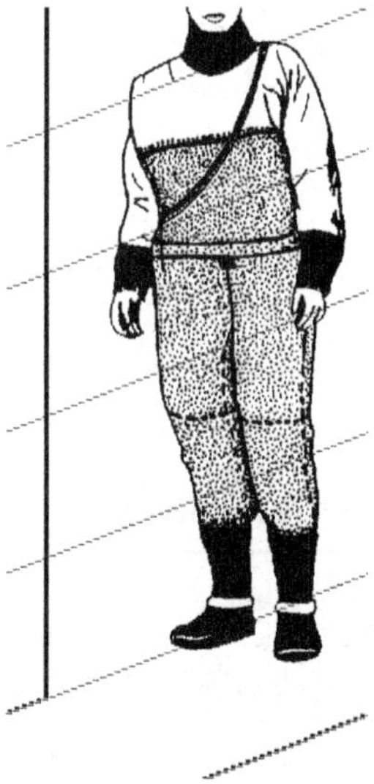

Figure 6-6
Dry Suit

Wet Suit

B.17. Description

The wet suit may be worn by cutter surface swimmers when entering the water. (see **Figure 6-7**) The wet suit is not authorized for use by boat crewmembers. It provides protection from exposure to cold water, but will not keep the user dry. A dry suit or anti-exposure coverall provides more out-of-water protection.

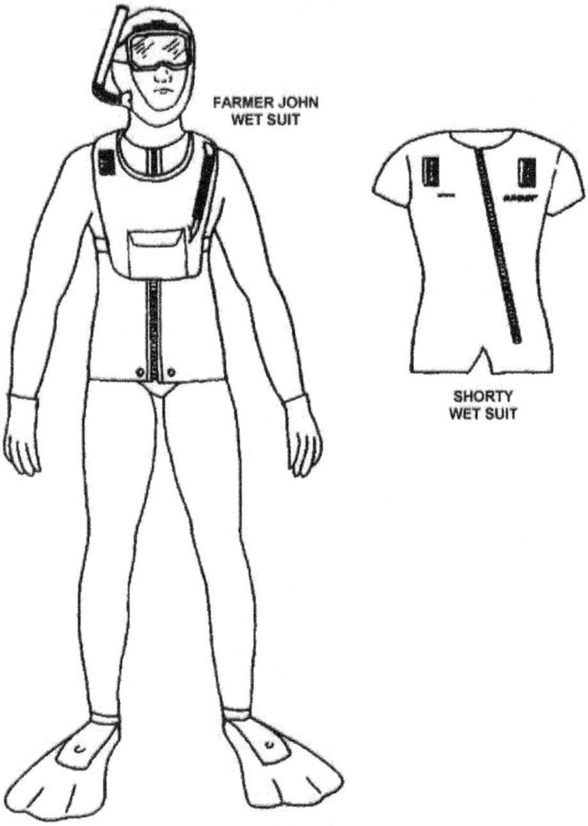

Figure 6-7
Wet Suit (Typical Neoprene)

B.18. Characteristics

The standard wet suit is fabricated of $\frac{3}{16}$" neoprene foam, an elastic material with high-flotation characteristics. The surface swimmer's wet suit ensemble consists of a custom fitted two-piece farmer-john style wet suit, a custom fitted one-piece shorty wet suit, hood, gloves and boots. Refer to the *Rescue and Survival Systems Manual*, COMDTINST M10470.10 (series) for procurement and inspection.

B.19. Use

Units should issue a wet suit to personnel designated as surface swimmers. It should be individually fitted. For added comfort and warmth, the suit may be worn over polypropylene cold weather underwear. Units shall issue custom-fitted wet suits as non-returnable items.

NOTE

> Wet suits are not authorized for crewmembers operating boats. Surface swimmers may wear either a dry suit or a wet suit when in the water, depending on water temperature.

B.20. Donning

When properly worn and with all fasteners closed, a wet suit should fit almost skin-tight.

Immersion Suit

B.21. Description

The immersion suit (also know as a survival suit) is worn when abandoning ship. They provide flotation as well as excellent hypothermia protection. (see **Figure 6-8**)

B.22. Characteristics

The immersion suit is a one-piece international orange garment constructed of nylon-lined neoprene or polyvinyl chloride foam. It is also equipped with an inflatable pillow to help keep the wearer's head out of the water. The suit has a built-in hood, boots, and gloves. The immersion suit is designed as one size fits all.

B.23. Use

The immersion suit is used when extended exposure to the elements is expected. It is the recommended PFD when abandoning ship. Even if boarding the life raft directly from the ship is possible, the immersion suit should still be worn. It is not to be used as a working outfit due to the wearer's limited dexterity when wearing the suit.

B.24. Donning

The immersion suit is similar to a regular pair of coveralls with a central zipper closing the one opening. Before putting on the immersion suit, care should be taken to ensure all sharp objects (knives, pens, collar devices) are stowed to prevent puncturing the suit. Footwear should also be removed before donning to reduce the possibility of tearing. Donning an immersion suit may be awkward and is best done in pairs with another crewmember.

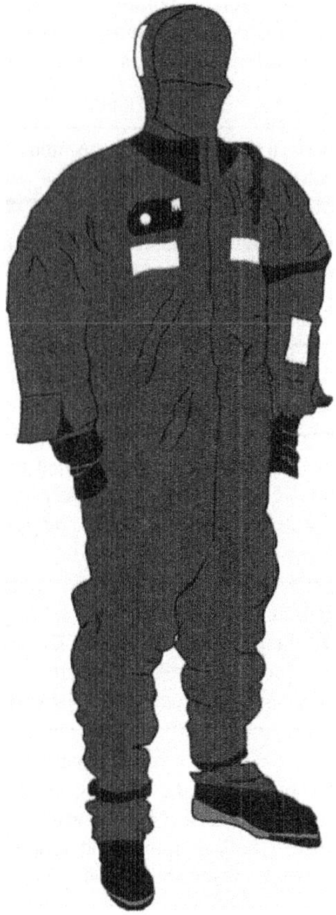

Figure 6-8
Immersion Suit

Section C. Headgear

Introduction

Boat crew personnel wear headgear for protection in cold weather conditions and during other hazardous conditions such as heavy weather and high-speed operations.

C.1. Thermal Protection

The Navy standard wool watch cap is worn for thermal protection. However, under extreme weather conditions it offers little protection to the face and neck. When operating in a cold environment, the polypropylene or fleece balaclava should be worn in conjunction with the wool watch cap or protective helmet.

For units that operate in dry suits, a neoprene hood shall be part of the crewmember's outfit. This orange hood will be stored in the front leg pocket of the dry suit and donned anytime a crewmember enters water that is 50° F or lower.

C.2. Protective Helmet

The wearing of helmets on boats under hazardous conditions, such as heavy weather and helicopter operations, is mandatory for Coast Guard crews and strongly recommended for auxiliarists. A lightweight kayaker-type helmet is the best.

NOTE The use of helmets by boat crews is recommended during high-speed operations.

Section D. Boat Crew Survival Vest

CAUTION ! Do not wear the boat crew survival vest over any inflatable PFD!

Introduction

The equipment in the boat crew survival vest provides crewmembers a means to signal their position on the surface of the water, day or night. The vest is worn over all PFDs with the exception of Type V inflatables. The vest does not interfere with wearing a PFD or hypothermia protective clothing. If using a Type V inflatable, the equipment normally stored in the boat crew survival vest will be tethered to the PFD's storage pocket/pouch. The components of the boat crew survival vest shall not be removed to other devices/individual PFDs. Auxiliary survival equipment requirements are outlined in the *Auxiliary Operations Policy Manual*, COMDTINST M16798.3 (series).

In this section

This section contains the following information:

Contents of the Boat Crew Survival Vest

CAUTION !

A boat coxswain is responsible for ensuring that each boat crewmember wears the appropriate PFD for the weather conditions/operations they will be performing. In addition to the PFD, each crewmember must also be outfitted with either a boat crew survival vest, or if wearing a Type V inflatable PFD, the same contents found in the survival vest stored in the PFD's pocket/pouch.

D.1. Description

Boat crew survival vests contain the equipment listed in **Table 6-1**, with their use, characteristics, and operation described later in this section.

Figure 6-9 shows the boat crew survival vest and the proper storage location for each item.

NOTE

The PML is not an authorized substitute for the distress signal light.

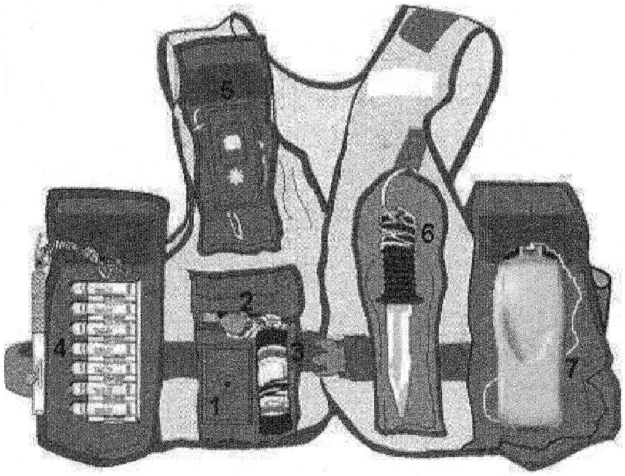

Figure 6-9
Boat Crew Survival Vest

Table 6-1
Contents of the Boat Crew Survival Vest

Item #	Equipment	Quantity
1	Emergency Signaling Mirror	1
2	Signal Whistle	1
3	Marine Smoke and Illumination Signal	1
4	Illumination Signal Kit	1
5	Distress Signal Light	1
6	Survival Knife	1
7	Personal Locator Beacon (PLB)	1

CH-1

NOTE To prevent losing signal kit equipment overboard while being handled, each item shall be tethered to the vest with a lanyard.

Emergency Signaling Mirror

D.2. Description The emergency signaling mirror is a pocket-sized mirror with a sighting hole in the center and a lanyard attached. (see **Figure 6-10**) However, any common mirror is useful as an emergency signaling device.

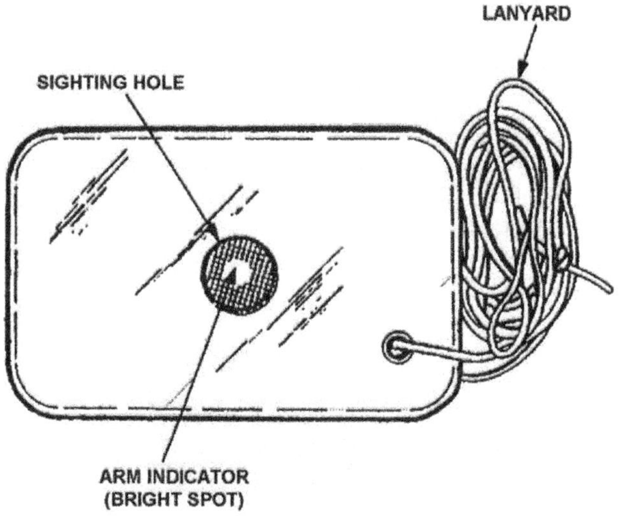

Figure 6-10
Emergency Signaling Mirror, MK-3

D.3. Use The mirror is used to attract the attention of passing aircraft, boats, or ground rescue teams by reflecting light at them.

D.4. Characteristics Light reflected in this manner can be seen at a great distance from the point of origin. Practice is the key to effective use of a signal mirror.

D.5. Operation

Instructions for using the mirror are printed on its backside. If these instructions have been worn away or are unreadable, the mirror shall be replaced. The following procedures describe how to properly use this accessory:

Step	Procedure
1	Face a point about halfway between the sun and an object you wish to signal.
2	Reflect sunlight from the mirror onto a nearby surface such as the raft, your hand, etc.
3	Slowly bring the mirror up to eye-level and look through the sighting hole. You will see a bright light spot, this is the aim indicator.
4	Hold the mirror near your eye and slowly turn and manipulate it so the bright light spot is on target.

Signal Whistle

D.6. Description

The whistle is a small, hand-held device that produces a loud sound when it is blown. (see **Figure 6-11**) The standard whistle is constructed of plastic and resembles a police officer's whistle.

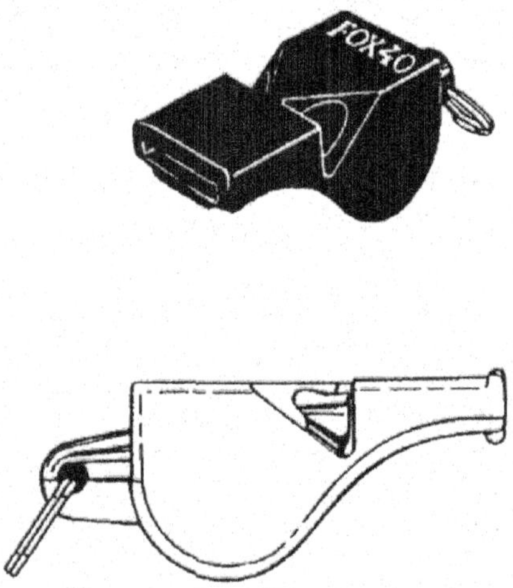

Figure 6-11
Signal Whistle

D.7. Use

The sound produced by a whistle will attract the attention of rescuers and guide them to the whistle's origination. During periods of restricted visibility, fog, and darkness, rescuers may hear the sound it produces before they sight the distress signal light.

D.8. Characteristics

Depending on weather conditions, a whistle's audible sound may be heard up to 1,000 meters/1,100 yards. Any wind has the effect of carrying the sound downwind.

D.9. Operation

To operate the signal whistle, perform the following procedures:

Step	Procedure
1	Place the reed part of a whistle between the lips and blow.
2	If the whistle does not produce a distinct whistle-like tone, quickly turn the whistle over and blow the water out the bail air relief hole and try again.

Smoke and Illumination Signal, MK-124 MOD 0

D.10. Description

The MK-124 MOD 0 is a pyrotechnic smoke and illumination signal used day or night as a distress signal at sea or on land. (see **Figure 6-12**) One end produces orange smoke as the day signal and the other end produces a red flare as the night signal. Because of its weight, about 8 ounces, and size, it may be carried in a PFD, vest, anti-exposure coverall, or life raft.

NOTE

Auxiliary crewmembers may use commercially available Coast Guard approved survival equipment while operating an Auxiliary facility. See the *Auxiliary Operations Policy Manual*, COMDTINST M16798.3 (series) for specific requirements.

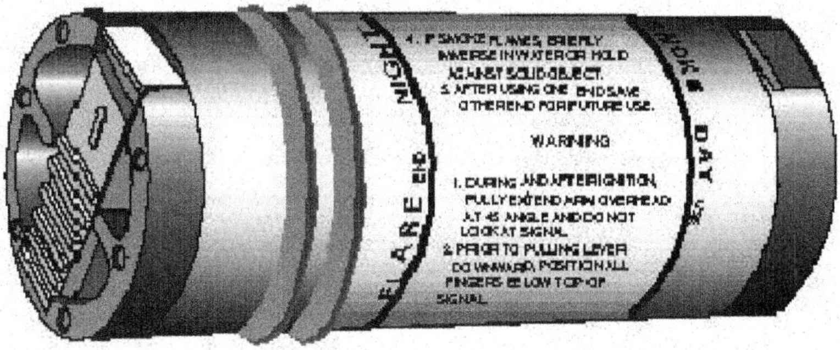

Figure 6-12
Smoke and Illumination Signal, MK-124 MOD 0

WARNING

Under no circumstances shall personnel ignite both ends simultaneously.

D.11. Use

These signals are used to attract vessels, aircraft, and ground rescue teams day or night. The signal may also be used to indicate wind direction for helicopter hoists. It is labeled with the following operating instructions:

- Do not dispose of the signal until both ends have been used.
- Only when signals misfire should it be disposed of over the side. Misfires are a safety hazard if kept onboard a vessel.
- When both ends of the signal have been discharged, properly dispose of it. In an actual distress situation, spent signals may be tossed over the side.

D.12. Characteristics

As mentioned above, both ends of the device produce a signal and each end burns for about 20 seconds. The night end produces a red flare (similar to a road flare) and the day end produces orange smoke.

D.13. Operation

The device has two raised bands around its circumference on its night end (flare). These bands positively identify the night end by sense of touch. Also, a label on the case identifies the day (smoke) and night (flare) ends and provides instructions for use.

After choosing which end to use, perform the following procedures:

Step	Procedure
WARNING	After ignition, the outer case may overheat and burn the hand. Dropping the signal on land will not decrease its effectiveness.
WARNING	Do not look directly at the light of a night flare close up. The intensity of the lights could burn the eyes.
WARNING	Do not direct either end of a signal toward another person.
1	Remove the black rubber protective cap from the end to be ignited.
2	Slide the plastic lever in the direction of the arrow until fully extended.
3	Hold the signal downwind and overhead at a 45° angle from the horizon over the side of the raft or away from dry debris to prevent burns from hot drippings.
WARNING	Prior to pulling lever downward, position all fingers below top of signal.
4	Using the thumb, pull down on the extended tab to ignite signal. (see **Figure 6-13**)
5	If the smoke signal end flames up, briefly immerse it in water or hold it against a solid object.
6	After using one end, douse in water to cool it, or if on land, place it on the ground to cool. Save the signal to use the other end when needed.

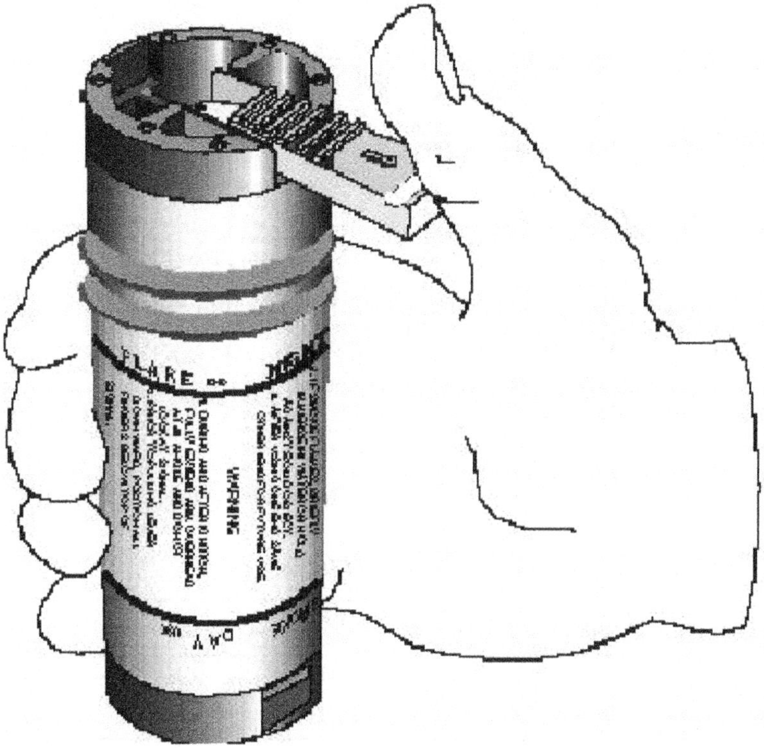

Figure 6-13
Operating the MK-124 MOD 0 Signal Flare

Illumination Signal Kit, MK-79 MOD 0

D.14. Description	The MK-79 MOD 0 is a pyrotechnic illumination signal kit that contains seven screw-in cartridge flares and one pencil-type projector. The projector in this kit is used to aim and fire a signal cartridge. (see **Figure 6-14**)

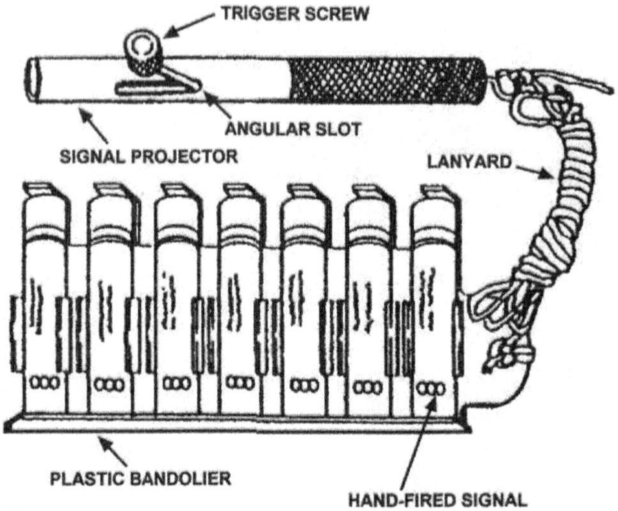

Figure 6-14
Illumination Signal Kit, MK-79 MOD 0

D.15. Use	The MK-79 MOD 0 is used to attract vessels, aircraft, and ground rescue teams.
D.16. Characteristics	These signals produce a red star display at an altitude of 250-650 feet for a minimum time of 4.5 seconds. Their luminous intensity is about 12,000 candle power.
D.17. Operation	The following are procedures for operating the MK-79 MOD 0:

Step	Procedure
WARNING	Failing to cock the firing pin back may result in the cartridge firing prematurely when attaching to the projector.
1	Remove the bandolier and projector from the plastic envelope.
2	Cock the firing pin of the projector by moving the trigger screw to the bottom of the vertical slot and slipping it to the right so that it catches at the top of the angular (safety) slot.
WARNING	The plastic tabs over signals in the bandolier protect percussion primers on the cartridges from being struck accidentally. They should be kept intact until just before loading into the projector.
3	Bend protective plastic tab away from signal in bandolier to allow attachment to projector.
WARNING	Keep the projectile-end of the flare pointed in a safe direction while loading the flare in the projector. Ensure Step 2 is completed prior to "loading". Accidental firing may occur if projector is not cocked.
4	Mate a signal flare with the projector and rotate clockwise until signal is seated.
5	Hold projector overhead with arm fully extended. The projector should be pointed at a slight angle away from the body.
6	While firmly gripping the projector, fire the signal by slipping the trigger screw to the left out of the safety slot and into the firing slot.
7	If the signal fails to fire, try again twice by depressing the trigger screw to the bottom of the firing slot with the thumb and releasing it quickly. If it still fails to fire, wait 30 seconds before unscrewing, to eliminate possibility of hang fire.
NOTE	This action should be one continuous movement so that the thumb does not interfere with the upward motion of the trigger screw when it is brought into the firing slot. The trigger screw must "snap" upward.
WARNING	Do not aim at personnel, aircraft, or other objects.
8	Unscrew the spent signal case or signal that has failed to fire. Discard by throwing overboard.
9	To fire another signal, repeat the procedures above.

Distress Signal Light

D.18. Description

The distress signal light is a lightweight, compact, battery-operated strobe light that emits a high intensity visual distress signal. (see **Figure 6-15**) The strobe light model that is currently in use is the battery-operated SDU-5/E or CG-1 strobe light. Some lights are also Coast Guard-approved as PMLs.

Figure 6-15
Distress Signal Light, CG-1

D.19. Use

The distress signal light is used to attract the attention of aircraft, ships, or ground parties. One side is equipped with hook tape so that it can be attached to the pile tape found on the boat crew safety helmet, inflatable PFD, or survival vest. This eliminates the need to hold the distress signal light, freeing up hands to operate other signaling equipment.

D.20. Characteristics

The SDU-5/E and the CG-1 distress signal lights emit approximately 50 flashes per minute. At the peak of each flash, the luminous intensity is 100,000 candlepower. Under continuous operation, they will flash for 9 hours, or 18 hours when operated intermittently. On a clear night, the distress signal light has a minimum visual range of five miles. However, the range of visibility will be determined by the height of eye of the observer. For an observer low on a boat, the range will most likely be much less than the advertised five miles.

D.21. Operation

The following are the procedures to operate the distress signal light:

Step	Procedure
1	Turn *on*. SDU-5/E: Push the button switch in until a click is heard, then release. CG-1: Slide the switch into the *on* position. Light should begin flashing within seconds.
2	Turn *off*. SDU-5/E: Push the button switch in until click is heard, then release. CG-1: Slide the switch back into the *off* position. The light should stop flashing.
3	If this light is tested and it fails to perform within operational limits, replace the battery. If it still does not operate properly, remove it from service.

Survival Knife

D.22. Description

The survival knife (see **Figure 6-16**) is a basic tool used to free the crewmember from entangling lines. It is also used to cut material blocking a path in escaping a capsized or sinking boat. It should be a fixed blade design made of corrosion-resistant material. The blade should be checked periodically for sharpness.

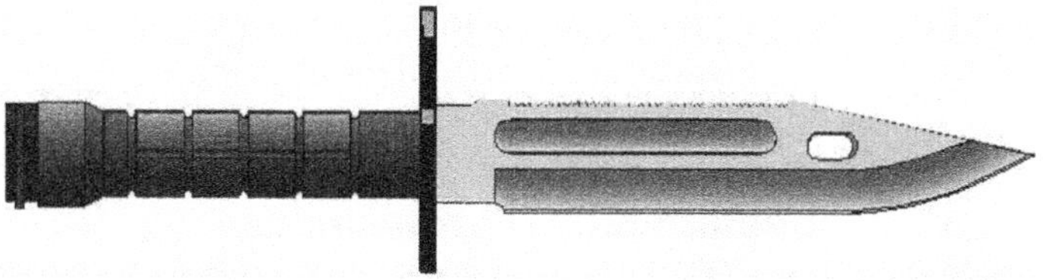

Figure 6-16
Survival Knife

Personal Locator Beacon (PLB)

D.23. Description

The PLB is the newest addition to the boat crew survival vest. It is a smaller version of the common ship mounted EPIRB that is used on military, commercial, and recreational vessels. This personal transmitter is capable of broadcasting a distress signal that can be received and tracked world-wide guiding emergency response resources to the transmitting position for rescue.

D.24. Use

The PLB is for emergency use only. This device is the primary distress signal and should be activated immediately to signal for help. Once activated, do not turn it off. Once search vessels or aircraft have reached the transmitting position area, use other signaling equipment (radio, signal mirror, flares, etc.) to vector them to the position.

D.25. Characteristics

The PLB is a personal transmitter capable of broadcasting on both 406 MHz and 121.5 MHz. The international satellite based search and rescue system (COSPAS SARSAT) monitors 406 MHz and is able to provide a position accurate to within three nautical miles within 90 minutes. Once the rescue platform is in the vicinity, the 121.5 MHz transmitter provides a signal allowing the resource to home in on the vessel or individual in distress particularly if the individual is equipped with flares and a strobe light.

CH-1

D.26. Operation

Since PLBs may vary in style and operation, as new models are produced, each crewmember shall read and understand the PLB owner's manual. Prior to getting underway with the PLB for the first time, each crewmember shall demonstrate the test sequence and explain the activation procedure to a qualified member. An appropriate entry shall be made in the boat crew training record documenting this training.

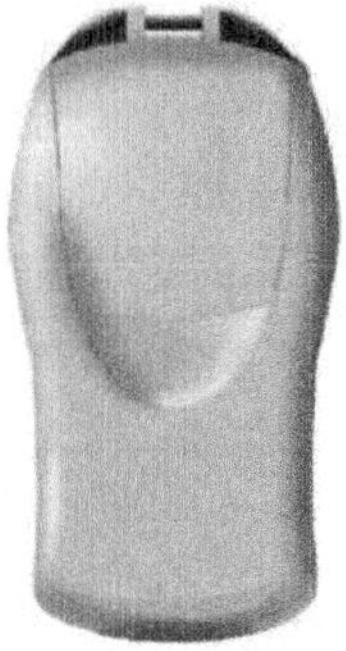

Figure 6-17
Personal Locator Beacon(PLB)

Section E. Pyrotechnics

Introduction

If the boat becomes disabled during a mission, its crew must have some means of signaling aircraft or vessels for assistance. Signaling devices include pyrotechnics. The smoke and illumination signal, Marine MK-124 MOD 0 and the MK 79 MOD 0 signal kits were discussed earlier in this chapter. Additional pyrotechnics can be found in a boat's pyrotechnics kit and are explained in this section. Visual distress signals, in general, are discussed in *Chapter 11, Communications.*

E.1. Requirements

Stowage, allowance, and handling of pyrotechnics is performed in accordance with the *Ordnance Manual*, COMDTINST M8000.2 (series) and the Navy publication NAVSEA SW050-AB-MMA-010. Coast Guard Unit Commanders will outfit their boats with the required pyrotechnics. All Auxiliary boats must carry visual distress signals that meet facility requirements. The pyrotechnic devices carried in the survival vest or inflatable PFD's storage pocket/pouch should be small enough to be carried comfortably and be well protected from the elements. The following are Coast Guard-approved visual distress signal devices typically used by the Auxiliary:

NOTE Pyrotechnic devices should not be used until a rescue craft is actually in sight.

CFR No. Marked on Device	Device Description	Quantity
160.021	Hand-held, red flare distress signals, day and night.	3
160.022	Floating, orange smoke distress signals, day only	3
160.024	Pistol-projected, parachute red flare distress signals, day and night	3
160.037	Hand-held, orange smoke distress signals, day only	3
160.057	Floating, orange smoke distress signals, day only	3
160.066	Distress signal for boats, red aerial pyrotechnic flare, day and night	3

E.2. Parachute Illumination Signal, MK-127A1

The parachute illumination signal, MK-127A1 is a night time illumination-signaling device. When fired, it climbs to an altitude of 650 to 700 feet before igniting. Upon ignition, it produces a parachute-suspended white star flare that burns for about 36 seconds with 125,000 candlepower. The signal descends at a rate of 10 to 15 feet per second. (see **Figure 6-18**)

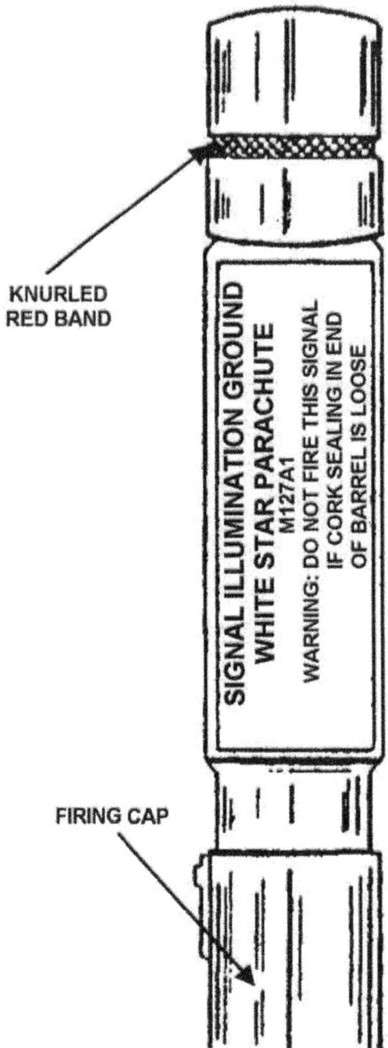

Figure 6-18
Parachute Illumination Signal, MK-127A1

E.2.a. Firing Instructions

The following are procedures for firing the parachute illumination signal:

Step	Procedure
1	Do not remove a signal from its sealed container until just before use.
2	Remove a signal from the container in accordance with instructions printed on the container.
3	In all handling, avoid striking the signal primer.
4	Do not use signals that are dented, cracked, or otherwise damaged.
5	Hold the signal in left hand with the RED band of the signal FACING UP. Align left thumb and forefinger along the red band.
6	Withdraw the firing cap from the lower end of the signal.
7	Point the ejection end of the signal (the end opposite the red knurled band) away from the body and away from other people, equipment, and materials. Slowly push the cap onto the primer (red band) end until the cap meets the edge of the knurled band. DO NOT PERMIT THE CAP TO GO BEYOND THE RED BAND.
CAUTION !	Exercise due care to prevent the expended rocket body from falling on people, watercraft, and structures.
8	Hold the signal FIRMLY at arm's length with the left hand, with the ejection end facing straight up. The signal should be held in a vertical position (90° elevation) when firing.
9	Strike the firing cap bottom sharply with the palm of the right hand, keeping the left arm rigid and pointing straight up.
10	If a signal misfires while on land, place it in a secure position to prevent people from being hurt should the signal fire. The signal must not be approached for at least 30 minutes. If a misfire occurs while underway, toss it overboard.

WARNING If a signal is fired at an angle less than 90° elevation (directly overhead), the altitude reached is reduced and the altitude of candle burnout is lessened. If the firing angle is 60° or less, the candle will, in almost all cases, still be burning when it strikes the surface.

WARNING When conducting SAR operations with a helicopter, extreme caution and coordination must be used by surface units using pyrotechnics. Do not fire pyrotechnics without permission and instructions from the Aircraft Commander.

E.2.b. Firing Angles

Firing a signal at angles other than a vertical position may be necessary under the following circumstances:

- To compensate for high wind velocities.
- To gain maximum illumination of the area.

Section F. Rescue and Survival Raft

Introduction

The six-person rescue and survival raft is a multipurpose raft designed for crew survival or rescue and assistance to persons in distress. It is usually carried on Coast Guard boats greater than 30 feet in length. The discussion here applies to a Coast Guard procured raft, but the general procedures apply to almost any commercially available raft. The Auxiliary may use commercially available Coast Guard-approved life rafts that may typically be less complete but still serve the same purpose. The instructions for use and maintenance of any life raft should always be reviewed.

F.1. Automatic Inflation and Deployment

When properly stowed, this life raft is designed to automatically float free from its storage rack and inflate in the event of capsizing or sinking. As the raft container is released and drifts away, the inflation cable, attached to the raft-end of the 50-foot painter line, is pulled tight. When this occurs, the CO_2 cylinder will automatically discharge and inflate the life raft. The painter line will remain attached to the rack by a weak link, which requires 500 pounds of force to separate. Separation will also occur by heaving around on the painter line or by the stress exerted on it from the raft's buoyancy if the boat sinks to a depth greater than 50 feet.

F.2. Manual Deployment

To manually deploy the rescue and survival raft, perform the following procedures (see **Figure 6-19**):

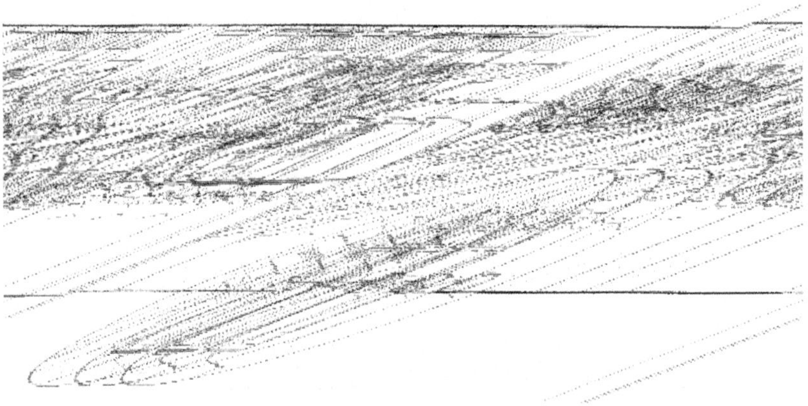

Figure 6-19
Manual Deployment of Survival Raft

Step	Procedure
1	Cut/untie painter line or disconnect shackle from the weak link.
2	Disconnect the shock retaining cord and remove the raft container from the stowage rack.
3	Attach the painter line to a cleat on the boat.
4	Drop the raft into the water on the leeward side of the boat.
NOTE	In the event of a fire on your vessel, drop the raft into the water on the windward side of the vessel to stay upwind of harmful smoke, fumes and fire.
5	Pull the remaining painter line (approximately 50 feet) from the raft container to actuate the inflation assembly. As the raft inflates, tend the painter line to keep the raft close. Fend off the inflating raft to prevent damage to the raft from the boat.
6	Time permitting; place extra equipment and supplies aboard the raft such as signals, portable radios, immersion suits, water, and food.
7	If practical, pull the raft alongside the boat and board the raft directly from the boat.
8	Deploy sea anchor.
9	Pull the canopy over the support tubes and secure in place.
10	Set a watch on the boat and painter line. If the boat begins to sink, cut the painter line to free the raft to drift.

CAUTION ! If possible, board the raft directly from the sinking vessel. Avoid entering the water.

F.3. Boarding a Raft

The boat crew should try to remain in the general area of the boat. If the boat does not sink immediately, the operating painter line should be left attached to the cleat. If the boat sinks rapidly, the painter line should be cut before it starts to pull the life raft down.

F.4. Tasks Onboard a Raft

Upon boarding a raft, complete the following procedures as soon as possible:

CAUTION ! Be careful not to snag the raft with your shoes or with sharp objects.

Step	Procedure
1	Account for everyone and search for survivors.
2	If more than one raft is deployed, tie them together.
3	Check the physical condition of all people aboard. Give first aid as necessary. Weather permitting, wash any oil or gasoline from clothing and body. These substances will not only burn skin, but also pose a fire hazard. Additionally, they may be transferred from skin to the raft, deteriorating the rubber surfaces.
4	Salvage any floating equipment that may be useful. Inventory, stow, and secure all survival items.
5	If no longer attached to the vessel, deploy the sea anchor to reduce rate of drift and improve stability in heavy seas.
6	Check the raft for proper inflation and points of possible chafing (areas where equipment may wear a hole in the buoyancy tubes).
7	Bail out any water that may have entered the raft.
8	Inflate the floor immediately.
9	In cold water, put on hypothermia protective clothing, if available. Rig the entrance cover, close when necessary.
10	If other people are with you, huddle together for warmth.

F.5. Conduct in a Raft

The safety and survival of everyone in a raft depends on clear thinking and common sense. To protect those aboard and increase survival time, perform the following procedures:

Step	Procedure
1	Maintain a positive attitude.
2	Inventory all equipment. Ration water and food. Assign lookout and other necessary duties to crewmembers.
3	Do not rely on memory. If materials are available, keep a written log. Record the following: • Time of entry into the water. • Names and physical condition of survivors. • Ration schedule. • Winds. • Weather. • Direction of swells. • Times of sunrise and sunset. • Other navigation data.

WARNING

Although the raft is ballasted and very stable in most sea states, it may capsize in large breaking waves. For this reason, consider other methods for rescue of people in breaking surf or seas. (e.g., helicopter rescue).

F.6. Using a Raft to Rescue Others

When it is impossible or too dangerous to maneuver close to a distressed vessel, the life raft may be used to ferry survivors to the boat. It may also be used to recover people from the water if a boat cannot get close enough to them. Use the following procedures when deploying a life raft during a rescue attempt: (see **Figure 6-20**)

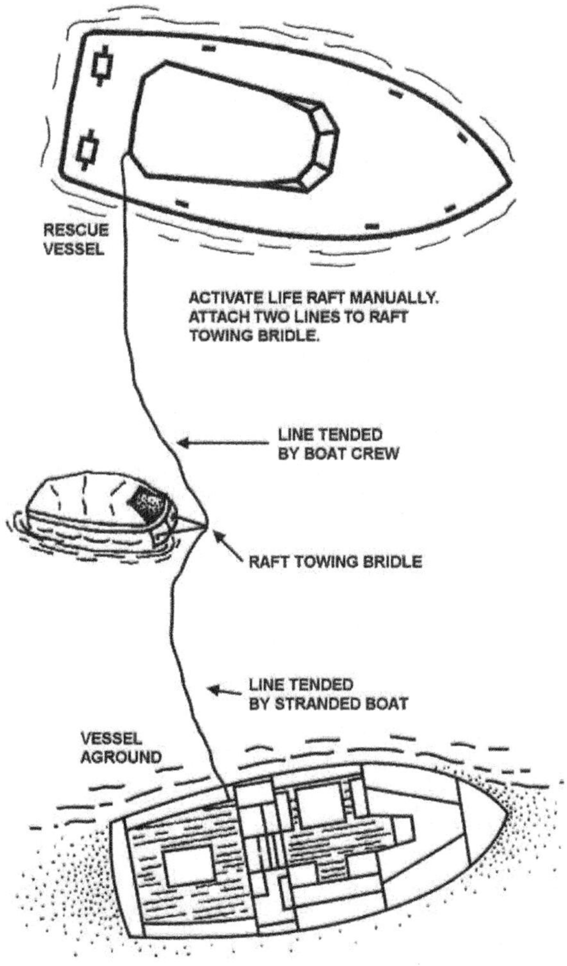

Figure 6-20
Life Raft as Rescue Ferry

Step	Procedure
1	Remove the raft container from its storage rack.
2	Do not manually or automatically inflate the life raft while removing the tape sealing the life raft case (half shells) together.
3	Roll the life raft out of the case and place it in the water on the leeward side of the boat.
4	Pull the 50' painter line from the raft container, manually inflate the raft, and hold it alongside your boat.
5	Attach two lines, each of a length longer than the maximum distance between your boat and the people in distress.
6	Use one line to tend the life raft from your boat during the evolution (NEVER LET GO OF THIS LINE).
7	Pass the other line to the people in distress with a heaving line or let the current float it down to them.
8	Tell the persons being assisted to haul the life raft to their position.
WARNING	Ensure each person is wearing a PFD. Do not permit more people to enter the raft than are allowed by the raft's specifications.
9	Once the life raft is alongside, direct the persons to board the life raft, one person at a time.
10	If the number of people being assisted is more than the carrying capacity of the raft, direct the people remaining to tend the line attached to the life raft from their location; haul back the maximum number of survivors and repeat the procedure.
11	After recovering all people, deflate the raft and bring it aboard the rescue boat. The raft may have taken on water during the rescue evolution. De-ballast the raft before bringing it aboard. Use the handles located on the ballast bags and slowly lift one side of the raft until all the water has run out.
12	Once the raft is aboard, do not repack the raft. Wash the raft and have it repacked at a certified packing station before returning it to service.

Section G. Emergency Procedures in the Event of Capsizing

Introduction

The key to surviving capsizing is to avoid it ever happening. If it cannot be avoided, then the crew must recognize when it could happen and be prepared. *Chapter 9, Stability, Chapter 10, Boat Handling, and Chapter 20, Heavy Weather Addendum*, all discuss situations and conditions where capsizing could result. These chapters also present warning signs and measures to take to minimize risk. The coxswain must continually assess the conditions to ensure the safety of the boat crew and of those in distress; however, all crewmembers have the responsibility to keep the coxswain advised if the situation changes.

G.1. Prevention

A boat is less likely to capsize in deep, open water. The chances of capsizing are greatest while operating in or near the surf or breaking seas. The force needed to capsize is most likely to come from heavy seas directly astern (following seas), or large breakers striking abeam. A boat should stay at sea until conditions change. The safest point for most boats to take heavy seas is nearly bow-on. A boat should not operate or tow in conditions beyond the capability of the boat or crew. In such conditions, the Operational Commander should be advised so that the proper resource (e.g., MLB, SRB, cutter, or helicopter) can respond. Conditions present in many capsizings include:

- Surf or breaking seas.
- Shallow water depth (less than 20 feet).
- Going against a strong tidal current and with steep following seas.
- Escorting or towing another boat through an inlet.
- Restricted visibility due to darkness, rain, or fog.
- Stability reduced by low fuel in the tank, excessive amounts of water in bilges, icing of topsides, or too many people onboard.

G.2. Precautions

If the hull is intact after capsizing, it will not sink for some time, even in rough seas. The crew will have time to escape if panic is avoided. Precautions ahead of time include:

- Learn the boat's interior. Initially the crew will be disoriented due to being upside down and with a lack of lighting.
- Stow all loose gear, and have all equipment and doors operating properly for ease in escaping.
- Know the location and use of all survival equipment. Check it regularly to be sure that it is adequate, in good repair, and that all signaling devices work.
- Be ready to grab a sturdy support to prevent being thrown about.

G.3. Escape Procedures

If trapped in or under the boat, crewmembers should seek out an air pocket near the top (inverted bottom). The crew should be gathered together in the air pocket. Everyone should settle down and focus on planning a safe escape. The escape route and objects of reference along the route should be discussed. Everyone should look down; light may be visible and escape immediate.

- Make every effort to escape. The boat may sink or the air will eventually escape through hull fittings, cracks, or holes, or become unfit to breathe (fuel vapors, bilge waste, or lack of oxygen due to survivors breathing).
- Before attempting to escape, check for needed survival equipment, especially flotation and signaling devices.
- Activate Personal Marker Light (PML) to assist in locating other survivors particularly at night. If PML does not activate due to salt water intrusion or impact, activate emergency strobe. Extinguish if it becomes too disorienting.
- PFDs may have to be removed temporarily for people to fit through spaces or to go underwater to reach an exit. If necessary, tie a line to the PFD and pull it out after exiting.
- Avoid the stern if the engines are still running.
- If caught in an open cockpit area, swim down below the gunwales and surface alongside the boat.

G.3.a. Escape from an Enclosed Compartment

Escape from an enclosed compartment will require additional planning. Advice includes:

- All exits are upside down when the boat capsizes. Locate an exit route and reference points from the compartment to open water.
- PFDs may have to be removed temporarily for people to fit through spaces or to go underwater to reach an exit. If necessary, tie a line to the PFD and pull it out after exiting.
- Swim underwater through the exit and out from the boat. If a line is available, the best swimmer should exit first through a cabin door or window, carrying the line. If no line is available, have the best swimmer go first, followed by a poorer swimmer and lastly a good swimmer. (If the poorer swimmers are left alone inside, they are likely to panic and not escape.) The first swimmer, when free, should tap on the hull to signal success in getting out to the others.
- Cold water decreases the length of time anyone can hold his or her breath underwater. Immersion in cold water may also give a sensation of tightness in the chest. Experiment inside the compartment before attempting to escape. This will decrease the possibility of panic during the escape attempt.

G.3.b. Alongside a Capsized Boat

Survivors from a capsized boat should attempt to stay with the boat or other visible floating debris.

- Get onboard a life raft if available.
- If a life raft is not available, climb onto the boat, if possible. Otherwise, hold onto the largest floating object available.
- Generally, everyone should stay with the boat and not swim for shore. Distances to the beach can be deceiving, and strenuous activities such as swimming in cold water can hasten the onset of hypothermia.

Survivors should consider tying themselves to the boat if there is a rapid means of untying or cutting free, in case the boat shifts or sinks. Most people are likely to become tired or develop hypothermia.

G.3.c. Remaining Inside a Capsized Boat

If someone cannot exit the capsized boat:

- Remain calm and stay within an air pocket.
- Trap the air in the compartments (e.g., close any hull valves that can be located).
- When hearing rescuers, attempt to communicate to them by shouting or tapping on the hull.
- Conserve oxygen by remaining calm and minimizing physical activity. If possible, get out of the water to reduce hypothermia.
- Remember that rescuers should arrive soon.

This page intentionally left blank.

Chapter 7
Marlinespike Seamanship

Introduction

Marlinespike seamanship is the art of handling and working with all kinds of line or rope. It includes knotting, splicing, and fancy decorative work. There is no better measure of a sailor's worth than skill in marlinespike seamanship. Much practice is required to become proficient in this skill. Knowledge of line handling terminology, phrases, and standard communication among the crew is necessary. To be less than proficient may be costly when the safety of life and property depends on the crew's knowledge of marlinespike seamanship.

This chapter discusses the following information:

- Types, characteristics, and care of line.
- Definitions.
- Safety practices.
- Line handling commands.
- Directions for tying knots and making splices commonly used on Coast Guard boats and Auxiliary facilities.
- Instructions about basic boat line handling.
- Technical information for determining which line, hooks, and shackles are safe to use.

In this chapter

This chapter contains the following sections:

WARNING

The wearing of jewelry, including rings, wristwatches, necklaces or other items not consisting of organizational clothing, PPE, or uniform articles by boat crew members engaged in hoisting, towing, or other deck evolutions where the potential for snagging exists **is prohibited**. OICs and coxswains will address this during all pre-underway briefs and coxswains shall ensure jewelry is removed prior to beginning all deck evolutions.

Section A. Types and Characteristics of Line

Introduction

The uses for a particular line will depend heavily upon the type and characteristics of the line. This section includes information regarding the different types of line used during boat operations.

In this section

This section contains the following information:

Line Characteristics

A.1. Composition

Lines are made of natural or synthetic fibers twisted into yarns. The yarns are grouped together in such a way as to form strands. Finally, the strands are twisted, plaited, or braided, in various patterns, to form line.

A.2. Coast Guard Line

Line used on Coast Guard boats is classified in two different ways:

- Material used.
- Size.

A.2.a. Material Used

Lines are categorized as natural fiber or synthetic fiber. Refer to **Table 7-1** for fiber line characteristics. The characteristics of the natural and synthetic fiber lines will be explained further in this section.

A.2.b. Size

No matter what the line is made of (natural or synthetic), it is measured the same way, by its circumference or distance around the line. This makes it different from wire rope, which is measured by diameter.

Depending on its size, the line is placed into one of the following three categories:

- Small stuff – Up to 1.5" in circumference
- Line – 1.5" to 5" in circumference
- Hawser – Everything over 5" in circumference

Table 7-1
Fiber Line Characteristics

LINE CHARACTERISTICS	NATURAL FIBER LINE			SYNTHETIC FIBER LINE			
	Manila	Sisal	Cotton	Nylon	Polyester	Polypropylene	Polyethylene
Strength:							
Wet strength compared to dry strength	Up to 120%	Up to 120%	Up to 120%	85-90%[1]	100%[1]	100%	105%
Shock load absorption ability	Poor	Poor	Poor	Excellent	Very good	Very good	Fair
Weight:							
Specific gravity	1 38	1 38	1 54	1 14	1 38	91	95
Able to float	No	No	No	No	No	Yes	Yes
Elongation:							
Percent at break	10-12%	10-12%	5-12%	15-28%	12-15%	18-22%	20-24%
Creep (extension under sustained load)	Very low	Very low		Moderate	Low	High	High
Effects of Moisture:							
Water absorption of individual fibers	Up to 100%	Up to 100%	Up to 100%	2 0-6 0%	<1 0%	None	None
Resistance to rot, mildew, and deterioration due to marine organisms	Poor	Very poor	Very poor	Excellent	Excellent	Excellent	Excellent
Degradation:							
Resistance to UV in sunlight	Good	Good	Good	Good	Excellent	Fair[2]	Fair[2]
Resistance to aging for property store rope	Good	Good	Good	Excellent	Excellent	Excellent	Excellent
Rope Abrasion Resistance:							
Surface	Good	Fair	Poor	Very good[3]	Very good[1]	Good	Fair
Internal	Good	Good	Good	Very good[3]	Excellent[1]	Good	Good
Thermal Properties:							
High temperature working limit	300° F	300° F	300° F	250° F	275° F	200° F	150° F
Low temperature working limit	-100° F	-100° F	-100° F	-70° F	-70° F	-20° F	-100° F
Melting point			Chars 300° F	490-500° F	490-500° F	330° F	285° F
Chemical Resistance:							
Effect of acid	Will disintegrate in hot diluted and cold concentrated acids	Same as manila	Same as manila	Decompose by strong mineral acids; resistant to weak acids	Resistant to most mineral acids; disintegrate by 95% sulfuric acid	Very resistant	Very resistant
Effect of alkalis	Poor resistance will lose strength where exposed	Same as manila	May swell but will not be damaged	Little or none	No effect cold; slowly disintegrate by strong alkalis at the boil	Very resistant	Very resistant
Effect of organic solvents	Fair resistance for fiber, but hydrocarbons will remove protective lubricants on rope	Good resistance	Poor resistance	Resistant Soluble in some phenolic compounds and in 90% formic acid	Generally unaffected; soluble in some phenolic compounds	Soluble in chlorinated hydrocarbons at 160° F	Same as polypropylene

[1] Grades with special over finishes are available to enhance wet strength and abrasion properties

[2] For non-UV stabilized product, consult manufacturer

[3] Dry condition Under wet condition: Good

A.2.c. Construction

Strands are twisted to either the right or the left. This twisting is the "lay" of the line. Line may have either a left lay or a right lay depending upon how the strands are twisted together. Line is usually constructed as plain-laid, plaited, and double-braided lines. **Figure 7-1** illustrates fiber rope components and construction. The type of construction will depend upon the intended use of the line. The following describes line types:

Line Type	Characteristics
Plain-laid	Made of three strands, right- or left-laid. Most common is right-hand laid.
Cable-laid	Made of three, right-hand, plain-laid lines laid together to the left to make a larger cable.
Plaited	Made of eight strands, four right-twisted and four left-twisted. Strands are paired and worked like a four strand braid.
Braided	Usually made from three strands (sometimes four) braided together. The more common braided lines are hollow-braided, stuffer-braided, solid-braided, and double-braided.
Double-braided	Made of two hollow-braided ropes, one inside the other. The core is made of large single yarns in a slack braid. The cover is also made of large single yarns but in a tight braid that compresses and holds the core. This line is manufactured only from synthetics, and about 50% of the strength is in the core.

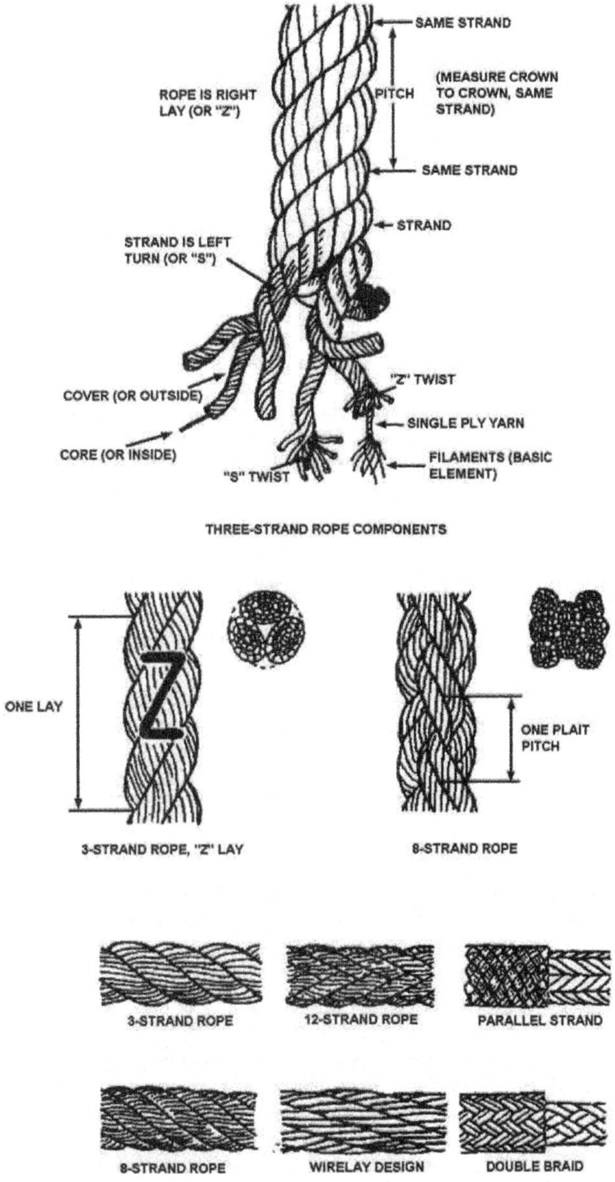

Figure 7-1
Fiber Rope Components and Construction

Natural Fiber Line

A.3. Composition

Natural fiber line is made from organic material, specifically, plant fiber. The following describes the various natural fiber lines:

Natural Fiber Line Type	Characteristics
Manila	Made from fibers of the abaca plant and is the strongest and most expensive of the natural fibers.
Sisal	Made from the agave plant and is next in strength to manila, being rated at 80% of manila's strength.
Hemp	Made from the fiber of the stalk of the hemp plant, is now rarely used.
Cotton	Made from natural fibers of the cotton plant, may be three-stranded, right-lay or of braided construction used for fancy work and lashings.

A.4. Uses of Natural Fiber Line

Natural fiber line, usually manila, hemp or sisal, are used for tying off fenders, securing chafing gear, and doing other small projects where line strength is not a major concern.

Braided line is most commonly used for signal halyard, heaving lines, and lead lines.

Plain-laid line may be used for securing loose gear, fender lines, and fancy work.

CAUTION ! Do not use natural fiber line as a towline.

A.5. Limitations

Natural fiber line has a lower breaking strength than synthetic fiber line of an equal size, and unlike synthetic line, natural fiber line does not recover after being stretched (elasticity). In the Coast Guard, it is not used for load-bearing purposes on boats. Another limitation of natural fiber line is the likelihood of rotting if stowed wet.

A.6. Construction

A close look at a natural fiber line will reveal that the strands are twisted together. They will have either a right or left lay.

A.7. Plain-Laid Lines

Plain-laid line is the most common type of natural fiber line used in the Coast Guard. In plain-laid, three strands are twisted together to the right in an alternating pattern. Because of the number of strands, this line is sometimes called "three-strand" line. The yarns making up the strands are laid in the opposite direction of the strands. These are twisted together in the opposite direction to make the line. The direction of the twist determines the lay of the line. In the case of plain-laid lines, the yarns are twisted to the right. They are then twisted together to the left to make the strands. The strands are twisted together to the right to make the line. (see **Figure 7-1**)

Synthetic Fiber Line

A.8. Composition

Synthetic fiber line is made of inorganic (man-made) materials. The characteristics of synthetic fiber line are considerably different from natural fiber line. The differences will vary depending on the type of material from which the line is made. The following identifies the various types of synthetic fiber line used:

Type	Characteristics
Nylon	A synthetic fiber of great strength, elasticity, and resistance to weather. It comes in twisted, braided, and plaited construction, and can be used for almost any purpose where its slippery surface and elasticity is not a disadvantage.
Dacron	A synthetic fiber of about 80% of the strength of nylon that will only stretch 10% of its original length.
Polyethylene and Polypropylene	A synthetic fiber with about half the strength of nylon, 25% lighter than nylon making it easier to handle, and it floats in water.

A.9. Commonly Used Types

The most common types of synthetic line used on Coast Guard boats are nylon and polypropylene. Because of its superior strength and elasticity, nylon is used where the line must bear a load.

A.9.a. Double-Braided Nylon Line

Double-braided nylon line is the only line used for towlines on Coast Guard boats. However, privately owned Auxiliary facilities might have towlines other than double-braided construction. When double-braided line is made, the yarns are woven together much like the individual yarns in a piece of cloth are woven. The actual line consists of two hollow braid lines, an inner core and an outer cover. The core is woven into a slack, limp braid from large single yarns. The cover is woven from even larger yarns into a tight braid to cover and compress the core.

A.9.a.1. Advantages

Double-braided nylon has two other characteristics that increase its strength, elongation and elasticity. Elongation refers to the stretch of the line and elasticity refers to the ability of the line to recover from elongation. Synthetic line will stretch farther and recover better than natural line. Because of this, synthetic line can absorb the intermittent forces and surges resulting from waves or seas much better than natural fiber line.

A.9.a.2. Limitations

While its superior strength makes double-braided nylon line the preferred choice for load bearing, there are disadvantages. Because it will stretch further (elongate) and still recover (elasticity), the snap back potential if the line parts is greater than with natural fiber line. Also, if nylon line is doubled and placed under excessive strain, there is a danger that the deck fittings might fail. If that happens, the line will snap back like a rubber band, bringing the deck fitting with it. Additionally, damage to the engine or deck fittings could occur if the bollard pull is exceeded.

CAUTION !

Never double a line or use a single line that can withstand more pulling force than the bollard pull of the towing bitt.

A.9.a.4. Bollard Pull

Bollard pull is the point where the static pulling force becomes such that any increase in engine load could lead to damage to the engine or the towing bitt.

A.9.b. Plain-Laid Polypropylene Line

Orange-colored polypropylene line is used on Coast Guard boats for life rings and heaving lines.

A.9.b.1. Advantages

The advantages to this line are high visibility and flotation.

A.9.b.2. Limitations

The main disadvantage of plain-laid polypropylene line is lack of strength compared to nylon line of equal size. Its loose, course weave makes it easy to splice but susceptible to chafing. Aggravating this is polypropylene's characteristic of deteriorating rapidly when exposed to continuous sunlight. It can, in fact, lose up to 40% of its strength over three months of exposure. For this reason, the line is best kept covered when not in use, and inspected and replaced on a regular basis.

A.10. Slippage

Synthetic line slips much easier than natural line. Because of this, it will slip through deck fittings and will not hold knots as well. Care should be taken when bending synthetic line to an object or to another line to ensure the knot will not slip out. One way to help prevent this is to leave a longer tail on the running or bitter end than with natural fiber line.

CAUTION !

To minimize the hazard of being pulled into a deck fitting when a line suddenly surges, ensure all crewmembers stand as far as possible from the equipment. Work the lines with hands at a safe distance from the fittings. This is particularly important during towing operations.

A.11. Considerations

When using synthetic lines consider the following:

- Synthetic line will slip more easily than natural fiber line. Use caution when paying it or surging it from deck fittings.
- Beware of slippage when bending synthetic line together or securing.
- Never stand in a position where exposed to the dangers of snap back if the line parts.
- Do not double up the line during a towing operation.
- Keep working surfaces of bitts free of paint and rust.
- Do not stand in the bight of a line or directly in line with its direction of pull.

A.12. Cutting

The use of a hot knife is the preferred method for cutting nylon and polypropylene line. Using a hot knife eliminates the need for burning the ends. Commercial electric knives, used by sail makers, are available. Some soldering irons can be fit with blades for cutting line. One of the more common methods is to heat an old knife or scraper using a propane torch.

When cutting the line, the blade or saw should not be forced through the line, as the heat will do the job The best method is to work from the outside in. First, an incision is made around the circumference of the line, and then a cut is made through the center.

NOTE

Remember, when a piece of rope is cut, it will fray. Always finish the end of the line whether before or immediately after cutting the line.

Section B. Inspection, Handling, Maintenance, and Stowage of Line

Introduction

Proper maintenance and inspection of line is vital to the completion of the mission as well as the safety of the crew. If a line is damaged or not properly maintained, it could fail, resulting in possible damage to property and/or injury to personnel. This section provides the necessary information regarding basic inspection, uncoiling and unreeling, maintenance, and stowage of line.

In this section

This section contains the following information:

Inspection

B.1. Description

A periodic inspection of all lines used should be made, paying special attention to the following items:

- Aging.
- Fiber wear.
- Fiber damage.
- Chafing.
- Kinks.
- Cockles.
- Cutting.
- Overloading or shockloading.
- Rust/foreign materials.
- Eye splices.

CAUTION ! Synthetic double-braided line should not be taken apart for internal inspection.

B.2. Aging

Aging affects natural fibers more severely than synthetic. Cellulose, the main component in natural fibers will deteriorate with age, getting more brittle and turning yellow or brownish. When bent over bitts or cleats, the fibers easily rupture and break. During bending, line strength may decrease up to five times. Crewmembers can check for aging by opening the lay of the line and noting the color of the interior fibers. In an old line, they will be gray or dark brown. Aging is not a significant problem for nylon line, though it will change its color with age. As stated before though, polypropylene line does deteriorate rapidly when exposed to sunlight.

B.3. Fiber Wear

When natural fiber line is under strain, the friction of the fibers, yarns and strands against each other, causes internal wear. Also, internal wear is a good indication of aging. Upon opening the lay of the line, any presence of a white powdery substance indicates small particles of line worn off by friction.

B.4. Fiber Damage

Damage to internal natural fibers occurs when a line under a strain exceeds 75% of its breaking strength. Although this load is not enough to part the line, it is enough to cause some of the internal fibers to break. Internal fiber damage indicates aging and internal wear. Internal broken fibers indicate that the line has been damaged. With synthetic line, some of the individual synthetic fibers of the line may break if overloaded. These will be visible on the outer surface of the line.

B.5. Chafing

Chafing is wear affecting the outer surface of a line, caused by the friction of the line rubbing against a rough surface. To check for chafing, the outer surface of the line should be visually inspected for frayed threads and broken or flattened strands. With synthetic line, chafing can also cause hardening and fusing of the outer layer.

B.6. Kinks

A kink (see **Figure 7-2**) is a twist or curl caused when the line doubles back on itself. A line with a kink in it should never be placed under strain. The tension will put a permanent distortion in the line. All kinks should be removed before using a line.

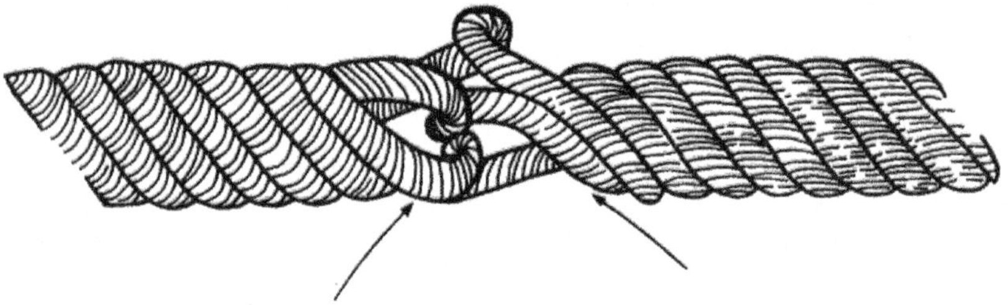

Figure 7-2
Line with a Kink

B.7. Cockles

A cockle (or hockle) is actually a kink in an inner yarn that forces the yarns to the surface. Cockles can be corrected by stretching the line and twisting the free end to restore the original lay. A cockle can reduce line strength by as much as a third.

NOTE

Braided line will not kink or cockle.

B.8. Cutting

Cutting damage found on line is similar to chafing, but occurs when the line rubs against a sharp edge rather than a rough surface. This will give the appearance as if the line was cut with a knife. Cutting damage to yarns and threads will greatly reduce the effectiveness of the line and can cause failure under strain.

WARNING

> **DO NOT** stand directly in line behind a line under strain! If the line were to part, it could snap back and cause injury.

B.9. Overloading or Shock-Loading

Signs that a line was overloaded are elongation and hardness. Line stretched to the point where it will not come back has a decreased diameter. To determine this, the crewmember should place the line under slight tension and measure the circumference of a reduced area and of a normal area. If the circumference is reduced by five percent or more, the line should be replaced.

Another indication of synthetic line overloading is hardness to the touch. This can be noticed while gently squeezing the line. Overloaded line shall not be used.

A line under strain is dangerous. If it parts, it will do so with a lot of force, depending on the size and type of line, and how much strain it is under when it parts. As a general rule, when a line is under stress, it is important to always keep an eye on it. Standing in line with the strain may cause serious injury if the line parts and snaps back.

B.10. Rust/Foreign Material

Rust stains, extending into the cross-section of natural fiber and nylon fiber yarns can lower line strength as much as 40%.

Foreign materials (sand, dirt, paint chips, etc.) can get lodged inside the fibers of a line. Once inside the line and under stain, these materials can cause abrasive damage to the line. Care should be taken to cover up lines to prevent foreign materials from entering if they are stowed or in use near work areas.

B.11. Eye Splices (Double-Braided Nylon Line)

Prior to each use, all eye splices should be inspected on working lines (towline, anchor rode, mooring lines, etc.). Crewmembers should pay particular attention to the area of the line that is tucked back in on itself, ensuring there are no "flat spots" or areas where the inner core has slipped away leaving only the outer cover. The entire eye should be inspected for chafing and cuts. (see *Section D* of this chapter for illustrations)

Uncoiling and Unreeling

B.12. Description

Proper use and care will significantly extend the lifetime of the lines used. Everyone should be responsible for protecting lines from damage. Along with good inspections, some of the ways to accomplish this are proper breakout, stowage, and care.

NOTE

> Never permanently cover natural fiber line with anything that will prevent the evaporation of moisture.

B.13. Uncoiling Natural Fiber Laid Line

To uncoil natural fiber laid line, perform the following procedures:

Step	Procedure
1	Look inside the center tunnel of the coil to locate the end of the line.
2	Position the coil so the inside line end is at the bottom of the center tunnel.
3	Start uncoiling the line by drawing the inside end up through the top of the tunnel. (see **Figure 7-3**)
4	Do not pull on any kinks that develop, as they will develop into permanent strand cockles. If kinks develop, lay the line out straight and remove them before use.

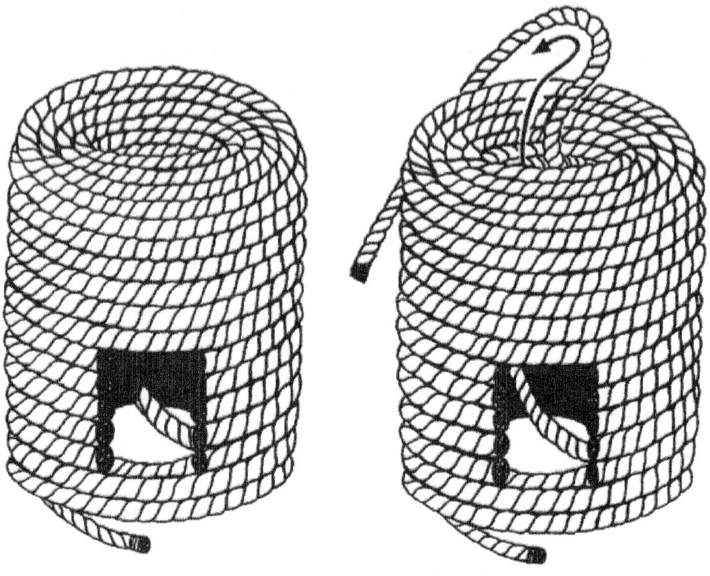

Figure 7-3
Opening a New Coil of Line

B.14. Unreeling Synthetic Fiber Line

The recommended method for unreeling synthetic fiber lines is to:

- Insert a pipe through the center and hang the reel off the deck.
- Draw the line from the lower reel surface.

Twisted fiber lines must not be "thrown" off the reel, as this will cause tangles and kinks. It is recommended that three-strand synthetic lines be faked down on deck and allowed to relax for twenty-four hours. Lengths less than 50 feet will relax in one hour when laid out straight. Fake down double-braided line in figure eight patterns. (see **Figure 7-4**)

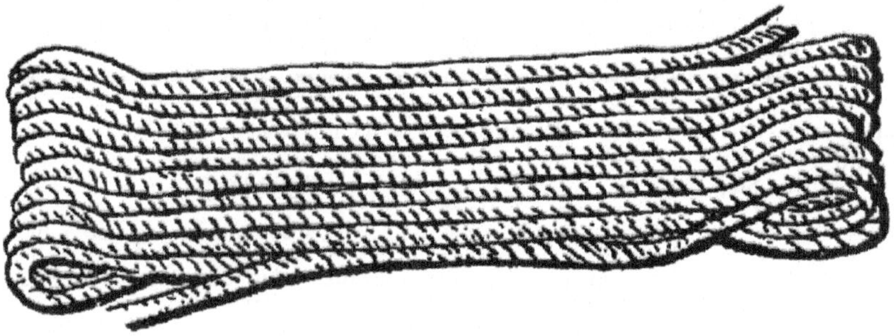

Figure 7-4
Line Faked Down

Maintenance

B.15. Description

While there is nothing that can be done to restore bad line, precautions can be taken to extend the life of lines.

B.16. Keeping Lines Clean

Lines should be kept free from grit or dirt. Gritty material can work down into the fibers while a line is relaxed. Under tension, the movement of the grit will act as an abrasive and will cause serious damage to the fibers.

B.17. Using Chafing Gear

Chafing gear can be made of old hoses, leather, or heavy canvas. It is used to protect short pieces of line where they run over taff rails, chocks, or other surfaces. (see **Figure 7-5**)

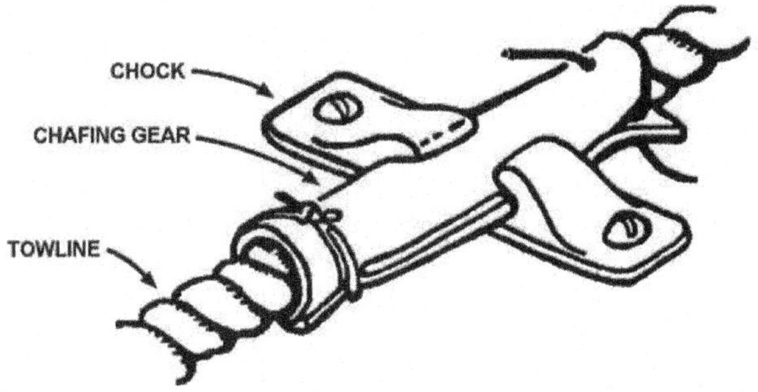

Figure 7-5
Chafing Gear

B.18. Keeping Deck Fittings Clean and Smooth

Bitts, cleats, and chock surfaces should be kept smooth to reduce line abrasion.

B.19. Watching for Frozen Water

Crewmembers should ensure that water does not freeze on lines. Ice is abrasive and can cut fibers.

B.20. Avoiding Crushing or Pinching Lines

Crewmembers should avoid walking on, placing loads on, dragging loads over, or in other ways crushing or pinching a line.

B.21. Being Cautious of Sharp Bends

Bending under a load causes internal abrasion between the strands of the line. If a line has to go around something, a fair lead should be used. A fair lead is any hole, bull's-eye, lizard, suitably placed roller, sheave, etc., serving to guide or lead a rope in a desired direction. It is important to remember that if a fair lead is not used, the bigger the bend, the less the abrasive effect.

B.22. Care of Natural Fiber Line

The practices that should be avoided or observed in the maintenance of natural fiber line are as follows:

DOs	DON'Ts
• Dry line before stowing it. • Protect line from weather when possible. • Use chafing gear (canvas, short lengths of old fire hose, etc.) where line runs over sharp edges or rough surfaces. • Slack off taut lines when it rains. Wet lines shrink and if the line is taut, the resulting strain may be enough to break some of the fibers. • Reverse turns on winches periodically to keep out the kinks. • Lay right-laid lines clockwise on reels or capstans and left-laid lines counterclockwise until they are broken in. • Inspect lines for fiber damage and other wear conditions before each use. • Try to tie knots or hitches in new places as much as possible so as not to wear out the line. • Occasionally end-for-ending (swap one end for the other) to help reduce excessive wear at certain points.	• Stow wet or damp line in an unventilated compartment or cover it so that it cannot dry. Mildew will form and weaken the fibers. • Subject the line to intense heat or unnecessarily allow it to lie in the hot sun. The lubricant will dry out, thus shortening the useful life of the line. • Subject a line to loads exceeding its working load limit. Individual fibers will break, reducing the strength. • Allow line to bear on sharp edges or run over rough surfaces. • Scrub line. The lubricant will be washed away, and caustics in strong soap may harm the fibers. • Try to lubricate line. The lubricant added may do more harm than good. • Put a strain on a line with a kink in it. • Let wear become localized in one spot. • Unbalance line by continued use on winch in same direction.

B.23. Care of Synthetic Fiber Line

Most of the practices in the maintenance of natural fiber line are the same for synthetic fiber line. However, the differences are as follows:

- Nylon is not subject to mildew, and it may and should be scrubbed if it becomes slippery because of oil or grease. Spots may be removed by cleaning with a 10% solution of mild detergent/degreaser and water.
- Synthetic line stretches when put under a load. Allow plenty of time for the line to recover to its original length before coiling on a drum or reel.

Stowing Lines

B.24. Description

To prevent the deteriorating effects of sunlight, chemicals, paints, soaps, and linseed or cottonseed oils, lines should be stored to prevent contact with harmful items or conditions.

B.25. Natural Fiber Lines

Natural fiber lines can be damaged by contact with just about anything. They are especially susceptible to the rotting and mildewing effects of moisture. After use, natural fiber line should be allowed to dry thoroughly and stowed in a cool, dark, well-ventilated space.

B.26. Synthetic Fiber Lines

Synthetic fiber lines are not as susceptible to the effects of moisture as natural fiber lines. They are, however, affected by all of the other conditions and materials that will hurt line. The boat's towline and other synthetic lines should be kept covered or stored in a dark area, when not in use.

Synthetic line should not be constantly coiled in the same direction, as doing this tends to tighten the twist. Three-strand synthetic line is often coiled clockwise to reduce a natural tendency to tighten up. It can be coiled in figure eights to avoid kinks when paying out. (see **Figure 7-6**)

Whereas synthetic line stretches when put under a load, allow plenty of time for the line to recover to its original length before coiling on a drum or reel.

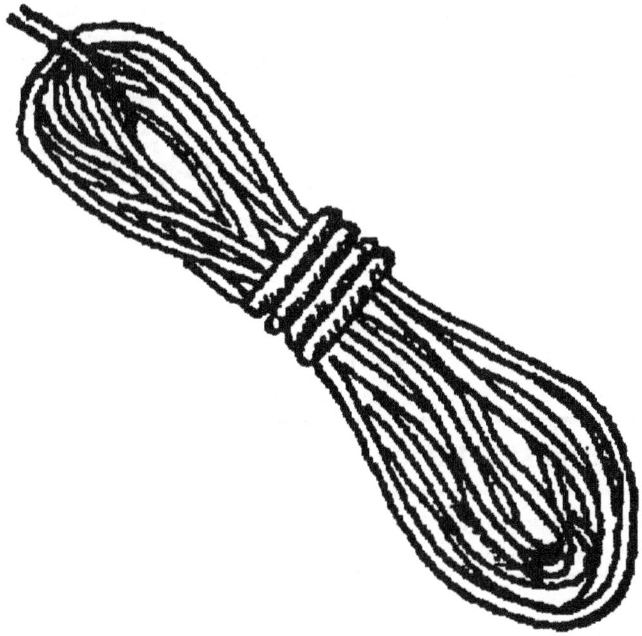

Figure 7-6
Figure Eight Coils

B.27. Towline

See *Chapter 17, Towing* for procedures to stow towlines.

B.28. Coiling

The most common method of stowing the extra line on deck or on the dock after making fast to a cleat is to coil it.

B.29. Flemishing a Line

Flemishing a line consists of coiling a line clockwise against the deck. It is used for appearance (e.g., inspections, seaman-like appearance). (see **Figure 7-7**)

Figure 7-7
Flemishing a Line

Section C. Breaking Strength (BS) and Working Load Limit (WLL)

Introduction

This section provides the necessary information to determine the breaking strength (BS) and working load limit (WLL) of a line.

In this section

This section contains the following information:

Breaking Strength (BS) and Working Load Limit (WLL) of a Line

C.1. Description

A line stretches as it takes on a load. It will continue to do so as tension increases until it reaches its breaking point. Then it will part and snap back. There have been many injuries and deaths caused by lines snapping when working under tension. Safe line handling is a combination of knowledge and skill. The ability to determine the BS and WLL of a line is an important factor in safe line handling.

C.2. Breaking Strength (BS)

The BS of a line is measured in the number of pounds of stress a line can take before it parts. It is a part of the technical information provided to a purchaser. The number comes from stress tests conducted by the manufacturer of the line and is an average of all the lines tested. BS is not exact for any specific line. A safety factor must be applied to determine the WLL of a line.

C.3. Working Load Limit (WLL)

Line should be selected with its intended usage, or working load, in mind. A common seamanship practice says that the WLL of a line should be not more than one-fifth of its BS, or that the BS should be five times the weight of the object attached to the line. This five-to-one safety factor allows for sudden strains, shock-loading, and normal deterioration as the line ages.

C.4. Various Types of Line

Table 7-2 provides the BS and WLL in pounds for various types of line used on Coast Guard boats. In the table, each size of line is classified as "good," "average" or "poor."

The WLL and BS of the lines below were figured mathematically based on the circumference of each line. Line procured through government supply sources is measured in circumference. Commercially procured line, however, is measured in diameter. The formula for converting circumference to diameter and vice versa is contained below. For simplicity, both the diameter and the circumference of the most commonly used Coast Guard lines are provided below.

Table 7-2
Minimum Breaking Strengths and Safe Working Loads for Natural and Synthetic Lines

		Manila				Nylon (Double-Braided)			
Size	Size	BS	WLL by Line Condition			BS	WLL by Line Condition		
Diam. (inches)	Cir. (inches)	Lbs.	Good	Average	Poor	Lbs.	Good	Average	Poor
5/8	2	3,600	720	360	240	9,000	3,000	2,250	1,500
11/16	2½	5,625	1,125	562	375	14,062	4,687	3,515	2,343
7/8	2¾	6,806	1,361	680	454	17,015	5,671	4,253	2,835
1	3	8,100	1,620	810	540	20,250	6,750	5,062	3,375

		Polypropylene/Polyethylene				Polyester (Dacron)			
Size	Size	BS	WLL by Line Condition			BS	WLL by Line Condition		
Diam. (inches)	Cir. (inches)	Lbs.	Good	Average	Poor	Lbs.	Good	Average	Poor
5/8	2	5,040	1,008	840	630	7,200	2,400	1,800	1,200
11/16	2½	7,875	1,575	1,312	984	11,250	3,750	2,812	1,875
7/8	2¾	9,528	1,905	1,588	1,191	13,612	4,537	3,402	2,268
1	3	11,340	2,268	1,890	1,417	16,200	5,400	4,050	2,700

Three-Strand Nylon					
Size	Size	BS	WLL by Line Condition		
Diam. (inches)	Cir. (inches)	Lbs.	Good	Average	Poor
5/8	2	9,000	3,000	2,250	1,500
11/16	2½	14,062	4,687	3,515	2,343
7/8	2¾	17,015	5,671	4,253	2,835
1	3	20,250	6,750	5,062	3,375

NOTE

The only type of synthetic line authorized by the Coast Guard for towing is double-braided nylon. The other lines listed in the table are for comparison purposes.

C.5. Three-Strand Nylon Line

The Auxiliary may use three-strand nylon line for towing. Typical line size and average breaking strength are summarized above. The working load limit condition and specific values can be calculated as shown below.

Estimating the Breaking Strength and Working Load Limit of Lines

C.6. Description

The following paragraphs provide a detailed explanation of how to estimate the breaking strengths of particular types of lines. It also explains how to use this number to figure the WLL. Each type of line has a different BS, and a different WLL.

C.7. Breaking Strength of Natural Line+

The estimated BS of a piece of manila line can be found by squaring the circumference (C) of the line and then multiplying that number by 900 pounds. The formula for this is: BS = C2 x 900 pounds.

Example:

Suppose the circumference of a piece of manila line is 3 inches. The breaking strength of that line can be determined as follows:

Step	Procedure
1	BS = C2 x 900 pounds
2	C2 = 3 x 3 = 9
3	BS = 9 x 900 pounds
4	BS = 8100 pounds

C.8. Breaking Strength of Synthetic Line

The same basic formula should be used to estimate the breaking strength of synthetic lines by the addition of one more step. Because synthetic lines are stronger than manila line, the number of pounds representing their breaking strengths is multiplied by their comparison factors (CFs).

C.9. Comparison Factors

Comparison factors (CFs) are based on the strength of a synthetic line in comparison to natural manila line. The CFs given in **Table 7-3** reveal that synthetic line is stronger than manila line.

Table 7-3
Comparison Factors (CF) for Synthetic Line

Line Name	CF to Manila Line
Polypropylene	1.4
Polyethylene	1.4
Polyester (Dacron)	2.0
Nylon	2.5

C.10. Estimating BS of Synthetic Line

The formula for estimating the BS of synthetic line is BS = C2 x 900 x CF.

Step	Procedure
1	BS = C2 x 900 x CF
2	C2 = 3 x 3 = 9
3	BS = 9 x 900 pounds x CF
4	BS = 8100 pounds x CF
5	CF = 2.0 for polyester (Dacron) line (taken from **Table 7-3**.)
6	BS = 8100 pounds x 2
7	BS = 16,200 pounds

C.11. WLL of Natural and Synthetic Line

BS is the tension, measured in pounds, a line can absorb before it breaks. To be on the safe side, a line should not be stressed anywhere near its breaking point. The WLL of the line is considerably less than its BS.

As a line wears, stretches, or is spliced, its BS decreases. Quite naturally, this also causes a decrease in the WLL of the line. By making a quick inspection of a piece of line and determining whether it is in good, average, or poor condition, the approximate WLL of a line can be calculated. Once the condition of the line is determined, **Table 7-4** can be utilized to enter and apply the safety factor (SF) into its BS using the formula: WLL = BS/SF.

Table 7-4
SFs for Natural and Synthetic Lines

Condition	Manila	Nylon & Polyester	Polypropylene Polyethylene
Good	5	3	5
Average	10	4	6
Poor	15	6	8

C.11.a. WLL of Manila Line

Utilize the following procedures to figure the WLL of a 3-inch manila line, in average condition, with a BS of 8100 pounds:

Step	Procedure
1	Determine the condition of the line and extract the appropriate SF from **Table 7-4**. In this case SF = 10.
2	WLL = BS/SF
3	WLL = 8,100 pounds/10
4	WLL = 810 pounds

C.11.b. WLL of Polyester Line

Utilize the following procedures to figure the WLL of a 2-inch polyester (Dacron) line in poor condition:

Step	Procedure
1	BS = C2 x 900 pounds x CF
2	C2 = 2 x 2 = 4
3	BS = 4 x 900 x CF
4	BS = 3,600 x CF
5	CF = 2 (**Table 7-3**)
6	BS = 3,600 x 2
7	BS = 7,200 pounds
8	SF = 6 (**Table 7-4**, polyester in poor condition)
9	WLL = BS/SF
10	WLL = 7,200/6
11	WLL = 1,200 pounds

C.12. Determining the Diameter of a Line

The following formulas will help when determining the diameter of a line using two methods:

- Converting diameter to circumference.
- Converting circumference to diameter.

C.12.a. Converting Diameter to Circumference

Some sources of supply measure line by diameter. Sailors measure and refer to line by circumference. The formula to convert diameter to circumference is C = D x 3.1416.

Utilize the following procedures to convert a diameter of ½ inch into circumference:

Step	Procedure
1	C = ½" x 3.1416
2	C = 1.5708"
3	C = 1½" (rounded off)

C.12.b. Converting Circumference to Diameter

For converting circumference to diameter, just turn the formula over. Use D = C/3.1416.

Utilize the following procedures to convert a circumference of 3" into a diameter.

Step	Procedure
1	D = 3"/3.1416
2	D = .955"
3	D = 1" (rounded off)

BS and WLL for Shackles and Hooks

C.13. Description

Given a choice between the hardware breaking and the line parting, it is usually safer for the line to part. The BS of shackles is up to six times greater than their WLL.

CAUTION !

Never use a shackle or hook with a WLL **less than** the WLL of the line being used.

C.14. Determining WLL

Since shackles and hooks are made of different materials (stainless, forged, tempered steel) and they come in many different shapes and sizes, their BS and WLL will vary. There is no single set formula to determine the BS or WLL for all shackles and hooks. In most cases, the WLL will be stamped or molded directly into the hardware. Crewmembers should always refer to the manufacturer's specifications before use. A shackle or hook with a WLL less than the WLL of the line being used should never be used.

Estimating the WLL of Shackles

C.15. Description

As mentioned earlier in this chapter, there is no one formula to determine the BS of shackles. The manufacturer's specifications must always be followed and damaged, bent or severely rusted shackles will not be used. All shackles will be inspected before use.

C.16. Estimating the WLL

The best method for obtaining the WLL of a shackle is to use the manufacturer's specifications. Most shackles will have the WLL stamped or forged into the shackle. Because shackles are made of different materials, shackles of the same size will have different WLLs.

If the manufacturer's information is not available, the WLL can be estimated by the following method:

- First measure the diameter (D) of the shackle at the point on the shackle shown in **Figure 7-8**. Technically, this is referred to as the wire diameter. The estimated WLL of a shackle, in tons, is calculated by using the formula WLL = 3 x D2.
- Use 3 tons as a constant and apply it to all usable shackles.

Utilize the following procedures to calculate the WLL of a shackle with a 2-inch wire diameter:

Step	Procedure
1	WLL = 3 tons x D2
2	D2 = 2 x 2 = 4
3	WLL = 3 tons x 4
4	WLL = 12 tons

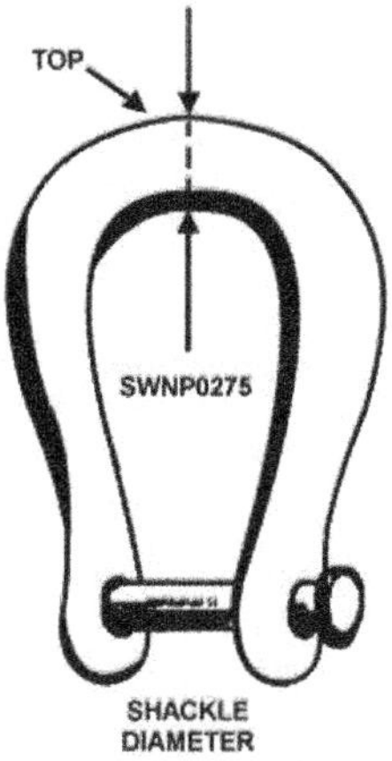

Figure 7-8
Shackle Diameter

Estimating the WLL of Hooks

C.17. Description

Like shackles, the WLL of hooks is either found stamped or forged in the hook itself or from manufacturer's specifications. Damaged, bent, or severely rusted hooks will not be used. All hooks shall be inspected for wear, deformity and cracks before lifting a load.

C.18. Estimating the WLL

If the manufacturer's information is not available, the WLL can be estimated by the following method:

- Measure the diameter (D) as shown in **Figure 7-9**.
- Use a ⅔ of a ton as a constant factor and apply it to all usable hooks by using the formula WLL = ⅔ ton x D2.

Utilize the following procedures to calculate the WLL of a hook with a 2-inch diameter:

Step	Procedure
1	WLL = ⅔ ton x D2
2	D2 = 2 x 2 = 4
3	WLL = ⅔ (0.6666) ton X 4
4	WLL = 2.66 tons

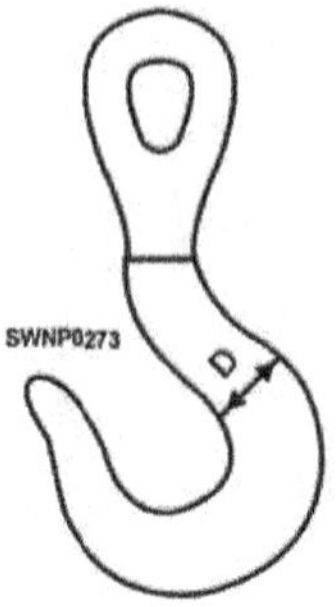

Figure 7-9
Hook Diameter

Considerations and Limitations

C.19. Description

Even though the WLL of lines, shackles and hooks may be correctly determined, there are many variables affecting the equipment. In actual use, it is not always possible to operate within the WLL. Sometimes appropriate hardware cannot be matched with particular lines.

C.20. Keeping Alert

It is necessary to keep a constant eye on a line under stress. Crewmembers should always remain on guard to prepare for the unpredictable, unforeseen and often dangerous forces in the marine environment. By using good judgment, timely adjustments can usually be made to correct for these adverse forces.

C.21. Staying Within Limits

The tension on line and equipment should be kept well within their WLL. It is difficult to tell when the WLL is reached or surpassed. A sudden surging (pulling) of a towline may cause the tension on the line and hardware to approach their breaking points. This is when the danger of parting becomes a safety hazard.

C.22. Unknown BS and WLL

The moment the towline is connected to a distressed vessel's deck fittings, the entire towing system assumes an unknown BS and WLL factor. A reliable estimate of BS and WLL often cannot be achieved even when the proper equipment is attached to the disabled craft. Because this is the weak link in towing, the towline and the boat in tow must be kept under constant observation.

C.23. Measuring Percentage of Elongation

The device used to measure the percentage of elongation is called a tattletale cord or a strain gauge. A tattletale cord is a bight of heavy cord or light small stuff that is cut to a specific length depending on the type of synthetic line it is used with (see **Table 7-5**). The ends of the tattletale cord are secured at a specified distance apart on the line, again, depending on the type of synthetic line. As the line elongates under strain, the tattletale cord stretches with it. If the tattletale parts, it signals that the main line is not far behind. This warning system allows actions to be taken to prevent the parting of larger lines.

Dimensions for tattletale cords can be summarized as follows:

NOTE Navy studies have shown that tattletales will give warning for a line that has been shock-loaded. Their position of placement on mooring and towlines should be where they can be easily seen from the deck.

Table 7-5
Tattletale Specifications

Type of Synthetic Line	Length of Tattletale	Distance Cord	Critical Stretch
Nylon (3-strand)	40 inches	30 inches	40%
Nylon (double-braided)	48 inches	40 inches	20%
Nylon (plaited)	40 inches	30 inches	40%
Polyester (3-strand)	34 inches	34 inches	20%
Polypropylene (3-strand)	36 inches	30 inches	20%

Section D. Knots and Splices

Introduction This section details the procedures regarding the art of knots and splices.

In this section This section contains the following information:

Estimating the Length of a Line

D.1. Procedure Estimating the length of a line can be a useful skill. One method of doing so is as follows:

Step	Procedure
1	Hold the end of a length of line in one hand.
2	Reach across with the other hand and pull the line through the first hand, fully extending both arms from the shoulder.

The length of line from one hand to the other, across the chest, will be roughly six feet (one fathom). Actually, this distance will be closer to the person's height, but this measure is close enough for a rough and quick estimate of line needed.

If more line is needed, the process should be repeated keeping the first hand in place on the line as a marker until the length of line required has been measured off. For example, if 36' of line is needed, the procedure should be repeated six times.

Breaking Strength

D.2. Knots and Splices

Knots are used for pulling, holding, lifting, and lowering. When using line for these purposes, it is often necessary to join two or more lines together. Knots and bends are used for temporary joining, and splices provide a permanent joining. In either case, the BS of the joined line is normally less than the BS of the separated lines.

The weakest point in a line is the knot or splice. They can reduce the BS of a line as much as 50 to 60 percent. A splice, however, is stronger than a knot. **Table 7-6** lists each of the commonly used knots and splices. It provides their percent of line BS lost and percent of line BS remaining.

Table 7-6
Percent of Line BS Loss

Knots or Splice Remaining	Percent of Line BS Lost	Percent of Line BS Remaining
Square	46	54
Bowline	37	63
Two Bowlines (Eye-in-Eye)	43	57
Becket Bend	41	59
Double-Becket Bend	41	59
Round Turn	30-35	65-70
Timber Hitch	30-35	65-70
Clove Hitch	40	60
Eye Splice	5-10	90-95
Short Splice	15	85

Basic Knots

D.3. Temporary Knots

Knots are the intertwining of the parts of one or more lines to secure the lines to themselves, each other (bends), or other objects (hitches). Because knots decrease the strength of the line, they should always be treated as temporary. If something permanent is needed, a splice or seizing can be used.

D.4. Definitions

In making knots and splices, the crewmember must know the names for the parts of a line and the basic turns employed. Refer to **Figure 7-10** and **Figure 7-11** for an example of the following knots.

Knot	Description
Running End (Bitter End)	The running end (bitter end) or the free end of a line. It is the end of the line that is worked with.
Standing Part	The standing part is the long unused or belayed end of a line. It is the remaining part of the line, including the end that is not worked.
Overhand Loop	The overhand loop is a loop made in a line by crossing the bitter end over the standing part.
Underhand Loop	The underhand loop is a loop made in the line by crossing the bitter end under the standing part.

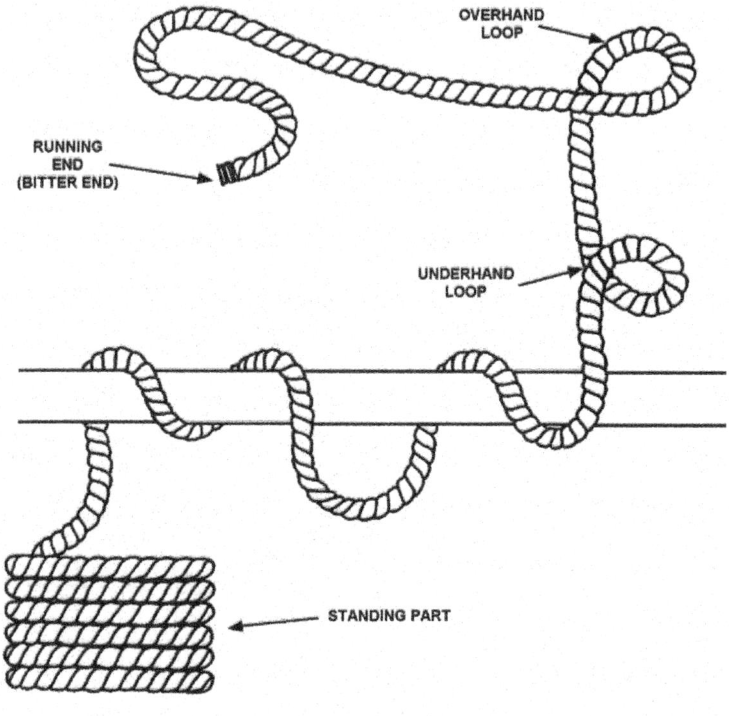

Figure 7-10
Basic Parts and Loops

Knot	Description
Bight	A bight is a half loop formed by turning the line back on itself.
Turn	A turn is a single wind or bight of a rope, laid around a belaying pin, post, bollard, or the like.
Round Turn	A round turn is a complete turn or encircling of a line about an object, as opposed to a single turn.

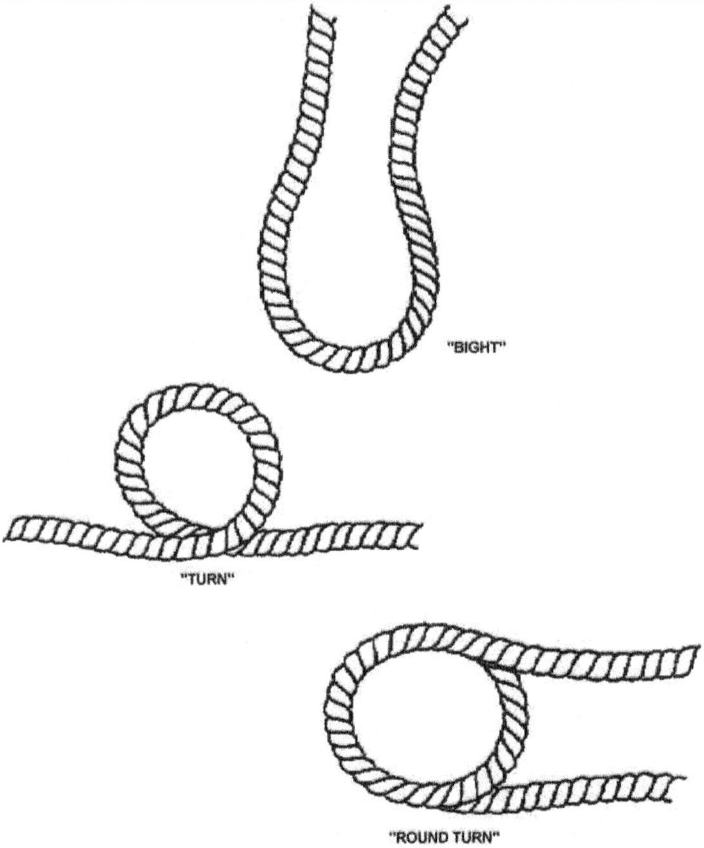

Figure 7-11
Bight and Turns

D.5. Anatomy of a Knot

Good knots are easy to tie, are easy to untie, and hold well. A good knot will not untie itself. In sailing vernacular, a knot is used to tie a line back upon itself, a bend used to secure two lines together, and a hitch is used to tie a line to a ring, rail or spar. A knot used to secure a line to an object, such as a ring or eye, is a hitch. The knots listed below are those most commonly used in boat operations. Crewmembers should learn to tie them well, for the time may come when the skill to do so could decide the outcome of a mission.

D.5.a. Bowline

The bowline is a versatile knot and can be used anytime a temporary eye is needed in the end of a line. It also works for tying two lines securely together, though there are better knots for this. An advantage of bowlines is that they do not slip or jam easily. Refer to **Figure 7-12** while performing the following procedures:

Step	Procedure
1	Make an overhand loop in the line the size of the eye desired.
2	Pass the bitter end up through the overhand loop.
3	Bring the bitter end around the standing part and back down through the overhand loop.
4	Pull the knot tight by holding the bitter end and the loop with one hand, and pulling on the standing part with the other.

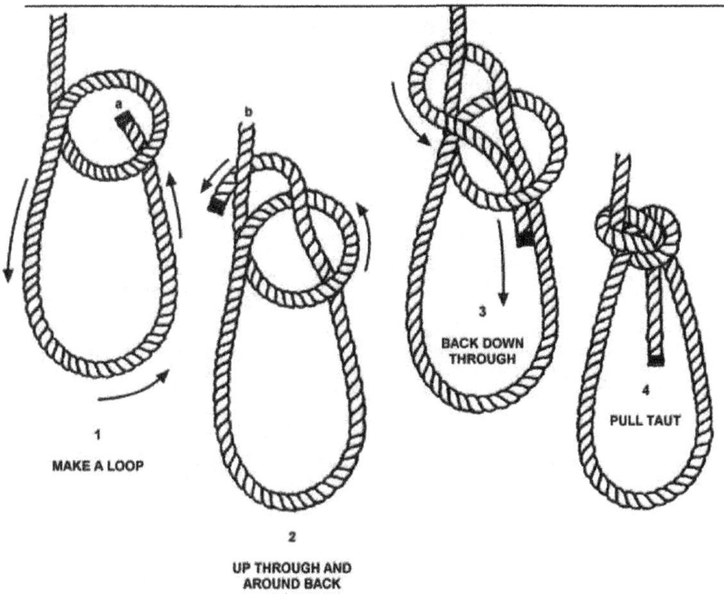

Figure 7-12
Bowline

D.5.b. Half Hitches

Hitches are used for temporarily securing a line to objects such as a ring or eye. One of their advantages is their ease in untying. The half hitch is the smallest and simplest hitch. It should be tied only to objects having a right-hand pull. Since a single half hitch may slip easily, care should be taken in cases where it will encounter stress. Refer to **Figure 7-13** while performing the following procedures:

Step	Procedure
1	Pass the line around the object.
2	Bring the working end "a" around the standing part and back under itself.

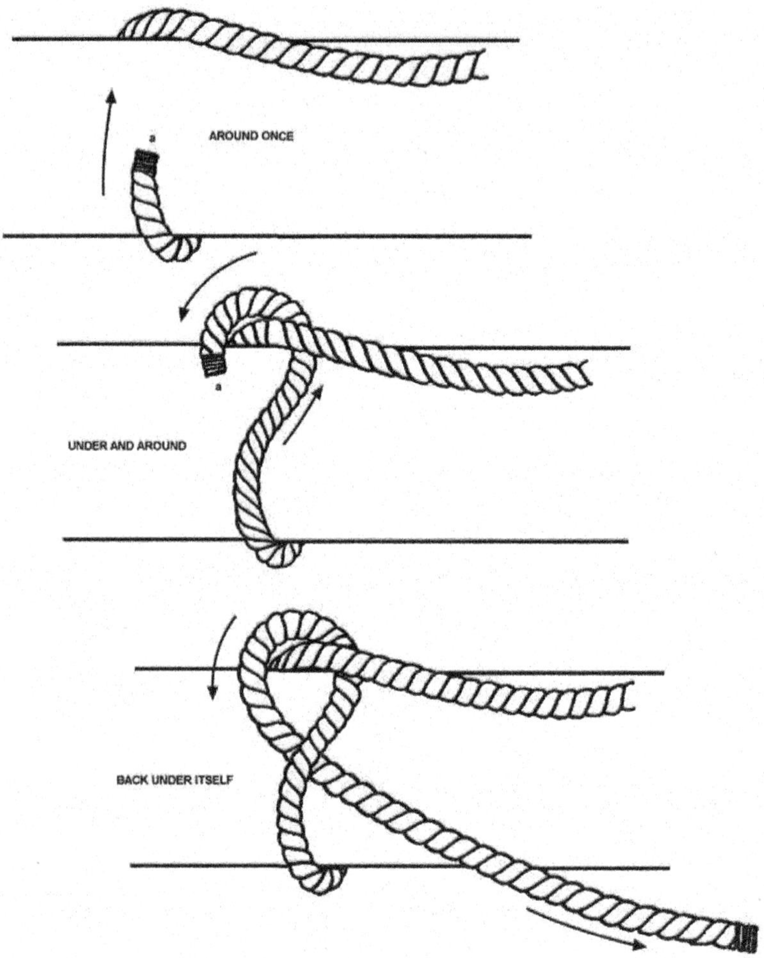

Figure 7-13
Half Hitch

D.5.c. Two Half Hitches

To reinforce or strengthen a single half hitch, the rope can be tied once more. Two half hitches make a more reliable knot than a single half hitch and can be used to make the ends of a line fast around its own standing part. A round turn or two, secured with a couple of half hitches, is a quick way to secure a line to a pole or spar. Two half hitches are needed to secure a line at an angle where it might slide vertically or horizontally. Refer to **Figure 7-14** while performing the following procedures:

Step	Procedure
1	Take a turn around the object.
2	Bring the running end (bitter end) under and over the standing part and back under itself.
3	Continue by passing bitter end under and over the standing part and back under itself.

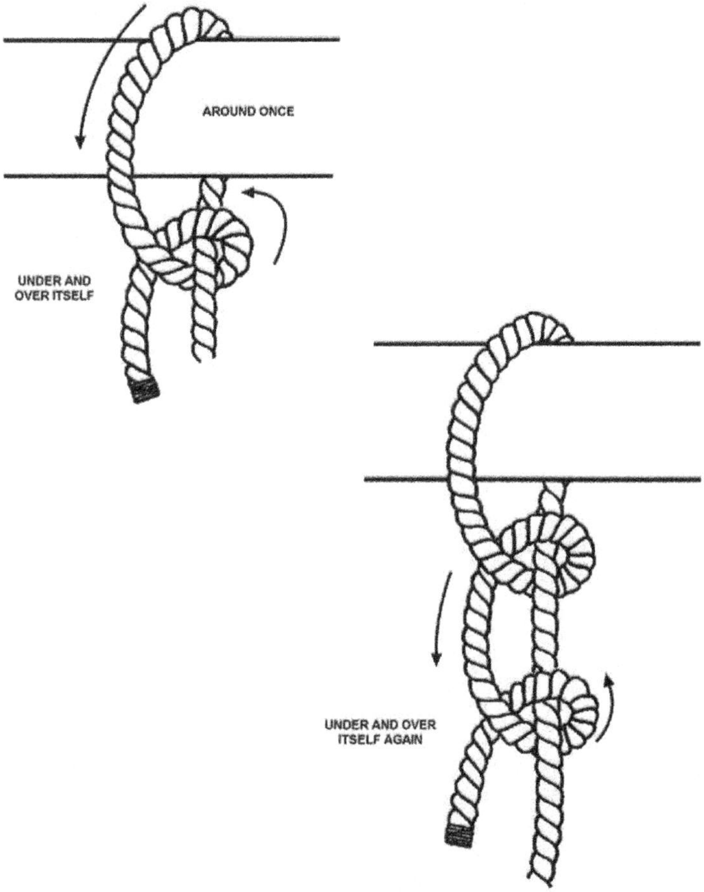

Figure 7-14
Two Half Hitches

D.5.d. Rolling Hitch (Stopper)

A rolling hitch is used to attach one line to another, where the second line is under a strain and cannot be bent. Refer to **Figure 7-15** while performing the following procedures:

Step	Procedure
1	With the bitter end "a", make a turn over and under the second line "b" and pass the link over itself.
2	Pass "a" over and under "b" again bringing "a" through the space between the two lines on the first turn.
3	Pull taut and make another turn with the bitter end "a" taking it over, then under, then back over itself.
4	Pull taut and tie a half hitch.

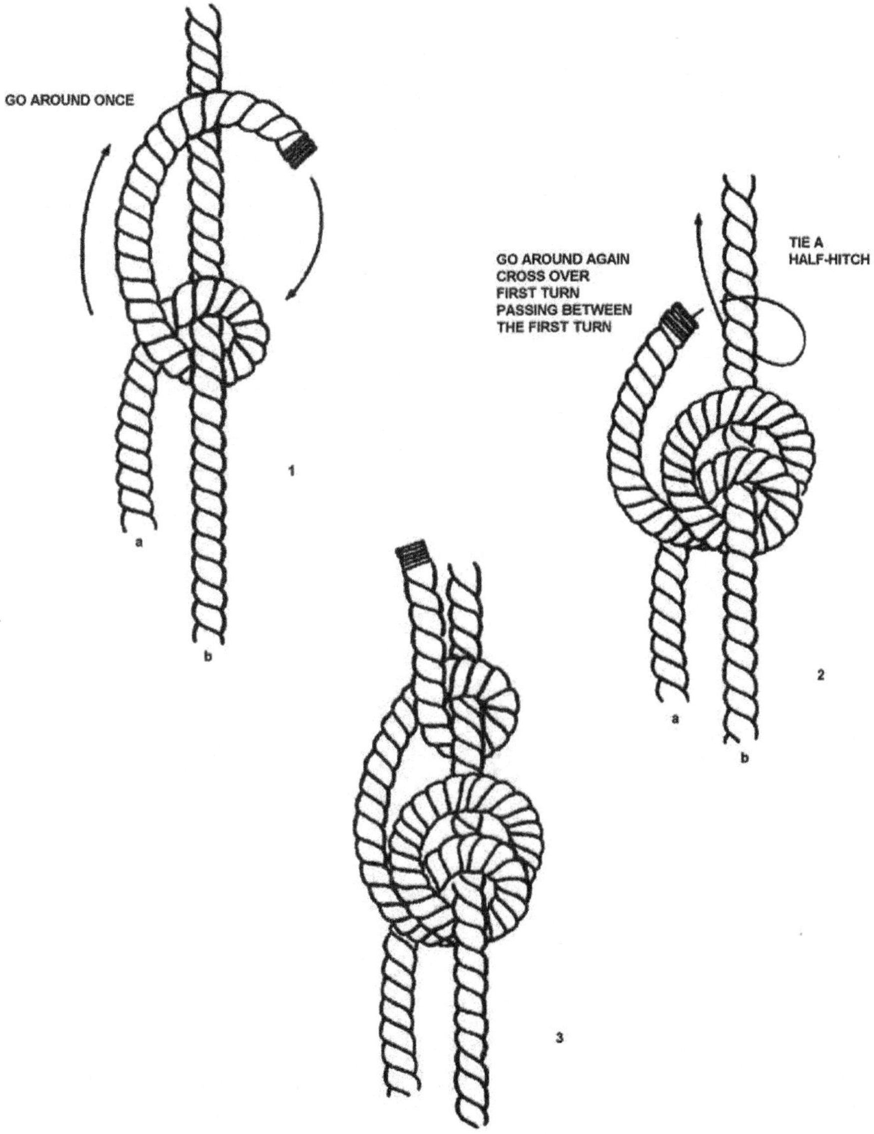

Figure 7-15
Rolling Hitch

D.5.e. Clove Hitch

A clove hitch is preferred for securing a heaving line to a towline. It is the best all-around knot for securing a line to a ring or spar. Correctly tied, a clove hitch will not jam or loosen. However, if it is not tied tight enough, it may work itself out. Reinforcing it with a half hitch will prevent this from happening. Refer to **Figure 7-16** while performing the following procedures:

Step	Procedure
1	Pass the bitter end "a" around the object so the first turn crosses the standing part.
2	Bring the bitter end "a" around again and pass it through itself.
3	Pull taut.
4	Reinforce by tying a half hitch.

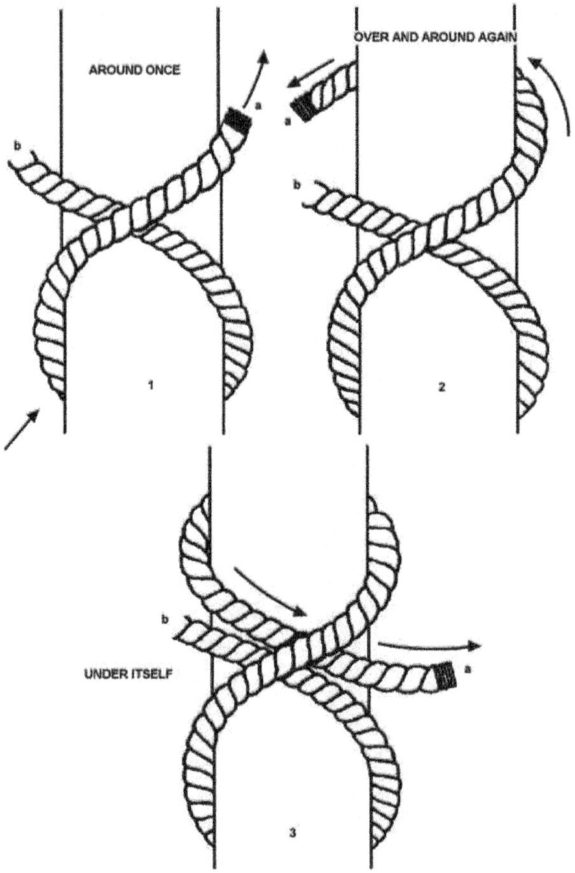

Figure 7-16
Clove Hitch

D.5 f. Slip Clove Hitch

A slip clove hitch should be used in lieu of a clove hitch when a quick release is required. It should be tied in the same manner as the clove hitch but finish it with a bight to allow for quick release. (see **Figure 7-17**) It is sometimes used for stowing lines and fenders. It should not be used when working with the line.

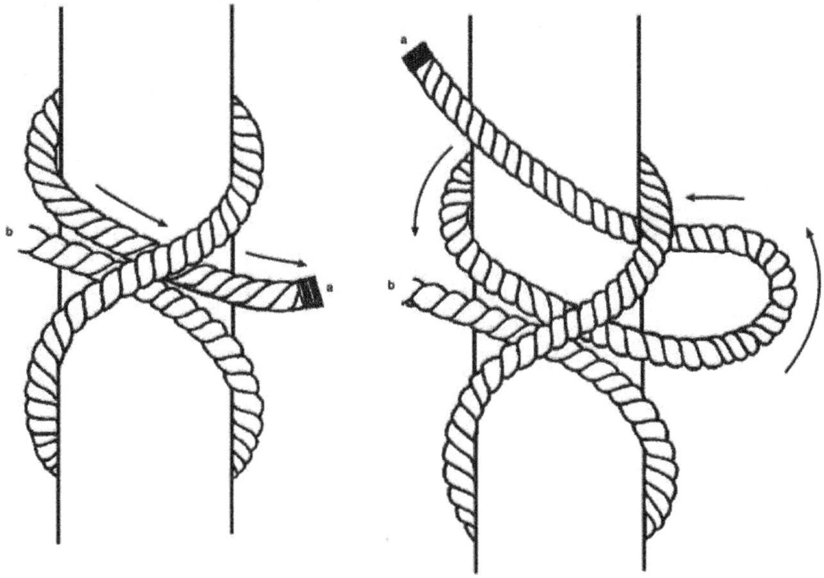

Figure 7-17
Slip Clove Hitch

D.5.g. Timber Hitch

Timber hitches are used to secure a line to logs, spars, planks or other rough-surfaced material, but should not be used on pipes or other metal objects. Refer to **Figure 7-18** while performing the following procedures:

Step	Procedure
1	Tie a half hitch.
2	Continue taking the bitter end "a" over and under the standing part.
3	Pull the standing part taut.
4	Add two half hitches for extra holding, if necessary. (see **Figure 7-19)** Unless the half hitch can be slipped over the end of the object, tie it before making the timber hitch.

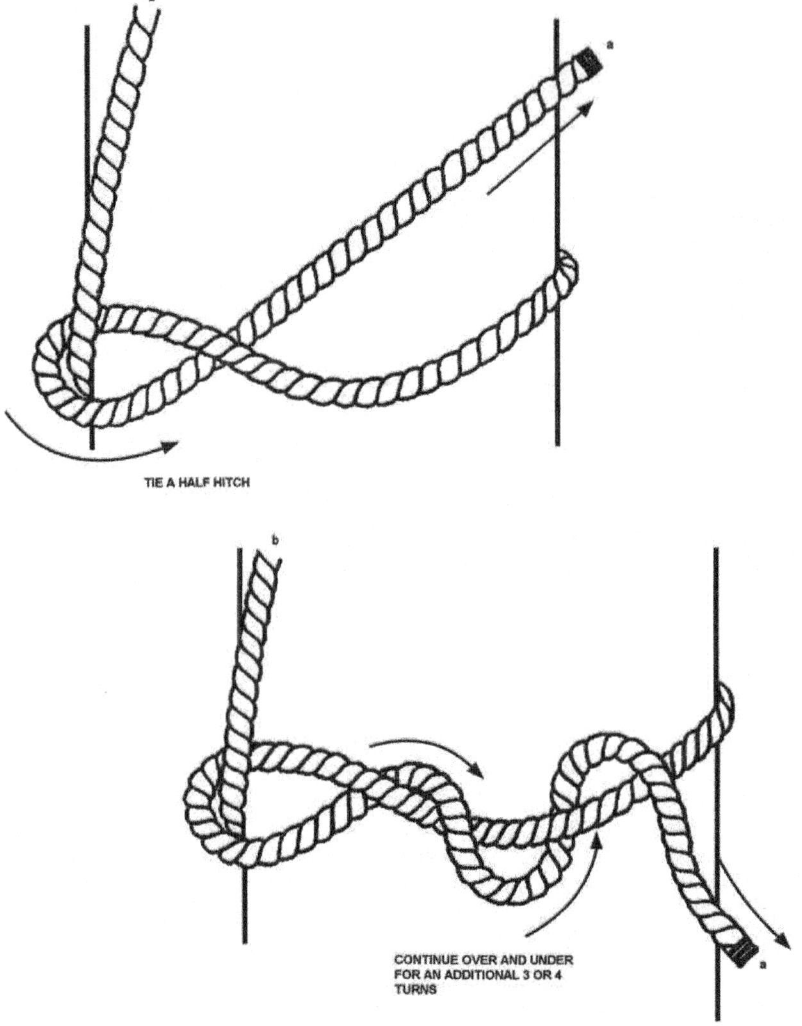

Figure 7-18
Timber Hitch

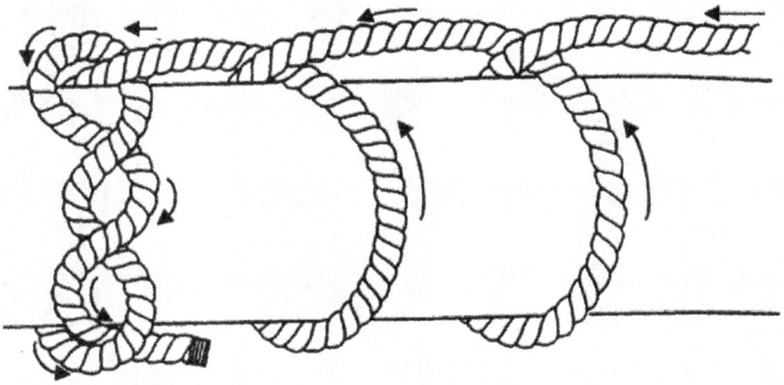

Figure 7-19
Timber Hitch with Two Half Hitches

D.5 h. Single Becket Bend (Sheet Bend)

Lines can be lengthened by bending one to another using a becket bend. It is the best knot for connecting a line to an eye splice in another line. It can be readily taken apart even after being under a load. Single becket bends are used to join line of the same size or nearly the same size. It is intended to be temporary. Refer to **Figure 7-20** while performing the following procedures:

Step	Procedure
1	Form a bight in one of the lines to be joined together, line "a".
2	Pass the bitter end of the second line "b" up through the bight formed by the first line "a."
3	Wrap the end of line "b" around the bight in "a."
4	Pass the end of "b" under its own standing part.
5	Pull taut.

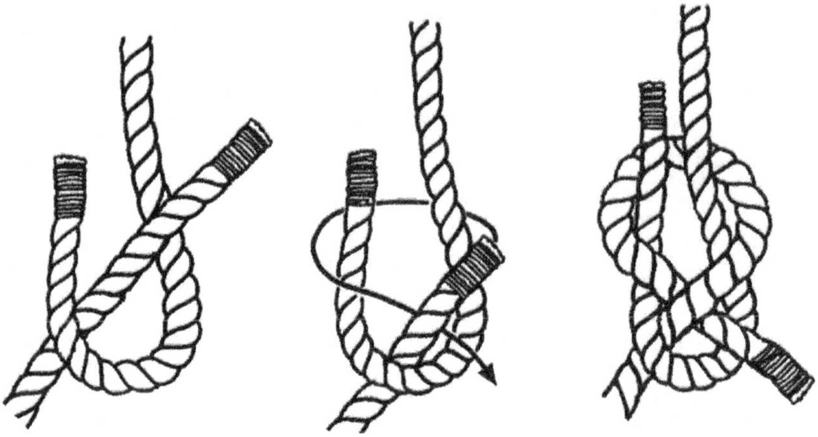

Figure 7-20
Single Becket Bend/Sheet Bend

D.4.i. Double Becket Bend (Double Sheet Bend)

The double becket bend works for joining lines of unequal size. It is tied in the same manner as the single becket bend except for the following variation in step 4 above: Pass line "b" around and under its standing part twice. (see **Figure 7-21**)

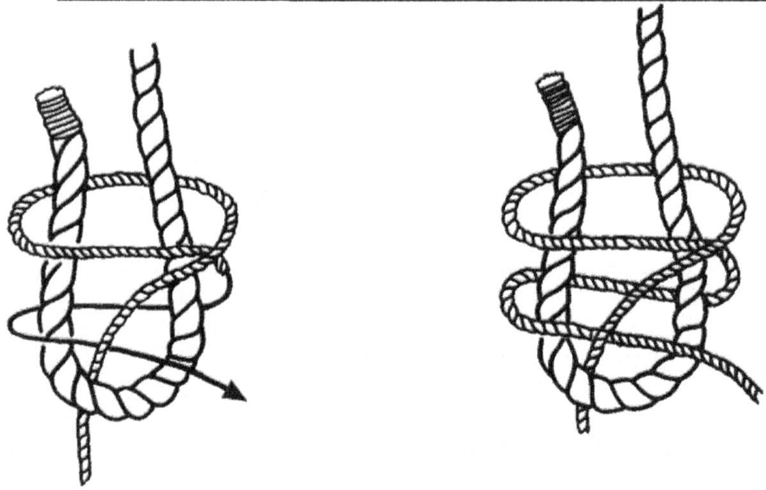

Figure 7-21
Double Becket Bend/Sheet Bend

D.5.j. Reef Knot (Square Knot)

Called a square knot by Boy Scouts, the reef knot is one of the most commonly used knots in marlinespike seamanship. Reef knots are primarily used to join two lines of equal size and similar material. Caution should be used if the line is going to be under heavy strain since the reef knot can jam badly and become difficult to untie afterwards. Reef knots are best used to finish securing laces (canvas cover, awning, sail to a gaff, etc.), temporary whippings, and other small stuff. Refer to **Figure 7-22** while performing the following procedures:

Step	Procedure
1	Tie a single overhand knot.
2	Tie a second overhand knot on top so it mirrors (right and left reversed) the first one. The ends should come out together.
3	Draw tight.

Figure 7-22
Reef Knot (Square Knot)

D.5 k. The Monkey's Fist

Because some lines, such as towlines, are too heavy and awkward to throw any distance, a smaller line called a "heaving line" which is weighted at one end is used to pass the towline to a disabled vessel. Most heaving lines today are between 75 and 100 feet long and use a softball sized rubber ball at the end to provide the additional weight needed during the throw. Another option would be to tie a monkey's fist at one end of the heaving line. Placing pieces of metal (lead or steel), as additional weight in the monkey's fist, will not be used since it could cause damage to personnel or property upon impact. Scrap pieces of line, leather, or cloth can be used instead to provide additional weight needed to throw the heaving line. Refer to **Figure 7-23** while performing the following procedures:

Step	Procedure
1	Lay a bight of the line across the fingers of the left hand, about three and one-half feet from the end, holding the standing part with the left thumb.
2	With fingers separated, take three turns around them.
3	Next take three turns around the first three and at right angles to them.
4	Take the knot off fingers and take an additional three turns around the second three, and inside the first three.
5	Take additional care at this step. Place the core weight (pieces of line, leather, or cloth) into the knot and tighten it down carefully.
6	After tightening, there should be about 18 inches of line left on the bitter end. This can be brought up and seized alongside to the standing part.

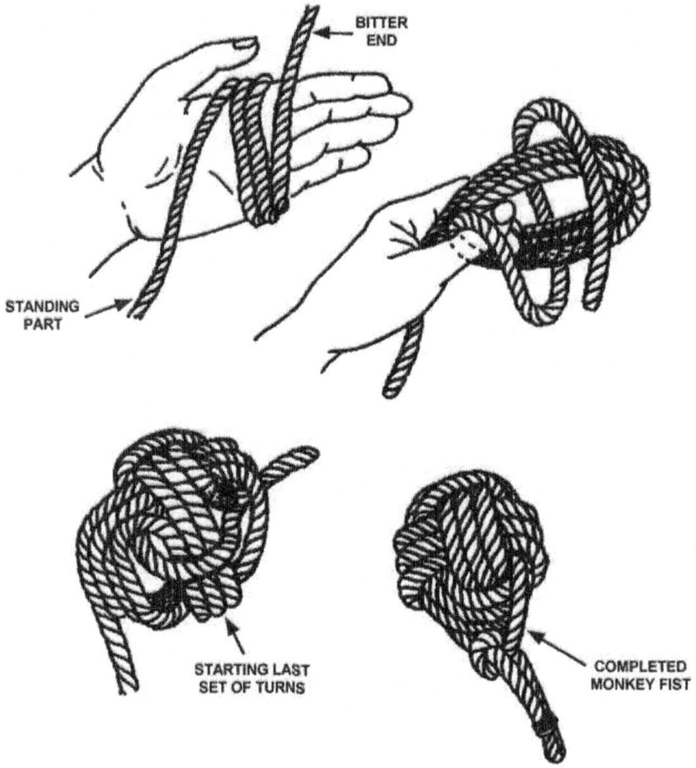

Figure 7-23
Monkey's Fist

D.5.1. Figure Eight (Stopper)

A figure eight knot is an overhand knot with an extra twist. It will prevent the end of a line from feeding through a block or fairlead when loads are involved. It is also easier to untie and does not jam as hard as the over hand knot. (see **Figure 7-24**)

Figure 7-24
Figure Eight Knot

D.5 m. Sheepshank

The sheepshank hitch is used for temporarily shortening a piece of line. It consists of two bights of line, side-by-side, with a half hitch at either end. (see **Figure 7-25**)

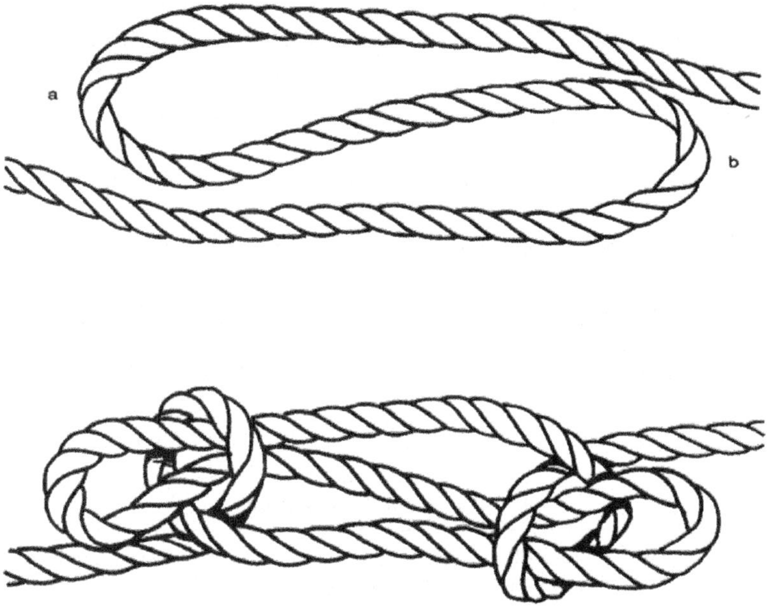

Figure 7-25
Sheepshank

D.5 n. Fisherman's or Anchor Bend

The fisherman's, or anchor bend is used to secure a line to a ring in an anchor or mooring buoy. It can also be tied around a spar. Refer to **Figure 7-26** while performing the following procedures:

Step	Procedure
1	Pass the bitter end through the ring and around twice creating two loops spiraling downward.
2	Wrap the bitter end up around the standing end and pass back through the loops at the top.
3	Tie a half hitch.
4	Pull taut.

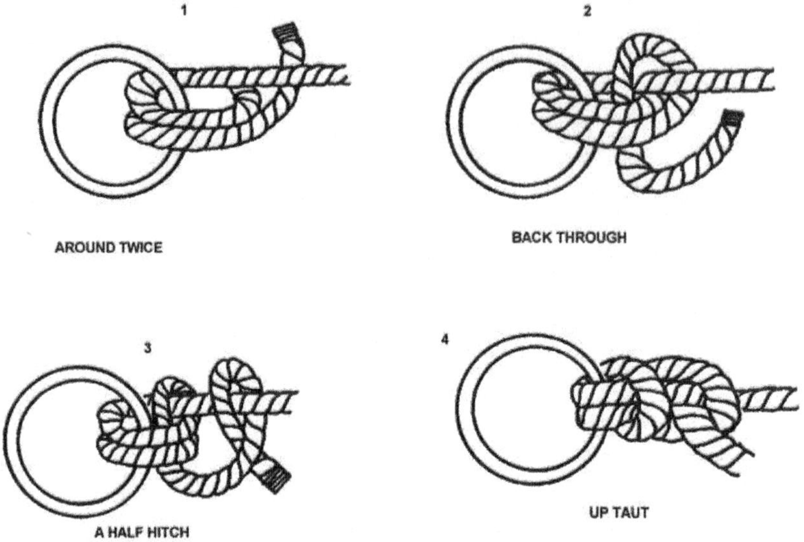

Figure 7-26
Fisherman's or Anchor Bend

D.5.o. Crown Knot

A crown knot may be used to prevent an unwhipped line from unlaying. Refer to **Figure 7-27** while performing the following procedures:

Step	Procedure
1	Unlay the strands of the line about 12".
2	Separate the strands and hold them up, facing the with the middle strand.
3	Bend the middle strand "a" away and form a loop.
4	Bring the right strand "b" around behind the loop, placing it between strands "a" and "c".
5	Bring strand "c" over strand "b" and through the loop formed by strands "a".
6	Pull taut by heaving on each of the three strands.
7	Lay the back splice by tucking each strand backup the line. The splicing is done as if making an eye splice.

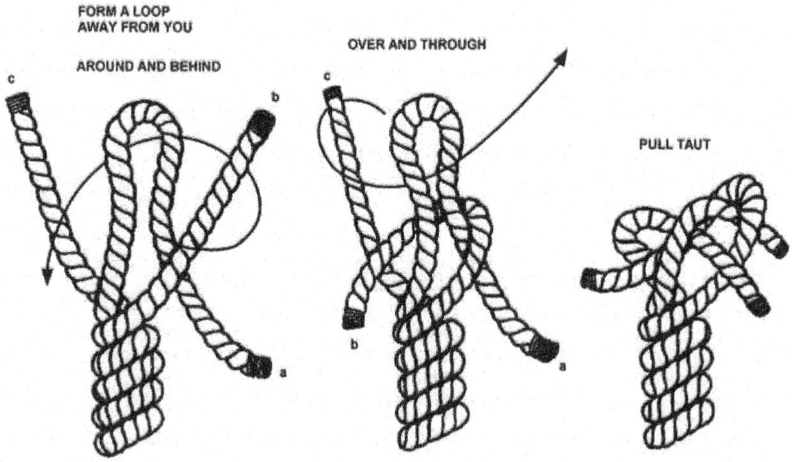

Figure 7-27
Crown Knot

Splices

D.6. Procedure

Splices form a more permanent joining of two lines or two parts of a line. Splicing can be done with many different styles of line including three-strand and doubled-braided. Three-strand lines are unlayed and woven back into themselves or into another line. Double-braided lines go through a series of core/cover removals and tucks in order to complete the splice. Splices are preferred over knots since they allow the line to retain more of its original working strength. The type of splice used depends on the type of joint and the type of line. On Coast Guard boats, the most common splices are eye splices at the working end of the towline, side lines, and mooring lines. Eye, back, and short splices will be illustrated for plain laid three-strand line and eye and short (end-for-end) splices will be illustrated for double-braided nylon.

D.7. Eye Splice in Three-Strand Plain-Laid Line

The eye splice makes a permanent loop (the eye) in the end of a line. Refer to **Figure 7-28** while performing the following procedures:

Step	Procedure
1	Unlay the strands of the line about 12".
2	Make a bight the size of the eye required.
3	Hold the strands up so the middle strand is facing you.
4	Tuck the middle strand "a."
NOTE	Always tuck the middle strand first, and keep the right-hand strand of the side of the line that is facing toward you. All tucks are made from outboard toward the person tying.
5	Cross-strand "b" over the strand just tucked and then under the strand just below it.
6	Turn the entire eye splice over and tuck strand "c."
7	Pull all strands tight.
8	Pass each strand over the adjacent strand and under the next strand (over & under). The number of tucks depends on the material of the line being worked with. Natural fiber lines should be tucked a minimum of three times. Synthetic fiber lines require four or more tucks to ensure they do not slip.

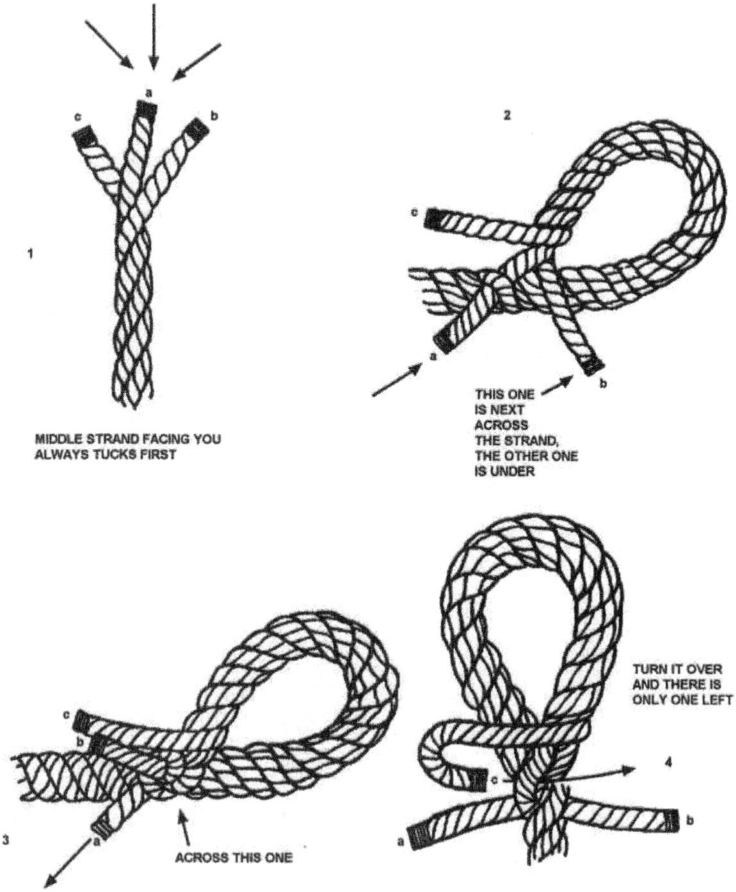

Figure 7-28
Three-Stranded Eye Splice

D.8. Back Splice in Three-Strand Plain-Laid Line

A back splice is commonly used to finish off the end of a line. On Coast Guard boats, it can be used on the ends of fender lines. Care should be used when selecting a back splice to finish off a line. The splice will increase the diameter of the line that may cause it to jam or foul when running through a block or deck fitting. If the line must be able to run free, a permanent whipping (see **Figure 7-32**) on the end is preferred to prevent unraveling. Crewmembers should starting with unlaying the strands at the end, then bending them back on the line, and then interweaving them back through the strands of the standing part. Refer to **Figure 7-29** while performing the following procedures:

Step	Procedure
1	Begin the back splice by tying a crown knot (see **Figure 7-29**). Each strand goes under and out from its neighbor in the direction of the lay.
2	Pass each strand under itself, just beneath the crown knot. Do not pull these first tucks too tight.
3	Proceed with three more rounds of tucks - over one, under one, as in an eye splice.
4	If preferred, it can be finished by trimming the ends of the strands.

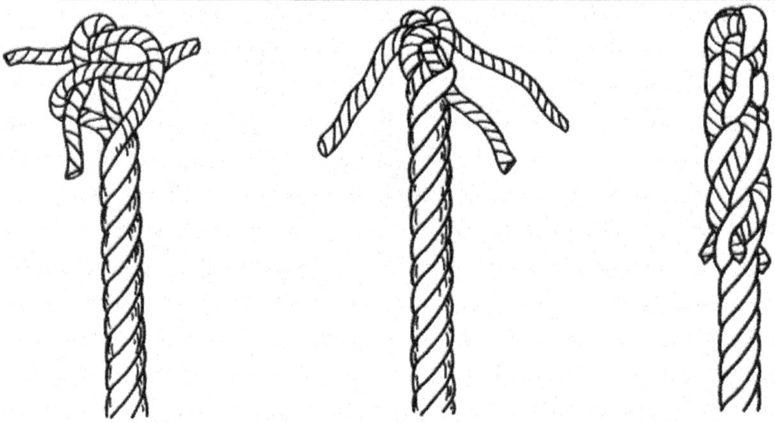

Figure 7-29
Back Splice (Three-Strand)

D.9. Short Splice

A short splice is used to permanently connect two ends of a line. It is important to note that a short splice is never used in a line that must pass over a pulley or sheave. Refer to **Figure 7-30** while performing the following procedures:

Step	Procedure
1	Unlay the strands of the lines to be spliced, about 12".
2	Bring the ends together by alternating strands.
3	Slide the two ends together, that is, butt them and temporarily seize them with sail twin or tape.
4	Tuck each strand over and under three times, the same way as in eye splicing. (Synthetic line requires an additional tuck.)
5	Remove the seizing.

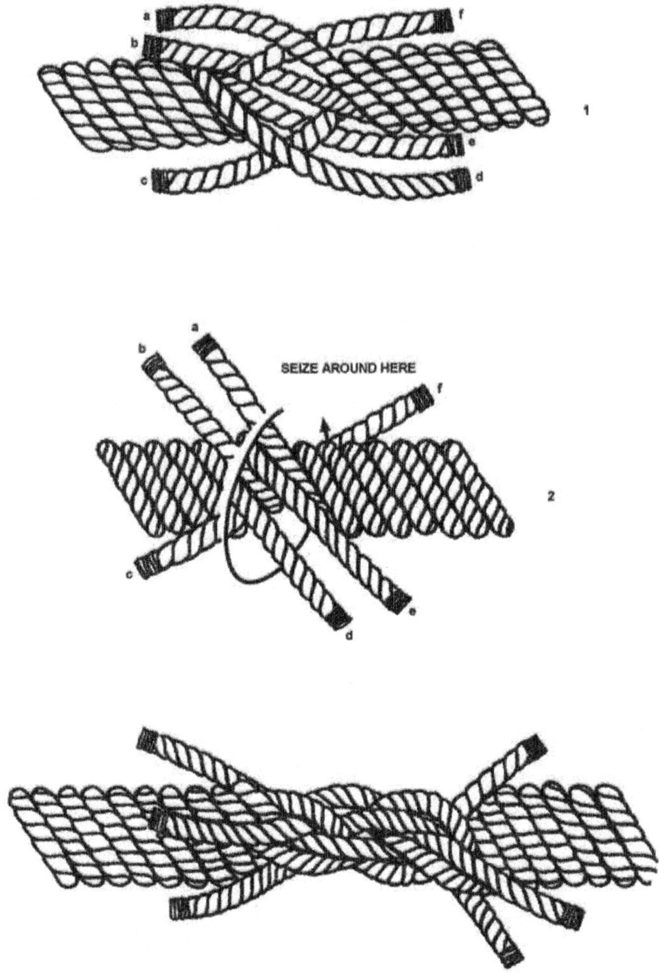

Figure 7-30
Short Splice

D.10. Eye Splice in Double-Braided Line

Splicing a double-braided line entails pulling the core out of the cover and then putting the line back together to make the splice. The basic principle for putting it back together is:

- The cover goes into the core.
- Then the core goes back into the cover.

Splicing a double-braided line requires the use of special equipment. The "pusher" and "fid" are especially designed to splice a certain size of line. The correct measurements supplied by the manufacturer must be used before starting the splice. One mistake in a measurement can result in an improper and dangerous splice. Utilize the following instructions for splicing a double-braided line:

NOTE

The following series of steps (which is under copyright by Samson Ocean Systems, Inc.) is reprinted here by permission. Other manufacturers of double-braided line provide splicing instructions. Specific information for splicing should be requested from the appropriate manufacturer.

Standard Eye – NEW ROPE

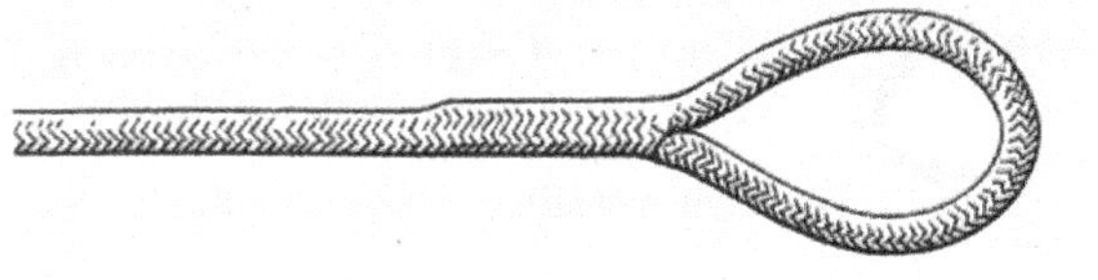

This Samson Eye Splice is for new rope only. It retains approximately 90% of the average new rope strength.

For splicing used rope, start with Step 1B, on Page 29.

MARKING THE MEASUREMENTS . . . STEP 1A

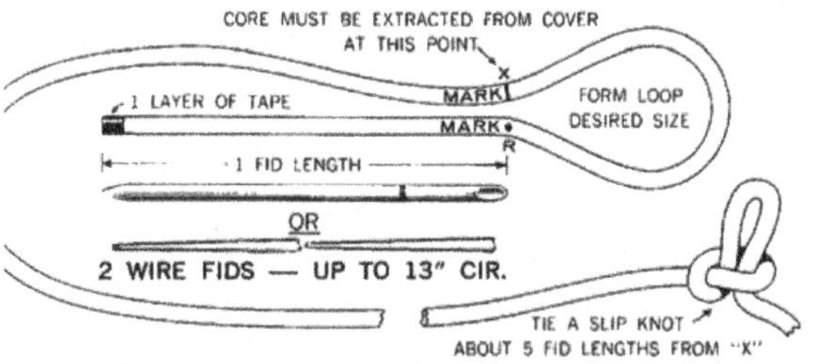

On rope over 1" diameter, it is often easier to pass a spike or similar object through the rope instead of tying a slipknot.

Tape end to be spliced with one thin layer of tape. Then, measure one tubular fid length (2 wire fid lengths because wire fid is ½ size) from end of rope and mark. This is Point R (Reference).

From R form a loop the size of the eye desired and mark. This is Point X where you extract core from inside the cover. If using a thimble, form the loop around the thimble. (See Special Tips, for more information on installing a thimble).

Tie a tight slip knot approximately five fid lengths from X. **THIS MUST BE DONE.**

In the event you require the rope with the finished splice(s) to be a certain overall length, refer to Special Tips.

STEP 2A . . . NEW ROPE: EXTRACTING THE CORE

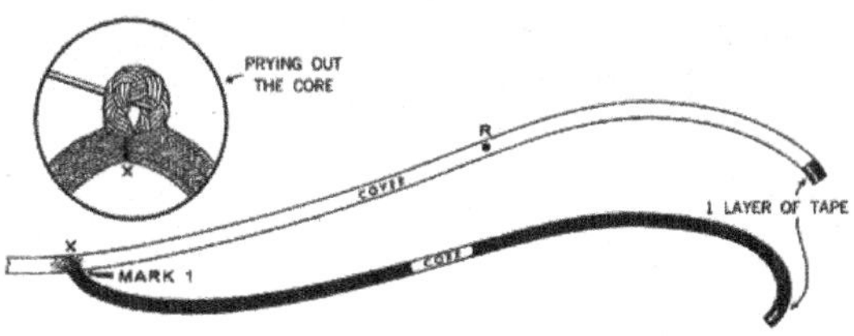

Bend rope sharply at X. With the pusher or any sharp tool such as an ice pick, awl, or marlin spike, spread the cover strands to expose core. First pry, then, pull the core completely out of cover from X to the taped end of the rope. Put one layer only of tape on end of core.

Note: DO NOT pull cover strands away from rope when spreading cover as this will distort rope unnecessarily.

To assure correct positioning of Mark #1 do the following.

Holding the exposed core, slide cover as far back towards the tightly tied slipknot as you can. Then, firmly smooth the cover back from the slip knot towards taped end. Smooth again until all cover slack is removed.

Then, mark the core where it comes out of the cover.

THIS IS MARK #1.

NEW ROPE: MARKING THE CORE . . . STEP 3A

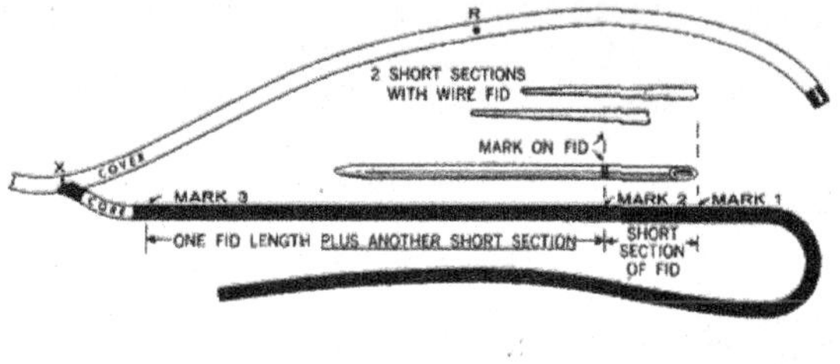

Again slide cover toward slipknot to expose more core.

From Mark #1, measure along core towards X a distance equal to the short section of tubular fid (2 short sections with wire fid) and make two heavy marks.

THIS IS MARK #2.

From Mark #2 measure in the same direction one fid length plus another short section of the fid. (With wire fid, double measurements) make 3 heavy marks.

THIS IS MARK #3.

STEP 4A . . . NEW ROPE: MARKING THE COVER FOR TAPERING

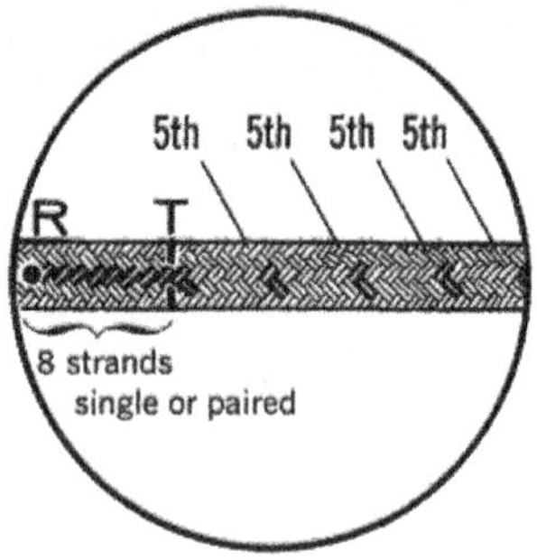

Note nature of cover braid. It is made up of strands — either one or two (pair). By inspection you can see half the strands revolve to the right around rope and half revolve to the left.

Beginning at "R" and working toward taped end of the cover, count 8 consecutive strands (single or pairs) which revolve to the right (or left). **MARK THE 8th STRAND.**

This is Point T. (See Insert). Make Mark T go completely around cover.

Starting at T and working toward the taped cover end, count and mark every fifth right and left strand (single or paired) until you have progressed down to end of taped cover.

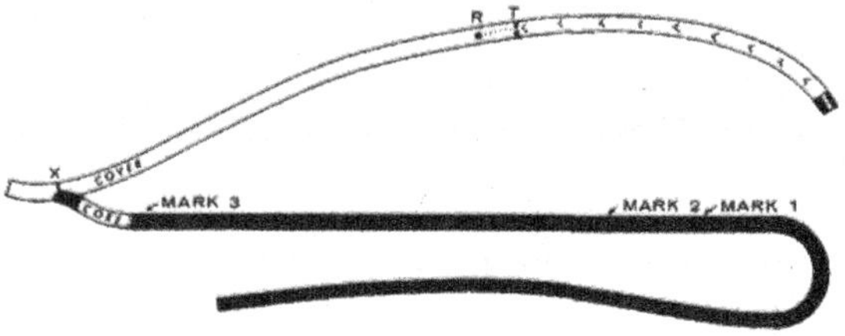

NEW ROPE: PUTTING THE COVER INSIDE CORE . . . STEP 5A

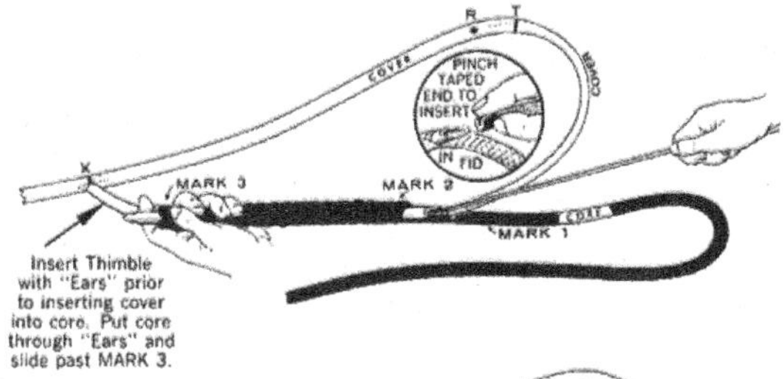

Insert fid into core at Mark #2. Slide it through and out at Mark #3.

Add extra tape to cover end; then jam it tightly into the hollow end of fid (See Insert). Hold core lightly at Mark #3, place pusher joint into taped end, and push fid and cover through from Mark #2 and out at Mark #3.

With wire fid first press prongs into cover, then tape over (see "Tools Needed"). Then after fid is on, milk braid over fid while pulling fid through from Mark #2 to Mark #3.

Take the fid off the cover. Continue pulling cover tail through the core until Mark R on the cover emerges from Mark #3. Then remove tape from end of cover.

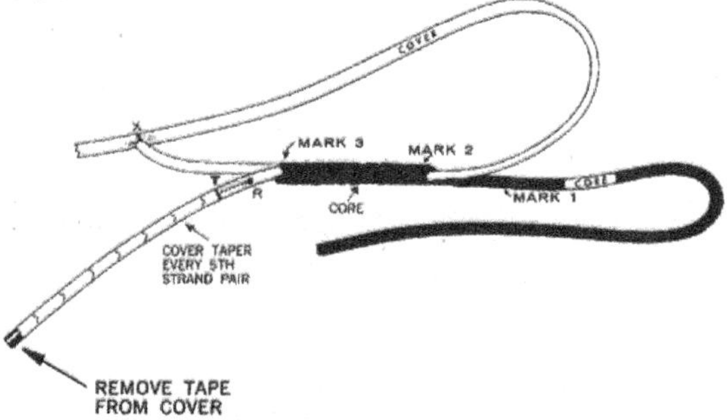

STEP 6A . . . NEW ROPE: PERFORMING THE TAPER

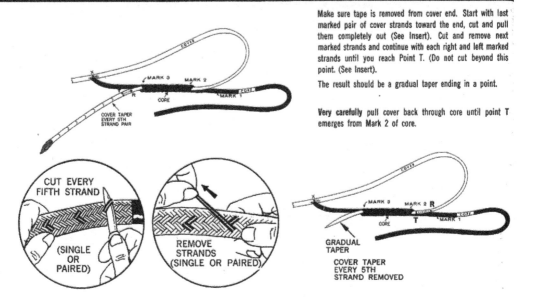

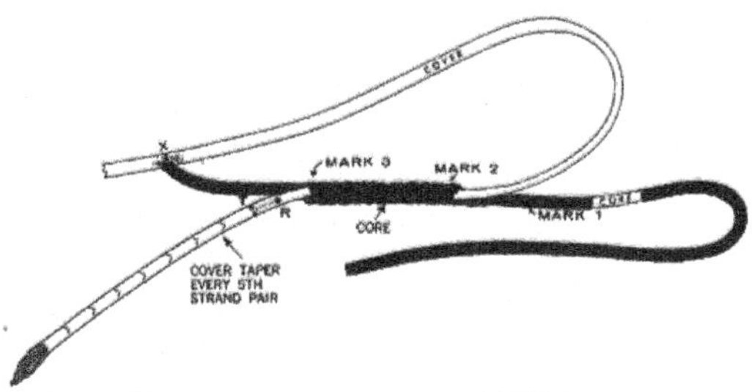

Make sure tape is removed from cover end. Start with last marked pair of cover strands toward the end, cut and pull them completely out (See Insert). Cut and remove next marked strands and continue with each right and left marked strands until you reach Point T. (Do not cut beyond this point. (See Insert).

The result should be a gradual taper ending in a point.

Very carefully pull cover back through core until point T emerges from Mark 2 of core.

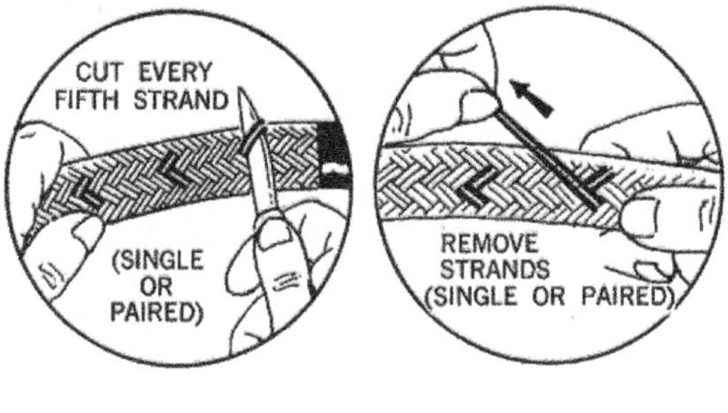

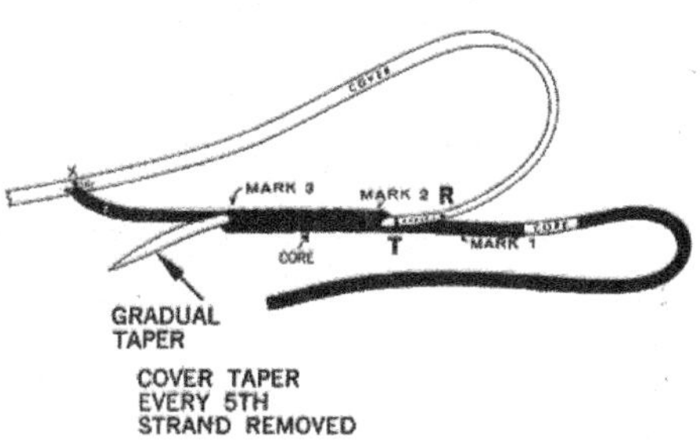

NEW ROPE: REINSERTING THE CORE INTO COVER . . . STEP 7A

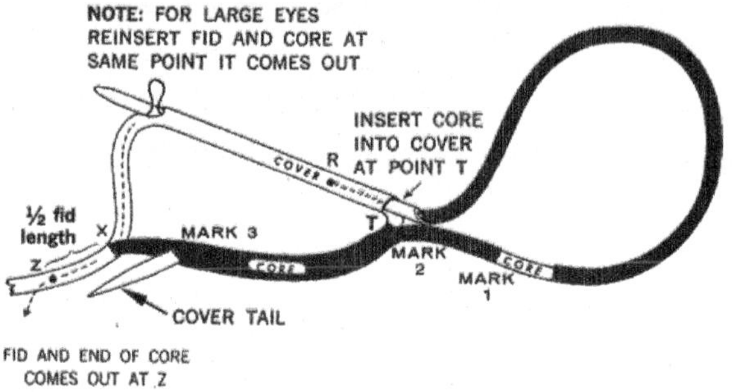

From point X on cover measure approximately ½ fid length toward slip knot on rope and mark this as point Z.

You are now ready to put core back into cover from T to Z. Insert fid at T, jam the taped core end tightly into end of fid. With pusher, push fid and core through cover "tunnel", past X, to, and through cover at Z.

When using wire fid, attach fid to taped core. After fid is on, milk braid over fid while pulling through from T to Z.

When pushing fid past X to Z **make sure** fid does not catch any internal core strands.

NOTE:
Depending on eye size, fid may not be long enough to reach from T to Z in one pass. If not, bring fid out through cover, pull core through and reinsert fid into exact hole it came out of. Do this as many times as needed to reach Z.

STEP 8A . . . NEW ROPE: MARKING THE REDUCED VOLUME TAIL CORE

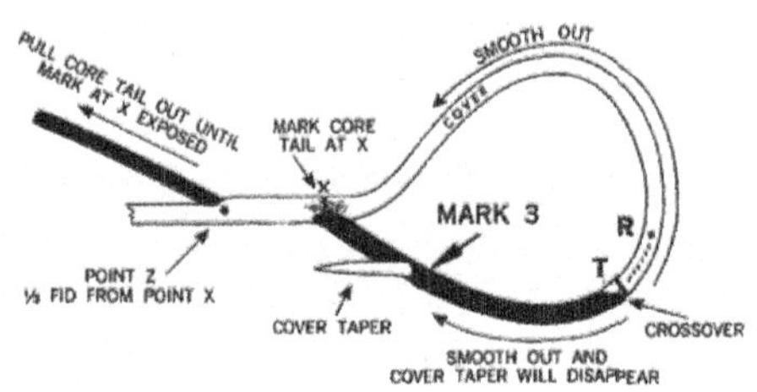

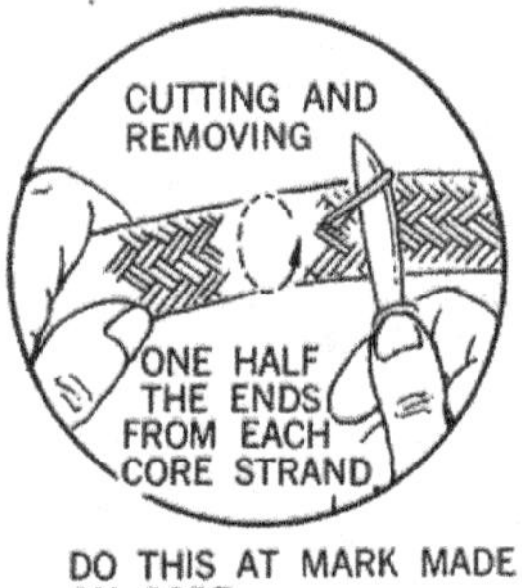

DO THIS AT MARK MADE ON CORE (THROUGH COVER AT X)

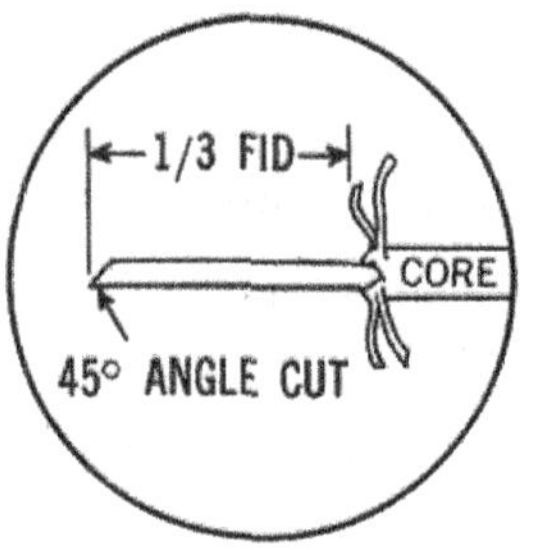

Alternately pull on core tail at Z, then pull on tapered cover at **Mark 3**. The crossover should be tightened until crossover is approximately equal to diameter of rope.

Smooth out cover of eye completely, from crossover (T) toward X, to get all slack out of eye area.

MARK CORE TAIL THROUGH COVER AT POINT X.

Pull core tail out until mark on core just made is exposed at Z.

Reduce core volume at this point by cutting and removing one strand at each group, progressing around the circumference of the rope (see insert).

Measure 1/3 fid from start of reduction cuts (mark) toward end and mark. Cut off remaining tail at this point. Make cut on a 45° angle to prevent a blunt end (see insert).

With one hand, hold crossover — **MARK T.**

Smooth cover section of eye out firmly and completely from crossover toward X; Reduced volume core tail should disappear into cover at Z.

Smooth out core section from crossover towards MARK 3 and cover taper will disappear into core.

16

NEW ROPE: BURYING THE EXPOSED CORE . . . STEP 9A

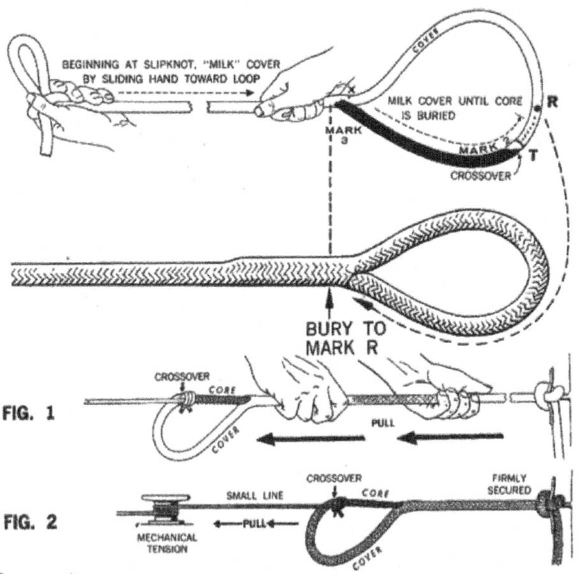

FIG. 1

FIG. 2

Hold rope at slipknot and with other hand milk cover toward splice, gently at first, then more firmly. Cover will slide over Mark #3, Mark #2, the crossover, and T and R. (It may be necessary to occasionally smooth out eye during milking to prevent reduced volume tail catching in throat of splice).

If bunching occurs at cross-over preventing full burying, smooth cover from T to X. Grasp crossover at T with one hand and then firmly smooth cover slack (female side of eye) with other hand towards throat (X). Repeat as necessary until bunching disappears.

Continue milking until all cover slack between knot and throat of eye has been removed.

TIP:
Before burying the cover over the crossover:

A. Anchor loop of slip-knot by tying it to stationary object before starting to bury. You can then use both hands and weight of body to more easily bury cover over core and crossover. (See Fig. 1 & 2).

B. Holding the crossover tightly milk all the excess cover from R to X.

Flex and loosen the rope at the crossover point during the final burying process. Hammering cover at point X will help loosen strands.

With larger ropes it is helpful to securely anchor slip-knot, attach a small line to the braided core at the crossover and mechanically apply tension with either a block and tackle, capstan, come-a-long, or power winch. Tension will reduce diameter of core and crossover for easier burying. (See Fig. 2).

17

STEP 10A . . . NEW ROPE: FINISHING THE SPLICE WITH LOCK-STITCH

Stitch locking is advantageous on splices to prevent no-load opening due to mishandling.

Material Required — About one (1) fid length of Nylon or Polyester Whipping Twine approximately the same size of the strands in the size rope you are stitch locking. The same strands cut from the rope you are stitch locking may also be used.

Step 1

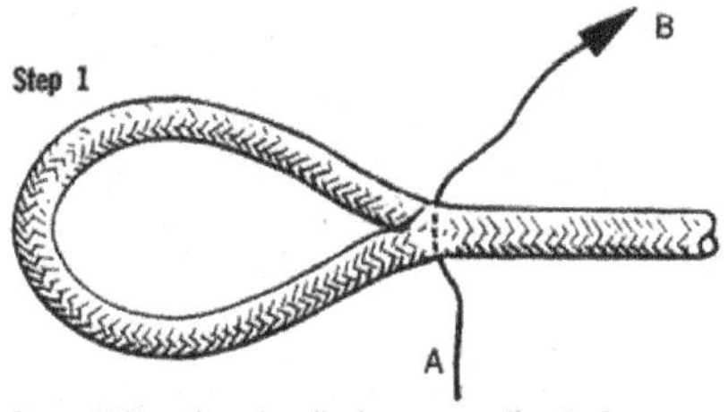

Pass stitching through spliced area near throat of eye as shown.

Step 2

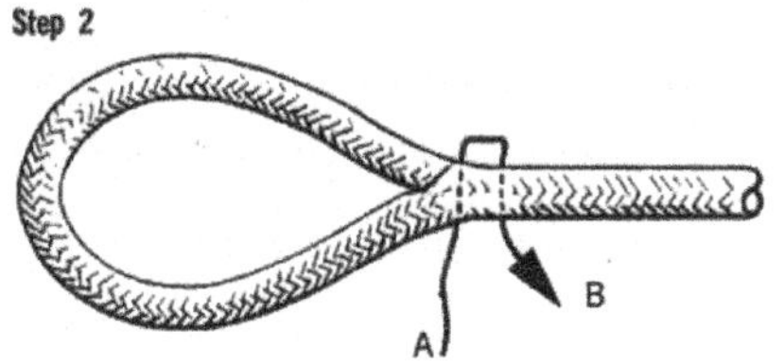

Re-insert as shown pulling snug but not tight.

NEW ROPE: LOCK-STITCH PROCEDURE . . . STEP 11A

Step 3

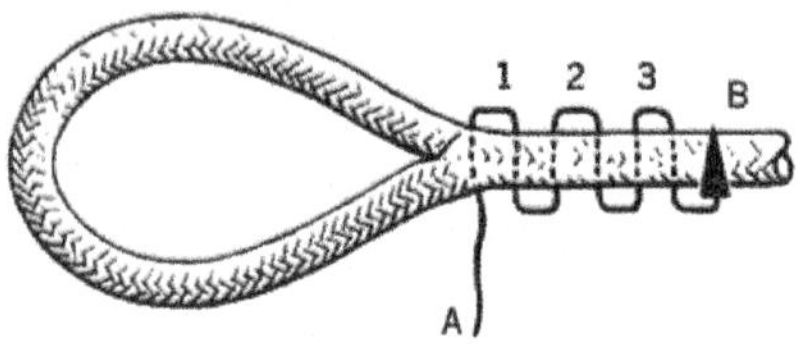

Continue to re-insert as shown until you have at least three (3) complete stitches.

Step 4

After completing Step #3, rotate spliced part of rope 90° and re-insert end "A" into splice area in the same fashion as in steps #1, #2, and #3. The splice will now be stitched on two planes perpendicular to each other. Make sure you do not pull stitching too tight.

Configuration of cross section after completing Step #4.

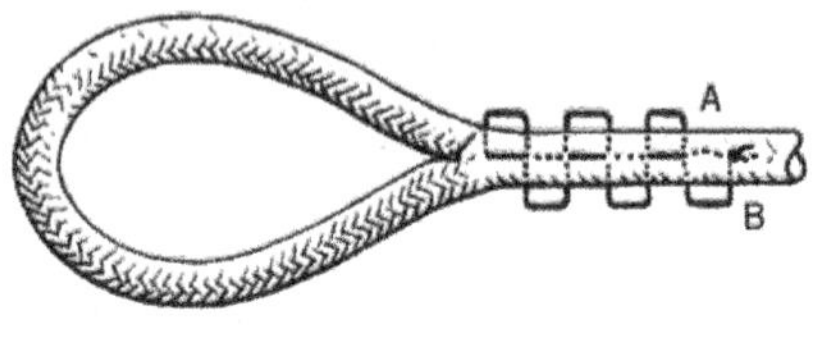

Step 5

After stitching at least three (3) complete stitches as in step #3, extract two ends A & B together through the same opening in the braid. Tie them together with a square knot and re-insert back into braid between cover and core.

End-For-End Double Braid

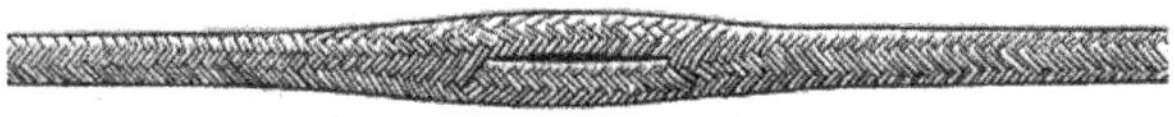

The Samson Standard End-for-End Splice can be performed on new and used rope. This is an all-purpose splice technique designed for people who generally splice used rope as frequently as new rope. It retains up to 85% of average new rope strength and in used rope up to 85% of the remaining used rope strength.

Before splicing used rope, study the Special Tips shown on Page 7.

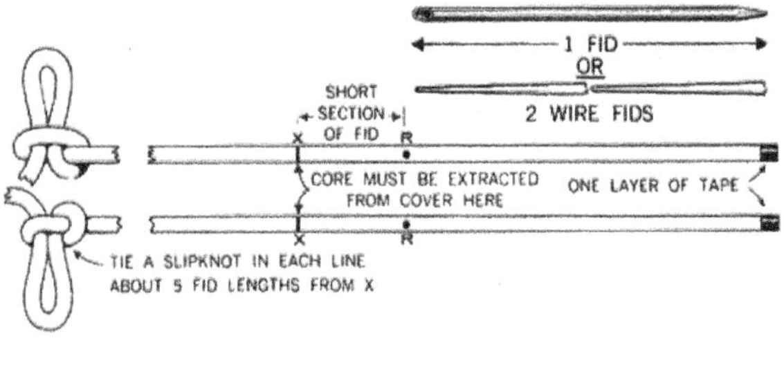

Tape the end of each rope with one thin layer of tape. Lay two ropes to be spliced side by side and measure one tubular fid length (2 wire fid lengths because wire fid is ½ size) from end of each rope and make a mark. This is Point R (Reference).

From R measure one short fid section length as scribed on the fid; then, mark again. This is Point X where you should extract core from inside cover. Be sure both ropes are identically marked.

Tie a tight slipknot approximately 5 fid lengths from X.

If you require the rope with the finished splice to be a certain overall length, refer to Special Tips Page 5.

EXTRACTING THE CORES . . . STEP 2

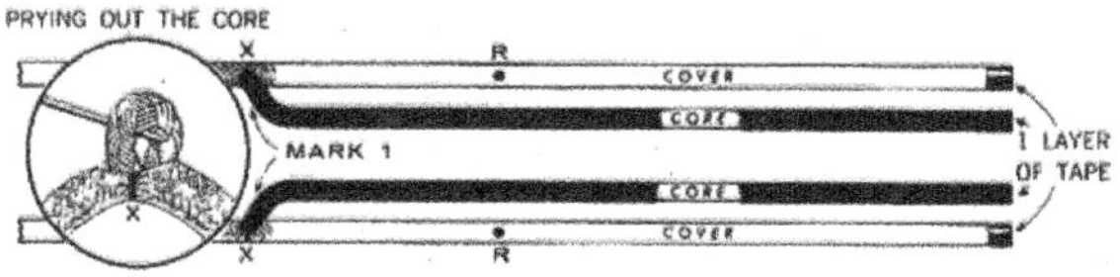

DO NOT PULL COVER STRANDS AWAY FROM ROPE AS THIS WILL DISTORT COVER UNNECESSARILY

Bend rope sharply at X. With the pusher or any sharp tool such as an ice pick, awl, or marlin spike, spread cover strands to expose core. First pry; then, pull core completely out of cover from X to the end of rope. Put one layer only of tape on end of core.

To assure correct positioning of Mark #1 do the following. Holding the exposed core, slide cover as far back towards the tightly tied slip knot as you can. Then, firmly smooth cover back from the slip knot towards taped end. Smooth again until all cover slack is removed. Then, mark core where it comes out of cover. This is Mark #1. Do this to both ropes.

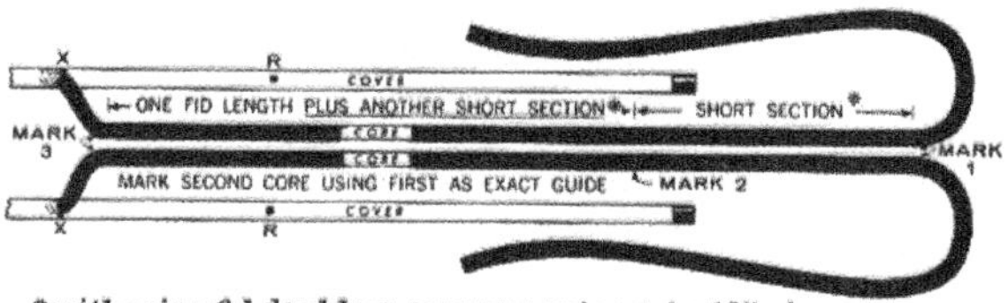

**with wire fid double measurements up to 13" cir.*

Hold one core at Mark #1 and slide cover back to expose more core.

From Mark #1, measure along core towards X a distance equal to the short section of fid *and make two heavy marks. This is Mark #2.

From Mark #2, measure in the same direction **one fid length plus another short section** *and make three heavy marks. This is Mark #3.

Mark second core by laying it alongside the first and using it as an exact guide.

STEP 4 . . . MARKING THE COVER FOR TAPERING

51

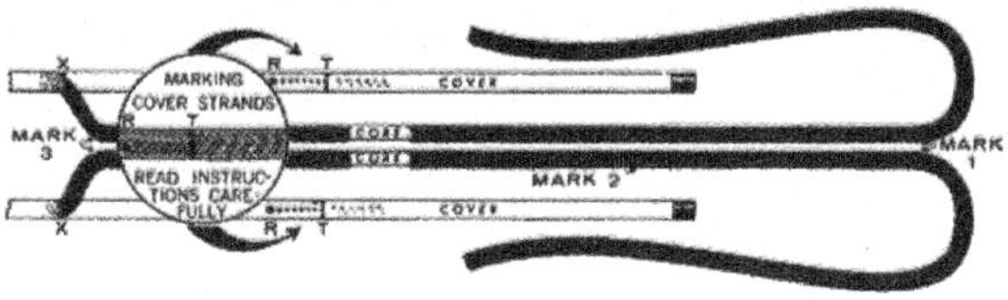

Note nature of the cover braid. It is made up of strands. By inspection you can see that half the strands revolve to the right around the rope and half revolve to the left.

Beginning at R and working toward the taped end of cover, count 8 consecutive pairs of cover strands which revolve to the right (or left). Mark the 8th pair. This is Point T (See Insert). Make Mark T go completely around cover.

Starting at T and working toward taped cover end **count** and **mark every second right pair** of strands for a total of **6.** Again, starting at T, count and mark every second left pair of strands for a total of 6. (See Insert).

Make both ropes identical.

PERFORMING THE TAPER . . . STEP 5

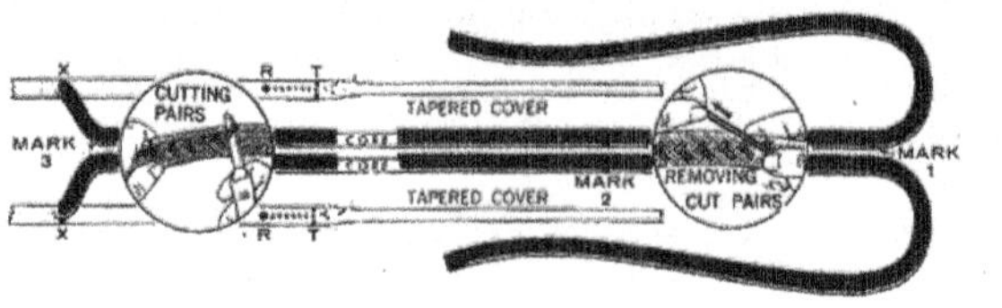

First remove tape from cover end. Starting with last marked pair of cover strands toward the end, cut and pull them completely out (See Insert). Cut and remove next marked strands and continue with each right and left marked strands until you reach Point T. **Do not cut beyond this point.** (See Insert)

Retape tapered end.

Cut and remove marked strands on the other marked cover, again stopping at T. Retape tapered end.

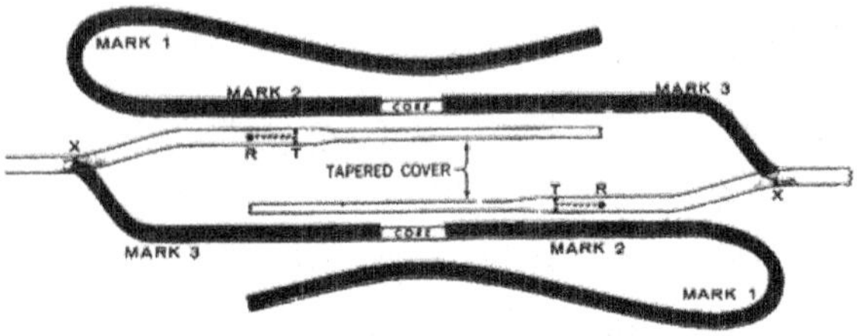

Reposition ropes for splicing according to diagram. Note how cover of one rope has been paired off with core of the opposite line. **Avoid twisting.**

STEP 7 . . . PUTTING THE COVER INSIDE CORE

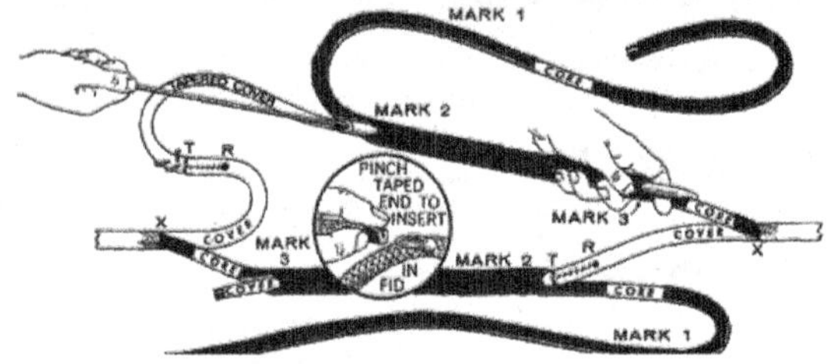

Insert fid into one core at Mark #2 and bring it out at Mark #3. Add extra tape to tapered cover end then jam it tightly into hollow end of fid (see insert). Hold core lightly at Mark #3, place pusher point into taped end pushing fid and with cover in it from Mark #2 out at Mark #3. When using wire fid, attach fid to cover. Then pull fid through from Mark #2 to Mark #3. Pull cover tail through core until Mark T on cover meets Mark #2 on core. Insert other cover into core in same manner.

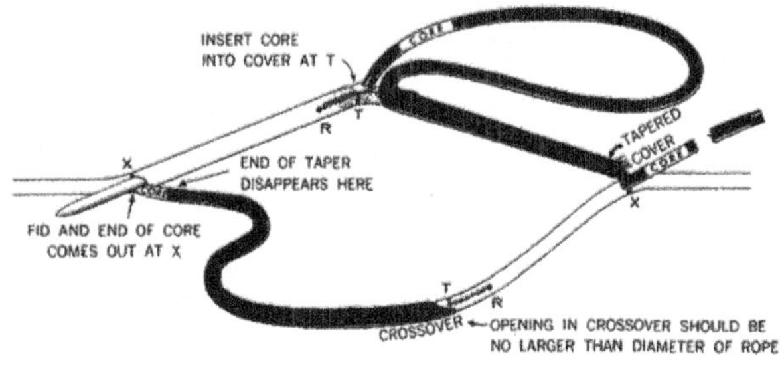

Now put core back into cover from T to X. Insert fid at T, jam taped core tightly into end of fid. With pusher, push fid and core through cover bringing out at Point X. When using wire fid attach fid to taped core. Then pull fid and braid through from T to X. Do this to both cores. Remove tape from end of cover. Bring crossover up tight by pulling on core tail and on tapered covered tail. Hold crossover tightly smoothing out all excess braid away from crossover in each direction. Trim end of Tapered cover on an angle to eliminate blunt end. Tapered cover tail will disappear at Mark #3. Cut core tail off close to Point X at an angle.

BURYING THE EXPOSED CORE . . . STEP 9

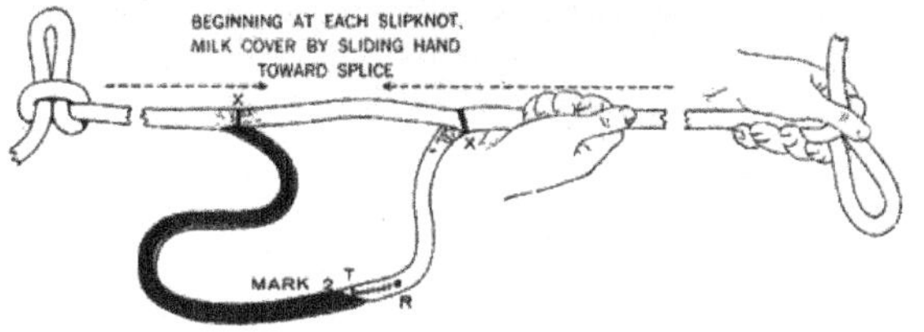

Hold rope at slipknot and with other hand milk cover toward the splice, gently at first, and then more firmly. The cover will slide over Mark #3, Mark #2 the crossover and R. Repeat with the other side of the splice.

Continue burying until all cover slack between the knot and the splice has been removed.

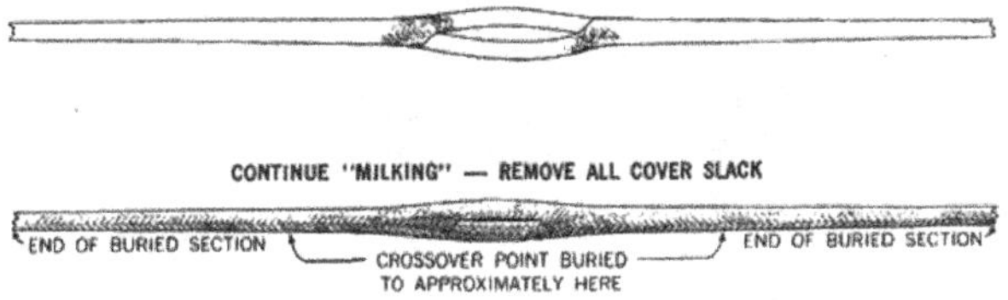

The splice is done when all cover slack has been removed and there is an opening in the splice approximately equal in length to the diameter of rope. If at the opening one side of the splice is noticeably longer than the other side, something is wrong. Check Steps 1-9 and remake if necessary.

Now untie the slip knots.

Whipping

D.11. Importance

The end of a cut line will unravel and fray if not secured with a whipping or back splice. Whippings may be permanent or temporary.

D.12. Temporary Whipping

Sometimes called the common whipping, temporary whippings make temporary repairs and secure strands of lines while splicing. They are not very durable and unravel easily if snagged. Whippings are normally made using sail twine, although almost any small stuff will do. Refer to **Figure 7-31** while performing the following procedures:

Step	Procedure
1	Cut a piece of sail twine or small stuff, in length about ten times the circumference of the line being seized.
2	Lay the sail twine or small stuff alongside the line to be whipped. (see **Figure 7-31**)
3	Form an overhand loop in the sail twine or small stuff such that the loop extends about ½" beyond the end.
4	Holding end "a", make a series of turns over the loop toward the bitter end of the line. Make enough turns so that the length of turns is almost equal to the diameter of the line.
5	Slip end "a" through the loop "c".
6	Secure by pulling loop end from sight by pulling on "b".
7	Cut off excess whipping ends or secure them by tying them together with a reef or square knot.

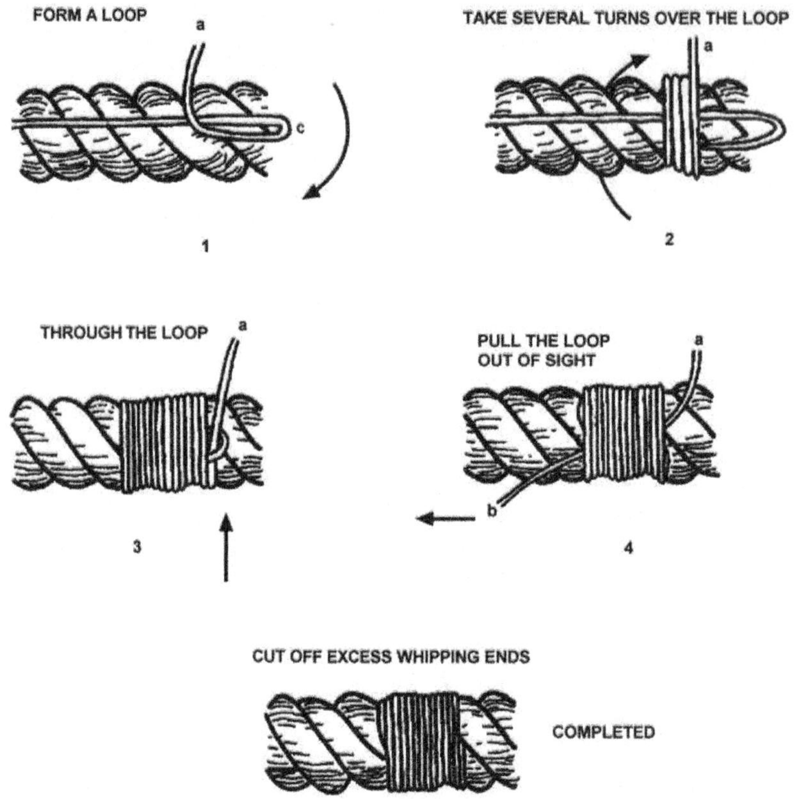

Figure 7-31
Temporary Whipping

D.13. Permanent Whipping

Permanent whippings are made to last. To make one, several wraps are made around the line using shot line or waxed nylon. The ends of the whipping line are then sewn across the whipping and through the line. Refer to **Figure 7-32** while performing the following procedures:

Step	Procedure
1	Cut enough of the whipping line to allow for 15 to 20 wraps, with at least a foot of line left over.
2	Secure the whipping line by sewing it through the line. If desired, add strength by sewing through more than once.
3	Wind the whipping line around the line 15 to 20 times, working toward the end of the line. Make sure the body of the whipping covers the secured end of the whipping line.
4	Secure the whipping by sewing through the line. Then bring the line across the whipping and sew it through the line. Do this three or more times, depending on the size of the line.
5	Finish the whipping by sewing through the line a couple more times and cutting the whipping line off close. A pull on the line will pull the end of the whipping line inside, hiding it from view.

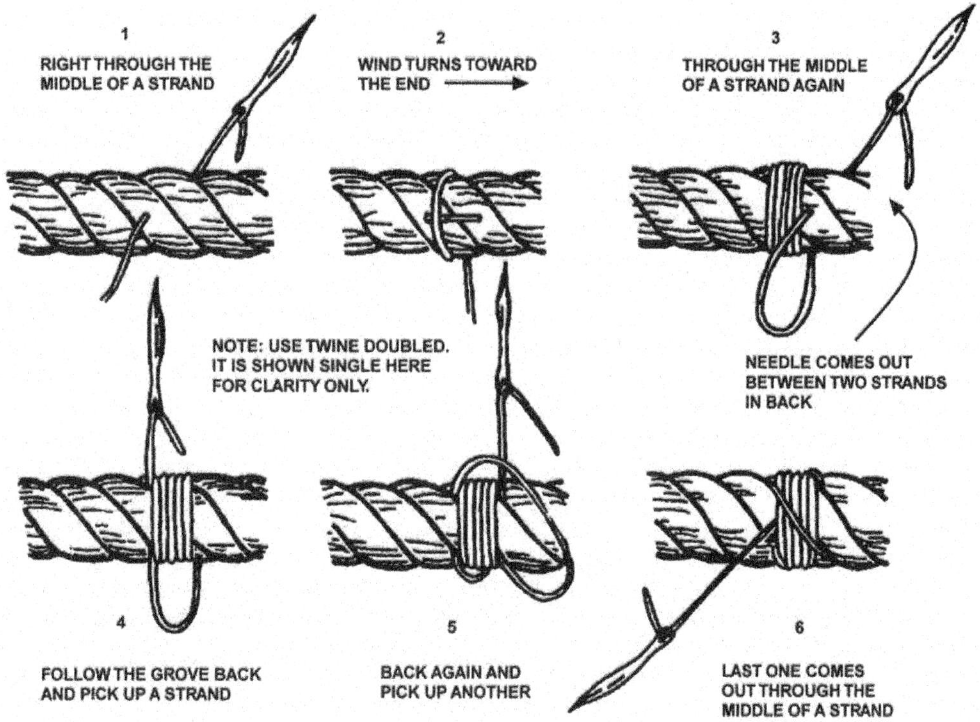

Figure 7-32
Permanent Whipping

Mousing Hooks and Shackles

D.14. Mousing Hooks

A hook is moused to keep slings and straps from slipping out or off the hooks. This is accomplished by either mechanical means or by seizing the hook, using seizing wire or small stuff, from opposite sides. (see **Figure 7-33**)

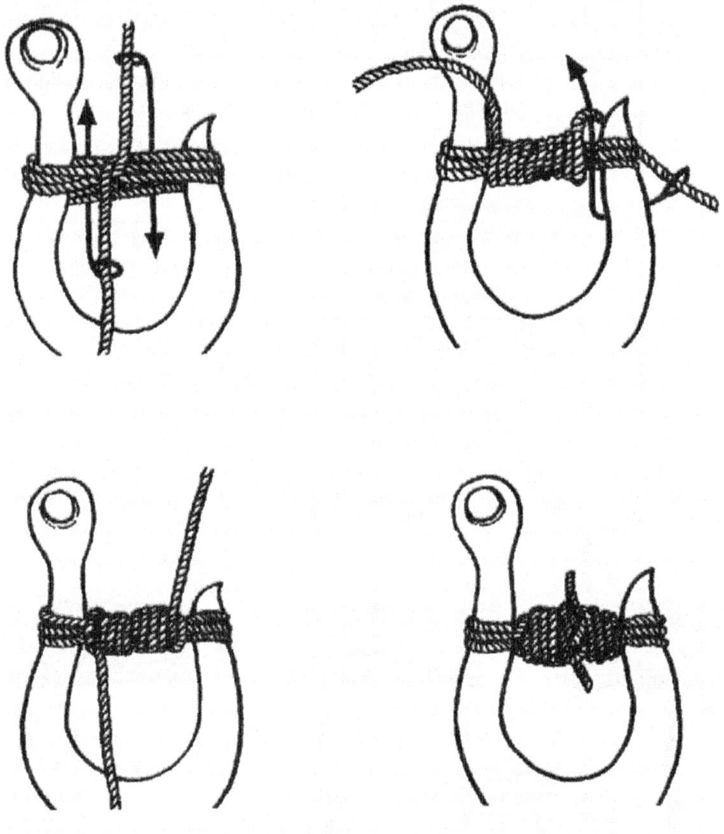

Figure 7-33
Mousing a Hook

D.15. Shackles

Shackles are moused to prevent the pin from backing out. This is usually done on screw-pin shackles. Mousing is accomplished by taking several turns, using seizing wire or small stuff, through the pin eye and around the shackle itself in such a way so the pin cannot turn. (see **Figure 7-34**)

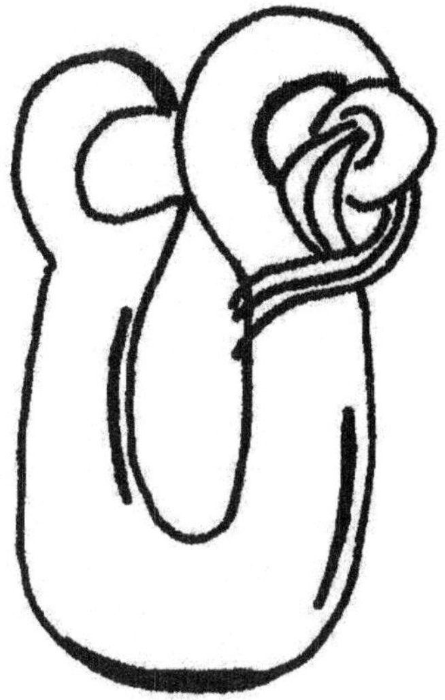

Figure 7-34
Mousing a Shackle

Section E. Deck Fittings and Line Handling

Introduction

This section explains the procedures for securing lines to the various types of deck fittings.

E.1. Deck Fittings

Deck fittings are attachments or securing points for lines. They permit easy handling and reduce wear and friction on lines. There are three basic types of deck fittings:

- Bitts.
- Cleats.
- Chocks.

Several types of deck fittings are shown in **Figure 7-35**.

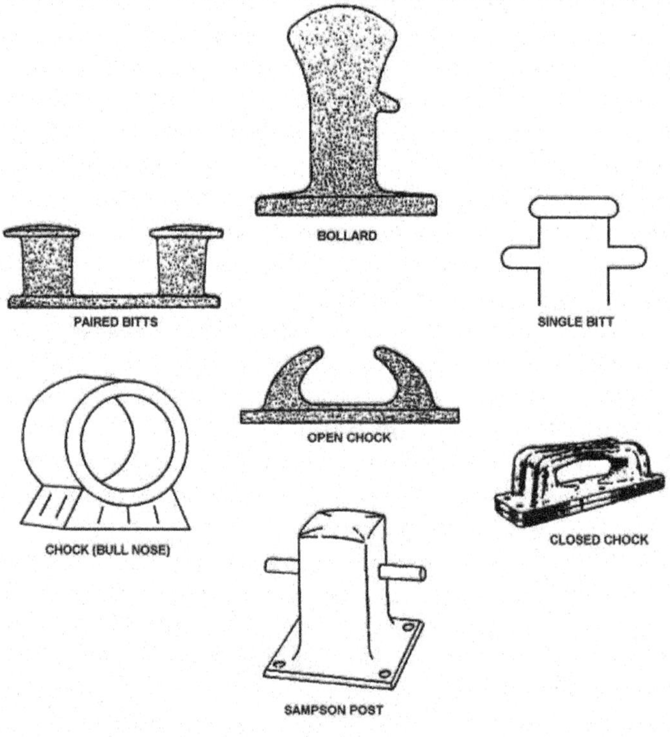

Figure 7-35
Types of Deck Fittings

E.2. Line Handling

Most Coast Guard standard boats have a towing bitt and a bow bitt. Cleats may be found on the decks next to the gunwales on each side of a boat used with bitts and cleats to help prevent chafing of the line. The chock provides a smooth surface for the line to run over or through. Because of the difference in the structural design of nonstandard boats, the strength of their deck fittings will vary widely.

E.2.a. Using Properly Sized Line

The size of the deck hardware depends on the size of line to be used for mooring, docking and towing. Cleats are sized by length, and the rule of thumb is the line should be $\frac{1}{16}$" in diameter for each inch of cleat ($\frac{3}{8}$" line = 6" cleat, ½" line = 8" cleat.

NOTE ☞ On auxiliary operational facilities (as a rule of thumb) no tow should be attempted with smaller than $\frac{3}{8}$" line; therefore, the smallest size cleat on a facility should be 6".

E.2.b. Using Backup Plates

All deck hardware that is used for towing should have backup plates to distribute the load over a wide area. (see **Figure 7-36**) The backup plate can be made of pressure treated hardwood or exterior grade plywood, at least twice as thick as the largest bolt diameter. Bolts, not screws should be used. A flat washer and a lock washer must be used with the bolt. The flat washer is three times the bolt diameter. If metal is used, the thickness should be at least the same as the bolt diameter. The use of aluminum is not recommended.

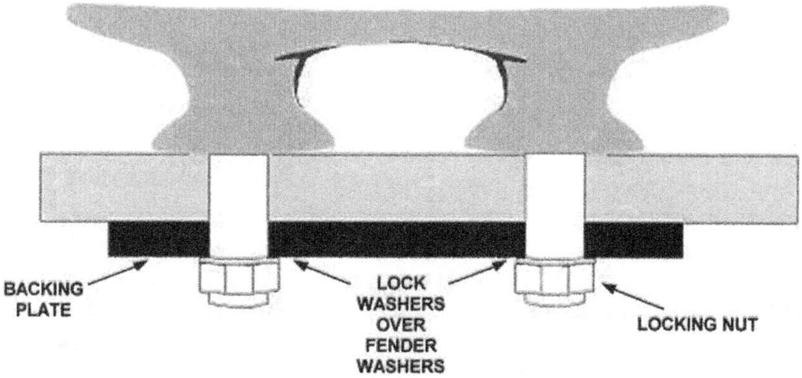

Figure 7-36
Backup Plate

E.2.c. Securing a Line to a Bitt

The following procedures describe how to secure a line to a set of bitts (see **Figure 7-37**):

Step	Procedure
1	Make a complete turn around the near horn.
2	Make several figure eights around both horns. (Size of line and cleats may restrict the number of turns. Minimum of 3 turns is the standard).
3	Finish off with a round turn.

NOTE ☞ Avoid the use of half hitches, weather hitches, and lock hitches on standard boats.

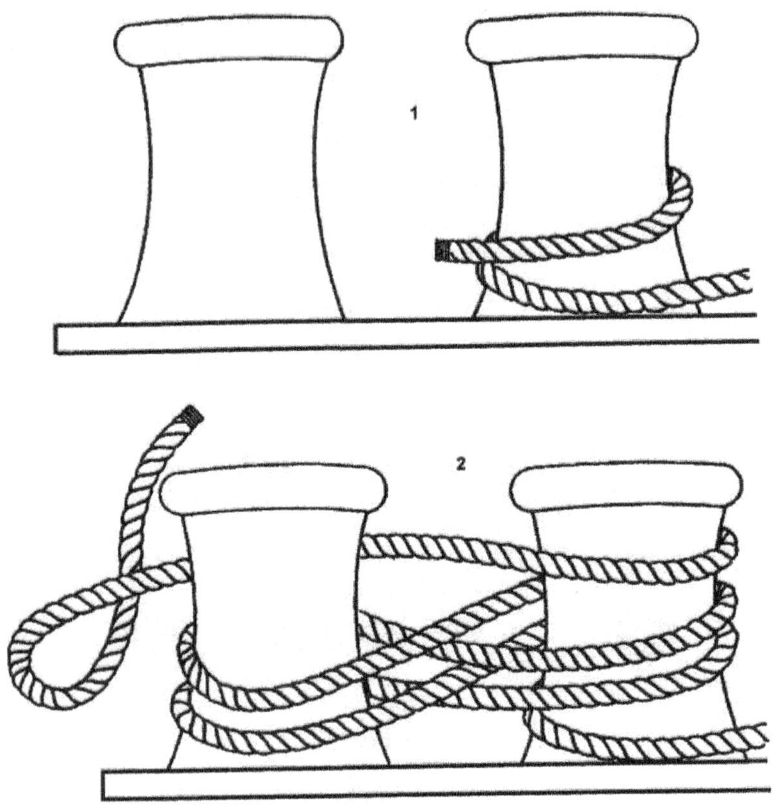

Figure 7-37
Securing a Line to a Bitt

E.2.d. Securing a Line to a Sampson Post

A sampson post is a vertical timber or king post on the forward deck of a boat. It is used as a bow cleat or bitt. The following procedures describe how to secure a line to a Sampson post (see **Figure 7-38**):

Step	Procedure
1	Make a complete turn around the base of the sampson post.
2	Form several figure eights around the horns of the sampson post. (Standard is 3 turns.)

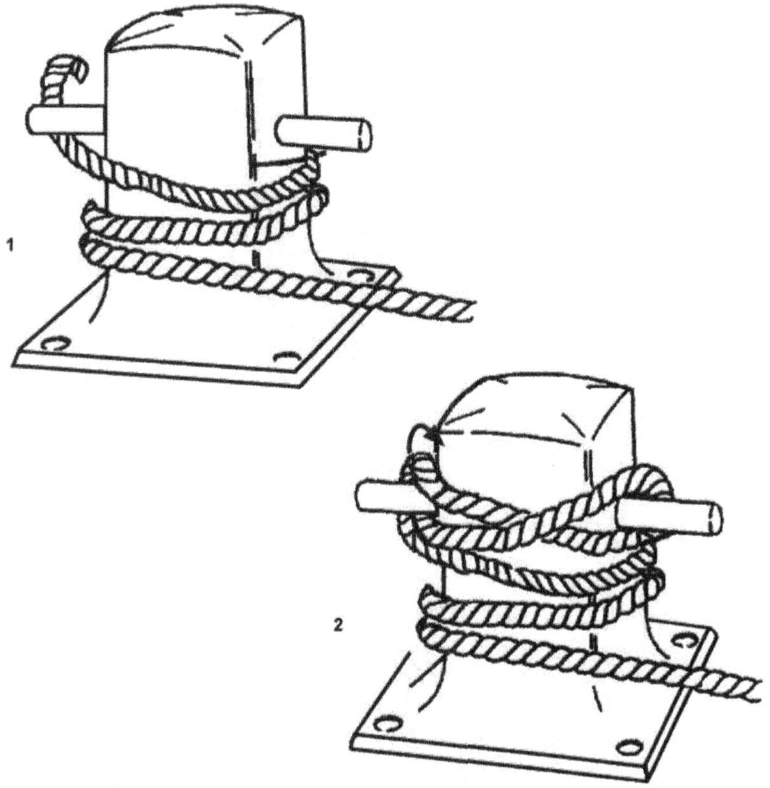

Figure 7-38
Securing a Line to a Sampson Post

NOTE The figure does not show extra figure eights.

E.2.e. Securing a Line to a Standard Cleat

The following procedures describe how to secure a line to a standard cleat (see **Figure 7-39**):

Step	Procedure
1	Make a complete turn around the cleat.
2	Lead the line over the top of the cleat and around the horn to form a figure eight.
3	If possible, make two more figure eights.

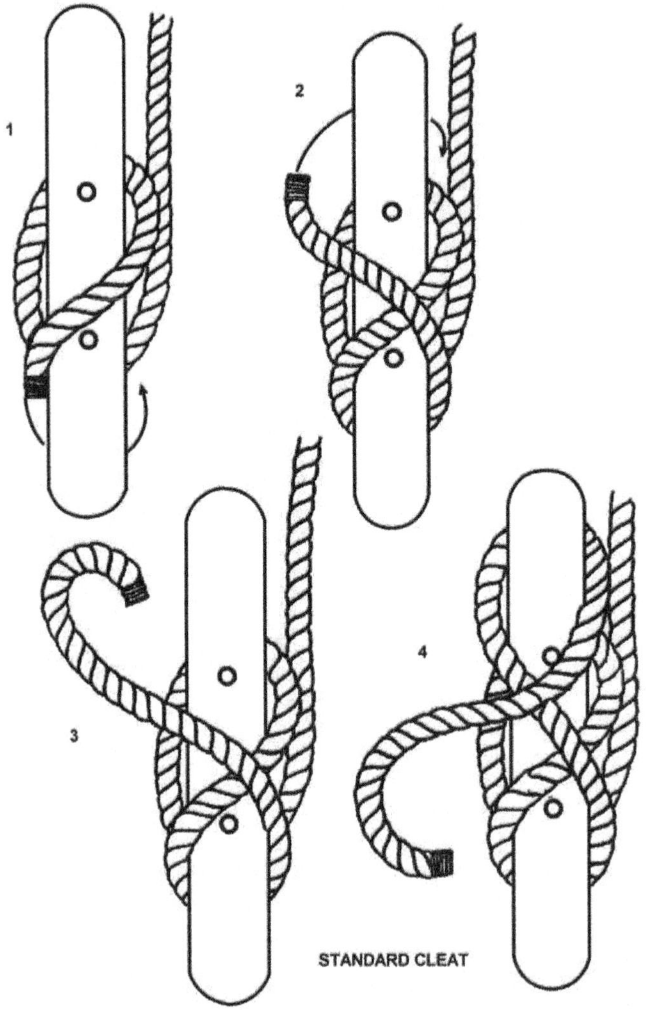

Figure 7-39
Securing a Line to a Standard Cleat

NOTE The figure does not show extra figure eights.

E.2 f. Securing a Line to a Mooring Cleat

The following procedures describe how to secure a line to a mooring cleat (see **Figure 7-40**):

Step	Procedure
1	Feed the eye of the line through the opening.
2	Loop the line back over both horns and pull the line taut.

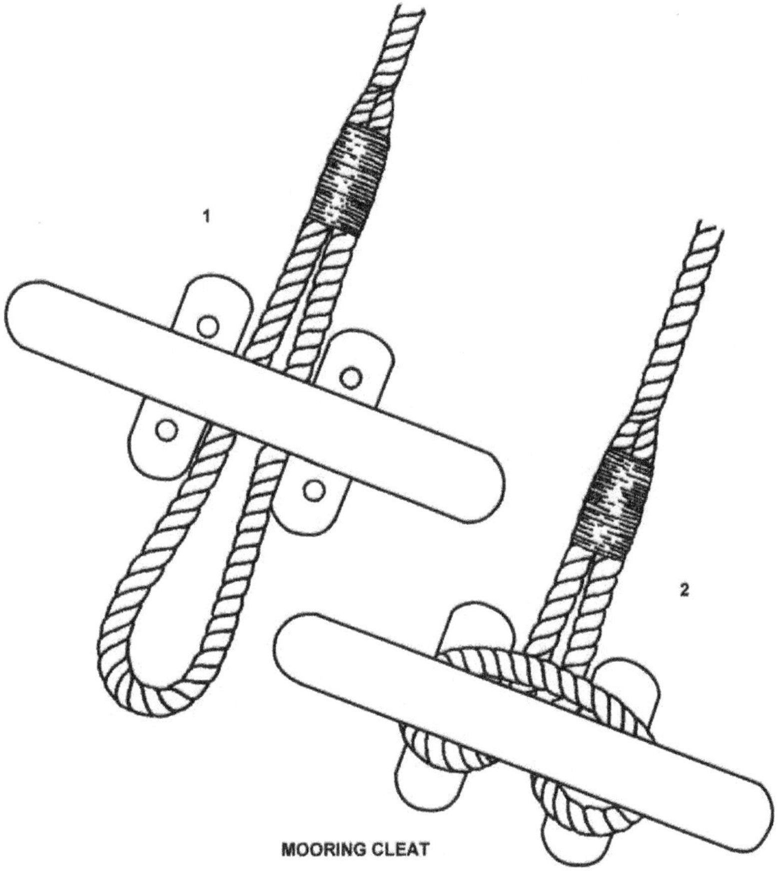

Figure 7-40
Securing a Line to a Mooring Cleat

E.2.g. Dipping the Eye

When two lines with eye splices are placed on a bollard, it may not be possible to remove the bottom line until the top line is removed. By dipping the eye, both lines can be placed for easy removal. The following procedures describe how to dip the eye (see **Figure 7-41**):

Step	Procedure
1	Place the eye of one mooring line over the bollard.
2	Take the eye of the second line up through the eye of the first line.
3	Place the eye of the second line over the bollard.

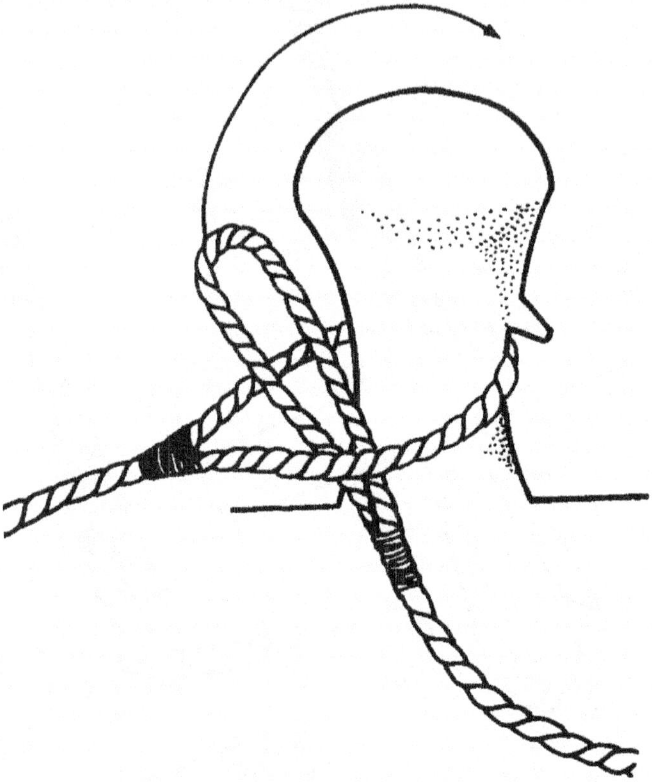

Figure 7-41
Dipping the Eye

E.2 h. Securing a Towline

The towline is probably the hardest worked line on a boat. Able to handle tremendous strain, it still is a possible danger to anyone working near it. Towlines should be made up so slack can be paid out at any time or so the line can be slipped (cast off) in an emergency. Coast Guard boats have different styles of tow bitts and must be made up securing the tow while allowing for easy adjustment. Additional information on the use of towlines is provided in *Chapter 17, Towing.*

Chapter 8
Boat Characteristics

Introduction

Knowledge of a boat's characteristics is crucial in performing safe boat operations. All crewmembers must be able to recognize and correctly apply boat related terminology. They must also be able to locate any piece of gear quickly and to operate all equipment efficiently, even in the dark. To accomplish these tasks, crewmembers must be familiar with the boat's layout. Each boat has specific operational characteristics and limitations. These are outlined in the boat's standard manuals or for non-standard boats, in the owner's/operator's manual. Some types of characteristics that the boat crew should be familiar with include:

- Maximum speed.
- Economical cruising speed.
- Maximum range at various speeds.
- Maximum endurance of boat at cruising speed.
- Minimum required crew size.
- Maximum number of people that can be safely carried.
- Maximum load capacity.

This chapter covers the basic knowledge needed to know a boat. For additional definitions, see *Appendix Glossary*.

In this chapter

This chapter contains the following sections:

Section A. Boat Nomenclature and Terminology

A.1. Definitions

As with any profession or skill, there are special terms that mariners use. Many of these terms have a fascinating history. Fellow mariners will expect that these terms will be used in routine conversation. Many of these words will be discussed within this chapter.

The following are common terms used for location, position and direction aboard a boat. **Figure 8-1** provides a diagram of a boat with the more common terms noted.

A.2. Bow

The front end of a boat is the bow. Moving toward the bow is going forward; when the boat moves forward, it is going ahead. When facing the bow, the front right side is the starboard bow, and the front left side is the port bow.

A.3. Amidships

The central or middle area of a boat is amidships. The right center side is the starboard beam, and the left center side is the port beam.

A.4. Stern

The rear of a boat is the stern. Moving toward the stern is going aft. When the boat moves backwards, it is going astern. Standing at the stern looking forward, the right rear section is the starboard quarter and the left rear section is the port quarter.

A.5. Starboard

Starboard is the entire right side of a boat, from bow to stern.

A.6. Port

Port is the entire left side of a boat, from bow to stern.

A.7. Fore and Aft

A line, or anything else, running parallel to the centerline of a boat is fore and aft.

A.8. Athwartships

A line or anything else running from side to side is athwartships.

A.9. Outboard

Outboard is from the centerline of the boat toward either port or starboard side.

A.10. Inboard

Inboard is from either side of the boat toward the centerline. However, there is a variation in the use of outboard and inboard when a boat is tied up alongside something (e.g., pier or another vessel). In this example, the side tied up is inboard; the side away is outboard.

A.11. Going Topside

Going topside is moving from a lower deck to a weather deck or upper deck.

A.12. Going Below

Going below is moving from an upper deck to a lower deck.

A.13. Going Aloft

Going aloft is going up into the boat's rigging.

A.14. Weather Deck

The weather deck is the deck exposed to the elements (weather).

A.15. Lifelines

Lifelines or railings, erected around the edge of weather decks, are all technically called lifelines, although they may have different proper names.

A.16. Windward

Windward is moving in the direction from which the wind is blowing; toward the wind.

A.17. Leeward

Leeward is the opposite point from which the wind is blowing; away from the wind. The term is pronounced "loo-urd".

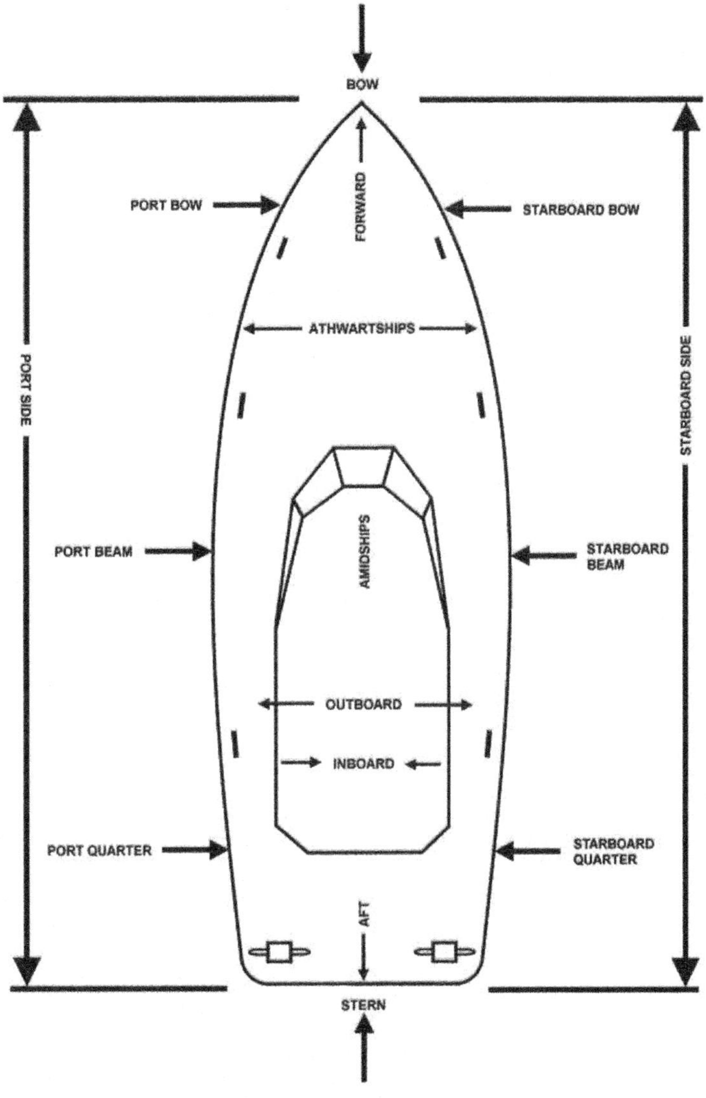

Figure 8-1
Position and Direction Aboard Boats

Section B. Boat Construction

Introduction

Boat construction covers terms that the boat crew will use on a daily basis in normal conversations and in operational situations. Proper understanding of these terms and concepts has importance that an inexperienced sailor may overlook.

In this section

This section contains the following information:

Hull Types

B.1. Three Types

The hull is the main body of a boat. It consists of a structural framework and a skin or shell plating. The hull may be constructed of many different materials, the most common being metal or fiberglass. A metal skin is usually welded to the structural framework, although riveting is sometimes used. A vessel could be monohull or multi-hull, such as catamarans and trimarans. The three basic types of hull forms based on vessel speed are:

- Displacement hull.
- Planing hull.
- Semi-displacement hull.

B.2. Factors Influencing Hull Shapes

Many factors influence hull shapes and affect the boat's buoyancy (its ability to float) and stability (its ability to remain upright). Factors that influence hull shapes are discussed as follows:

Factor	Description
Flare	Flare is the outward turn of the hull as the sides of the hull come up from the waterline. As the boat is launched into the water, the flare increases the boat's displacement and creates a positive buoyant force to float the boat.
Tumble home	Tumble home is the reverse of flare and is the shape of the hull as it moves out going from the gunwale to the waterline. This feature is most noticeable when viewing the transom of an older classic cruiser.
Camber	A deck usually curves athwartships, making it higher at the centerline than at the gunwales so the water flows off the deck. This curvature is called camber.

Factor	Description
Sheer	Sheer is the curvature of the main deck from the stem to the stern. When the sheer is pronounced and the bow of the boat is higher than the main deck at amidship, additional buoyancy is provided in the bow. This additional flotation, known as reserve buoyancy, is provided by flare and sheer.
Chine	The turn of the boat's hull below the waterline is called the chine. It is "soft" if it is rounded, and "hard" if it is squared off. Chine affects the boat's speed on turning characteristics.
Transom	The transom at the stern of the boat is either wide, flat, or curved. The shape of the stern affects the speed, hull resistance, and performance of the boat.
Length on waterline	The boat's length on waterline (LWL) is the distance from the bow to the stern, measured at the waterline when the boat is stationary. Note that this length changes as the boat rides high or low in the water.
Length overall	The boat's length overall (LOA) is the distance from the foremost to the aftermost points on the boat's hull measured in a straight line. It does not change according to the way the boat sits in the water.
Beam and breadth	Beam and breadth are measures of a boat's width. Beam is the measurement of the widest part of the hull. Breadth is the measurement of a frame from its port inside edge to its starboard inside edge. Molded beam is the distance between outside surfaces of the shell plating of the hull at its widest point. Extreme breadth is the distance between outside edges of the frames at the widest point of the hull.
Draft	Draft is the depth of the boat from the actual waterline to the bottom of its keel.
Draft appendage	Draft appendage is the depth of the boat from the actual waterline to the bottom of its keel or other permanent projection (e.g., propeller, rudder, skeg, etc.), if such a projection is deeper than the keel. The draft is also the depth of water necessary to float the boat. The draft varies according to how the boat lies in the water.
Trim	Trim is a relative term that refers to the way the boat sets in the water and describes generally its stability and buoyancy. A change in trim may be defined as the change in the difference between drafts forward and aft. A boat is trimmed by the bow when the draft forward increases and the draft is greater than the stern draft. A boat is trimmed by the stern if it is down by the stern.

Displacement

B.3. Measurement Displacement is the weight of a boat and is measured in long tons (2,240 lbs) or pounds.

B.4. Gross Tons

A gross ton is the entire cubic capacity of a boat expressed in tons of 100 cubic feet.

B.5. Net Tons

A net ton is the carrying capacity of a boat expressed in tons of 100 cubic feet. It is calculated by measuring the cubic content of the cargo and passenger spaces.

B.6. Deadweight

Deadweight is the difference between the light displacement and the maximum loaded displacement of a boat and is expressed in long tons or pounds.

B.6.a. Light Displacement

Light displacement is the weight of the boat excluding fuel, water, outfit, cargo, crew, and passengers.

B.6.b. Loaded Displacement

Loaded displacement is the weight of the boat including fuel, water, outfit, cargo, crew, and passengers.

CAUTION !

When towing a vessel, be careful not to tow beyond the vessel's design speed.

B.7. Displacement Hull

A displacement hull boat pushes away (displaces) water allowing the hull to settle down into the water. Underway, the hull pushes out this water, creating waves. (see **Figure 8-2**) The water separates at the bow and closes at the stern. Tremendous forces work against a displacement hull as the power pushing it and the boat's speed both increase. At maximum displacement speed, there is a distinct bow and stern wave. The length of these waves depends upon the boat's length and speed. (The longer the boat, the longer the wave length.) The bow and the stern ride lower in the water while increasing speed, and the water level alongside, amidships becomes lower than that of the surrounding water.

This lower water level is caused by the increase in the velocity of the water flowing under the boat and its interaction with the bow and stern wave. As the boat travels along, it rides in a depression created by its own passage. The displacement hull vessel's maximum speed is determined by the vessel's waterline length. Heavy displacement hulls cannot exceed a speed of 1.34 times the square root of their waterline length without requiring excessive power. This speed is known as critical speed. When towing a vessel, care must be taken not to tow beyond that vessel's critical speed. For details on towing displacement hulls, see *Chapter 17, Towing.*

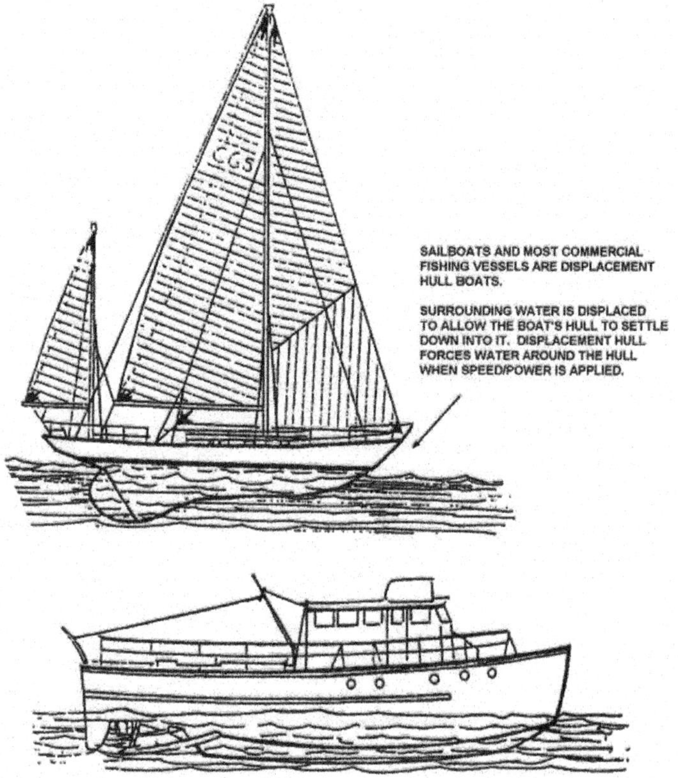

SAILBOATS AND MOST COMMERCIAL FISHING VESSELS ARE DISPLACEMENT HULL BOATS.
SURROUNDING WATER IS DISPLACED TO ALLOW THE BOAT'S HULL TO SETTLE DOWN INTO IT. DISPLACEMENT HULL FORCES WATER AROUND THE HULL WHEN SPEED/POWER IS APPLIED.

Figure 8-2
Displacement Hulls

B.8. Planing Hull

At rest, the planing hull and the displacement hull both displace the water around them. The planing hull reacts nearly the same as a displacement hull when it initially gets underway - it takes considerable power to produce a small increase in speed. However, at a certain point, external forces acting on the shape cause an interesting effect - the hull is lifted up onto the surface of the water. (see **Figure 8-3**) The planing hull skims along the surface of the water whereas the displacement hull always forces water around it. This is called planing.

Once "on-plane," the power/speed ratio is considerably altered-very little power increase results in a large increase in speed. Crewmembers must apply or reduce power gradually when going from the displacement mode to the planing mode or from the planing mode to the displacement mode. When the power is decreased gradually, the hull makes an even, steady transition, like slowly moving the hand from above the water's surface, through it, and into the liquid below. However, if power is rapidly decreased, the transition will be a rough one, for the hull will slap the surface of the water like the slap resulting by hitting a liquid surface with the hand.

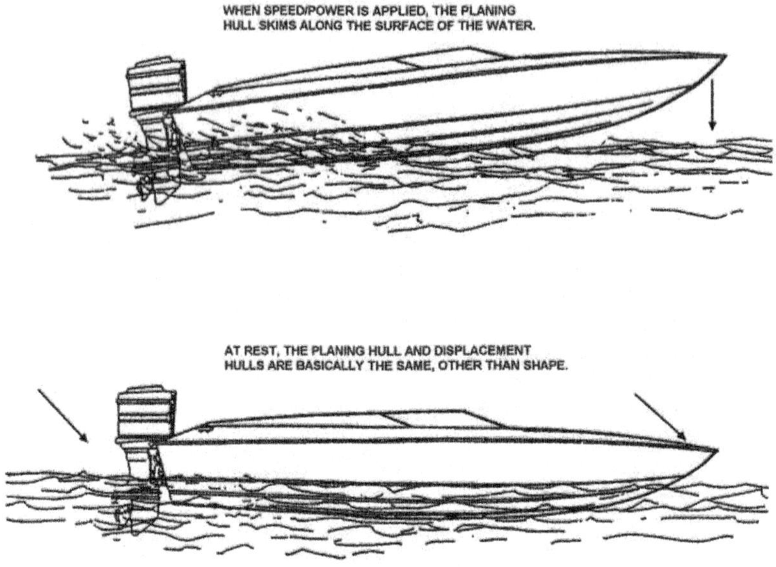

WHEN SPEED/POWER IS APPLIED, THE PLANING
HULL SKIMS ALONG THE SURFACE OF THE WATER.
AT REST, THE PLANING HULL AND DISPLACEMENT
HULLS ARE BASICALLY THE SAME, OTHER THAN SHAPE.

Figure 8-3
Planing Hulls

Additionally, the rapid "re-entry" into the displacement mode from above the surface, through the surface, and back into the water causes rapid deceleration as the forces in the water exert pressure against the hull. The effect is like rapidly braking an automobile.

B.9. Semi-Displacement Hull

The semi-displacement hull is a combination of characteristics of the displacement hull and the planing hull. Many Coast Guard boats are this type. This means that up to a certain power level and speed (power/speed ratio), the hull remains in the displacement mode. Beyond this point, the hull is raised to a partial plane. Essentially, the semi-displacement hull, like the displacement hull, always remains in the water; it never gets "on-plane." When in the displacement mode, the power/speed ratio is similar to the power/speed ratio described above for the displacement hull. When in the semi-planing mode, it is affected by a combination of forces for the displacement mode and some for the planing mode. Thus, while a small power increase will increase speed, the amount of resulting speed will not be as great as the same power increase would produce for a planing hull.

Keel

B.10. Location

The keel is literally the backbone of the boat. It runs fore and aft along the center bottom of the boat.

B.11. Keel Parts

The following are all integral parts of the keel:

- Frames.
- Stem.
- Sternpost.

B.11.a. Frames

Frames are attached to the keel, which extend athwartships (from side to side). The skin of the boat is attached to the frames. The keel and the frames strengthen the hull to resist external forces and distribute the boat's weight.

B.11.b. Stem

The stem is an extension of the forward end of the keel. Although there are a number of common stem shapes, all are normally slanted forward (raked) at an upward angle to reduce water friction.

B.11.c. Sternpost

The sternpost is a vertical extension of the aft end of the keel.

B.12. Keel Types

There are many types of keels. However, in metal boats, there are two types of particular interest:

- Bar keel.
- Flat plate keel.

B.12.a. Bar Keel

The bar keel is popular because its stiffeners (vertical or upright members which increase strength) protect the boat's hull plating if the boat grounds on a hard bottom. It also reduces rolling. A disadvantage of the bar keel is that, because it extends below the bottom of the boat, it increases the boat's draft.

B.12.b. Flat Plate Keel

The flat plate keel has a plate that is perpendicular to the centerline of the hull. A vertical center keel that runs internal to the hull at the centerline typically supports the flat plate keel. The vertical center keel is often provided with a flange top so that when combined with the flat plate keel the section resembles an "I" beam.

Principle Boat Parts

B.13. Bow

The shape of a boat's bow, its profile, form, and construction determine hull resistance as the boat advances through the water. Hull resistance develops from friction and from the wave the hull makes as it moves in the water. Wave-making resistance depends on the boat's speed.

The bow of a boat must be designed with enough buoyancy so it lifts with the waves and does not cut through them. The bow flare provides this buoyancy.

Boats intended for operation in rough seas and heavy weather have "full" bows. The bow increases the buoyancy of the forward part of a boat and deflects water and spray. When a boat is heading into a wave, the bow will initially start to cut into the wave. It may be immersed momentarily if the seas are rough. As the bow flare cuts into the wave, it causes the water to fall away from a boat's stern, shifting the center of buoyancy to move forward from the center of gravity. The bow lifts with the wave and the wave passes under the boat, shifting the center of buoyancy aft. This action causes the bow to drop back down and the vessel achieves a level attitude.

B.14. Stern

The shape of the stern affects the speed, resistance, and performance of the boat. It also affects the way water is forced to the propellers.

The design of the stern is critical in following seas where the stern is the first part of a boat to meet the waves. If the following waves lift the stern too high, the bow may be buried in the sea. The force of the wave will push the stern causing it to pivot around toward the bow. If this is not controlled, the result can be that a boat broaches or pitch poles.

B.14.a. Rounded Cruiser-Type Stern

The rounded, cruiser-type stern presents less flat surface area for a following sea to push upon and tends to split the waves of a following sea, allowing it to pass forward along each side of the boat. Thus, the wave has minimum impact on the attitude of the vessel and provides additional buoyancy for the stern. Crewmembers should always steer into any sideways movement of the stern. For example, when the stern slips to starboard, turn to starboard. It is particularly important that these corrections be made quickly and accurately in short, choppy following seas. (see **Figure 8-4**)

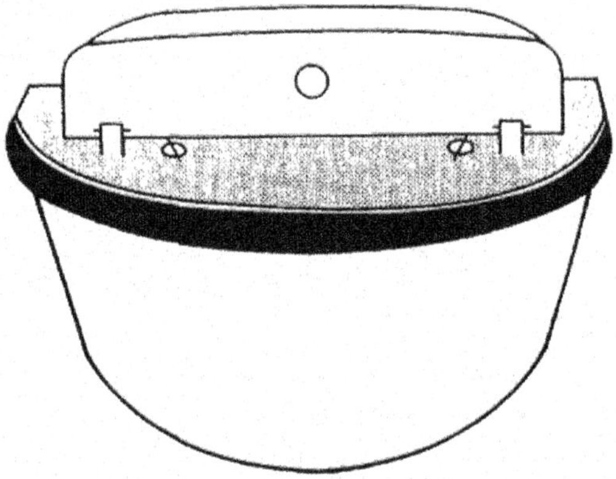

Figure 8-4
Rounded, Cruiser-Type Stern

B.14.b. Transom Stern

The transom stern provides a larger surface area for the seas to push upon and should not be exposed to heavy following seas or surf conditions. (see **Figure 8-5**)

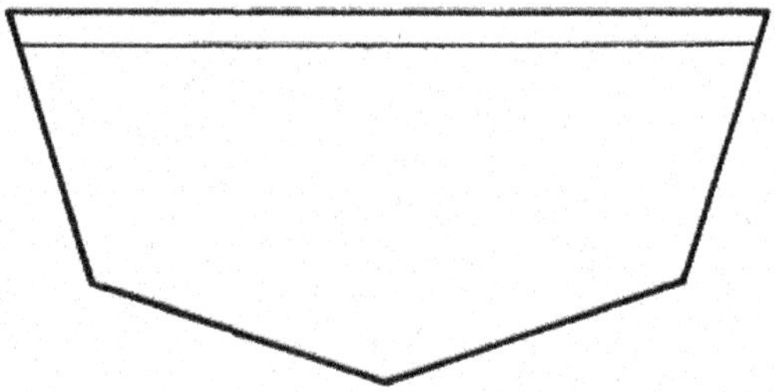

Figure 8-5
Transom Stern

B.15. Rudder

The rudder controls the direction of the boat and may vary widely in size, design, and method of construction. The shape of the stern, the number of propellers, and the characteristics of the boat determine the type of rudder. The following rudder types are shown in **Figure 8-6**:

- Balanced: blade about half forward and half aft of the rudder post.
- Semi-balanced: more than half of the blade aft of the rudder post.
- Unbalanced: blade entirely aft of the rudder post.

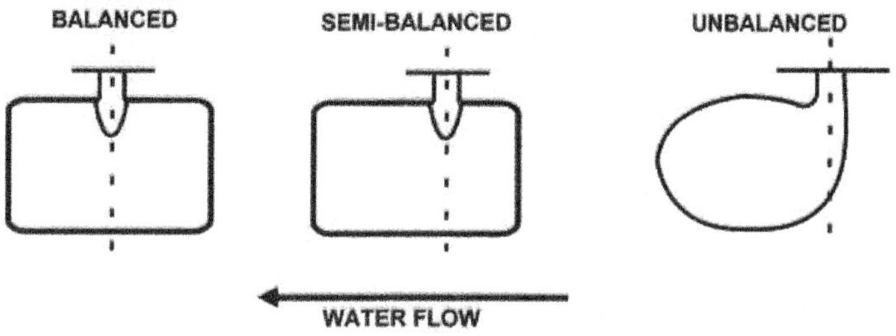

Figure 8-6
Rudder Types

B.16. Propeller

Most boats are driven by one or more screw propellers, which move in spirals somewhat like the threads on a screw. That is why the propeller is commonly referred to as a screw. The most common propellers are built with three and four blades. The propeller on a single-screw boat typically turns in a clockwise direction (looking from aft forward) as the boat moves forward. Such screws are referred to as right-handed. On twin-screw boats, the screws turn in opposite directions, rotating outward from the centerline of the boat. The port screw is left-handed and turns counterclockwise. The starboard screw is right-handed and turns clockwise.

B.16.a. Propeller Parts

A propeller consists of blades and a hub. The area of the blade down at the hub is called the root, and its outer edge is called the tip. (see **Figure 8-7**)

B.16.b. Propeller Edge

The edge of the blade that strikes the water first is the leading edge; the opposite is the following edge. The diameter of the screw, the circle made by its tips and its circumference, is called the tip circle. Each blade has a degree of twist from root to tip called pitch. (see **Figure 8-7**)

B.16.c. Pitch

Pitch is the distance a propeller advances in one revolution with no slip. (see **Figure 8-7**) Generally, less pitch in the same diameter propeller makes it easier for the engine to reach its preferred maximum RPM; thus, like putting a car in first gear, more power, and sometimes more speed, is available. Similarly, like third gear in a car, more pitch may give more speed, but lower RPMs gives less power. Optimum performance is obtained when pitch is matched to the optimum design speed (RPM) of the engine.

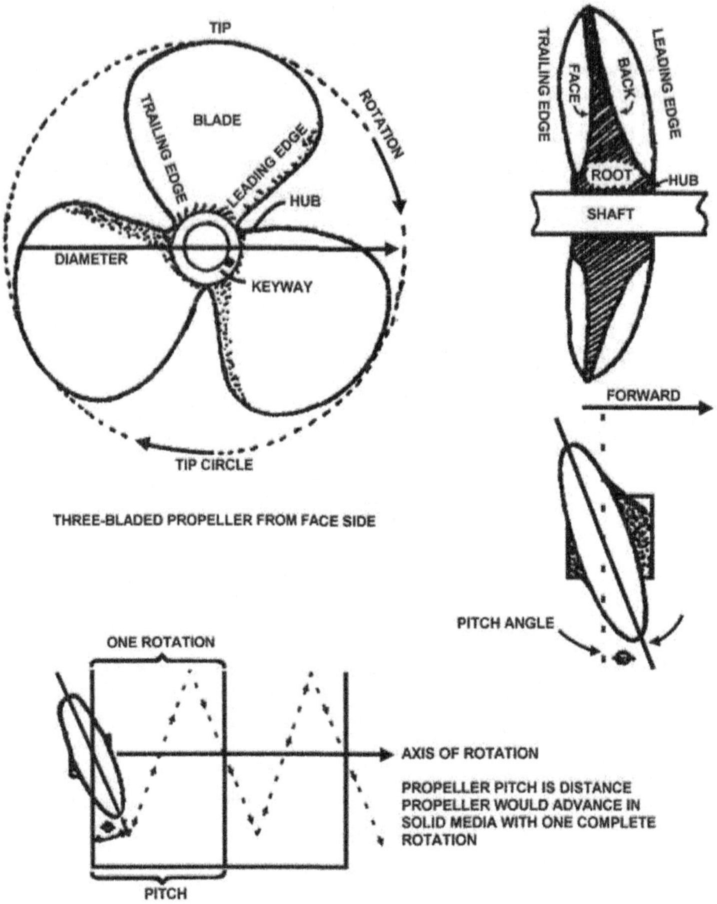

Figure 8-7
Parts of a Propeller

B.17. Frames

As previously stated, it is the framing that gives the hull its strength. Frames are of two types:

- Transverse.
- Longitudinal.

B.17.a. Transverse Frames

Watertight bulkheads or web frames are located at certain points in the hull to further increase the strength of the hull. Just as the keel is the backbone of the hull, transverse frames are often referred to as ribs. Transverse frames extend athwartships and are perpendicular (vertical or upright) to the keel and are spaced at specified distances. (see **Figure 8-8**). They vary in size from the bow to the stern giving the boat hull its distinct shape when the skin is attached. They are numbered from the bow to the stern, except the 47' MLB which is numbered stern to bow, to help quickly identify a particular location in the interior and, in the event of damage to the hull, to isolate the area of damage.

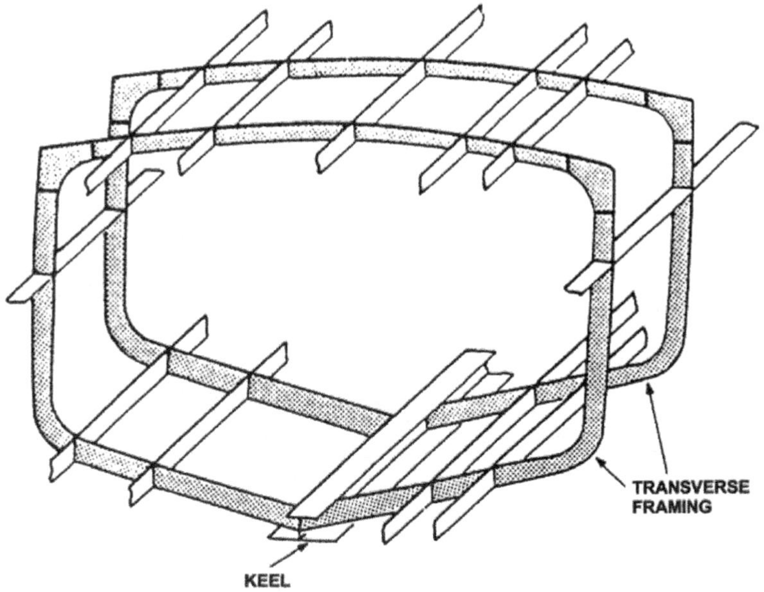

Figure 8-8
Transverse Framing System

B.17.b. Longitudinal Frames	Longitudinal frames provide hull strength along the length of the hull (fore and aft). (see **Figure 8-9**). They run parallel to the keel and at right angles to the transverse frames. In addition to strengthening the hull, the top longitudinal frames provide a skeletal structure over which deck plating is laid.

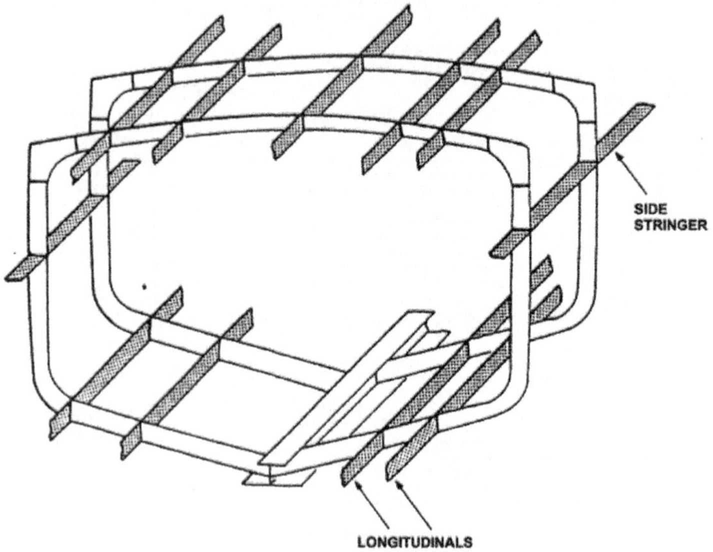

Figure 8-9
Longitudinal Framing System

B.18. Decks

A deck is a seagoing floor and provides strength to the hull by reinforcing the transverse frames and deck beams. The top deck of a boat is called the weather deck because it is exposed to the elements and is watertight. In general, decks have a slight downward slope from the bow. The slope makes any water taken aboard run aft. A deck also has a rounded, athwartship curve called camber. The two low points of this curve are on the port and starboard sides of the boat where the weather deck meets the hull. Water that runs aft down the sheer line is forced to the port or starboard side of the boat by the camber. When the water reaches one of the sides, it flows overboard through holes, or scuppers, in the side railings.

Hatches and Doors

B.19. Hatches

In order for a deck with a hatch in it to be watertight, the hatch must be watertight. A weather deck hatch is made watertight by sealing it into a raised framework called a coaming. Hatches operate with quick-acting devices such as wheels or handles, or they may be secured with individual dogs. (see **Figure 8-10**)

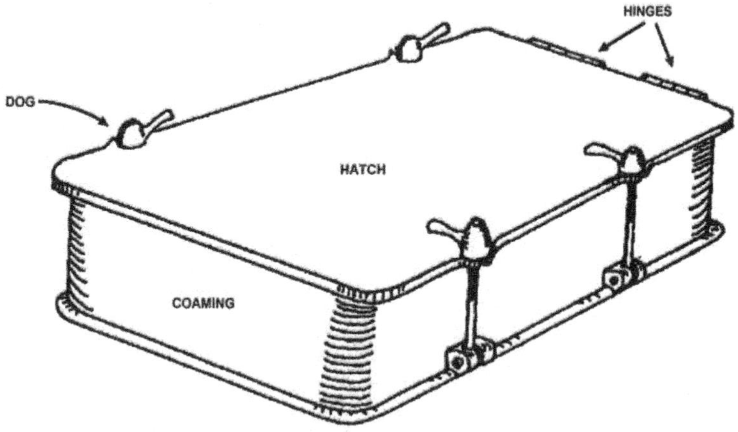

Figure 8-10
Watertight Hatch

B.20. Scuttles Scuttles are small openings. A scuttle cover, fitted with a gasket and dogs, is used to secure the scuttle. A tool called a "T-handle wrench" is used to tighten down the scuttle cover dogs.

B.21. Doors Watertight doors are designed to resist as much pressure as the bulkheads through which they provide access. Some doors have dogs that must be individually closed and opened; others, called "quick-acting watertight doors" have handwheels or a handle, which operate all dogs at once.

B.22. Gaskets Rubber gaskets form tight seals on most watertight closure devices. These gaskets, mounted on the covering surface of the closure device (e.g., door, hatch, scuttle cover), are pressed into a groove around the covering. The gaskets are sealed tight by pressing against a fixed position "knife edge."

CAUTION ! Scuttles must be secured at all times to maintain watertight integrity except when they are open for inspection, cleaning, or painting. They must never be left open overnight or when crewmembers are not actually working or passing through them.

B.23. Knife Edges Watertight closures must have clean, bright, unpainted, smooth knife edges for the gaskets to press against. A well-fitted watertight closure device with new gaskets will still leak if knife edges are not properly maintained. On some boats, such as the 47' MLB, some of the watertight closures have a sealing surface instead of a knife edge.

B.24. Interior

The interior of a boat is compartmentalized by bulkheads, decks, and hatches. With the doors and hatches closed, the space between them becomes watertight and is called a watertight compartment. (see **Figure 8-11**) These watertight compartments are extremely important. Without them, the boat has no watertight integrity and a hole anywhere in the hull will cause it to sink. By dividing the hull into several watertight compartments, the watertight integrity of the boat is significantly increased. One or more of these compartments may flood without causing the boat to sink. A boat could be made unsinkable if its hull could be divided into enough watertight compartments. Unfortunately, excessive compartmentation would interfere with the engineering spaces and restrict movement in the interior spaces.

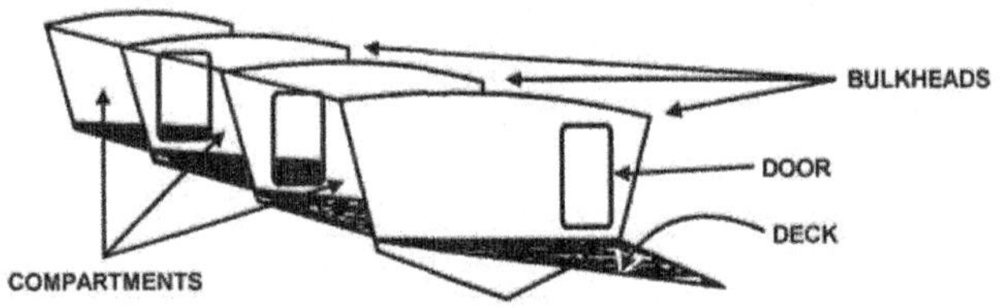

Figure 8-11
Watertight Compartment

Section C. Watertight Integrity

Introduction

Watertight integrity describes a compartment or fitting that is designed to prevent the passage of water into it. An important concern in boat operations is to ensure the watertight integrity of the vessel. A boat may sustain heavy damage and remain afloat if watertight integrity is maintained. Doors, hatches, and scuttle covers must be securely dogged while the boat is underway and while it is moored and unattended by crewmembers.

C.1. Closing and Opening Watertight Doors and Hatches

Watertight doors and hatches will retain their efficiency longer and require less maintenance if they are properly closed and opened as described below.

C.1.a. Closing

The procedures for closing a watertight door are as follows:

Step	Procedure
1	Begin by tightening a dog that is opposite the hinges.
2	Place just enough pressure on the dog to keep the door shut.
3	Tighten up the other dogs evenly to obtain uniform pressure all around the closing device.

For quick-acting watertight doors, the wheels or handles are turned in the correct direction (clockwise).

C.1.b. Opening

If the dogs on watertight doors and hatches open individually, the dog nearest the hinge is opened first. This keeps the closing device from springing and makes loosening the other dogs easier.

For quick-acting watertight doors, the wheels or handles are turned in the correct direction (counterclockwise).

CAUTION !

Extreme caution is always necessary when opening compartments below the waterline near hull damage.

C.2. Entering a Closed Compartment After Damage

Watertight doors, hatches, and scuttle covers on a damaged boat must not be opened until the following is determined:

- Flooding did not occur or, if flooded,
- Further flooding will not occur if the closure is opened.

NOTE

Suspect flooding if air escapes when the dogs on a door or hatch are released.

Section D. General Boat Equipment

Introduction

All boats should carry basic equipment for the routine procedures, such as tying up, or anchoring. There is also equipment that is needed to conduct specific operations, such as SAR, towing, or pollution response. Crewmembers must be familiar with the use of the equipment carried onboard and where it is located. A complete listing of required equipment is contained in the Boat Outfit List. Each type of boat has its own outfit list. Outfit lists for all standard Coast Guard boats will be found in their boat type operator's handbooks. Each Auxiliary vessel should have a boat outfit of the types of items listed below.

D.1. General Boat Equipment List

The general equipment found on Coast Guard boats and a brief statement of the purpose of each item is provided in **Table 8-1**.

Table 8-1
General Boat Equipment List

Item	Purpose
Anchors	For anchoring in calm, moderate, and heavy weather.
Anchor Lines	Provides scope to prevent the anchor from dragging. Enables retrieval of the anchor. Serves as an additional towline if necessary.
Chafing Chain	Assists in preventing chafing of the anchor line on the bottom.
Screw Pin Shackle	Attaches chafing chain to shank of anchor.
Swivel	Allows anchor line to spin freely.
Thimble	Prevents chafing of anchor line at connection point with associated hardware.
Towline	Used for towing astern.
Alongside Lines	Used for alongside towing, joining to kicker hooks, passing a pump, etc.
Heaving Lines (75' to 100')	Used for passing a towline when a close approach is not possible.
Grapnel Hook with 100' of Line	Used for recovering objects from the water.
Boat Hook	For reaching dockside lines, fending boat from boat, and recovering objects from water.
Kicker Hook	Attaches to trailer eyebolt on small boats for towing or weighing anchor of disabled boats, etc.
Shackles	For weighing a disabled boat's anchor, attaching towing bridles to towlines, attaching towlines to trailer eyebolt, etc.
Lead Line (Sounding Pole)	Used in determining water depth and bottom type.
First Aid Kit	For emergency treatment of injuries suffered by crewmembers or survivors.
Personnel Survival Kits	Used by crewmembers in the event of a capsizing or person overboard.

Table 8-1 (continued)
General Boat Equipment List

Item	Purpose
Heavy Weather Crew Safety Belt	For personnel safety during heavy weather or surf operations. Secures a crewmember to the boat.
Type I PFDs, each with a distress signal light, a whistle, and retroreflective tape	Provides personal flotation support. Keeps the head of an unconscious or injured person out of the water. Worn by crewmembers and given to survivors who are brought onboard. Also worn by survivors who remain on their own boat when it is in tow.
Ring Buoy, 30" diameter	Used during person overboard emergencies.

Section E. Troubleshooting Basic Mechanical Problems

Introduction

Troubleshooting mechanical problems is typically the responsibility of the boat engineer, if one is assigned. However, not all Coast Guard boats or Auxiliary facilities deploy with a dedicated boat engineer. Boats without engineers should be able to provide basic troubleshooting for themselves and those vessels that they are trying to assist. Often, a simple mechanical fix can avoid a long tow or other loss of use of a Coast Guard boat. The primary source for a boat's maintenance and repair requirements should be the manufacturer's service manuals that come with the boat.

NOTE

In all casualties, keep the Station/unit command advised of the problem and updates of changing status. If in restricted water, consider anchoring.

In this section

This section contains the following information:

Troubleshooting Diesel Engines

E.1. Problems, Causes, and Solutions

Diesel engines are very common as inboard engines for boats. They are very reliable when properly maintained. Typical problems, their possible causes, and potential solutions are provided in **Table 8-2**.

Table 8-2
Diesel Engine Problems, Causes, and Solutions

Problem	Cause	Solution
Engine will not turn over when starter button is pushed	Main power switch *off*.	• Turn main power switch *on*.
	Battery cable loose or corroded.	• Tighten, clean, or replace cable, terminals.
	Starter motor cable loose or corroded.	• Tighten, clean, or replace cable.
	Batteries are low or dead.	• Charge or replace batteries.
	Engine seized due to hydraulic lock (fuel or water in cylinders).	• Remove injectors, bar engine over by hand after (to relieve pressure and prevent internal damage).
	Misalignment of controls, neutral safety switch.	• Make appropriate adjustment, realign controls.
	Non-operation or chattering solenoid switch.	• Replace, repair cable. Replace solenoid. Check battery voltage.
Irregular engine operation (engine runs unevenly or stalls)	Strainers and fuel filter clogged.	• Clean, replace, or purge air (bleed).
	Lines and fittings leaking.	• Check fuel lines and fittings for leaks; tighten or replace.
	Insufficient fuel/aeration of fuel.	• Sound tanks-shift suction, refuel if necessary.
	Binding fuel control linkages.	• Inspect and adjust.
	Insufficient intake of air.	• Inspect intake for obstructions from air silencer. Check emergency air shutdown for possible restriction.

Table 8-2 (continued)
Diesel Engine Problems, Causes, and Solutions

Problem	Cause	Solution
Engine overspeeds or overruns	Loose or jammed linkage.	• Tighten or free linkage.
	If engine RPMs increase, an internal engine malfunction has occurred. A stuck injector, a clutch that slipped into *neutral*, a lost prop or a ruptured lube oil seal could be the cause. Most engines overspeed after someone has performed maintenance. For this reason, it is most important that the operator promptly assess what is occurring. Regardless, when the engine overspeeds, follow the procedures in the next column.	• If an engine appears to be operating normally at *cruising* speed but fails to slow down as the throttle is being returned to *neutral*, do not place the throttle in *neutral* until a determination is made that the engine is in fact out of control (i.e., check for throttle linkage that became detached). Keeping the engine in gear will prevent it from being destroyed. Secure the engine by following the steps below: ➢ If overspeed continues pull engine stops, (kill switch). ➢ If engine RPMs still overspeed, shut off fuel supply. ➢ If problem continues, stuff rags against air silencer. ➢ As a last resort, shoot CO_2 into the air intake.
Engine oil pressure high	Incorrect grade of oil.	• Monitor, and if pressure becomes too high, secure engine.
	Oil filters dirty.	• Change oil filters.
	Cold engine not up to operating temperature.	• Warm up engine.
	Relief valve stuck.	• Adjust, remove and clean, or replace.
	External oil leaks.	• Check and correct leaks. • Add oil, monitor and secure engine if necessary.
	Internal oil leaks.	• Secure engine.
	Worn or damaged engine parts.	• Monitor, add oil, and secure engine if excessive oil consumption continues.
Engine surges	Air in fuel system.	• Secure engine. • Bleed air out of fuel system. • Check and correct leaks.
	Clogged fuel strainers/filters.	• Switch/replace fuel filters.
	Governor instability.	• Adjust the buffer screw (G.M.). • Check free movement of flyweights.
	Loose throttle linkage.	• Tighten linkage.

Table 8-2 (continued)
Diesel Engine Problems, Causes, and Solutions

Problem	Cause	Solution
Marine (reduction) gear fails to engage	Loss of gear oil.	• Add gear oil. • Check and correct leaks.
	Strainer/filter clogged.	• Clean strainer, replace filter.
	Loose, broken maladjusted linkage.	• Inspect and correct, as necessary.
Unusual noise in reduction gear	Loss of gear oil.	• Secure engine, check gear oil. • Refill and resume operation for trial.
	Worn out reduction gear.	• Secure engine.
	Misalignment of gear.	• Secure engine.
Loss of gear oil pressure to reduction gear	Loss of gear oil.	• Inspect all high-pressure lines for leaks and repair. • If unable to repair, secure engine.
Temperature of engine coolant higher than normal	Thermostat faulty, expansion tank cap faulty, leaky hoses, etc.	• Inspect all lines for leaks and repair. • For tank cap, replace if possible; and monitor coolant level. • For thermostat, secure engine.
Engine smokes		
Black or gray smoke	Incompletely burned fuel.	• High exhaust backpressure or a restricted air inlet causes insufficient air for combustion and will result in incompletely burned fuel. • High exhaust backpressure is caused by faulty exhaust piping or muffler obstruction and is measured at the exhaust manifold outlet with a manometer, a meter gauge which measures differential pressure. • Replace faulty parts. • Restricted air inlet to the engine cylinders is caused by clogged cylinder liner ports, air cleaner, or blower air inlet screen. Clean these items. • Check the emergency stop to make sure that it is completely open and readjust if necessary.
	Excessive fuel or irregular fuel distribution.	• Check for improperly timed injectors and improperly positioned injector rack control levers. Time the fuel injectors and perform the appropriate tune-up. • Replace faulty injectors if this condition continues. Avoid lugging the engine as this will cause incomplete combustion.
	Improper grade of fuel.	• Check for use of an improper grade of fuel.

Table 8-2 (continued)
Diesel Engine Problems, Causes, and Solutions

Problem	Cause	Solution
Blue smoke	Lubricating oil being burned (blow by valves/seals).	• Check for internal lubricating oil leaks. • Conduct compression test. • Check valve and rings. • Check for use of improper grade of fuel.
	Bad oil seals in the turbocharger. Faulty intercooler. Faulty after cooler.	• Throttle engine back, notify engineer and/or unit. • Monitor engine (secure if necessary). • Return to unit.
White smoke	Misfiring cylinders.	• Check for faulty injectors and replace as necessary.
	Cold engine.	• Allow engine to warm under a light load.
	Water in the fuel.	• Drain off strainers/filters. • Strip fuel tanks.

Troubleshooting Gasoline Inboard Engines

E.2. Indicators

Normal operation indicators are:

- Ease of starting.
- Engine reaches specified RPMs at full throttle.
- Correct shift and reverse RPMs.
- Smooth idle.
- Correct operating temperatures.
- Adequate cooling water discharge and kill switch.
- Smooth acceleration from idle to full RPMs.

E.3. Basic Troubleshooting

An initial quick check of the following may reveal a simple fix for a problem that does not appear simple at first:

- Visually inspect for obvious damage.
- Check the spark plugs for fouling.
- Check ignition system for spark.
- Check linkages for adjustments.
- Check NEUTRAL/START switch.
- Check gear case and lubricants in the engine.

E.4. Repairs

The manufacturer's technical manual should be consulted for all adjustments and specifications. Use the following examples in **Table 8-3** as a guide, but always follow the specific engine's technical manual.

Table 8-3
Repair Advice

Problem	Check
Engine stops suddenly after a period of operation	• Inspect for obvious damage of engine components such as loose wires, leaking fuel lines, leaking of coolant, excessive heat. • Check ignition system for broken or loose parts such as wiring, distributor cap, points, or coil. • Check for clogged fuel filters, quality/quantity of fuel.
Engine stops suddenly with no spark to spark plugs	• Inspect for obvious damage, check the ignition system for broken or loose parts such as wiring, distributor cap, points, or coil.
Engine stops, restarts when cool and stops again when hot	• Have the ignition coil and condenser checked out; they may be breaking down when hot.
Engine stops after a period of rough, uneven operation	• Inspect for obvious damage. • Check the ignition system for broken or loose parts such as wiring, distributor cap, points, or coil. • Check the battery, ignition timing, and the fuel filter.
Engine runs by spurts, and stops with the fuel filter clean	• Check the fuel tank and fuel lines. • Check the ignition system for obvious damage. • Check ignition timing and points. • Check the fuel pump for proper operation.
Engine runs by spurts and stops, water is present in the fuel filter	• Drain, clean or replace fuel filter. • Check the fuel tank for presence of water and drain if necessary. • If the carburetor is filled with water, it must also be drained. • Take appropriate safety precautions to avoid fire or explosion.
WARNING	Beware of fuel vapors before starting engine.
Engine misses, gallops, spits, backfires, and has a loss of power	• Inspect for obvious damage. • Carburetor may be dirty. • Check ignition system for broken or loose parts such as wiring, distributor cap, rotor points and coil. • Check fuel filter and fuel lines. • Check for plugged vent.
Engine starts hard, especially in cold weather	• Battery voltage may be low. • Check ignition timing and points. • Check ignition system for obvious damage. • Exhaust valves may be burned. • May have to change to a lighter engine oil.
Engine pops and pings in exhaust pipe at all speeds	• Exhaust valves may be burned, worn piston rings or worn valve guides. • Timing may be off. • Fuel octane may be too low. • Time for engine overhaul.

Table 8-3 (continued)
Repair Advice

Problem	Check
Starter turns engine, but engine will not start	• Check fuel level. • Inspect for obvious damage to ignition system, broken or loose parts such as wiring, distributor cap, rotor points, or coil. • Check ignition timing and points. • Check fuel pump.

Casualties Common to Both Diesel and Gasoline Engines

E.5. Problems, Causes, and Solutions

Diesel and gasoline engines, though both run on a type of petroleum, operate in different ways. Common problems, causes, and solutions that apply to both are provided in **Table 8-4**.

Table 8-4
Diesel and Gasoline Engine Problems, Causes, and Solutions

Problem	Cause	Solution
Starter whines, engine doesn't crank over or doesn't engage, starter relay may chatter	Defective starter. Bendix is not engaged. Defective starter relay.	• Call for assistance. • Replace or repair starter or relay. • Check bendix on return to dock.
	Low battery voltage.	• Check battery cables for loose connection (or corrosion) to starter. • Clean or replace cables. • Charge or replace battery.
Engine fails to start with starter turning over	Fuel stop closed.	• Open fuel stop.
	Fuel shutoff valve closed.	• Open fuel shutoff valve.
	Clogged air cleaner.	• Remove and clean or replace air cleaner.
	Fuel supply exhausted.	• Refill fuel tanks, bleed and prime system.
	Clogged strainer.	• Shift strainer and clean, bleed off.
	Fuel filters clogged.	• Shift and replace filters, bleed air off.
	Clogged/crimped restricted fuel line.	• Replace or repair fuel line.
	Inoperable fuel pump.	• Replace fuel pump.
	Emergency air shutdown tripped (type specific).	• Reset shutdown trip mechanism.
	Clogged air intake.	• Remove, clean, or replace.
	Low battery voltage causes slow cranking.	• Charge or replace battery.
	Cold engine.	• Check hot start.

Table 8-4 (continued)
Diesel and Gasoline Engine Problems, Causes, and Solutions

Problem	Cause	Solution
Engine temperature high	Closed or partially closed sea suction valve.	• Check raw water overboard discharge; if little or none, check sea suction valve. • Open valve.
WARNING	Let the engine cool down before working on it to avoid being burned or getting splashed by fluids that may be under pressure. Never work on a pressurized fluid system. Use appropriate PPE.	
NOTE	For all high temperature situations, the immediate action is to place the throttle in neutral then look for the probable cause. When an overheated engine must be secured, turn the engine over periodically to keep it from seizing.	
	Dirty, plugged raw water strainer. (Especially in shallow water.)	• Replace strainer. • Check all strainers, clean as necessary.
	Broken raw water hose.	• Secure engine, replace hose.
	Broken or loose raw water pump drive belt.	• Secure engine, replace or tighten belt.
	Faulty raw water pump.	• Secure engine.
	Clogged heat exchanger.	• Inspect heat exchanger, clean as necessary.
	No/low water in expansion tank (fresh water system).	• Handle the same as for a car radiator-open with caution releasing pressure before removing cap. • With engine running add fresh water.
	Broken fresh water hose.	• Secure engine, replace hose, add fresh water.
	Broken belts/drive fresh water system.	• Treat same as raw water system.
	Faulty water pump, fresh water system.	• Secure engine.
	Water in lube oil.	• Check lube oil for "milky" color. If found, secure engine.
	Blown head gasket.	• Secure engine, lock shaft, return to mooring.
	Engine overloaded (towing too big a vessel or towing too fast.)	• Reduce engine speed.
	Ice clogged sea strainers (especially during operation in slush ice.)	• Shift sea strainer, open deicing valve.
	Air bound sea chest.	• Open/clear sea chest vent valve.
	Rubber impeller on raw water pump is inoperable.	• Replace impeller.

Table 8-4 (continued)
Diesel and Gasoline Engine Problems, Causes, and Solutions

Problem	Cause	Solution
Engine lube oil pressure fails (loss or increase)	Lube oil level low.	• If above parameters, check oil, add if needed. • If below parameters, secure engine.
	External oil leak.	• Do not tighten fittings under pressure. Secure engine. Tighten fittings if possible.
	Lube oil dilution.	• Secure engine if fuel dilution is beyond 5% or 2.5% [type specific; refer to Specific Boat Type Operator's Handbook, COMDTINST M16114 (series)].
	Lube oil gauge defective.	• Take load off engine, if applicable, check to confirm if gauge appears to operate normally.
	Mechanical damage to engine.	• Secure engine.
No oil pressure	Lube oil pump failure.	• Secure engine.
	Defective gauge.	• Verify that failure is only in gauge. Otherwise, secure engine.
Loss of electrical power	Short circuit/loose connections causing tripped circuit breaker or blown fuse.	• Check for shorts/grounds. Reset circuit breakers, replace fuses as necessary.
	Corroded wiring connections.	• Clean or replace cables/wires.
	Overloaded circuit.	• Secure all unnecessary circuits, reset circuit breakers, replace fuses.
	Dead battery.	• Replace battery.
Alternator indicator light *on*	Loose/broken belt.	• Replace/tighten belt.
	Loose terminal connections.	• Inspect and tighten as necessary.
	Defective alternator or regulator.	• Replace defective item.
REGARDLESS OF CAUSE, FOLLOW PROCEDURES BELOW.		

Table 8-4 (continued)
Diesel and Gasoline Engine Problems, Causes, and Solutions

Problem	Cause	Solution
Shaft packing overheats	Packing too tight.	• Reduce speed, but do not secure engine or shaft.
	Bent shaft.	• Reduce speed, check hull for damage or leaks. • Loosen packing nuts by turning the two nuts securing spacer plate. • In cases where nuts will not back, use raw water from a bucket, wet a rag, and place it on the shaft packing housing. • When the housing is cool, tighten the two nuts on the space plate until a discharge of about 10 drops of water per minute is obtained. • Maintain watch on water flow (step #3) and adjust discharge as needed. • Check coolness by carefully placing the back of the hand near or on the packing gland housing. • Return to unit.
REGARDLESS OF CAUSE, FOLLOW PROCEDURES BELOW.		
Shaft vibration	Damaged or fouled propeller.	• Place throttles in *neutral* if possible.
	Bent shaft.	• Reduce speed, check hull for damage or leaks.
	Cutlass bearing worn.	• Check for line fouled in the propeller or shaft.
	Engine or shaft out of alignment.	• Slowly increase speed on engine. On twin-propeller boats, do one engine at a time to figure out which shaft is vibrating. • If vibration continues even at low speeds, secure the engine or engines involved. • If engines are secured, lock the shafts.
FOR ALL FIRES, FOLLOW PROCEDURES BELOW.		
Engine room fire		
Petroleum based	Oil and grease in bilges.	• Secure engines, turn off fuel at the tank, if possible.
	Fuel or lube oil spill.	• Call for assistance immediately.
	Improper containers of flammable liquids.	• Secure electrical power to and from engine room.
	Improper venting of engine room before starting engine.	• Use any available portable fire extinguisher (PKP, CO_2, etc.) • Seal compartment.

Table 8-4 (continued)
Diesel and Gasoline Engine Problems, Causes, and Solutions

Problem	Cause	Solution
Electrical fires		• Secure electricity if possible. • Select the proper extinguishing agent and employ.
Engine stops suddenly and will not turn through a full revolution		• Check for obstructions within the cylinders. • Engine may require overhaul.
Engine stops firing hot and won't turn over when cool		• Engine seized, overhaul as necessary.
Engine stops with a loud clatter		• Inspect for obvious damage. Damage may be to internal parts such as valves, valve springs, bearings, piston rings, etc. Engine overhaul required.
Engine oil level rises, oil looks and feels gummy		• There may be coolant leaking into the engine oil. Check for internal leakage. • Repair the engine before continuing operation.
Engine oil rises or feels thin		• Fuel is leaking into the crankcase. • Check fuel pump. • After problem has been corrected, change oil and filters. • Check internal fuel connections.
Hot water in bilges		• Inspect the exhaust piping muffler, and/or cooling water level. It is probably leaking into the bilges. • Check all hoses.
Engine runs with a thumping or knocking noise		• Inspect for obvious damage to internal parts of the engine. They may be damaged. • Engine overhaul required.

Troubleshooting the Outboard

E.6. Problems and Corrections

Outboard motors are very common on recreational boats and many Coast Guard boats. The operator's manual provides the best guidance. Working over the transom of the boat poses a hazard to the operator and creates the potential for loss of parts and tools. General advice is provided in **Table 8-5**.

Table 8-5
Outboard Motor Troubleshooting

Problem	Possible Cause/Correction
Engine won't start	• Fuel tank empty. • Fuel tank vent *closed.* • Fuel line improperly connected or damaged; check both ends. • Engine not primed. • Engine flooded, look for fuel overflow. • Clogged fuel filter or line. • Spark plug wires reversed. • Loose battery connections. • Cracked or fouled spark plug. • Fuel pump not primed.
Starter motor won't work (electric starter)	• Gearshift not in *neutral.* • Defective starter switch (sometimes gets wet and corrodes if motor is mounted too low).
Loss of power	• Too much oil in fuel mix. • Fuel/air mix too lean (backfires). • Fuel hose kinked. • Slight blockage in fuel line or fuel filter. • Weeds or some other matter on propeller. • Water has condensed in fuel. • Spark plug fouled. • Magneto or distributor points fouled. • Clogged fuel filters.
Engine misfires	• Spark plug damaged. • Spark plug loose. • Faulty coil or condenser. • Spark plug type incorrect. • Spark plug dirty. • Choke needs adjusting. • Improper oil and fuel mixture. • Dirty carburetor filter. • Partially clogged water intake. • Distributor cap cracked.
Overheating	• Mud or grease on cooling system intakes. • Too little oil. • Water pump is worn or impeller (rubber) is broken. • Defective water pump.

Table 8-5 (continued)
Outboard Motor Troubleshooting

Problem	Possible Cause/Correction
Blue smoke	• Spark plugs are fouled, means too much oil.
Engine surges	• Outboard not properly mounted/propeller rides out of the water. • Carburetor needs adjustments.
Poor performance on boat	• Wrong propeller. • Engine improperly tilted compared with transom. Engine should be vertical when boat is underway. • Bent propeller-usually accompanied by high level of vibration. • Improper load distribution in boat. • Heavy marine growth on boat bottom. • Cavitation.

Steering Casualty

E.7. Problems and Corrections

A steering casualty may have a simple solution or require outside assistance. It may also test your boat handling skills if the boat has two propellers. General advice is provided in **Table 8-6**.

Table 8-6
Steering Casualties

Problem	Possible Cause/Correction
Broken or jammed cable	• Rig emergency steering as applicable. Advise Operational Commander.
Broken hydraulic line, or hydraulic system malfunction	• Inspect hoses for leaks, check fluid level, add if necessary. • Replace hose if spare is onboard. • Rig emergency steering, as applicable. • Notify controlling unit. • Steer with engines if twin propeller. • Try to center rudder amidships. • Anchor, if necessary.
"Frozen", damaged or blocked rudder, outdrive or outboard	• Attempt to free, if possible. • Center rudder, if possible, and block in place.

Basic Engine Maintenance for Auxiliary Facilities

E.8. Maintenance Logs

A very important maintenance procedure is to maintain a hull and engine maintenance log. Ideally, the log should be in two parts. One part would include a series of alphabetically arranged entries: battery, filters, oil, zincs, etc. This makes it easy, for example, to look up "S" for spark plugs or "P" for points. The other should contain several pages available for chronologically entering haul-outs and major maintenance work. To structure the log properly, the engine manufacturer's maintenance manual is needed. Also, a good practice is to buy a large ring binder and put in it every instruction or technical manual for electronics, instruments, heads, stoves, etc. that comes with the boat.

E.9. Basic Maintenance Actions

There is not enough space in this chapter to write a maintenance manual for each type of Auxiliary boat. The primary source for a boat's maintenance requirements should be the engine maintenance manual that came with the boat. However, any auxiliarist can accomplish the following engine maintenance actions:

- Change engine oil, oil filters, and fuel filters.
- Select, gap, and properly torque to specifications, new spark plugs.
- Check and change, if necessary, heat exchanger zincs (if equipped). In some areas this should be done monthly.
- Drain and replace hydraulic drive fluids.
- Replace and adjust engine belts.
- Adjust and tighten stuffing box fittings, steering cable or hydraulics, stuffing boxes, and hull fittings.
- Replace defective engine hoses.
- Clean the air cleaner and flame arrester.
- Check and charge batteries.
- Lube and maintain saltwater intakes/sea cocks.

NOTE

> Keep the tools needed to affect these repairs onboard. With the right spares onboard and the hand tools to install them, the chances of becoming a SAR case are reduced.

E.10. Advanced Maintenance Actions

The more experienced power boater can change ignition points, adjust timing, align engine coupling faces, etc.

E.11. Inboard Boats Kept in Salt Water

A selection of wire brushes, spray cans of primer, engine touch-up paint, and a small 5x7 mirror should be kept onboard. About twice a month, crewmembers should get in the bilges and inspect the engines (mounts, etc.) for rust and corrosion. When found, it should be wire-brushed clean and sprayed with touch-up paint. (There is no reason for engines to be lumps of rust.) Also, while minutely going over the engine, crewmembers should look for leaking hoses, gaskets, loose wires, etc. Many engine problems relate to electrical problems, including loss of electrical ground and oxidation of leads or connectors. These areas should be inspected regularly. The 5x7 mirror is for inspecting the blind side of the engine. Many occasions to be towed can be eliminated by following meticulous maintenance procedures.

E.12. Buying Engine Parts

Spark plugs, hoses, belts, ignition wires, and points can be purchased at auto supply stores. However, alternators, distributors, and carburetors used on boats must have certain marine safety features, screens, etc. Any attempt to replace them with automotive components increases the risk of fire and explosion.

NOTE

> Do not use auto parts on the boat.

Chapter 9
Stability

Introduction

Stability is defined as the ability of a vessel to return to an upright position after being heeled over. Many forces influence the stability of a vessel in the water, and each type of vessel reacts differently. Coxswains must be aware of how internal forces (those caused by the boat's design and loading) and external forces (those caused by nature) affect the boat. With practice and experience, coxswains learn to anticipate how a vessel being piloted and a vessel being assisted will react to various internal and external forces. Recognizing unstable vessel conditions will lead to safe operations for both the boat crew and persons on a craft in distress.

In this chapter

This chapter contains the following sections:

Section A. Understanding Stability

Introduction

When a vessel is heeled over in reaction to some external influence, other than damage to the vessel, it tends to either return to an upright position or continue to heel over and capsize. The tendency of a vessel to remain upright is its stability. The greater the tendency to remain upright, and the stronger the force required to heel the vessel over in any direction, the more stability the vessel achieves. The stability of a vessel in the water is very important to all members of a boat crew. Being able to anticipate how the crewmembers' vessel and the vessel that is being assisted will react in any given set of circumstances is dependent on the crew's knowledge of stability. Gravity and buoyancy are the two primary forces acting upon a floating vessel that affect stability. Gravity pushes the vessel down into the water, while buoyancy is the force that pushes up from the water to keep the vessel afloat. The interaction of these two forces determines the vessel's stability.

A.1. Center of Gravity

The center of gravity is the point at which the weight of the boat acts vertically downwards. Thus, the boat acts as though all of its weight were concentrated at the center of gravity. Generally, the lower the center of gravity, the more stable the vessel.

A.1.a. Changes in the Center of Gravity

The center of gravity of a boat is fixed for stability and does not shift unless weight is added, subtracted, or shifted. When weight is added (e.g., vessel takes on water), the center of gravity moves toward the added weight. When the weight is removed, the center of gravity moves in the opposite direction.

A.2. Buoyancy

The buoyancy is the upward force of water displaced by the hull. The force of buoyancy keeps the boat afloat; however, it may be overcome if too much weight is added.

A.2.a. Center of Buoyancy

The center of buoyancy is the center of gravity of displaced water. Similar to the center of gravity, this is the point on which all upward/vertical force is considered to act. It lies in the center of the underwater form of the hull. (see **Figure 9-1**)

A.3. Equilibrium

When a boat is at rest, the center of buoyancy acting upwards/vertically is below the center of gravity acting downwards. It is at this point that a boat is considered to be in equilibrium. Equilibrium is affected by movement of the center of gravity or center of buoyancy or by some outside forces, such as wind and waves. (see **Figure 9-1**)

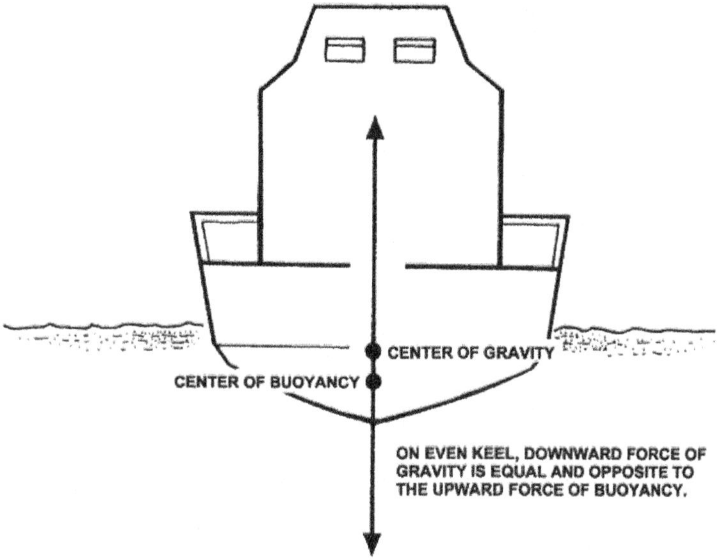

Figure 9-1
Stability in Equilibrium

A.3.a. Rolling

When a boat rolls, the force of the center of gravity will move in the same direction as the roll. The downward force of gravity is offset by the upward force of buoyancy and causes the boat to heel.

A.3.b. Heeling

In heeling, the underwater volume of the boat changes shape causing the center of buoyancy to move.

The center of buoyancy will move towards the part of the hull that is more deeply immersed. When this happens, the center of buoyancy will no longer be aligned vertically with the center of gravity. The intersection of the vertical line through the center of buoyancy and the vertical centerline is called the metacenter. When the metacentric height (the distance between center of gravity and metacenter) is positive, that is the metacenter is above center and gravity, the center of buoyancy shifts so that it is outboard of the center of gravity. Now the boat is considered to be stable, and the forces of buoyancy and gravity will act to bring the boat back to an upright position. If the center of buoyancy is inboard of the center of gravity, that is the metacentric height is negative, the forces of buoyancy and gravity will tend to roll the boat further towards capsize. (see **Figure 9-2**)

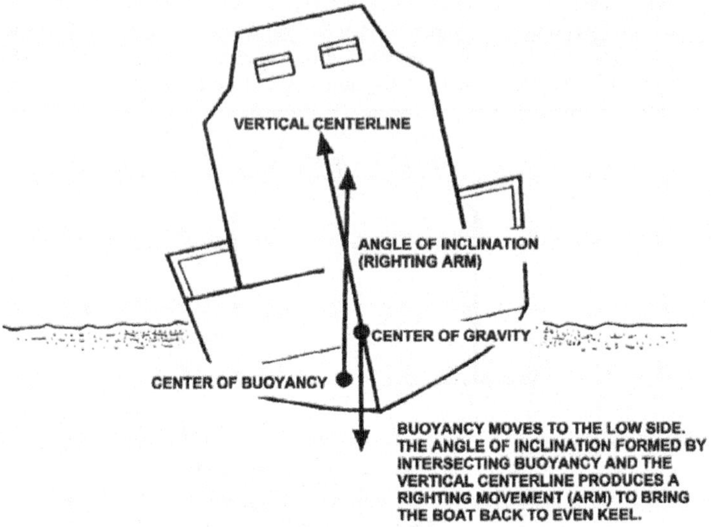

Figure 9-2
Heeling

A.3.c. Listing

If the center of gravity is not on the centerline of the boat, the boat will heel until equilibrium is reached with the center of buoyancy and center of gravity in alignment. This condition is referred to as listing.

NOTE

Heeling is a temporary leaning, listing is a permanent leaning, and both are different from rolling which is a side-to-side motion.

A.4. Types of Stability

A boat has two principle types of stability:

- Longitudinal.
- Transverse.

A boat is usually much longer than it is wide. Therefore, the longitudinal plane (fore and aft) is more stable than its transverse plane (beam).

A.4.a. Longitudinal (Fore and Aft) Stability

Longitudinal (fore and aft) stability tends to balance the boat, preventing it from pitching end-over-end (pitch poling). Vessels are designed with enough longitudinal stability to avoid damage under normal circumstances. However, differences in vessel design varies the longitudinal stability characteristics of different vessels depending on the purpose for which a vessel is designed. Some vessels can suffer excessive pitching and offer a very wet and uncomfortable ride during rough sea and weather conditions. Such an uncomfortable ride often affects the endurance and capability of the crew as well as the people on the vessels being assisted.

A.4.b. Transverse (Athwartships) Stability

Transverse (athwartships) stability tends to keep the boat from rolling over (capsizing). Additional weight above the center of gravity increases the distance from the center of gravity up to the center of buoyancy. As a result, stability is also decreased. Removal of weight from below the center of gravity also decreases stability. If the center of gravity is raised enough, the boat will become unstable.

A.5. Moment and Forces

The force that causes a vessel to return to an even keel, or upright position, is called the vessel's moment. Both static and dynamic forces can reduce stability and moment. Moments, and the internal and external forces that act to increase or decrease the righting moment, are important factors in determining the stability of a vessel at any given point in time.

A.5.a. Righting Moment and Capsizing

A righting moment is the force causing a vessel to react against a roll and return to an even keel. Generally, the broader a boat's beam, the more stable that boat will be, and the less likely it is to capsize. For any given condition of loading, the center of gravity is at a fixed position. As a boat heels, the center of buoyancy moves to the lower side of the boat forming an angle of inclination. Larger changes in the movement of the center of buoyancy will result with any given angle of heel. This change provides greater righting movement up to a maximum angle of inclination.

Too much weight added to the side of the vessel that is heeled over can overcome the forces supporting stability and cause the vessel to capsize. (see **Figure 9-3**)

A boat may also capsize when aground as the volume of water beneath the vessel decreases and the vessel loses balance. As the amount of water supporting the vessel is reduced, there is a loss of buoyancy force being provided by that water. In addition, the upward force acting at the point of grounding will increase and cause the unsupported hull to fall to one side.

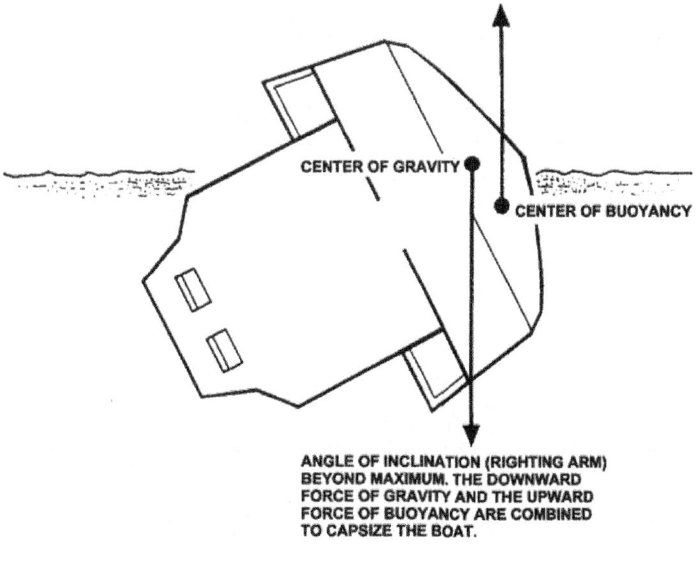

Figure 9-3
Righting Moment and Capsizing

A.5.b. Static and Dynamic Forces

Unless acted upon by some external force, a boat that is properly designed and loaded remains on an even keel. The two principle forces that affect stability are static and dynamic forces.

- Static forces are caused by placement of weight within the hull. Adding weight on one side of a boat's centerline or above its center of gravity usually reduces stability. Flooding or grounding a boat makes it susceptible to static forces which may adversely affect stability.
- Dynamic forces are caused by actions outside the hull such as wind and waves. Strong gusts of wind or heavy seas, especially in shallow water, may build up a dangerous sea tending to capsize a boat.

For a boat crewmember this understanding is useful when approaching a vessel to provide assistance. Observing the vessel's roll can provide some initial indications about the stability of the vessel.

- Watch the time required for a complete roll from side to side. The time should remain about the same regardless of the severity of the angle or roll.
- If the time increases significantly or the boat hesitates at the end of the roll, the boat is approaching or past the position of maximum righting effect. Take immediate steps to decrease the roll by changing course or speed, or both.

A.5.c. Vessel Design

General vessel design features that influence stability include:

- Size and shape of the hull.
- Draft of the boat (the distance from the surface of the water to the keel).
- Trim (the angle from horizontal at which a vessel rides).
- Displacement.
- Freeboard.
- Superstructure size, shape, and weight.
- Non-watertight openings.

Many of these features are discussed *in Chapter 8, Boat Characteristics.*

Section B. Losing Stability

Introduction

A vessel may be inclined away from its upright position by certain internal and external influences such as:

- Waves.
- Wind.
- Turning forces when the rudder is put over.
- Shifting of weights onboard.
- Addition or removal of weights.
- Loss of buoyancy (damage).

These influences exert heeling moments on a vessel causing it to list (permanent) or heel (temporary). A stable boat does not capsize when subjected to normal heeling moments due to the boat's tendency to right itself (righting moment).

B.1. Stability After Damage

When assisting a damaged vessel, any change in stability may result in the loss of the vessel. The added weight of assisting personnel or equipment may cause the vessel to lose its righting moment, lose stability, and capsize. This consequence, and the danger involved, must be considered when determining risk to avoid harm to the crew and further damage or loss of a vessel.

WARNING

When a vessel is visibly unstable (i.e., listing, trimmed to the bow/stern or when downflooding occurs), never make the vessel fast to or tow the distressed vessel. A flooded vessel may appear stable when it in fact is not. Compare the boat's reaction to sea conditions with your own boat's

B.1.a. Stability Risk Management Plan

The entire crew must constantly watch for any loss of stability in their own vessel and that of the distressed craft. Crewmembers should not assume that the coxswain has been able to observe all of the warning signs. They should advise the coxswain of stability concerns that may have been overlooked and any warning signs. The following warning signs should be used as a guideline for a Stability Risk Management Plan:

- Observe the roll of your own boat and, for a distressed vessel, observe its roll upon approaching and when under tow.
- Be aware of external forces - wind, waves, and water depth.
- Be aware of control loading, amount of weight and placement, on own and the distressed craft.
- If necessary, attempt to keep your equipment aboard your vessel when dewatering the vessel.
- Attempt to tow the distressed vessel only after any loss of stability has been corrected.
- Adjust course, speed, or both as necessary to decrease rolling or listing.
- Avoid sharp turns or turns at high speed when loss of stability is possible.

B.2. Free Surface Effect

Compartments in a vessel may contain liquids as a matter of design or as a result of damage. If a compartment is only partly filled, the liquid can flow from side to side as the vessel rolls or pitches. The surface of the liquid tends to remain parallel to the waterline. Liquid that only partly fills a compartment is said to have free surface and water in such a compartment is called loose water. When loose water shifts from side to side or forward and aft due to turning, speed changes, or wave action, the vessel does not want to right itself. This causes a loss of stability. This can cause the vessel to capsize or sink. (see **Figure 9-4** and **Figure 9-5**)

Corrective actions include:

- Minimize the number of partially filled tanks (fuel, water, or cargo); ballast with seawater as necessary.
- Prevent cargo such as aids to navigation equipment and rescue gear from rolling back and forth on the deck.
- If possible, store cargo low and close to the centerline.

NOTE

Note that the area of free surface is very important, and in particular its width. If the free surface area doubles in width, its adverse effect on stability will change by a factor of four.

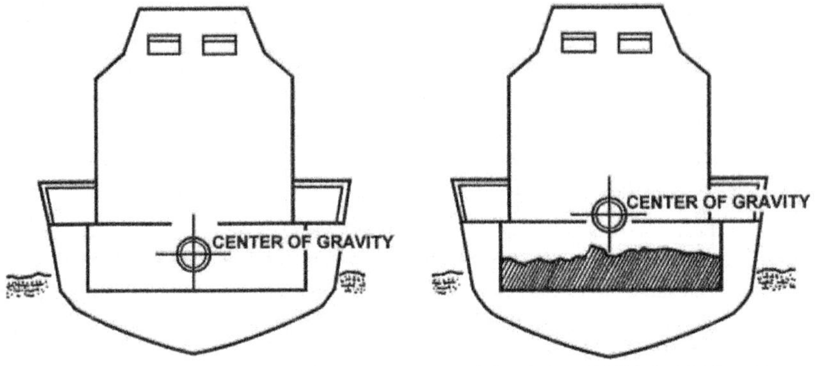

Figure 9-4
Effects of Free Surface

CAUTION !

Special caution should be used when dealing with fishing vessels that use fish wells to store their catch. If these fish wells are not emptied or kept full, they could have a serious affect on the vessels stability.

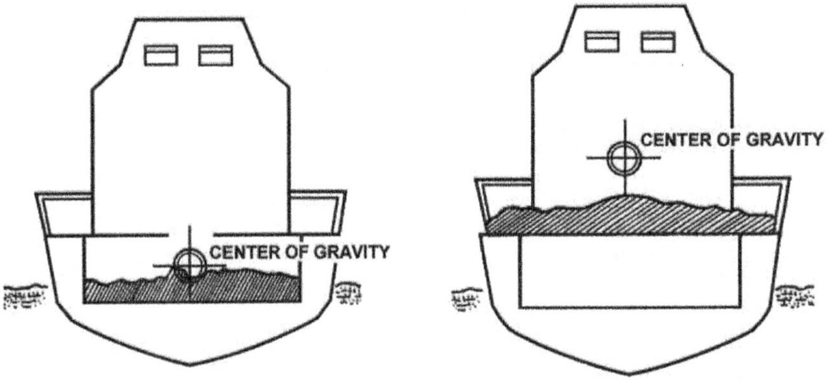

Figure 9-5
Effects of Load Weight

B.3. Free Communication with the Sea

Damage to the hull of a vessel can create free communication with the sea, which is the unobstructed movement of seawater into and out of the vessel.

Corrective actions include:

- Patch the hull opening.
- Place weight on the high side to decrease the list toward the damaged side.
- Remove weight above the center of gravity on the damaged side.

B.4. Effects of Icing

Icing can increase the displacement of a boat by adding weight above the center of gravity causing the center of gravity to rise. This can cause a vessel to heel over and greatly reduce stability. Sea swells, sharp turns, or quick changes in speed can capsize a vessel that has accumulated ice on its topside surfaces. (see **Figure 9-6**)

Corrective actions include:

- Change course, speed, or both to reduce freezing spray and rolling.
- Physically remove the ice.

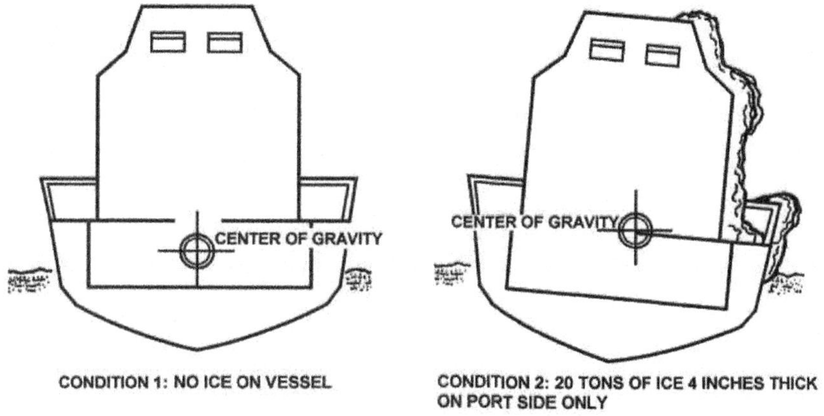

Figure 9-6
Effects of Icing

B.5. Effects of Downflooding

Downflooding is the entry of water into the hull, resulting in progressive flooding and loss of stability. Vessels are designed with sufficient stability and proper righting moments as long as they are not overloaded. These design features cannot compensate for the carelessness of a boat crew who fails to maintain the watertight integrity of a vessel and allows it to needlessly take on water. (see **Figure 9-7**)

Corrective actions include:

- Keep all watertight fittings and openings secured when a vessel is underway.
- Pump out the water.

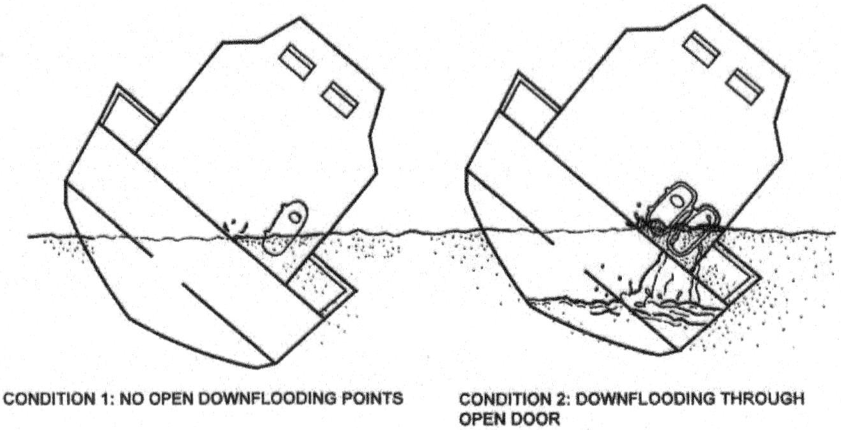

Figure 9-7
Effects of Downflooding

B.6. Effects of Water on Deck

Water on deck can cause stability problems by (see **Figure 9-8**):

- Increasing displacement (increasing draft and decreasing stability and trim).
- Contributing to free surface effect.
- Amplifying the rolling motion of the vessel which may result in capsizing.

Corrective actions include:

- Decrease trim, increase freeboard.
- Change course, speed or both.
- Ensure drain openings are unobstructed.

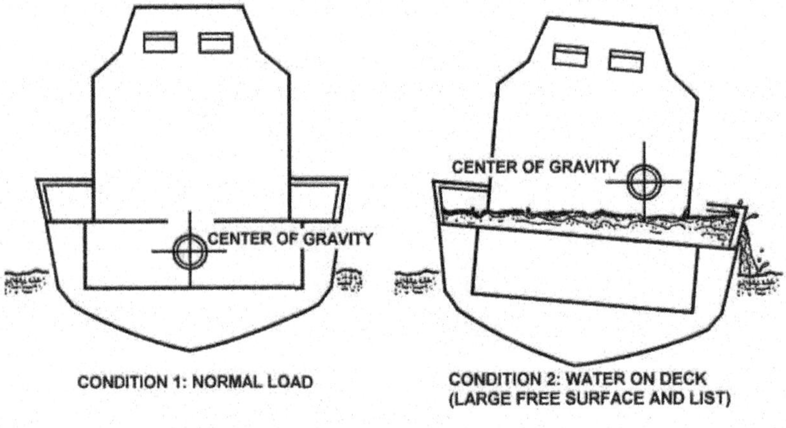

Figure 9-8
Effects of Water on Deck

Chapter 10
Boat Handling

Introduction

This chapter covers handling vessels under power. Vessels under sail and personal watercraft are not addressed. Topics include:

- Forces that move or control a vessel.
- Basic maneuvering and boat operating.
- Maneuvering techniques for general categories of vessels.
- Purpose-based boat handling evolutions and procedures.

Boat handling requires an understanding of many variables. The coxswain must understand how to balance those forces they have control over (power, steering, etc.) and those they don't have control over (wind, waves, etc.) to complete the mission. Though boat handling skills can only be developed through hands-on experience, the information in this chapter provides a basic description of principles and practices.

The Best Coxswains

Though good coxswains are familiar with the characteristics of their boat and how it operates, the best coxswains are knowledgeable in the operation of all types of small craft, including sailboats and personal watercraft. They know how varying weather and sea conditions affect the operation of not just their vessel, but are also keenly aware of the limitations that the weather and sea impose on other vessels. They have a thorough knowledge of navigation, piloting and characteristics of their operating area. Above all, the best coxswains understand how to mesh the capabilities of their vessel to weather and sea conditions to conduct the safest possible boat operations.

In this chapter

This chapter contains the following sections:

Section A. Forces

Introduction

Different forces act on a vessel's hull, causing it to move in a particular direction or to change direction. These forces include environmental forces, propulsion, and steering.

In this section

This section contains the following information:

Environmental Forces

A.1. Safe Boat Handling

Environmental forces that affect the horizontal motion of a vessel are wind, seas, and current. The coxswain has no control over them and must take the time to observe how the wind, seas, and current, alone and together, affect the vessel. The coxswain should also determine how these forces cause the vessel to drift, and at what speed and angle. Coxswains must use environmental forces to their advantage and use propulsion and steering to overcome the environmental forces. Usually, a good mix of using and overcoming environmental forces results in smooth, safe boat handling.

A.2. Winds

The wind acts upon any portion of the vessel that is above the waterline. This includes the hull, superstructure, and on smaller boats, the crew. The amount of surface upon which the wind acts is called sail area. The vessel will make "leeway" (drift downwind) at a speed proportional to the wind velocity and the amount of sail area. The "aspect" or angle the vessel takes due to the wind will depend on where the sail area is centered compared to the underwater hull's center of lateral resistance. A vessel with a high cabin near the bow and low freeboard aft (see **Figure 10-1**) would tend to ride stern to the wind. If a vessel's draft were shallower forward than aft, the wind would affect the bow more than the stern. A sudden gust of wind from abeam when mooring a vessel like this might quickly set the bow down on a pier.

Figure 10-1
High Cabin Near Bow, Low Freeboard Aft

A.3. Close Quarters

Knowledge of how the wind affects a vessel is very important in all close quarters situations, such as mooring, recovery of an object in the water, or maneuvering close aboard another vessel. If maneuvering from a downwind or leeward side of a vessel or pier, the coxswain should look for any wind shadow the vessel or pier makes by blocking the wind. (see **Figure 10-2**) The coxswain should also account for the change in wind by planning maneuvers with this wind shadow in mind.

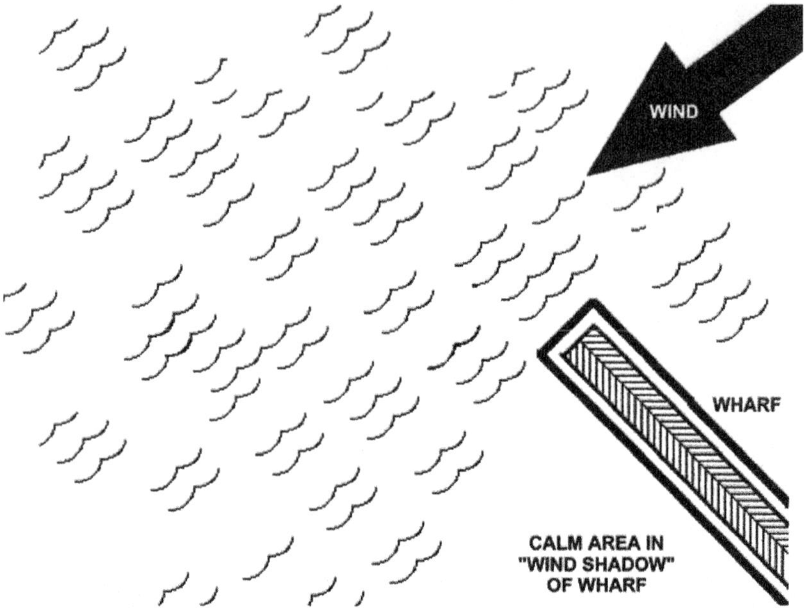

Figure 10-2
Wind Shadow

A.4. Seas

Seas are a product of the wind acting on the surface of the water. Seas affect boat handling in various ways, depending on their height and direction and the particular vessel's characteristics. Vessels that readily react to wave motion, particularly pitching, will often expose part of the underwater hull to the wind. In situations such as this, the bow or stern may tend to "fall off" the wind when cresting a wave, as less underwater hull is available to prevent this downwind movement.

Relatively large seas have the effect of making a temporary wind shadow for smaller vessels. In the trough between two crests, the wind may be substantially less than the wind at the wave crest. Very small vessels may need to make corrective maneuvers in the trough before approaching the next crest.

A.5. Current

Current acts on a vessel's underwater hull in the same manner as wind pushes on a vessel's superstructure. The amount of draft a vessel has will determine how much affect current will have. A one-knot current may affect a vessel to the same degree as a 30-knot wind. A strong current will easily move a vessel upwind.

The coxswain should learn to look for the signs of current flow so as to be prepared when current affects the vessel, and should be particularly aware of instances where current shear is present. As with wind, a large, stationary object like a breakwater or jetty will cause major changes in the amount and direction of current. (see **Figure 10-3**) Crewmembers should note the amount of current around floating moorings or those with open pile supports. Caution should be used when maneuvering in close quarters to buoys and anchored vessels. Crewmembers should observe the effect of current by looking for current wake or flow patterns around buoys or piers and should watch how currents affect other vessels.

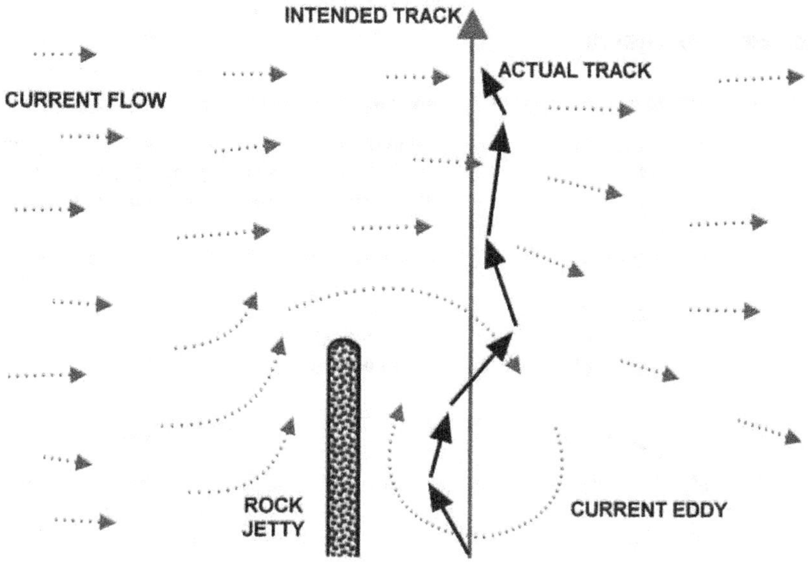

Figure 10-3
Effects of Current

A.6. Combined Environmental Forces

Environmental conditions can range from perfectly calm and absolutely no current to a howling gale and spring tides. Chances are that even if operation does not occur at either extreme, some degree of environmental forces will be in action.

A.7. Knowing the Vessel's Response

The coxswain should know how the vessel responds to combinations of wind and current, and should determine which one has the greatest effect on the vessel. It may be that up to a certain wind speed, current has more control over a given vessel, but above that certain wind speed, the boat sails like a kite. The coxswain should know what will happen if a sudden gust of wind is encountered; will the boat immediately veer, or will it take a sustained wind to start it turning?

When current goes against the wind, the wave patterns will be steeper and closer together. The coxswain should be particularly cautious where current or wind is funneled against the other. Tide rips, breaking bars, or gorge conditions frequently occur in these types of areas and may present a challenge to even the most proficient coxswain.

On the other hand, making leeway while drifting downstream (down current) requires a change in approach to prevent overshooting the landing.

NOTE Stay constantly aware of conditions, how they may be changing, and how they affect the vessel.

Forces Acting on a Vessel

A.8. Assumptions

For this discussion of propulsion, the following assumptions are made:

- If a vessel has a single-shaft motor or drive unit, it is mounted on the vessel's centerline.
- When applying thrust to go forward, the propeller turns clockwise (the top to the right or a "right-handed" propeller), viewed from astern, and turns counterclockwise viewed from astern when making thrust to go astern.
- If twin propulsion is used, the propeller to starboard operates as above (right-hand turning), while the port unit turns counterclockwise when making thrust to go forward when viewed from astern (left-hand turning). (see **Figure 10-4**)
- Be aware that some propeller drive units rotate in only one direction, and changing the propeller blade angle of attack controls ahead or astern thrust (controllable pitch propeller).

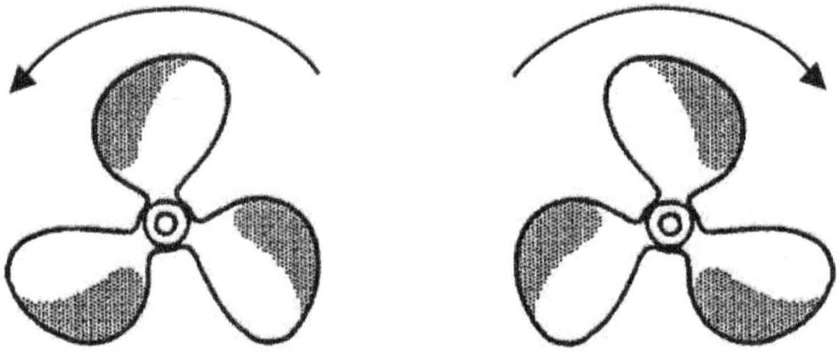

VIEWED FROM ASTERN, TURNING FOR PROPULSION TO GO AHEAD. PROPELLER ON RIGHT (STARBOARD SHAFT) TURNS CLOCKWISE AND IS CALLED A RIGHT-HANDED PROPELLER. WHEN BACKING, ROTATION IS OPPOSITE.

Figure 10-4
Twin Propulsion

A.9. Propulsion and Steering

The key to powered vessel movement is the effective transfer of energy from the source of the power (an internal combustion engine) to the water through a mechanism that turns the engine's power into thrust. This thrust moves the boat. There must also be an element of directional control, both fore and aft, and from side to side.

Propulsion and steering are considered together here for two reasons. Applying thrust has no use if the vessel's direction cannot be controlled, and often the device providing the propulsion also provides the steering.

There are three common methods to transfer power and provide directional control:

- Rotating shaft and propeller with separate rudder.
- A movable (steerable) combination as an outboard motor or stern drive.
- An engine-driven pump mechanism with directional control, called a waterjet.

All three arrangements have their advantages and disadvantages from the standpoint of mechanical efficiency, ease of maintenance, and vessel control. Using one type of propulsion instead of another is often a matter of vessel design and use parameters, operating area limitations, life cycle cost and frequently, personal preference. There is no single "best choice" for all applications. Regardless of which type you use, become familiar with how each operates and how the differences in operation affect vessel movement.

NOTE

On almost every boat, propulsion and steering arrangement is designed to operate more efficiently and effectively when going ahead than when going astern. Also, every vessel rotates in a transverse direction about a vertical axis on its pivot point. (see **Figure 10-5**) The fore and aft location of the pivot point varies from boat to boat, but is generally just forward of amidships when the boat is at rest. As a hull moves either ahead or astern, the effective position of the pivot point moves either forward or aft, respectively.

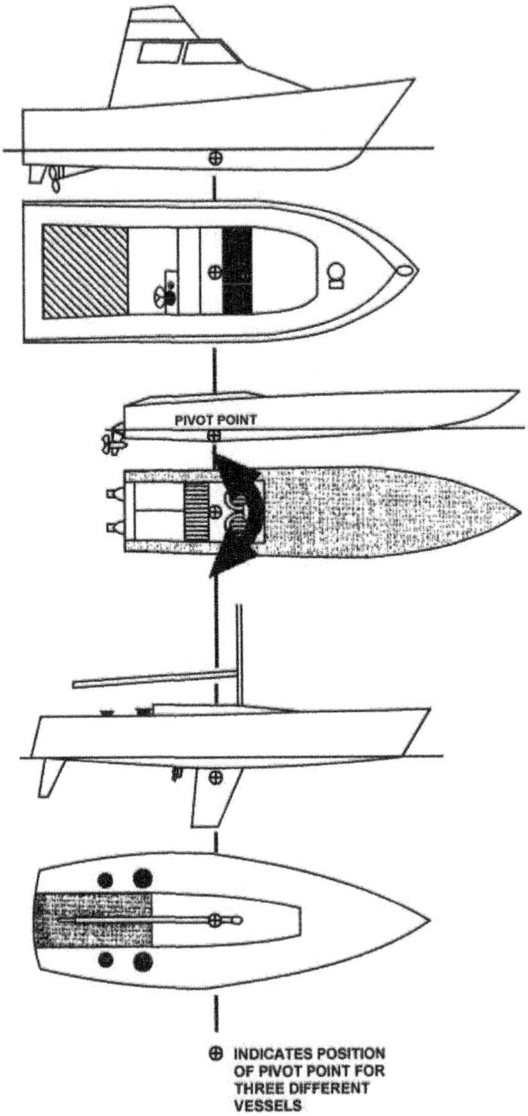

Figure 10-5
Pivot Point

Shaft, Propeller, and Rudder

A.10. Shaft

In small craft installations, the propeller shaft usually penetrates the bottom of the hull at an angle to the vessel's designed waterline and true horizontal. The practical reason for this is because the engine or marine gear must be inside the hull while the diameter of the propeller must be outside and beneath the hull. Additionally, there must be a space between the propeller blade arc of rotation and the bottom of the hull. For single-screw vessels, the shaft is generally aligned to the centerline of the vessel. However, in some installations, a slight offset (approximately 1°) is used to compensate for shaft torque. To finish the installation, the rudder is usually mounted directly astern of the propeller.

For twin-screw vessels, both shafts are parallel to the vessel's centerline (or nearly so), rudders are mounted astern of the propellers, and the rudders turn on vertical rudder posts.

A.11. Propeller Action

When rotating to move in a forward direction, a propeller draws its supply of water from every direction forward of and around the blades. Each blade's shape and pitch develop a low-pressure area on the forward face of the blade and a high-pressure area on the after face of the blades, forcing it in a stream toward the stern. This thrust, or dynamic pressure, along the propeller's rotation axis is transmitted through the shaft, moving the boat ahead as the propeller tries to move into the area of lower pressure.

A.11.a. Screw Current

Regardless of whether the propeller is turning to go ahead or astern, the water flow pattern into the propeller's arc of rotation is called suction screw current, and the thrust flow pattern out of the propeller is called discharge screw current. (see **Figure 10-6**) The discharge screw current will always be stronger and more concentrated than the suction screw current.

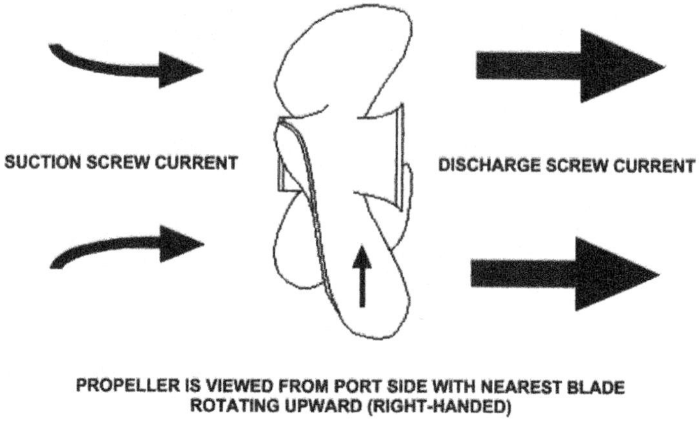

Figure 10-6
Screw Current

A.11.b. Side Force

In addition to the thrust along the shaft axis, another effect of propeller rotation is side force. Explanations for side force include:

- How the propeller reacts to interference from the vessel hull as the hull drags a layer of water along with it (the propeller encounters boundary layer "frictional wake").
- How the discharge screw current acts on the rudder.
- The propeller blade at the top of the arc transfers some energy to the water surface (prop wash) or to the hull (noise) and that the blade at the top of the arc either entrains air or encounters aerated water.

Due to the angle of the propeller shaft, the effective pitch angle is different for ascending and descending propeller blades, resulting in an unequal blade thrust. (The descending blade has a higher effective pitch angle and causes more thrust.) This net effect is sometimes referred to as sideways blade pressure.

The important facts to know: for a right-handed screw turning ahead, the stern will tend to move to starboard (see **Figure 10-7**), and for a right-handed screw when backing, the stern will tend to move to port. For a left-handed screw (normally the port shaft on a twin-screw boat), the action is the opposite.

An easy way to remember how side force will push the stern is to think of the propeller as a wheel on the ground. As the wheel rolls clockwise, it moves to the right. As a propeller turns clockwise when viewed from astern, the stern moves to starboard.

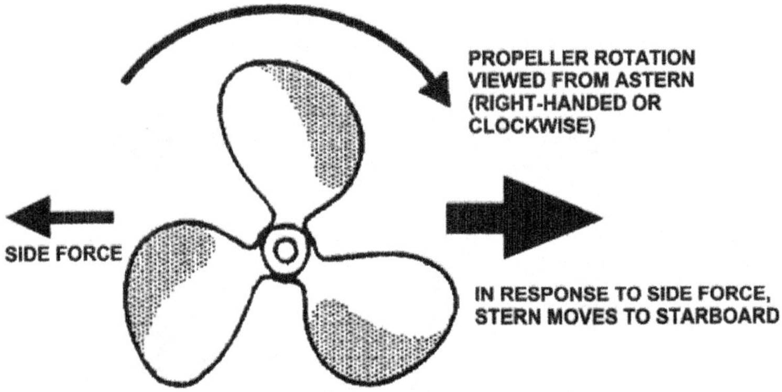

Figure 10-7
Side Force

A.11.c. Cavitation

Cavitation usually occurs when the propeller rotates at very high speed and a partial vacuum forms air bubbles at the tips of the propeller blades. Cavitation can also occur when trying to get a stopped propeller to spin at maximum speed, rapidly going from ahead to astern (or vice-versa), or by operating in aerated water where bubbles are dragged into the propeller flow.

Cavitation occurs more readily when trying to back, as the suction screw current draws water from behind the transom, and air at the waterline mixes with the water and is drawn into the propeller. Cavitation frequently occurs when backing with outboard motors. In this case, through-hub exhaust gas bubbles are also drawn forward into the propeller blade arc.

NOTE ☞ A small degree of cavitation is normal and defined as when effective thrust is lost and the propeller just spins and makes bubbles. The easiest way to regain thrust is to reduce propeller revolutions and as the bubbles subside, gradually increase RPMs.

A.12. Rudder Action

When a vessel moves through the water (even without propulsion), the rudder is normally used to change the vessel's heading. As a hull moves forward and the rudder is held steady, amidships, pressure on either side of the rudder is relatively equal and the vessel will usually keep a straight track. When turning the rudder to port or starboard, pressure decreases on one side of the rudder and increases on the other. This force causes the vessel's stern to move to one side or the other. As noted above, because a vessel rotates about its pivot point, as the stern moves in one direction, the bow moves in the other direction. (see **Figure 10-8** (a) and (b))

The speed of the water flowing past the rudder greatly enhances the rudder's force. The thrust or screw discharge current from a propeller while operating ahead increases the water flow speed past the rudder. Also, while turning the rudder to a side, it directs about one-half of the propeller's thrust to that side, adding a major component of force to move the stern. (see **Figure 10-8** (c) and (d))

When operating astern, the rudder is in the screw suction current. The rudder cannot direct any propeller thrust, and since the screw suction current is neither as strong nor as concentrated as the screw discharge current, water flow past the rudder does not increase as much. The combined effects of screw current and rudder force when operating astern are not nearly as effective as when operating ahead.

As rudder force is determined by water flow along it, a rudder loses some of its effectiveness if the propeller cavitates and aerated water flows along the rudder.

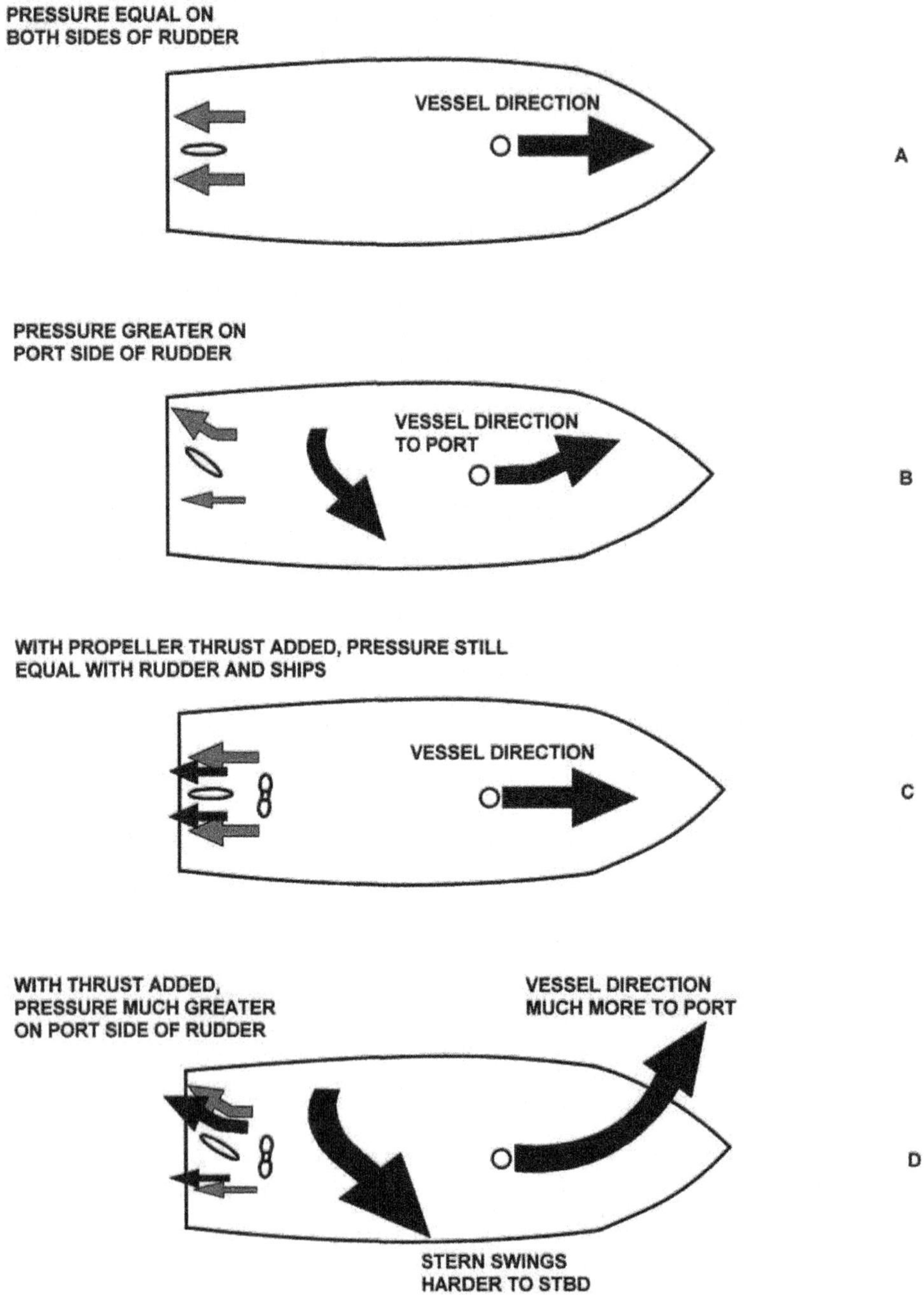

Figure 10-8
Effect of Rudder Action

Outboard Motors and Stern Drives

A.13. Major Differences

Outboard motors and stern drives will be considered together, as both include a pivoting gear case and propeller drive unit (called a lower unit on an outboard). The difference between these drive arrangements and the shaft/propeller/rudder arrangement is that the screw currents and thrust from an outboard or stern drive can be developed at an angle to the vessel centerline. Also, the point where thrust and steering are developed is usually aft of the vessel hull.

The lower unit contains drive gears, a spline connection, and on many set-ups, through-the-propeller hub exhaust. Many lower unit gear housings are over six inches in diameter. Where an inboard engine powers the stern drive attached through the transom to the drive unit (the outdrive) and is commonly referred to as an inboard/outdrive or I/O. The outboard "powerhead" (engine) is mounted directly above the lower unit. Both outboards and stern drives can usually direct thrust at up to 35° to 40° off the vessel centerline. Also, both types generally allow the coxswain some amount of trim control. Trim control adjusts the propeller axis angle with the horizontal or surface of the water.

The major difference in operation between the I/O and outboard is that the outboard motor, operating with a vertical crankshaft and driveshaft, develops a certain degree of rotational torque that could cause some degree of "pull" in the steering, usually when accelerating or in a sharp turn to starboard. If caught unaware, the coxswain could have difficulty stopping the turning action. The easiest way to overcome this torque-lock is to immediately reduce RPMs before trying to counter-steer.

A.14. Thrust and Directional Control

Outboards and stern drives have a small steering vane or skeg below the propeller. The housing above the gearcase (below the waterline) is generally foil shaped. Though these features help directional control, particularly at speed, the larger amount of steering force from an outboard or stern drive is based upon the ability to direct the screw discharge current thrust at an angle to the vessel's centerline. (see **Figure 10-9**) This directed thrust provides extremely effective directional control when powering ahead. When making way with no propeller RPMs, the lower unit and skeg are not as effective as a rudder in providing directional control.

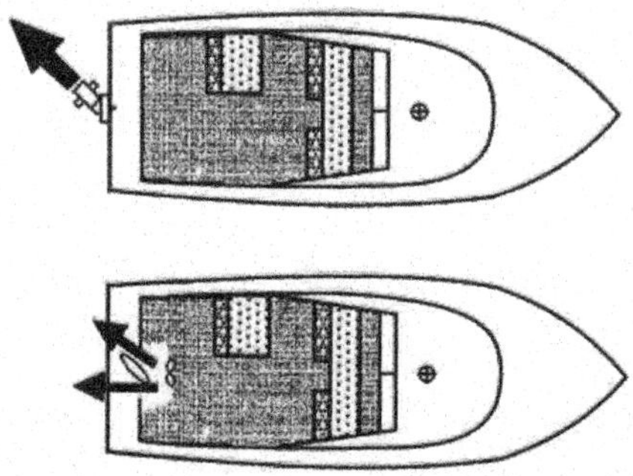

THE OUTBOARD OR OUTDRIVE (TOP) DIRECTS ALL THE THRUST IN THE DIRECTION THE HELM IS TURNED WHERE THE INBOARD, WITH SEPARATE PROPELLER AND RUDDER (BOTTOM), DIRECTS ONLY 60-70% OF THE THRUST TO THE SIDE.

Figure 10-9
Lower Unit/Outdrive Directed Thrust

NOTE

The propeller forces discussed above in A.11 also apply to the propellers on outboards or outdrives. However, because these drives can be directed, side force can be countered. The steering vane/skeg angle is usually adjustable, also assisting in countering side force.

A.15. Propeller Side Force

When backing, it is possible to direct outboard/outdrive thrust to move the stern to port or starboard. When backing with the unit hard over to port, propeller side force introduces an element of forward motion (see **Figure 10-10**), but can be countered through less helm. When backing to starboard, the side force tends to cause an element of astern motion and also tries to offset the initial starboard movement. Many lower units are fitted with a small vertical vane, slightly offset from centerline, directly above and astern of the propeller. This vane also acts to counter side force, particularly at higher speeds.

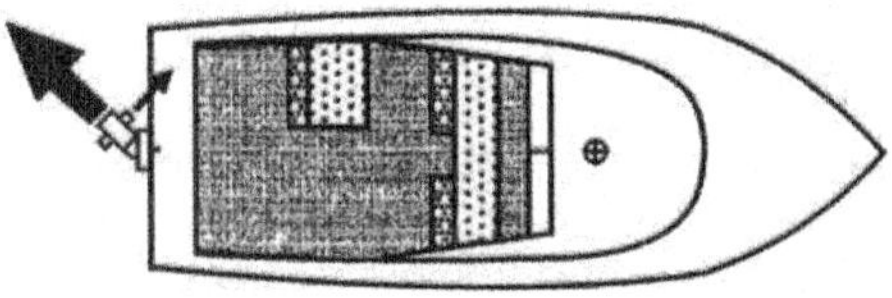

WITH HELM OVER, THE PROPELLER SIDE FORCE (SMALL ARROW) HAS A FORE AND AFT COMPONENT.
THIS EXAMPLE SHOWS THE EFFECT OF SIDE FORCE WHEN BACKING WITH AN OUTDRIVE.
WITH HELM TO PORT, THE BOAT'S TRANSOM WILL MOVE BOTH TO PORT AND FORWARD (SMALL ARROW).

Figure 10-10
Lower Unit/Outdrive Side Force

A.16. Vertical Thrust

Outboards and stern drive usually allow a level of vertical thrust control. Trim controls the angle of attack between the propeller's axis of rotation and both the vessel waterline and the surface of the water. Vertical thrust control, especially applied aft of the transom, changes the attitude the vessel hull will take to the water. (see **Figure 10-11**) Small amounts of trim should be used to offset for extreme loading conditions or to adjust how the vessel goes through chop.

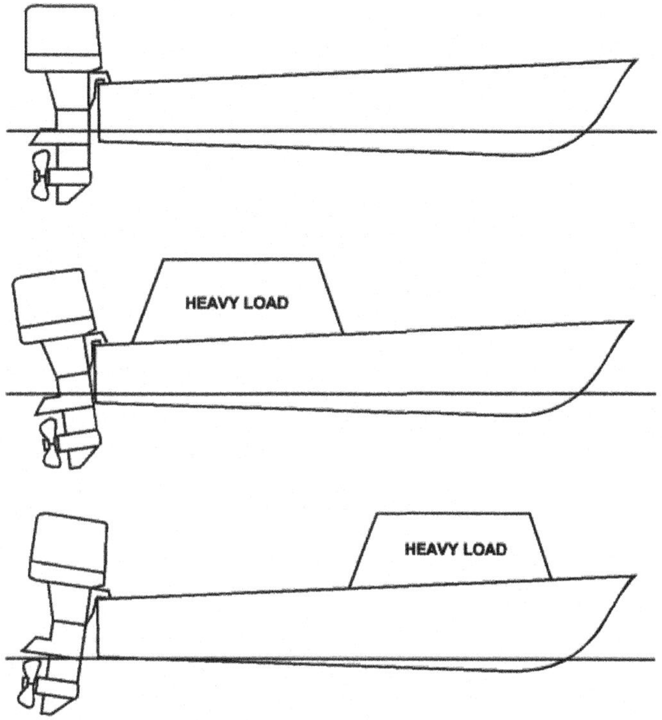

Figure 10-11
Trim to Offset Loading Condition

In addition to trim, a vertical component of thrust develops in another situation. Depending on the type of hull, if a vessel is forced into an extremely tight turn with power applied, thrust is directed sideways while the vessel heels, actually trying to force the transom up out of the water, causing a turn to tighten even more.

WARNING

In lightweight or highly buoyant outboard powered boats, use of full power in tight turns can cause loss of control or ejection of crew, coxswain or both. It is mandatory that the helmsmen attach the engine kill switch lanyard to themselves.

A.17. Cavitation

As noted earlier, cavitation frequently occurs when backing with outboard motors. As through-hub exhaust gas bubbles are drawn forward into the propeller blade arc, the aerated water increases the possibility of cavitation. Though outboards and stern-drives are fitted with an anti-cavitation plate above the propeller, the coxswain should always take care to limit cavitation, particularly when backing or maneuvering using large amounts of throttle.

Waterjets

A.18. Operation

A waterjet is an engine-driven impeller mounted in housing. The impeller draws water in and forces it out through a nozzle. The suction (inlet) side of the waterjet is forward of the nozzle, usually mounted at the deepest draft near the after sections of the hull. The discharge nozzle is mounted low in the hull, exiting through the transom. The cross-sectional area of the inlet is much larger than that of the nozzle. The volume of water entering the inlet is the same as being discharged through the nozzle, so the water flow is much stronger at the nozzle than at the intake. This pump-drive system is strictly a directed-thrust drive arrangement. A waterjet normally has no appendages, nor does it extend below the bottom of the vessel hull, allowing for operation in very shallow water.

A.19. Thrust and Directional Control

Vessel control is through the nozzle-directed thrust. To attain forward motion, the thrust exits directly astern. For turning, the nozzle pivots (as a stern drive) to provide a transverse thrust component that moves the stern. For astern motion, a bucket-like deflector drops down behind the nozzle and directs the thrust forward. Some waterjet applications include trim control as with a stern drive or outboard. With this, thrust can be directed slightly upward or downward to offset vessel loading or improve ride.

In most cases the only vessel control is by the nozzle-directed thrust, but occasionally a waterjet with a small steering vane will be seen. If a waterjet craft is proceeding at high speed, power brought down quickly to neutral, and the helm put over, no turning action will occur. Of the three drive arrangements discussed; the waterjet alone has no directional control when there is no power.

A.20. No Side Force

Since the waterjet impeller is fully enclosed in the pump-drive housing, no propeller side force is generated. The only way to move the stern to port or starboard is by using the directed thrust.

A.21. Cavitation

Waterjet impeller blades revolve at an extremely high speed. A much higher degree of cavitation normally occurs than associated with external propellers without a loss of effective thrust. In fact, a telltale indicator of waterjet propulsion is a pronounced aerated, water discharge frequently seen as a rooster tail astern of such craft.

As the impeller rotation does not change with thrust direction, frequent shifting from ahead to astern motion does not induce cavitation. However, as the thrust to make astern motion reaches the waterjet inlet, the aerated water is drawn into the jet, causing some reduction of effective thrust. As with all types of propulsion, slowing the impeller until clear of the aerated water reduces cavitation effects.

Section B. Basic Maneuvering

Introduction

To learn the basic handling and maneuvering characteristics of a vessel, a trainee must first observe a skilled coxswain. Also, one must first learn to operate the vessel in relatively open water, away from fixed piers and moored vessels.

In this section

This section contains the following information:

Learning the Controls

B.1. Description

When stepping up to the controls of any vessel for the first time, the coxswain should immediately become familiar with any physical constraints or limitations of the helm and engine controls. Ideally, controls should be designed and mounted to allow for a wide range of operators of different arm length and hand size, though this is not always so.

B.1. Obstructions/ Hazards

The coxswain should determine if anything obstructs hand or arm movement for helm and throttle control. Checks should be made for the following obstructions and hazards:

- A firm grasp of the wheel through 360°.
- Anything that prevents use of the spokes.
- Awkward position of throttle/gear selector.
- Layout that prevents use of heavy gloves.
- Inaccessible engine shutdown handles.
- An easily fouled outboard kill-switch lanyard.
- Other commonsense items.

The coxswain should also learn where all the controls are and know their function before snagging a sleeve while maneuvering in close quarters or banging a knee or elbow in choppy seas.

NOTE

Check control operation while moored with engines secured. Some larger vessels require engine operation to operate controls, such as engine-assisted hydraulic steering. If so, check throttle controls with engines secured.

B.3. Helm Limits

The following are some guidelines for determining the helm limits:

Step	Procedure
1	Determine the amount of helm from full right rudder to full left rudder.
2	Check for any binding, play, or slop in the helm and rudder control, and at what angle it occurs.
3	Ensure that the helm indicates rudder amidships.
4	Ensure that a rudder angle indicator accurately matches rudder position and matches a centered helm.

B.4. Engine Control Action Check

The following are some items to check when checking engine control action:

Step	Procedure
1	Is throttle separate from shifting/direction mechanism?
2	Any detent, notch, or stops that separate *neutral*, *ahead* and *astern*.
3	Force required to shift from *neutral* to *ahead* or *astern*.
4	Binding or excessive looseness at any stage of the throttle control.
5	Is NEUTRAL easily found without looking at the control handle?
6	Do the controls stay put or do they tend to slide back?
7	Does the kill-switch lanyard allow adequate but not excessive range of motion?
8	Does an engine shut down handle work properly?
9	Is idle speed adjusted properly?

NOTE Perform these steps as part of every getting-underway check.

WARNING Smooth, positive operation of helm and engine controls is absolutely necessary for safe boat operation. Do not accept improper control configuration, mismatched equipment, or improper maintenance as a reason for poorly operating controls. Poor control operation causes unsafe boat operations.

B.5. Engine Control Recheck

After checking all controls while moored with engines secured, the coxswain should recheck their operation with engines running while securely moored. It may not be safe to apply full ahead to astern throttle, however, a note should be made anytime there is a lag between throttle shift and propulsion, from *neutral* to *ahead*, *neutral* to *astern*, *ahead* to *astern*, and *astern* to *ahead*.

CAUTION ! When going from the *ahead* position to the *astern* position, and when going from the *astern* position to the *ahead* position, pause briefly at the *neutral* position.

When training, an experienced individual should get the vessel underway and into open water before turning control over to anyone not familiar with the particular boat's operation. Once in open water, control may be turned over to the new coxswain who should recheck helm and engine control operation at clutch speed.

Moving Forward in a Straight Line

B.6. Description

When moving forward in a straight line, throttle should be advanced gradually and firmly. If the vessel is single-screw, outboard, or outdrive, propeller side force will tend to move the stern slightly to starboard. (see **Figure 10-12**) The side force should be offset with slight starboard helm. If twin-engine, throttles should be advanced together. The vessel should not yaw in either direction if power is applied evenly. Engine RPMs should be checked so both engines turn at the same speed. Some vessels have a separate indicator to show if engine RPMs match, but also compare tachometer readings.

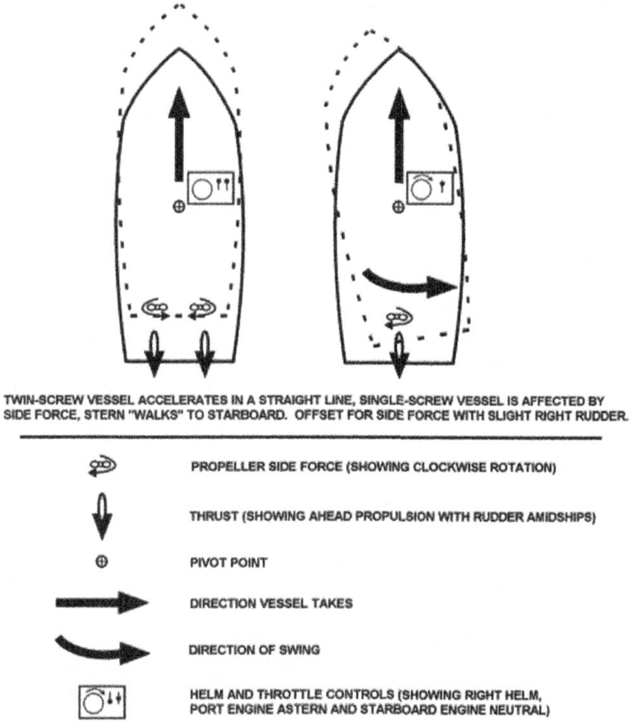

Figure 10-12
Accelerated Ahead

NOTE

Do not ram throttles forward when starting up. As the engines try to transfer the excessive power, the stern will squat, raising the bow and decreasing visibility (see **Figure 10-13**), and propellers or impellers may cavitate.

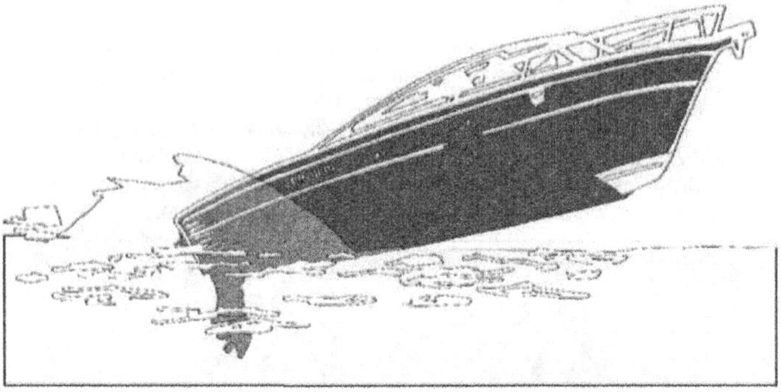
EXCESSIVE POWER APPLIED CAUSES STERN TO SQUAT. LARGE STERN WAVE AND RAISED BOW RESULT. COXSWAIN LOSES FORWARD VISIBILITY UNTIL CRAFT ATTAINS PLANING MODE.

Figure 10-13
Pronounced Squat on Acceleration

B.7. Direction Control

Small amounts of helm should be used to offset any propeller side force or the effects of winds and seas. Compass course should always be noted and corrected frequently to stay on course. It is important to develop a practiced eye and steer on a geographic point or range such as a point between buoys. Small, early helm corrections should be applied to stay on course, rather than large corrections after becoming well off course. Oversteering, leaving a snake-like path, should be avoided. At low speeds, helm correction will be more frequent and require more rudder than at higher speeds.

B.8. Planing

For planing or semi-displacement hulls, the boat will gradually gain speed until planing. If fitted with trim control (including trim tabs on inboard boats), slight, bow-down trim may lessen the amount of time needed to get on plane or "on step."

B.9. Appropriate Speed

Running at full speed all of the time should be avoided. This wastes fuel and can cause excessive wear on the boat and crew. Many vessels will not exceed or will only marginally exceed a given speed, regardless of the power applied. At some point, the only effect of applying additional throttle is increased fuel consumption with no speed increase. Finding a speed that offers a comfortable ride as well as allows mission completion is advised.

B.9.a. Margin of Power

A margin of power should always be left available for emergencies. The best speed for the vessel should be determined. A good normal operating limit for semi-displacement vessels is usually 80 percent maximum power, allowing the remaining 20 percent for emergency use.

B.9.b. Safe Speed

A boat at high speed has a large amount of force. With an untrained operator, this force can be dangerous. The following different factors should be considered to determine safe speed.

- High seas: Slow down as winds and seas increase; the boat will handle more easily. Pounding or becoming airborne fatigues the hull and could injure the crew or cause them chronic skeletal problems. If it takes tremendous effort just to hang on, the crew will be spent and not able to perform their jobs. Minimize taking spray and water on deck.

NOTE

Find the most comfortable, secure location for the entire crew. For many vessels, this means in the immediate vicinity of the helm.

WARNING

Being "on plane" will not allow crossing a shoal that would ground the vessel in the displacement mode. At high planing speed, the stern will squat as it gets in shallow water, possibly grounding at a very damaging speed.

- Traffic density: Do not use high speed in high traffic density areas. A safe speed allows response to developing situations and minimizes risk of collision, not only with the nearest approaching vessel, but with others around it.
- Visibility: If conditions make it difficult to see, slow down. Fog, rain, and snow are obvious limits to visibility, but there are others. Geographic features and obstructions (river bends, piers, bridges and causeways), along with heavy vessel traffic, can limit the view of "the big picture." Darkness or steering directly into the sun lessens ability to see objects or judge distances. Prevent spray on the windscreen (particularly salt spray or freezing spray) as much as possible and clean it regularly. Spray build-up on the windscreen is particularly hazardous in darkness or in glare.
- Shoal waters: In shallow water, the bottom has an effect on the movement of the vessel. Slow down in shallow water. In extremely shallow water, the vessel's stern tends to "squat" and actually moves closer to the bottom.

CAUTION !

Do not overcompensate for bank cushion and bank suction. Too much helm in the direction of the bank could cause the bow to veer into the bank. Then, a subsequent large helm movement to turn the bow away from the bank may cause the stern to swing into the bank.

B.10. Bank Cushion and Bank Suction

In extremely narrow channels, a vessel moving through the water will cause the "wedge" of water between the bow and the nearer bank to build up higher than on the other side. This bank cushion tends to push the bow away from the edge of the channel.

As the stern moves along, screw suction and the movement of water to "fill-in" where the boat was creates bank suction. This causes the stern to move towards the bank. The combined effect of momentary bank cushion and bank suction may cause a sudden shear toward the opposite bank. Bank cushion and bank suction are strongest when the bank of a channel is steep. They are weakest when the edge of the channel shoals gradually and extends in a large shallow area. When possible, a trainee should stay exactly in the center of an extremely narrow channel to avoid these forces. (see **Figure 10-14**) Slower speed also reduces the amount of cushion and suction. Some rudder offset towards the closer bank will help to avoid continuous cushion and suction effects by.

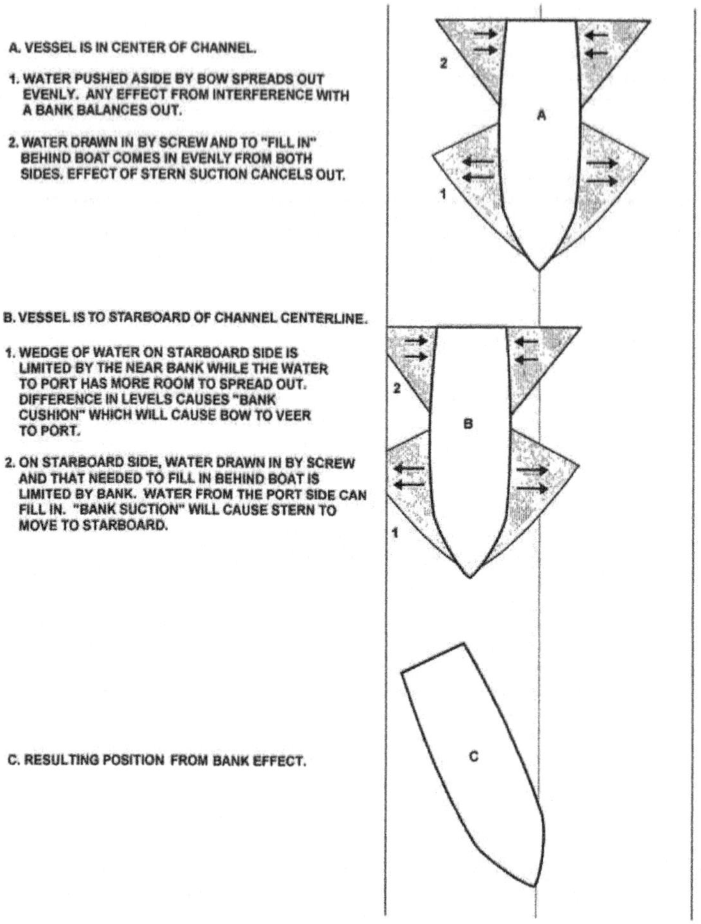
A. VESSEL IS IN CENTER OF CHANNEL.
1. WATER PUSHED ASIDE BY BOW SPREADS OUT EVENLY. ANY EFFECT FROM INTERFERENCE WITH A BANK BALANCES OUT.
2. WATER DRAWN IN BY SCREW AND TO "FILL IN" BEHIND BOAT COMES IN EVENLY FROM BOTH SIDES. EFFECT OF STERN SUCTION CANCELS OUT.
B. VESSEL IS TO STARBOARD OF CHANNEL CENTERLINE.
1. WEDGE OF WATER ON STARBOARD SIDE IS LIMITED BY THE NEAR BANK WHILE THE WATER TO PORT HAS MORE ROOM TO SPREAD OUT. DIFFERENCE IN LEVELS CAUSES "BANK CUSHION" WHICH WILL CAUSE BOW TO VEER TO PORT.
2. ON STARBOARD SIDE, WATER DRAWN IN BY SCREW AND THAT NEEDED TO FILL IN BEHIND BOAT IS LIMITED BY BANK. WATER FROM THE PORT SIDE CAN FILL IN. "BANK SUCTION" WILL CAUSE STERN TO MOVE TO STARBOARD.
C. RESULTING POSITION FROM BANK EFFECT.
A
B
C
1
2

Figure 10-14
Bank Cushion and Bank Suction

B.11. Bow Cushion and Stern Suction

When meeting another vessel close aboard, bow cushion and stern suction occur between the vessels much the same as bank cushion and suction. Helm corrections should be used to compensate. As both vessels move through the water, the combined effect is greater than what a single vessel encounters from bank interaction. Caution should be used so the bow does not veer too far from the intended track and the stern swings into the path of the other vessel.

A port-to-port meeting situation is assumed. Before vessels are bow-to-bow, a small amount of right rudder should be used to ensure the bow is clear. The bow cushion will increase separation. As the vessels near bow-to-beam, using left rudder will enable the vessel to keep away from the right-hand bank and to stay parallel to the channel. When the vessels are bow-to-quarter, the bow cushion will be offset by the stern suction, and bank cushion may need to be offset by some right rudder. Finally, as the vessels are quarter-to-quarter, stern suction will predominate, and will require left rudder to keep the sterns apart.

NOTE

The following bow cushion and stern suction considerations apply when meeting another vessel in a narrow channel and when operating near a bank:

- The deeper the vessel's draft, the greater the cushion and suction effect, particularly if draft approaches water depth.
- The closer to a bank or another vessel, the greater the cushion and suction.
- In very narrow waterways, slow down to decrease cushion and suction effects, but not to the point of losing adequate steerage.

When meeting another vessel in a narrow channel, the bow cushion and stern suction effects caused by the other vessel should be balanced with the bank cushion and suction effects due to the channel.

WARNING

While maneuvering, keep the crew informed, especially if rapidly accelerating, turning or slowing. A quick warning shout could prevent injury.

B.12. Wake Awareness

As a vessel proceeds, a combination of bow and stern waves move outward at an angle to the vessel track. The wake height and speed depend on vessel speed and hull type. Relatively large, semi-displacement hulls, proceeding at cruising speed, cause some of the largest wakes. Some lighter craft actually make less wake at top speed in the planing mode rather than at a slower speed. Displacement craft make the largest wake at hull speed. The coxswain should determine how to make the vessel leave the least wake; it might require slowing appreciably.

All vessels are responsible for their wake and any injury or damage it might cause. Only an unaware coxswain trails a large wake through a mooring area or shallows, tossing vessels and straining moorings. "Get-home-itis" and a false sense of urgency are two reasons coxswains forget to watch their wake. A large, unnecessary wake, particularly in enclosed waters or near other smaller vessels, ruins the credibility of a professional image.

Turning the Boat with the Helm

B.13. Description

To move in a straight line, small, frequent, momentary helm inputs adjust the position of the stern and bow to head in the desired direction. To intentionally change the vessel heading, larger, more sustained helm movement should be used.

B.14. Pivot Point

As noted earlier, the direction of the bow may be changed by moving the stern in the opposite direction. As the stern swings a certain angle, the bow swings the same angle. Depending on the fore and aft position of the pivot point, the stern could swing through a larger distance than the bow, at the same angle. When a hull moves forward through the water, the effective pivot point moves forward. The higher the forward speed, the farther the pivot point moves forward.

B.15. Propulsion Type and Turning

Because outboards, stern drives, and waterjets use propulsion thrust for directional control, they can make a much tighter turn (using helm alone) with a given hull shape than if the same hull had shaft, propeller, and rudder. With extended outboard mounting brackets, the directed, lower-unit thrust is farthest aft of the pivot point compared to the other configurations. Some brackets move the thrust three to four feet aft of the hull. The location aft of the pivot point, along with the amount of directed thrust determines how much the stern will kick away from the direction of the turn. With directed thrust, the stern will usually skid outward more than with shaft, propeller and rudder, making the bow describe a very tight arc. (see **Figure 10-15**)

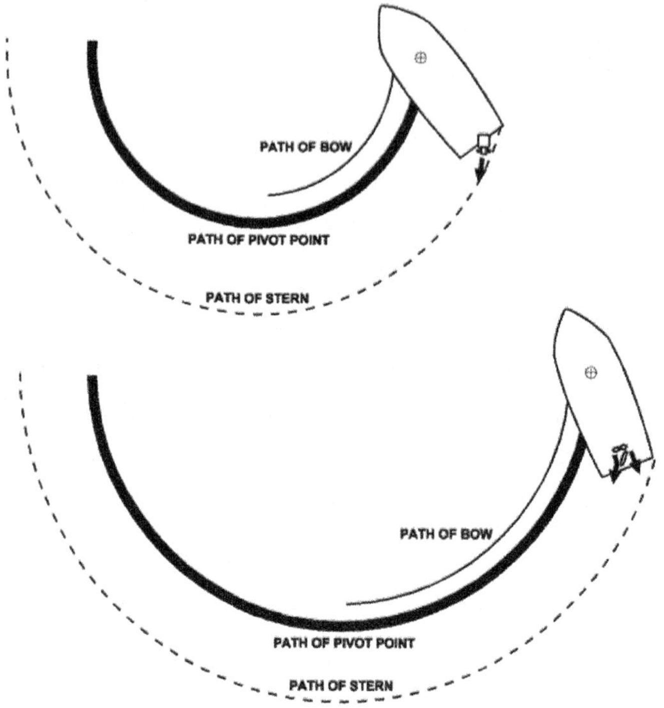

Figure 10-15
Pivot Point, Skid, Kick, Inboard vs. Outboard

B.16. Vessel's Turning Characteristics

When proceeding on a steady heading, putting the helm over to one side or the other, begins to turn the boat. Up to the time the boat turns through 90°, the boat has continued to advance in the original direction. By the time the boat has turned through 90°, it is well off to the side of the original track. This distance is transfer. As the boat continues through 180°, its path has defined its tactical diameter. If the vessel holds the turn through 360°, the distance it takes to reach the point where it first put the helm is referred to as its final diameter. For a particular vessel, these values vary for speed and rudder angle. (see **Figure 10-16**)

Developing a working knowledge of the vessel's turning characteristics will enable decision-making such as whether to make a particular maneuver in a certain space solely with the helm or whether other maneuvering tactics are needed. Learning when to ease the helm will help to prevent oversteering a course.

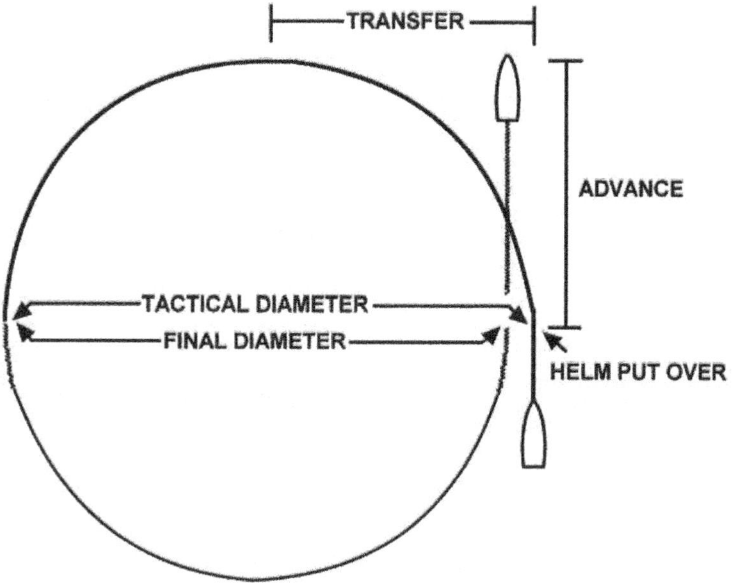

Figure 10-16
Turning Characteristics

WARNING

With light-displacement, high-powered craft, maximum helm at high speed will quickly stop a boat's progress in the original direction of movement. Though such a turning action is effective to avoid contact with an immediate hazard, the violent motion could eject unsuspecting crewmembers. Use this technique only as an emergency maneuver. Do not use this maneuver to demonstrate the boat's capability.

B.17. Loss of Speed

Some planing hulls and most semi-displacement craft will slow appreciably when turning at high speeds. As the boat heels into a turn, the hull provides less buoyancy to keep the vessel on plane at a given speed. Also, as the aft part of the hull skids across the water while in a heel, it presents a flat shape in the original direction of movement and pushes water outward. The bottom becomes a braking surface.

B.18. Making Course Changes and Turns in Channels

Bank suction, bank cushion (see B.10 above), and currents will all affect a boat navigating a sharp bend in a narrow channel. Where natural waterways have bends or turns, the water is always deepest and the current is always strongest on the outside of the bend. This is true for 15° jogs in a tidal estuary and for the "s" shaped meanders on the Mississippi River. This happens because the water flow has a great degree of momentum and resists having its direction changed. As it strikes the outside of the bank, it erodes the earth and carries the particles with it. The particles fall out farther downstream in areas of less current (the inside of a turn or bend) and cause shoaling. In some turns or bends, there may be circular currents (eddies) in either the deep outside of the bend or the shallow inside. Back currents also sometimes occur near eddies on the inside of the bend. When eddies or back currents occur, those near the shallows are much weaker than eddies or main current flow at the outside of the bend.

Because bank cushion and suction are strongest when the bank of a channel is steep and weakest when the edge of the channel shoals gradually, bank effect is stronger on the outside of bends or turns. The coxswain should be aware of the mix of current and bank effect and use these forces to the fullest extent.

B.18.a. Countering a Head Current Through a Bend

The effect of a head current is minimized by steering along the inside quarter of the channel, making sure to avoid shoaling. If the bow gets into the area of greater current, it may begin to sheer towards the outside of the bend. It can be countered through helm towards the inside of the bend and by getting the stern directly down current from the bow. The vessel can then be gradually worked back to the inside quarter of the channel.

If the starting point is the outside of the bend, the full force of the current will be encountered. Bank cushion should keep the bow from the outside edge, but the stern is limited in its movement by bank suction. Initial helm towards the inside of the turn may allow the current to cause the bow to rapidly sheer away from the outside, but this is immediately offset with power and helm to keep the bow pointed upstream. Gradual helm with constant power should be used to get out of the main force of the current, and work across to the inside quarter of the channel.

B.18.b. Navigating a Turn with a Following Current

The turn on a course should be approached just to the outside of the middle of the channel. This will avoid the strongest currents at the outside edge while still getting a reasonable push. While turning, the strongest current will accentuate the swing of the stern quarter to the outside of the channel. Because of this, and because the following current tends to carry the boat toward the outside, the turn should begin early in the bend. The amount of sideways movement or if the boat tends to "crab" in the channel should be constantly monitored. If the boat starts to move too close to the outside of a bend, more helm and power should be constantly monitored to maneuver the boat back into the middle. Once through the turn, the vessel can be gradually worked back to the inside quarter of the channel.

- If the boat stays too far to the outside of the bend, timing the turn is difficult. Turning too early with stern suction on one quarter with the strongest current on the other quarter may cause an extreme veer to the inside of the turn. Any bow cushion will accentuate the sheer. Turning too late with stern suction and the quartering current could cause grounding.
- If trying to hug the inside of the turn, both current and bank effect will be lessened. Use a small amount of rudder toward the inside bank to enter the turn. As the channel begins to bend, use less rudder while the boat starts to move from the inside bank. Use caution as the current under the quarter affects the stern, giving it an increase in sheer towards the inside bank. Slack water or an eddy down current on the inside will increase this sheer while bow cushion may not be enough to prevent grounding.

Stopping the Boat

B.19. Description

Pulling back the throttle to *neutral* will cause the vessel to begin to lose forward motion. For a heavy-displacement vessel, once propulsion is stopped, the vessel will continue to move forward for some distance. The vessel carries its momentum without propulsion. For a semi-displacement hull or planing hull, retarding the throttle and reduce power will cause the boat to quickly come off plane. As the vessel reverts to displacement mode, the resistance of the hull going through the water instead of on top of the water slows the boat. The vessel still carries some way, but at only a fraction of the original speed. The coxswain should experiment with the vessel and see how rapidly the boat slows after going from cruising speed to *neutral* throttle. Knowing the distance the vessel will travel when stopping (also known as head reach) from different speeds is very important when maneuvering.

WARNING

> The crash stop is an emergency maneuver. It may damage the drive train and stall the engine(s). In most cases, with high levels of crew professionalism, skill and situational awareness, it is not necessary.

B.20. Using Astern Propulsion to Stop the Vessel

Slowing the vessel's forward movement is not always enough. In an emergency situation, a complete and quick stop to dead-in-the-water or crash stop may be required. This is done by applying astern propulsion while still making forward way. The first step is to slow the vessel by retarding throttle. After the vessel begins to lose way, astern propulsion should be applied firmly and forcefully. Power must be higher than that available at clutch speed to prevent engine stall. On a single-screw vessel, the stern will want to swing to port. After all way is off, the throttle should be placed in *neutral*.

At low forward speeds, astern propulsion is frequently used to maneuver, both to check forward way and to gain sternway.

With a waterjet, reverse thrust is immediate. There is no marine gear or drive unit that requires the shaft and propeller to change rotation directions. The clamshell or bucket-shaped deflector plate drops down and redirects thrust forward. As with other drives, enough astern engine power should be used to overcome potential engine stall.

Though many vessels are tested and capable of immediately going from full speed ahead to full reverse throttle, this crash stop technique is extremely harsh on the drive train and may cause engine stall. Though much of the power goes to propeller cavitation, this technique can be effective in an emergency.

WARNING

> As with the crash stop, a full-helm, high-speed stop is an emergency maneuver. The violent motion could eject crewmembers. Do not use this maneuver in choppy waters as a chine could "trip" and cause the vessel to snap-roll and capsize.

B.21. Using Full Helm to Stop Forward Way

As noted above, with light-displacement, high-powered craft, maximum helm at high speed will quickly stop a boat's progress in the original direction of movement. To fully stop, the throttle should be placed down to *neutral* after entering the skid. If done properly, no astern propulsion is required.

NOTE

> With a jet drive, no directional control will be available without thrust. The boat must be in a skid before reducing power. If thrust is reduced before trying to turn, the boat will slow on the original heading.

Backing the Vessel

CAUTION !

Do not back in a way that allows water to ship over the transom. Be careful with boats of very low freeboard aft. Outboard powered vessels, with low cut-out for motor mounting and a large portion of weight aft are susceptible to shipping water while backing, particularly in a chop. If shipped water does not immediately drain, it jeopardizes stability.

CAUTION !

Most inboard engines exhaust through the transom. Outboard motors exhaust astern. Backing could subject the crew and cabin spaces to a large amount of exhaust fumes. Limit exposure to exhaust fumes. If training, frequently change vessel aspect to the wind to clear fumes. After backing, ventilate interior spaces.

B.22. Description

Control while making sternway is essential. Because vessels are designed to go forward, many vessels do not easily back in a straight line. Due to higher freeboard and superstructure forward (increased sail area), many vessels back into the wind. Knowledge of how environmental forces affect a boat is critical when backing.

Besides watching where the stern goes, the coxswain should keep track of the bow. The stern will move one direction and the bow the other direction around the pivot point. As a vessel develops sternway, the apparent pivot point moves aft and the bow may swing through a greater distance. Firm control of the helm should be maintained to prevent the rudder or drive from swinging to a hard-over angle.

B.23. Screw and Rudder

While backing, the rudders are in the weaker, less concentrated screw suction current, and most steering control comes from flow across the rudder due to sternway.

B.23.a. Single-Engine Vessels

Propeller side force presents a major obstacle to backing in the direction desired. The rudder does not have much effect until sternway occurs, and even then, many boats will back into the wind despite a best effort to do otherwise. If backing to the wind, the coxswain should know at what wind speed the boat will back into the wind without backing to port.

- Before starting to back, apply right full rudder to get any advantage available.
- A quick burst of power astern will cause the stern to swing to port, but use it to get the boat moving.
- Once moving, reduce power somewhat to reduce propeller side force and steer with the rudder. As sternway increases, less rudder will be needed to maintain a straight track astern.
- If more sternway is needed to improve steerage, increase power gradually. A strong burst astern will quickly swing the stern to port.
- If stern swing to port cannot be controlled by the rudder alone, use a burst of power ahead for propeller side force to swing the stern to starboard. Do not apply so much power as to stop sternway or to set up a screw discharge current that would cause the stern to swing farther to port. (As the vessel backs, it uses sternway water flow across the rudder to steer).
- If this fails, use a larger burst of power ahead, with helm to port. Sternway will probably stop, but propeller side force and discharge current across the shifted rudder will move the stern to starboard. Now try backing, again.

B.23.b. Twin-Engine Vessels

Both engines should be backed evenly to offset propeller side force. Using asymmetric power (one engine at higher RPM than the other) will help steer the stern. Asymmetric power will also give unequal propeller side force that will help steer.

- Apply astern power evenly, keeping rudders amidships.
- If the stern tends to one side, first try to control direction with slight helm adjustment. If not effective, either increase backing power on the side toward the direction of veer or decrease power on the opposite side.

B.24. Stern Drives and Outboards

The coxswain shall use the directed thrust to pull the stern to one side or the other. As the power is applied aft of the transom he/she should, use care to keep the bow from falling off course due to winds, avoiding cavitation that can easily occur when backing with a lower unit. Propeller side force is present, but is offset through helm. A lower unit that is not providing thrust is not efficient when trying to steer while backing. It is better to keep steady, slow RPMs than to vary between high power and *neutral.*

B.24.a. Single-Outboard/ Outdrive

For single-outboard/outdrive, propeller side force is offset by turning the helm slightly to the right. Astern power is then applied gradually, but care should be taken not to cause propeller cavitation.

B.24.b. Twin-Outboard/ Outdrive

If astern power is matched, propeller side forces will cancel. As with twin inboards, offsetting any stern swing with helm should be attempted before using asymmetric power.

If less thrust than that provided by both drives at clutch speed is needed, one motor or engine should be used. This will keep speed low but will keep thrust available for steering, rather than shifting one or both engines from *reverse* to *neutral*. If using one unit, compensate with helm for propeller side force and the increased, off-centered drag caused by the other lower unit.

B.25. Waterjets

There is no propeller side force and thrust is directed as with an outboard. Going from *forward* to *reverse* thrust has no marine gear or drive train to slow things. Thrust is simply redirected with the "bucket." Unless thrust is applied and being directed, there is no directional control at all. The power must be on and applied to steer either *forward* or in *reverse*.

Bursts of power astern when backing should be avoided. Bursts of power when making astern thrust will excessively aerate the waterjet intake flow ahead of the transom.

Using Asymmetric or Opposed Propulsion (Twin-Screw Theory)

B.26. Description

Asymmetric propulsion while backing was covered in previous paragraphs. The techniques presented here are additional methods of maneuvering that capitalize on twin-engine vessel capability to differ the amount or direction of thrust produced by the two engines. Any difference in thrust affects the boat's heading. The amount of this difference can vary from that needed to hold a course at cruising speed to turning a boat 360° in its own length by opposing propulsion (splitting throttles). The concept of asymmetric or opposed propulsion can be likened to "twisting" the boat, but the forces and fundamentals discussed earlier still apply and affect vessel response. Pivot point, propeller side force, and turning characteristics remain important. Because the drives are offset from vessel centerline on a twin-engine vessel, they apply a turning moment to the hull. Twin outboard motors on a bracket apply this twist aft of the hull (and well aft of the hull pivot point), while twin inboards apply most of this twist to the hull at the first thrust-bearing member of the drive train (usually the reduction gear or v-drive, much closer to the pivot point). With inboards, propeller side force is transferred through a strut and stern tube to the hull.

Up to a point, the greater the difference in RPMs, the greater the effect on the change in heading. Above that point, specific for each boat, type of propulsion, sea conditions and operating speed, cavitation or aeration will occur, and propulsion efficiency will decrease, at least on one drive.

NOTE As with all boat handling techniques, learn these first in calm weather, in open water, and at low speeds.

B.27. Holding a Course

Depending on a vessel's topside profile, wind conditions might make the bow continually fall off to leeward. Though the helmsman can compensate for this by steering with constant pressure to hold desired course, a less taxing way is to adjust the throttles so the leeward engine turns at more RPMs than the windward engine. The difference in RPMs can be fine-tuned until pressure is off the helm.

B.28. Changing Vessel Heading

The following techniques cause a faster change in heading by increasing both skid and kick, reducing advance and transfer, and if the heading change is held long enough, the overall tactical diameter.

B.28.a. Rotating about the Pivot Point

Rotating about the pivot point is a low-speed maneuver. It is important because situations will occur when the boat's heading needs to be changed (to the weather or another vessel) or the bow or stern moved in a limited area. The engines should be opposed to turn in an extremely tight space. This maneuver is first performed at *clutch* speed in calm conditions to learn how the vessel reacts and what type of arcs the bow and stern describe. With no way on, there is no initial advance and transfer, so depending on the boat; this maneuver might yield a tactical diameter of zero if the heading is changed 360° (rotating the vessel in its own length).

The forces involved should be considered. Vessels with propellers will develop side force from both drives during this maneuver. The rudder, where equipped, can use screw discharge current from the ahead engine to help pivot the stern. Because boats operate more efficiently ahead, some headway may develop.

B.28.a.1. Helm Amidships

With helm amidships, perform the following procedures:

Step	Procedure
1	At dead-in-the-water and throttles in *neutral*, simultaneously *clutch ahead* with starboard engine, and *clutch astern* with port engine (keep both engine RPMs the same, though in opposite direction).
2	Note the arcs described by bow and stern as the vessel swings through 360° to determine vessel pivot point.
3	If vessel moved forward (along its centerline) during the rotation, slightly increase astern RPM to compensate.
4	Now, simultaneously shift throttles so port is *clutch ahead* and starboard is *clutch astern*; note how long it takes to stop and reverse direction of swing.
5	Again, check bow and stern arcs as vessel swings through 360°, and then stop the swing.

B.28.a.2. Helm Over Hard-to-Port

Put the helm over hard-to-port by performing the following procedures:

Step	Procedure
1	Perform the same procedures as with helm amidships. When stopping and reversing direction of swing, shift the helm to starboard.
2	In addition to the observations made with helm amidships, note whether the sizes of the arcs were smaller (due to directed thrust by lower unit or rudder).

CAUTION ! All crewmembers must pay close attention to throttle changes and vessel movements. Firmly hold onto the vessel during these maneuvers.

B.28.a.3. Developing Skills

With the basic skill in hand, practice controlling the amount of swing by performing the following procedures:

Step	Procedure
1	Use the compass and gradually limit the degree of rotation down to 30° each side of the original heading.
2	Increase amount of throttle applied.
3	Note the effect on vessel movement especially as to the rate of swing.
4	Develop boat handling knowledge and skills to know the degree of throttle splitting or asymmetric thrust for best effect in any situation. Maneuvering near the face of a breaking wave may require opposing engines at one-third or more of their available RPM, while maneuvering near the pier might only require a short, small burst on one engine to bring the bow through the wind.

NOTE

Experiment with the vessel.

- Though rudder use should help increase the rate of swing, the increase in turn rate might not be worth the workload increase (stop-to-stop helm use). Due to rudder swing rate, full helm use may not be as effective as leaving the helm centered.
- At some level of power for each vessel and drive train arrangement, cavitation will occur with split throttles. Know at what throttle settings cavitation occurs. More power will not increase turning ability and might cause temporary loss of maneuverability until cavitation subsides. In critical situations, loss of effective power could leave a vessel vulnerable.

B.28.b. Reducing Tactical Diameter at Speed

An emergency maneuver at cruising speed may require a turn with reduced tactical diameter.

B.28.b.1. Turn and Drag Propeller

An effective technique for a twin-propeller boat is to have one propeller act as a brake. This creates drag on the side with that propeller and reduces the turning diameter.

Step	Procedure
1	Put helm hard over.
2	Bring throttle on the engine in the direction of the turn to *clutch ahead.*

NOTE

Do not put throttle to *neutral* position. In *neutral*, the propeller will "free-wheel" and rotate without any resistance. Keeping the engine in *clutch ahead* will keep the propeller from spinning freely and start "braking" the vessel on the inboard side.

WARNING

As with the crash stop, this maneuver is extremely hard on the engine and drive train. The backing engine's power must be higher than that available at clutch speed to prevent engine stall.

B.28.b.2. Turn and Split Throttles

This practice is also more effective with shaft, propeller, and rudder arrangement than with directed thrust drives. One propeller will still be providing forward thrust while the other will be backing. As with opposing thrust in low speed maneuvering, propeller side force is multiplied. Cavitation will be pronounced on the backing screw, but the vessel's forward motion keeps advancing this screw into relatively undisturbed (or non-aerated) water.

Step	Procedure
1	Put helm hard over.
2	Bring throttle on the engine in the direction of the turn firmly to and through *neutral*, then past the *clutch astern position*, and gradually increase astern RPM.

Performing Single-Screw Compound Maneuvering (Single-Screw Theory)

B.29. Description

Basic maneuvering techniques should be applied in combination with a single propeller at low speed to further boat handling skills. Practice these maneuvers in calm, no-current situations before learning to overcome environmental forces.

A single-screw vessel never has the ability to use asymmetric or opposed propulsion, and its coxswain must develop boat handling skills with this in mind. The operator of a twin-engine vessel could easily become limited to use of one drive due to engine failure or fouling a screw, and must also become a proficient, single-screw boat handler.

For the discussion here, the case of a single-engine propeller vessel with right-hand turning screw is used. When maneuvering a twin-engine vessel on one drive, the coxswain must account for the propeller rotation and side force for the particular drive used (normally starboard: right-hand turning, port: left-hand turning), and the offset of the drive from centerline.

B.30. Back and Fill (Casting)

The back and fill technique, also known as casting, provides a method to turn a vessel in little more than its own length. At some point, anyone who operates a single-screw vessel will need to rely on these concepts when they operate a boat, particularly in close-quarters maneuvering. To back and fill, the coxswain should rely on the tendency of a vessel to back to port, and then use the rudder to direct thrust when powering ahead to starboard. The coxswain should also decide the radius of the circle in which to keep the vessel (at most, 25 to 35 percent larger than the vessel's overall length), and the intended change in direction (usually no more than 180°) before starting. For initial training, the vessel should be turned through at least 360°.

From dead-in-the-water position, perform the following procedures to back and fill:

Step	Procedure
1	Put helm at right full and momentarily throttle ahead, being careful not to make much headway. (Rudder directs screw discharge current thrust to starboard, more than offsetting propeller side force and moves stern to port).
2	Before gaining much headway, quickly throttle astern and shift helm to left full. (With throttle astern, side force is much stronger than screw suction, rudder to port takes advantage of any sternway).
3	Once sternway begins, simultaneously shift helm to full right and throttle ahead as in step 1.
4	Repeat procedures until vessel has come to desired heading, then put helm amidships and apply appropriate propulsion.

NOTE

- A firm grasp of the vessel's maneuvering characteristics is necessary to know whether to back and fill rather than just maneuver at full rudder.
- The amount of steps used will depend on size of the turning area and the desired change in heading. The smaller the area, the more backing and filling required.
- Winds will play a factor in casting. If the vessel's bow is easily blown off course, the vessel probably has a tendency to back into the wind. Set up the maneuver (including direction of turn) to take advantage of this in getting the bow to change direction. Strong winds will offset both propeller side force and any rudder effect.
- A quick helm hand is a prerequisite for casting with an outboard or stern drive. To get full advantage of the lower unit's directed thrust, fully shift the helm before applying propulsion. With helm at left full, the propeller side force when backing will have an element that tries to move the stern "forward" around the pivot point.

Section C. Maneuvering Near Other Objects

Introduction

This section applies basic maneuvering principles to control a vessel with respect to other objects. Later sections will cover mooring, unmooring, and coming alongside other vessels or objects.

This section covers maneuvering your vessel near, but not next to, another object.

C.1. Station Keeping

Coxswains must learn to manage the effects of environmental forces by using power and helm to maintain their position next to an object. Station keeping is defined as maintaining distance, position and aspect to or from an object. With twin propulsion, coxswains need to develop the skills required to maintain any aspect to an object during most conditions. Though many single-drive boats are thought to be less maneuverable, coxswains should fully develop single-drive station keeping skills should the need arise. Station keeping should be practiced during various levels of wind, seas, and current.

NOTE

All coxswains of twin-drive vessels must frequently train for single-drive operation. This includes station keeping.

C.1.a. Maneuvering Zone

Each situation requires a safe maneuvering zone to reach an optimal position near the object so an evolution can safely occur and can be done effectively (i.e., equipment transfer, object recovery, surveillance, etc.)

Before station keeping perform the following procedures to determine a safe and effective maneuvering zone:

CAUTION ! When station keeping, always have a safe escape route to get clear of the object or any hazard. While station keeping, ensure the escape route stays clear. This may require changing position to establish a new escape route.

Step	Procedure
1	Evaluate environmental conditions and how they affect the situation.
2	Determine if obstructions on the object or in and above the water limit your safe maneuvering zone.
3	Account for these obstructions and keep the environmental forces in mind.
4	Avoid vessel outriggers, hull protrusions, loose pier camels, broken pilings, ice guards, shoals, low overhead cables, bridge spans, and rocks or other submerged obstructions.
5	Define the maneuvering zone by distance, position, and aspect. Put limits on each element and maneuver to stay within those limits.

C.1.b Distance

The coxswain should station keep close enough to complete a mission or evolution, yet far enough to prevent collision or allision. Minimum distance to the object will probably vary around the object or along its length. Environmental conditions and boat maneuverability play a major role in determining distance. The coxswain should perform the following procedures:

Step	Procedure
1	Use a practiced eye and ranging techniques to keep distance.
2	When able, use identifiable keys, such as a boat length. Unless well practiced, each crewmember will probably differ in how they view 25 feet or 25 yards.
3	Use knowledge of the vessel. If it has a twelve-foot beam at the transom, transpose that measurement to the gap between the boat and an object.
4	If the coxswain station does not allow a clear view of the object, use points on the vessel (windscreen brackets, antennae, or fittings) to set up range-keeping clues.
5	Position the angle from the object to the vessel (or the reciprocal). To keep station on another vessel, particularly one that is disabled and adrift, determine the angle from the other vessel's centerline; on a moored or fixed object, use a geographic or compass bearing.
6	Aspect: the relative angle the vessel makes to the other object (bow, beam, quarter, etc.). It may be necessary to keep the object at a certain aspect to pass equipment or a towline, or to maintain surveillance or to train a fire hose.

C.1.c. Differences in Objects

Differences in objects determine the maneuvering situation. The coxswain should become fully capable of station keeping in a variety of situations with both different types of objects and different environmental conditions.

C.1.c.1. Free-Drifting Object

Object type and size ranges from small items floating in the water to other vessels. No two items will drift at the same speed through the water. Free-drifting objects will present a different drift rate from the vessel. The coxswain should develop station keeping techniques by first comparing your drift rate to the object, and then overcoming the difference.

While another vessel maintains a steady course at low speed, the coxswain should pace his/her vessel to the other vessel and then maneuver around it. Pacing movement to the other vessel is critical before safely going alongside. The following are procedures for station keeping on a free-drifting object:

Drift Rate	Procedure
No Leeway	Practice with a floating (but ballasted) item that does not drift with the wind. A weighted mannequin with PFD or weighted duffel bag with a float in one end will work. The object's drift will be limited to the surface current, while vessel will respond to currents and winds. This type of object simulates a person-in-the-water.
Leeway	Wind-drift is the main consideration here. Practice with paired fenders, a partially filled 6-gallon bucket or a small skiff. Though wind will have a measurable effect on object drift, current will play little role. As above, the vessel will be subject to both wind and current.
Other Vessel	Become proficient at station keeping on a variety of vessel types. Different vessels react differently to environmental forces. Learn how other vessels drift, see how other vessels lie to the wind, and then maneuver the vessel to an optimal position for observation, coming alongside or passing a tow rig.

C.1.c.2. Anchored Object

Station keeping on an anchored object limits much of the object's movement due to wind and current, but the object will often surge and swing. A vessel will react freely to the wind and current. The object will ride with its moored end into the strongest environmental force affecting it, while the combination of forces on a vessel may cause it to take a different aspect.

Station keeping on an anchored object helps determine where to and where not to maneuver. Upstream of a buoy, strong current could easily carry the vessel. On the other hand, the only safe approach to a disabled vessel, anchored off a lee shore, may be from dead-to-weather. The following are procedures for station keeping on an anchored object:

Object	Procedure
Buoy or Float	In general, approach a moored buoy or float from down current or downwind, bow to the object. If servicing a floating aid to navigation, the approach may require centering the stern on the buoy. To train, keep station at various distances and angles to an object. Pick something totally surrounded by safe water. Next, maneuver up current or upwind.
A Vessel at Anchor	Surveillance, personnel or equipment transfer, or fire fighting may require station keeping on an anchored vessel. Develop skills to keep station at all distances and angles. Different sizes and types of vessels will ride their anchors differently. Deep draft or a large underbody will make a vessel ride with the current, while high freeboard and superstructure may make the vessel tend downwind. Evaluate the combination of forces while station keeping.
Note vessel interaction.	If close aboard and upwind, a small, light vessel may ride the anchor differently than if another vessel were not there. A larger vessel may affect the forces of a smaller vessel by making a lee. Watch a vessel's motions while it "rides" anchor. Some vessels don't "steady out," but veer back and forth. Observe and plan accordingly.
Fixed Object	Keep station on a pier, seawall, or breakwater. View this as a step before mooring. Also, these skills may be necessary to transfer someone to a fixed aids to navigation or to remove a person stranded on rocks. Station keeping on fixed objects makes the coxswain deal with forces that affect him/her and not the object. Often, the fixed object affects the environmental forces by funneling, blocking, or changing direction of the current or wind.

C.2. Maneuvering

Station keeping will usually require frequent to near-continuous applications of power and helm to stay in the safe maneuvering zone. While station keeping and trying to stay within the maneuvering zone limits, adjusting for one of the parameters (distance, position, aspect) will almost always involve a change to one or both of the other two. While using power and helm to compensate for and to overcome wind and current, the wind and current should be used to the fullest extent.

C.2.a. Stem the Forces

To stem the forces means to keep the current or wind directly on the bow or stern and hold position by setting boat speed to equally oppose the speed of drift.

C.2.b. Crab the Boat Sideways

To crab the boat sideways, environmental forces should be used to move the boat at a right angle to the forces. The coxswain should put the bow at a shallow angle (20° to 30°) to the prevailing force and use ahead propulsion and helm to keep from getting set backward, while staying at the shallow angle to the prevailing environmental force.

C.2.e. Open and Close

Make a vessel "open" and "close" the distance on the object at various angles, both to leeward and to weather. With an object on the bow or stern, directly up-drift or down-drift from you, opening and closing requires only to compensate for the fore and aft drift rate and to maintain a steady heading. A combination of control and environmental forces should be used:

- Side force.
- Ahead and astern thrust.
- Rudder force.
- Leeway.
- Current.
- Drift.

The more difficult scenario is opening or closing distance abeam.

Section D. Maneuvering to or from a Dock

Introduction

The most challenging and probably most frequent maneuvering encountered is that associated with getting in and out of slips, dock areas, piers, boat basins or marinas.

D.1. General Considerations

When maneuvering to or from a dock, the coxswain should keep the following points in mind and brief the crew on procedures to be used especially when mooring at a new location.

Step	Procedure
1	Check the conditions before maneuvering. Always take advantage of wind and current when docking or mooring. To maintain best control, approach against the wind and current and moor on the leeward side of a mooring when possible. Chances are that when mooring, conditions are not the same as when getting underway.
2	Rig and lead mooring lines and fenders well before the approach. Have everything ready on deck before the coxswain must concentrate and maneuver to the dock. Though common practice is to leave mooring lines attached to the home pier, always have a spare mooring line and moveable fender on the boat and at the ready while approaching any dock, including the home pier.
3	Emphasize control, not speed, when docking. Keep just enough headway or sternway to counteract the winds and currents and allow steerage while making progress to the dock. Keep an eye on the amount of stern or bow swing. With a high foredeck, the wind can cause the bow to swing much easier, making it harder to control. In higher winds, a greater amount of maneuvering speed may be needed to lessen the time exposed to the winds and currents, but be careful not to overdo it.
4	Line handling is extremely important when docking. Coxswains must give specific line-handling instructions in a loud, clear voice. If mooring at a different location, brief the crew before starting the approach to where the lines will be secured. Avoid using civilians to handle lines on the dock since their knowledge of line handling is not known and they may not be wearing the appropriate safety equipment.

D.2. Basic Maneuvers

Often, the presence of other craft or obstructions will complicate the clearing of a berth, or any simple maneuver. Wind and/or current can also become a factor. Before maneuvering, the options should be evaluated in order to take full advantage of the prevailing conditions.

This section covers some basic examples of mooring and unmooring. Again, actual hands-on practice of different approach styles and maneuvers during different weather conditions with different boat styles are highly recommended.

D.2.a. Clearing a Slip

Clearing a slip assumes that there is no wind or current, and that the vessel is a single-screw. (see **Figure 10-17**)

Step	Procedure
1	Set rudder amidships.
2	Apply slight right rudder to offset propeller side force.
3	Use throttle and move ahead slowly (b).
4	As the boat gains headway, apply additional helm to turn (c). Remember that the rudder causes the stern to swing in the opposite direction of the bow around the pivot point. Before starting a turn, make sure the stern will clear the pier.

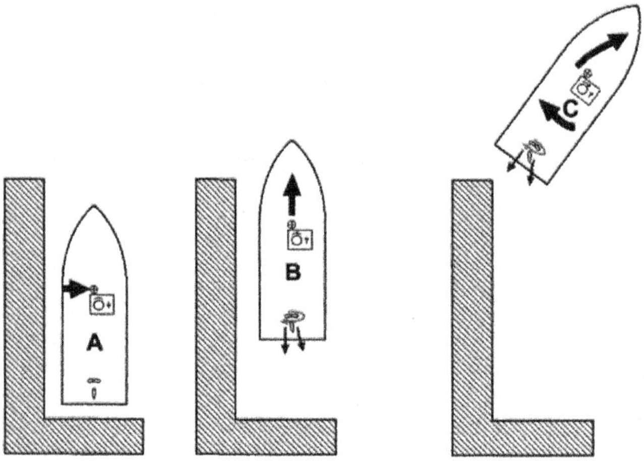

Figure 10-17
Clearing a Slip (No Wind or Current, Single-Screw)

D.2.b. Backing into a Slip

Backing into a slip assumes that there is no wind or current and the vessel is a single-screw, outboard or I/O. (see **Figure 10-18**)

Step	Procedure
1	Approach at low speed, perpendicular to slip, approximately one-half to one boat-length away.
2	As the amidship section is even with the nearest edge of the slip, apply hard left rudder and "bump" throttle ahead to swing the stern to starboard.
3	As bow swings to port, go to neutral throttle and aim lower unit at the back corner of the slip. Immediately apply astern throttle to stop headway and acquire sternway. Side force will stop swing.
4	Steer lower unit towards slip, just aft of desired final position, offsetting for side force as necessary, using astern clutch speed and neutral to keep speed down.
5	When almost alongside, apply slight left rudder and "bump" throttle ahead, then go to neutral.

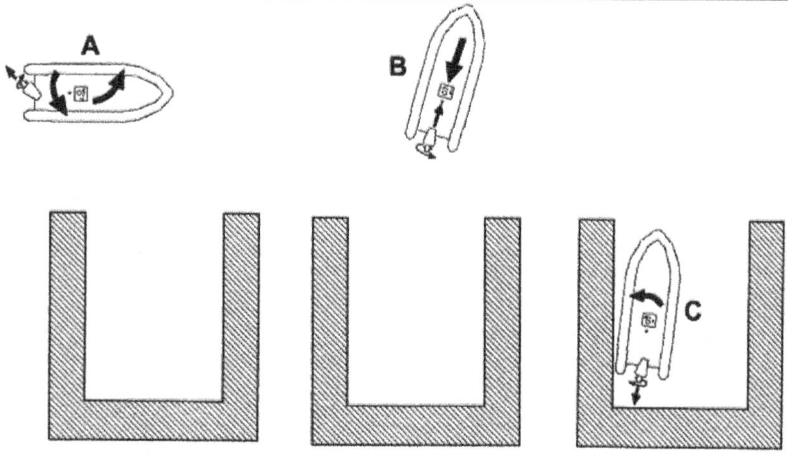

Figure 10-18
Backing Into a Slip (No Wind or Current, Single Outboard/Stern Drive)

D.2.c. Identifying Mooring Lines

Before using mooring lines to help maneuver at the dock, crewmembers need to first know their names and what they do (see **Figure 10-19**):

- The bow line (#1) and stern line (#4) are used to keep the vessel secured to the dock.
- The after bows spring (#2) and forward quarter spring (#3) are used to keep the vessel from surging forward or aft at the dock.

Normally, only these four lines are required when mooring. During times of foul weather, breast lines (#5) may be used to provide additional holding strength. Fenders should be used at strategic points along the hull to prevent chafing against the dock or float.

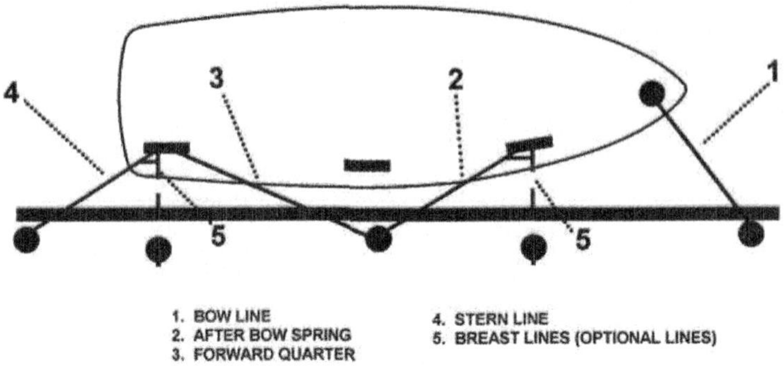

Figure 10-19
Mooring Lines

CAUTION !

> Ensure there is adequate and properly placed fenders between the boat and the dock before attempting a spring maneuver.

D.2.d. Using Spring Lines

If it becomes necessary to hold position alongside a dock, but swing the bow or stern out in order to clear another vessel or obstacle, using a spring line can help to accomplish this.

The forward quarter spring, or stern spring (#3) should be used to "spring out" or move the bow away from the dock. By backing down on a boat's engine with just the forward quarter spring attached to the dock, the bow will move away from the dock.

The after bow spring, or bow spring (#2) should be used to "spring out" or move the stern away from the dock. The stern will move away with the rudder full toward the dock and the engines ahead. With the rudder turned the other direction or away from the dock, the stern will move towards the dock or "spring in". (see **Figure 10-20**)

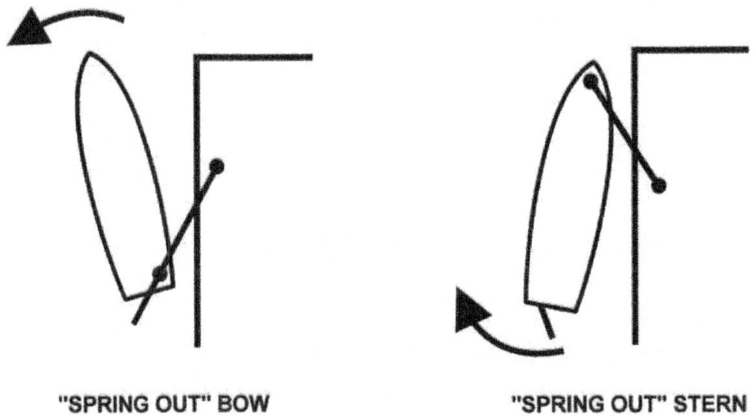

Figure 10-20
Basic Spring Line Maneuvers

D.2.e. Rigging Mooring Lines to "Slip"	Knowing how to rig mooring lines to "slip" can be helpful, particularly when no shore-side line handlers are available. Both bitter ends should be aboard the boat with a bight around the shore-side attachment point. Then the spring line may be let go, or cast off, releasing one end and hauling in the other. A spring line should be carefully tended so that it does not foul the rudder or screw or get caught on the dock. When maneuvering, a line tied to a bitt or cleat should always be watched and never left unattended.
D.3. Rules of Thumb	The following rules of thumb should be adhered to when maneuvering to or from a dock.
D.3.a. Responsibility	The coxswain is always responsible for the boat regardless of the existing environmental conditions and situations. Care must be exercised before assigning newly qualified coxswains to missions in extreme weather conditions.
D.3.b. Slow Speeds	On single-screw vessels maneuvering at slow speeds alongside another object, the coxswain should use full left (or right) rudders for better maneuverability. On twin-screw boats, the coxswain should leave the rudders amidships and use the engines at *clutch* (*idle*) speed to maneuver.
D.3.c. Alongside	When maneuvering alongside, speed should be kept to a minimum. Power should be applied in short bursts (with rudder at left or right full for single-screw boats) to get changes in heading; but the bursts should be kept short enough so as not to increase speed.
D.3.d. Port Side	Port side moorings are the easiest for single-screw boats with "right-hand" props (see *Section A* of this chapter for information regarding forces acting on a vessel).
D.3.e. Backing and Filling	Slow speed maneuvers to starboard are best for single-screw boats with "right-hand" props in restricted areas. The procedures for backing and filling are covered in *Section B* of this chapter.
D.3 f. Precise Control	When requiring precise control, the boat's heading should be kept into the predominate wind or current, or as close as possible. The boat should be maneuvered so that the set from the wind or current is either on the starboard or port bow allowing the boat to "crab" (move sideways) in the opposite direction.
D.3.g. Wind and Current	Wind and current are the most important forces to consider in maneuvering. The operator should use them to their advantage, if possible, rather than attempting to fight the elements.
D.3 h. Spring Lines	Spring lines are very useful when mooring with an off-dock set or when unmooring with an on-dock set. The spring lines should be used to spring either the bow or stern in or out. (see **Figure 10-21** and **Figure 10-22**).

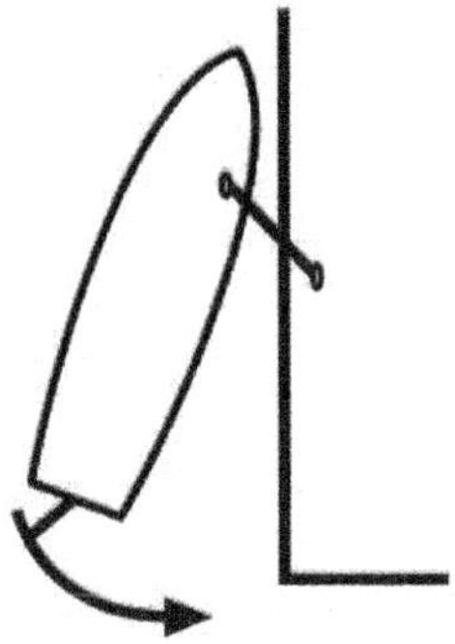

Figure 10-21
Going Ahead With Left Rudder Use of Spring Line

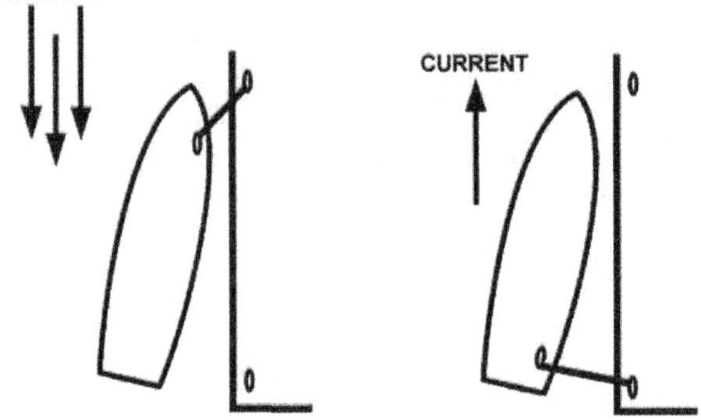

Figure 10-22
Making Use of Current

D.3.i. Thrusting Away from Another Boat	To thrust away from another boat, a camel, or a ship, the coxswain should use the prop wash or "screw knuckle." By applying full power astern in a short burst then returning to *neutral*, the prop wash will move forward between the boat and the surface alongside, pushing the boat away.
D.3.j. Fenders	The coxswain should never attempt to fend a boat off a pier, float, etc., by hand or by foot, but should always use a fender. The proper sized fenders should be kept at hand.
D.3 k. Mooring/ Off-Dock Wind	When mooring with an off-dock wind, the approach should be made at a sharp angle - 45° or more.
D.3.l. Mooring/On-Dock Wind	When mooring with an on-dock wind, the approach should be made parallel with the intended berth and the fender should be rigged in appropriate positions. The coxswain should ensure that the boat has no fore and aft movement when contacting the dock.

D.3 m. Tying Down

Except for using the forward quarter spring, (see **Figure 10-19**) the stern of a boat should never be tied down while maneuvering beside a dock. This restricts maneuverability.

D.3 n. Pivot Point

The pivot point of a boat is approximately one-third of the way aft of the bow when the boat is underway at standard speed. This point moves forward as speed is increased and aft as speed is decreased.

D.3.o. Protecting the Stern

The stern should be kept away from danger. If propellers and rudder become damaged, the boat is crippled. If the stern is free to maneuver, usually the boat can be worked out of trouble.

D.3.p. Controlling the Boat

The greatest amount of control over the boat is gained by maneuvering into the prevailing face of the wind or sea. Boats turn more slowly into the wind and sea than away from them. A single-screw boat will generally back into the wind when the boat has more "sail" area forward of the boat's pivot point than aft.

D.3.q. The Wake

Coxswains are responsible for their boat's wake.

D.3 r. Informing the Crew

The coxswain must keep the crew informed. The coxswain should never assume the crew knows everything he or she is thinking.

D.3.s. Sea Conditions

All coxswains should know the sea conditions in which they can and cannot operate. All coxswains should immediately notify their Operational Commander if they are approaching their comfortable operating limits. It is better to return to the Station for a more suitable platform or a more experienced coxswain/crew than push the limits and possibly injure someone or cause damage to property.

D.3.t. Forethought

Coxswains should always think ahead and not take chances.

Section E. Maneuvering Alongside Another Vessel

Introduction

Many missions will require going alongside and making contact with another vessel. Activity can vary from a RIB going alongside a large merchant vessel to a large twin-screw boat going alongside a small canoe. Comparative vessel size, mission requirements, and prevailing conditions all dictate maneuvering practices. For many recreational and commercial mariners, maneuvering alongside their vessel is often the first; "up close and personal" look they get of the Coast Guard.

In this section

This section contains the following information:

Determining Approach

CAUTION ! Do not approach from leeward if it will put the vessel and crew in jeopardy, whether from shoal water or obstructions farther to leeward, or from smoke or hazardous fumes.

E.1. Conditions

When determining approach, the following conditions should be considered:

- Prevailing weather.
- Currents.
- Location.
- Vessel conditions.
- Vessel sizes.
- Traffic density.

The coxswain should discuss intentions with the other vessel's master.

NOTE If going alongside a disabled vessel or one that is underway but dead-in-the water, compare relative drift rates. When approaching a larger vessel with a low drift rate, approach from leeward. If approaching a smaller vessel, determine if vessel makes a wind shadow that will slow the other vessel's drift. In this case, an approach from windward may be better, and the smaller vessel will then be protected from winds and waves by the larger vessel. See *Chapter 17, Towing*, for more information.

E.2. Course and Speed

If possible and prudent, the vessel should maintain a course and speed to make the approach as smooth as possible for both vessels.

E.2.a. Large Vessels

Most large vessels will not be able to alter course significantly in a limited area to provide ideal alongside conditions. If it is not practical for the large vessel to change course, the coxswain should request that it reduce speed so the effects of bow and stern waves are reduced.

E.2.b. Small Vessels

Small vessels do not ride well when not making way in any kind of winds or seas. Unless the weather is perfectly calm or the vessel is disabled, a small vessel should maintain a course and speed that makes for safe, comfortable navigation while allowing mission completion. Speed should be slow enough to safely come alongside, but fast enough for both vessels to maintain steerageway when alongside one another.

CAUTION ! Make sure the other vessel does not change course while approaching or coming alongside. If this happens, break off and start the approach over again once the other vessel is on a steady course. Inform the master to maintain course and speed until the transfer is complete.

E.2.c. Stability

Many sailing vessels are much more stable while under sail than when powering or drifting. The coxswain should consider coming alongside while the other vessel is under sail, but should ensure that spars, standing or running rigging, or control lines do not foul either vessel. The situation should be discussed with the other vessel's master.

E.3. Approach From Leeward and Astern

A large vessel will create a wind shadow and block most of the seas allowing a smoother approach on the leeward side of a vessel. Coxswains should take advantage of this as in mooring to the leeward side of a pier.

When approaching smaller vessels, the coxswain should first determine the smaller vessel's rate of drift. The coxswain can then determine if an approach on the leeward side (better control over approach) or windward side (a wind shadow will be created) would be better.

NOTE

If an approach from leeward is not possible (due to sea room or other condition like smoke or hazardous vapors), use caution during a windward approach to prevent being pinned up against the side of another vessel. If approaching on the windward side is a must, a bow-in approach might provide the most maneuverability.

E.4. Line and Fenders

Lines and fenders should be rigged as needed. Remember that with fenders, too many is much better than too few.

Going Alongside

WARNING

Pick a contact point well clear of a larger vessel's propeller (including in the area of suction screw current), rudder, and quarter wave. Forces from these could cause loss of control.

E.5. Contacting and Closing In

After completing approach preparations, the coxswain should go alongside and determine where to make contact on both vessels. Perform the following procedures to close in on another vessel:

Step	Procedure
1	Conditions permitting, match speed to the other vessel, and then start closing in from the side.
2	Close at a 15° to 30° angle to the other vessel's heading. This should provide a comfortable rate of lateral closure at no more than one-half the forward speed.

NOTE

If initial heading was parallel to the other vessel, increase speed slightly when starting to close at an angle.

E.6. Using a Sea Painter

In some instances, a sea painter may be used in coming alongside a larger vessel underway. The sea painter is a line used to sheer a boat clear of a ship's side when underway or to hold a boat in position under shipboard hoisting davits and occasionally to hold the boat alongside a ship in order to embark or disembark personnel. It leads from the larger vessel's deck well forward of where the boat will come alongside.

Perform the following procedures when securing a sea painter to the boat:

Step	Procedure
1	Choose a position for attachment of the painter just aft of the bow on the side of the boat that will be alongside the larger vessel. Normally, the first deck fitting aft of the bull nose works well.
2	Lead it outboard of handrails, stanchions, and fittings. It makes a pivoting point on the "inboard" bow of the boat.
3	Never secure the sea painter to the boat's stem nor to the side of the boat away from the ship. If secured to the "outboard" side of the boat, capsizing could result.

As both the boat and ship have headway, the pressure of water on the boat's bow will cause it to sheer away from the ship. The coxswain should use this force by a touch of the helm to control sheer, in or out or, by catching the current on one side of the bow or the other. Riding a sea painter helps maintain position and control of the boat.

Perform the following procedures if using a sea painter:

NOTE When sheering in or out, apply rudder slowly and be prepared to counteract the tendency of the boat to close or open quickly.

Step	Procedure
1	Go alongside of the vessel, matching its course and speed. When close aboard the larger vessel, and forward of the desired contact point, ask the ship to pass the sea painter.
2	The sea painter is usually passed by use of a heaving line. Quickly haul in the heaving line and adjust the boat's heading and speed to control slack in the sea painter so that these lines do not get into the boat's propeller.
3	Once the sea painter is onboard, secure it to an inboard cleat just aft of the bow.
4	Reduce speed slowly and drift back on the painter (ride the painter).
5	Use helm to hold the boat at the desired position alongside or at some distance off the ship.
6	If set toward the ship, apply rudder to sheer the bow out. If too far away, apply rudder to sheer the bow in. The forward strain on the painter will pull the boat and provide steerage.

NOTE If approaching a vessel anchored in a strong current, the sea painter can be used to provide a means to lie alongside. Procedures are the same as if the vessel is making way. Approach from leeward, against the current.

E.7. Making and Holding Contact

Perform the following procedures to make and hold contact with a vessel:

Step	Procedure
1	Make contact with the forward sections of the boat (about halfway between the bow and amidships).
2	Use helm and power (if not on a sea painter) to hold the bow into the other vessel, at the same forward speed.
3	Do not use so much helm or power that the other vessel is caused to change course.

E.8. Conducting the Mission

When alongside and conducting the intended missions, the coxswain should:

Step	Procedure
1	Minimize time alongside.
2	If necessary, "make-up" to the other vessel rather than relying on helm and power to maintain contact.

CAUTION !

Never back down when clearing alongside. Always pull away parallel to the other vessel that is making way.

E.9. Clearing

Getting set toward the side or stern of the vessel should be avoided. Perform the following procedures to clear the side of a vessel:

Step	Procedure
1	Sheer the stern in with helm to get the bow out.
2	Apply gradual power to gain slight relative speed.
3	Slowly steer away from the vessel while applying gradual power.
4	Ensure stern is clear of the other vessel before applying a large amount of rudder.

NOTE

If on a sea painter, use enough speed to get slack in the line, then cast off once clear. Ensure the sea painter is hauled back aboard the larger vessel immediately to prevent it from catching in the screws.

If operating a twin-screw boat, go ahead slowly on the inboard engine. This also helps to keep the boat clear of the ship's side.

Section F. Maneuvering in Rough Weather

WARNING Do not exceed any vessel's operating limits as specified in the Specific Boat Operator's Handbooks, COMDTINST M16114 (series) or through district-use guidelines for other vessels.

Introduction

At some time, every boat and crew will encounter wind or sea conditions that challenge safe, successful boat operation. Due to size and design differences, extreme weather for one vessel is not necessarily challenging for another. Also, crew training, experience, and skill more often than not make the difference between safety and danger, regardless of the vessel.

Size, stability, and power are vessel characteristics that enhance safety and allow some forgiveness in large waves and high winds or due to the occasional lapse in skill or judgment. On the other hand, lightweight, speed, and agility give a means to avoid or to outrun conditions, but offer little protection or forgiveness for the slightest miscalculation.

The coxswain should learn to operate a vessel through the full range of conditions possible, beginning in light winds and small waves and working up to varied conditions that build knowledge and confidence.

In this section

This section contains the following information:

Using Caution

F.1. Description

Caution should be used at all times. The power of winds and waves and what they can do to a vessel or crew should never be underestimated. The following concepts will increase the level of safety of operation.

F.2. Vessel Operating Characteristics and Limitations

Crewmembers should be familiar with the vessel's operating characteristics and limitations to safely and confidently handle conditions that approach those limits including:

- Learning the vessel's motions and peculiarities.
- Knowing the vessel's limits.
- Ensuring proper operational readiness.
- Utilizing only capable vessels.

F.2.a. Learning Vessel Motions and Peculiarities

Operate the vessel frequently and develop a working knowledge of its response to waves and winds. Excessive boat motion is very fatiguing and could cause motion sickness.

- Learn the motions the boat makes in response to varying sea conditions. Find out if the vessel has any distinctive tendencies, for instance, attaining a dangerous heel while cresting a wave in high winds, burying the bow in all but the longest swells, or "lightness" to the stern in quartering conditions.
- Learn and develop techniques to minimize vessel motion in all conditions. A small tweak of the throttle or a smooth helm-hand can make the ride much smoother and less fatiguing.
- On smaller vessels, keep crew weight centered around the helm position. This is usually near the boat's center of gravity. It will make the ride more comfortable for the crew and will allow the hull to ride as designed.

Common Motions	Description
Pitch	Pitch is the up and down motion of the bow (and stern). In small waves at high speeds, pitch can be very small and barely noticeable. As seas increase, the bow might rise up when it meets a wave, and fully clear the water. As it comes back down, it immerses to a point on the hull above the designed waterline, sometimes with a heavy slam. Pitch is usually experienced when heading into the seas. Reduce pitch by reducing speed or by taking head seas at more of an angle.
Roll	Roll is the side-to-side motion as each side goes up and down. This is associated with beam seas. A round-bottomed vessel will roll even in near-calm conditions. Reduce roll by setting a course that does not have the seas directly on the beam.
Heave	Heave is the vertical motion the entire boat makes. Though frequently hidden by combined pitch and roll, it is felt as a boat encounters large waves or a heavy swell.

F.2.b. Vessel Limits

Knowing the maximum wind speed and wave height in which the vessel is allowed to operate is a must. Every attempt should be made to avoid exceeding these conditions. However, learning how to ride out the worst winds or seas is recommended before the need arises.

F.2.c. Operational Readiness

A vessel must not be used in rough weather when it is not operationally ready. A small discrepancy can lead to serious consequences. All required gear should be properly stowed and everything else should be removed.

F.2.d. Capable Vessel

When conditions exceed a particular vessel's limits, a more capable vessel should be used. If one is not available, OPCON must be notified and a waiver granted before launching on the mission.

- Do not use the wrong vessel or tool for a job.
- Always apply risk assessment.

F.3. Knowledge of Area Conditions

Operators should learn to handle the vessel in the types of winds and seas found in their specific area and learn their interaction with local geography and hydrography.

F.3.a. Area Conditions

Learn the area's tide rips, bars, gorges, coastal currents, and local waters before maneuvering there in rough weather by performing the following procedures:

Step	Procedure
1	Find out where wind funnels between headlands or in a river constriction.
2	Get the "big picture," if possible. Spend time in a watch tower or on an overlook, map the patterns of waves, where and when they break.
3	Follow the tracks of severe storms or squall lines. Learn how local geography affects their motion, winds or intensity.
4	Pay attention to forecasts, then frequently compare to actual conditions in the area.
5	Know location of points, capes, bars, hazards to navigation (i.e., piers, wrecks, submerged piles, etc.)

F.3.b. On-Scene Conditions

Evaluate on-scene conditions before committing to a maneuver by performing the following procedures:

Step	Procedure
1	Time the series of waves. Note relative lulls between large waves, any place where the waves do not curl and break with intensity, or where they seem to peak and break continuously.
2	Note if an approaching thunderstorm has a wall cloud or if a "downburst" is visible.
3	Determine the best way to lessen the effect of a sudden, extreme gust of wind.

F.4. Crew Limitations

Knowing the crew limitations as well as being aware of the human factors and clues associated with risk management is essential. False bravado or over-confidence in rough weather will not compensate for inexperience or fear. The following are common sense guidelines to follow:

- When in doubt, DON'T. Experience helps hone good judgment in risk assessment.
- Understand responsibility. Rough weather is not a game or a sport.
- Know when to end an evolution. This is particularly true in training. Damage or injury during training removes resources and people from operational availability.
- Perform as a team. While the coxswain concentrates on the detailed maneuvering, the crew must act as additional eyes and ears.

Negotiating Head Seas

F.5. Description

The operator should use the vessel's inherent capabilities. Bow flare provides additional buoyancy to help lift the bow, but larger seas must be met much slower than smaller ones. A slower speed of approach gives the bow time to rise and meet the waves.

NOTE The following information on maneuvering is general in nature. Remember that each specific boat type will perform differently.

NOTE

Keep in mind that aerated, broken, sloughing, or "white" water will not provide as much buoyancy as "green" water. Also, propulsion and helm response will be sluggish. Aerated water favors cavitation.

F.6. Maneuvering Constantly

Operators should always look and drive for the path of least resistance. The best way to get through waves is to avoid as many as possible. Anticipating patterns and taking advantage of them is key.

F.6.a. Breaking Waves

Pick ways around breaking waves as follows:

- Take advantage of any lulls between the higher series of waves.
- Look for gaps or windows in the breaking waves, but watch them to see if they close out before the vessel approaches.
- Do not try to steer a perfectly straight course; steer the smoothest course if navigation allows.

F.6.b. Crests

Operators should avoid the highest crests, staying away from waves that begin to peak in a triangular fashion. A "square" wave leaves no room to maneuver, and the trough behind is much deeper than others.

WARNING

If the vessel is a single-screw, do not attempt this if originally planning to take the wave on the port bow. Backing down will throw the stern to port and the vessel could end up beam-to the crashing wave.

CAUTION !

Do not use so much power to cause cavitation when backing away from a wave. If cavitation occurs, all thrust and maneuverability will be lost.

F.7. Working Over Waves

Operators should work over each wave individually, varying speed and angle of approach to account for differences in each wave. The following procedures apply:

NOTE

If going through a breaking wave, keep headway. Just as the breaking sea hits the bow, increase power to lift the bow so the sea will not spill on deck, then immediately reduce power.

Step	Procedure
1	Slow down, approach at an angle. Too much speed could "launch" a boat as it leaves a crest and result in a severe drop. Approach at a 10° to 25° angle to the wave rather than straight into it. Cross the crest at this angle to stay in the water and keep the propellers and rudders working.
2	Stay ready to maneuver. It may be necessary to straighten out quickly or to "fall off" to avoid a forming break.
3	Continually adjust boat speed. Increase speed to keep the screw and rudder or drive in the water and working, but then immediately reduce it to minimize wave impact.
4	Do not drive the bow into the wave.

NOTE

If the sea is about to break directly ahead and plunge onto the bow, back down squarely and quickly to avoid the plunging water. The boat will settle as the aerated froth passes, and propulsion and steering will lose some effectiveness until the white water passes.

F.8. Managing Power

Operators should always keep one hand constantly on the throttle control(s).

F.8.a. Heavier Vessels

Use the following procedures when managing the power of heavier vessels:

Step	Procedure
1	Use only enough power to get the bow sections safely over or through the crest.
2	Let momentum carry, and cut back power to let the boat slide down the backside of the swell. When the stern is high, gravity pulls the boat downward and the engines may race somewhat, but stay in gear. Do not decrease RPMs to the point where the engines need time to "spool up" to regain enough power to deal with the next wave.
3	Increase speed in the trough to counteract the reversed water flow and maintain directional control as the next wave approaches.
4	Slow down again and approach the next wave.

F.8.b. Lighter Craft (Including RIBs)

Use the following procedures when managing the power of light craft:

Step	Procedure
1	Use enough power to get the entire boat safely over or through the crest. Lighter craft will not carry momentum so constant application of power is necessary.
2	Keep a slight, bow-up angle at all times.
3	Once through the crest, a slight, bow-up angle, will let the after sections provide a good contact surface if the boat clears the water. A bow up attitude will help to approach the next wave.
4	Increase speed in the trough to counteract the reversed water flow and maintain directional control as the next wave approaches.
5	Slow down again and approach the next wave.

F.9. Staying in the Water

"Flying through" the crest should be avoided at all costs.

- If a large vessel becomes airborne at the top of a wave, the crew is threatened with serious injury and could damage the vessel when it lands.
- With lighter craft, ensure the after sections stay in contact with the water, but do not let the bow sections get too high. If the bow sections get too high while going through a crest, the apparent wind or the break can carry the bow over backward. On the other hand, if forward way is lost with the stern at the crest, the bow might fall downward, requiring to redeveloping speed and bow-up attitude before the next wave approaches.

F.10. Holding On

Crewmembers should keep a firm grasp on controls or hand holds, but should not brace rigidly. Staying rigid and tense will quickly sap strength. If standing, the knees should be kept flexed.

Running Before a Sea

F.11. Description

A following sea does not present the high relative closure rate of head seas, but keeping vessel control and stability is more challenging.

Operation in a following sea, especially a breaking sea, involves the risk of having the stern lifted up and forced forward by the onrushing swell or breaker. Surfing down the face of a wave is extremely dangerous and nearly impossible to control. Quite often, surfing will force the boat to "broach" and capsize or to "pitchpole" end over end. Through proper boat handling, a skilled coxswain may be able to keep a vessel ahead of breaking seas while maintaining control of both direction and speed. Only specially designed vessels, like motor lifeboats, have balanced buoyancy and sea keeping abilities to handle extremely rough weather, including large, breaking, following seas. Motor lifeboats also have the ability to quickly re-right themselves after capsizing.

F.12. Using Extreme Caution

Coxswains should be very careful when running in a large following sea. Some boats slip down the back of seas and heel strongly. In large stern seas, the rudder may get sluggish. Depending on the vessel, down-swell heading should be made anywhere from directly down-swell to a 15° angle to the swells.

NOTE

A great deal of skill is needed to maintain a heading in large, quartering seas (30-45 degrees off the stern), especially in restricted waters. In addition to the action from astern, the forces from abeam will set up a rolling action that causes large changes in the vessel's underwater hull shape (on anything except a round-bottomed, displacement hull). This causes asymmetric forces that increase steering difficulty, could set up "chine-riding," loss of effective helm, and a pronounced veer to the side as the vessel begins to surf along the face of the wave. Even in open water, quartering seas present a challenge.

CAUTION !

Avoid letting waves break over the transom of the boat. Be extremely careful in small craft with outboard motors, the relatively low transom-well offers little protection from even a small, breaking wave. A wave that breaks over the transom could fill the cockpit with water and swamp the boat. Without self-bailing, the vessel is vulnerable to capsize.

F.13. Riding the Backs of the Swells

In waves with a wide regular pattern, coxswains should ride the back of the swell, never riding on the front of a wave. On most vessels, wider and flatter after-hull sections are more buoyant than the bow. On the front of a wave, the boat may begin to surf, pushed along by the wave. As the bow nears the wave trough, it will tend to "dig in" while the stern continues to be pushed. This sets up either a broadside "broach" or an end-for-end "pitchpole" as the breaking crest acts on the boat.

F.13.a. Where to Look

The coxswain should keep an eye both ahead and astern. If the coxswain concentrates completely on the wave ahead, he/she will not be aware of waves from astern. Since larger waves travel faster than smaller ones, one much larger than the present wave may move up quickly from astern and catch the crew unaware.

WARNING

Many small craft can travel faster than the largest waves. Do not keep climbing the back of a large wave ahead to its crest. The boat could go over the crest just as it breaks and fall into the trough under the plunging water.

F.13.b. Speed

The coxswain should adjust the speed to stay on the back of the swell and pay extremely close attention to the way the crest ahead breaks. If the vessel keeps gaining on the crest ahead, the coxswain should slow down.

F.14. Reserve Power

Large seas run at over 20 knots. If the boat is being pulled back towards a following sea, the coxswain should open the throttle. If the boat is still being pulled back, the coxswain should watch for "mushy" helm response and engine racing. If either happens, reducing throttle, then applying full throttle will help to kick out of the wave.

WARNING

Coming about in large seas can be dangerous. It puts the boat beam-to the seas. Do not try this unless well trained and experienced. Any close, steep swells will test all skills. Sluggish rudder, sail area, and irregular waves may cause the stern to slew off and result in a broach.

CAUTION !

If it is necessary to come about before a wave, use judicious helm and throttle. Too much throttle, especially when splitting throttles, could easily result in cavitation and leave no positive control in the face of the oncoming sea.

F.15. Slow, Back or Come About

If running with the seas and a wave is gaining astern, avoid it breaking on the transom by using the following procedures:

Step	Procedure
1	Slow Down: With a well-found vessel, it may be possible to just slow enough so the crest passes by before it breaks. This will cause some loss of positive steering and propulsion control as the crest passes because the water in the crest will be moving forward faster than the boat.
2	Back Down: It may be necessary to back and gain sternway to steer before the crest reaches the screws and rudder, particularly if the wave breaks and aerated water will slough past.
3	Come About: The safest point for most vessels to take a breaking sea is nearly bow-on. Always stay aware of the time and distance between crests. If time and distance allow, come about and present the bow to the sea with headway.

Traversing Beam Seas

F.16. Description

In large beam seas, the wave action will cause the boat to roll. The rolling will cause asymmetric hydrodynamic forces and will affect steering. If this occurs, drive and rudder should be kept immersed.

F.17. Breaking Waves

The number of breaking waves encountered should be minimized. If traversing near a surf zone, going into deeper water will help to avoid breaking waves.

F.18. Using Local Knowledge

Avoid areas that break when no other areas do. Offset your transit from areas of shifting bars.

NOTE

If it is necessary to operate in the surf zone, complete wave avoidance is not possible. The coxswain must be totally involved in operating the boat while the crew carries out the details of the mission (search, recovery, etc.).

F.19. Keeping a Weather-Eye to the Waves

As with head seas and following seas, the boat will be pulled towards the next, oncoming wave while in the trough, and set down-swell by the crest. Perform the following procedures to keep a weather-eye to the waves:

Step	Procedure
1	Look for a lull in the series to cross-seas. If necessary, slow to allow a large series of waves to cross ahead.
2	Use caution to avoid a forming break. Watch how the waves break. Plan to cross an oncoming wave well before it begins to break. Do not get caught racing a break to cross at a particular point. Use procedures for negotiating head seas to cross oncoming waves. As with head seas, cross them at the lowest part.
3	Never get caught broadside to a breaking sea. A breaking swell taken on the beam can easily capsize the vessel.
4	Do not get trapped. If the boat gets into seas that are spaced closer together, look for an out. If shallow water or a current against the seas is on one side, work toward the other direction.

Transiting Harbor Entrances, Inlets, or River Entrances

F.20. Description

When transiting harbor entrances, inlets, or river entrances in rough weather, there will be times when the vessel must either leave or enter port in challenging conditions. Though certain locations have extreme conditions much more often than others, learning how rough weather affects the various harbors and entrances throughout the local area is essential. Methods covered above for maneuvering in head, following, and beam seas still apply, but the entrance areas add additional consideration.

F.21. Knowing the Entrance

Though mentioned above, local knowledge is key. Knowing as much as possible before transiting an entrance in rough weather will help guard against potential problems. Utilize the following procedures and considerations to assess entrances areas:

Step	Procedure
1	Watch where waves break. Know how far out into the channel, whether near jetties or shoals, or directly across the entrance the waves break.
2	Pay close attention to how the entrance affects wave patterns. A jettied entrance may reflect waves back across an entrance where they combine with the original waves.
3	Some entrances have an outer bar that breaks, and then additional breaks farther in. Others are susceptible to a large, heaving motion that creates a heavy surge as it hits rocks or structures.
4	Know where the channel actually is. If shoaling has occurred, room to maneuver may be significantly reduced.
5	Know the actual depths of the water. Account for any difference between actual and charted depth due to water stage, height of tide, recent rainfall, or atmospheric pressure effects.

F.22. Transiting When Current Opposes the Seas

Transiting when the current opposed the seas presents the most challenging situation near an entrance. In opposition to the seas, a current has the effect of shortening the wavelength, and increasing the wave height. This makes waves much more unstable and much closer together. Utilize the following procedures and considerations to transit when the current opposes the seas:

Step	Procedure
1	When going into the seas, the current behind will push the boat into them, at a relatively higher speed.
2	Reduce the effect (which will also give more time to react between waves) by slowing, but because the current is behind, keep enough headway to ensure effective steering.
3	Do not let the current push the boat into a large cresting wave or combined waves peaking together. In an entrance, maneuvering room is often limited. The only safe water may be the area just left. Be ready to back down and avoid a breaking crest.
4	The situation can be critical in following seas and a head current. The waves will overtake at a higher rate; they become unstable more quickly, and will break more often. The current reduces the boat's progress over the ground, subjecting the vessel to more waves.
5	As with all following seas, stay on the back of the wave ahead. Because the waves become unstable and break more quickly, use extra caution to not go over the crest ahead. Concentrate both on the crest ahead and the waves behind.
6	Keep a hand on the throttle and adjust power continuously. In many entrances, there is not enough room to come about and take a breaking wave bow-on. Anticipate. If a wave looks to break, the only out may be to back down before it gets to the vessel.
7	Stay extremely aware of any wave combinations and avoid spots ahead where they tend to peak. If they peak ahead in the same place, chances are they will peak there when the vessel is closer. However, do not let a slightly different wave or wave combination catch the crew by surprise.
8	The crew must keep an eye on the situation and pass information freely.

F.23. Transiting When Current and Seas Coincide

In a situation of transiting when current and seas coincide, a current has the effect of lengthening the waves. Longer waves are more stable, with the crests farther apart, but caution is still needed. Utilize the following procedures and considerations to transit when current and seas collide:

Step	Procedure
1	When going into the seas and current, progress over the ground will be lessened, so more time will be spent in the entrance. Increasing boat speed may be warranted.
2	Do not increase boat speed so that negotiating waves becomes hazardous. The waves are just as high, so if overall speed was increased, reduce speed to negotiate each crest individually.
3	With following seas and current, speed over the ground will be increased. Because the waves are farther apart, the task of riding the back of the wave ahead should be easier. Because the current is behind, more forward way will be required to maintain steering control.
4	As with all following seas, stay on the back of the wave ahead. Do not be lulled into a false sense of security. With higher speed over the ground and less maneuverability due to the following current, there is not as much time to avoid a situation ahead.
5	Keep a hand on the throttle and adjust power continuously.
6	Because less time will be spent in the entrance, stay extremely aware of any spots ahead to avoid. Maneuver early, as the current will carry the boat.
7	The crew must keep an eye on the situation and pass information freely.

Coping with High Winds

F.24. Description

Though preceding discussions dealt with encountering severe wave action, high winds do not always accompany large swells. Also, there will be instances when extreme winds occur without sufficient duration to make large waves. Much of the time, though, high winds and building seas will coincide.

F.25. Crabbing Through Steady Winds

Depending on the vessel's sail area, it may be necessary to steadily apply helm or asymmetric propulsion to hold a course in high winds. Coxswains should learn to "read" the water for stronger gusts. The amount of chop on the surface will increase in gusts, and extremely powerful gusts may even blow the tops off waves. The effect of a gust should be anticipated before it hits the vessel.

NOTE

> Boats that show extreme motion and minimal control in high winds and seas, regardless of size and power, are not well-suited for missions in these conditions. If caught in marginal conditions, safety of the vessel and crew must be the only concern. Other, more capable resources must conduct the mission.

Utilize the following procedures and considerations when crabbing through steady winds:

Step	Procedure
1	In large waves, the wave crest will block much of the wind when the boat is in the trough. Plan to offset its full force at the crest. The force of the wind may accentuate a breaking crest, and require steering into the wind when near the crest in head seas. Depending on the vessel, winds may force the bow off to one side while crossing the crest.
2	For light vessels, the force of the wind at the wave crest could easily get under the bow sections (or sponson on a RIB), lift the bow to an unsafe angle, or force it sideways. Though a light vessel must keep some speed to get over or through the crest of a large wave, do not use so much speed that the vessel clears the crest, most of the bottom is exposed to a high wind. Be particularly cautious in gusty conditions and stay ready for a sudden large gust when clearing a wave.
3	With twin-engined craft, be ready to use asymmetric propulsion to get the bow into or through the wind. As with all other maneuvers, early and steady application of power is much more effective than a "catch-up" burst of power.
4	Vessels with large sail area and superstructures will develop an almost constant heel during high winds. In a gust, sudden heel, at times becoming extreme, may develop. This could cause handling difficulties at the crest of high waves. If the vessel exhibits theses tendencies, exercise extreme caution when cresting waves. Learn to safely balance available power and steering against the effects of winds and waves.

F.26. Avoiding Severe Weather

Thunderstorms, downbursts, squalls, and waterspouts should be avoided. Many areas regularly get severe weather with localized winds in excess of 50 knots. As these conditions often arise at peak times in the recreational boating season, chances are that the crew may find themselves underway in them. Since numerous cells can occur in one thunderstorm, the crew may be faced with maneuvering among many different storms, and therefore, should keep an eye on what is approaching.

NOTE

> If faced with a severe storm while on the water, reduce as much sail area as possible. Lower bimini tops, dodgers, outriggers, antennas, flags and ensigns. This significantly improves vessel stability and response to high winds. Also, stow all loose gear, close hatches and doors, and stay low.

F.26.a. Gusts

Coxswains should try to avoid the highest gusts. Some storm cells have their own gust fronts that precede them. These gust fronts appear as a layer of steam on the water. A 50-knot gust front will actually turn the surface of the water into spray, with the highest gusts mixing with the relative heat of the water to lift the spray vertically.

NOTE

> If sea room permits, move away from (perpendicular to) the direction of the gust.

F.26.b. Drifting Stern-To the Winds

Coxswains should consider drifting stern-to the winds. At the speed these gusts move, they often do not have time to develop much of a sea. If so, it may be possible to lie safely, stern-to the wind, engines in *neutral*. This way, it will not be necessary to fight the overpowering force to keep the bow directly into the wind.

CAUTION !

Laying stern-to is not safe if an approaching storm has enough open water to develop fetch and build seas. A strong thunderstorm needs as few as five miles of open water to build a three- to four-foot chop. In combination with 50-knot winds, this chop can easily swamp small vessels.

F.26.c. Getting Between a Storm and Shore

Getting between a severe storm and a near, lee shore should be avoided. The coxswain should attempt to move across a gust front, before it arrives, as best as possible to safe haven or open water.

Heaving-To

F.27. Description

If unable to reach safe haven in extreme weather, heaving-to might be the only option to ride out the foul weather while waiting for conditions to improve. Basically, heaving-to is putting the bow into the wind or seas, and holding it there with helm and throttle. For vessels with a large sail area or superstructure, this might not be possible. If the conditions are strong enough, large waves or strong gusts of wind may cause the vessel to "fall-off" and lay beam-to or stern-to the wind or seas.

WARNING

Only heave-to when there is adequate sea room to leeward. Drift will be downwind and down sea.

F.28. Maneuvering

Coxswains should maneuver only to keep a bow-on aspect to the weather. Heave-to only when the vessel cannot safely make progress in a desired direction, utilizing the following procedures:

Step	Procedure
1	Offset for the strongest force. Wind and seas might not be from the same direction.
2	Try to keep seas between 10° and 25° off the bow as if negotiating head seas and note the compass heading. Negotiate the seas will still occur, but no progress will be made. If the wind allows holding this angle, it will give the best ride. Determine a mix of helm and throttle to hold the heading. Try not to use full rudder or throttle as it leaves no reserve for an emergency maneuver.
3	If the winds are gusty and have frequent shifts, they can easily force the bow off the desired heading. Listen for signs of an approaching gust and start to counteract its effect before it actually strikes the boat.
4	If seas are not the strongest force, keep the bow directly into the wind.

F.29. Sea Anchor

Utilize the following procedures to employ a sea anchor, if necessary, to hold the vessel into the weather:

Step	Procedure
1	If unable to hold a heading, use a drogue as a sea anchor, made fast to the bow, to hold it into the weather.
2	Use as much scope as available up to 300 feet.
3	Let the rode pay out and see if the vessel motions settle down.
4	The bow may continue to "sail" back and forth. Counteract this by using some forward power and helm to hold the bow at a constant compass angle.
5	Maneuver with caution, keeping the sea anchor rode off the bow.

Section G. Maneuvering in Rivers

Introduction

This section discusses the techniques and hazards of maneuvering in narrow rivers.

In this section

This section contains the following information:

Operating in a Narrow Channel

G.1. Bank Cushion

Bank cushion occurs only when operating in close proximity to the bank and refers to a boat being pushed away from the nearest riverbank. As the boat moves ahead in the river, the water between the bow and the near riverbank builds up high on the side of the boat, causing the bow to move away from the bank. The bank cushion affect is especially prevalent if the draft of the boat is nearly equal to the depth of the water, or in narrow channels with steep banks.

G.2. Bank Suction

Bank suction refers to the stern of a boat being pulled toward the bank. As the boat moves ahead while near the riverbank, the unbalanced pressure of water on the aft quarter lowers the water level between the boat and the bank, forcing the stern to move toward the bank. This suction effect occurs most notably with a twin-screw boat.

G.3. Combined Effect

The combined effect of bank cushion and bank suction may cause a boat to take a sudden sheer toward the opposite bank. (see **Figure 10-23**)

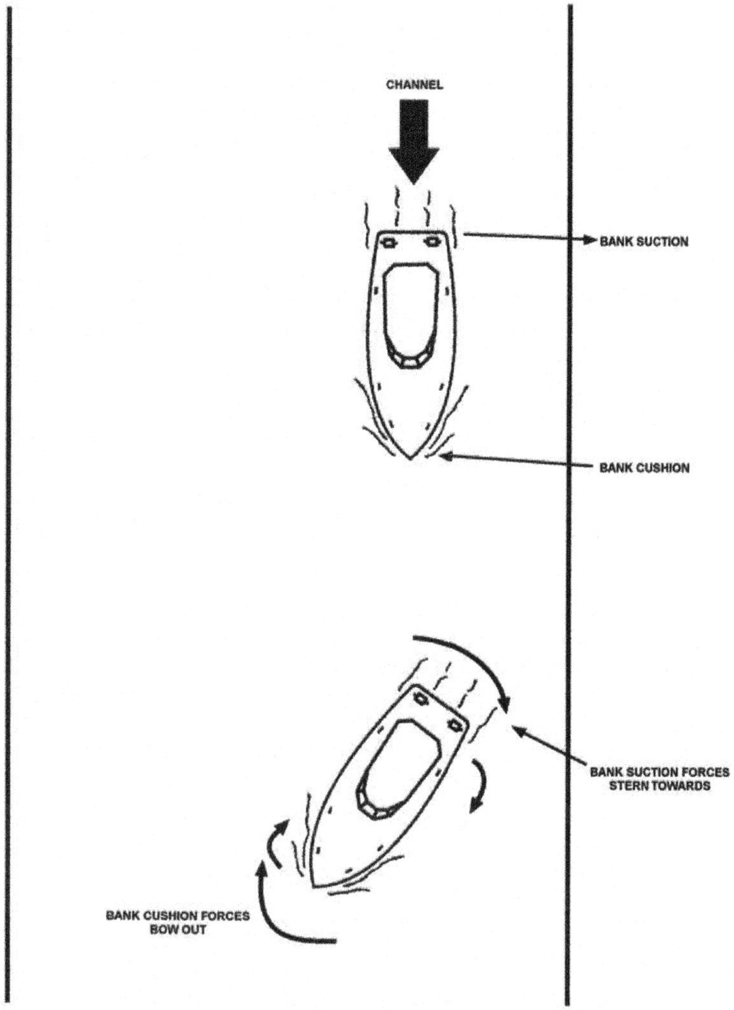

Figure 10-23
Bank Cushion and Bank Suction Affects in a Narrow Straight Channel

G.3.a. Single-Screw Boats	A single-screw boat going at a very slow speed with its port side near the left bank may lose control if sheer occurs. Increasing speed and adding a small amount of left rudder will bring the boat under control.
G.3.b. Twin-Screw Boats	A twin-screw boat, with its port side near the left bank, usually recovers from this sheer by increasing speed on the starboard engine, and adding left rudder.

G.4. Current

Current is the horizontal flow or movement of water in a river. Maximum current occurs during runoff and/or high water and the greatest velocity is in the area of the channel. Restricted or narrow channels tend to have a venturi effect, in that rushing water squeezes into a passage and accelerates. Current in a bend will tend to flow away from the inside point (to the outside), creating eddies, counter currents, and slack water immediately past the point. This effect will build shoals at the point or inside a bend. The prudent operator will be alert to the changing current within a waterway.

G.5. Extremely Narrow Channels

In extremely narrow channels where bank cushion and bank suction are expected, the coxswain should proceed at a very slow speed, keeping near the middle of the channel and passing other boats closer than normal. In a meeting situation in a narrow channel, headway should be reduced but not enough to lose steerage. On approaching the boat, a small amount of right rudder should be applied to head slightly toward the bank. Shortly after passing the other boat, the coxswain should reverse the rudder and straighten up. A little right rudder may be needed to hold course against the bank cushion effect. Because of wash from passing boats, extreme caution should be used.

Turning in a Bend

G.6. Strengths and Weaknesses

Bank suction, bank cushion, currents and wind are factors that affect a boat's turn in a sharp bend in a narrow channel. Bank cushion and bank suction are strongest when the bank of a channel is steep. They are weakest when the edge of a channel shoals gradually and extends into a large area. Bank suction and bank cushion increase with the boat's speed. Channel currents are usually strongest in the bend with eddies or counter-currents and shoaling on the lee side of the point. Speed of the current is greater in deeper water than in shallow water.

G.7. Following Current

In a following current, the boat makes good speed with little help from the engines. When making a sharp turn with a following current, it is possible to make the following maneuvers:

- Hugging the point.
- Staying in the bend.
- Proceeding on the bend side, middle of the channel.

An experienced operator can accomplish any of the three; however, the third choice, called the "bend side, middle of the channel," is the safest, and therefore, the preferred choice.

G.7.a. Hugging the Point

The operator carries a small amount of rudder toward the near bank to steer a straight course. As the channel begins to bend and the boat moves from the bank, less rudder will be necessary. This condition is a signal that it is time to begin the turn. However, slack water or eddies may be around the bend, making it difficult to prevent a sheer toward the near bank, especially in shallow water. The current under the quarter may affect the stern, and result in an increase in sheer. (see **Figure 10-24**) To correct for this, the coxswain should apply additional power and rudder to steer back towards the center of the channel, keeping the stern in the middle of the channel.

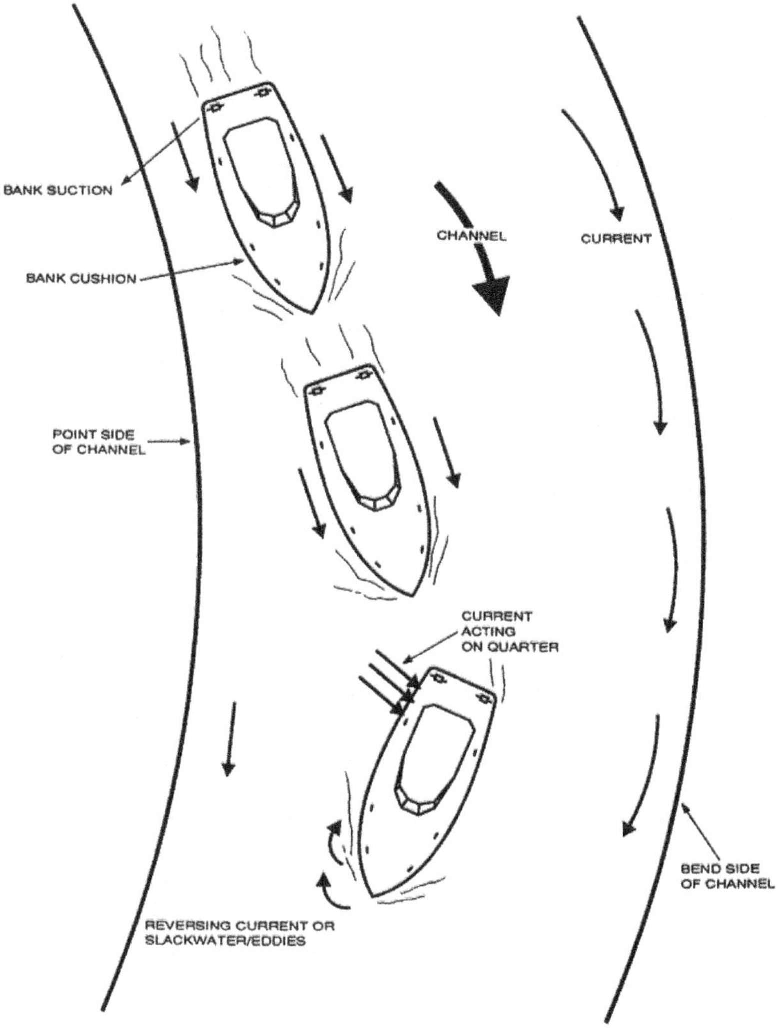

Figure 10-24
Hug the Point: Current Astern

G.7.b. Staying in the Bend

Staying in the bend is a turn in the bend away from the point that takes precise timing. If done too late, the boat may ground on the bank in the bend. If done too soon, there is extreme danger that a strong and sudden sheer will occur. The bank suction on one quarter combines with the current on the other quarter to give the boat the sheer. Also, the bank cushion under the bow will increase the sheer. (see **Figure 10-25**) Again, to correct for this situation, additional power and rudder should be applied to steer back towards the center of the channel.

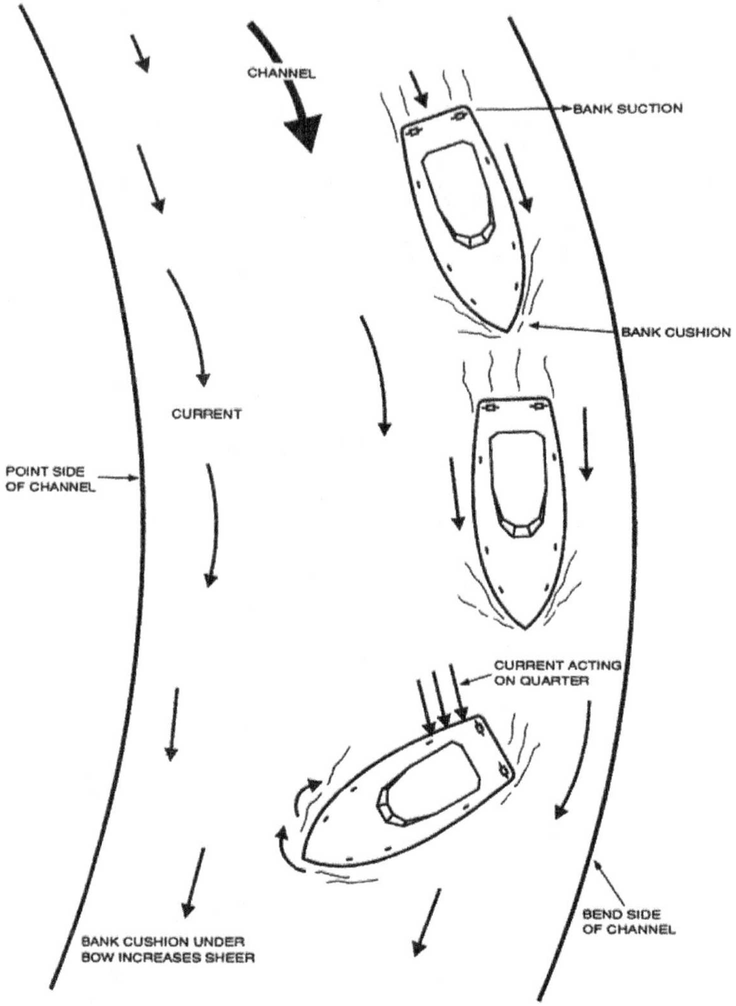

Figure 10-25
Stay in the Bend: Current Astern

G.7.c. Bend Side, Middle of the Channel

Approaching the turn steering a course toward the bend side of the middle of the channel is the safest method when the current is following. By doing this, the boat avoids any eddies under the point and the increase in currents in the bend. The operator can also use the force of the current against the quarter to help in the turn. A following current will force a boat toward the bend side; consequently, the turn should be commenced early in the bend. Additional power and rudder should be applied as needed to stay in the middle of the channel. (see **Figure 10-26**).

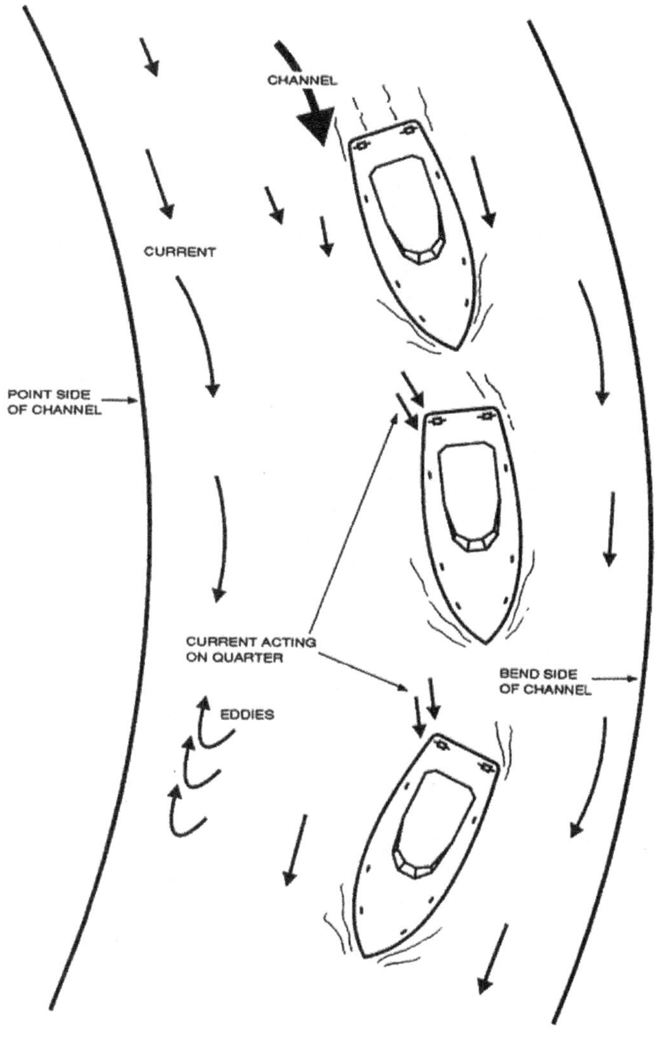

Figure 10-26
Approaching Slightly on the Bend Side, Middle of the Channel: Current Astern

G.7.d. Head Current

It is always easier to pilot the vessel into the current rather than have the current off the stern. When making a turn into a head current, the coxswain should apply power and rudder as needed to stay in the middle of the channel. Caution should be used when starting a turn. If started too soon, the head current could catch the bow and force the vessel down on the point side of the channel. If this happens, the coxswain should apply power and steer back towards the center of the channel and wait until later in the bend to commence the turn. Care should be taken not to wait too long before starting the turn. If the turn is started too late, the current could catch the bow and push the vessel towards the bend side of the channel. The stern should always be kept in the middle of the channel. (see **Figure 10-27**)

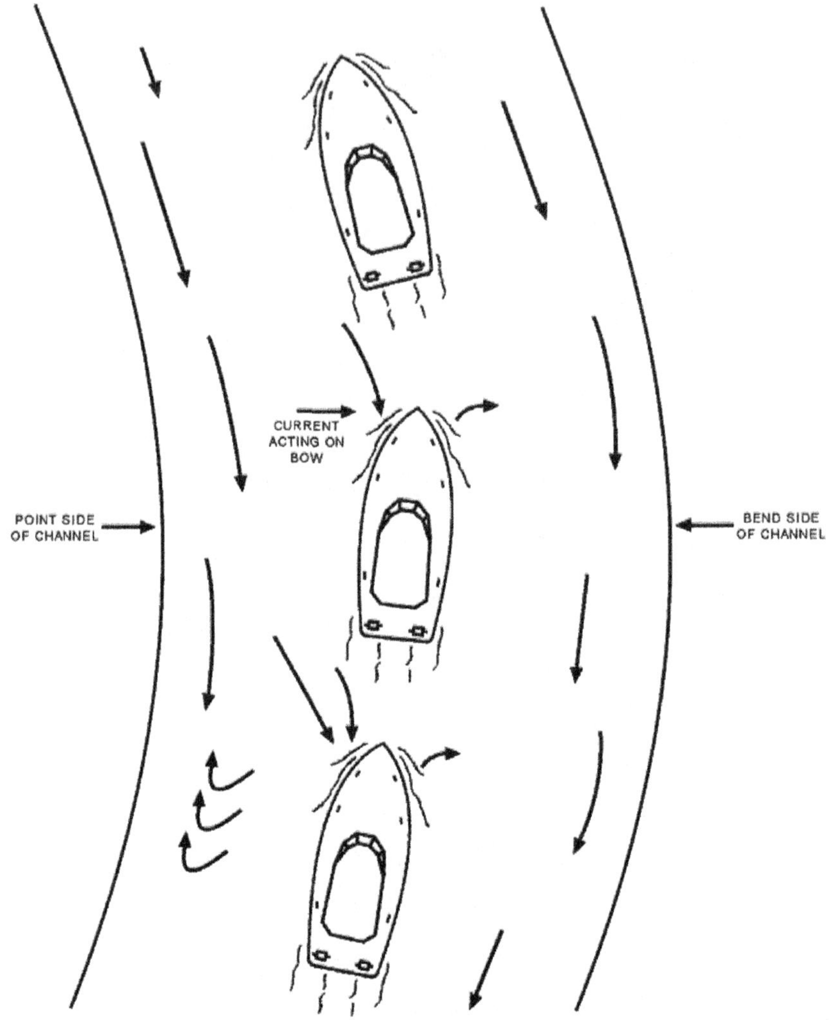

Figure 10-27
Heading into Current

Section H. Anchoring

Introduction

Anchoring must be performed correctly in order to be effective. This section discusses the techniques necessary to properly anchor a boat.

In this section

This section contains the following information:

Proper Anchoring

H.1. Elements

The basic elements of proper anchoring include:

- Proper equipment availability.
- Knowledge to use that equipment.
- Ability to select good anchoring areas.

H.2. Terms and Definitions

The anchoring system is all the gear used in conjunction with the anchor. The table below defines several of the terms used to describe the different parts of most modern types of anchors.

Term	Definition
Anchor	A device designed to engage the bottom of a waterway and through its resistance to drag maintain a vessel within a given radius.
Anchor chocks	Fittings on the deck of a vessel used to stow an anchor when it is not in use.
Bow chocks	Fittings, usually on the rail of a vessel near its stem, having jaws that serve as fairleads for anchor rodes and other lines.
Ground tackle	A general term for the anchor, anchor rodes, fittings, etc., used for securing a vessel at anchor.
Hawspipe	A cylindrical or elliptical pipe or casting in a vessel's hull through which the anchor rode runs.
Horizontal load	The horizontal force placed on an anchoring device by the vessel to which it is connected.
Mooring bitt	A post or cleat through or on the deck of a vessel used to secure an anchor rode or other line to the vessel.

Term	Definition
Rode	The line connecting an anchor with a vessel.
Scope	The ratio of the length of the anchor rode to the vertical distance from the bow chocks to the bottom (depth plus height of bow chocks above water).
Vertical load	The lifting force placed on the bow of the vessel by its anchor rode.

H.3. Reasons for Anchoring

There are many reasons to anchor; the most important is for safety. Other reasons for anchoring are:

- Engine failure.
- Need to stay outside of a breaking inlet or bar.
- To weather a storm.
- To hold position while passing gear to a disabled vessel.

H.4. Anchor Types

There are different types of anchors with specific advantages of each type. The type of anchor and size (weight) of anchor a boat uses depends upon the size of the boat. It is advisable for each boat to carry at least two anchors (see **Table 10-1**).

- A working, or service anchor should have the holding power to equal to approximately 6% of the boat's displacement.
- A storm anchor should be at least 150-200% as effective as the service anchor.

Table 10-1
Suggested Anchor Weights for Danforth Anchors

Maximum Boat Length	Working Anchor	Storm Anchor
20 feet (approx. 7 meters)	5 lbs.	12 lbs.
30 feet (approx. 10 meters)	12 lbs.	18 lbs

H.5. Danforth Anchor

Since most small boats use a Danforth type anchor because of their excellent holding strength compared to their overall weight, it is described below (see **Figure 10-28):**

Part #	Part Name	Description
1	Shank	Aids in setting and weighing the anchor. Attachment point for the anchor line.
2	Flukes	Dig in the bottom and bury the anchor, providing holding power.
3	Crown	Lifts the rear of the flukes, and forces the flukes into the bottom.
4	Stock	Prevents the anchor from rolling or rotating

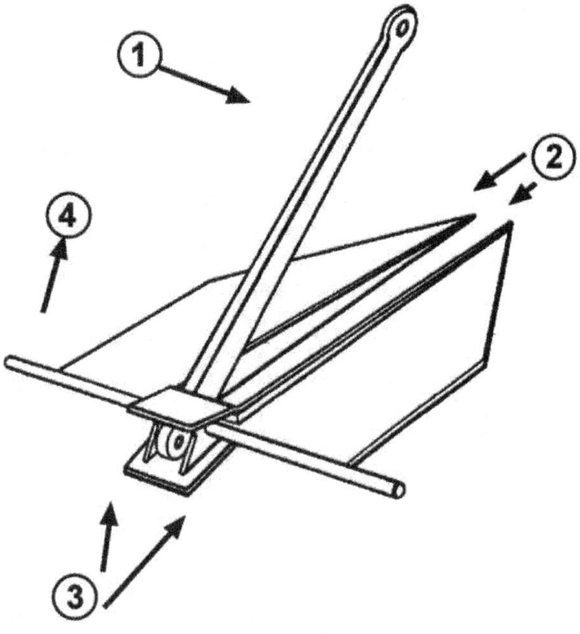

Figure 10-28
Main Parts of a Danforth Anchor

Ground Tackle

H.6. Anchor System	The complete anchor system consists of the anchor, the rode, and the various fittings connecting the rode to the anchor.
H.7. Anchor Rode	The rode is the line from the boat to the anchor and is usually made up of a length of line plus a short length of chain. Large vessels may use an all-chain rode. Each element of the system must be connected to its neighbor in a strong and dependable manner.
H.7.a. Line Type	The most commonly used line for rode is nylon. The line may be either cable laid or braided, and must be free of cuts and abrasions. Foot or fathom markers may be placed in the line to aid in paying out the proper amount of anchor rode.
H.7.b. Nylon and Chain	Chain added with the rode has several advantages: • Lowers the angle of pull (the chain tends to lie on the bottom). • Helps to prevent chafing of the line on a coral or rocky bottom. • Sand has less chance to penetrate strands of the fiber line higher up. • Sand does not stick to the chain. • Mud is easily washed off (without the chain, nylon gets very dirty in mud). The chain should be galvanized to protect against rust.

Fittings

H.8. Securing the Rode

There are various methods for securing the rode to the anchor ring. With fiber line, the preferred practice is to place an eye splice with thimble and swivel at the end of the line. If the thimble does not allow the swivel to be attached before the splice, a shackle is used to attach the swivel to the thimble. Then shackles are used to attach the swivel to one end of the chain and the other end of the chain to the anchor's shank. (see **Figure 10-29**)

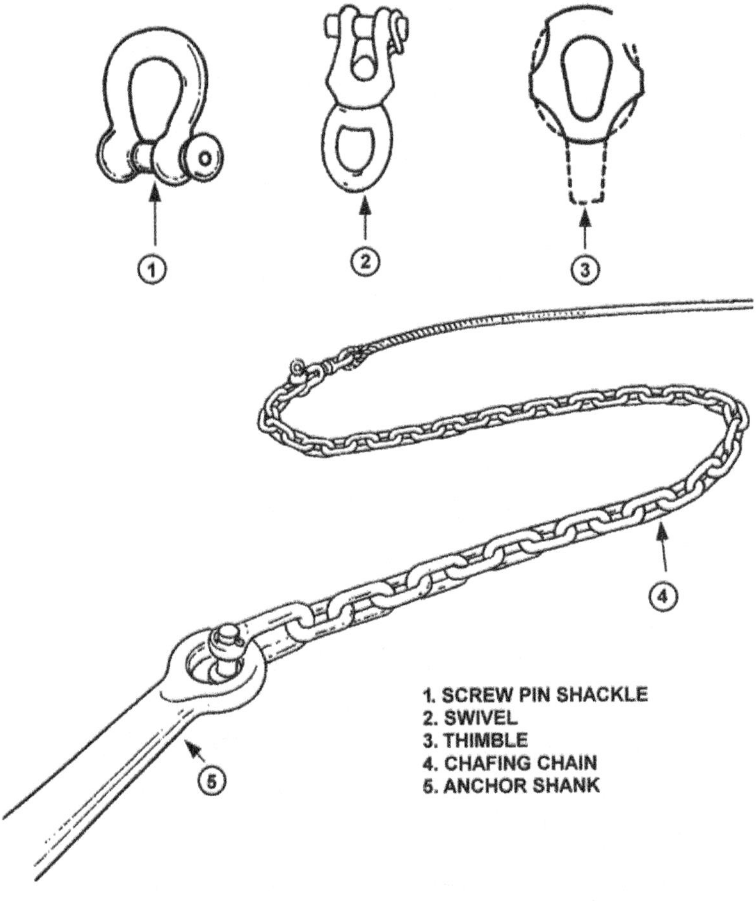

Figure 10-29
Anchor Fittings

H.9. Description

The following describes the different fittings used to connect the rode to the anchor:

Part	Description
Shackle	Bends the length of chafing chain to the shank of the anchor. Can also be used to connect other pieces of ground tackle together (swivels, thimbles, etc.).
Swivel	Allows the vessel to rotate around the anchor without twisting the line/chain.
Thimble	Protects the anchor line from chafing at the connection point. Use synthetic line thimbles for lines 2¾" in circumference (⅞" diameter) and larger.
Chafing chain	Tends to lower the angle of pull of the anchor and assists in preventing chafing of the anchor line on the bottom.
Detachable link	Attaches the anchor and associated ground tackle to the anchor line (not mandatory).
Eye splice	Used at the end of the line to permanently attach the thimble.

Anchoring Techniques

H.10. Procedure

Before the need arises, the coxswain should brief the crewmembers on procedures for anchoring.

Anchoring involves good communication between the coxswain and the crew. With noise from the engine(s) and the wind, it is difficult to hear voice communication. The coxswain should ensure a pre-arranged set of hand signals that the crew understands. Keep the signals as simple as possible.

NOTE

PFDs must be worn during the anchoring evolution.

CAUTION !

Never anchor by the stern especially with small boats. Weather and seas may swamp the craft.

H.11. Precautions for Selecting Anchorage Area

Sometimes it may be possible to choose a sheltered anchorage area in shallow water (40' or less).

- Check charts to ensure that the anchorage area avoids any submerged cables or other obstructions.
- If other boats are in the same area, be careful not to anchor too close to another vessel.
- Never drop within the swing area of another boat. (see **Figure 10-30**)
- Always approach the anchorage into the wind or current. (see **Figure 10-31**)

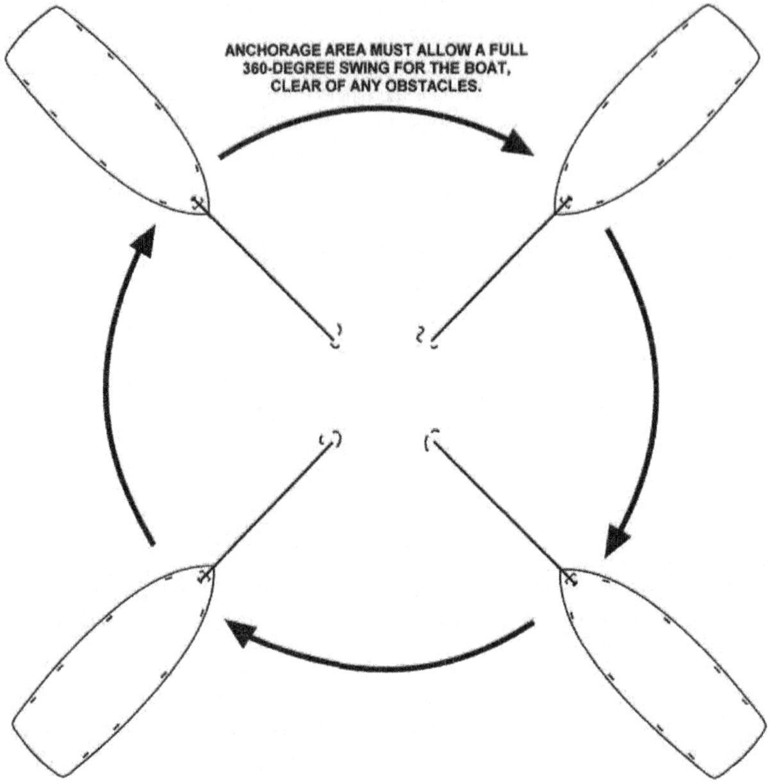

Figure 10-30
Anchorage Swing Area

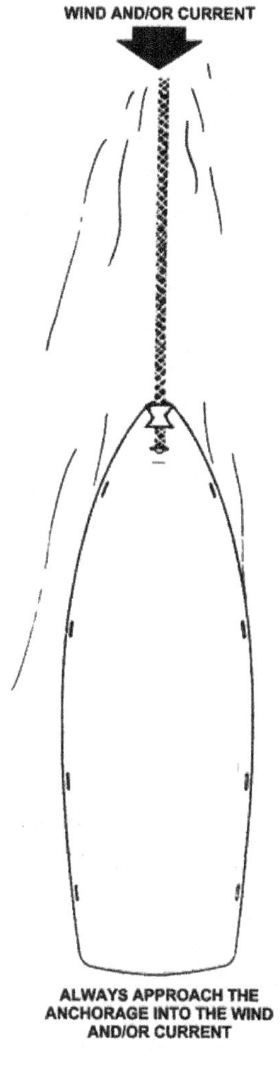
WIND AND/OR CURRENT
ALWAYS APPROACH THE ANCHORAGE INTO THE WIND AND/OR CURRENT

Figure 10-31
Approaching an Anchorage

H.12. Approaching the Anchorage

Having selected a suitable spot, the coxswain should run in slowly, preferably on some range ashore selected from marks identified on the chart, or referring to the vessel's position to radar ranges or GPS data to aid in locating the chosen spot. Use of two ranges will give the most precise positioning. Later these aids will be helpful in determining whether the anchor is holding or dragging.

Bottom characteristics are of prime importance. The following characteristics of the bottom are normally shown on charts:

Type	Description
Firm sand	Excellent holding quality and is consistent.
Clay	Excellent holding quality if quite dense, and sufficiently pliable to allow good anchor engagement.
Mud	Varies greatly from sticky, which holds well, to soft or silt that has questionable holding power.
Loose sand	Fair, if the anchor engages deeply.
Rock and coral	Less desirable for holding an anchor unless the anchor becomes hooked in a crevice.
Grass	Often prevents the anchor from digging into the bottom, and so provides very questionable holding for most anchors.

H.13. Lowering the Anchor

As the anchor is lowered into the water, it is important to know how much rode is paid out when the anchor hits the bottom. It is advisable to take a working turn on the forward bitt or cleat to maintain control of the rode. If anchoring in a strong wind or current, the anchor rode may not be held with hands alone.

NOTE Never stand in the coils of line on deck and do not attempt to "heave" the anchor by casting it as far as possible from the side of the boat.

Step	Procedure
1	Station two persons on the forward deck (if available).
2	Haul out enough line from the locker and fake it on deck so as to run freely without kinking or fouling. If previously detached, the line must be shackled to the ring, and the stock set up (if of the stock type) and keyed.
3	On the coxswain's command, lower the anchor over the side hand-over-hand until it reaches bottom.
4	Once the anchor is on the bottom, take a working turn on the forward bitt to control how fast and how much anchor rode is released.
5	Once the desired length is paid out, make up the anchor rode to the forward bitt.

Many an anchor has been lost for failure to attach the rode properly. If anchoring for an extended period, the pin should be seized on all shackles to prevent the pin from coming out. Rodes as well, have gone with the anchor when not secured properly to the vessel.

Lightweight anchors are always ready for use and do not have to be set up, but a check should always be made to see that the shackle is properly fastened.

H.13.a. Length of Rode (Scope)

The scope is a ratio of the length of rode paid out to the depth of the water. Enough rode should be paid out so the lower end of the rode forms an angle of 8° (or less) with the bottom. This helps the anchor dig-in and give good holding power.

NOTE Scope of the anchor rode should have a ratio range between 5:1 and 7:1. For heavy weather use 10:1. (Example: For the 5:1 ratio, anchoring in 20 feet of water would require 100 feet of rode.)

H.13.b. Markers

Markers along the line, show the amount of rode that is out. It also helps to decide the scope necessary for good holding of the anchor.

H.14. Setting the Anchor

An anchor must be set properly if it is to yield its full holding power. The best techniques for setting an anchor will vary from type to type; only general guidelines can be given here. Experimenting will help determine the best procedures for the boat, the anchors, and the cruising waters.

Step	Procedure
1	With the anchor on the bottom and the boat backing down slowly, pay out line as the boat takes it with a turn around the bitt or cleat.
2	When the predetermined scope has been paid out, hold the line quickly and the anchor will probably get a quick bite into the bottom.
3	If the anchor becomes shod with mud or bottom grass adhering to the flukes, lift it, wash it off by dunking at the surface, and try again.

H.15. After Anchor is Set

After the anchor is set, perform the following procedures:

Step	Procedure
1	Pay out or take in rode to the proper length for the anchorage, accounting for the prevailing and expected weather conditions.
2	The scope must be adequate for holding, but in a crowded anchorage consider the other boats in the vicinity.
3	Attach chafing gear to the rode at the point where it passes through the chocks and over the side to prevent abrasion and wear-and-tear on the rode and boat.

H.16. Checking the Anchor Holding

There are several ways to make a positive check to ensure the anchor is holding, and not dragging.

- If the water is clear enough to see the bottom, movement may be detected easily.
- If the anchor rode is jerking, or vibrating, the anchor is most likely not holding.
- Monitor bearings taken on at least two landmarks (if available) that are a minimum of 45° apart, or use radar ranges and bearings. Small changes usually mean that the wind, tide, or current has caused the boat to swing around the anchor. If the compass heading is constant, but the bearings change, the anchor is dragging.
- If using a buoyed trip line from the crown of the anchor, apply reverse power to test the anchor's holding. The float on this line should continue to bob up and down in one spot unaffected by the pull on the anchor rode.
- Some electronic navigation units (GPS/DGPS) have anchoring features that will warn if the vessel has drifted out of its swing circle. These can be used, but should not replace visual and radar methods.

H.17. Making Fast

After the anchor has gotten a good bite and the proper scope has been paid out, the line should be made fast to the connection fitting (bitt, cleat, etc.). A check should be made to ensure the vessel is not dragging anchor before shutting off the motor. The fundamental idea in making fast is to secure in such a manner that the line can neither slip nor jam.

H.17.a. Forward Bitt

On boats with a forward bitt (sampson post), the best way to secure the anchor line is with one full round turn followed by three figure eights around the pin. The final figure eight can finish off with a weather hitch around the pin.

H.17.b. Stout Cleat

Where a stout cleat is used to make fast, a full turn is taken around the base, followed by three figure eights around the horns. The final figure eight can finish off with a weather hitch around one horn.

H.18. Anchor Watch

Maintain a live watch whenever anchored to monitor the conditions and equipment. Things to watch for are:

- Dragging anchor.
- Changes in the weather.
- Other vessels dragging their anchor or anchoring near your vessel.
- Connection of the anchor rode to the fitting.

See *Chapter 1, Section C, Watchstanding Responsibilities* for a complete description of the anchor watch.

H.19. Weighing Anchor

When it is time to weigh anchor and get underway, perform the following procedures:

Step	Procedure
1	Go forward slowly and take in the anchor rode to prevent fouling the screws.
2	Fake the line on the deck as it comes onboard.
3	When the boat approaches the spot directly over the anchor, and the rode is tending straight up and down, the anchor will usually free itself from the bottom.

H.20. Clearing a Fouled Anchor

If the anchor refuses to break free, perform the following procedures:

Step	Procedure
1	Snub the anchor line around the forward bitt or cleat and advance the boat a few feet.
2	Sometimes even this will not free the anchor, and the operator should run in a wide circle, slowly, to change the angle of pull.
3	Take extreme care to ensure the anchor line does not tangle in the screws during this operation. (see **Figure 10-32**)

Another way to break out an anchor is with a "trip line" (if one was rigged before anchoring). A trip line is a line strong enough to stand the pull of a snagged anchor (a ⅜-inch line is a typical size). Perform the following procedures if a trip line is needed:

Step	Procedure
1	Attach one end of the trip line to the crown of the anchor (some anchors have a hole for this purpose). The trip line should be long enough to reach the surface in normal anchoring waters, with allowance for tidal changes.
2	Secure the other end of the trip line to a float that can be retrieved with a boathook.
3	If the anchor does not trip in the normal manner, pick up the trip line and haul the anchor up crown first.

Besides helping recover a fouled anchor, a trip line helps determine where the anchor is on the bottom in relation to the vessel. This may help prevent other boaters from anchoring in the area as well as help make the approach back to the anchor during recovery.

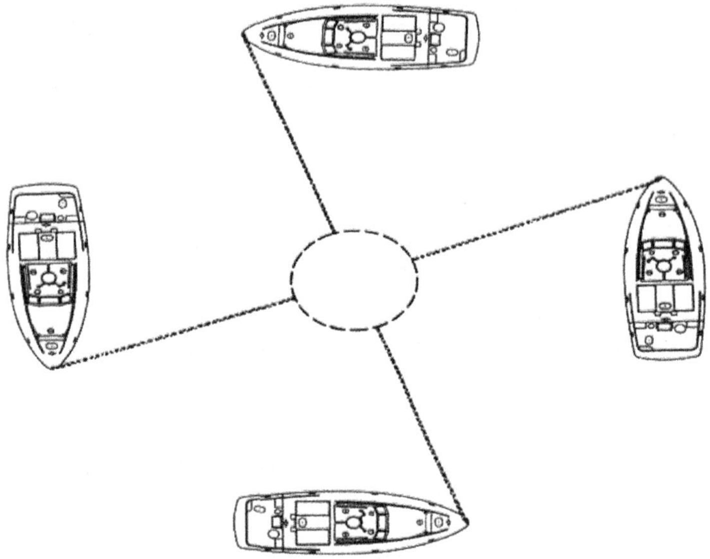

Figure 10-32
Freeing a Fouled Anchor

H.21. Cleaning the Anchor

The anchor should be cleaned before bringing it onboard, as it may have some "bottom" on it. Perform the following procedures to clean the anchor:

Step	Procedure
1	Either dunk the anchor up and down in the water or make the rode off to your connection point so that the anchor is just below the surface of the water.
2	Back down slowly and drag the anchor through the water till clean.
3	Check the condition of the equipment and, before departure from the area, be sure the anchor is adequately secured to prevent shifting and damage to the boat.

Anchor Stowage

H.22. Boat Size

Stowage of ground tackle depends upon the size of the boat. In smaller boats, it may be on deck, with the anchor secured in chocks to prevent shifting as waves cause the boat to roll. Some boats have the working anchor attached to a pulpit and the rode in a forward locker. The ground tackle should always be ready for use when the boat is underway.

H.23. Maintenance

After anchoring in salt water, ground tackle should be rinsed off with fresh water before stowing it, if possible.

- Nylon: Nylon rode dries quickly and can be stowed while damp.
- All-chain rode: If using an all-chain rode, drying on deck before stowing will help to prevent rust.
- Natural fiber: A natural fiber, like manila, must be thoroughly dried before stowage to prevent rot.

H.24. Second Anchor

Some boats carry a second anchor to use as a storm anchor. It is stowed securely, but in a readily accessible place with a rode nearby. The second anchor should be inspected from time to time to make sure it is in good condition.

This page intentionally left blank.

Chapter 11
Communications

Introduction

Communication between mariners has long been recognized as a necessity. Using the radio proficiently and knowing proper radio protocol reflects well upon the boat crew's and the radio operator's professionalism. It is essential that each boat crewmember is completely aware of the common distress signals and how they are used in emergencies. This chapter will provide basic knowledge of voice communication conventions, procedures, and the various distress signals.

Most marine communications are done by using voice radio transmissions. These are very much like two people talking on the telephone, but with significant differences that boat crewmembers must understand.

Typically, voice radio communications are "simplex," or one way at a time - when one person is speaking, the second person must wait. This differs from face-to-face and telephone conversations where voices may overlap. Simplex communication is the reason for many of the procedural regulations for voice radio communications.

NOTE For additional information on Coast Guard communications, refer to the *Telecommunications Manual (TCM)*, COMDTINST M2000.3 (series).

NOTE All operators should check all of their radio equipment for proper operation before getting underway and immediately report any malfunctions.

In this chapter

This chapter contains the following sections:

Section A. Radio Signal Characteristics

Introduction

Types of modulation and frequencies are the two basic characteristics shared by radio signals. To understand radio communications, it is fundamental for all crewmembers who use the radio to know about types of modulation, use of the different radios, and frequencies.

In this section

This section contains the following information:

Modulation and Frequency

A.1. Types of Modulation

Modulation is a variation in radio wave amplitude or frequency. The Coast Guard uses the common types of modulation:

- Amplitude Modulation (AM) - Single Side Band (SSB) Medium Frequency/High Frequency (MF/HF), some Very High Frequency (VHF) systems and Ultra High Frequency (UHF)
- Frequency Modulation (FM) - Very High Frequency (VHF) systems

A.2. Frequencies, Types, and Ranges

The Coast Guard uses several types of modulation, among them SSB and FM. For maritime use, the most commonly used radio frequencies are in the following ranges:

Band	Frequency Range
MF	0.3 to 3 MHz
HF	3 to 30 MHz
VHF	30 to 300 MHz
UHF	300 to 3000 MHz

Radio Systems

A.3. Description

There are several basic types of voice radios. On boats, they are frequently MF/HF and VHF-FM, and usually, are identified by the radio's mode of transmission. Understanding the basic differences of the types of radios and their use will assist crewmembers in using them most effectively and professionally.

A.4. Use and Performance

Every Coast Guard boat carries a VHF-FM radio; many will also carry an MF-HF radio. There are several differences in usage and performance of MF/HF SSB and VHF-FM radios.

A.4.a. VHF Line of Sight Radio

VHF-FM (156-162 MHz) is used for local, short-range marine communications. Frequencies in this band operate on the line-of-sight (LOS) principle. Effective communications range depends mainly on the height of antennas of both the receiving and transmitting stations, and somewhat on the power output of the transmitting station. VHF equipment is called "line-of-sight radio" because its radio waves travel in nearly a straight line, meaning, if one antenna can "see" another antenna, communications between the two is possible. Occasionally, atmospheric conditions allow VHF signals to bounce or bend in their line of travel, increasing the transmission's range farther than normal.

A.4.b. VHF-FM National Distress System

The Coast Guard VHF-FM National Distress System (NDS) provides distress, safety, and command and control communications coverage in most areas of boating activity (including inland waters) in which the Coast Guard has SAR responsibilities. It is designed to provide coverage for, or "see," a radio with an antenna 6 feet above the water and up to 20 miles offshore for most areas in U.S. coastal waters. (see **Figure 11-1**)

Figure 11-1
Line-of-Sight

A.4.c. MF and HF Bands

Boats use the MF band typically to communicate when out of VHF radio range. The MF band uses low frequencies, so the ground wave travels along the surface of the earth, permitting communications at distances up to 200 miles during daylight hours. The low frequency also makes communications at much greater distances at night easier. MF and HF radios of any modulation type always have greater range than VHF. The operating range for MF and HF radios can shift as conditions change, and the conditions that affect the operating range will typically vary from hour to hour. As a consequence, communications between two vessels can be lost due to a number of factors, including changing weather.

A.4.d. VHF-FM and MF/HF Comparison

The following summarizes the major advantages and disadvantages of the radio systems discussed above:

Radio System	Advantages	Disadvantages
VHF-FM	• Relatively static-free signal transmission. • Offers a wide range of frequencies.	• Limited range. • Overcrowding causing interruptions.
MF and HF	• Greater range. • Interference (caused by atmospheric conditions). • Less traffic and less interruptions than VHF-FM.	• Interference (caused by atmospheric conditions).

Radio Frequencies

A.5. Description

The following are the most common frequencies for VHF-FM and MF/HF bands and the purpose assigned to each.

A.6. VHF-FM

Table 11-1 is a list of the most common VHF-FM channels used for marine operations. It is organized by channel and frequency in MHz, followed by their use.

Table 11-1
Commonly Used VHF-FM Channels

Channel	Frequency (MHz)	Use
6	156.300	Intership safety and SAR communications for ships and aircraft.
9	156.450	Alternate calling channel for non-commercial vessels (only 9th district high level radio sites have Channel 9 capability).
12	156.600	Port operations.
13	156.650	Bridge-to-bridge VHF-FM frequency. Transmissions on this frequency are limited to one-watt output, with few exceptions. This frequency is to clarify a vessel's intent in meeting and passing situations, as described in the International Regulations for Preventing Collisions at Sea (COLREGS). Do not use for communications between Coast Guard boats and Stations.
16	156.800	International calling and distress frequency used by vessels in emergencies or to establish contact with others. Shore Stations use it to announce broadcasts of general information occurring on other frequencies. Boat crews use Channel 16 to: • Transmit/receive distress calls and distress messages. • Transmit/receive urgent marine information broadcasts. • Identify vessel traffic concerns. • Place a preliminary call to other units in order to establish communications and shift to a working frequency to after contact. • Announce safety marine information broadcasts. Do not use this channel to deliver general information messages.
21A	157.05	Intra-Coast Guard VHF-FM working frequency for units in maritime mobile operations.
22A	157.100	Primary VHF-FM liaison frequency for communications between Coast Guard units and civilian Stations. It is also used for making Coast Guard marine information and marine assistance request broadcasts (MARBs).
23A	157.15	Intra-Coast Guard VHF-FM working frequency used for communications between Coast Guard units working in maritime mobile operations.

Table 11-1 (continued)
Commonly Used VHF-FM Channels

Channel	Frequency (MHz)	Use
67	156.375	Bridge-to-bridge VHF-FM frequency. Transmissions on this frequency are limited to one-watt output, with few exceptions. This frequency is to clarify a vessel's intent in meeting and passing situations, as described in the International Regulations for Preventing Collisions at Sea (COLREGS). Do not use for communications between Coast Guard boats and Stations. Used the same as Channel 13 in the Gulf of Mexico and the Mississippi River.
81A	157.075	Intra-Coast Guard VHF-FM working frequency for units in maritime mobile operations.
83A	157.175	Intra-Coast Guard VHF-FM working frequency for units in maritime mobile operations.

NOTE All vessels equipped with a VHF-FM radio are required to monitor Channel 16. Use this channel only when unsuccessful in establishing contact with units on a working frequency.

A.7. MF/HF-(SSB)

Table 11-2 is a list of common MF/HF frequencies used for marine operations followed by their use.

Table 11-2
Commonly Used MF/HF Frequencies

Frequency (kHz)	Use
2182	International distress and calling frequency used worldwide for distress calls and for urgent message traffic. Also, ship and shore Stations may use it to establish initial contact, and then shift to a proper working frequency for passing operational traffic. All units must maintain radio silence on this frequency for three minutes, twice each hour; radio silence should begin on the hour and half hour, except for transmitting distress, or urgency messages, or vital navigation warnings.
2670	Coast Guard working frequency used to broadcast urgent safety messages. Precede messages on 2670 kHz with a preliminary announcement on 2182 kHz. Primary MF/HF Coast Guard/civilian liaison frequency.
3023.5 and 5680	International SAR on-scene frequencies. Use either of these frequencies to conduct communications at the scene of an emergency or as the SAR control frequency.
5692	Helo working frequency.
5696	Coast Guard aircraft primary frequency (air to ground).

Section B. Prowords and Common Abbreviations

Introduction

Prowords speed the handling of radio messages by abbreviating a single word or phrase to replace common words, phrases, sentences, and even paragraphs. Among other things, knowing and using prowords helps to reduce radio traffic by performing radio transmissions efficiently. **Table 11-3** contains the most common prowords used.

Table 11-3
Prowords

Proword	Meaning
AFFIRMATIVE	Yes.
ALL AFTER	The portion of the message to which I make reference is all that follows.
ALL BEFORE	The portion of the message to which I make reference is all that comes before.
BREAK	I hereby indicate the separation of text from other portions of the message.
CORRECT	You are correct, or what you have transmitted is correct.
CORRECTION	An error has been made in this transmission. Transmission will continue with the last word correctly sent. The correct version is...
ETA	Estimated time of arrival.
ETD	Estimated time of departure.
ETR	Estimated time of return or repair.
FIGURES	Indicates numbers or numerals to follow. Used when numbers occur in the text of a message.
FROM	The originator of this message.
I SPELL	I shall spell the next word phonetically.
OPS NORMAL	Used to say the patrol is normal in all respects, "operations normal".
OUT	Used following the last line of the message transmitted, signifying the end of the transmission and nothing follows. No reply is required or expected.
OVER	Used following a transmission when a response from the other Station is necessary. It is an invitation to the other Station to transmit.
NEGATIVE	No.
ROGER	I have received your transmission satisfactorily.
I SAY AGAIN, or REQUEST YOU SAY AGAIN	I am repeating transmission or the portion indicated, or you should repeat your transmission or the portion indicated.
SILENCE (Spoken 3 times and pronounced SEE LONS)	Cease all transmissions immediately. Silence will be maintained until lifted. Used to clear routine transmissions from a channel only when an emergency is in progress.
SILENCE FINI (Pronounced SEE LONS FEE NEE)	Silence is lifted. Indicates the end of an emergency and resumption of normal traffic.

Table 11-3 (continued)
Prowords

Proword	Meaning
THIS IS	This transmission is from the Station whose designator immediately follows.
TO	The addressees immediately following are addressed for action.
UNKNOWN STATION	The identity of the Station which you are trying to establish communications with is unknown.
WAIT	I must pause for a few seconds.
WAIT OUT	I must pause longer than a few seconds.
WILCO	Will comply with your last order or request.
WORD AFTER	The word to which I have referenced is that which follows.
WORD BEFORE	The word to which I have referenced is that which precedes.
WRONG	Your last transmission was not correct. The correct version is...

Section C. Verbal Communications

Introduction

Letters and numbers spoken over a radio are often difficult for others to understand. Spelling out words and numbers that may be easily confused over a radio helps clarify their meaning. Knowing how to pronounce the phonetic alphabet and numbers over the radio increases the chance that all voice communications between the vessel and other vessels are successful.

In this section

This section contains the following information:

The Phonetic Alphabet

C.1. Speaking the Phonetic Alphabet

The phonetic alphabet is based on the assumption that it is easier to understand a word than a letter. The phonetic alphabet is a series of words, each standing for a letter in the alphabet. Boat crewmembers should memorize each word of the phonetic alphabet listed in **Table 11-4** and always be ready to pair them to the correct letter in the alphabet.

Table 11-4
Phonetic Alphabet

Alphabet	Phonetic Alphabet	Pronounced
A	ALPHA	AL-FA
B	BRAVO	BRAH-VOH
C	CHARLIE	CHAR-LEE

D	DELTA	DEL-TAH
E	ECHO	ECK-O
F	FOXTROT	FOKS-TROT
G	GOLF	GOLF
H	HOTEL	HOH-TEL
I	INDIA	IN-DEE-AH
J	JULIETT	JEW-LEE-ETT
K	KILO	KEY-LOH
L	LIMA	LEE-MAH
M	MIKE	MIKE
N	NOVEMBER	NO-VEM-BER
O	OSCAR	OSS-CAR
P	PAPA	PAH-PAH

Table 11-4 (con't)
Phonetic Alphabet

Q	QUEBEC	KAY-BECK
R	ROMEO	ROW-ME-OH
S	SIERRA	SEE-AIR-RAH
T	TANGO	TANG-GO
U	UNIFORM	YOU-NEE-FORM
V	VICTOR	VIK-TAH
W	WHISKEY	WISS-KEY
X	XRAY	ECKS-RAY
Y	YANKEE	YANG-KEY
Z	ZULU	ZOO-LOO

C.2. Using the Phonetic Alphabet

To use the phonetic alphabet to spell out difficult words within a message, the actual spelling should always be preceded with the procedural words (prowords) "I spell."

Example: "Search from Saugatuck, I spell, Saugatuck - SIERRA, ALPHA, UNIFORM, GOLF, ALPHA, TANGO, UNIFORM, CHARLIE, KILO - Saugatuck to King's Point."

Numbers and Decimal Points

C.3. Using Numbers and Decimal Points

Numbers and the term "decimal point" can be misunderstood when spoken over a radio. To reduce confusion, crewmembers should pronounce numbers differently over the radio than when speaking in normal conversation. **Table 11-5** contains the radio pronunciation.

Table 11-5
Number Pronunciation

Numeral	Spoken As
0	ZE-RO
1	WUN
2	TOO
3	THUH-REE
4	FO-WER
5	FI-YIV
6	SIX
7	SEVEN
8	ATE
9	NIN-ER
Decimal	DAY-SEE-MAL

C.3.a. Prowords

Numbers should always be preceded with the proword "FIGURES," except in the heading of a message.

Example: "The master indicates he has figures WUN, ZERO persons onboard, including self."

C.3.b. Multiple Numbers

When a number consists of more than one numeral or digit, one numeral at a time should be pronounced with a short pause between numerals.

Example: 52 - Say, "Figures FI-YIV, TOO"; do not say, "FIFTY-TWO."

C.3.c. Decimals

Decimals should be included in a spoken number by saying the word decimal ("DAY-SEE-MAL") in the proper location.

Example: 156.8 is pronounced: "Figures WUN, FI-YIV, SIX, DAY-SEE-MAL, ATE," not "ONE FIFTY-SIX DECIMAL EIGHT."

Section D. Radio Operating Procedures

Introduction

As a boat crewmember, operating a voice radio will be a frequent task, so it is important to be familiar and comfortable with using a radio. It is also important to learn basic procedures and ways for properly using the radio so that messages are sent and received in the most effective and professional manner.

D.1. Basic Radio Discipline

Learning and understanding the following will help to use voice radios effectively:

Item	Procedure
Check setting.	Be certain the radio is set on the proper frequency.
Squelch control.	Squelch control blocks out weak signals. Adjust the squelch control until the noise (static) can be heard, then adjust it slightly in the opposite direction until the noise stops. Setting the squelch control adjusts the receiver so only signals strong enough to pass the level selected will be heard and reduces the amount of static noise on the speaker.
CAUTION !	This is a critical setting. Ensure that the setting is properly made. Setting the squelch too high will prevent the reception of desired signals.
Do not interrupt others.	Before beginning a transmission, listen for a few seconds to avoid interrupting other communications that are already in progress.
Microphone placement.	Keep the microphone about 1 to 2 inches from lips. When transmitting, shield the microphone by keeping head and body between noise generating sources (such as engine noise, wind, helicopter, etc.) and the microphone.
Know what to say.	Before keying the transmitter, know how to say what is going to be said. Keep all transmissions short and to the point. Never "chit-chat" or make unnecessary transmissions on any frequency.
Speaking.	Speak clearly, concisely, and in a normal tone of voice, maintaining a natural speaking rhythm.
Phonetic alphabet.	Use the phonetic alphabet to spell out a word or a group of letters.
Speak slow so others can write.	Send transmitting messages only as fast as the receiving operator can write.
Proper prowords.	Use proper prowords, ending each transmission with "over" and the last with "out." Never say "over and out."
Proword for pauses.	In cases where a pause for a few seconds between transmissions is necessary, use the proword "wait." If the pause is to be longer than a few seconds, use prowords "wait, out." Do not use "wait one" or "stand by."
Messages are not private.	Remember, transmissions may be heard by anyone with a radio or scanner.

NOTE When transmitting, the microphone may pick up the conversations of people talking near by.

D.2. Use of Appropriate Radio Language

The following is a list of things not to do while using the radio. Items on this list either are not protocol, they are illegal, or they cause misunderstandings of messages.

Do not:

- Break radio silence! Break it only for emergencies or ensuring safe navigation under the Bridge-to-Bridge Radiotelephone Act.
- Use profane or obscene language.
- Use unauthorized prowords, abbreviations, and procedures.
- Speak using extremes of voice pitch. This will cause distortion.
- Slur syllables or clip speech. They are hard to understand.
- Use phrases such as "would you believe," "be informed," or "be advised". They are unprofessional and not correct procedure.
- Key the microphone unless ready to transmit. Keying the microphone also transmits a signal, causing interference on that frequency.
- Use "10 Codes" such as those used by many law enforcement agencies.

Section E. Communicating Between Coast Guard Facilities

Introduction

Communicating with other units within the Coast Guard is a common task required. Knowing proper call signs and reporting procedures will become "second-nature", even so, crewmembers should be careful to always use the military message formats. Radio communications are an official record. They reflect upon the ability of the entire boat crew. The information reported to other units is important, especially in emergencies.

In this section

This section contains the following information:

Coast Guard Voice Call Signs and Ops Normal Reports

E.1. Voice Call Signs

Voice call signs are used to identify the craft that is calling or being called over voice radio. A Coast Guard boat's number or an Auxiliary boat's number serves as voice call sign for radio communications. The following summarizes the different Coast Guard facilities and how to state each call sign that may be encountered in the field.

Facility	Call Sign
Coast Guard boat	"COAST GUARD FO-WER WUN THUH-REE ZE-RO ZE-RO" (41300)
Auxiliary boat	"COAST GUARD AUXILIARY VESSEL TOO TOO SEVEN ATE TOO" (22782)
Cutter	"COAST GUARD CUTTER DILIGENCE"
Shore radio facilities	"COAST GUARD" followed by the type of facility air, radio, or Station, and the geographical location if necessary. (e.g., COAST GUARD GROUP KEY WEST)
Aircraft	"COAST GUARD SIX FI-YIV ZE-RO ATE" (6508)
Aircraft involved in SAR	"RESCUE" shall be included as part of the call sign, "COAST GUARD RESCUE SIX FI-YIV ZE-RO ATE." (6508)

NOTE

"COAST GUARD" may be dropped once establishing communications with other Coast Guard units on Coast Guard frequencies. Number call signs may be shortened to the last three digits, if it does not cause confusion. For example, Coast Guard Boat 41357, already communicating with another Coast Guard unit, could refer to themselves simply as "THUH-REE FI-YIV SEVEN".

E.2. Ops Normal Reports

When underway, boat crews are required to provide an operations normal (Ops Normal) report every 30 minutes or according to local policy. The information to report is:

- Current position.
- Operational status.
- Significant changes in weather, wind, and sea conditions.

Example: "Coast Guard Station Neah Bay, this is Coast Guard Four Seven Three One Five. Operations normal. My position is one mile north of Tatoosh Island. Wind has increased to 25 knots; seas have increased to 6 feet. Over."

NOTE

Depending on what type of patrol is being conducted, the information sent during an operations check might change. For example, if conducting a law enforcement patrol, giving position over a clear radio frequency might provide vital information to those targets of interdiction. Always review what to say and how it might affect the mission before saying it.

E.3. Lost Communications

In most instances, Coast Guard boats should check in with their operational command (Ops and position report) every 30 minutes. If the conditions are such that more frequent checks are desired by the operational command (heavy weather, darkness, etc.), then they should be performed as needed.

Every means available should be used to ensure contact with the operational command is maintained. At times, the primary means of communication might not work and alternate methods will need to be taken. These may include:

- Relaying information through another unit.
- Using cellular telephones (if available).

If after 60 minutes communications have not been established with the boat, the operational command should contact its parent group and have them try to contact the boat using other stations in the area and more powerful transmitting sites controlled by the group. If this proves ineffective, an underway search from their last know position may be required.

NOTE

> Even when maintaining "radio silence" because of a sensitive mission, use a predetermined method (secure voice radio, cell phone, different working frequency, etc.) to maintain communications with the operational command.

Bridge-to-Bridge Communications

E.4. Description

Coast Guard boats shall follow the requirements of the Bridge-to-Bridge Radiotelephone Act of 1971 ("bridge" meaning the bridge or conning station of a ship). This act was written mainly for ships but the *Telecommunications Manual (TCM),* COMDTINST M2000.3 (series) discusses those requirements that apply to boats.

E.5. Applicable Boats

Both the Radiotelephone Act and the *Telecommunications Manual (TCM),* COMDTINST M2000.3 (series) require the following boats to use bridge-to-bridge communications:

- Every buoy boat and AtoN, or any other boat 26 feet or greater in length, when operating in or near a channel or fairway and conducting operations likely to restrict or affect navigation.
- Every towing vessel 26 feet or greater in length while navigating.

E.6. Other Boats

All other Coast Guard boats shall use Channel 13 for the exchange or monitoring of navigational information. This information includes only that necessary for mission requirements or necessary to assure safe navigation.

E.7. Limiting Transmission Power

For bridge-to-bridge communications, the transmission power should be limited to one watt or less except in the following situations, when use of more power may be considered:

- Any emergency situation.
- When the vessel called fails to respond to a second call at low power.

When making a broadcast in the blind (e.g., rounding a bend in a river).

Cell Phone Communications

E.8 Description

Many Coast Guard units have replaced radio communications with cell phone communications. Standard communications are not limited or regulated by standard radio protocol such as pro-words. Units should include cell phone communications in their radio logs and all the components of the reports shall stay consistent. (For example: Ops and Position reports.)

E.9 Consideration

Cell phone communications appear to be more secure than radio communications. However, the relays from a cell phone are easily intercepted by simple police-type scanners. Operational Security should be kept in mind when engaged in these communications. As with radio transmissions, names of crew as well as operationally sensitive information should not be passed.

Section F. Emergency Voice Communications and Distress Signals

Introduction

Whether the vessel is providing emergency assistance or in need of it itself, knowledge of the correct procedures and available equipment can save lives.

In this section

This section contains the following information:

Standard Voice Radio Urgency Calls

F.1. Description

When an emergency occurs, the proper prowords should be used to show the degree of urgency. Hearing one of these urgency calls should trigger specific responses in a listener, such as, preparing to collect information on an emergency or refraining from transmitting on the frequency until all is clear. The meaning of each urgency call is outlined below.

F.2. MAYDAY

MAYDAY is a distress call of the highest priority. Spoken three times, it shows that a person, boat, or aircraft is threatened by grave or imminent danger and requires immediate assistance. Broadcast on 2182 kHz or Channel 16.

F.2.a. Priority

A MAYDAY call has absolute priority over all other transmissions and shall not be addressed to a particular station.

F.2.b. Station Responses

All units hearing a MAYDAY call should immediately cease transmissions that may interfere with the distress traffic, and continue to listen on the distress message's frequency.

NOTE If the unit transmitting the distress call is determined to be some distance away, pause a few moments to allow ships or stations nearer the scene to answer.

NOTE When working a distress situation on Channel 16, do not attempt to change (shift) to a working channel until enough information is obtained to handle the distress in case communications are lost during the act of shifting. (For more information on the necessary SAR incident information required to assist a vessel in distress, see *Chapter 15, Search and Rescue.*

F.3. PAN-PAN

Broadcast on 2182 kHz or Channel 16, this urgency signal consists of three repetitions of the group of words "PAN-PAN" (*pahn-pahn*). It means that the calling Station has a very urgent message to transmit concerning the safety of a ship, aircraft, vehicle, or person.

F.4. SECURITÉ

"SECURITÉ" (*SEE-CURE-IT-TAY*) is a safety signal spoken three times and transmitted on 2182 kHz or Channel 16. It indicates a message concerning the safety of navigation, or important weather warnings will be transmitted on 2670 kHz or Channel 22.

F.5. Radio Alarm Signal

The radio alarm signal consists of two audible tones of different pitch sent alternately, producing a warbling sound. If used, the alarm continuously sends the signal for not less than 30 seconds or more than one minute, and the originator of the signal should follow the signal by the radio distress signal and message. There are two primary reasons to use a radio alarm signal:

- To attract the attention of listeners on the frequency.
- To activate the automatic listening devices found on large ships and occasionally at shore Stations.

F.6. Receipt of Distress Messages

When a distressed unit is in the vicinity, receipt for the message should be acknowledged immediately. However, if the unit is determined to be some distance away, crewmembers should pause a few moments to allow ships or Stations nearer the scene to answer. In the areas where communications with one or more shore Stations are practicable, ships should wait a short period of time to allow them to acknowledge receipt.

F.6.a. Receipt Procedure

The receipt of distress messages should be in the following manner.

- The distress signal MAYDAY.
- The call sign of the unit in distress (spoken three (3) times).
- The words THIS IS (spoken once).
- The call sign of the unit (spoken three (3) times).
- The words RECEIVED MAYDAY.
  - Use SAR incident check-off sheet found in the *U.S. Coast Guard Addendum to the United States National Search and Rescue Supplement (NSS) to the International Aeronautical and Maritime Search and Rescue Manual*, COMDTINST M16130.2 (series).
  - Request essential information needed to render assistance (position, number of people onboard, nature of distress, vessel's description). Obtain less important information in a later transmission.
- The proword OVER.

F.6.b. CG Assistance

Inform the distressed unit of any Coast Guard assistance being dispatched and to stand by.

F.6.c. Vessel and Shore Stations

Vessels and shore Stations receiving distress traffic should do so by the most rapid means:

- Forward the information to the OPCEN.
- Set a continuous radio watch on frequencies of the distress unit.
- Maintain communications with the distressed unit.
- Maintain distress radio log.
- Keep the OPCEN informed of new developments in the case.
- Place additional people on watch, if necessary.
- Obtain radio direction finder bearing of distressed unit if equipment and conditions permit.

F.6.d. Transmitting Information

Every Coast Guard ship or aircraft which acknowledges receipt of distress messages, ensuring it will not interfere with Stations in a better position to render immediate assistance, shall on the order of the CO/OIC, transmit as soon as possible the following information to the unit in distress:

- Acknowledgment of unit's name and position.
- Speed of advance of assisting unit to scene.
- Estimated time of arrival at scene.

CAUTION !

Needless shifting of frequencies by the boat crew or the distressed unit may end in a loss of communications.

F.6.e. Keeping Distressed Unit Informed

The distressed unit should be kept informed of any circumstances that may affect assistance, such as speed, sea conditions, etc. Coast Guard units should speak in a tone of voice that expresses confidence. After receiving a distress call or information pertaining to one, Coast Guard units shall, within equipment capabilities, set a continuous radio guard on the frequency of the distressed unit and set up a radio schedule if the distressed unit is unable to stand a continuous watch.

Emergency Position Indicating Radio Beacon (EPIRB) and Emergency Locator Transmitter (ELT)

F.7. Description

The emergency position indicating radio beacon (EPIRB) is carried on vessels to give a distress alert. Aircraft have a similar device called an emergency locator transmitter (ELT). The original EPIRB and ELT transmitted on the frequency 121.5 MHz. However, the 406.025 MHz EPIRB and ELT were developed for satellites to detect these distress alerts. A global satellite detection network, COSPAS-SARSAT, has been established for detecting both 121.5 and 406 MHz distress beacons. (see **Figure 11-2**). The 121.5 MHz can be detected by facilities that tune into that frequency, typically aircraft and their support facilities. Coast Guard boats carry the 406 MHz EPIRB. Requirements to carry EPIRBs vary:

- All Coast Guard cutters and most boats have been equipped.
- Optional for Coast Guard Auxiliary vessels.
- Encouraged for recreational vessels.
- Required for U.S. commercial vessels and many commercial fishing vessels.

NOTE

Additional information on EPIRBs, ELTs, and the COSPAS-SARSAT system, are found in the *U.S. Coast Guard Addendum to the United States National Search and Rescue Supplement (NSS) to the International Aeronautical and Maritime Search and Rescue Manual*, COMDTINST M16130.2 (series).

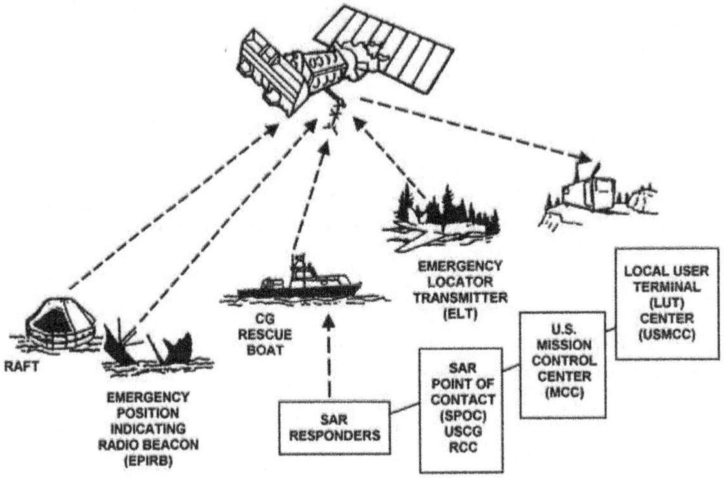

Figure 11-2
EPIRB System Operation

F.8. Types of EPIRBs

There are two main types of EPIRBs.

- 121.5 MHz.
- 406 MHz.

F.8.a. 121.5 MHz

These beacons transmit anonymously and their signals (once interpreted and plotted) are accurate to within approximately 15 nautical miles. 121.5-MHz coverage is limited by the locations of sites selected for ground stations. 121.5-MHz beacons are plagued by a high false alarm rate. 121.5 MHz EPIRBs are categorized as follows:

- Class A, 121.5-MHz EPIRBs are designed to float free and may be activated automatically or manually.
- Class B, 121.5-MHz EPIRBs must be manually activated.

NOTE Satellite-based monitoring of 121.5-MHz EPIRBs is expected to be terminated on 01 February 2009.

F.8.b. 406 MHz

The EPIRB transmits a digital signal with a beacon-unique identifier. Owner registration allows automatic distressed vessel identification and provides case prosecution critical information. 406-MHz EPIRBs generate positions accurate to within about 3 nautical miles. 406-MHz EPIRBs have a 121.5-MHz homing signal and strobe. The false alarm rate is much lower for 406-MHz EPIRBs and registration makes it possible to identify false alarms, often before resources launch. 406-MHz EPIRBs are categorized as follows:

- Category I, 406-MHz EPIRBs are designed to float free and may be activated automatically or manually.
- Category II, 406-MHz EPIRBs must be manually activated.

F.9. EPIRB Testing

Different models exist, so the EPIRB should be tested by following manufacturer instructions printed on the beacon. Any test emitting a 121.5-MHz signal must be performed within the first five minutes after the hour and be limited to not more than ten seconds.

Global Marine Distress and Safety System

F.10. Description

The Global Maritime Distress and Safety System (GMDSS) was developed mainly for larger vessels. However, there will be times that boats have to respond and assist these vessels or to contact them. GMDSS has three key elements which assist SAR:

- Reliable, timely distress alerting.
- Accurate position indicating.
- Efficient locating (visual and electronic).

F.11. GMDSS System Concept

GMDSS relies on ship-to-shore as well as ship-to-ship distress alerts by satellites and land-based radio systems. GMDSS defines four worldwide sea areas. These areas are:

- **Sea Area A1:** VHF-FM range - Coastal area within the radiotelephone coverage of at least one VHF coast station with continuous DSC alerting capabilities (approximately 20 miles offshore). Sea Area A1 must be declared effective by a signatory nation. The United States will declare Sea Area A1 when the National Distress and Response System Modernization Project (NDRSMP) is completed in 2006.
- **Sea Area A2:** MF range - The area beyond VHF-FM coverage, within the radiotelephone coverage of at least one MF station with continuous digital selective calling (DSC) alerting capabilities (approximately 200 miles offshore). Sea Area A2 must be declared effective by a signatory nation. The United States will declare A2 for the continental United States and selected OUTCONUS areas as soon as practicable.
- **Sea Area A3:** HF range (INMARSAT Satellite coverage) - Generally defined as the area between 70N and 70S. Sea Area A3 includes Sea Areas A1 and A2 if those areas are not declared effective by the signatory nation.
- **Sea Area A4:** Beyond areas A1, A2, and A3. Generally defined as the polar region north of 70N and south of 70S.

Ships operating in these areas are required to have two separate means to send a distress message. They could include:

- 406 MHz EPIRB.
- Satellite communications (SATCOM).
- HF voice radio.
- Error correcting teletype.
- Digital selective calling capability.

Distress Signals

F.12. Description

If voice communication is not possible or not effective, other means of communication will have to be used. These may include signals using pyrotechnics, flag hoist signals, hand signals, or a flashing light S-O-S. (see **Figure 11-3**) These signals can be found in the *Navigation Rules, International – Inland,* COMDTINST M16672.2 (series).

F.13. Pyrotechnics

The following are some pyrotechnic emergency signals that may be encountered:

- Gun or explosive signal fired at one-minute intervals.
- Red flare fired one at a time in short intervals.
- Red parachute flare.
- Smoke (orange or red).
- Any flame on a vessel may be used for signaling.

F.14. Flag Hoists

Flag hoists are a quick way of emergency signaling, but can only be used in the daytime. These are some of the best known examples:

- A square black flag with a black ball, or ball-shaped object below the flag.
- Hoisting an orange flag with a black square and ball.
- Signal code flags "November" over "Charlie".

F.15. Hand Signals

Possibly the oldest form of signaling is hand signals, but like other methods of visual communications, the signals are not standardized and can be easily misunderstood. Boat crewmembers must be constantly alert for hand signals from other mariners that are not standard distress signals, but that may be attempts to indicate an emergency situation. These are three standard hand signals that are used as distress signals:

- Slowly raising and lowering an outstretched arm.
- Signaling with an oar raised in the vertical position.
- Holding a life jacket aloft.

F.16. Flashing Light/Strobe (50-70/Minute)

The Morse Code symbols "SOS" (Save our Ship) transmitted by a flashing light may be used to communicate distress.

S O S
... --- ...
A strobe light (may be attached to a personal flotation device).

NOTE

> Any unusual signal or action seen could be a signal that a craft is in trouble. Investigate any peculiar or suspicious signals such as, the U.S. flag flown upside down or continuous sounding of a horn or fog-signaling device.

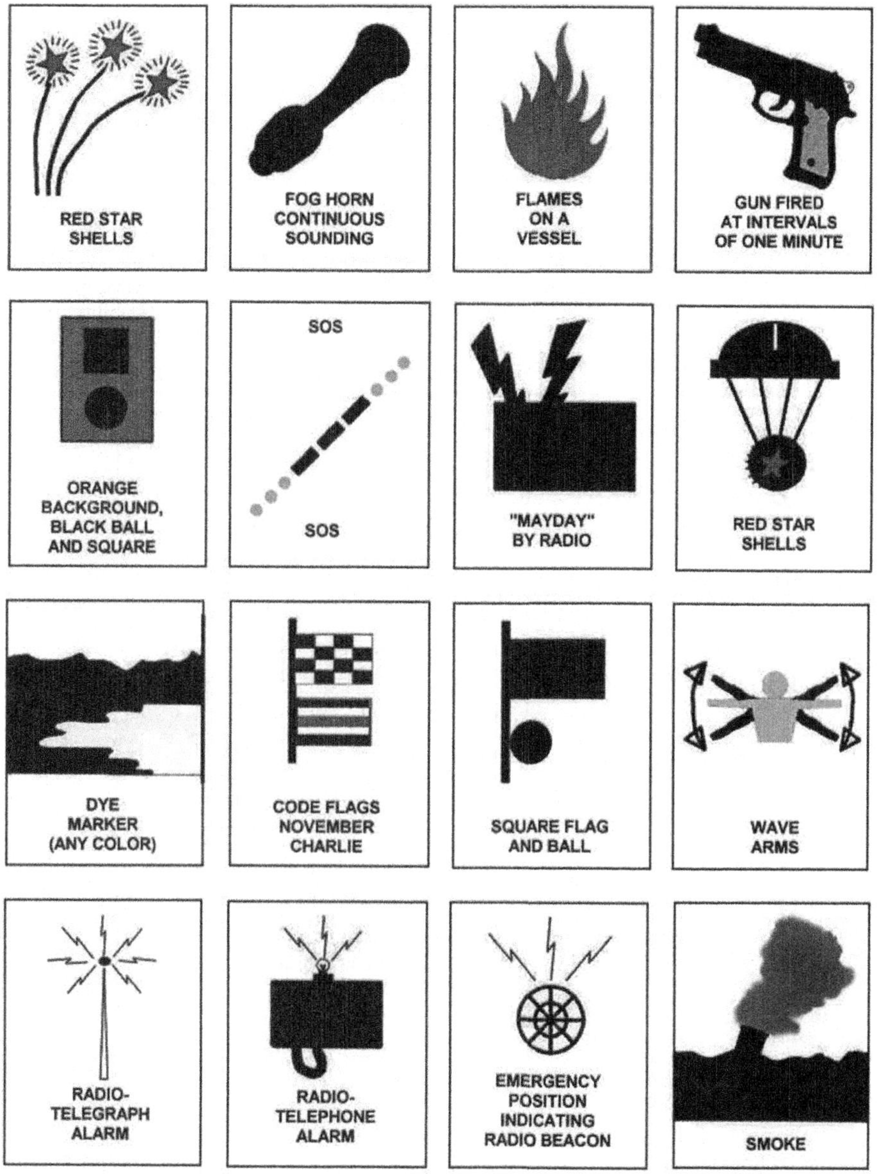
RED STAR SHELLS
FOG HORN CONTINUOUS SOUNDING
FLAMES ON A VESSEL
GUN FIRED AT INTERVALS OF ONE MINUTE
ORANGE BACKGROUND, BLACK BALL AND SQUARE
SOS
SOS
"MAYDAY" BY RADIO
RED STAR SHELLS
DYE MARKER (ANY COLOR)
CODE FLAGS NOVEMBER CHARLIE
SQUARE FLAG AND BALL
WAVE ARMS
RADIO-TELEGRAPH ALARM
RADIO-TELEPHONE ALARM
EMERGENCY POSITION INDICATING RADIO BEACON
SMOKE

Figure 11-3
Distress Signals

Section G. Radio Checks

Introduction

Radio checks test the signal strength and readability of transmitted radio signals. Checks are a simple way to determine that the radio used to send and receive messages is working properly. This is accomplished by transmitting a request for a radio check and receiving a response from any other Station that provides a standardized description of the strength and readability of a transmitted signal. If ever in doubt about the readability of the signal being sent, a radio check should be initiated to confirm the strength and readability of the signal.

G.1. Reporting Procedures

Any Station transmitting voice traffic assumes that its signal is clearly readable unless another Station responds and reports that the signal strength and readability is less than loud and clear. Responses to requests for a radio check should always be concise and a combination of the following standard terms should be used:

Signal Strength	Meaning
Loud	Signal is strong.
Good	Signal is readable.
Weak	Signal is poor, but readable.
Very Weak	Signal is unreadable.

Signal Readability	Meaning
Clear	Excellent quality.
Readable	Satisfactory.
Distorted	Having difficulty in reading the transmission because of signal distortion.
Unreadable	The quality of the transmission is so bad it cannot be understood.
With Interference	Having great difficulty in reading the transmission because of interference.

Section H. Rescue 21

Introduction

The future of Coast Guard communications is the Rescue 21 program. Rescue 21 is a modernization of the National Distress and Response System (NDRS). Currently, the NDRS consists of a network of VHF-FM antenna high sites with analog transceivers that are remotely controlled by regional communications centers and rescue boat stations providing coverage out to approximately 20 nautical miles from shore. The current system lacks several important features and uses outdated technology.

Rescue 21 will bring the NDRS into the 21st Century as the nation's primary maritime "911" system for the coastal waters of the continental United States, Alaska, Hawaii, Guam, Puerto Rico, and the navigable rivers and lakes within the United States.

The Rescue 21 system will reduce response time by providing effective communications for maritime distress and rescue coordination. Rescue 21 will also assist the Coast Guard in enforcing laws, preventing terrorism and security threats, and reducing damage to the marine environment.

H.1. Description

The present NDRS consists of approximately 300 VHF-FM antenna high sites with analog transceivers. The operation of these high sites is controlled by the local group's communication center. Much of the existing equipment was installed in the 1970's and is no longer commercially available and becoming increasingly difficult to support. The present system does not provide complete coverage of the continental U.S. coastal areas, bays, inlets, and river systems. Only some of these sites have been enhanced with multi-channel recorders, instant playback recorders, and localized direction finding equipment. All of these factors have contributed to an overall lack of system integration and standardization.

The National Distress Response System Modernization Project (NDRSMP) or "Rescue 21" system will update all of these sights and provide the Coast Guard with the means to:

- Monitor the international VHF-FM distress frequencies of Channel 16 and Channel 70 digital selective calling (DSC).
- Coordinate SAR response operations.
- Communicate with commercial and recreational vessels.
- Provide command and control for Coast Guard units (active, Auxiliary, and reserve) performing various missions.

The NDRSMP will provide essential communications between Coast Guard facilities (e.g., Activities, Groups, Sections, MSOs, Stations, cutters, boats, selected vehicles, and detached personnel), the Coast Guard's customers (e.g., recreational and commercial mariners), and partners like other federal (including the other military services), state, and local agencies.

H.2. Capabilities

The core function of the NDRSMP is to provide reliable two-way voice and data communications between shore Stations, vessels, and vehicles in the coastal maritime environment.

Capabilities of the "Rescue 21" system include:

- Communications coverage.
- Position localization.
- DSC.
- Automatic asset tracking.
- Recordable communications.
- Data communications.

H.2.a. Communications Coverage

The system will provide coverage out to 20 nautical miles seaward of the territorial sea baseline of the contiguous U.S. Coast, Hawaii, Puerto Rico, Virgin Islands, Guam and Gulf of Alaska coastal zone. Coverage also includes the Great Lakes, navigable waters of the Intracoastal Waterway System, and the Western Rivers. Coverage is based on a transmission from a low-power, one-watt omni directional transmitter at two-meters of elevation. This is the minimum transmit strength for a VHF radio. However, it is important to note that the standard VHF marine radio transmits at 25 watts, resulting in a considerably greater coverage area.

H.2.b. Position Localization

Direction finding (DF) equipment that is accurate within plus or minus 2° will be installed throughout the entire communications coverage area. At a minimum, the DF equipment will provide one line-of-bearing (LOB) to a voice transmission. The maximum search area to locate mariners, with a single LOB, is 25 square nautical miles. In many regions, the system will receive more than one LOB, which will reduce the search area. Furthermore, a DSC radio equipped with GPS will provide a pinpoint location.

H.2.c. Digital Selective Calling (DSC)

The modernized system will include DSC send and receive capability in the entire coverage area. Low cost DSC radios are capable of instantly transmitting exact location, name of vessel, nature of distress and other vital information when used in conjunction with an integrated GPS receiver and properly registered Maritime Mobile Service Identity (MMSI) number.

H.2.d. Automatic Asset Tracking

The new system will be capable of automatically tracking the position of all Coast Guard mobile assets (i.e. vessels, aircraft, etc). This will enhance the Coast Guard's ability to coordinate all mission activities.

H.2.e. Recordable Communications

The new system will digitally record, time stamp, and provide the instant playback and archiving of unclassified communications, both voice and data.

H.2 f. Data Communications

The new system will send and receive data on one communication channel at 9.6 Kbs.

The modernized system will also provide automated marine information broadcasts, protected communications, increased channel capacity, and will demonstrate a high state of operational readiness (99.5%) for all critical functions.

H.3. Implementation

The proposed plan for establishing Rescue 21 in the field starts in FY03 with select areas in the Mid-Atlantic, Gulf Coast, and Northwest Pacific. The deployment for the remaining coastal waters of the continental U.S. will be completed by September 2005 with all regions completed by September 2006.

Chapter 12
Weather and Oceanography

Introduction

Boat crews operate in constantly changing environments. Weather and sea conditions interact causing many different types of situations. It is important to understand these conditions and how to operate in them. The information in this chapter will concentrate on the effects the environment has on the water and the problems these effects can cause. It will not provide an explanation of advanced meteorology or oceanography.

Wind, fog, rain, and cold temperatures (sea and air) can be very dangerous. Any of these can complicate the simplest mission, not only increasing the danger, but also lessening the survival probability of persons in distress.

Effects of wind, current, and tide can also dramatically affect a boat's behavior. A coxswain must understand how outside influences cause the boat to react in different ways.

In this chapter

This chapter contains the following sections:

Section A. Weather

Introduction

One of the greatest hazards to the boat crew occurs when its members must work close inshore or in heavy weather. The waves, seas, and surf can present the greatest challenges to seamanship and survival skills. The operating AOR will provide its own unique weather characteristics. Some major distinct conditions occur in various regions of the United States in predictable patterns. For example:

- Bermuda High: A semipermanent high-pressure area off of Bermuda. It affects the general wind circulation and the weather of the East Coast, especially summer heat waves.
- Santa Ana Wind: On the southern California coast, a dry, warm wind that blows through a pass and down the Santa Ana Valley. It may blow so strongly that it threatens small craft near the coast.
- Taku Wind: A strong east-northeast wind, in the vicinity of Juneau, Alaska, between October and March, that can threaten small craft near the coast. It sometimes reaches hurricane force at the mouth of the Taku River.

In this section

This section contains the following information:

Wind

A.1. Air

High winds account for considerable destruction in the marine environment every year. Everyone knows water seeks its own level; the same is true with air. Air tends to equalize its pressure by flowing from a high-pressure area to a low-pressure area, producing wind.

A.2. Afternoon Wind Increases

Members of the boating public often get underway in the calm waters of the cool early morning. By afternoon, when they try to get home, the bay or ocean is so choppy that they may find themselves in need of assistance. The wind changes so drastically because the sun warms the earth. The land warms faster than the surface of the water and radiates heat to the overlying air, warming it. This warm air rises, reducing the atmospheric pressure in that area. The air offshore over the ocean is cool, and cool air is dense and heavy.

The cool air from offshore flows inland in an attempt to equalize the pressure differential caused by the rising warm air. This flow produces wind, known as sea breeze. After sunset, the inland area cools more quickly than the water, and the wind diminishes.

Sea breezes typically reach their highest speeds during the period of maximum heating (i.e., during mid-afternoon). In some areas a land breeze can be established late at night or early in the morning. For this breeze to occur, the sea surface temperature must be higher than the air temperature over land, along with weak winds prior to the breeze.

NOTE Wind direction is the compass heading from which the wind blows.

A.3. Beaufort Wind Scale

The Beaufort Wind Scale (see **Table 12-1**) numbers define a particular state of wind and wave. The scale allows mariners to estimate the wind speed based on the sea state.

NOTE The Beaufort Wind Scale extends to force 18. For boat operating purposes, **Table 12-1** is limited to force 10.

Table 12-1
Beaufort Wind Scale

Beaufort Scale	Wind Speed (Knots)	Indications	Approximate Wave Height		Davis Sea State
			(Feet)	(Meters)	
0	Calm	Mirror like.	0	0	0
1	1-3	Ripples with appearance of scales.	0.25	0.1	0
2	4-6	Small wavelets that do not break. Glassy appearance.	0.5-1	0.2-0.3	1
3	7-10	Large wavelets. Some crests begin to break. Scattered whitecaps.	2-3	0.6-1	2
4	11-16	Small waves becoming longer. Fairly frequent whitecaps.	3.5-5	1-1.5	3
5	17-21	Moderate waves. Pronounced long form. Many whitecaps.	6-8	2-2.5	4
6	22-27	Large waves begin to form. White foam crests are more extensive. Some spray.	9.5-13	3-4	5
7	28-33	Sea heaps up. White foam from breaking waves begins to blow in streaks along the direction of the waves.	13.5-19	4-5.5	6
8	34-40	Moderately high waves of greater length. Edges of crests break into spindrift foam blown in well-marked streaks in the direction of the waves.	18-25	5.5-7.5	6
9	41-47	High waves. Dense streaks of foam. Sea begins to roll. Spray affects visibility.	23-32	7-10	6
10	48-55	Very high waves with over-hanging crests. Foam in great patches blown in dense white streaks. Whole surface of sea takes on a white appearance. Visibility affected.	29-41	9-12.5	7

A.4. Weather Warning Signals

The National Weather Service provides radio weather broadcasts. Although no longer required to be displayed, various shore activities may still use a system of flag and light signals to announce weather warnings. These weather warnings and their flags and lights signals are summarized in **Table 12-2**.

Table 12-2
Marine Advisories and Warnings Included in Coastal and Offshore Forecasts

Marine Advisories and Warnings	Winds	Day Signal Onshore	Night Signal Onshore
Special Marine Warning	A severe local storm warning affecting coastal water areas, or a warning of potentially hazardous weather conditions usually of short duration (2 hours or less) and producing wind speeds of 34 KT or more, that is not adequately covered by existing marine warnings.		
Small Craft Advisory (conditions dangerous to small craft operations)	An advisory in coastal waters for winds from approximately 18 to 33 KT inclusive (lower limit may vary by region) or for sea conditions, either predicted or occurring, that are considered potentially hazardous to small boats. There is no legal definition for "small craft."	Red pennant	Red-over-white light
Gale Warning	A warning of sustained winds in the range 34 to 47 KT inclusive either predicted or occurring, not associated with tropical cyclones.	Two red pennants	White-over-red lights
Storm Warning	A warning of sustained winds of 48 KT or more, not associated with a tropical cyclone.	Square red flag with black center	Two red lights
Hurricane Force Wind Warning	A warning for sustained winds of 64 KT or greater either predicted or occurring, not associated with a tropical cyclone.		
Tropical Storm Warning	A warning of sustained winds from 34 to 63 KT inclusive either predicted or occurring, associated with tropical cyclones.		
Hurricane Warning	A warning for sustained winds of 64 KT or greater either predicted or occurring, associated with a tropical cyclone.	Two square red flags with black centers	Three vertical lights - red, white, red

A.5. Coastal Warning Display Program

The U.S. Government has formally terminated its Coastal Warning Display program. However, private sector groups, such as marinas, can continue to maintain such displays as a source of marine advisory and warning information. These organizations shall be solely responsible for obtaining up-to-date and accurate information for their displays through such sources as NWR, NWWS, USCG circuits and broadcasts, or local emergency service organizations. They shall also assume all financial responsibilities for purchasing and maintaining displays such as flags, pennants, lights, and other equipment.

Thunderstorms and Lightning

A.6. Thunderstorms

Thunderstorms have violent vertical movement of air. They usually form when air currents rise over locally warmed areas or a cold front forces warm moist air aloft. Thunderstorms are dangerous not only because of lightning, but also because of the strong winds and the rough, confused seas that accompany them. Sharp intermittent static on the AM radio often indicates a thunderstorm.

A.7. Lightning

Lightning is a potentially life-threatening phenomenon associated with some storms. Not all storms are thunderstorms, but all thunderstorms have lightning. Lightning occurs when opposite electrical charges within a thundercloud, or between a cloud and the earth, attract. It is actually a rapid equalization of the large static charges built up by air motion within the clouds. Lightning is very unpredictable and has immense power. A lightning "bolt" usually strikes the highest object on the boat, generally the mast or radio antenna. A mast with a full grounding harness affords excellent protection.

WARNING

Fiberglass radio antennas are not suitable protection, and antennas with loading coils offer protection only to the height of the loading coil. (see **Figure 12-1** through **Figure 12-3**) Underwriters' texts such as the National Fire Protective Association manuals describe a proper grounding system.

A.7.a. Grounding Systems

Coast Guard standard boats have a grounding system (most commercially available vessels do not). A boat can minimize being struck by lightning by staying in port (assuming there are higher objects about) during thunderstorms and by installing a grounding system similar to those found on buildings and other land structures. The grounding system provides lightning a path to reach ground without causing damage or injury. **Figure 12-1** and **Figure 12-2** show the lightning protected zone for a motorboat and a sailboat. **Figure 12-3** diagrams how a grounding system can be installed on a boat.

NOTE

A grounding system on a boat provides lightning with a path to reach the water without causing severe damage or injury. Despite the high number of boats on the water, reports of lightning strikes on boats are rare.

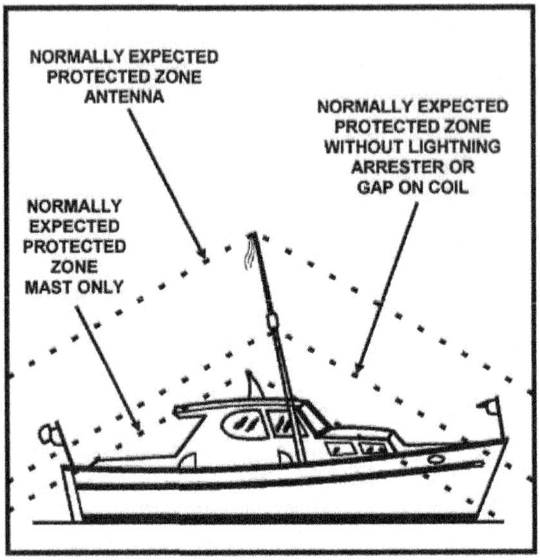

Figure 12-1
Lightning Protected Zone on a Motorboat

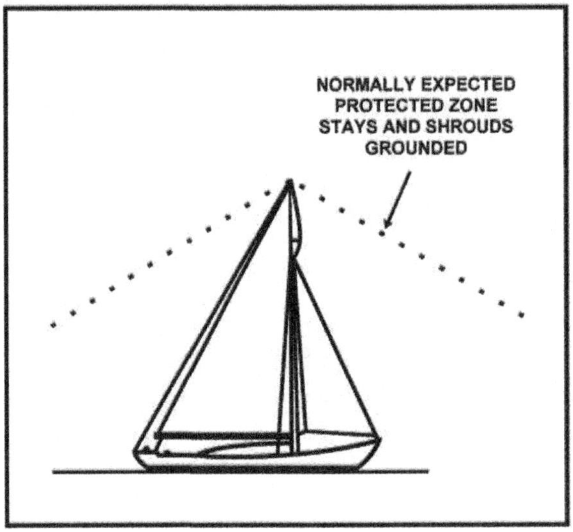

Figure 12-2
Lightning Protected Zone on a Sailboat

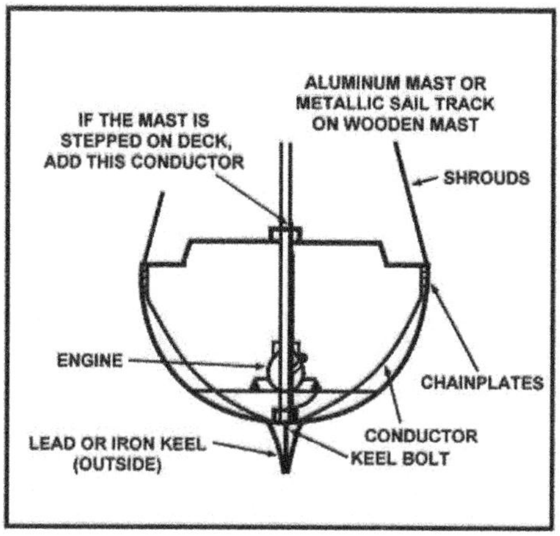

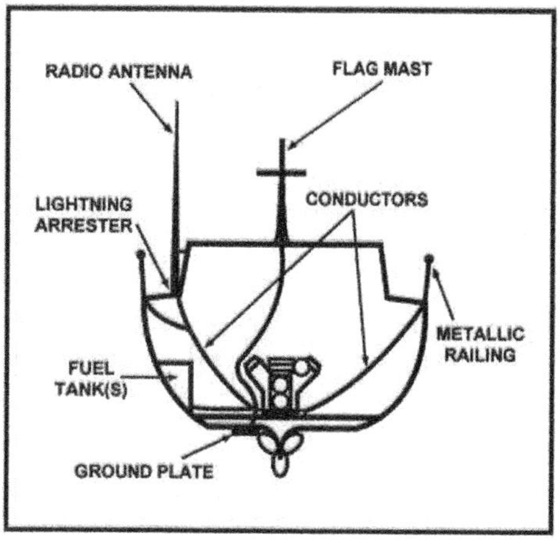

Figure 12-3
Grounding System on a Sailboat and a Motorboat

A.8. Distance From a Thunderstorm

The boat's distance from a thunderstorm can be estimated by knowing it takes about five seconds for the sound of thunder to travel each mile.

- Observe the lightning flash.
- Count the number of seconds it takes for the sound of its thunder to arrive.
- Convert to miles by dividing the number of seconds by 5.

NOTE Counting "one thousand one, one thousand two, one thousand three, one thousand four, one thousand five" will aid in correctly counting seconds.

A.9. Safety

If caught in a lightning strike area, the following procedures apply:

Step	Procedure
1	Head for shore or the nearest shelter.
2	While underway, stay inside the boat, keep crewmembers low, and stay dry.
3	Avoid touching metal, such as metal shift and throttle levers and metal steering wheels.
4	Avoid contact with the radio.
5	If lightning strikes, expect the compass to be inaccurate and onboard electronics to suffer extensive damage.

A.10. Waterspouts

A waterspout is a rotating column of air, usually pendant from a cumulus or cumulonimbus cloud, that forms over water and whose circulation extends to the surface. There are two types of waterspouts:

- Violent convective storms over land moving seaward (tornadoes).
- Storms formed over sea with fair or foul weather (more common than tornadoes).

Waterspouts develop as a funnel-shaped cloud and when fully developed extend from the water's surface to the base of a cumulus cloud. The water in a waterspout is mostly confined to its lower portion. The air in waterspouts may rotate clockwise or counterclockwise, depending on the manner of formation. Waterspouts vary in diameter, height, strength and duration, and are found most frequently in tropical regions.

NOTE While waterspouts are found more frequently in tropical areas, they are not uncommon in higher latitudes.

Fog

A.11. Description

Fog is a multitude of minute water droplets suspended in the atmosphere, sufficiently dense to scatter light rays and reduce visibility. Fog makes locating anything more difficult and also makes the voyage to and from the scene more hazardous.

A.12. Advection Fog

The most troublesome type of fog to mariners is advection fog. Advection means horizontal movement. This type of fog occurs when warm, moist air moves over colder land or water surfaces. The greater the difference between the air temperature and the underlying surface temperature, the denser the fog. Sunlight hardly affects advection fog. It can occur during either the day or night. An increase in wind speed or change in direction may disperse advection fog; however, a slight increase in wind speed can actually make the fog layer thicker.

A.13. Radiation (Ground) Fog

Radiation fog occurs mainly at night/early morning with the cooling of the earth's surface, which cools faster than the surrounding air. The air near the surface is stagnated by light winds, then cooled to its dew point by the colder surface, producing a shallow layer of fog. It is most common in middle and high latitudes, near the inland lakes and rivers, which add water vapor to the fog. It clears slowly over water because the land heats and cools three times faster from night to day than water. Sunlight burns off radiation fog by warming the air. Surface winds break up the fog by mixing the air.

A.14. Fog Frequency

The United States' Pacific Coast fog appears most frequently in areas from the northern tip of Washington State to around Santa Barbara, California. The nation's Atlantic Coast fog is most common from the northern tip of Maine to the southern tip of New York. Fog appears, on the average, more than 10% of the time in these waters. Off the coasts of Maine and Northern California it averages more than 20%. The fog frequency near Los Angeles, California, on the other hand, is about three times that of Wilmington, North Carolina.

A.15. Operating in Fog

When operating in fog, utilize the following procedures:

Step	Procedure
1	Slow down to allow enough time to maneuver or stop (i.e., operate the boat at a safe speed).
2	Display the proper navigation lights and sound appropriate sound signals.
3	Employ all available navigation aids.
4	Station a lookout well forward and away from the engine sounds and lights, to listen and look for other signals. Navigation rules require the use of a proper lookout.
5	Besides listening for other boats, the lookout should listen for surf in case the navigational plot is incorrect.
6	If the facility has dual steering stations, one inside and one exposed, use the exposed one in restricted visibility conditions. Being outside allows the lookout and operator the best chance to hear dangers to the boat.

NOTE

Consider anchoring to await better visibility, especially if transiting congested areas or narrow channels. Remember, fog increases the chance of a collision or grounding.

Ice

A.16. Salinity

Temperature and salinity govern the freezing point of water; however, winds, currents, and tides can slow the formation of ice by mixing in warmer water from below the surface. Fresh water freezes at 0° C/32° F, but the freezing point of seawater decreases to -2° C/28° F because of its salinity, which is the concentration of the dissolved solutes (often referred to as salt) in the water.

Shallow bodies of low-salinity water freeze more rapidly than deeper basins because a lesser volume must be cooled. Once the initial cover of ice has formed on the surface, no more mixing can take place from wind/wave action, and the ice will thicken. As a result, the first ice of the season usually appears in the mouths of rivers that empty over a shallow continental shelf. During the increasingly longer and colder nights of late autumn, ice forms along the shorelines as a semi-permanent feature and widens by spreading into more exposed waters. When islands are close together, ice can cover the sea surface between the land areas.

A.17. Topside Icing

One of the most serious effects of subfreezing air temperatures is that of topside icing, also known as ice accretion, particularly if the ice continues to accumulate. This icing is caused by freezing spray, which is an accumulation of freezing water droplets on a vessel, caused by some combination of cold seawater, wind, or vessel movement. Precipitation may freeze to the vessel as well. Ice will continue to accumulate as long as freezing spray continues to occur, in turn, causing increased weight on decks, superstructures, and masts. Ice also produces complications with the handling and operation of equipment, and creates slippery deck conditions. The ice accumulation causes the boat to become less stable and may lead to capsizing.

NOTE ✍ The easiest and most effective way to minimize icing is to slow down.

NOTE ✍ Ice can be broken away by chipping it off with mallets, clubs, scrapers, and even stiff brooms. Use special care to avoid damage to electrical wiring and finished surfaces.

Forecasting

A.18. Sources of Weather Information

Listening to either a news media broadcast meteorologist or NOAA Weather Radio, coupled with local knowledge, should make everyone informed weather-wise. Also, many old common weather "hunches" are often correct, but should not be the only source without some basic weather knowledge and a tool (e.g., barometer or thermometer) with which to crosscheck the belief. Using multiple sources to confirm personal hunches is recommended.

A.19. Weather Indicators

Even experts are far from 100% correct. However, the following generalized table, **Table 12-3**, can assist in forecasting weather changes:

Table 12-3
Generalized Weather Indicators

Condition	Deteriorating Weather	Impending Precipitation	Clearing Weather	Continuing Fair Weather	Impending Strong Winds
CLOUDS					
Clouds lowering and thickening	X				
Puffy clouds beginning to develop vertically and darkening	X				
Sky is dark and threatening to the west					X
Clouds increasing in numbers, moving rapidly across sky	X				X
Clouds moving in different directions at different heights	X				X
Clouds moving from east or northeast toward the south	X				
Transparent veil-like cirrus clouds thickening; ceiling lowering		X			
Increasing south wind with clouds moving from the west		X			
Cloud bases rising			X		
Rain stopping, clouds breaking away at sunset			X		
Clouds dotting afternoon summer sky				X	
Clouds not increasing, or instead decreasing				X	
Altitude of cloud bases near mountains increasing				X	
SKY					
Western sky dark and threatening	X				
A red sky in morning	X				X
Red western sky at dawn		X			
Gray early morning sky showing signs of clearing			X		X

Table 12-3 (continued)
Generalized Weather Indicators

Condition	Deteriorating Weather	Impending Precipitation	Clearing Weather	Continuing Fair Weather	Impending Strong Winds
Red eastern sky with clear western sky at sunset				X	
Clear blue morning sky to west				X	
PRECIPITATION					
Heavy rains occurring at night	X				
Rain stopping, clouds breaking away at sunset			X		
Temperatures far above or below normal for time of year	X				
A cold front passing in the past four to seven hours (in which case the weather has probably already cleared)			X		
FOG, DEW, AND FROST					
Morning fog or dew			X		
Early morning fog that clears				X	
Heavy dew or frost				X	
No dew after a hot day		X			
WIND					
Wind shifting north to east and possibly through east to south	X				
Strong wind in morning	X				
Increasing south wind with clouds moving from the west		X			
Gentle wind from west or northwest				X	
Bright moon and light breeze				X	
Winds (especially north winds) shifting to west and then to south		X			
BAROMETER					
Barometer falling steadily or rapidly	X				

Table 12-3 (continued)
Generalized Weather Indicators

Condition	Deteriorating Weather	Impending Precipitation	Clearing Weather	Continuing Fair Weather	Impending Strong Winds
Steadily falling barometer		X			
Barometer rising			X		
Barometer steady or rising slightly				X	
VISUAL PHENOMENA					
A ring (halo) around the moon	X				
Distant objects seeming to stand above the horizon		X			
If on land, leaves that grow according to prevailing winds turnover and show their backs					X
Halo around sun or moon		X			
Smoke from building stacks rising			X		
Smoke from building stacks lowering	X				X
Bright moon and light breeze				X	
AUDIBLE PHENOMENA					
Very clear sounds that can be heard for great distances		X			
Dull hearing, short-range of sound				X	
Static on AM radio	X				

Section B. Oceanography

Introduction

Oceanography is a broad field encompassing the study of waves, currents, and tides. It includes the biology and chemistry of the oceans and the geological formations that affect the water. Boat crewmembers must have an appreciation of all these factors to safely operate in an ever-changing environment. Some major distinct conditions occur in various regions of the United States. For example:

- The freezing over of the Great Lakes.
- The Gulf Stream: A powerful, warm ocean current flowing along the East Coast. In the straits of Florida, it greatly affects the speed of advance of vessels underway and drifting objects; off of Cape Hatteras, North Carolina, it "collides" with weather systems and can cause dangerous wave conditions.
- The West Coast, in general, has a narrow continental shelf (a gentle bottom slope) followed by a sharp drop into great ocean depth.

In this section

This section contains the following information:

Waves

B.1. Description

By understanding how waves form and behave, boat crewmembers know what to expect and how to minimize danger to both boat and crew.

B.2. Definitions

The following definitions will help in understanding waves:

Term	Definition
Breaker	A breaking wave.
Breaker Line	The outer limit of the surf. All breakers may not present themselves in a line. Breakers can occur outside the breaker line and seem to come from nowhere.
Comber	A wave on the point of breaking. A comber has a thin line of white water upon its crest, called feathering.
Crest	The top of a wave, breaker, or swell.
Fetch	The distance over water in which seas are generated by an unobstructed wind of a constant direction and speed.
Foam Crest	Top of the foaming water that speeds toward the beach after the wave has broken, popularly known as white water.
Frequency	The time interval between successive wave crests passing a fixed point.
Interference	Waves refracted or reflected can interact with other waves. This action may increase or decrease wave height, often resulting in unnaturally high waves. Interference may even result in standing-wave patterns (waves that consistently appear to peak in the same spot). Interference can be of particular concern because it may result in a boat being subjected to waves from unexpected directions and of unexpected size.
Period	The time, in seconds, it takes for two successive crests to pass a fixed point.
Seas	The combination of waves and swells, generally referred to as seas.
Series	A group of waves that seem to travel together, at the same speed.
Surf	Several breakers in a continuous line.
Surf Zone	The area near shore in which breaking occurs continuously in various intensities.
Swell	Swells are waves that have moved out of the area in which they were created. The crests have become lower, more rounded and have a longer period than waves. They can travel for thousands of miles across deepwater without much loss of energy. Generally, a swell's direction of travel differs from the wind direction by at least 30°.
Trough	The valley between waves.

Term	Definition
Wave Height	The height from the bottom of a wave's trough to the top of its crest; measured in the vertical, not diagonal.
Wave Length	The distance from one wave crest to the next in the same wave group or series.
Wave Reflection	Any obstacle can reflect part of a wave. This includes underwater barriers (e.g., submerged reefs or bars), although the main waves may seem to pass over them without change. These reflected waves move back towards the incoming waves. When the obstacles are vertical or nearly so, the waves may be reflected in their entirety.
Wave Refraction	Refraction means bending. Wave refraction occurs when the wave moves into shoaling water, interacts with the bottom and slows. The first part of the wave slows, causing the crest of the wave to bend toward the shallower water. As a result, the waves tend to become parallel to the underwater contours. The key to the amount of refraction that occurs is the bottom terrain. This can also occur when a wave passes around a point of land, jetty, or an island. While different segments of the wave travel in different depths of water, the crests bend and the waves change direction constantly. This is why wave fronts become parallel to the underwater contours and the shoreline, and why an observer on the beach sees larger waves coming in directly toward the beach, while offshore they approach at an angle. Waves refracted off shoals can produce very dangerous seas. As the waves pass on each side of the shoal, they refract from their original line of travel toward each other. The angle from where they meet behind the shoal produces a pyramid-type sea where the wave crests meet. (see **Figure 12-4**)
Waves	Local waves generated from the action of the wind on the water's surface (and sometimes by earthquakes). Waves usually have a shorter period than swells.

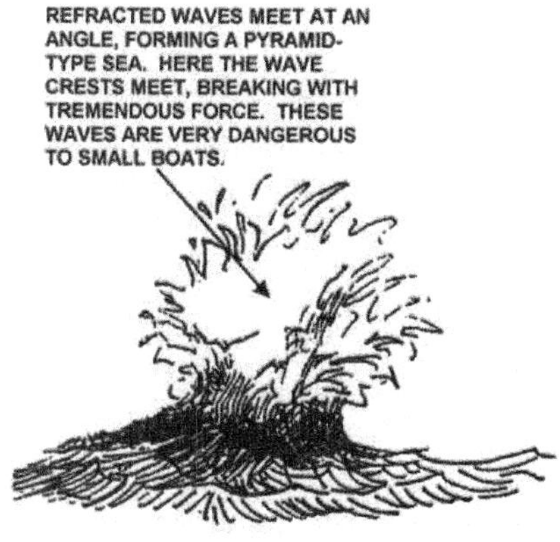

REFRACTED WAVES MEET AT AN ANGLE, FORMING A PYRAMID-TYPE SEA. HERE THE WAVE CRESTS MEET, BREAKING WITH TREMENDOUS FORCE. THESE WAVES ARE VERY DANGEROUS TO SMALL BOATS.

Figure 12-4
Wave Refraction

B.3. Wave Types

The wind generates waves by moving over the water's surface. As wind speed increases, white caps appear. As the wind continues from a constant direction and speed over a given area (fetch), the waves become higher and longer. The Beaufort Wind Scale (**Table 12-1**) shows the size of waves in open water for a given wind strength. There are two major types of waves:

- More choppy waves found in shallow water (e.g., in bays and inland lakes).
- Broad, rounded waves associated with deepwater. (see **Figure 12-5**)

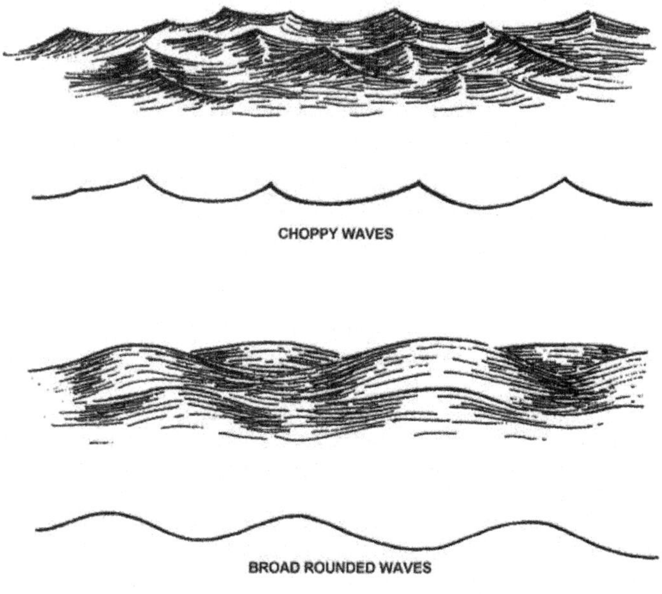

Figure 12-5
Two Major Types of Waves

WARNING

> A 6-meter/20-foot breaker will drop 1,362,000 kilograms/1500 tons of water on a boat and can swamp and/or severely damage it.

B.4. Breaking Waves

Breaking waves are the most dangerous kind of wave for boat operations. How dangerous the wave is depends on the ratio of wave height to length, and on wave frequency. Steep sloped waves are the most dangerous. There are three main types of breaking waves:

- Plunging waves.
- Spilling breakers.
- Surging breakers.

More information on operating in heavy weather and surf is listed in *Chapter 20, Heavy Weather Addendum.*

B.4.a. Plunging Waves

Plunging waves result when there is a sudden lack of water ahead of the wave, such as in a steep rise of the ocean floor. This situation prevents the wave from traveling along, and causes the crest to be hurled ahead of the front of the wave and break with tremendous force. (see **Figure 12-6**)

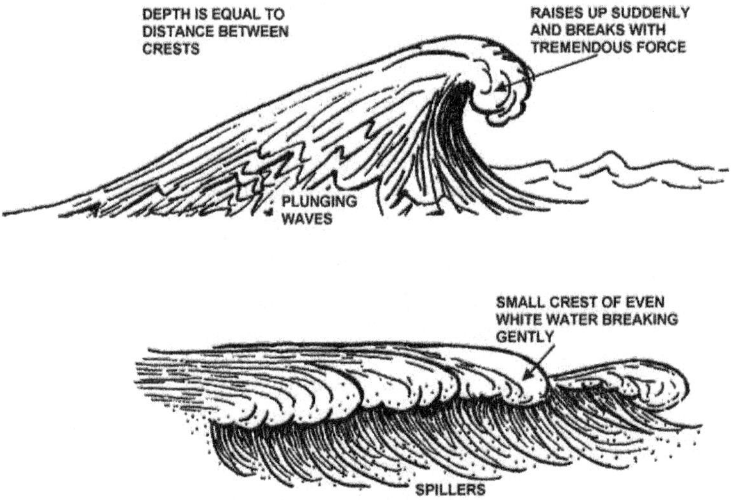

Figure 12-6
Plunging and Spilling Waves

B.4.b. Spilling Breakers

Spilling breakers result from waves of low steepness moving over a gentle sloping ocean floor. They normally have a small crest of white water spreading evenly down the wave, and break slowly without violence. (see **Figure 12-6**)

B.4.c. Surging Breakers

A surging breaker occurs on very steep beaches. The wave builds very quickly and expends its energy on the beach. It is very unlikely that a surging breaker will be encountered while aboard a boat unless beaching it on a very steep beach.

B.5. Deepwater Wave

A deepwater wave is a wind wave where the depth of the water is greater than one-half the wavelength.

B.6. Shallow Water Wave

A shallow water wave travels in water where the depth is less than one-half the wavelength. If the depth of water is small in comparison to the wavelength, the bottom will change the character of the wave.

NOTE As the waves travel out from their origin, they become swells developing into a series of waves equidistant apart which track more or less at a constant speed. Consequently, it is possible to time series of breakers.

B.7. Wave Series

Wave series are irregular because of constant shifting of wind direction and speed. Storms at sea create masses of waves that build up in groups higher than other waves. Breakers vary in size and there is no regular pattern or sequence to their height. But while the space or interval between series of breakers may vary, it is fairly regular. Despite the interval, breakers tend to stay the same for hours at a time.

The height and period of a wave depends on:

- The speed of the wind.
- The amount of time the wind has been blowing.
- The distance over water which the wind travels unobstructed, known as fetch. Nearness to land will limit fetch, if the wind is blowing offshore.

The lifecycle of a wave consists of its:

- Generation by wind.
- Gradual growth to maximum size.
- Distance traveled across the sea.
- Dissipation as wind decreases or when the wave impacts against the shore or an object.

NOTE Tidal currents going against the waves will make the waves steeper.

B.8. Surf

Irregular waves of deepwater become organized by the effects of the contact with the bottom. They move in the same direction at similar speeds. As the depth of water decreases to very shallow, the waves break and the crests tumble forward. They fall into the trough ahead usually as a mass of foaming white water. This forward momentum carries the broken water forward until the wave's last remaining energy becomes a wash rushing up the beach. The zone where the wave gives up this energy and the systematic water motions is the surf. (see **Figure 12-7**)

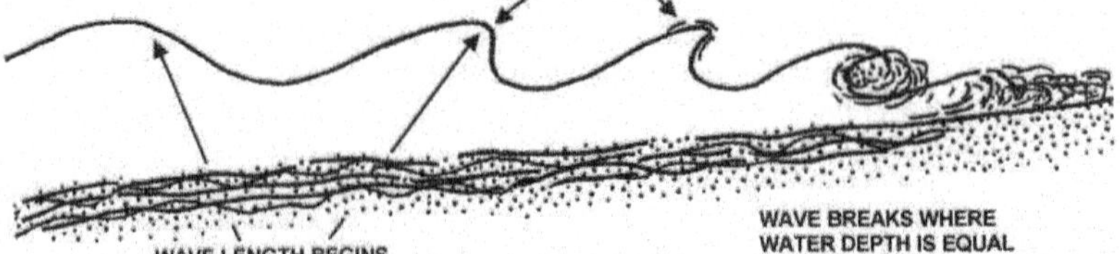

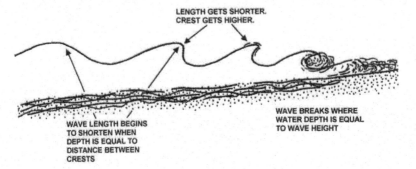

Figure 12-7
Surf

WARNING

> Stay out of the wave's curl. Coast Guard utility boat operations are not permitted in breaking surf or bar conditions. Auxiliarists are not authorized to operate in surf.

Sometimes there are two breaks of surf between the beach and the outer surf line. These breaks result from an outer sand bar or reef working against the wave causing the seas to pile up. The movement of water over such outer bars forms the inner surf belt as the water rolls toward the shore. The surf that forms around an inlet depends on the size of approaching swells and the bottom contours. The waves' speed and shape change as they approach shallow coastal waters. They become closer together (as their speed slows) and steeper as they contact the bottom. This change typically happens at a point where the water is approximately one half as deep as the wave's length.

As a wave steepens, its momentum will cause it to fall forward or curl. It is this momentum that gives a curl of breakers its tremendous force.

NOTE

> Operators can size up the surf situation by comparing the swell height and length with the water depth.

Currents

B.9. Description

Tide is the vertical rise and fall of the ocean water level caused by the gravitational attraction of the sun and moon. A tidal current is the horizontal motion of water resulting from the change in the tide. It is different from ocean currents, river currents, or those created by the wind. Tidal currents are of particular concern in boat operations.

NOTE

> Current direction is the compass heading toward which the water moves.

B.10. Flood, Ebb, and Slack Currents

Flood current is the horizontal motion of water toward the land, caused by a rising tide. Ebb current is the horizontal motion away from the land, caused by a falling tide. Slack water is the period that occurs while the current is changing direction and has no horizontal motion.

An outgoing or ebb current running across a bar builds up a more intense sea than the incoming or flood current. The intense sea results because the rush of water out against the incoming ground swell slows the wave speed and steepens the wave prematurely.

CAUTION !

Pay close attention to longshore currents. They can cause a boat to broach or the object of a search to move further than expected.

B.11. Longshore Currents

Longshore currents run parallel to the shore and inside the breakers. They are the result of the water transported to the beach by the waves.

CAUTION !

Watch for and avoid eddies. They can abruptly change speed and steering control of boats.

B.12. Eddy Currents

Eddy currents (eddies) occur at channel bends, near points of land, and at places where the bottom is uneven.

B.13. Wind Effects on Current

Wind affects the speed of currents. Sustained wind in the same direction as the current increases the speed of the current by a small amount. Wind in the opposite direction slows it down and may create a chop. A very strong wind, blowing directly into the mouth of an inlet or bay, can produce an unusually high tide by piling up the water. Similarly, a very strong wind blowing out of a bay can cause an unusually low tide and change the time of the high or low tide.

B.14. Effects on Boat Speed

When going with the current, a boat's speed over ground is faster than the speed/RPM indication. When going against the current, a boat's speed over ground is slower than the speed/RPM indication.

B.15. Effects on Boat Maneuverability

When working in current, the boat's maneuverability depends on its speed through the water. Although a boat has significant speed in relation to fixed objects (e.g., a pier) when going with the current, a boat lacks maneuverability unless there is sufficient water flow past the rudder. When going into the current, maneuverability is usually improved as long as enough headway is maintained. However, at slow speeds, even a small change in course can have the bow swing greatly as the water flow pushes on one side of the bow.

B.16. Crossing the Current

When crossing the current to compensate for the set, a boat may be put into a crab (i.e., the boat may be forced off course by the current or wind). Because of this maneuver, the boat heading and the actual course made good will be different. When the boat is crabbing, the heading will not be the intended course of the boat. Therefore, navigate the current or wind by sighting on a fixed object (such as a range) or by marking the bearing drift on an object in line with the destination. Piloting in currents is covered in more detail in *Chapter 14, Navigation*.

B.17. Tide and Tidal Current Changes

The change of direction of the tidal current always lags behind the turning of the tide. This difference occurs by a time period that varies according to the physical characteristics of the land around the body of water, as well as the bottom topography. For instance, with a straight coast and only shallow indentations, there is little difference between the time of high or low tide and the time of slack water. However, where a large body of water connects with the ocean through a narrow channel, the tide and the current may be out of phase by as much as several hours. In a situation such as this, the current in the channel may be running at its greatest velocity when it is high or low water outside.

B.18. Tidal Current Tables

It is important for each operator operating in tidal waters to know the set (direction toward) and drift (speed expressed in knots) of the tidal currents in the area. This information can be obtained from the *Tidal Current Tables*. The National Ocean Service (NOS) annually publishes the *Tidal Current Tables*. It contains a table for reference stations and a table for subordinate stations.

B.18.a. Table 1

Table 1 lists the daily times of slack water and the times and velocities of maximum flood and ebb at the reference stations. (see **Figure 12-8**).

B.18.b. Table 2

Table 2 includes the latitude and longitude of each subordinate station (and reference stations). It also includes the time and differences for slack water and maximum current, the speed ratios for maximum flood and ebb, and the direction and average speed for maximum flood and ebb currents. (see **Figure 12-9**).

Bay of Fundy Entrance (Grand Manan Channel), 1995

F–Flood, Dir. 032° True E–Ebb, Dir. 212° True

April

Day	Slack h m	Maximum h m	knots
1 Sa	0035	0345	3.1E
	0640	0940	3.0F
	1250	1555	2.8E
	1845	2150	3.2F
2 Su	0105	0415	3.0E
	0715	1010	3.0F
	1325	1625	2.6E
	1915	2220	3.1F
3 M	0130	0445	2.9E
	0745	1040	2.8F
	1355	1655	2.4E
	1945	2250	2.9F
4 Tu	0200	0515	2.7E
	0820	1110	2.6F
	1425	1725	2.1E
	2015	2320	2.6F
5 W	0225	0545	2.4E
	0850	1145	2.4F
	1455	1800	1.8E
	2050	2350	2.3F
6 Th	0255	0615	2.1E
	0925	1220	2.1F
	1535	1835	1.4E
	2125		
7 F		0030	2.0F
	0330	0655	1.8E
	1005	1305	1.8F
	1625	1920	1.1E
	2210		
8 Sa		0115	1.6F
	0420	0745	1.4E
	1100	1400	1.5F
◐	1730	2035	0.9E
	2320		
9 Su		0215	1.3F
	0525	0905	1.2E
	1210	1515	1.4F
	1900	2210	0.9E
10 M	0045	0340	1.2F
	0700	1035	1.3E
	1325	1640	1.5F
	2025	2330	1.3E
11 Tu	0210	0510	1.4F
	0825	1145	1.6E
	1435	1750	1.9F
	2120		
12 W		0025	1.8E
	0320	0620	1.8F
	0930	1245	2.0E
	1535	1845	2.4F
	2210		
13 Th		0115	2.3E
	0410	0710	2.4F
	1020	1330	2.5E
	1620	1930	2.9F
	2250		
14 F		0200	2.8E
	0455	0755	2.9F
	1105	1415	2.8E
	1705	2015	3.4F
	2330		
15 Sa		0240	3.3E
	0540	0840	3.3F
	1150	1455	3.1E
○	1750	2055	3.7F
16 Su	0005	0320	3.6E
	0620	0920	3.6F
	1230	1535	3.3E
	1830	2135	3.8F
17 M	0045	0400	3.7E
	0700	1000	3.7F
	1310	1615	3.3E
	1910	2215	3.8F
18 Tu	0125	0440	3.6E
	0745	1040	3.6F
	1355	1700	3.1E
	1955	2255	3.6F
19 W	0205	0520	3.4E
	0825	1125	3.4F
	1440	1745	2.8E
	2040	2340	3.2F
20 Th	0250	0605	3.1E
	0915	1210	3.1F
	1530	1835	2.4E
	2130		
21 F		0030	2.8F
	0340	0700	2.6E
	1005	1305	2.6F
◐	1630	1935	2.0E
	2225		
22 Sa		0125	2.3F
	0435	0800	2.2E
	1105	1405	2.3F
	1740	2045	1.7E
	2335		
23 Su		0230	1.8F
	0550	0915	1.9E
	1215	1520	2.0F
	1905	2205	1.8E
24 M	0055	0355	1.6F
	0715	1035	1.8E
	1325	1645	2.0F
	2020	2320	1.8E
25 Tu	0215	0520	1.7F
	0835	1145	1.9E
	1435	1755	2.2F
	2125		
26 W		0025	2.1E
	0320	0630	2.0F
	0940	1245	2.1E
	1535	1850	2.4F
	2210		
27 Th		0115	2.4E
	0415	0720	2.3F
	1030	1330	2.3E
	1625	1935	2.6F
	2255		
28 F		0200	2.6E
	0500	0805	2.5F
	1115	1415	2.5E
	1705	2015	2.8F
	2330		
29 Sa		0240	2.8E
	0540	0840	2.7F
	1155	1455	2.5E
●	1740	2050	2.9F
30 Su	0000	0315	2.9E
	0615	0910	2.8F
	1225	1530	2.5E
	1815	2120	2.9F

May

Day	Slack h m	Maximum h m	knots
1 M	0030	0345	2.8E
	0645	0945	2.8F
	1300	1600	2.4E
	1850	2150	2.8F
2 Tu	0100	0415	2.7E
	0720	1015	2.7F
	1330	1630	2.2E
	1920	2220	2.7F
3 W	0130	0445	2.6E
	0750	1045	2.6F
	1400	1705	2.0E
	1955	2255	2.5F
4 Th	0200	0515	2.4E
	0825	1120	2.5F
	1435	1735	1.8E
	2030	2330	2.3F
5 F	0235	0550	2.2E
	0900	1200	2.3F
	1515	1815	1.6E
	2110		
6 Sa		0010	2.1F
	0310	0635	1.9E
	0945	1245	2.1F
	1605	1905	1.4E
	2200		
7 Su		0100	1.8F
	0400	0725	1.7E
	1035	1335	1.9F
◐	1705	2015	1.3E
	2305		
8 M		0200	1.6F
	0505	0835	1.5E
	1135	1440	1.8F
	1815	2130	1.3E
9 Tu	0020	0310	1.5F
	0625	0955	1.5E
	1245	1555	1.9F
	1930	2240	1.6E
10 W	0135	0430	1.6F
	0745	1105	1.7E
	1355	1705	2.1F
	2035	2345	2.0E
11 Th	0240	0540	2.0F
	0855	1205	2.0E
	1455	1805	2.5F
	2125		
12 F		0040	2.4E
	0340	0640	2.4F
	0950	1300	2.4E
	1550	1900	2.9F
	2215		
13 Sa		0125	2.8E
	0430	0730	2.9F
	1040	1345	2.7E
	1640	1945	3.2F
	2300		
14 Su		0210	3.2E
	0515	0815	3.2F
	1130	1430	3.0E
○	1725	2030	3.5F
	2340		
15 M		0255	3.5E
	0600	0900	3.5F
	1215	1515	3.1E
	1810	2115	3.6F
16 Tu	0025	0340	3.6E
	0645	0945	3.6F
	1300	1600	3.1E
	1855	2200	3.5F
17 W	0105	0425	3.5E
	0725	1025	3.5F
	1345	1645	3.0E
	1940	2240	3.4F
18 Th	0150	0510	3.3E
	0810	1110	3.4F
	1430	1735	2.8E
	2030	2325	3.1F
19 F	0235	0555	3.0E
	0900	1200	3.1F
	1520	1825	2.5E
	2120		
20 Sa		0015	2.7F
	0325	0645	2.6E
	0950	1250	2.8F
	1615	1925	2.2E
	2215		
21 Su		0110	2.3F
	0425	0745	2.3E
	1045	1345	2.4F
◐	1720	2025	1.9E
	2320		
22 M		0210	1.9F
	0530	0850	1.9E
	1145	1450	2.1F
	1830	2135	1.8E
23 Tu	0030	0325	1.7F
	0645	1000	1.7E
	1250	1600	2.0F
	1940	2245	1.8E
24 W	0140	0440	1.6F
	0800	1105	1.7E
	1355	1710	2.0F
	2040	2345	1.9E
25 Th	0245	0550	1.8F
	0910	1205	1.8E
	1455	1810	2.1F
	2135		
26 F		0040	2.1E
	0340	0645	2.0F
	1005	1300	1.9E
	1545	1900	2.2F
	2220		
27 Sa		0125	2.3E
	0430	0730	2.2F
	1050	1345	2.0E
	1630	1940	2.3F
	2255		
28 Su		0210	2.4E
	0510	0810	2.3F
	1130	1425	2.0E
	1710	2020	2.4F
	2330		
29 M		0245	2.5E
	0545	0845	2.5F
	1205	1505	2.1E
●	1750	2050	2.5F
30 Tu	0005	0320	2.5E
	0620	0920	2.5F
	1240	1540	2.1E
	1825	2125	2.5F
31 W	0035	0350	2.6E
	0655	0955	2.6F
	1310	1615	2.1E
	1900	2200	2.5F

June

Day	Slack h m	Maximum h m	knots
1 Th	0105	0425	2.5E
	0725	1025	2.7F
	1345	1645	2.1E
	1935	2235	2.5F
2 F	0140	0500	2.5E
	0805	1105	2.7F
	1420	1725	2.0E
	2015	2315	2.4F
3 Sa	0215	0535	2.3E
	0840	1140	2.6F
	1500	1805	2.0E
	2100	2355	2.3F
4 Su	0300	0620	2.2E
	0925	1225	2.5F
	1545	1850	1.9E
	2150		
5 M		0045	2.2F
	0350	0710	2.0E
	1010	1315	2.4F
	1635	1945	1.8E
	2245		
6 Tu		0140	2.0F
	0445	0805	1.9E
	1105	1410	2.3F
◐	1735	2050	1.8E
	2345		
7 W		0240	1.9F
	0555	0910	1.8E
	1205	1515	2.2F
	1840	2155	1.9E
8 Th	0055	0350	1.9F
	0705	1020	1.8E
	1310	1620	2.3F
	1945	2300	2.1E
9 F	0200	0500	2.1F
	0820	1125	2.0E
	1415	1725	2.4F
	2045		
10 Sa		0000	2.4E
	0305	0605	2.4F
	0925	1230	2.2E
	1515	1825	2.7F
	2140		
11 Su		0100	2.7E
	0400	0705	2.7F
	1020	1325	2.5E
	1615	1920	2.9F
	2235		
12 M		0150	3.0E
	0455	0755	3.0F
	1115	1415	2.7E
	1705	2010	3.1F
	2325		
13 Tu		0240	3.3E
	0540	0845	3.3F
	1200	1505	2.9E
○	1755	2100	3.3F
14 W	0010	0325	3.4E
	0630	0930	3.5F
	1250	1550	3.0E
	1845	2145	3.3F
15 Th	0055	0410	3.4E
	0715	1015	3.5F
	1335	1640	3.0E
	1935	2230	3.2F
16 F	0140	0455	3.3E
	0800	1100	3.4F
	1420	1725	2.9E
	2020	2315	3.0F
17 Sa	0225	0545	3.0E
	0845	1145	3.2F
	1510	1815	2.7E
	2110		
18 Su		0005	2.8F
	0315	0630	2.7E
	0930	1230	3.0F
	1555	1905	2.4E
	2200		
19 M		0050	2.5F
	0405	0720	2.4E
	1015	1320	2.6F
◐	1650	2000	2.2E
	2250		
20 Tu		0145	2.1F
	0500	0815	2.0E
	1105	1410	2.3F
	1745	2055	1.9E
	2350		
21 W		0240	1.8F
	0605	0915	1.7E
	1200	1510	2.0F
	1845	2155	1.8E
22 Th	0055	0350	1.6F
	0715	1020	1.4E
	1300	1610	1.8F
	1945	2300	1.7E
23 F	0200	0500	1.5F
	0830	1125	1.4E
	1405	1715	1.7F
	2045		
24 Sa		0000	1.7E
	0300	0605	1.6F
	0930	1225	1.4E
	1505	1815	1.7F
	2135		
25 Su		0050	1.9E
	0355	0700	1.7F
	1025	1320	1.5E
	1600	1905	1.8F
	2225		
26 M		0140	2.0E
	0440	0745	2.0F
	1110	1405	1.6E
	1645	1950	2.0F
	2305		
27 Tu		0220	2.2E
	0520	0825	2.2F
	1150	1445	1.8E
●	1730	2030	2.1F
	2340		
28 W		0300	2.3E
	0555	0900	2.4F
	1220	1520	2.0E
	1810	2105	2.3F
29 Th	0015	0335	2.5E
	0630	0935	2.6F
	1255	1600	2.2E
	1845	2145	2.5F
30 F	0050	0410	2.8E
	0705	1010	2.8F
	1330	1635	2.3E
	1925	2220	2.6F

Time meridian 60° W. 0000 is midnight. 1200 is noon.

Figure 12-8
Table 1 of the Tidal Current Tables

TABLE 2 – CURRENT DIFFERENCES AND OTHER CONSTANTS

No.	PLACE	Meter Depth	POSITION Latitude	POSITION Longitude	TIME DIFFERENCES Min. before Flood	TIME DIFFERENCES Flood	TIME DIFFERENCES Min. before Ebb	TIME DIFFERENCES Ebb	SPEED RATIOS Flood	SPEED RATIOS Ebb	Minimum before Flood knots	Minimum before Flood Dir.	Maximum Flood knots	Maximum Flood Dir.	Minimum before Ebb knots	Minimum before Ebb Dir.	Maximum Ebb knots	Maximum Ebb Dir.
		ft	North	West	h m	h m	h m	h m										
	BAY OF FUNDY Time meridian, 60° W				on Bay of Fundy Entrance, p.4													
1	Brazil Rock, 6 miles east of		43° 22'	65° 18'	−2 02	−2 00	−1 56	−2 00	0.4	0.4	0.0	– –	1.0	275°	0.0	– –	1.0	050°
6	Cape Sable, 3 miles south of		43° 20'	65° 38'	−3 02	−2 10	−1 21	−2 10	1.0	0.8	0.0	– –	2.2	275°	0.0	– –	2.0	095°
11	Cape Sable, 12 miles south of		43° 11'	65° 37'	−1 12	−1 00	−0 46	−1 00	0.7	0.7	0.0	– –	1.7	285°	0.0	– –	1.8	090°
16	Blonde Rock, 5 miles south of		43° 15'	65° 59'	−1 02	−0 50	−0 36	−0 50	0.9	0.8	0.0	– –	2.0	310°	0.0	– –	2.0	125°
21	Seal Island, 13 miles southwest of		43° 16'	66° 15'	−0 17	+0 10	+0 39	+0 10	1.1	0.7	0.0	– –	2.6	325°	0.0	– –	1.6	140°
26	Cape Fourchu, 17 miles southwest of		43° 34'	66° 24'	+0 38	+0 45	+0 44	+0 45	0.5	0.5	0.0	– –	1.2	355°	0.0	– –	1.2	145°
31	Cape Fourchu, 4 miles west of		43° 47'	66° 15'	−0 12	0 00	+0 09	0 00	0.9	0.7	0.0	– –	2.0	000°	0.0	– –	1.7	175°
36	Lurcher Shoal, 6 miles east of		43° 52'	66° 21'	+0 08	+0 30	+0 39	+0 30	0.9	0.8	0.0	– –	2.0	355°	0.0	– –	1.8	175°
41	Lurcher Shoal, 10 miles west of		43° 46'	66° 42'	+0 23	+0 30	−0 34	+0 30	0.6	0.7	0.0	– –	1.4	000°	0.0	– –	1.6	160°
46	Lurcher Shoal, 10 miles northwest of		43° 59'	66° 37'	−0 02	+0 30	+0 49	+0 30	0.8	0.5	0.0	– –	1.8	005°	0.0	– –	1.2	175°
51	Brier Island, 5 miles west of		44° 13'	66° 30'	+0 43	+0 50	+0 54	+0 50	1.2	1.0	0.0	– –	2.7	005°	0.0	– –	2.5	185°
56	Brier Island, 15 miles west of		44° 17'	66° 44'	−0 42	−0 15	+0 14	−0 15	0.8	0.5	0.0	– –	1.4	060°	0.0	– –	1.2	250°
61	Gannet Rock, 5 miles southeast of		44° 29'	66° 41'	+0 38	+0 30	+0 09	+0 30	1.1	1.6	0.0	– –	2.6	040°	0.0	– –	3.9	230°
66	Boars Head, 10 miles northwest of		44° 31'	66° 23'	+0 48	+0 55	+0 59	+0 55	0.8	0.8	0.0	– –	1.9	020°	0.0	– –	2.0	205°
71	Prim Point, 20 miles west of		44° 44'	66° 15'	+0 38	+0 45	+0 54	+0 45	0.7	0.6	0.0	– –	1.6	040°	0.0	– –	1.4	235°
76	Cape Spencer, 14 miles south of		44° 58'	65° 57'	+0 51	+0 55	+0 57	+0 55	0.7	0.7	0.0	– –	1.7	050°	0.0	– –	1.6	245°
81	BAY OF FUNDY ENTRANCE		44° 45.2'	66° 55.9'	Daily predictions						0.0	– –	2.3	032°	0.0	– –	2.4	212°
	MAINE COAST Time meridian, 75° W																	
86	Eastport, Friar Roads		44° 54'	66° 59'	0 00	0 00	0 00	0 00	1.2	1.2	0.0	– –	3.0	210°	0.0	– –	3.0	040°
91	Western Passage, off Kendall Head		44° 55.9'	67° 00.0'	+0 27	+0 11	+0 13	+0 40	1.4	1.3	0.0	– –	3.2	319°	0.0	– –	3.1	142°
96	Western Passage, off Frost Ledge		44° 57.9'	67° 01.9'	+0 33	+0 04	−0 16	+0 15	0.9	0.7	0.0	– –	2.1	330°	0.0	– –	1.7	150°
101	Pond Point, 7.6 miles SSE of		44° 20.1'	67° 30.2'	+0 13	−0 20	−1 33	−0 05	0.2	0.5	0.0	– –	0.5	015°	0.0	– –	1.2	215°
106	Moosabec Reach, east end		44° 31.71'	67° 34.36'	−2 45	−3 08	−3 13	−3 39	0.4	0.4	0.0	– –	1.0	110°	0.0	– –	1.0	258°
111	Moosabec Reach, west end		44° 31.25'	67° 39.00'	−1 43	−1 43	−2 00	−1 44	0.4	0.5	0.0	– –	1.0	092°	0.0	– –	1.2	253°
116	Bar Harbor, 1.2 miles east of <1>		44° 23.0'	68° 10.0'	– – –	+0 30	– – –	+0 48	0.1	0.3	0.0	– –	0.2	328°	0.0	– –	0.7	148°
121	Casco Passage, east end, Blue Hill Bay		44° 11.7'	68° 27.9'	−1 49	−1 44	−1 02	−1 58	0.3	0.3	0.0	– –	0.7	086°	0.0	– –	0.7	284°
126	Hat Island, SE of, Jericho Bay		44° 08.0'	68° 29.7'	−1 02	−0 35	−0 50	−1 20	0.4	0.5	0.0	– –	0.9	318°	0.0	– –	1.3	124°
131	Clam I., NW of, Deer I. Thorofare	14	44° 09.87'	68° 36.23'	−2 14	−0 15	−0 57	−2 46	0.1	0.1	0.0	– –	0.2	004°	0.0	– –	0.2	199°
136	Grog Island, E of, Deer Island Thorofare	14	44° 09.72'	68° 37.23'	−2 16	−2 22	−2 27	−3 31	0.1	0.1	0.0	– –	0.2	020°	0.1	302°	0.3	235°
141	Russ Island, N of, Deer Island Thorofare	14	44° 09.18'	68° 38.78'	−2 12	−2 10	−2 29	−3 16	0.2	0.2	0.0	– –	0.4	074°	0.0	– –	0.6	265°
146	Crotch Island–Moose Island, between <58>	14	44° 08.85'	68° 40.58'	Currents are unidirectional													
151	Isle au Haut, 0.8 mile E of Rich's Pt	11	44° 05'	68° 35'	−0 53	−1 07	−1 07	−1 19	0.6	0.6	0.0	– –	1.4	336°	0.0	– –	1.5	139°
	East Penobscot Bay																	
156	Mark Island, north of	14	44° 08.20'	68° 42.17'	−0 18	−1 01	−2 27	−0 22	0.1	0.2	0.0	– –	0.3	013°	0.1	300°	0.4	164°
161	Widow Island–Stimpson Island, between	14	44° 07.95'	68° 49.50'	−0 43	−0 49	+0 04	−1 08	0.3	0.2	0.0	– –	0.8	302°	0.0	– –	0.5	118°
166	Eagle Island, 0.4 nautical mile S of	14	44° 11.63'	68° 46.93'	−0 18	−0 55	−2 20	−1 48	0.4	0.4	0.2	030°	0.9	336°	0.3	050°	1.0	147°
171	Burnt Island–Oak Island, between	14	44° 11.47'	68° 49.13'	−0 18	−1 19	−2 22	−0 57	0.3	0.5	0.1	347°	0.7	290°	0.0	– –	1.3	098°
176	Butter I., 0.3 nautical mile SE of	14	44° 13.33'	68° 46.67'	−2 43	−2 14	−0 25	−1 36	0.1	0.3	0.0	– –	0.3	050°	0.1	150°	0.6	194°
						−1 31			0.1				0.2	032°				
						−0 23			0.2				0.4	077°				
181	Bradbury Island, ESE of	14	44° 14.03'	68° 44.07'	+0 11	−0 17	−0 53	−0 56	0.2	0.3	0.2	305°	0.5	025°	0.1	304°	0.7	225°
186	Compass Island, 0.4 nmi. ENE of	14	44° 13.00'	68° 51.33'	−1 44	−1 22	−1 25	−1 01	0.1	0.1	0.2	092°	0.3	015°	0.0	– –	0.3	175°
191	Scrag Island, 0.3 nautical mile SW of	14	44° 13.33'	68° 50.62'	−0 45	−0 27	−0 55	−0 55	0.2	0.1	0.0	– –	0.4	010°	0.1	078°	0.3	197°
196	Great Spruce Head Island, west of	14	44° 14.30'	68° 50.18'	−1 14	−0 54	−0 26	−1 19	0.2	0.1	0.0	– –	0.3	003°	0.0	– –	0.3	174°
201	Horse Head Island, 0.2 nmi. ENE of	14	44° 15.07'	68° 50.67'	See Rotary tidal currents, table 2.													
206	Pickering Island, south of	14	44° 15.63'	68° 45.38'	−2 45	−1 37	−1 56	−2 37	0.2	0.2	0.2	203°	0.6	300°	0.3	201°	0.6	150°
211	Little Eaton Island, NNE of	14	44° 16.45'	68° 43.87'	−0 43	+0 12	+0 02	−0 19	0.2	0.1	0.0	– –	0.4	300°	0.2	224°	0.3	106°
216	Pickering Island, north of	14	44° 16.48'	68° 45.28'	See Rotary tidal currents, table 2.													
221	Hog Island, ESE of	14	44° 16.52'	68° 46.87'	−0 13	−0 02	−0 33	−0 51	0.1	0.2	0.0	– –	0.3	024°	0.2	105°	0.5	180°
226	Little Deer I.–Sheep I., between	14	44° 16.78'	68° 43.43'	−0 13	−0 37	+0 33	−0 52	0.2	0.2	0.1	231°	0.6	310°	0.0	– –	0.6	124°
231	Swains Ledge, WSW of	14	44° 16.97'	68° 45.28'	See Rotary tidal currents, table 2.													
236	Swains Ledge, 0.3 nautical mile SW of	14	44° 17.13'	68° 43.87'	−0 46	−0 22	−0 55	−1 07	0.2	0.2	0.0	– –	0.5	358°	0.0	– –	0.4	170°
241	Pond Island–Western Island, between	14	44° 17.58'	68° 49.00'	−1 44	−1 13	−1 56	−1 34	0.2	0.2	0.0	– –	0.4	356°	0.0	– –	0.6	172°

Endnotes can be found at the end of table 2.

Figure 12-9
Table 2 of the Tidal Current Tables

B.18.c. Time and Speed

Boat crews should select the station closest to their area of concern. (sometimes it may be a reference station, which means no calculating is needed). If using a subordinate station, its time differences should be applied to the time of slack and maximum current at the reference station to obtain the corresponding times at the subordinate station.

The maximum speed at the subordinate station is calculated by multiplying the maximum speed at the reference station by the appropriate flood or ebb ratio.

B.18.d. Current Velocity

Flood direction is the approximate true direction toward which the flooding current flows. Ebb direction is generally close to the reciprocal of the flood direction. Average flood and ebb speeds are averages of all the flood and ebb currents. Table 3 is used to find the velocity of the current at a specific time. (see **Figure 12-10**)

B.18.e. Actual vs. Predicted Conditions

NOS also publishes the *Tide Tables* for determining height and times of the tides. Their procedures are similar to those for tidal current calculations. In using both the *Tide Tables* and the *Tidal Current Tables*, actual conditions frequently vary considerably from predicted conditions in the tables. Changes in wind force and direction, or variations in atmospheric pressure, produce variations in the ocean water level, especially the high-water height. The actual heights of both high-water and low-water levels are higher than the predicted heights with an on-shore wind or a low barometer. With a high barometer or offshore wind, those heights usually are lower than predicted.

When working with the Current Tables, the actual times of slack or maximum current sometimes differ from the predicted times by as much as half an hour. Occasionally, the difference may be as much as half an hour. However, a comparison between predicted and observed times of slack shows that more than 90% of slack water predictions are accurate to within half an hour. To get the full advantage of a favorable current or slack water, the navigator should plan to reach an entrance or strait at least half an hour before the predicted time of the desired condition of the current.

TABLE 3.—SPEED OF CURRENT AT ANY TIME

TABLE A

Interval between slack and desired time	Interval between slack and maximum current													
	h. m. 1 20	h. m. 1 40	h. m. 2 00	h. m. 2 20	h. m. 2 40	h. m. 3 00	h.m. 3 20	h.m. 3 40	h.m. 4 00	h.m. 4 20	h.m. 4 40	h.m. 5 00	h.m. 5 20	h.m. 5 40
h. m.	ft.	ft.	ft.	ft.	ft.	ft.	ft.	ft.	ft.	ft.	ft.	ft.	ft.	ft.
0 20	0.4	0.3	0.3	0.2	0.2	0.2	0.2	0.1	0.1	0.1	0.1	0.1	0.1	0.1
0 40	0.7	0.6	0.5	0.4	0.4	0.3	0.3	0.3	0.3	0.2	0.2	0.2	0.2	0.2
1 00	0.9	0.8	0.7	0.6	0.6	0.5	0.5	0.4	0.4	0.4	0.3	0.3	0.3	0.3
1 20	1.0	1.0	0.9	0.8	0.7	0.6	0.6	0.5	0.5	0.5	0.4	0.4	0.4	0.4
1 40	----	1.0	1.0	0.9	0.8	0.8	0.7	0.7	0.6	0.6	0.5	0.5	0.5	0.4
2 00	----	----	1.0	1.0	0.9	0.9	0.8	0.8	0.7	0.7	0.6	0.6	0.6	0.5
2 20	----	----	----	1.0	1.0	0.9	0.9	0.8	0.8	0.7	0.7	0.7	0.6	0.6
2 40	----	----	----	----	1.0	1.0	1.0	0.9	0.9	0.8	0.8	0.7	0.7	0.7
3 00	----	----	----	----	----	1.0	1.0	1.0	0.9	0.9	0.8	0.8	0.8	0.7
3 20	----	----	----	----	----	----	1.0	1.0	1.0	0.9	0.9	0.9	0.8	0.8
3 40	----	----	----	----	----	----	----	1.0	1.0	1.0	0.9	0.9	0.9	0.9
4 00	----	----	----	----	----	----	----	----	1.0	1.0	1.0	1.0	0.9	0.9
4 20	----	----	----	----	----	----	----	----	----	1.0	1.0	1.0	1.0	0.9
4 40	----	----	----	----	----	----	----	----	----	----	1.0	1.0	1.0	1.0
5 00	----	----	----	----	----	----	----	----	----	----	----	1.0	1.0	1.0
5 20	----	----	----	----	----	----	----	----	----	----	----	----	1.0	1.0
5 40	----	----	----	----	----	----	----	----	----	----	----	----	----	1.0

TABLE B

Interval between slack and desired time	Interval between slack and maximum current													
	h. m. 1 20	h. m. 1 40	h. m. 2 00	h. m. 2 20	h. m. 2 40	h. m. 3 00	h. m. 3 20	h. m. 3 40	h. m. 4 00	h. m. 4 20	h. m. 4 40	h. m. 5 00	h. m. 5 20	h. m. 5 40
h. m.	ft.	ft.	ft.	ft.	ft.	ft.	ft.	ft.	ft.	ft.	ft.	ft.	ft.	ft.
0 20	0.5	0.4	0.4	0.3	0.3	0.3	0.3	0.3	0.2	0.2	0.2	0.2	0.2	0.2
0 40	0.8	0.7	0.6	0.5	0.5	0.5	0.4	0.4	0.4	0.4	0.3	0.3	0.3	0.3
1 00	0.9	0.8	0.8	0.7	0.7	0.6	0.6	0.5	0.5	0.5	0.4	0.4	0.4	0.4
1 20	1.0	1.0	0.9	0.8	0.8	0.7	0.7	0.6	0.6	0.6	0.5	0.5	0.5	0.5
1 40	----	1.0	1.0	0.9	0.9	0.8	0.8	0.7	0.7	0.7	0.6	0.6	0.6	0.6
2 00	----	----	1.0	1.0	0.9	0.9	0.9	0.8	0.8	0.7	0.7	0.7	0.7	0.6
2 20	----	----	----	1.0	1.0	1.0	0.9	0.9	0.8	0.8	0.8	0.7	0.7	0.7
2 40	----	----	----	----	1.0	1.0	1.0	0.9	0.9	0.9	0.8	0.8	0.8	0.7
3 00	----	----	----	----	----	1.0	1.0	1.0	0.9	0.9	0.9	0.9	0.8	0.8
3 20	----	----	----	----	----	----	1.0	1.0	1.0	1.0	0.9	0.9	0.9	0.9
3 40	----	----	----	----	----	----	----	1.0	1.0	1.0	1.0	0.9	0.9	0.9
4 00	----	----	----	----	----	----	----	----	1.0	1.0	1.0	1.0	0.9	0.9
4 20	----	----	----	----	----	----	----	----	----	1.0	1.0	1.0	1.0	0.9
4 40	----	----	----	----	----	----	----	----	----	----	1.0	1.0	1.0	1.0
5 00	----	----	----	----	----	----	----	----	----	----	----	1.0	1.0	1.0
5 20	----	----	----	----	----	----	----	----	----	----	----	----	1.0	1.0
5 40	----	----	----	----	----	----	----	----	----	----	----	----	----	1.0

Use table A
for all places except those listed below for table B.
Use table B for Cape Code Canal, Hell Gate, Chesapeake and Delaware Canal, and all stations in table 2 which are referred to them.

1. From predictions find the time of slack water and the time and velocity of maximum current (flood or ebb), one of which is immediately before and the other after the time for which the velocity is desired.
2. Find the interval of time between the above slack and maximum current, and enter the top of table A or B with the interval which most nearly agrees with this value.
3. Find the interval of time between the above slack and the time desired, and enter the side of table A or B with the interval which most nearly agrees with this value.
4. Find, in the table, the factor corresponding to the above two intervals, and multiply the maximum velocity by this factor. The result will be the approximate velocity at the time desired.

Figure 12-10
Table 3 of the Tidal Current Tables

Chapter 13
Aids to Navigation

Introduction

This chapter introduces the aids to navigation (AtoN) used in the United States. AtoN are devices or marks that assist mariners in determining their vessel's position, or course, or to warn of dangers, obstructions, or regulatory requirements affecting safe navigation. In the U.S., the Coast Guard is responsible for servicing and maintaining AtoN under federal jurisdiction. This includes both short and long-range navigation systems found in the navigable waters, along the U.S. coast, Intracoastal Waterway (ICW) system, and the Western Rivers system.

Lakes and inland waterways that fall under state jurisdiction use the Uniform State Waterway Marking System (USWMS).

In this chapter

This chapter contains the following sections:

Section A. U.S. Aids to Navigation System

Introduction

Buoys, beacons, and other short-range AtoN are used the same way signs, lane separations, and traffic lights guide motor vehicle drivers. Together, these AtoN make up the short-range AtoN system, which uses charted reference marks to provide information for safely navigating waterways. In the U.S., short-range aids conform to the International Association of Lighthouse Authorities (IALA) Region B. This is called System B, the U.S. Lateral System, or the U.S. Aids to Navigation System. The Coast Guard maintains short-range aids to provide:

- Daytime visual system of daymarks, beacons and buoys.
- Nighttime visual system of lights and retroreflective signals.
- Radar system of radar reflectors and RACONs (radar beacons).
- A sound system of various non-directional sound producing devices, though not required by IALA.

Section F through *Section I* of this chapter provide color representations of AtoN for the various U.S. systems and how it would appear on a nautical chart.

NOTE Not all U.S. aids are in the IALA B System. Aids in Guam, Tinian and other outlying areas are in the IALA A System.

NOTE "Natural AtoN" are charted prominent structures or landmarks that supplement the short range AtoN system. They are not a part of IALA System B, and are not a Coast Guard responsibility to service or maintain.

In this section

This section contains the following information:

Lateral and Cardinal Significance

A.1. IALA-A and IALA-B

Prior to the mid-1970's, there were over 30 different navigation systems in use around the world. To reduce confusion, IALA established two systems of buoyage for conveying navigation information to mariners. The IALA System A and B were established, with the U.S. complying with the IALA B System.

The IALA-A and IALA-B systems use the Lateral and Cardinal Systems to define the conventions of buoyage, and to mark channels with AtoN. "Lateral significance" or "cardinal significance" means that the rules for the Lateral or Cardinal System apply in that instance. However, if something has no lateral or cardinal significance, the respective system's rules do not apply to the situation. The differences between the markings and conventions used in the Lateral and Cardinal Systems are discussed in the following paragraphs. **Table 13-1** briefly describes the IALA Systems A and B:

Table 13-1
IALA-A and IALA-B Systems

	Buoyage System	
	IALA-A System	**IALA-B System**
Location	Europe, Africa, Australia, New Zealand, and most of Asia	North and South America, Japan, South Korea, and the Philippines
Information shown by	Buoy shapes, colors, and if lighted, rhythm of flashes and colored lights	
Topmarks	Small distinctive shapes above the basic aid that assist in identification of the aid.	
Marks	Cardinal and lateral marks	Mostly lateral, some cardinal in the Uniform State Waterway Marking System (USWMS)
Cardinal marks have black and yellow horizontal bands regardless of the IALA system.		
When entering from seaward:		
Keep red buoys to	Port	Starboard, "red, right, returning"
Keep green buoys to	Starboard	Port

A.2. Lateral System

In the lateral system, buoys and beacons indicate the sides of the channel or route relative to a conventional direction of buoyage (usually upstream). They also mark junctions, a point where two channels meet when proceeding seaward; or bifurcations, the point where a channel divides when proceeding from seaward, or the place where two tributaries meet.

In U.S. waters, AtoN use the IALA-B system of lateral marks with few exceptions (see A.3 below), arranged in geographic order known as the "conventional direction of buoyage" (see **Figure 13-1**). Under this, the memory aid 3R rule of "red, right, returning" applies when a vessel is returning from seaward. This means, when returning from sea, keep red markers to the right of the vessel from:

- North to south along the Atlantic Coast.
- South to north and east to west along the Gulf Coast.
- South to north and east to west along the Pacific Coast.
- East to west in the Great Lakes except for Lake Michigan which is north to south.

A.3. Cardinal System

The Cardinal System uses a buoy to indicate the location of a danger relative to the buoy itself. In the U.S., the USWMS uses cardinal marks on waters where a state exercises sole jurisdiction. The colors of these marks differ from those of IALA. For instance, a white buoy with a black top indicates unsafe water to the south and west. Various countries throughout the world, including Canada, Bermuda, and the Bahamas, also use Cardinal marks along with lateral marks. Cardinal marks are not used on waters where the U.S. Coast Guard maintains short-range AtoN.

Figure 13-1
Proceeding From Seaward

General Characteristics of Short-Range AtoN

A.4. Description

Aids to navigation have many different characteristics. An aid's color, size, light, or sound signify what mariners should do when they see it. Characteristics of short-range aids used in the U.S. are described in the following paragraphs.

NOTE While reading the following section, refer to *Section F* through *Section I* of this chapter to see how the characteristics of color, numbering, lighting, and light rhythms are used on AtoN to mark a waterway.

NOTE All aids mentioned in this chapter (buoys/beacons) are described as they would appear in the IALA B marking system.

A.5. Type

The location and the intended use determine which one of the two types of AtoN will be placed in a spot or waterway:

- Floating (buoy).
- Fixed (beacon).

A.6. AtoN Identification (Numbers and Letters)

Solid red AtoN buoys and beacons bear even numbers and all solid green AtoN bear odd numbers. No other AtoN are numbered. When proceeding from seaward toward the direction of conventional navigation, the numbers increase. Numbers are kept in approximate sequence on both sides of the channel. Letters may be used to augment numbers when lateral AtoN are added to channels with previously completed numerical sequences. For instance, a buoy added between R"4" and R"6" in a channel would be numbered R"4A". Letters will also increase in alphabetical order.

Not every buoy or beacon is numbered. Preferred channel, safe water marks, isolated danger, special marks, and information/regulatory AtoN use only letters."

A.7. Color

During daylight hours, the color of an AtoN indicates the port or starboard side of a channel, preferred channels, safe water, isolated dangers, and special features. Only red or green buoys, or beacons fitted with red or green dayboards, have lateral significance.

A.8. Shape

Shapes of buoys and beacons help identify them from a distance or at dawn or dusk, when colors may be hard to see. Like other characteristics of AtoN, mariners should not rely solely on shape to identify an aid.

A.8.a. Cylindrical Buoys (Can)

Cylindrical buoys, often referred to as "can buoys," are unlighted AtoN. When used as a lateral mark, they indicate the left side of a channel or of the preferred channel when returning from seaward. They are painted solid green or have green and red horizontal bands; the topmost band is always green. Can buoys are also used as unlighted special marks and will be colored based on their use. (see **Figure 13-2**)

A.8.b. Conical Buoys (Nun)

Conical buoys, often referred to as "nun buoys," are unlighted AtoN. When used as a lateral mark, nun buoys indicate the right side of a channel or of the preferred channel when returning from seaward. They are painted solid red or red and green with horizontal bands and always with a red topmost band. Nun buoys are also used as unlighted special marks and will be colored based on their use. (see **Figure 13-2**)

NOTE

> Buoys other than a can and nun or buoys fitted with a top mark, such as isolated danger or safe-water buoys, have no shape significance. Their meanings are shown by numbers, colors, top marks, lights, and sound signal characteristics.

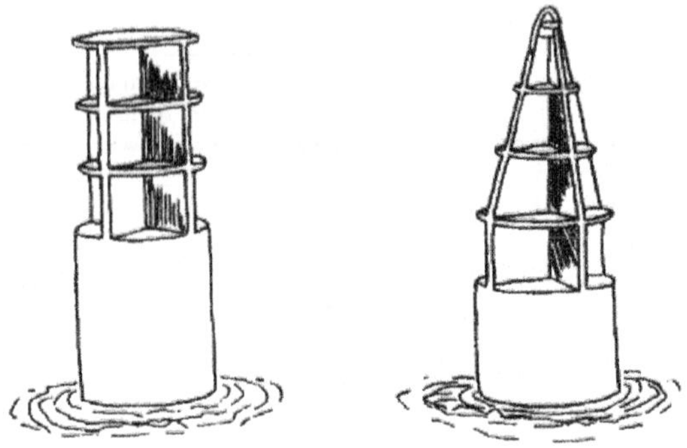

Figure 13-2
Can and Nun Buoys, "When Returning From Sea"

A.8.c. Miscellaneous Buoys

The Coast Guard and other agencies place (Station) specialty buoys for operational and developmental uses, and for research purposes. In many instances, the buoy used is a standard buoy modified for specialized use. There are several examples of specialty buoys:

- Fast water buoys.
- Discrepancy buoys.
- Weather/oceanographic buoys.
- Mooring buoys.

A.8.d. Beacons

Beacons have dayboards attached to a structure. When returning from sea, a triangular shaped dayboard marks the starboard side, and a rectangular shaped dayboard marks the port side of the channel. (see **Figure 13-3**)

Figure 13-3
Daybeacon, "When Returning From Sea"

A.9. Light Colors

Though there are white and yellow lights, only AtoN with green or red lights have lateral significance. When proceeding in the conventional direction of buoyage, AtoN will display the following light colors:

- Green.
- Red.
- White and yellow.

A.9.a. Green

Green lights mark port sides of channels and wrecks or obstructions. When proceeding from seaward, these aids are passed by keeping them on the port side. Green lights are also used on preferred channel marks where the preferred channel is to starboard. When proceeding along the conventional direction of buoyage (from seaward), a preferred channel mark fitted with a green light would be kept on the port side.

A.9.b. Red

Red lights mark starboard sides of channels and wrecks or obstructions. When proceeding from seaward, these aids would be passed by keeping them on the starboard side. Red lights are also used on preferred channel marks where the preferred channel is to port. When proceeding along the conventional direction of buoyage (from seaward), a preferred channel mark fitted with a red light would be kept on the starboard side.

A.9.c. White and Yellow

White and yellow lights have no lateral significance. However, the characteristic (rhythm) of the light does give information such as safe water, danger, or special purpose. The publication called *Light List*, discussed in *Section E* of this chapter, provides more details.

A.10. Light Signals

Lights are installed on AtoN to provide signals to distinguish one navigation light from another, or from the general background of shore lights.

A.10.a. Light Characteristics

Lights displayed from AtoN have distinct characteristics which help in identifying them. (see **Figure 13-4**) AtoN with lateral significance display flashing, quick, occulting, or isophase light rhythms.

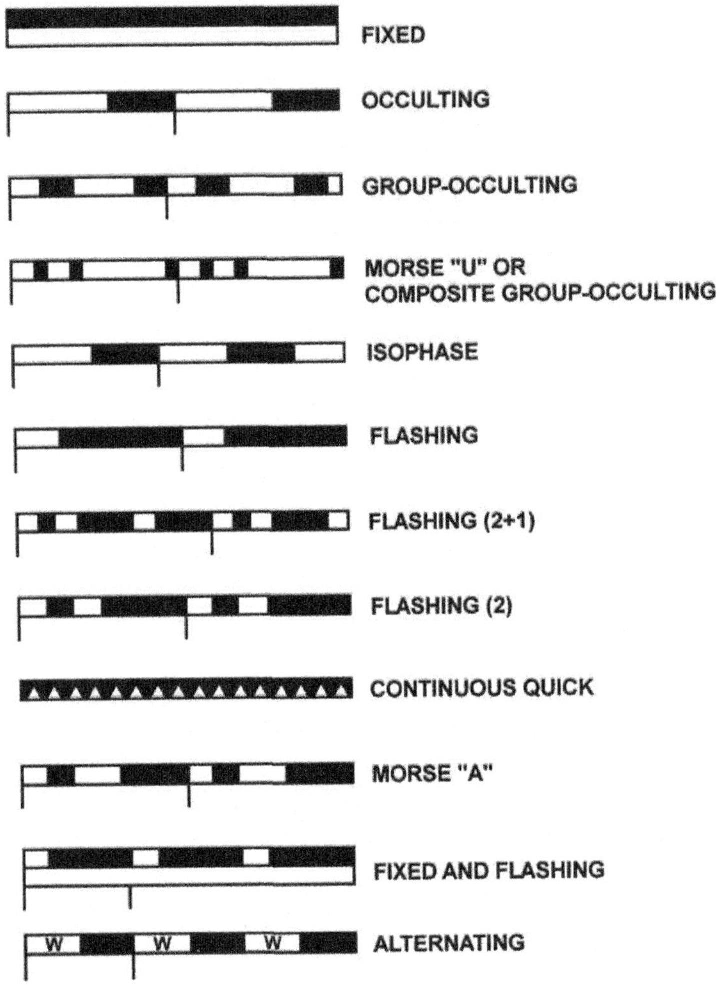

Figure 13-4
Light Characteristics

A.10.b. Light Identification

To identify a light, the following information should be determined:

Color	Color of the light beam (color of its lens).
Characteristic	Pattern of flashes or eclipses (dark periods) observed from the start of the one cycle to the start of the next cycle.
Duration	Length of time for the light to go through one complete cycle of changes.
Example: Buoy "8" displays one single flash of red every 4 seconds. That light color and rhythm information is indicated on the chart as shown below (it is underlined here for ease of identification, it is not underlined on a chart): R"8" Fl R 4s	

A.11. Sound Signals

Though not a requirement of IALA B system, in the U.S., some AtoN have sound signals to provide information to mariners during periods of restricted visibility. Different types of devices are used to produce these sounds. Sound signals may be activated as follows:

- Continuously (bell, gong, or whistle buoy).
- Manually.
- Remotely.
- Automatically (when equipped with a fog detector).

Sound signals can be identified by their tone and phase characteristics. Horns, sirens, whistles, bells, and gongs produce distinct sound signals. The sound signal characteristics for specific AtoN are briefly described on the chart, and in length in Column 8 of the *Light List*. Unless it is specifically stated that a signal "Operates Continuously" or the signal is a bell, gong, or whistle, signals will only operate in fog, reduced visibility, or adverse weather.

NOTE A bell, gong, or a whistle buoy may not produce a sound signal in calm seas.

Device	Characteristic
Tone Characteristics	
Electronic horns	Pure tone
Sirens	Wail
Whistle buoys	Loud moaning sound
Bell buoys	One tone
Gong buoys	Several tones
Phase Characteristics	
Fixed structures	Produce a specific number of blasts and silent periods every minute.
Buoys with a bell, gong, or whistle	Are wave actuated and do not produce a regular characteristic.
Buoys with electronic horn	Operate continuously.

NOTE

> Distance and direction cannot be accurately determined by sound intensity. Occasionally, sound signals may not be heard in areas close to their location.

A.12. Retroreflective Material

Most minor AtoN (buoys and beacons) are fitted with retroreflective material to increase their visibility at night. While this material does not produce light on its own, when illuminated by a light source (searchlight), it reflects the light back towards the operator with great intensity.

In most cases, the color of the reflective material panel is the same as the surface it covers (red on red, green on green). Numbers and letters found on buoys will be silver/white. Daybeacons are outlined with retroreflective material and will be identified with numbers or letters made of the same color as the beacon. Exceptions are found on some aids. (see *Section F* of this chapter).

Summary of Lateral Significance of Buoys and Beacons

A.13. Direction of Buoyage

While proceeding in the conventional direction of buoyage in IALA System B, boat crews will see the following AtoN:

MEMORY AID

> Red, right, returning.

A.14. Marking Starboard Side

Red buoys and beacons with triangular shaped red dayboards mark the starboard side of a channel when returning from seaward. This is the red, right, returning rule. AtoN displaying these characteristics are kept to starboard when returning from seaward.

A.15. Marking Port Side

Green buoys and beacons with square shaped green dayboards mark the port side of a channel when returning from seaward.

A.16. Marking Channel Junction or Bifurcation

Red and green, or green and red, horizontally banded buoys and beacons are called preferred-channel marks. They are used to indicate a channel junction or bifurcation (point where a channel divides or where two tributaries meet). They may also mark wrecks or obstructions and may be passed on either side. When returning from sea, and the topmost band is:

- Green: keep the aid to port to follow the preferred channel.
- Red: keep the aid to starboard to follow the preferred channel.

A.17. Safe Water Marks

Safe water marks are buoys with alternating red and white vertical stripes, and beacons with red and white vertically striped dayboards. (see **Figure 13-5**) They also mark a mid-channel, fairway, channel approach points and the "In" and "Out" channels of a "Traffic Separation Scheme." See buoy "N" in **Figure 13-5**. If lighted, they will display a white light with the characteristic Morse Code "A". Safe water buoys (lighted or not) should be fitted with a red sphere as a visually distinctive top mark. Safe water marks are not laterally significant.

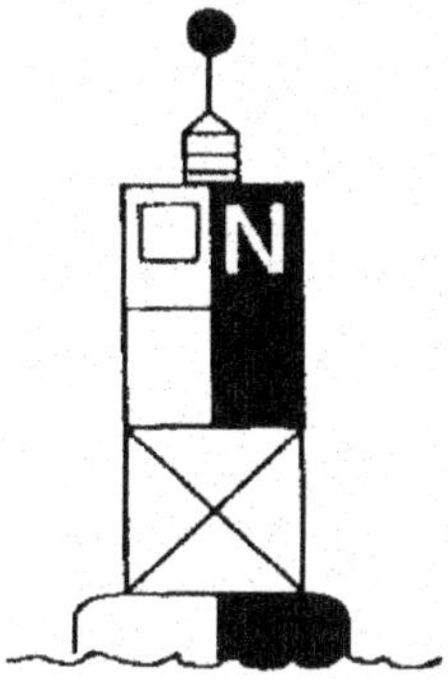

Figure 13-5
Safe-Water Mark

A.18. Isolated Danger Marks

Black and red horizontally banded buoys are called "Isolated Danger Marks". They are used to mark isolated dangers (wrecks or obstructions) which have navigable water all around. Isolated danger marks display a white light with a "group-flashing" characteristic; and are fitted with a visually distinctive topmark, consisting of two black spheres, one above the other. (see *Section F* of this chapter)

NOTE This buoy marking system is not used in the Western River System.

A.19. Special Marks

Yellow buoys and beacons are called "special marks". They mark anchorages, dredging/spoil areas, fishnet areas, and other special areas or features. When lighted, special marks will display a yellow light with a Fixed ("F") or Flashing ("Fl") characteristic. Special marks may also be used to mark the center of the traffic separation scheme. (see **Figure 13-6**)

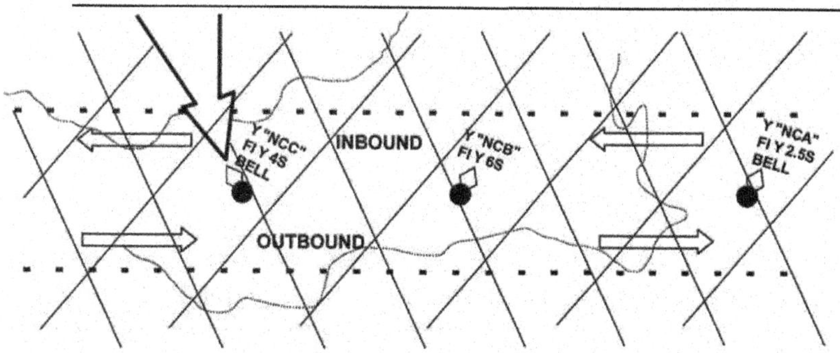

Figure 13-6
Traffic Separation Scheme

A.20. Marking Regulated Areas

Information and regulatory buoys and beacons indicate various warnings or regulatory matters. They are colored with white and orange shapes. (see *Section F* of this chapter) They will only display a white light and may display any light rhythm except quick flashing.

A.21. Marking Outside Normal Channels

Beacons with no lateral significance may be used to supplement lateral AtoN outside normal routes and channels. Daymarks for these aids are diamond shaped and will either be red and white, green and white, or black and white. (see *Section G* of this chapter)

Buoys

A.22. Identification Markings

Buoys are floating AtoN anchored at a given position to provide easy identification by mariners. The significance of an unlighted buoy can be determined by its shape. These shapes are only laterally significant when associated with laterally significant colors such as green or red. Buoys are useful AtoN, but should never be relied upon exclusively for navigation.

When a buoy is "watching properly", it is marking its charted position "on Station" and properly displaying all other distinguishing characteristics. Heavy storms, collisions with ships, and severe ice conditions may move a buoy "off Station". Heavy storms may also shift the shoal a buoy marks into the channel. It is important to remember, even heavily anchored buoys fail.

NOTE As printed on nautical charts, "The prudent mariner will not rely solely on any single aid to navigation, particularly a floating aid."

NOTE *United States Coast Guard Regulations 1992*, COMDTINST M5000.3 states: "Coxswains shall make every effort to observe and report any AtoN that is out of order or off station within a unit's area of operations."

Beacons

A.23. Types

Beacons are fixed AtoN structures attached directly to the earth's surface. The design, construction, and characteristics of these beacons depend on their location and relationship to other AtoN in the area. Strictly defined, a beacon is any fixed unlighted AtoN (daybeacon) or minor light (lighted) AtoN of relatively low candlepower. The following types of beacons are used in the U.S.:

- Daybeacons.
- Lighted beacons (minor lights).
- Major lights.
- Light towers.

NOTE Fixed aids (beacons) have a more accurate position than floating aids (buoys).

A.24. Daybeacons

Daybeacons are unlighted fixed structures fitted with a dayboard for daytime identification. To increase their visibility in darkness, dayboards are fitted with retroreflective material. Daybeacons are built on different types of structures:

- Single pile with a dayboard on the top.
- Multi-pile structure.
- Tower.
- Structure of masonry or steel.

A.25. Lighted Beacons (Minor Lights)

Just as daybeacons are sometimes substituted for unlighted buoys, lighted beacons are substituted for lighted buoys. Their structures are similar to daybeacons. (see **Figure 13-7**) Lighted beacons are used with other lateral aids (buoys) marking a channel, river, or harbor. In most instances, the lights have similar candlepower to those lights on buoys in the same area. They can also be used to mark isolated dangers.

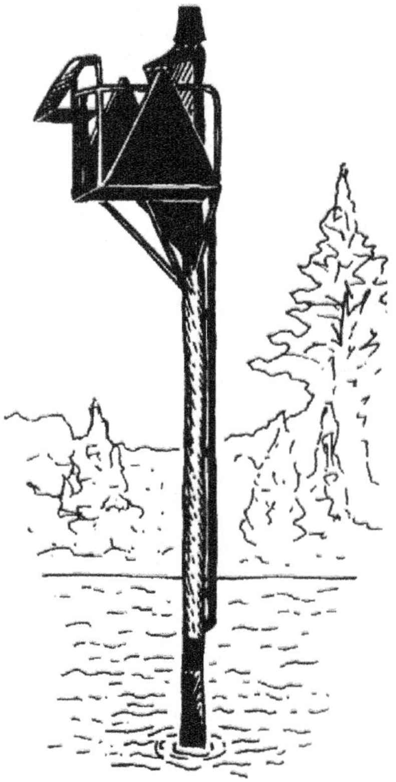

Figure 13-7
Lighted Beacon (Minor AtoN)

A.26. Major Lights

Major lights display a light of moderate to high candlepower. They may also have high intensity audible signaling devices, radiobeacons and radar beacons (RACONs). Major light structures, lighthouses for instance, enclose, protect, and house their signaling devices. In their surroundings, major light structures have visually distinctive appearances. (see **Figure 13-8**) Determining whether a light is major, or minor, depends upon its candlepower and the luminous range of the light. A light's category may change if fitted with a higher or lower candlepower light.

Major lights rarely have lateral significance and fall into two broad categories. They are used as coastal or seacoast lights and are often referred to as primary AtoN. They mark headlands and landfalls and are designed to assist vessels during coastal navigation or when approaching from seaward. They are also used as "Inland Major Lights" and are found in bays, sounds, large rivers, and coastal approaches. As an inland major light, they serve a variety of functions:

- Obstruction mark.
- Sector light.
- Reference mark from which a visual bearing or range can be obtained.

Figure 13-8
Lighthouse and Light Tower

A.27. Features

Besides the main signal light, additional features found on some major lights help provide more detailed information concerning the surrounding area (colored light sectors) or provide a secondary light source should the primary lantern fail.

A.27.a. Sector Lights

Sector lights are sectors of color that are displayed on lantern covers of certain lighthouses to indicate danger bearings. Sector bearings are true bearings and are expressed as "bearings from the vessel towards the light." A red sector indicates a vessel would be in danger of running aground on rocks or shoals while in the sector. Red sectors may be only a few degrees in width when marking an isolated obstruction. (see **Figure 13-9**)

A.27.b. Emergency Lights

Reduced intensity emergency lights are displayed if the primary lights are extinguished. They may or may not have the same characteristics as the primary lights. The characteristics of emergency lights are listed in Column 8 of the *Light List*. (see **Figure 13-9**)

(1) No	(2) Name and Location	(3) Position	(4) Characteristic	(5) Height	(6) Range	(7) Structure	(8) Remarks
	SEACOAST (Virginia) - Fifth District						
	OCEAN CITY INLET TO CAPE HATTERAS (Chart 12200)	N/W					
365	*Navy SESEF Lighted Buoy A*	36 55.0 75 38.3	**Fl Y** 2.5s		5	Yellow	
370	**Cape Henry Light**	36 55.6 76 00.4	**Mo (U) W** 20s **(R sector)** 1s fl 2s ec. 1s fl 2s ec. 7s fl 7s ec.	164	W 17 R 15	Octagonal pyramidal lower upper and lower half of each face alternately black and white. 163	Red from 154° to 233° covers shoals outside Cape Charles and Middle Ground inside bay. Emergency light of lower intensity will be displayed when main light is extinguished.

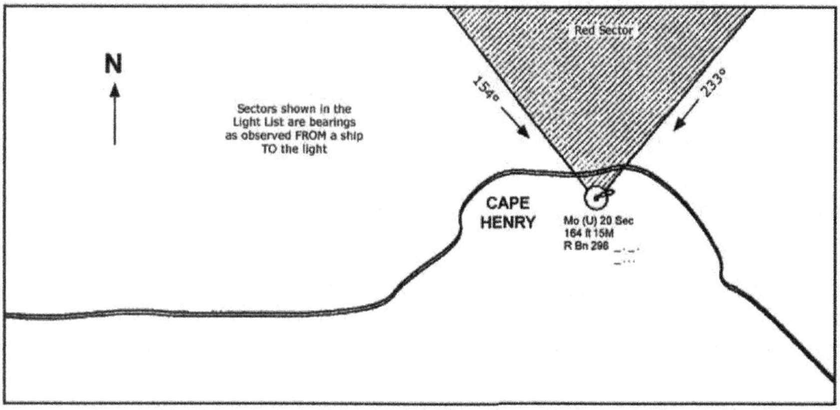

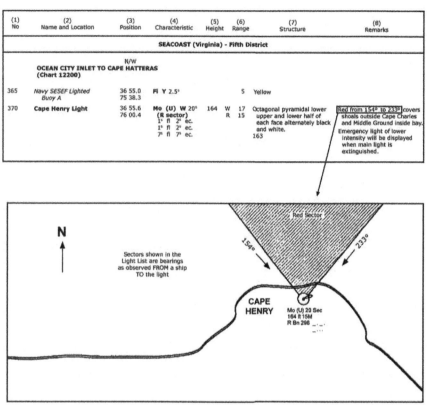

Figure 13-9
Sector Light

A.28. Light Towers

Light towers replaced lightships and are located in deepwater to mark shoals and heavily traveled sea lanes. The foundation or legs of these towers are fixed to the bottom. They are equipped with signals comparable to major lights.

A.29. Ranges

Ranges are pairs of beacons located to define a line down the center of a channel or harbor entrance. They are usually lighted and arranged so that one mark is behind and higher than the other mark. When both markers of the range are in line, a vessel's position is along a known LOP. Ranges are located on specially built structures, existing AtoN structures, or structures such as buildings or piers. Ranges are found in entrance channels to harbors, piers, or successive straight reaches. Again, range marks are located so that when viewed from the channel the upper mark is above, and a considerable distance beyond, the lower mark.

If...	Then...
the two marks are vertically aligned	the upper (rear) mark appearing directly above the lower (front) mark, the vessel is in the center of the channel. (see **Figure 13-10**)
the upper mark is seen to the left of the lower mark,	the vessel is to the left of the center of the channel.
the upper mark is to the right of the lower mark	the vessel is to the right of the center of the channel.

CAUTION !

The limits of a range can only be determined by checking the chart. They show the fairway or reach of the channel marked by the range. This area will be marked by a leading line (solid line) on the chart. At the turn, the range will be marked by a spaced line. (see **Figure 13-10**)

A.29.a. Range Characteristics

Ranges are considered to be non-lateral AtoN. Some ranges have rectangular daymarks that are striped in various colors (see *Section F* of this chapter). Most are lit 24 hours per day and may display either red, green, or white lights or combinations of the same. The *Light List* should be consulted for the light characteristics and color combinations displayed on the daymarks.

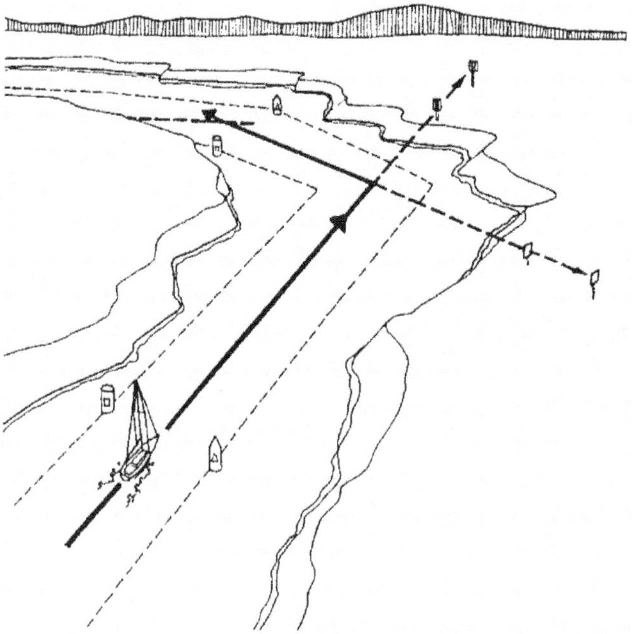

Figure 13-10
Using Range Lights

A.30. Directional Lights

Some structures have a directional light, a single light with a special lens, with a narrow white light beaming in a specific direction. On either side of the white beam is a red or green light. The width of the sector varies with the particular location. The *Light List* and chart should be checked for specific information.

Section B. U.S. AtoN System Variations

Introduction

Though the system of AtoN used in the U.S. and its territories consists of buoys and beacons conforming to IALA System B requirements; the waterway systems in the U.S. have variations that are exclusively used in the U.S. system. Some of these variations can be seen in the following sections located at the end of this chapter.

- *Section F*: U.S. Aids to Navigation System on Navigable Waters, except Western Rivers.
- *Section G*: Visual Buoyage Guide.
- *Section H*: How the Visual Guide Would Appear on a Nautical Chart (Fictitious Nautical Chart).
- *Section I*: U.S. Aids to Navigation System Used on the Western River System and the Uniform State Waterway Marking System.

In this section

This section contains the following information:

Intracoastal Waterway and Western Rivers

B.1. Intracoastal Waterway

Extending some 2,400 miles along the Atlantic and Gulf coasts of the U.S., the Intracoastal Waterway (ICW) is a largely sheltered waterway, suitable for year-round use. AtoN used to mark the ICW use the same coloring, numbering, and conventional direction of buoyage found in the U.S. AtoN System with the following additional characteristics:

- Special markings consisting of yellow squares and triangles are used so that vessels may readily follow the ICW.
- The yellow square shows that the aid should be kept on the left side when traveling north to south/east to west.
- The yellow triangle shows that the aid should be kept on the right side when traveling north to south/east to west.
- Non-lateral aids in the ICW, such as ranges and safe-water marks, are marked with a yellow horizontal band.

NOTE ✍

> Where the U.S. AtoN System (IALA B) and Intracoastal Waterway coexist, the yellow triangle and square denote the ICW's direction of travel, which may be counter to the color/shape of the aid marking the main wayerway (see *Section G* of this chapter).

B.2. Western Rivers

The western rivers marking system is used on the Mississippi River and tributaries above Baton Rouge, Louisiana, and certain other rivers which flow towards the Gulf of Mexico. The western rivers system varies from the U.S. AtoN System as follows:

- Buoys are not numbered.
- Lighted beacons and daybeacons are numbered but have no lateral significance. (The numbers relate to the distance up or downstream from a given point in statute miles).
- Red and green diamond-shaped daymarks, as appropriate, are used to show where the channel crosses from one side of the river to the other.
- Lights on green buoys and beacons are colored green or white (for crossings) and have a flashing (Fl) characteristic.
- Lights on red buoys and beacons are colored red or white (for crossings) and have a group flashing (Gp Fl) characteristic.
- Isolated danger marks are not used.

Uniform State Waterway Marking System

B.3. Categories of Aid

The Uniform State Waterway Marking System (USWMS) is designed for use by many types of operators and small vessels on lakes and inland waterways not shown on nautical charts. The conventional direction of buoyage in the USWMS is considered upstream or towards the head of navigation. This system has two categories of aids:

- System of AtoN compatible with and supplements the U.S. lateral system in states' waters, not federal jurisdiction.
- System of regulatory markers that warn of danger or provide general information and directions. (see *Section I* of this chapter)

NOTE

> USWMS marks may be used by the state or private individuals on waters where both state and federal governments have jurisdiction. These marks are classified as "Private" AtoN and require Coast Guard authorization prior to establishment.

NOTE

> The USWMS is scheduled to merge with the U.S. Aids to Navigation System and will be discontinued on December 31, 2003. Vessel operators may encounter both types of systems during this transitional period.

B.4. USWMS Variations

There are three USWMS variations to the U.S. AtoN System:

- On a well-defined channel, solid-colored red and black buoys are established in pairs (gate buoys), marking each side of the navigable channel.
- The color black is used instead of green.
- The shape of the buoy has no significance.

B.5. USWMS Cardinal Marks

When there is no well-defined channel or when there is an obstruction whose nature and location allows it to be approached by a vessel from more than one direction, AtoN with cardinal marks may be used. The USWMS provides for three aids with marks that have cardinal significance:

- A white buoy with a red top represents an obstruction and the buoy should be passed on the south or west.
- A white buoy with a black top represents an obstruction and the buoy should be passed to the north or east.
- A red and white vertically striped buoy indicates an obstruction exists between that buoy and the nearest shore.

B.6. USWMS Regulatory Marks

USWMS regulatory marks are white with two international orange horizontal bands completely around the buoy circumference. One band is near the top of the buoy while the second band is just above the waterline. Geometric shapes are placed on the buoy's body and are colored international orange. (see **Figure 13-11**) There are four basic geometric shapes authorized for these marks and each one has a specific meaning associated with it. These are:

- A vertical open-faced diamond shape having a cross centered in the diamond means that vessels are excluded from entering the marked area.
- A vertical open-faced diamond shape means danger.
- A circular shape indicates a control zone where vessels in the area are subject to certain operating restrictions.
- A square or rectangular shape is used to display information such as direction and/or distances to a location. (Information and regulatory marks can also be used in waters outside USWMS waters (e.g., federal channels which use the U.S. AtoN system.)

NOTE Regulatory marks are displayed on beacons as well as buoys.

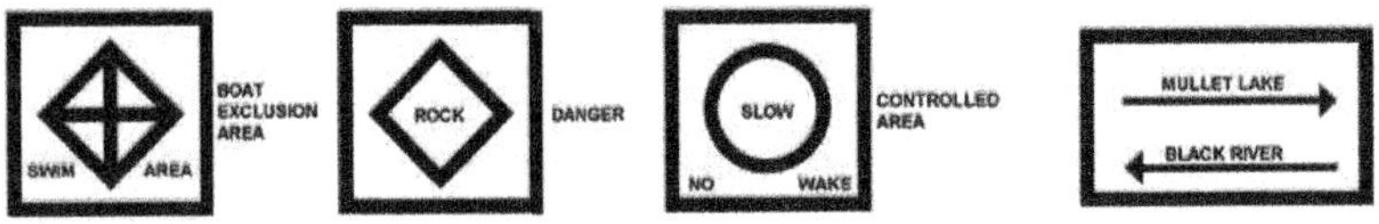

Figure 13-11
Regulatory Mark Information

B.7. USWMS Mooring Buoys

Mooring buoys in USWMS are white with a horizontal blue band midway between the waterline and the top of the buoy, and display a slow-flashing white light when lighted. Mooring buoys in federal waters (U.S. AtoN system) also display white with a horizontal blue band.

Section C. Short-Range Electronic Aids

Introduction

The science of locating position on the water is under constant change and improvement. The use of electronic signals to assist the mariner has come a long way in the last decade. With the development of improved methods of finding position on the water, older short-range electronic systems like radio beacons have been discontinued. One short-range system that remains in effect though is the Radar Beacon or RACON.

NOTE

> All navigation systems are not perfect, so a rhyme for the wise: "A mariner who relies solely on one navigation system, may soon find they are way off position."

C.1. Radar Beacons

RACON is an acronym for Radar Beacon. These beacons transmit a Morse Code reply when triggered by a boat's radar signal. This reply "paints" the boat's radar screen in the shape of dashes and dots representing a specific Morse Code letter, always beginning with a dash. The "paint" signal appears on the radar screen showing the Morse Code signal beginning at a point just beyond the location of the RACON transmitter location and extending radially for one to two nautical miles.

Transmission characteristics of RACONs may be found in the appropriate *Light List*. RACONs are shown on nautical charts with the letters "RACON" and a circle. RACONs are especially useful when trying to distinguish navigation aids from other contacts in congested areas. They can be found on both buoys and fixed structures.

Section D. Radionavigation Systems

Introduction

Radionavigation systems are used by mariners for obtaining a position fix. Depending upon their range and accuracy, some systems can be used in the middle of an ocean, or while entering a difficult harbor approach. All of the systems transmit a signal from a land or space-based transmitter to a shipboard receiver, allowing mariners to determine their position. The most recognizable systems are:

- LORAN-C.
- Global Positioning System (GPS).
- Differential Global Positioning System (DGPS).

D.1. LORAN-C

Derived from the words long-range navigation, LORAN-C is a navigation system network of transmitters consisting of one master station and two or more secondary stations. LORAN-C is a pulsed, hyperbolic (uses curved lines) system. LORAN-C receivers measure the time difference (TD) between the master transmitter site signal and the secondary transmitter site signal to obtain a single LOP. A second pair of LORAN-C transmitting stations produces a second LOP. Plotting positions using TDs requires charts overprinted with LORAN-C curves. However, most LORAN-C receivers can convert LORAN-C signals into a readout of latitude and longitude. The mariner then can use a standard nautical chart without LORAN-C curves.

D.1.a. Accuracy

LORAN-C is accurate to better than 460 meters and available better than 99.9% of the time for each station. When used to return to a position with known TDs, LORAN-C can produce an accuracy to within 20 meters (60 feet).

D.1.b. Area Coverage

U.S. and Canadian coastal areas are covered by LORAN-C transmitter sites controlled by the U.S. Coast Guard. LORAN-C is used by other countries and provides coverage for most of the North Atlantic, Europe, Mediterranean Sea, Japan, China, and Korea.

D.2. Global Positioning System (GPS)

The Global Positioning System (GPS) is a system of 24 satellites operated by the Department of Defense (DoD). It is available 24 hours per day, worldwide, in all weather conditions. Each GPS satellite transmits its precise location, meaning position and elevation. In a process called "ranging," a GPS receiver on the boat uses the signal to determine the distance between it and the satellite. Once the receiver has computed the range of at least four satellites, it processes a position that is accurate to within 13 meters horizontally. GPS provides two levels of service:

- Standard Positioning Service (SPS) for civilians users.
- Precise Positioning Service (PPS) for military users.

D.2.a. Standard Positioning Service

SPS is available on a continuous basis to any user worldwide. It is accurate to a radius within 13 meters of the position shown on the receiver about 99% of the time.

D.2.b. Precise Positioning Service

PPS provides positions fixes accurate to within 10 meters. This service is limited to approved U.S. Federal Government, allied military, and civil users.

D.3. Differential Global Positioning System (DGPS)

The Coast Guard developed DGPS to improve upon SPS signals of GPS. It uses a local reference receiver to correct errors in the standard GPS signals. These corrections are then broadcast and can be received by any user with a DGPS receiver. The corrections are applied within the user's receiver, providing mariners with a position that is accurate within 10 meters, with 99.7% probability.

The Coast Guard uses selected marine radiobeacons to send DGPS corrections to users. DGPS provides accurate and reliable navigation information to maritime users in Harbor Entrance and Approach (HEA), along U.S. coastal waters, the Great Lakes, navigable portions of the western rivers, Puerto Rico, Hawaii, and Alaska.

D.4. Radionavigation System Summary

The following is a summary of the different long-range AtoN used by mariners.

CAUTION ! System specifications noted here may change at any time.

System Parameters	LORAN-C	GPS	DGPS
Signal Characteristics	Pulsed hyperbolic (curved line), operating in the 90- to 110-kHz range.	Messages broadcast from satellites on two L-band frequencies: L1, 1575.42 MHz & L2, 1227.6 MHz.	Data messages broadcast from radiobeacon sites in 285 kHz to 325 kHz frequency band.
Predictable Accuracy	460 m	13 m	10 m
Availability	99.7%	99%	99.7%
Coverage	U.S. Coastal and continental areas and selected overseas areas.	Worldwide	U.S. coastal waters, Great Lakes, select areas of major inland rivers, P.R., HI, and AK.
Reliability	99.7% (triad reliability)	99.94%	99.7%
Fix Rate	10-20 fix/sec	1-20 per sec	1-20 per sec
Integrity	Steady monitoring: "stations" blink notifies pair is unusable, and detects flaws.	None	Yes, on-site monitor and 24-hour DGPS control center.
Advantages	Monitored, excellent integrity; some charts overlay LORAN lines.	Accurate; available worldwide.	Extremely accurate and monitored.
Common Interference	Electromagnetic irregularities.	Shadows, signals blocked due to natural or man-made obstructions.	Shadows, signals blocked due to natural or man-made obstructions.

Section E. The Light List

Introduction

The *Light List* is a seven-volume, annual publication providing information on AtoN maintained or authorized by the U.S. Coast Guard located on coastal and inland waters. The volumes cover the U.S. and its possessions, including the Intracoastal Waterway, Western Rivers, and the Great Lakes for both U.S. and Canadian waters. Each volume contains information on AtoN within its region maintained under the authority of the Coast Guard, including authorized private aids.

E.1. Contents

This publication includes detailed descriptions of both short-range AtoN and radionavigation systems, complete lists of lights for the area, LORAN-C chains not shown on a nautical chart, and more.

E.2. Numbering Sequence

The aids in the *Light List* are listed so that seacoast aids appear first, followed by entrance and harbor aids from seaward to the head of navigation. *Light List* numbers (LLNR) are assigned to aids for easy reference and appear in sequence from:

- North to south along the Atlantic Coast.
- South to north and east to west along the Gulf Coast.
- South to north along the Pacific Coast.

E.3. General Information Section

The general information section offers information about the layout and organization of the *Light List*. It describes the U.S. system of AtoN and its characteristics and provides a glossary of terms.

E.4. Example of Using the *Light List*

To determine the position and characteristic of Ocean City Inlet Jetty Light the following procedures should be taken to find this information in the *Light List*:

Step	Procedure
1	Use the *Light List* for that location (Volume II, Atlantic Coast).
2	Look up "Ocean City Inlet Jetty Light" in the index and note the LLNR. (see **Figure 13-12**) In this example, the LLNR is "225."
3	Find the correct page, listing LLNR 225. (see **Figure 13-13**) Each AtoN is listed numerically by LLNR.
4	Extract the information needed for the aid.

In this case, the position of the light is 38°19.5' N, 75°05.1' W; and the light characteristic is Isophase white 6 seconds.

NOTE ☞ Across the top of each page is a column heading which explains the information listed in the column.

In this example, the Ocean City Inlet Jetty Light has what appears to be two LLNRs, 225 and 4720. Having two LLNRs means that this aid will be listed as a "seacoast" aid using LLNR 225, and again as a "harbor entrance" aid under Ocean City Inlet Jetty Light using LLNR 4720. Seacoast AtoN are indexed in the beginning of the *Light List*.

Figure 13-12
***Light List* Index**

(1) No.	(2) Name and location	(3) Position	(4) Characteristic	(5) Height	(6) Range	(7) Structure	(8) Remarks
	SEACOAST (Maryland) – Fifth District						
	OCEAN CITY INLET TO CAPE HATTERAS (Chart 12200)						
225 4720	OCEAN CITY INLET JETTY LIGHT	38 19.5 75 05.1	**Iso W 6s**	28	8	NB on skeleton tower.	HORN: 1 blast ev 15s (2s bl).
230 4725	**Ocean City Inlet Radiobeacon**	38 19.5 75 05.3	**OC** (––– –•–•)		10		FREQ: 293 kHz. Antenna located on Ocean City Inlet Jetty Light.
235	Ocean City Research Buoy	38 20.8 75 01.1				Yellow.	Maintained by U.S. Army Corps of Engineers.

Figure 13-13
***Light List* Excerpt**

E.5. Corrections

Corrections to the *Light List* are made in the "Local Notice to Mariners" published by each Coast Guard district. These notices are essential for all navigators to keep their charts and *Light List*, current.

Section F. U.S. Aids to Navigation System on Navigable Waters, Except the Western River System

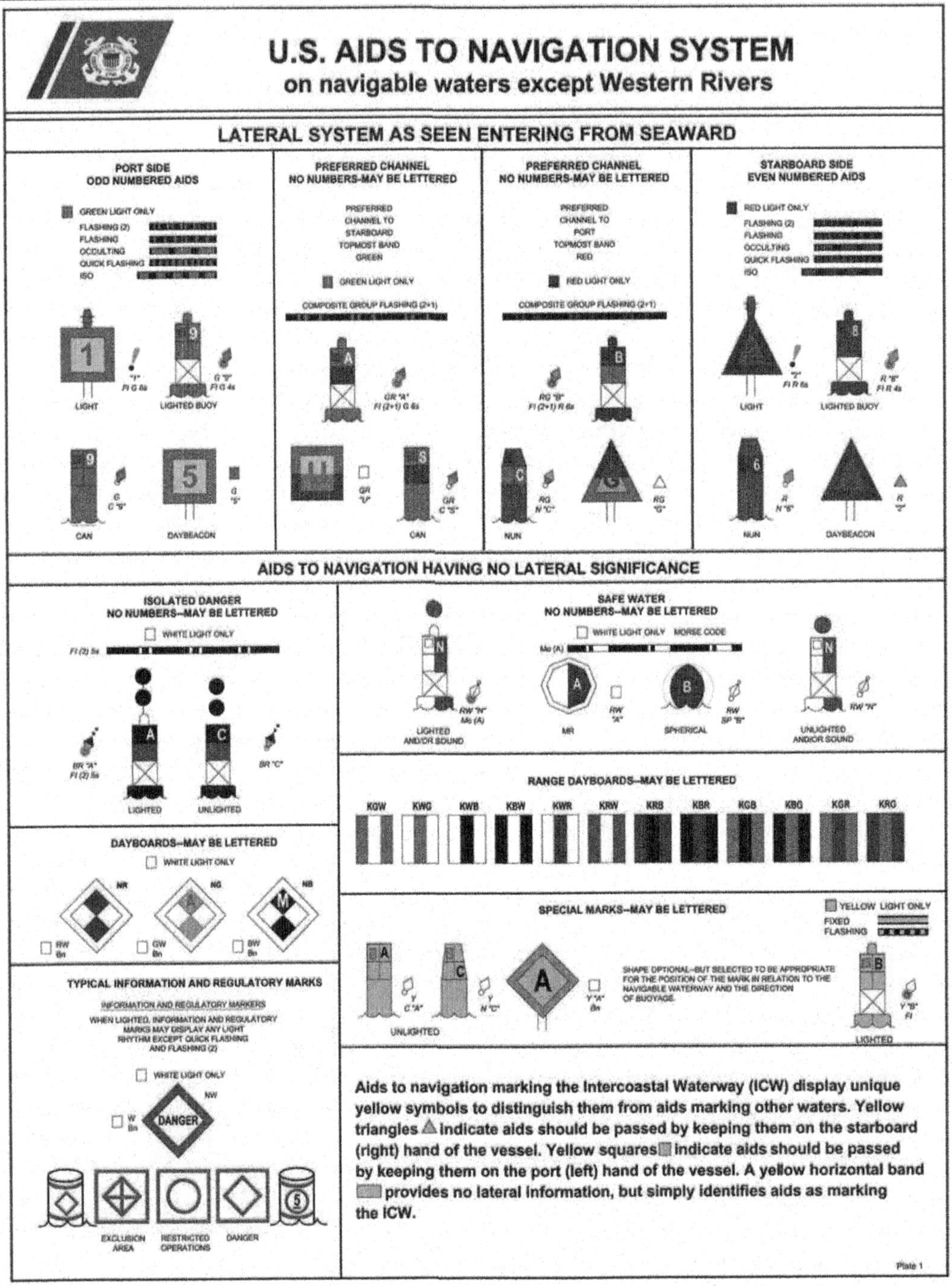

Section G. Visual Buoyage Guide

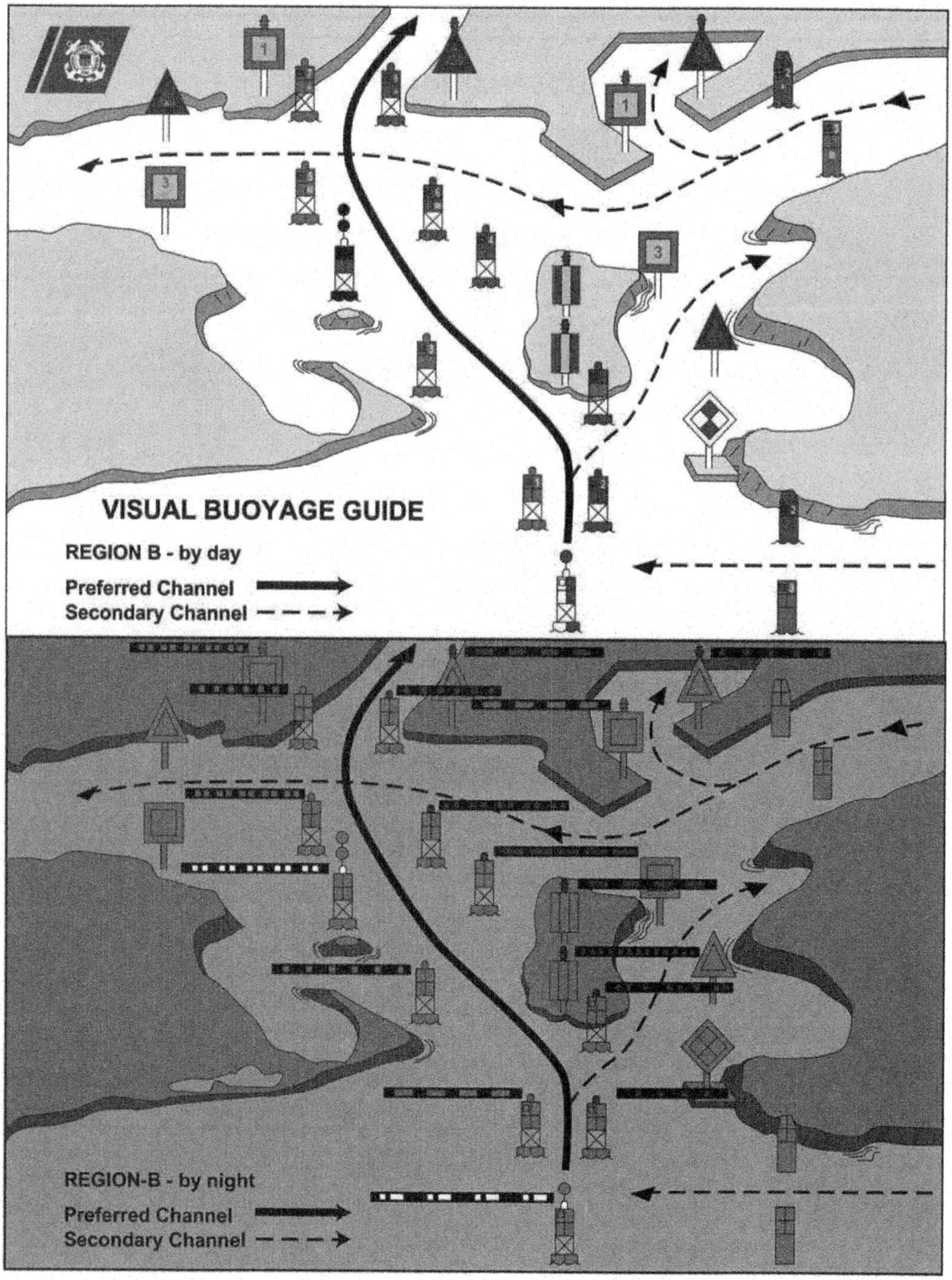

Section H. How the Visual Guide Would Appear on a Nautical Chart (Fictitious Nautical Chart)

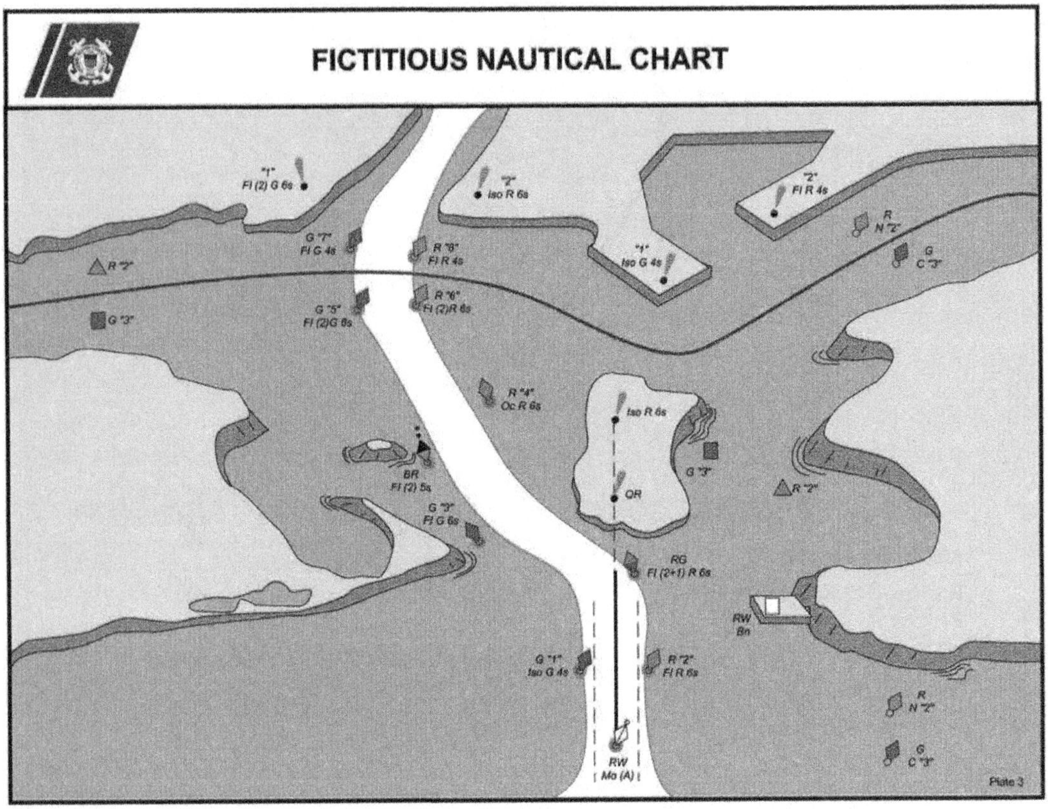

Section I. U.S. Aids to Navigation System on the Western River System and the Uniform State Waterway Marking System

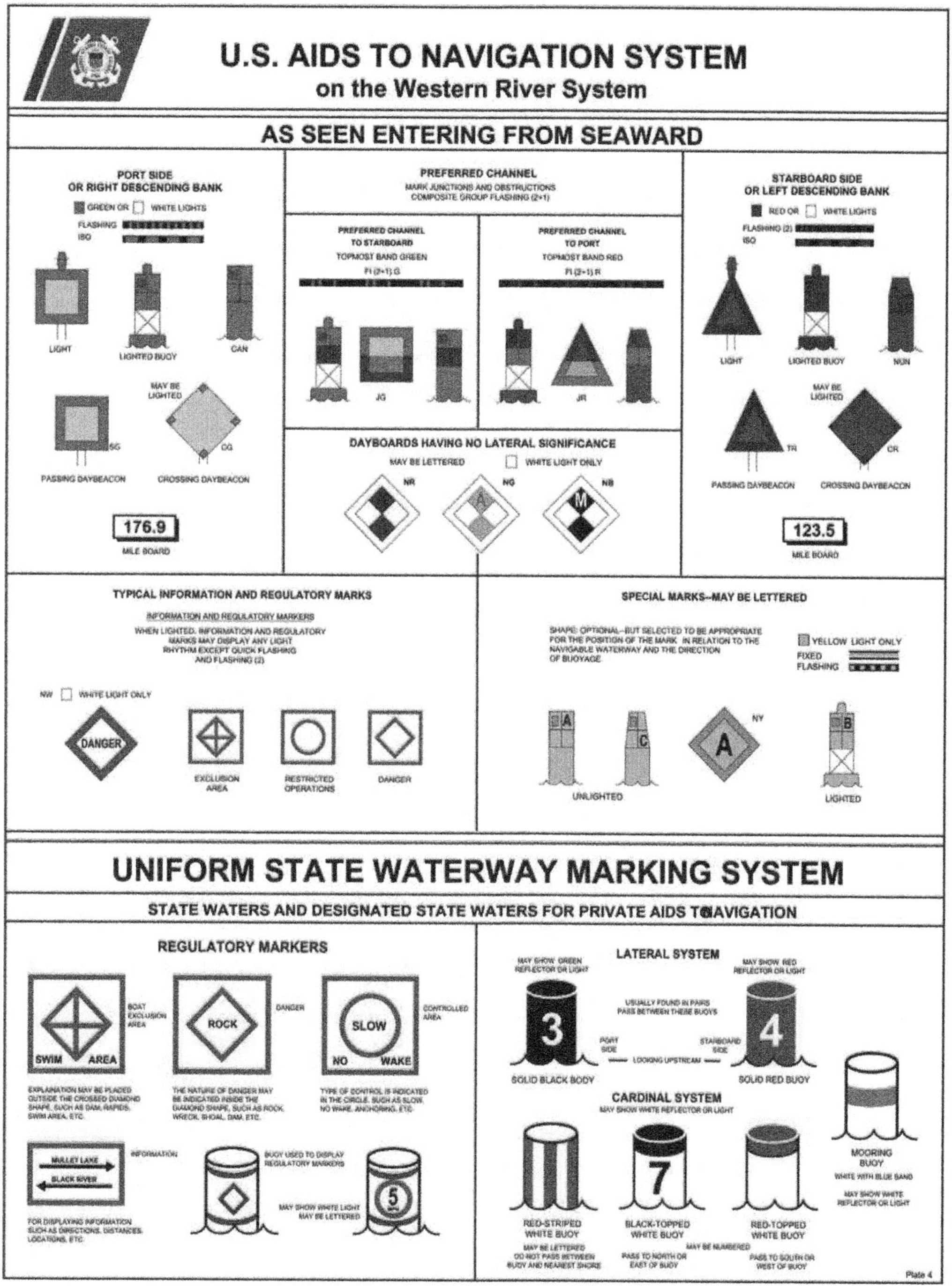

This page intentionally left blank.

Chapter 14
Navigation

Introduction

The art and science of navigation is an ancient skill. For thousands of years sailors navigated by using the stars as their guide. In the distant past only a select few were allowed access to the mysteries of navigation for possession of them gave one considerable power. A person who could safely follow the stars and navigate a ship - from one point to another - exercised significant influence over crewmembers who could not.

The art of navigation has expanded from using the stars and planets (celestial navigation) to sophisticated electronic systems (electronic navigation). The safe and confident navigation of the boat - is an absolute necessity, not only for the welfare of fellow crewmembers - but also for the welfare of those the crew is sent to assist. Boat navigation falls into three major categories:

- Piloting: use of visible landmarks and AtoN as well as by soundings.
- Dead Reckoning: by true or magnetic course steering and using speed to determine distance traveled from a known point in a known period.
- Electronic Navigation: by radio bearings, LORAN-C, GPS, and other electronic systems.

The coxswain is responsible for knowing the position of the boat at all times. Additionally, he/she has been entrusted with the safety of the boat, all crewmembers, and people from distressed vessels.

Each crewmember on a Coast Guard boat is a coxswain-in-training. A crewmember must learn all landmarks, charts and navigation aids used for the waters while operating. Through experience a crewmember will become proficient in the various skills necessary to perform any essential task in an emergency.

NOTE

> Additional information may also be found in the appropriate sections of the *Coast Guard Navigation Standards Manual*, COMDTINST M3530.2 (series).

In this chapter

This chapter contains the following sections:

Section A. The Earth and Its Coordinates

Introduction

Navigation is concerned with finding a position and calculating distances measured on the surface of the earth, which is a sphere. However, the earth is not a perfect sphere - the diameter through the equator is about 23 nautical miles longer than is the diameter through the North and South Poles. This difference is so small that most navigational problems are based on the earth being a perfect sphere. Charts are drawn to include this slight difference. Distance is figured from certain reference lines. Position at any given time, while underway, may be determined by location relative to these lines as well as visible landmarks in the local area. Knowing what these lines are and how to use them is essential.

A.1. Reference Lines of the Earth

The earth rotates around an axis; this axis may be defined as a straight line drawn through the center of the earth. The axis line meets the surface of the earth at the North Pole and at the South Pole. To determine location, a system of reference lines is placed on the surface of the earth as shown in **Figure 14-1**. This figure reveals the difficulty a boat navigator faces - the earth is curved as a sphere but navigation is typically done on a flat chart with straight reference lines running top to bottom and left to right.

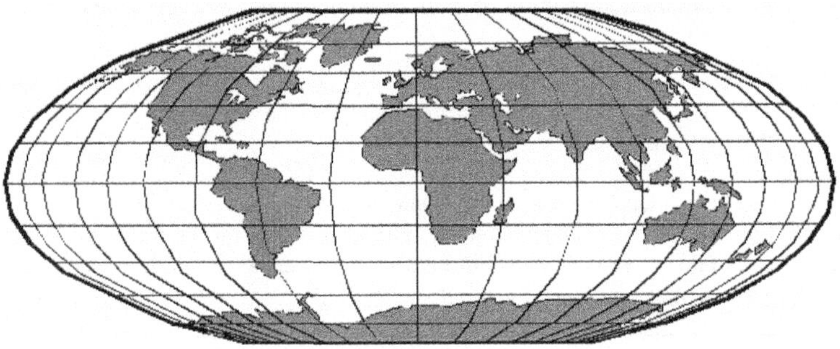

Figure 14-1
Earth with Reference Lines

A.2. Great Circles

A great circle is a geometric plane passing through the center of the earth, which divides the earth into two equal parts. A great circle always passes through the widest part of the earth. The equator is a great circle. All circles that pass through both the North and South Poles are great circles. The edge of a great circle conforms to the curvature of the earth, similar to seeing a circle when looking at a full moon.

NOTE

The earth's circumference is 21,600 nautical miles. Determine a degree of arc on the earth's surface by dividing the earth's circumference (in miles) by 360 degrees.

A.2.a. Circle Properties

The outline of the moon also reveals another fact about great circles which is a property of all circles: each circle possesses 360° around its edge, which passes through a sphere, as to divide the sphere into two equal half-spheres. There are an infinite number of great circles on a sphere.

A.2.b. Degrees

Great circles have 360° of arc. In every degree of arc in a circle, there are 60 minutes. Sixty (60) minutes is equal to 1° of arc, and 360° are equal to a complete circle. When degrees are written, the symbol (°) is used.

A.2.c. Minutes

For every degree of arc, there are 60 minutes. When minutes of degrees are written, the symbol (') is used; 14 degrees and 15 minutes is written: 14°15'.

When written, minutes of degrees are always expressed as two digits. Zero through nine minutes are always preceded with a zero. Three minutes and zero minutes are written as 03' and 00' respectively.

A.2.d. Seconds

For every minute of arc in a circle, there are 60 seconds of arc. Sixty (60) seconds is equal to one minute of arc, and 60 minutes is equal to 1° of arc.

For every minute of arc, there are 60 seconds. When seconds are written, the symbol (") is used; 24 degrees, 45 minutes, and 15 seconds is written: 24°45'15".

When seconds are written, they are always expressed as two digits. Zero through nine seconds are always preceded with a zero. Six seconds and zero seconds are written as 06" and 00" respectively.

Seconds may also be expressed in tenths of minutes; 10 minutes, 6 seconds (10'06") can be written as 10.1'.

The relationship of units of "arc" can be summarized as follows:

Circle =	360 degrees (°)
1 degree (°) =	60 minutes (')
1 minute (') =	60 seconds (")

Parallels

A.3. Parallels

Parallels are circles on the surface of the earth moving from the equator to the North or South Pole. They are parallel to the equator and known as parallels of latitude, or just latitude.

Parallels of equal latitude run in a west and east direction (left and right on a chart). They are measured in degrees, minutes, and seconds, in a north and south direction, from the equator. (0° at the equator to 90° at each pole).

The North Pole is 90° north latitude, and the South Pole is 90° south latitude. The equator itself is a special parallel because it is also a great circle. One degree of latitude (arc) is equal to 60 nautical miles (NM) on the surface of the earth; one minute (') of latitude is equal to 1 NM. The circumference of the parallels decreases as they approach the poles. (see **Figure 14-2**)

On charts of the northern hemisphere, true north is usually located at the top. Parallels are normally indicated by lines running from side to side. Latitude scales, however, are normally indicated along the side margins by divisions along the black-and-white border as shown in the upper left and the lower right margins of **Figure 14-2**.

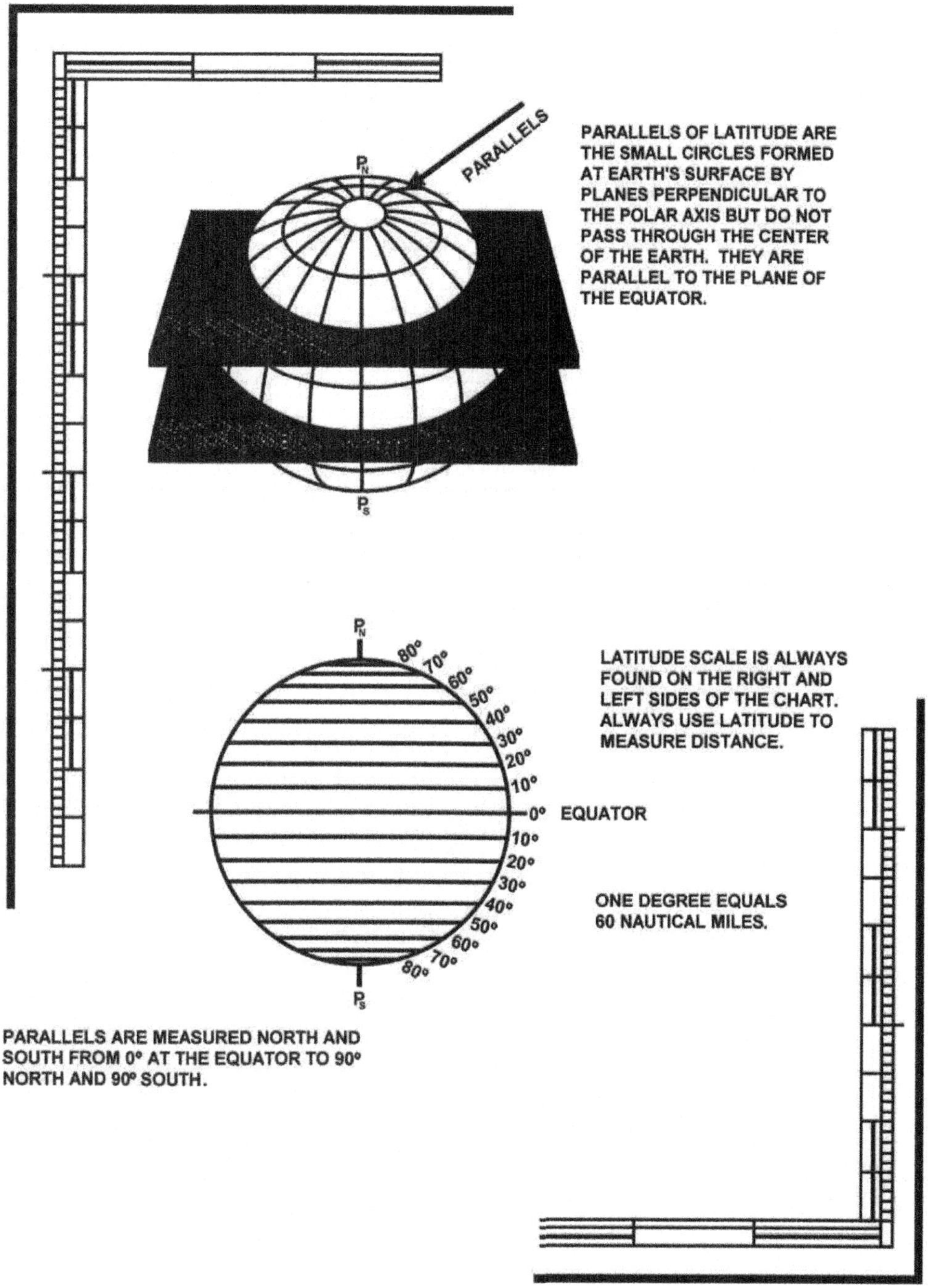
PARALLELS
P_N
P_S
PARALLELS OF LATITUDE ARE THE SMALL CIRCLES FORMED AT EARTH'S SURFACE BY PLANES PERPENDICULAR TO THE POLAR AXIS BUT DO NOT PASS THROUGH THE CENTER OF THE EARTH. THEY ARE PARALLEL TO THE PLANE OF THE EQUATOR.
P_N
80° 70° 60° 50° 40° 30° 20° 10°
0° EQUATOR
10° 20° 30° 40° 50° 60° 70° 80°
P_S
LATITUDE SCALE IS ALWAYS FOUND ON THE RIGHT AND LEFT SIDES OF THE CHART. ALWAYS USE LATITUDE TO MEASURE DISTANCE.
ONE DEGREE EQUALS 60 NAUTICAL MILES.
PARALLELS ARE MEASURED NORTH AND SOUTH FROM 0° AT THE EQUATOR TO 90° NORTH AND 90° SOUTH.

Figure 14-2
Parallels of Latitude

A.3.a. Measuring Latitude

To measure the latitudinal position of an object on a nautical chart, perform the procedures as follows:

Step	Procedure
1	Put one point of a pair of dividers on the parallel of latitude nearest to the object.
2	Place the other point of the dividers on the object.
3	Move the dividers to the nearest latitude scale, keeping the same spread on the dividers.
4	Place one point on the same parallel of latitude as used in step 1. The second point of the dividers will fall on the correct latitude of the object.
5	Read the latitude scale.

NOTE

- Always use the latitude scale to measure distance in navigation.
- A degree of latitude is measured up or down.

NOTE

On a Mercator projection chart (normally used for boat navigation), the scale varies along the latitude scale, but will always remain accurate in relation to actual distance within the latitude bounded by that scale.

CAUTION !

A degree of longitude is equal to 60 miles only at the equator. This is why parallels of latitude are used to measure distance in navigational problems.

A.4. Meridians

A meridian is a great circle formed by a plane, which cuts through the earth's axis and its poles. Such circles are termed meridians of longitude.

The meridian which passes through Greenwich, England, by international convention, has been selected as 000° and is called the Prime Meridian. From this point, longitude is measured both east and west for 180°.

The 180° meridian is on the exact opposite side of the earth from the 000° meridian. The International Date Line generally conforms to the 180th meridian. The great circle of the Prime Meridian and the International Date Line divide the earth into eastern and western hemispheres.

A degree of longitude equals 60 miles only at the equator and is undefined at the poles since all meridians meet there at one point. Meridians of Longitude run in a north and south direction (top to bottom on a chart) and are measured in degrees, minutes, and seconds, in an east or west direction. (see **Figure 14-3**)

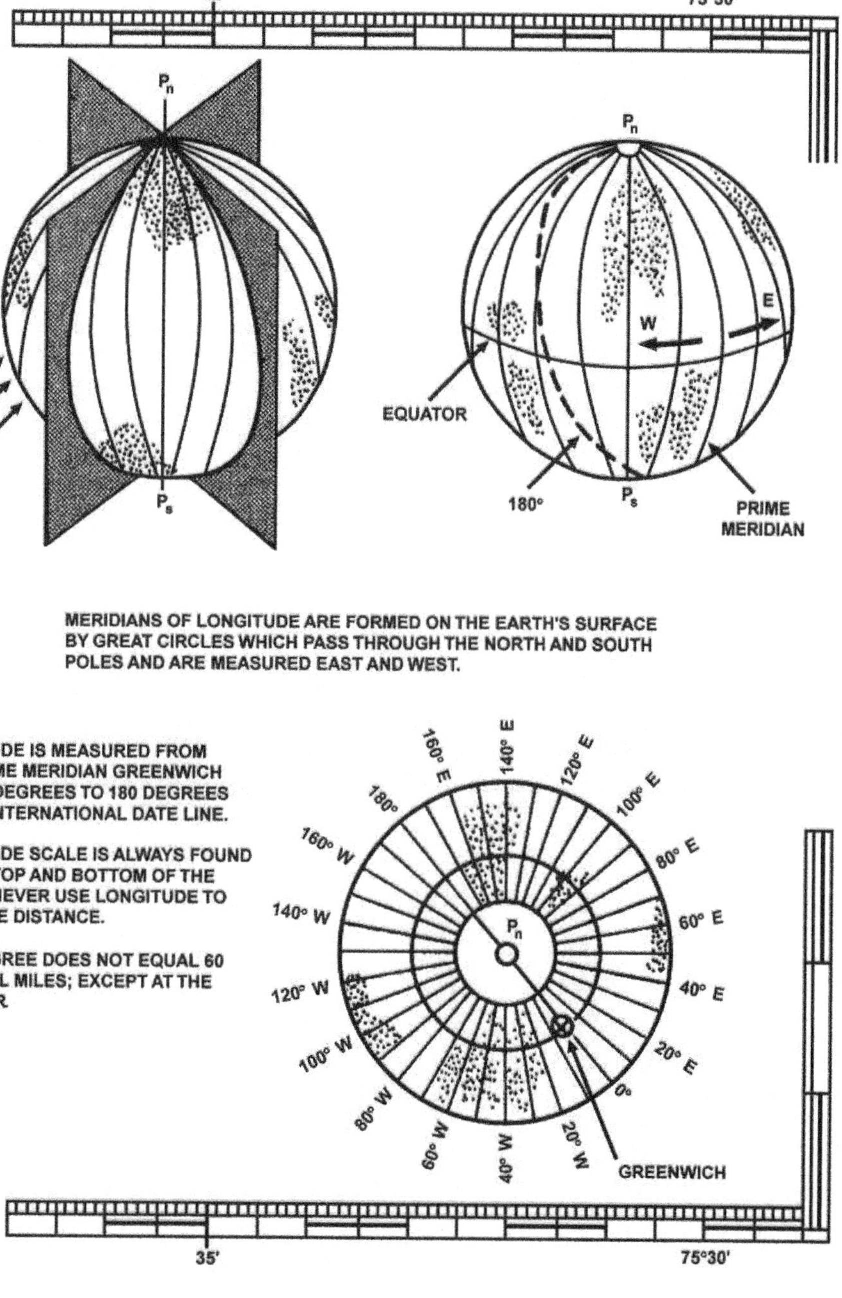
35'
75°30'
Pn
Ps
MERIDIANS
EQUATOR
W
E
180°
PRIME MERIDIAN
MERIDIANS OF LONGITUDE ARE FORMED ON THE EARTH'S SURFACE BY GREAT CIRCLES WHICH PASS THROUGH THE NORTH AND SOUTH POLES AND ARE MEASURED EAST AND WEST.
LONGITUDE IS MEASURED FROM THE PRIME MERIDIAN GREENWICH "ZERO" DEGREES TO 180 DEGREES AT THE INTERNATIONAL DATE LINE.
LONGITUDE SCALE IS ALWAYS FOUND ON THE TOP AND BOTTOM OF THE CHART. NEVER USE LONGITUDE TO MEASURE DISTANCE.
ONE DEGREE DOES NOT EQUAL 60 NAUTICAL MILES; EXCEPT AT THE EQUATOR.
160° E
140° E
120° E
100° E
80° E
60° E
40° E
20° E
0°
20° W
40° W
60° W
80° W
100° W
120° W
140° W
160° W
180°
GREENWICH
35'
75°30'

Figure 14-3
Meridians of Longitude

A.4.a. To Measure Longitude

To measure the longitude of an object on a nautical chart, the same procedures as in measuring a latitude position using the longitude scale shall be followed.

A.4.b. Rhumb Line

Typical boat navigation is done by plotting rhumb lines on a Mercator chart. A rhumb line is an imaginary line that intersects all meridians at the same angle. The rhumb line on the surface of a sphere is a curved line. On most nautical charts, this curved line (rhumb) is represented as a straight line.

A course line, such as a compass course, is a rhumb line that appears as a straight line on a Mercator chart. Navigating with a rhumb line course allows the helmsman to steer a single compass course.

A.5. Chart Projections

For the purpose of coastal navigation, the earth is considered to be a perfect sphere. To represent the features of the earth's spherical surface on the flat surface of a chart, a process termed "projection" is used. Two basic types of projection used in making piloting charts are:

- Mercator.
- Gnomonic.

A.5.a. Mercator Projection

Mercator charts are the primary charts used aboard boats. A Mercator projection is made by transferring the surface of the globe (representing the earth) onto a cylinder.

The equator is the reference point for accomplishing the projection from one geometric shape to another. The distinguishing feature of the Mercator projection is that the meridians are projected so they appear to be equal distance from each other and parallel. (see Error! Reference source not found.)

NOTE Only the latitude scale is used for measuring distance.

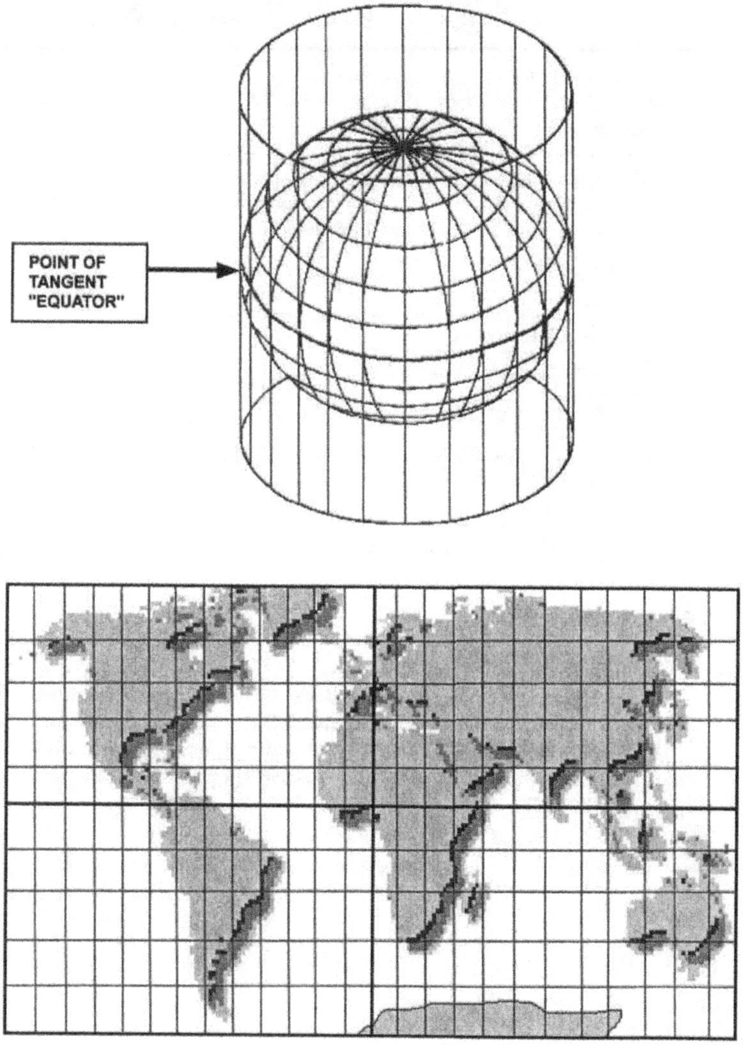

Figure 14-4
Mercator Projection

A.5.b. Gnomonic Projection

Gnomonic projections aid in long distance navigation by allowing navigators to use great circle courses. Meridians appear as straight lines that converge as they near the closest pole. The equator is represented by a straight line; all other parallels appear as curved lines.

NOTE Gnomonic charts are not normally used for boat navigation.

CH-1

Section B. Nautical Charts

Introduction

The nautical chart is one of the mariner's most useful and most widely used navigational aids. Navigational charts contain a lot of information of great value to you as a boat coxswain.

In this section

This section contains the following information:

Compass Rose

B.1. Description

Nautical charts usually have one or more compass roses printed on them. These are similar in appearance to the compass card and, like the compass card, are oriented with north at the top. Directions on the chart are measured by using the compass rose. (see **Figure 14-5**) Direction is measured as a straight line from the center point of the circle to a number on the compass rose. Plotting the direction and explanation of the terms is discussed later.

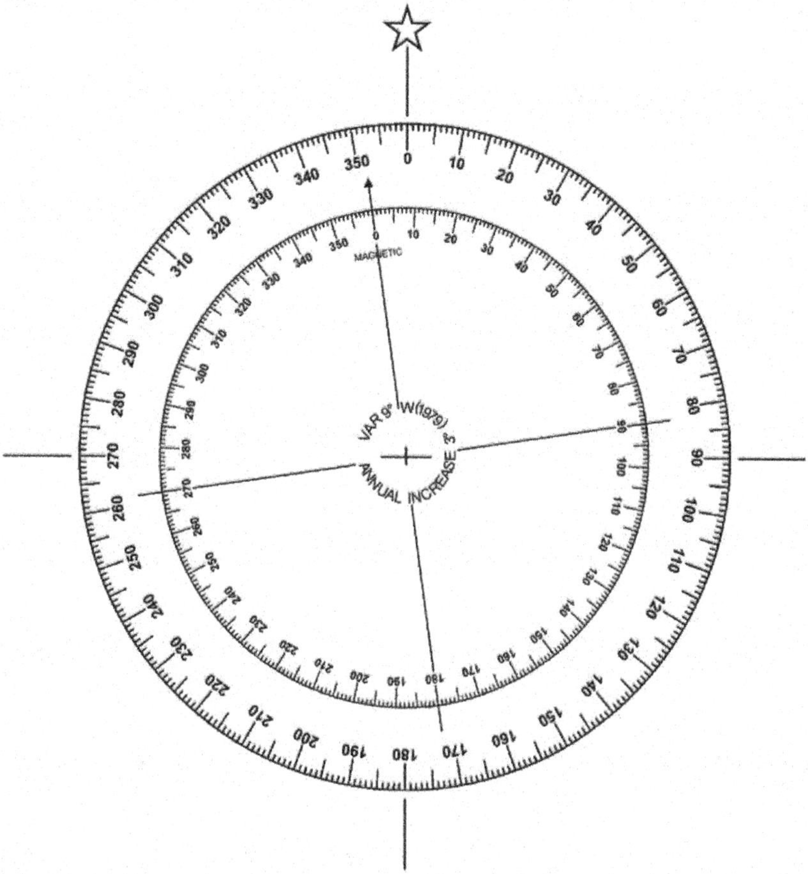

Figure 14-5
Compass Rose

B.2. True Direction

True direction is printed around the outside of the compass rose.

B.3. Magnetic Direction

Magnetic direction is printed around the inside of the compass rose. An arrow points to magnetic north.

B.4. Variation

Variation, the difference between true and magnetic north for the particular area covered by the chart, is printed in the middle of the compass rose (as well as any annual change).

Soundings

B.5. Description

One of the more vital services a chart performs is to describe the bottom characteristics to a boat operator. This is accomplished through the use of combinations of numbers, color codes, underwater contour lines, and a system of symbols and abbreviations.

B.6. Datum

The nautical chart water depth is measured downward from sea level at low water (soundings). Heights or landmarks are given in feet above sea level. In the interest of navigation safety, the mean, or average, of the lower of the two tides in the tidal cycle is used for soundings.

B.6.a. Mean Low Tide

Most of the numbers on the chart represent soundings of the water depth at mean low tide. Datum refers to a base line from which a chart's vertical measurements are made.

B.6.b. Mean Low Water

"Mean low water" is a tidal datum that is the average of all the low water heights observed over the National Tidal Datum Epoch (19 year average).

B.6.c. Average Low Tide

Since the greatest danger to navigation is during low tide, a number of the depths of low tide are averaged to produce the average low tide.

B.6.d. Mean Lower Low Water

"Mean lower low water" is a tidal datum that is the average of the lowest low water height of each tidal day observed over the National Tidal Datum Epoch (19 year average).

B.7. Color Code

Generally, shallow water is tinted darker blue on a chart, while deeper water is tinted light blue or white.

B.8. Contour Lines

Contour lines, also called fathom curves, connect points of roughly equal depth and provide a profile of the bottom. These lines are either numbered or coded, according to depth, using particular combinations of dots and dashes. Depth of water may be charted in feet, meters or fathoms (a fathom equals six feet). The chart legend will indicate which unit (feet, meters or fathoms) is used.

Basic Chart Information

B.9. Description

The nautical chart shows channels, depth of water buoys, lights, lighthouses, prominent landmarks, rocks, reefs, sandbars, and much more useful information for the safe piloting of the boat. The chart is the most essential part of all piloting equipment. Below are some basic facts to know about charts:

- Charts are oriented with north at the top.
- The frame of reference for all chart construction is the system of latitude and longitude.
- Any location on a chart can be expressed in terms of latitude or longitude. (see **Figure 14-6**)
  - The latitude scale runs along both sides of the chart.
  - The longitude scale runs across the top and bottom of the chart.
  - Latitude lines are reference points in a north and south direction with the equator as their zero reference point.
  - Longitude lines are the east and west reference points with the prime meridian as their zero reference point.

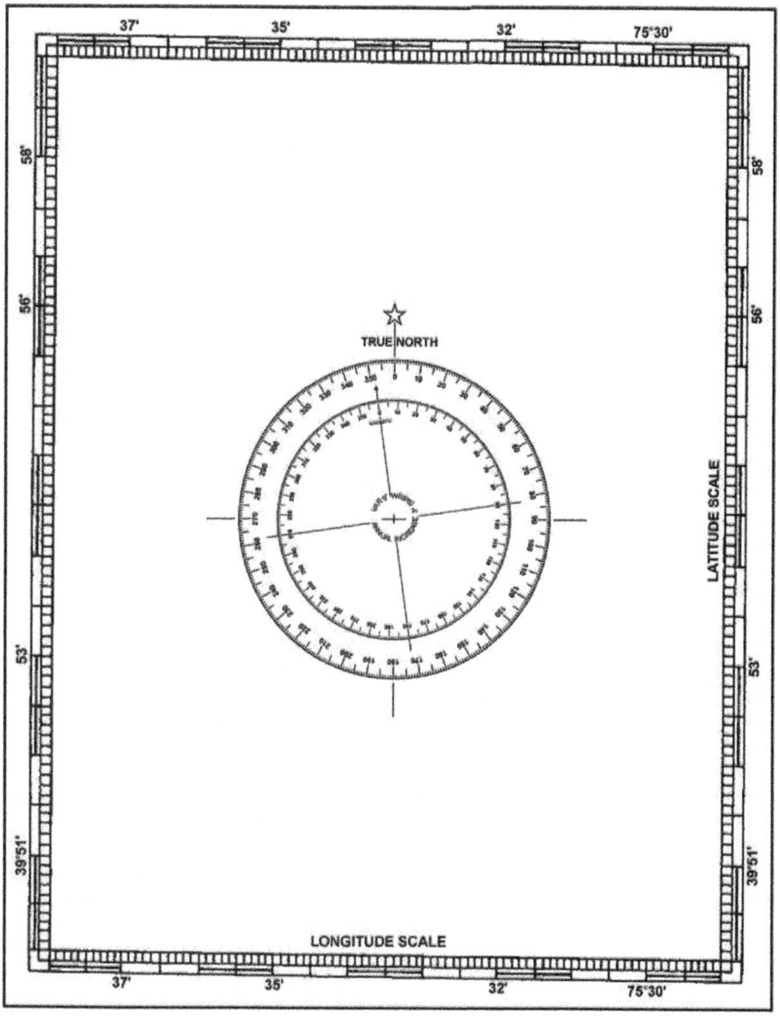

Figure 14-6
Chart Orientation

B.10. Title Block

The general information block (see **Figure 14-7**) contains the following items:

- The chart title which is usually the name of the prominent navigable body of water within the area covered in the chart.
- A statement of the type of projection and the scale.
- The unit of depth measurement, listed as soundings (feet, meters or fathoms).

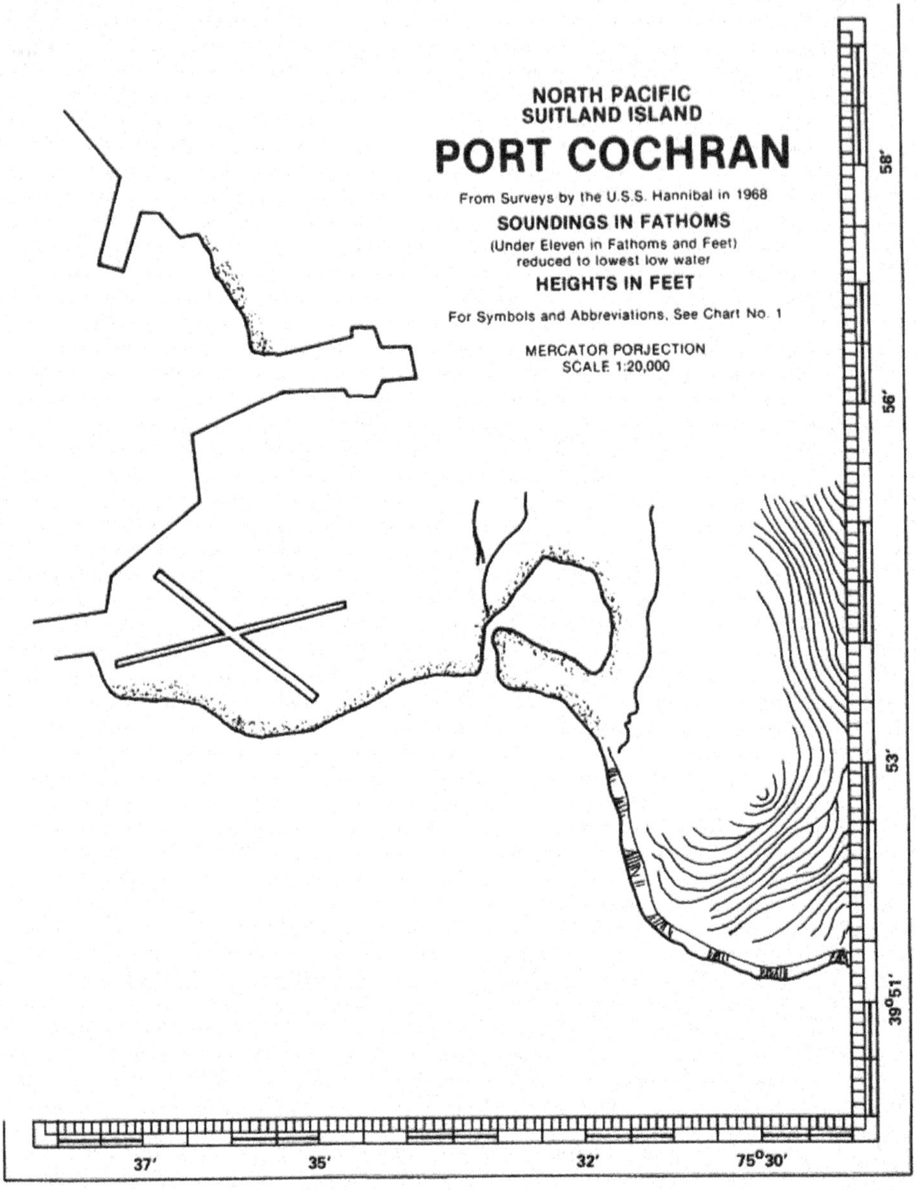

Figure 14-7
Title Block of a Chart

B.11. Notes

Notes are found in various places on the chart, such as along the margins or on the face of the chart. They may contain information that cannot be presented graphically, such as:

- The meaning of abbreviations used on the chart.
- Special notes of caution regarding danger.
- Tidal information.
- Reference to anchorage areas.

B.12. Edition Number

The edition number of a chart and latest revisions indicate when information on the chart was updated.

- The edition number and date of the chart is located in the margin of the lower left hand corner.
- The latest revision date immediately follows in the lower left hand corner below the border of the chart. Charts show all essential corrections concerning lights, beacons, buoys and dangers that have been received to the date of issue.

Corrections occurring after the date of issue are published in the Notice to Mariners and must be entered by hand on the chart of your local area upon receipt of the notice.

Scale of the Nautical Chart

B.13. Description

The scale of a nautical chart is the ratio comparing a unit of distance on the chart to the actual distance on the surface of the earth.

For example: The scale of 1:5,000,000 means that one of some kind of measurement of the chart is equal to 5,000,000 of the same kind of measurement on the earth's surface. One inch on the chart would equal 5,000,000 inches on the earth's surface. This would be a small scale, chart, since the ratio 1/5,000,000 is a very small number.

A large scale chart represents a smaller area than that of a small scale chart. There is no firm separation between large scale and small scale.

NOTE Remember large scale - small area, and small scale - large area.

For example: The scale of 1:2,500 (one inch on chart equals 2,500 inches on the earth's surface) is a much larger number and is referred to as a large scale chart.

NOTE Navigate with the largest scale chart available.

B.14. Sailing Charts

Sailing charts are produced at scales of 1:600,000 and smaller. They are used in fixing the mariners position for approach to the coast, from the open ocean, or for sailing between distant coastal ports.

On such charts, the shoreline and topography are generalized. Only offshore soundings, such as the principal lights, outer buoys and landmarks visible at considerable distances are shown.

B.15. General Charts

General charts are produced at scales between 1:150,000 and 1:600,000. They are used for coastwise navigation outside of outlying reefs and shoals when the ship or boat is generally within sight of land or AtoN and its course can be directed by piloting techniques.

B.16. Coastal Charts

Coastal charts are produced at scales between 1:50,000 and 1:150,000. They are used for inshore navigation, for entering bays and harbors of considerable width, and for navigating large inland waterways.

B.17. Harbor Charts

Harbor charts are produced at scales larger than 1:50,000. They are used in harbors, anchorage areas, and the smaller waterways.

B.18. Small Craft Charts

Small craft charts are produced at scales of 1:40,000 and larger. There are special charts of inland waters, including the intracoastal waterways. Special editions of conventional charts, called small craft charts, are printed on lighter weight paper than a normal chart and folded.

These "SC" charts contain additional information of interest to small craft operators, such as data on facilities, tide predictions, and weather broadcast information.

Chart Symbols and Abbreviations

B.19. Description

Many symbols and abbreviations are used on charts. It is a quick way to determine the physical characteristics of the charted area and information on AtoN.

These symbols are uniform and standardized, but may vary depending on the scale of the chart or chart series. These standardized chart symbols and abbreviations are shown in the Pamphlet 'CHART No. 1'; published jointly by the Defense Mapping Agency Hydrographic Center and the National Ocean Service.

B.20. Color

Nearly all charts employ color to distinguish various categories of information such as shoal water, deepwater, and land areas. Color is also used with AtoN to make them easier to locate and interpret.

Nautical purple ink (magenta) is used for most information since it is easier to read under red light normally used for navigating at night.

B.21. Lettering

Lettering on a chart provides valuable information. Slanted Roman lettering on the chart is used to label all information that is affected by tidal change or current (with the exception of bottom soundings). All descriptive lettering for floating AtoN is found in slanted lettering.

Vertical Roman lettering on the chart is used to label all information that is not affected by the tidal changes or current. Fixed aids such as lighthouses and ranges are found in vertical lettering. (see **Figure 14-8**)

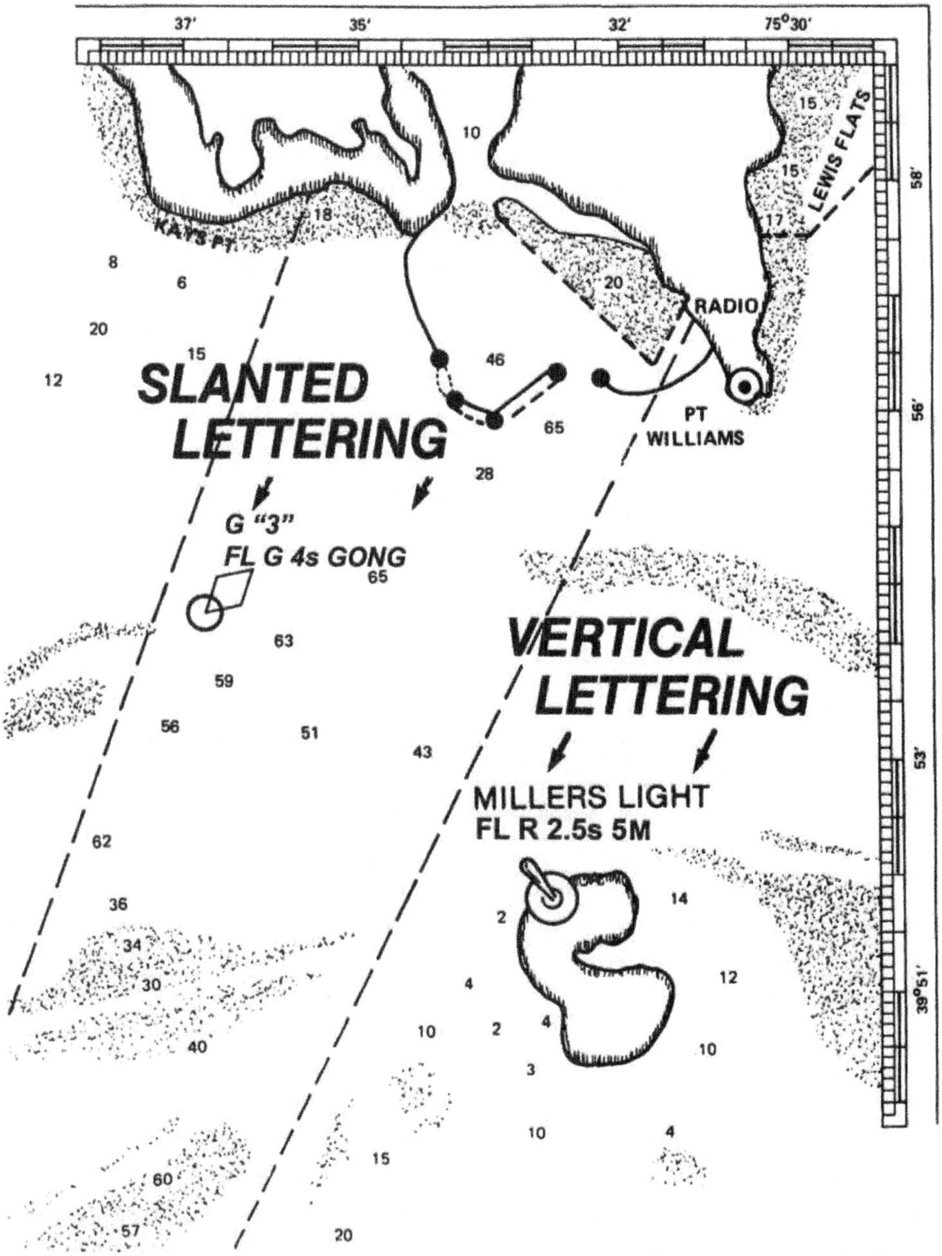

Figure 14-8
Chart Lettering

CH-1

Buoy Symbols

B.22. Description

Buoys are shown with the following symbols:

- The basic symbol for a buoy is a diamond and small circle.
- A dot will be shown instead of the circle on older charts.
- The diamond may be above, below or alongside the circle or dot.
- The small circle or dot denotes the approximate position of the buoy mooring.
- The diamond is used to draw attention to the position of the circle or dot and to describe the aid.

See *Chapter 13, Aids To Navigation* for AtoN chart symbols, additional information and color pictures of AtoN.

Other Chart Symbols

B.23. Lighthouses and Other Fixed Lights

The basic symbol is a black dot with a magenta "flare" giving much the appearance of a large exclamation mark (!). Major lights are named and described; minor lights are described only.

B.24. Ranges and Beacons

Chapter 13, Aids To Navigation, has chart symbols and color pictures of these AtoN.

B.24.a. Ranges

Ranges are indicated on charts by symbols for the lights (if lighted) and dashed line indicating the direction of the range.

B.24.b. Daybeacons

Daybeacons are indicated by small triangles or squares, which may be colored to match the aid. Daybeacons, also commonly called day marks, are always fixed aids. That is, they are on a structure secured to the bottom or on the shore. They are of many different shapes.

B.25. Prominent Landmarks

Prominent landmarks, such as water towers, smoke stacks, and flagpoles, are pinpointed by a standard symbol of a dot surrounded by a circle. A notation next to the symbol defines the landmark's nature. The omission of the dot indicates the location of the landmark is only an approximation. (see **Figure 14-9**)

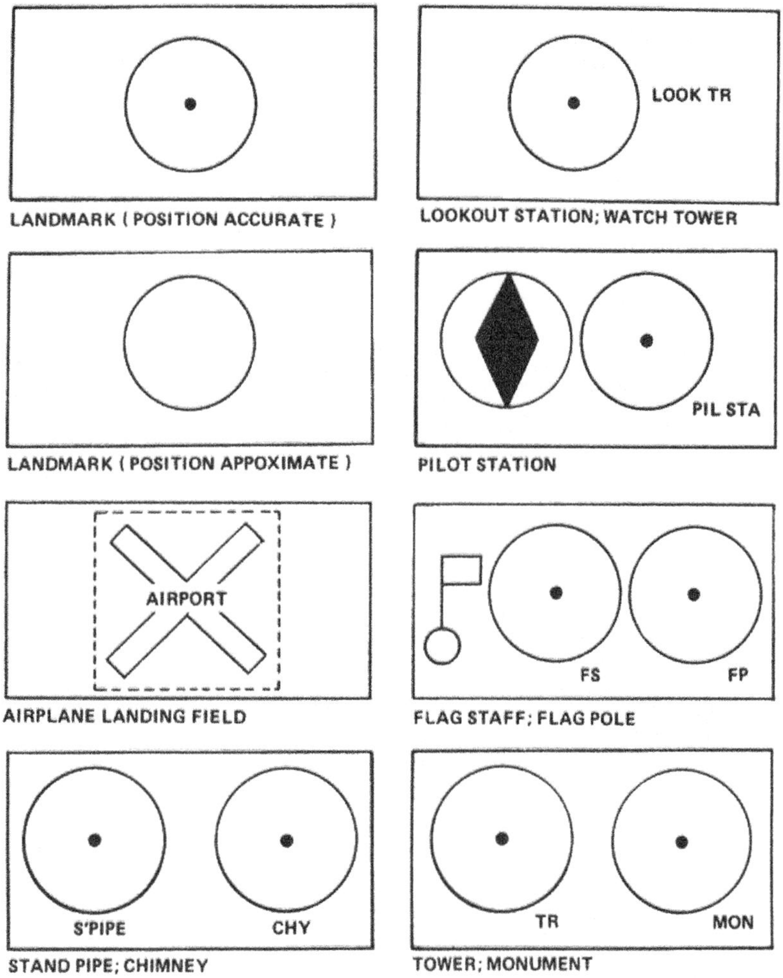

Figure 14-9
Symbols for Prominent Landmarks

B.26. Wrecks, Rocks, and Reefs

These are marked with standardized symbols, for example, a sunken wreck may be shown either by a symbol or by an abbreviation plus a number that gives the wreck's depth at mean low or lower low water. A dotted line around any symbol calls special attention to its hazardous nature. (see **Figure 14-10**)

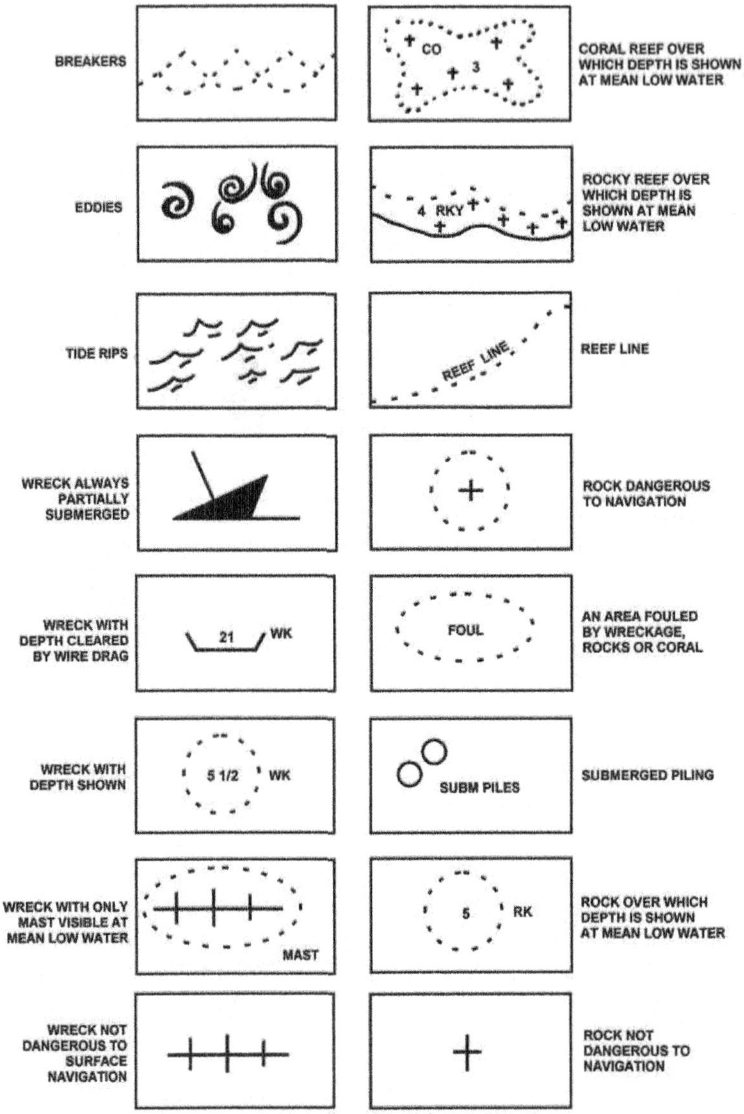

Figure 14-10
Breakers, Rocks, Reefs, Pilings

B.27. Bottom Characteristics

A system of abbreviations, used alone or in combination, describes the composition of the bottom allowing selection of the best holding ground for anchoring. (see **Table 14-1**)

NOTE Knowledge of bottom quality is very important in determining an anchorage.

Table 14-1
Bottom Composition

Abbreviation	Composition	Abbreviation	Composition
hrd	Hard	M	Mud; Muddy
Sft	Soft	G	Gravel
S	Sand	Stk	Sticky
Cl	Clay	Br	Brown
St	Stone	Gy	Gray
Co	Coral	Wd	Seaweed
Co Hd	Coral Head	Grs	Grass
Sh	Shells	Oys	Oysters

B.28. Structures

Shorthand representations have been developed and standardized for low-lying structures such as jetties, docks, drawbridges, and waterfront ramps. Such symbols are drawn to scale and viewed from overhead. (see **Figure 14-11**)

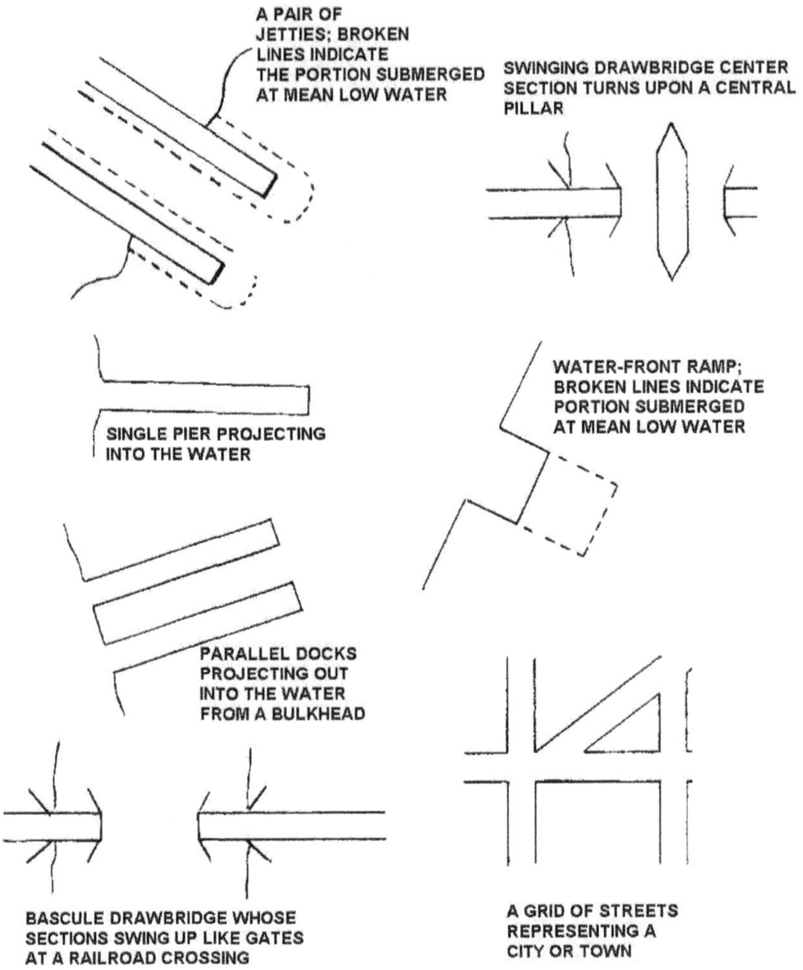
A PAIR OF JETTIES; BROKEN LINES INDICATE THE PORTION SUBMERGED AT MEAN LOW WATER
SWINGING DRAWBRIDGE CENTER SECTION TURNS UPON A CENTRAL PILLAR
WATER-FRONT RAMP; BROKEN LINES INDICATE PORTION SUBMERGED AT MEAN LOW WATER
SINGLE PIER PROJECTING INTO THE WATER
PARALLEL DOCKS PROJECTING OUT INTO THE WATER FROM A BULKHEAD
BASCULE DRAWBRIDGE WHOSE SECTIONS SWING UP LIKE GATES AT A RAILROAD CROSSING
A GRID OF STREETS REPRESENTING A CITY OR TOWN

Figure 14-11
Structures

B.29. Coastlines

Coastlines are viewed at both low and high water. Landmarks that may help in fixing position are noted and labeled. (see **Figure 14-12**)

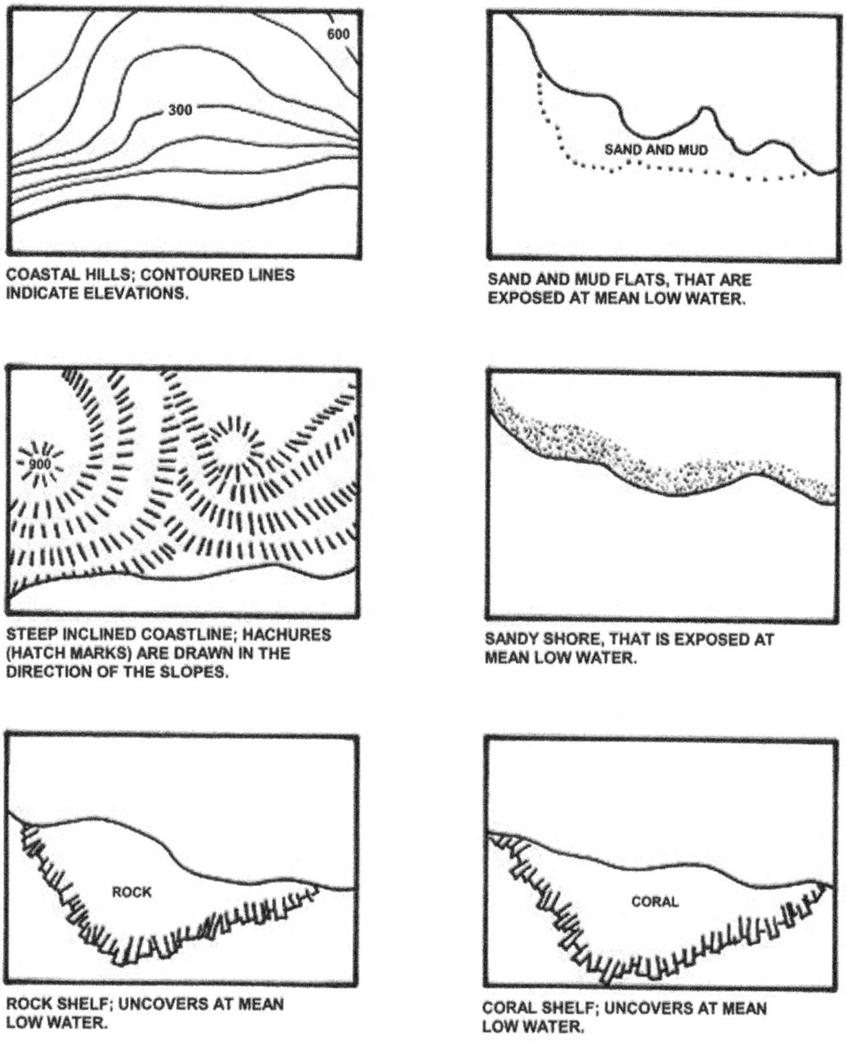

600
300
COASTAL HILLS; CONTOURED LINES INDICATE ELEVATIONS.
SAND AND MUD
SAND AND MUD FLATS, THAT ARE EXPOSED AT MEAN LOW WATER.
900
STEEP INCLINED COASTLINE; HACHURES (HATCH MARKS) ARE DRAWN IN THE DIRECTION OF THE SLOPES.
SANDY SHORE, THAT IS EXPOSED AT MEAN LOW WATER.
ROCK
ROCK SHELF; UNCOVERS AT MEAN LOW WATER.
CORAL
CORAL SHELF; UNCOVERS AT MEAN LOW WATER.

Figure 14-12
Coastlines

Accuracy of Charts

B.30. Description

A chart is only as accurate as the survey on which it is based. Major disturbances, such as hurricanes and earthquakes, cause sudden and extensive changes in the bottom contour. Even everyday forces of wind and waves cause changes in channels and shoals. The prudent sailor must be alert to the possibilities of changes in conditions and inaccuracies of charted information.

B.31. Determining Accuracy

Compromise is sometimes necessary in chart production as various factors may prevent the presentation of all data that has been collected for a given area. The information shown must be presented so that it can be understood with ease and certainty.

In order to judge the accuracy and completeness of a survey, the following should be noted:

- Source and date.
- Testing.
- Full or sparse soundings.
- Blank spaces among sounding.

B.31.a. Source and Date

The source and date of the chart are generally given in the title along with the changes that have taken place since the date of the survey. The earlier surveys often were made under circumstances that precluded great accuracy of detail.

B.31.b. Testing

Until a chart based on such a survey is tested, it should be regarded with caution. Except in well-frequented waters, few surveys have been so thorough as to make certain that all dangers have been found.

B.31.c. Full or Sparse Soundings

Noting the fullness or scantiness of the soundings is another method of estimating the completeness of the survey, but it must be remembered that the chart seldom shows all soundings that were obtained. If the soundings are sparse or unevenly distributed, it should be taken for granted, as a precautionary measure, that the survey was not in great detail.

B.31.d. Blank Spaces Among Soundings

Large or irregular blank spaces among soundings mean that no soundings were obtained in those areas. Where the nearby soundings are deep, it may logically be assumed that in the blanks the water is also deep. When the surrounding water is shallow, or if the local charts show that reefs are present in the area, such blanks should be regarded with suspicion. This is especially true in coral areas and off rocky coasts. These areas should be given wide berth.

Electronic Charts

B.32. Electronic Charts

Raster Charts and Vector Charts are the two types of electronic charts. Raster Charts are basically electronic photographs of an official, paper chart. Vector Charts are distillations of paper charts, but their presentation is different. Vector displays allow you to select "layers" of information to reduce clutter or add detail. Audible alarms can often be set to signal warnings based on the information in these layers such as depth sounding or distances off land.

Section C. Magnetic Compass

Introduction

The magnetic compass, even though it has been around for a long time, is still very important for safely navigating a boat. Whether steering a course out of sight of landmarks or in poor visibility, the magnetic compass is the primary tool for guiding the boat to its destination. Though used by larger vessels, the gyrocompass will not be discussed since it is not commonly used by boats.

In this section

This section contains the following information:

Components of the Magnetic Compass

C.1. Description

The magnetic compass is standard equipment on all boats. Mechanically, it is a simple piece of equipment. The magnetic compass is used to determine the boat's heading. A prudent seaman will check its accuracy frequently realizing that the magnetic compass is influenced, not only by the earth's magnetic field, but also by fields radiating from magnetic materials aboard the boat. It is also subject to error caused by violent movement as might be encountered in heavy weather.

C.2. Compass Card

The arc of the compass card is divided into 360 degrees (°) and is numbered all the way around the card from 000° through 359° in a clockwise direction. Attached to the compass card is a magnet that aligns itself with the magnetic field around it. The zero (north) on the compass card is in line with the magnet or needle attached to the card. When the boat turns, the needle continues to align itself with the magnetic field. This means the compass card stays stationary and the boat turns around it. (see **Figure 14-13**)

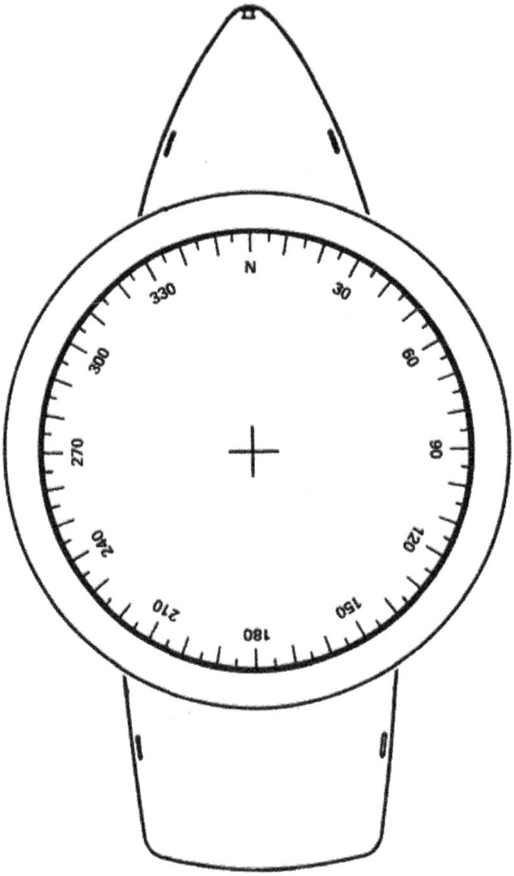

Figure 14-13
Compound Card

C.3. Lubber's Line

The lubber's line is a line or mark scribed on the compass housing to indicate the direction in which the boat is heading. The compass is mounted in the boat with the lubber's line on the boat's centerline and parallel to its keel. (see **Figure 14-14**)

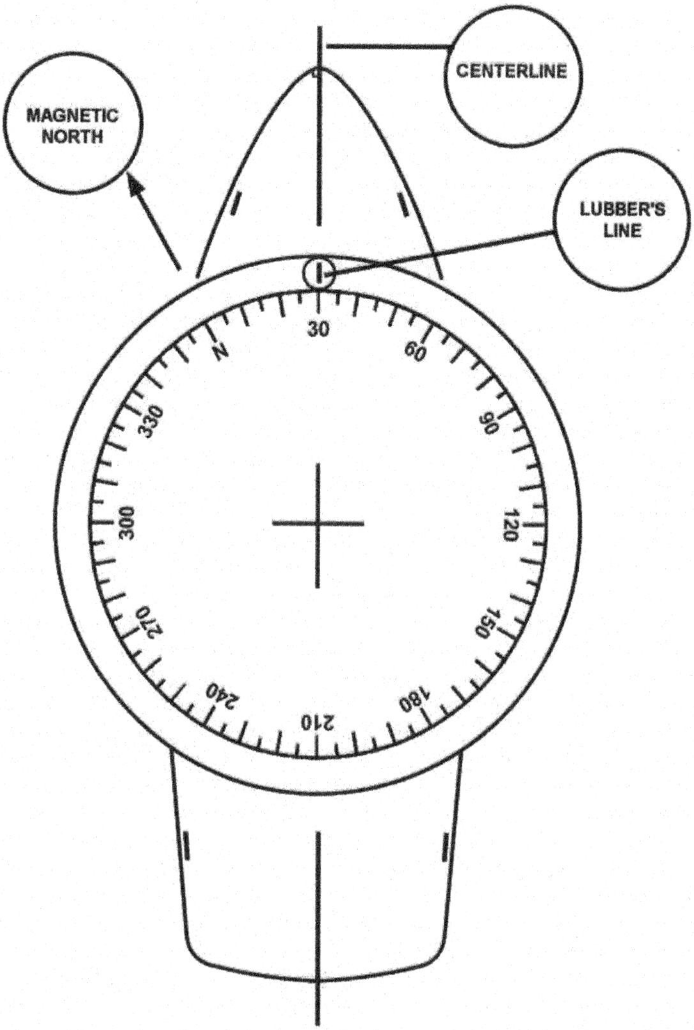

Figure 14-14
Lubber's Line and Magnetic North

Direction

C.4. Description

Direction is measured clockwise from 000° to 359°. When speaking of degrees in giving course or heading, three digits should always be used, such as 270° or 057°. The heading of 360° is always referred to or spoken as 000°.

C.5. True and Magnetic

Directions measured on a chart are in true degrees or magnetic degrees as follows:

- True direction uses the North Pole as a reference point.
- Magnetic direction uses the magnetic North Pole as a reference point.
- True direction differs from magnetic direction by variation.

Directions steered on the compass by the boat are magnetic degrees. (see **Figure 14-15**)

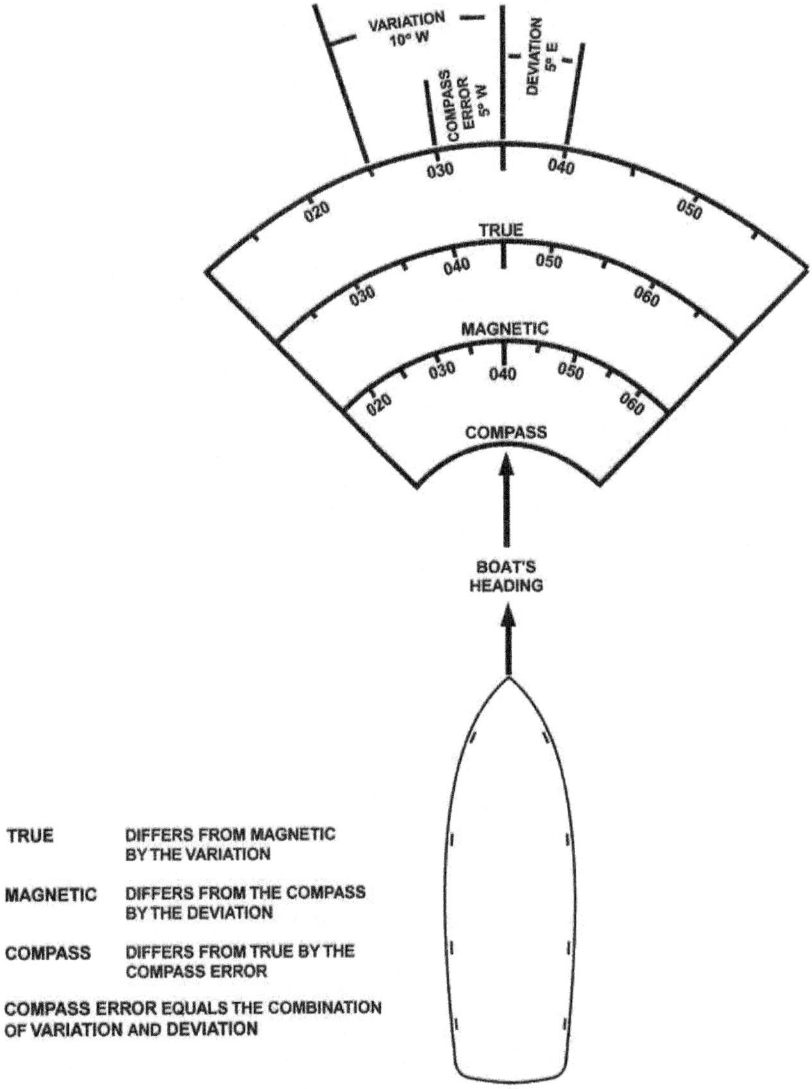
VARIATION 10° W
COMPASS ERROR 5° W
DEVIATION 5° E
020
030
040
050
TRUE
030
040
050
060
MAGNETIC
020
030
040
050
060
COMPASS
BOAT'S HEADING
TRUE DIFFERS FROM MAGNETIC BY THE VARIATION
MAGNETIC DIFFERS FROM THE COMPASS BY THE DEVIATION
COMPASS DIFFERS FROM TRUE BY THE COMPASS ERROR
COMPASS ERROR EQUALS THE COMBINATION OF VARIATION AND DEVIATION

Figure 14-15
True, Magnetic, and Compass Courses

Compass Error

C.6. Description

Compass error is the angular difference between a compass direction and its corresponding true direction. The magnetic compass reading must be corrected for variation and deviation.

Variation

C.7. Description

Variation is the angular difference, measured in degrees, between true and magnetic north. It varies according to geographic location.

C.8. Amount of Variation

The amount of variation changes from one point to the next on the earth's surface. It is written in degrees in either an easterly or a westerly direction. The variation is on the inside of the compass rose of the chart.

C.9. Variation Increases/ Decreases

Increases in variation may continue for many years, sometimes reaching large values, remaining nearly the same for a few years and then reverse its trends (decrease). Predictions of the change of variation are intended for short-term use, that is a period of only a few years. The latest charts available should always be used. The compass rose will show the amount of predicted change.

C.10. Calculating the Variation

Perform the following the procedures for determining the amount of annual increase or decrease of variation:

Step	Procedure
1	Locate the compass rose nearest to area of operation on the chart.
2	Locate the variation and annual increase/decrease from the center of the compass rose.
3	Locate the year from the center of the compass rose where variation and the year are indicated.
4	Subtract year indicated in the compass rose from the present year.
5	Multiply the number of years difference by the annual increase or decrease.
6	Add or subtract the amount from step 5 to the variation within the compass rose.

NOTE

Since variation is caused by the earth's magnetic field, its value changes with the geographic location of the boat. Variation remains the same for all headings of the boat.

Deviation

C.11. Description

Deviation is the amount of deflection influenced by a vessel and its electronics on the compass. It varies according to the heading of the vessel and can be caused by:

- Metal objects around the compass.
- Electrical motors.
- The boat itself.

Deviation creates an error in the compass course that a boat attempts to steer. For navigational accuracy and the safety of the boat and crew, the boat's compass heading must be corrected for deviation so that the actual magnetic course can be accurately steered.

NOTE Deviation changes with the boat's heading; it is not affected by the geographic location of the boat.

C.12. Deviation Table

Coast Guard regulations require Unit Commanders to ensure compass errors are accurately known and properly recorded and posted. This is accomplished for a magnetic compass by "swinging ship" to determine deviation. A deviation table may be created or the Coast Guard deviation table used by ships may be altered for use by boats. (Boats do not fill in the "Degaussing On" column since they do not carry this equipment.) Unit Commanders are also required to develop procedures to compensate or calibrate compasses as necessary.

A new deviation table must be completed and approved by the Unit Commander annually, after yard availabilities, and after addition or deletion of equipment or structural alterations that would affect the magnetic characteristics of the boat. The original deviation table shall be placed in the permanent boat record and a copy posted on the boat near the compass.

C.13. Preparing a Deviation Table

Since deviation varies from boat to boat, crewmembers should know the effect of deviation on the compass. The amount of deviation is normally determined by "swinging ship" (procedures are discussed later) and recording them on a deviation table. The table is tabulated for every 15° of the compass. Deviation varies for different courses steered and can be easterly (E), westerly (W), or no error. Deviation would then be applied to the boat's compass heading to determine the correct magnetic course.

C.14. Deviation By Running a Range

A commonly used practice to determine deviation is running a range. A range is a line of bearing made by two fixed objects. Sometimes, specific range marks are installed so that when they are lined up, the vessel is on the center of a channel (and a true or magnetic direction that can be read on the compass rose). Or, the chart may be checked for prominent landmarks that may line up as a natural range.

C.14.a. Finding Bearing of a Range

When obtaining the deviation, a position that will not interfere with normal shipping traffic should be selected. To find the magnetic bearing of the range:

- Align the edge of the parallel rulers (or course plotter) so that it passes through the charted positions of the two objects.
- Line up the edge of the parallel rulers with the center of the nearest compass rose.
- Read the magnetic bearing off of the inner ring of the compass rose.`

The correct side of the compass rose must be read. Going in the wrong direction will give the reciprocal bearing which is 180° in the wrong direction. To go in the correct direction, crewmembers should try to imagine the boat positioned in the center of the compass rose and looking out towards the range.

NOTE Man-made ranges may have their direction marked on the chart. If marked, the direction will be in degrees true, not magnetic.

C.14.b. Example

Example: The magnetic bearing (M) of the range measured on the chart is 272°. The bearing of the range read off of the magnetic compass (C) is 274°. (see **Figure 14-16**)

Answer: 2°W is the deviation.

The amount of deviation is the difference between C and M; this is 2°. The direction of deviation is based upon "compass best, error west". Since C is greater than M, the error is west. (This will be discussed in more detail later.)

NOTE To correct the compass - subtract easterly errors; add westerly errors.

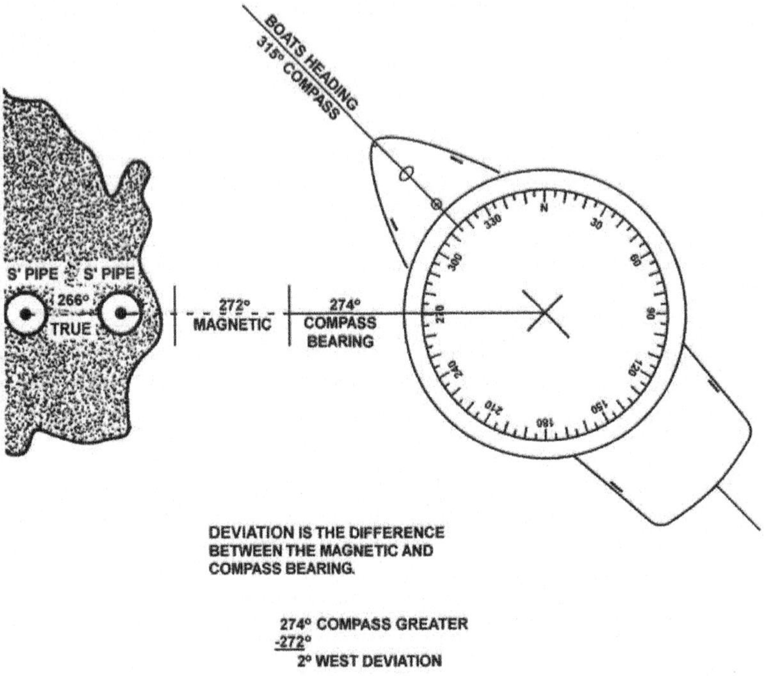

Figure 14-16
Obtaining Deviation Using Ranges

C.14.c. Exercise

The example above and **Figure 14-16** should be used for guidance in developing a deviation table. Prepare a work table using the procedures as follows:

NOTE Enter all compass bearings to the nearest whole degree.

Step	Procedure
1	Enter the boat's compass headings for every 15° in the first column.
2	Enter the range's magnetic bearing as measured on the chart (272°) in the third column. It is the same value for all entries.
3	Get the boat underway at slow speed and in calm water. Steer the boat's compass heading listed in the first column, normally starting with a compass heading of 000°. Steer a steady heading and cross the range.
4	Observe the compass bearing of the range at the instant the range is crossed. Use 266° for this exercise. Enter the range's bearing by compass in the second column on the same line as the boat's compass heading of 000°.
5	Come around to the boat's compass heading of 015°. Steer a steady heading and cross the range.
6	Observe the compass bearing of the range at the instant the range is crossed. Use 265° for this exercise. Enter the range's bearing by compass in the second column on the same line as the boat's compass heading of 015°.
7	Come around to the boat's compass heading of 030°. Steer a steady heading and cross the range.
8	Observe the compass bearing of the range at the instant the range is crossed. Use 265° for this exercise. Enter the range's bearing by compass in the second column on the same line as the boat's compass heading of 030°.
9	Continue changing course by 15° increments until the range is crossed and the compass bearing of the range for each for each boat's compass heading is noted. The table is already filled in for this exercise.
10	Having completed "swinging ship", determine deviation for each heading by taking the difference between the magnetic bearing and the compass bearing. (see **Table 14-2**)

Table 14-2
Completed Work Table, Deviation

Boat's Compass Heading	Compass Bearing of Range	Magnetic Bearing of Range	Deviation	Magnetic Course
000°	266°	272°	6° E	006°
015°	265°	272°	7° E	022°
030°	265°	272°	7° E	037°
045°	267°	272°	5° E	050°
060°	270°	272°	2° E	062°
075°	269°	272°	3° E	078°
090°	271°	272°	1° E	091°
105°	272°	272°	0°	105°
120°	267°	272°	5° E	125°
135°	273°	272°	1° W	134°
150°	268°	272°	4° E	154°
165°	275°	272°	3° W	162°
180°	274°	272°	2° W	178°
195°	277°	272°	5° W	190°
210°	278°	272°	6° W	204°
225°	279°	272°	7° W	218°
240°	275°	272°	3° W	237°
255°	279°	272°	7° W	248°
270°	279°	272°	7° W	263°
285°	277°	272°	5° W	280°
300°	270°	272°	2° E	302°
315°	274°	272°	2° W	313°
330°	269°	272°	3° E	333°
345°	266°	272°	6° E	351°

Step	Procedure
11	Prepare a smooth deviation table to be placed next to the boat's compass. The table must give the deviation for a magnetic course so the table may be used to correct courses. (see **Table 14-3**) As noted before, the deviation table used by ships can be altered for use by boats.

NOTE When the compass bearing is less than the magnetic bearing - deviation (error) is east. When the compass bearing is greater than the magnetic bearing - deviation (error) is west.

MEMORY AID Determining the direction of deviation compass least, error east; compass best, error west.

Table 14-3
Deviation Table (Mounted Close to Compass)

Compass Course	Deviation	Magnetic Course
000°	6° E	006°
015°	7° E	022°
030°	7° E	037°
045°	5° E	050°
060°	2° E	062°
075°	3° E	078°
090°	1° E	091°
105°	0°	105°
120°	5° E	125°
135°	1° W	134°
150°	4° E	154°
165°	3° W	162°
180°	2° W	178°
195°	5° W	190°
210°	6° W	204°
225°	7° W	218°
240°	3° W	237°
255°	7° W	248°
270°	7° W	263°
285°	5° W	280°
300°	2° E	302°
315°	2° W	313°
330°	3° E	333°
345°	6° E	351°

C.15. Deviation By Multiple Observations From One Position

To conduct a deviation by multiple observation from one position, an accurately charted object such as a solitary piling, with maneuvering room and depth around it, must be available. In addition, there must be charted and visible objects, suitable for steering on with accuracy, at a distance of greater than ½ mile. The largest scale chart possible should be used.

C.15.a. Preparation

To prepare for this task, perform the following procedures:

Step	Procedure
1	Determine and record the magnetic bearing from the chart (from piling to object) of various selected objects.
2	Ideally, the objects should be 15 ° apart. However, this is not necessary as long as a minimum of ten objects/bearings, evenly separated through the entire 360°, are available.
3	For ready reference, record this information as shown in columns (1) and (2) in the table below.

(1) Object (on chart)	(2) Magnetic Heading (plotted)	(3) Compass Heading (measured)	(4) Deviation (calculated)
Steeple	013°	014.0°	1.0° W
Stack	040°	041.5°	1.5° W
R. Tower	060°	062.0°	2.0° W
Lt. #5	112°	115.0°	3.0° W
Left Tangent Pier	160°	163.0°	3.0° W
Water Tower	200°	201.0°	1.0° W
Right Tangent Jetty	235°	235.0°	0.0° W
Light House	272°	271.0°	1.0° E
Flag Pole	310°	309.0°	1.0° E
Lookout Tower	345°	344.5°	0.5° E

C.15.b. Observation

To carry out this task, perform the following procedures:

Step	Procedure
1	With the above information (column (1) and (2)), proceed to and tie off to the piling.
2	With the piling amidships, pivot around it and steer on the objects that were identified, then record the compass heading in column (3). Comparing column (2) and (3) will yield the deviation for that heading (4).
3	Use the observed deviation (4) for the indicated magnetic heading (2) as reference points, then draw a deviation curve on the graph as is shown in **Figure 14-17**.

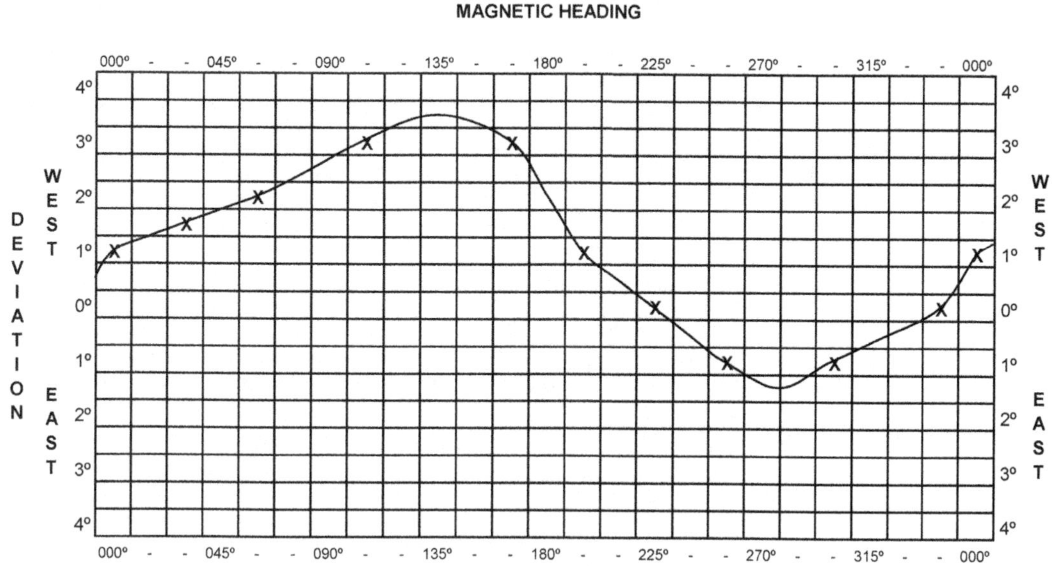

Figure 14-17
Example Deviation Curve

C.15.c. Determination

Deviations should be extracted from the deviation curve for any heading.

NOTE

> The graph is divided vertically in 15° increments and horizontally in half (for east and west deviation) and then further divided according to amount of deviation. This later subdivision may be greater than the 4° depicted. However, do not tolerate deviations of more than 3°. If excessive deviations are noted, the compass should be adjusted by the technique discussed later or by a professional compass adjuster.

C.16. Deviation by Multiple Ranges

The largest scale chart available covering the local area should be used. With parallel rulers, triangles, etc., crewmembers should identify as many terrestrial ranges as possible that will be visible when underway, and also provide lines of position (LOPs) across expanses of water with adequate maneuvering room and depth. As far as possible, the ranges should be in the same area, so that variation remains constant.

CAUTION !

Ensure that there are no local magnetic anomalies (such as wrecks, pipe lines, bridges or steel piers) near the boat that could affect the local variation indicated on the chart. Check the chart for any indication of local disturbances.

C.16.a. Preparation

The number of terrestrial ranges available may be limited. However, for each range, deviation will be for both the "steering toward" and the "steering away" (reciprocal) heading. To prepare for this task, perform the following procedures:

Step	Procedure
1	Be careful when "running" the reciprocal heading that the lubber's line of the compass aligns with the axis of the range.
2	Make every effort to identify no less than four ranges to yield deviation values for the cardinal points (N, S, E, W) and intercardinal points (NE, SE, SW, NW).
3	Determine the magnetic bearing from the chart. Record this information in the format shown below.

(1) Range (on chart)	(2) Magnetic Heading (plotted)	(3) Compass Heading (measured)	(4) Deviation (calculated)
Steeple -Jetty Lt. #4	015°/195°	014°/195°	1° E/0°
R. Tower - Tank	103°/283°	104°/282°	1° W/1° E
Flag Pole – Lt. #5	176°/356°	177°/355.5°	1° W/.5° E
Stack - Left Tangent Pier	273°/093°	272°/094°	1° E/1° W
Ent Channel Range	333°/153°	332°/154.5°	1° E/1.5° W

C.16.b. Observation

To carry out this task, perform the following procedures:

Step	Procedure
1	With the information from columns (1) and (2) get underway and "run" the various ranges.
2	Record the compass heading in column (3), as appropriate.
3	Take care not to become so preoccupied with running the range that the boat is in jeopardy of collision, grounding, etc.
4	Compare column (2) and (3) to yield the deviation from that heading (4).

C.16.c. Determination

The deviation for the indicated headings may be plotted on the deviation graph resulting in a deviation curve. With the resulting deviation curve, deviation for any heading is possible. (see **Figure 14-18**)

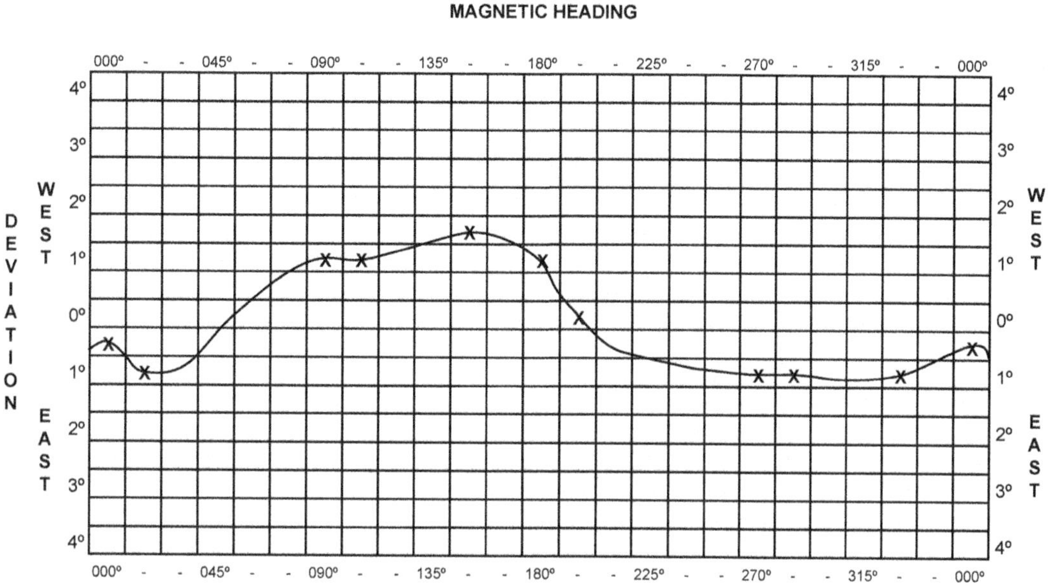

Figure 14-18
Example Deviation Curve

Compass Adjustment

C.17. Description

The following are the procedures for adjusting a small boat compass:

Step	Procedure
1	Steer a course in a northerly direction as close to magnetic north as possible as defined by the known objects on the chart. With a nonmagnetic tool, adjust the N/S compensating magnet to remove half the observed error. (Do not try to shortcut. Removing all the error in the first step will just overcompensate the error.)
2	Steer a course in a southerly direction. Again remove half the observed error.
3	Steer a course in an easterly direction. Adjust the E/W compensating magnet to remove half the observed error.
4	Steer a course in a westerly direction. Again remove half the observed error.
5	Repeat the above procedures, as often as needed, to reduce observed error to the minimum achievable.
6	Record the final observed instrument error for N, S, E, and W.
7	Determine the observed error for NE, SE, SW, and NW. Record these but do not try to adjust these errors manually.
8	Use the recorded values for compass corrections.

These simple procedures are sufficiently precise for most boats. To gain greater precision, a qualified compass adjuster should be used or a book on the subject should be consulted.

Applying Compass Error

C.18. Description

"Correcting" is going from magnetic direction (M) to true (T), or going from the compass direction (C) to magnetic (M). To apply compass error to correct course or direction:

- Take the compass course.
- Apply deviation to obtain the magnetic course.
- Apply variation to obtain true course.

The sequence of the procedure is outlined below: (see **Figure 14-19**)

- Compass (C).
- Deviation (D).
- Magnetic (M).
- Variation (V).
- True (T).

MEMORY AID

Applying compass error:
Can **D**ead **M**en **V**ote **T**wice **A**t **E**lection
(**C**ompass) (**D**eviation) (**M**agnetic) (**V**ariation) (**T**rue) (**A**dd) (**E**asterly error)
Add easterly errors - subtract westerly errors

C.19. Obtaining True Course

For **Figure 14-19**, the compass course is 127°, variation from the compass rose is 4° W, and the deviation from the boat's deviation table is 5° E. Then, the true course (T) is obtained as follows:

Step	Procedure
1	Write down the correction formula:
	• C = 127°
	• D = 5° E
	• M = 132°
	• V = 4° W
	• T = 128°
2	Compute the information opposite the appropriate letter in the previous step.
3	Add the easterly error of 5° E deviation to the compass course (127°) and obtain the magnetic course of 132°.
4	Subtract the westerly error of 4° W variation from the magnetic course (132°).
5	The true course is 128°.

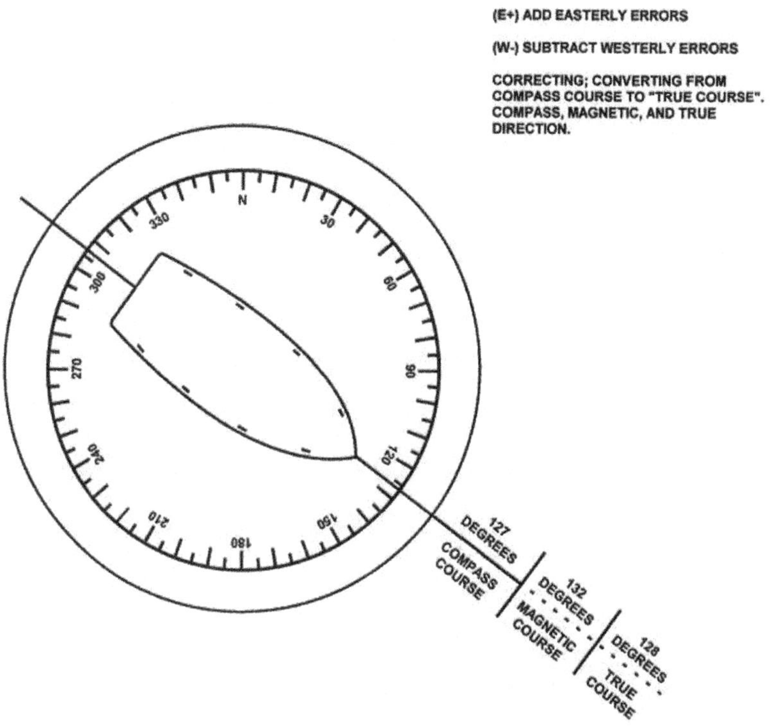

Figure 14-19
Applying Compass Error, Correcting

C.20. Converting True Course to Compass Course

Converting from true (T) direction to magnetic (M), or going from magnetic (M) to compass (C) is "uncorrecting". For converting from true course to compass course:

- Obtain the true course.
- Apply variation to obtain the magnetic course.
- Apply deviation to obtain the compass course.

The sequence of the procedure is outlined below:

- True (T).
- Variation (V).
- Magnetic (M).
- Deviation (D).
- Compass (C).

MEMORY AID

Converting true course to compass course:
True **V**irtue **M**akes **D**ull **C**ompany **A**fter **W**edding
(**T**rue) (**V**ariation) (**M**agnetic) (**D**eviation) (**C**ompass) (**A**dd) (**W**esterly error)
Subtract easterly errors - add westerly errors

C.21. Obtaining Compass Course

For **Figure 14-20**, by using parallel rulers, the true course between two points on a chart is measured as 221° T, variation is 9° E and deviation is 2° W. Then, obtain the compass course (C) is obtained as follows:

Step	Procedure
1	Write down the conversion formula: • T = 221° • V = 9° E • M = 212° • D = 2° W • C = 214°
2	Compute the information opposite the appropriate letter in the previous step.
3	Subtract the easterly error of 9° E variation from true course of 221° and obtain the magnetic course of 212°.
4	Add the westerly error of 2° W deviation to the magnetic course (212°).
5	The compass course (C) is 214°.

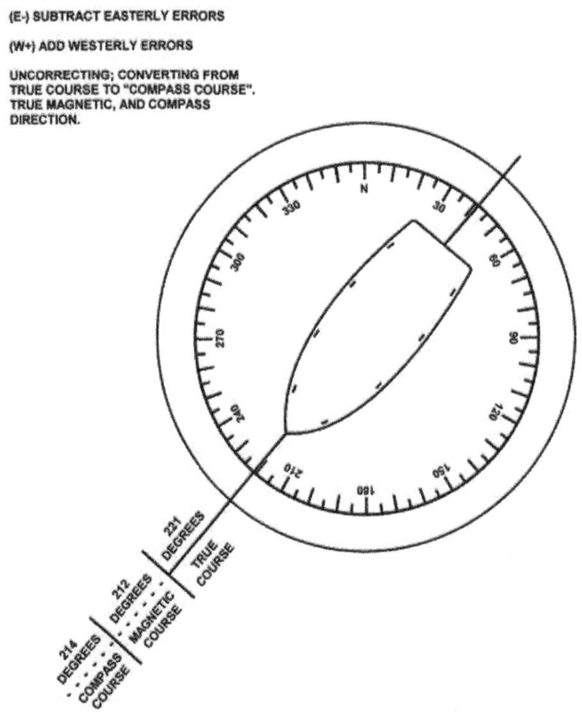

Figure 14-20
Applying Compass Error, Uncorrecting

Section D. Piloting

Introduction

Piloting is directing a vessel by using landmarks, other navigational aids, and soundings. Safe piloting requires the use of correct, up-to-date charts. Piloting deals with both present and future consequences. Therefore, it is important to be alert and attentive, and always be consciously aware of where the vessel is and where it soon will be.

In this section

This section contains the following information:

Basic Piloting Equipment

D.1. Description

Adequate preparation is very important in piloting a boat. Piloting is the primary method of determining a boat's position. In order for a boat coxswain to make good judgment on all decisions in navigation, tools such as compasses, dividers, stopwatches, parallel rulers, pencils, and publications must be available. (see **Figure 14-21**)

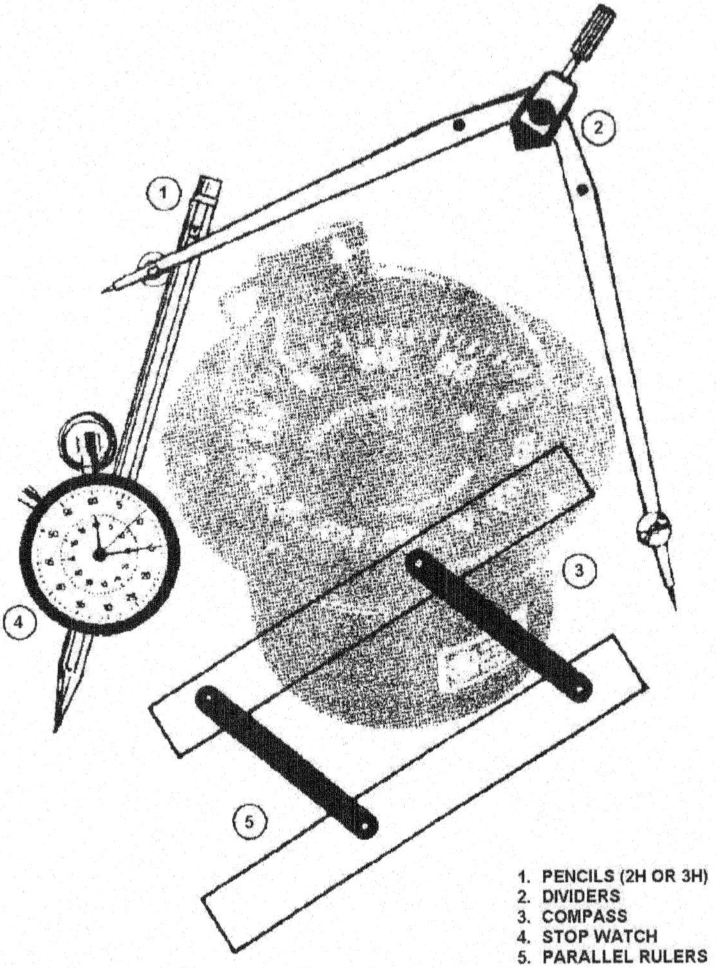

Figure 14-21
Basic Piloting Tools

D.2. Compass

For a boat, the magnetic compass is used:

- To steer the course.
- To give a constant report on the boat's heading.
- As a sighting instrument to determine bearings.

A mark called a "lubber's line" is fixed to the inner surface of the compass housing. Similar marks, called 90° lubber's lines, are usually mounted at 90° intervals around the compass card and are used in determining when an object is bearing directly abeam or astern. Centered on the compass card is a pin (longer than the lubber's line pins), which is used to determine a position by taking bearings on visible objects.

D.3. Parallel Rulers

Parallel rulers are two rulers connected by straps that allow the rulers to separate while remaining parallel. They are used in chart work to transfer directions from a compass rose to various plotted courses and bearing lines and vice versa. Parallel rulers are always walked so that the top or lower edge intersects the compass rose center to obtain accurate courses.

D.4. Course Plotter

A course plotter may be used for chart work in place of the parallel rulers discussed above. It is a rectangular piece of clear plastic with a set of lines parallel to the long edges and semi-circular scales. The center of the scales is at or near the center of one of the longer sides and has a small circle or bull's eye. The bull's eye is used to line up on a meridian so that the direction (course or bearing) can be plotted or read off of the scale. A popular model is the "Weems Plotter" that is mounted on a roller for ease of moving.

D.5. Pencils

It is important to use a correct type of pencil for plotting. A medium pencil (No. 2) is best. Pencils should be kept sharp; a dull pencil can cause considerable error in plotting a course due to the width of the lead.

D.6. Dividers

Dividers are instruments with two pointed legs, hinged where the upper ends join. Dividers are used to measure distance on a scale and transfer them to a chart.

D.7. Stopwatch

A stopwatch, or navigational timer, which can be started and stopped at will, is very useful to find the lighted period of a navigational aid. This is usually done for purposes of identification. Also, it is used to run a speed check.

D.8. Nautical Slide Rule

The nautical slide rule will be discussed in the Distance, Speed, and Time portion of this chapter.

D.9. Drafting Compass

The drafting compass is an instrument similar to the dividers. One leg has a pencil attached. This tool is used for swinging arcs and circles.

D.10. Speed Curve (Speed vs. RPMs)

A speed curve is used to translate tachometer readings of revolutions per minute (RPMs) into the boat's speed through the water. A speed curve is obtained by running a known distance at constant RPM in one direction and then in the opposite direction. The time for each run is recorded and averaged to take account for current and wind forces. Using distance and time, the speed is determined for the particular RPM. (see Error! Reference source not found.)

Table 14-4
Sample Speed vs. RPMs Conversion

Speed, Kts Calm Water	Approx. RPM	Fuel Gal/Hour	Consumption Gal/Mile	Cruise Radius/Miles
7.60	760	3.86	.51	882
7.89	1000	4.99	.63	712
9.17	1250	7.50	.82	550
9.48	1500	12.75	1.31	335
12.50	1750	16.80	1.35	333
15.53	2000	21.00	1.35	333
19.15	2250	33.00	1.72	261
21.34	2400	33.75	1.58	284

D.11. Charts

Charts are essential for plotting and determining your position, whether operating in familiar or unfamiliar waters. Boat crews should never get underway without the appropriate charts.

D.12. Depth Sounder

There are several types of depth sounders, but they operate on the same principle. The depth sounder transmits a high frequency sound wave that reflects off the bottom and returns to the receiver. The "echo" is converted to an electrical impulse and can be read from a visual scale on the depth sounder. It shows only the depth of water the vessel is in; it does not show the depth of water being headed for.

D.12.a. Transducer

The transducer is the part of the depth sounder that transmits the sound wave. The transducer is usually mounted through the hull and sticks out a very short distance. It is not mounted on the lowest part of the hull. The distance from the transducer to the lowest point of the hull must be known. This distance must be subtracted from the depth sounding reading to determine the actual depth of water available.

Example: Depth sounder reading is 6 feet. The transducer is 1 foot above the lowest point of the hull - the boat extends 1 foot below the transducer. This 1 foot is subtracted from the reading of 6 feet, which means the boat has 5 feet of water beneath it.

NOTE

Always consider the location of the transducer; it is usually mounted above the lowest point of the hull.

D.12.b. Water Depth

Water depth is indicated by a variety of methods:

- Indicator: A digital display or a flashing light that rotates clockwise around a scale on a visual screen in the pilothouse. In the flashing light type, the first "flash" is when the pulse goes out and the second flash is the "echo" back that indicates the depth.
- Recorder: Depths are recorded on paper tape.
- Video display screen: The display is similar to a small television set with brightness on the bottom of the screen indicating the sea floor.

NOTE

To determine the actual water depth below the boat's hull, subtract the distance between the transducer and the lowest point of the hull from all readings.

D.12.c. Bottom Conditions

With practice and experience, the bottom characteristics and conditions can be determined. Flashing light and video display sounders may be generally interpreted as:

- Sharp, clear flash - hard bottom.
- Broad, fuzzy flash - soft, muddy bottom.
- Multiple, fairly sharp flashes - rocky bottom.
- Additional flashes or displays at multiples of the least depth indicated may reveal the need to turn down the sensitivity control.

D.12.d. Adjustment Controls

Adjustment controls depend on the type of depth sounder. The equipment operator's manual should be reviewed for correct use. Typical adjustment controls include depth scales (which may include feet and fathoms) and a sensitivity control.

D.13. Lead Line

Depth of water is one of the most important dimensions of piloting. A hand-held lead line is used for ascertaining the depth of water when a depth sounder is not available, the depth sounder is not operational, or the crew is operating in known shallow water.

It consists of a line marked in fathoms and a lead weight of 7 to 14 pounds, hollowed at one end in which tallow is inserted to gather samples of the bottom. It is simple and not subject to breakdown. Lead line limitations include:

- Not useable in adverse sea conditions.
- Awkward to use.
- Usable only at slow speed.

NOTE Always keep a lead line neatly stowed and ready for use in the event the depth sounder becomes inoperative.

D.13.a. Lead Line Markings

Lead lines are marked as follows: (see **Figure 14-22**)

Depth	Lead Line Marking
2 Fathoms	Two (2) strips of leather
3 Fathoms	Three (3) strips of leather
5 Fathoms	One (1) white rag (usually cotton)
7 Fathoms	One (1) red rag (usually wool)
10 Fathoms	One (1) strip of leather with a hole
13 Fathoms	Three (3) strips of leather
15 Fathoms	One (1) white rag (usually cotton)
17 Fathoms	One (l) red rag (usually cotton)
20 Fathoms	Two (2) knots
25 Fathoms	One (1) knot

NOTE Lead lines should be wetted and stretched prior to marking. Lines should be checked periodically for accuracy of markings.

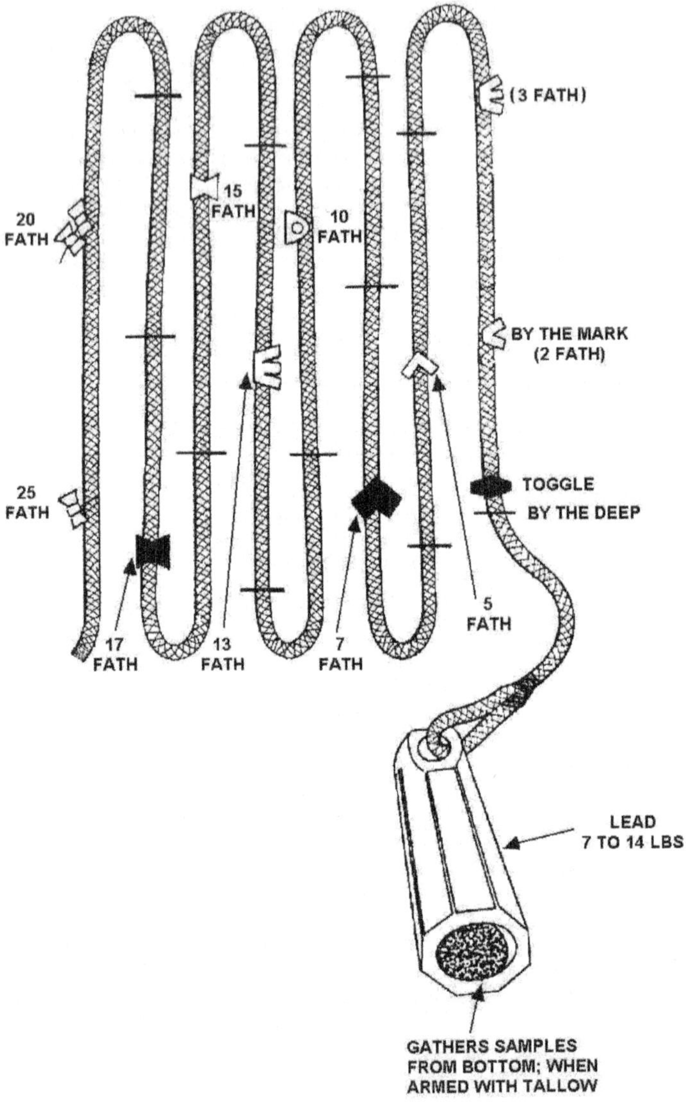

Figure 14-22
Handheld Lead Line

D.13.b. Casting the Hand-Held Lead Line

The following procedures should be used in casting a lead line:

Step	Procedure
1	Grasp the line by the toggle.
2	Swing the lead in a fore-and-aft arc.
3	When sufficient momentum is obtained and at shoulder level, throw the lead as far forward as possible. Keep hold of the bitter end of the line!
4	Pull the slack out of the line until the lead on the bottom is felt is felt.
5	When the line is straight up and down, read the sounding.

D.13.c. Reporting the Soundings

There are two ways to report soundings, depending upon where the watermark is located on the lead line.

- Depth that corresponds to any mark on the lead line is reported: "by the mark", that is, should the depth align with the two strips of leather, it would be reported "by the mark 2".
- All other unmarked whole fathoms are called deeps. This would be reported as "by the deep 6" for a depth of 6 fathoms.

Fractions of a fathom should be reported as halves and quarters, such as, "and a half seven" or "less a quarter ten".

D.14. RDF and ADF

A radio direction finder (RDF) will allow the users to take bearings on radio transmitters which are well beyond their visual range. One type of RDF requires manual operation to obtain bearings. The automatic radio direction finder (ADF) automatically takes and displays the bearings.

Radio bearings are not as accurate as visual bearings. It takes a great deal of experience to be able to effectively use the equipment. Care should be taken when plotting radio bearings, especially in the correct direction.

D.15. VHF-FM Homer

The VHF-FM homer (direction finder homing device) allows the users to home in on the source of any FM radio signals being received. This unit will also function as a backup VHF-FM receiver.

The VHF-FM homer measures the small difference in angle of a signal, from a known source and received by each antenna, then converts this signal into the angle of direction from the boat. This direction is shown on a swinging needle display screen mounted in the pilothouse. The source must continue to transmit to be able to track it.

The following procedures should be used for operating the homer:

NOTE

> A needle centered in the middle of the screen may indicate a source dead ahead, or dead astern. The homer cannot distinguish this since both signals would arrive at 90 degrees to each antenna. To determine which direction, turn off course 30 degrees and observe the needle. If it directs to return to the original heading, the source is ahead. If the needle points elsewhere, follow it. The indicator needle is affected by radio wave reflections and may bounce around when passing near large metal objects.

Step	Procedure
1	The homer has six channels (6, 12, 13, 14, 16, and 22) in addition to the weather channels. Set the channel switch to the channel receiving the signal.
2	Request a long count from the transmitting station.
3	Turn the squelch control fully counterclockwise.
4	Set volume to a comfortable level.
5	Rotate squelch control to remove speaker noise.
6	Push squelch control in for homing, out for monitoring.
7	Turn the boat in the direction of the pointer until it centers itself.
8	Turn 30° to be sure the source is ahead, not aft.
9	Change course as indicated by the needle and proceed to the source of the signals, giving due caution to navigation hazards that may be between the vessel and the destination.

D.16. Light List

Light Lists provide more complete information concerning aids to navigation than can be shown on charts. They are not intended to replace charts for navigation and are published in seven volumes, as follows:

Volume	Area of Coverage
I	Atlantic Coast, from St. Croix River, Maine to Toms River, New Jersey
II	Atlantic Coast, from Toms River, New Jersey to Little River Inlet, South Carolina
III	Atlantic Coast, from Little River Inlet, South Carolina, to Econfina River, Florida, and the Greater Antilles
IV	Gulf of Mexico, from Econfina River, Florida, to Rio Grande, Texas
V	Mississippi River System
VI	Pacific Coast and Pacific Islands
VII	Great Lakes

D.17. Tide Tables

Tide Tables give daily predictions of the height of water, at almost any place, at any given time, and are published annually in four volumes. Instructions for using the tables are provided within the publication. The four volumes are as follows:

Volume	Area of Coverage
I	Europe and West Coast of Africa (including the Mediterranean Sea)
II	East Coast of North and South America (including Greenland)
III	West Coast of North and South America (including the Hawaiian Islands)
IV	Central and Western Pacific Ocean and Indian Ocean.

D.18. Tidal Current Tables

Tidal current tables provide the times of maximum flood and ebb currents, and times of the two slack waters when current direction reverses. They also tell the predicted strength of the current in knots. The time of slack water does not correspond to times of high and low tide. The tide tables cannot be used for current predictions. The tables are published in two volumes. Instructions for using the tables are provided within the publication. The two volumes are as follows:

Volume	Area of Coverage
I	Atlantic Coast of North America
II	Pacific Coast of North America and Asia

D.19. Coast Pilots

The amount of information that can be printed on a nautical chart is limited by available space and the system of symbols that is used. Additional information is often needed for safe and convenient navigation. Such information is published in the *Coast Pilot*. These are printed in book form covering the coastline and the Great Lakes in nine separate volumes.

Each *Coast Pilot* contains sailing directions between points in its respective area, including recommended courses and distances. Channels with their controlling depths and all dangers and obstructions are fully described. Harbors and anchorages are listed with information on those points at which facilities are available for boat supplies and marine repairs. Information on canals, bridges, docks, and more, is included. The nine volumes are as follows:

Volume	Area of Coverage
	Atlantic Coast
No. 1	Eastport to Cape Cod
No. 2	Cape Cod to Sandy Hook
No. 3	Sandy Hook to Cape Henry
No. 4	Cape Henry to Key West
No. 5	Gulf of Mexico, Puerto Rico, and Virgin Islands
	Great Lakes
No. 6	Great Lakes and connecting waterways
	Pacific Coast
No. 7	California, Oregon, Washington, and Hawaii
	Alaska
No. 8	Dixon Strait to Cape Spencer
No. 9	Cape Spencer to Beaufort Sea

D.20. COLREGS

The Rules of the Road set forth regulations for navigable waters and are covered in *Navigation Rules, International – Inland*, COMDTINST M16672.2 (series).

Distance, Speed, and Time

D.21. Description

Distance, speed, and time are critical elements in navigational calculations. Each has its own importance and use in piloting. All three are closely associated in the way they are calculated. In planning the sortie or while underway, the typical navigation problem will involve calculating one of these elements based on the value of the other two elements.

D.22. Expressing Distance, Speed, and Time

Units of measurement are:

- Distance in nautical miles (NM) except statute miles on the western rivers.
- Speed in knots.
- Time in minutes.

In calculations and answers, express:

- Distance to the nearest tenth of a nautical mile.
- Speed to the nearest tenth of a knot.
- Time to the nearest minute.

D.23. Formulas

There are three basic equations for distance (D), speed (S), and time (T). Actually, they are the same equation rewritten to calculate each specific element. In each case, when two elements are known, they are used to find the third, which is unknown. The equations are:

- D = S x T/60
- S = 60D/T
- T = 60D/S

In the equation, 60 is for 60 minutes in an hour.

The following examples show how these equations work:

D.23.a. Example #1

If a boat is traveling at 10 knots, how far will you travel in 20 minutes? Solve for distance (D).

Step	Procedure
1	D = S x T/60
2	D = 10 x 20/60
3	D = 200/60 D = 3.3 NM

D.23.b. Example #2 At a speed of 10 knots, it took the boat 3 hours and 45 minutes to go from the Station to the shipping channel. What is the distance to the shipping channel?

Step	Procedure
1	Convert the hours to minutes for solving this equation. First, multiply the 3 hours by 60 (60 minutes in an hour), add the remaining 45 minutes, that is: 3 x 60 + 45 = 225 minutes
2	Write the equation. D = S x T/60
3	Substitute information for the appropriate letter and calculate the distance. D = 10 knots X 225 minutes/60
4	D = 2250/60 D = 37.5 NM (nearest tenth)

D.23.c. Example #3 A boat has traveled 12 NM in 40 minutes. What is its speed (S)?

Step	Procedure
1	S = 60D/T
2	S = 60 x12/40
3	S = 720/40 S = 18 knots

D.23.d. Example #4

Also, when distance and time are known, speed can be calculated. Departure time is 2030; the distance to the destination is 30 NM. Calculate the speed the boat must maintain to arrive at 2400.

Step	Procedure
1	Calculate the time interval between 2030 and 2400. To determine the time interval, convert time to hours and minutes and then subtract. 23 hours 60 minutes (2400) - 20 hours 30 minutes (2030) 3 hours 30 minutes
2	Distance - speed - time equations are computed in minutes. Convert the 3 hours to minutes, add the remaining 30 minutes. 3 x 60 = 180 minutes + 30 210
3	Write the equation. S = 60D/T
4	Substitute information for the appropriate letter and calculate the speed. S = 60D/T S = 60 x 30 NM/210 minutes
5	S = 1800/210 S = 8.6 knots

D.23.e. Example #5

The boat is cruising at 15 knots and has 12 NM more before reaching its destination. Determine how much longer before arriving at the destination.

Step	Procedure
1	T = 60D/S D= 12 NM S = 15 knots
2	T = 60 x 12/15
3	T = 720/15
4	T = 48 minutes

D.24. Nautical Slide Rule

The nautical slide rule was designed to solve speed, time and distance problems. Use of the slide rule provides greater speed and less chance of error than multiplication and division. There are several types of nautical slide rules but all work on the same basic principle.

The nautical slide rule has three scales that can rotate. The scales are clearly labeled for:

- Speed.
- Time.
- Distance.

By setting any two of the values on their opposite scales, the third is read from the appropriate index. See Error! Reference source not found. which is set for the approximate values of speed of 18.2 knots, time of 62 minutes and distance of 18.4 NM or 36,800 yards.

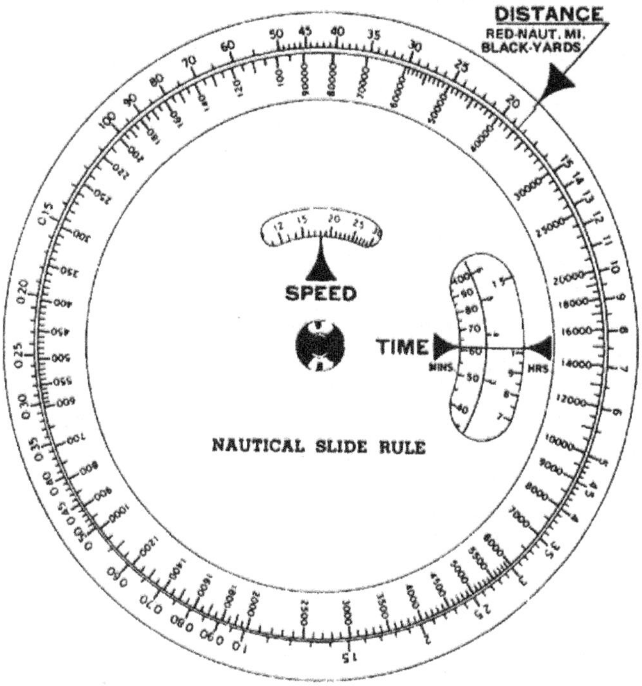

Figure 14-23
Nautical Slide Rule

Fuel Consumption

D.25. Description

In calculating solutions for navigation problems it is also important to know how much fuel the boat will consume. This is to ensure that there will be enough fuel onboard to complete the sortie. There must be enough fuel to arrive on scene, conduct operations, and return to base (or a refueling site).

D.26. Calculating Fuel Consumption

Calculating fuel consumption may be done by performing the following procedures:

Step	Procedure
1	Ensure fuel tank(s) are topped off.
2	Measure and record total gallons in fuel tank(s).
3	Start engine(s).
4	Record time engine(s) were started.
5	Set desired RPMs for engine(s).
6	Record set RPMs.
7	Maintain set RPMs.
8	Stop engine(s) at a specified time (usually one hour).
9	Record time.
10	Measure and record total gallons of fuel in tank(s).
11	Subtract total gallons in tank(s) after running one (1) hour from total gallons recorded on boat at beginning of underway period.
12	Record the difference.
13	Measure the distance traveled and record.
14	Compute boat speed and record.
15	Apply the equation: Time (T) multiplied by gallons per hour (GPH) equals total fuel consumption (TFC); or T x GPH = TFC.
16	Calculate TFC for other selected RPM settings. (Change RPM setting and repeat steps 6 through 15.)

Terms Used In Piloting

D.27. Description The following terms and their definitions (**Table 14-5**) are the most commonly used in the practice of piloting.

Table 14-5
Piloting Terms

Term	Abbreviation	Description
Bearing	B, Brg.	The horizontal direction of one terrestrial (earth bound) point from another (the direction in which an object lies from the vessel) is its bearing, expressed as the angular distance (degrees) from a reference direction (a direction used as a basis for comparison of other direction). A bearing is usually measured clockwise from 000° through 359° at the reference direction - true north, magnetic north or compass north.
Course	C	The intended horizontal direction of travel (the direction intended to go), expressed as angular distance from a reference direction clockwise from 000° through 360°. For marine navigation, the term applies to the direction to be steered. The heading of 360° is always referred to or spoken as 000°.
Heading	Hdg.	The actual direction the boat's bow is pointing at any given time.
Course line		Line drawn on a chart going in the direction of a course.
Current sailing		Current sailing is a method of allowing for current in determining the course made good, or of determining the effect of a current on the direction or motion of a boat.
Dead reckoning	DR	Dead reckoning is the determination of approximate position by advancing a previous position for course and distance only, without regard to other factors, such as, wind, sea conditions and current.
Dead reckoning plot		A DR plot is the plot of the movements of a boat as determined by dead reckoning.
Position		Position refers to the actual geographic location of a boat. It may be expressed as coordinates of latitude and longitude or as the bearing and distance from an object whose position is known.
DR position		A DR position is a position determined by plotting a single or a series of consecutive course lines using only the direction (course) and distance from the last fix, without consideration of current, wind, or other external forces on a boat.
Estimated position	EP	A DR position modified by additional information, which in itself is insufficient to establish a fix.
Estimated time of arrival	ETA	The ETA is the best estimate of predicted arrival time at a known destination.
Fix		A fix is a position determined from terrestrial, electronic or celestial data at a given time with a high degree of accuracy.
Line of position	LOP	A line of bearing to a known object, which a vessel is presumed to be located on at some point.

Table 14-5 (continued)
Piloting Terms

Term	Abbreviation	Description
Coast piloting		Coast piloting refers to directing the movements of a boat near a coast.
Range		There are two types of ranges used in piloting: • Two or more fixed objects in line. Such objects are said to be in range. • Distance in a single direction or along a great circle. Distance ranges are measured by means of radar or visually with a sextant.
Running fix	R Fix	A running fix is a position determined by crossing LOPs obtained at different times.
Nautical mile	NM	A nautical mile is used for measurement on most navigable waters. It is 6076 feet or approximately 2000 yards and is equal to one minute of latitude.
Knots	Kn or kt	A knot is a unit of speed equal to one nautical mile per hour.
Speed	S	The rate of travel of a boat through the water measured in knots is the speed. Speed of Advance (SOA) is the average speed in knots that must be maintained to arrive at a destination at any appointed time. Speed made good: Speed over ground (SOG) is the speed of travel of a boat along the track, expressed in knots. The difference between the estimated average speed (SOA) and the actual average speed (SOG) is caused by external forces acting on the boat (such as wind, current, etc.).
Track	TR	A track is the course followed or intended to be followed by a boat. The direction may be designated in degrees true or magnetic.
Set		The direction toward which the current is flowing expressed in degrees true.
Drift		The speed of the current usually stated in knots.
Course over ground/course made good	COG/CMG	The resultant direction of movement from one point to another.

Laying the Course

D.28. Description

The navigation plot typically includes several course lines to steer from the beginning point to arrival at the destination. The technique for laying each course line is the same and is summarized as follows: (see **Figure 14-24**)

NOTE Ensure the rulers do not slip. If they do, the original line of direction will be lost.

Step	Procedure
1	Draw a straight line from the departure point to the intended destination. This is the course line.
2	Lay one edge of the parallel rulers along the course line.
3	Walk the rulers to the nearest compass rose on the chart, moving one ruler while holding the other in place.
4	Walk the rulers until one edge intersects the crossed lines at the center of the compass rose.
5	Going from the center of the circle in the direction of the course line, read the inside degree circle where the ruler's edge intersects. This is the magnetic course (M).
6	Write the course along the top of the penciled trackline as three digits followed by the letter (M) magnetic, for example, C 068° M. **Figure 14-24** shows a course of 068° M between two buoys as measured by parallel rulers on a chart's compass rose.

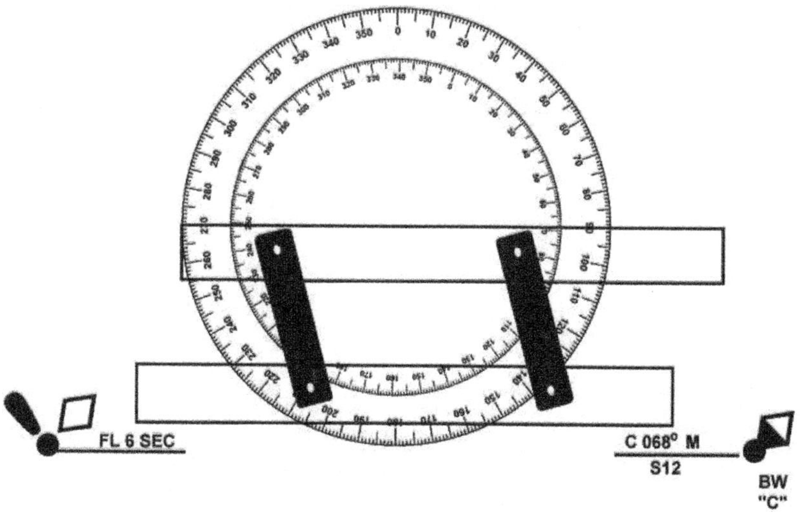

Figure 14-24
068° M Course Between Two Buoys

Dead Reckoning (DR)

D.29. Description

Dead reckoning (DR) is widely used in navigation. It is the process of determining a boat's approximate position by applying its speed, time, and course from its last known position.

D.30. Key Elements of Dead Reckoning

The key elements of dead reckoning are the course steered and the distance traveled without consideration to current, wind or other external forces.

D.30.a. Course Steered

Only courses steered are used to determine a DR. Course for a boat is normally magnetic (M) since it usually does not carry a gyrocompass, which gives true (T) direction.

D.30.b. Distance Traveled

Distance traveled is obtained by multiplying speed (in knots) by the time underway (in minutes).

$D = S \times T/60$

(On the western rivers, distance is in statute miles.)

D.31. Standardized Plotting Symbols

All lines and points plotted on a chart must be labeled. The symbols commonly used in marine navigation are standardized and summarized as follows:

- Labeling the fix: The plotter should clearly mark a visual fix with a circle or an electronic fix with a triangle. The time of each fix should be clearly labeled. A visual running fix should be circled, marked "R Fix" and labeled with the time of the second LOP. Maintain the chart neat and uncluttered when labeling fixes.
- DR position: A point marked with a semicircle and the time.
- Estimated position (EP): A point marked with a small square and the time.

See **Figure 14-25** for examples of the plotting symbols.

NOTE ✍

> Only standard symbols should be used to make it possible for every crewmember to understand the plot.

D.32. Labeling a DR Plot

The DR plot starts with the last known position (usually a fix). The procedures for labeling a DR plot are given below. (see **Figure 14-25**)

Figure 14-25 shows a DR plot starting in the upper left corner from a 0930 fix. (The compass rose is shown for information purposes and is not always so obvious on the chart.) At 1015 a fix is taken and a new DR plot started. Also, at 1015, the course is adjusted to C 134° M to get to the intended destination at the 1200 DR plot. Then, the 1200 fix is plotted and the new DR plot (C 051° M and S 16) is started.

Step	Procedure
1	Plot the course line, label it clearly and neatly. • Course: Above the course line, place a capital C followed by the ordered course in three digits. • Speed: Below the course line, place a capital S followed by the speed
2	Use standard symbols to label a DR plot: • Circle for a fix. • Semicircle for a DR position. • Square for an estimated position.
3	Plot a DR position: • At least every half hour. • At the time of every course change. • At the time of every speed change.
4	Start a new DR plot from each fix or running fix (plot a new course line from the fix).
5	Time is written as four digits.

The course can be magnetic (M), true (T) or compass (C) and is always expressed in three digits. If the course is less than 100°, zeros are prefixed to the number, for example, 009°.

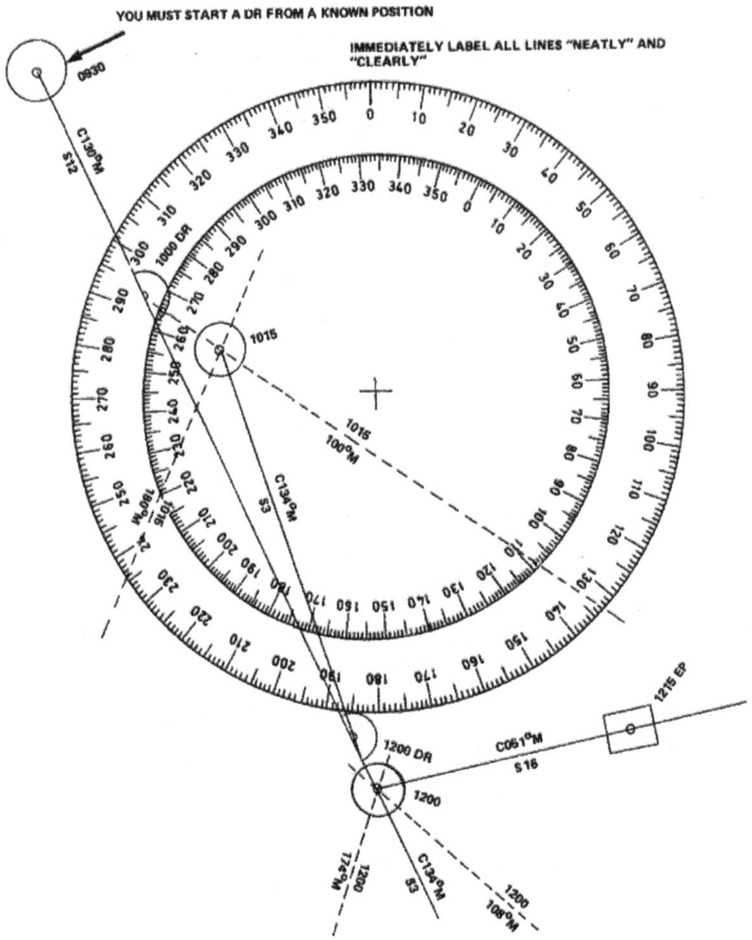

Figure 14-25
Labeling a DR Plot

Basic Elements of Piloting

D.33. Description Direction, distance, and time are the basic elements of piloting. With these elements, an accurate navigation plot can be maintained.

D.34. Direction Direction is the relationship of one point to another point (known as the reference point). Direction, referred to as bearing, is measured in degrees from 000 through 360°. The heading of 360° is always referred to or spoken 000°.

D.34.a. Reference Point/ Reference Direction

The usual reference point is 000°. The relationships between the reference points and reference directions are listed below:

Reference Direction	Reference Point
True (T)	Geographical North Pole
Magnetic (M)	Magnetic North Pole
Compass (C) *	Compass North
Relative (R) *	Boat's Bow

* Not to be plotted on a chart.

D.35. Bearings

Bearings are a direction, expressed in degrees from a reference point. Bearings may be true, magnetic, compass, or relative. All of the above reference directions may be used except relative direction to designate headings or courses. Relative direction, which uses the boat's bow as the reference direction, changes constantly.

In boat navigation, magnetic courses and bearings will usually be used, since true bearings are obtained from gyrocompasses, which are not normally found on boats.

D.35.a. Obtaining Bearings

Bearings are obtained primarily by using a magnetic compass (compass bearings) or radar (relative bearings). Bearings of fixed, known, objects are the most common sources for LOPs in coastal navigation. When using a compass to take bearings, the object should be sighted across the compass.

D.36. Compass Bearings

In the section on compass and compass error, how to convert from a compass course to magnetic and true courses by correcting the compass was discussed. A compass bearing must be corrected before it can be plotted.

NOTE

Deviation always depends upon the boat's heading. The bearing (compass or relative) of any object is not the course. Enter the deviation table with the compass heading being steered to obtain proper deviation.

D.36.a. Obtaining Compass Bearings

The vessel is on a heading of 263° M. The compass bearing to Kays Pt. Light is 060°. Deviation from the deviation table on the boat's heading of 263° M is 7° W. To obtain magnetic bearing of Kays Pt. Light perform the following procedures: (see **Figure 14-26**)

Step	Procedure
1	Correct the compass bearing of 60° magnetic. Write down the correction formula in a vertical line. C = 060° compass bearing of light. D = 7° W (+E, -W) from deviation table for boat's heading M = What is the magnetic bearing of the light?
2	Compute information opposite appropriate letter in step 1.
3	Subtract 7° W deviation, the westerly error, from the compass bearing (060°) to obtain magnetic bearing (053°). M = 053°

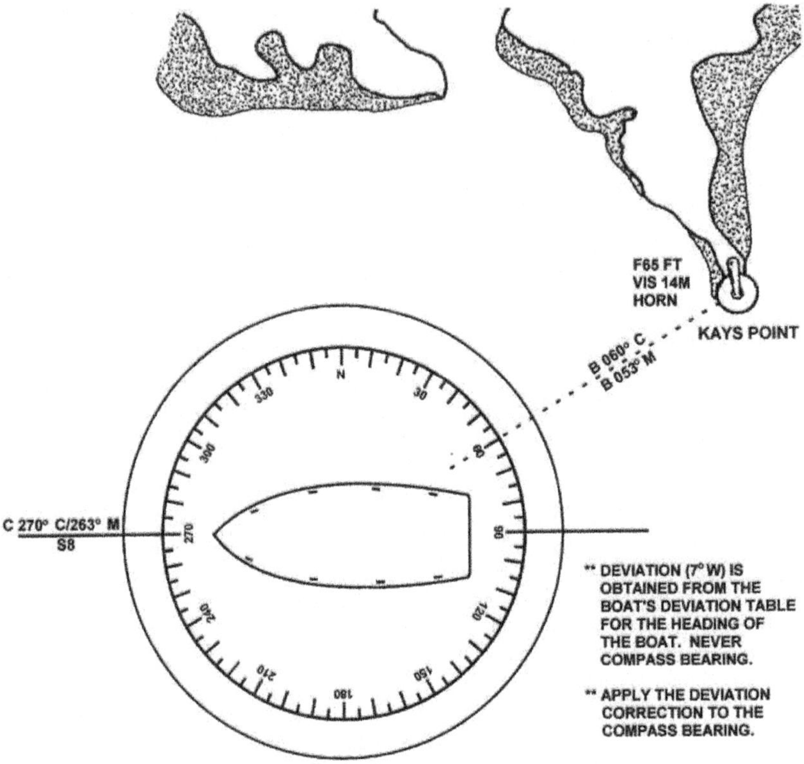

Figure 14-26
Converting Compass Bearing to Magnetic

D.37. Relative Bearings

Relative bearing of an object is its direction from the boat's bow at 000°, measured clockwise through 360°.

D.37.a. Converting to Magnetic Bearings

Relative bearings must be converted to magnetic bearings before they can be plotted. The procedures are as follows:

Step	Procedure
1	Convert heading to a magnetic course. Based on the boat's heading at the time the bearing was taken, use the deviation table to determine the deviation. (Deviation depends on the boat's heading, not that of the relative bearing.)
2	Add the relative bearing.
3	If this sum is more than 360°, subtract 360° to obtain the magnetic bearing.

Three examples follow to demonstrate these procedures.

D.37.a.1. Example #1

The boat is on a heading of 150°. The relative bearing to a standpipe is 125° relative. Deviation (from the boat's deviation table) on the boat's heading is 4° E. Obtain the magnetic bearing of the standpipe.

Step	Procedure
1	Correct heading of 150° to magnetic. Write down the correction formula in a vertical line. C = 150° D = 4° E (+E, -W) M = 154° V = Not applicable in this problem T = Not applicable in this problem
2	Compute information opposite appropriate letter in step 1.
3	Add the easterly error, 4° E deviation from the compass heading to obtain magnetic heading (154°).
4	Add the observed relative bearing (125°) and the magnetic heading (154°) to obtain magnetic bearing (279° M) of the standpipe.

D.37.a.2. Example #2

The boat is on a heading of 285°. The relative bearing to Williams Island Rock Light is 270° relative. The relative bearing to another light is 030° relative. Deviation (from the boats deviation table) on the boat's heading is 5° W. Obtain magnetic bearing of both lights. (see **Figure 14-27**)

Step	Procedure
1	Correct your heading of 285 to the magnetic heading. Write down the correction formula in a vertical line. C = 285° D = 5° W (+E, -W) M = 280° V = not applicable to this problem T = not applicable to this problem
2	Compute information opposite appropriate letter in step 1. Subtract the westerly error, 5° W deviation from the compass heading (285°) to obtain magnetic heading (280°).
3	Add each of the observed relative bearings (270° relative and 030° relative) to the magnetic heading (280°) to obtain the magnetic bearings. WILLIAMS IS ROCK 280° M + 270° relative bearing 550° (greater than 360°) -360 190° magnetic bearing OTHER LIGHT 280° M + 030° relative bearing 310° magnetic bearing

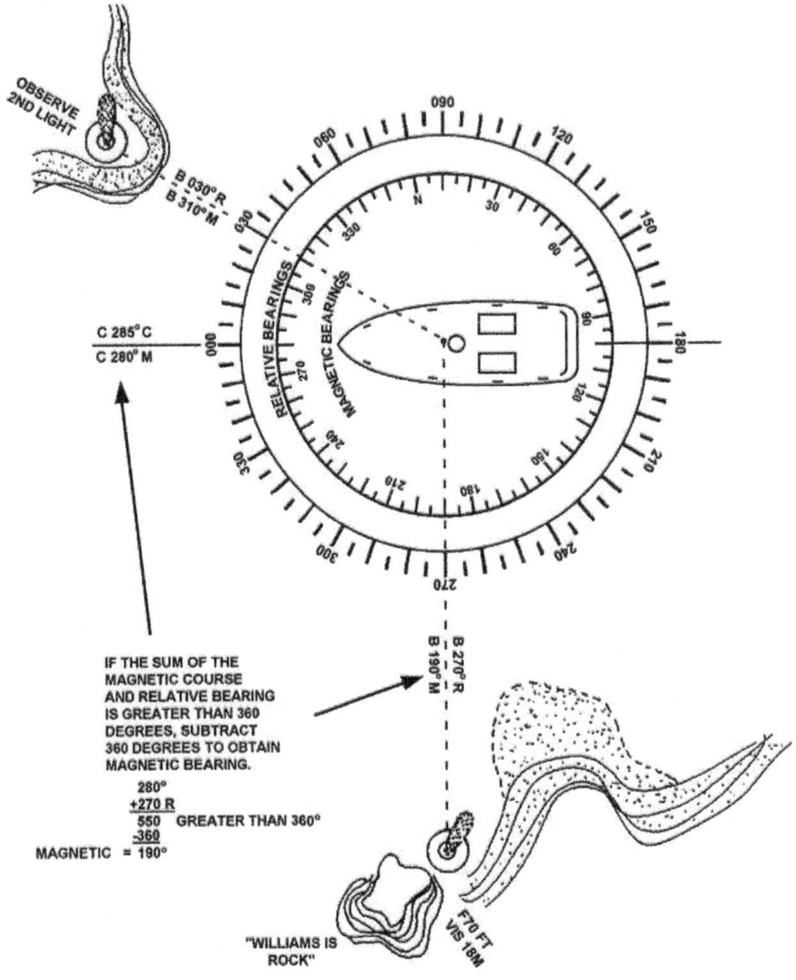

Figure 14-27
Converting Relative Bearings to Magnetic; Sums Greater than 360°

D.38. Distance

The second basic element in piloting is the special separation of two points measured by the length of a straight line joining the points without reference to direction. In piloting, it is measured in miles or yards. There are two different types of miles used:

- Nautical miles.
- Statute miles.

D.38.a. Nautical Mile

The nautical mile is used for measurement on most navigable waters. One nautical mile is 6076 feet or approximately 2000 yards and is equal to one minute of latitude.

D.38.b. Statute Mile

The statute mile is used mainly on land, but it is also used in piloting inland bodies of water such as the Mississippi River and its tributaries, the Great Lakes and the Atlantic and Gulf Intracoastal waterways.

CAUTION ! The longitude scale is never used for measuring distance.

D.38.c. Measuring Distance

Measure the distance by performing the following procedures:

Step	Procedure
1	Place one end of a pair of dividers at each end of the distance to be measured, being careful not to change the span of the dividers.
2	Transfer them to the latitude scale closest to the latitude being measured. Read the distance in minutes. (see **Figure 14-28**)
3	When the distance to be measured is greater than the span of the dividers, the dividers can be set at a minute or number of minutes of latitude from the scale and then "stepped off" between the points to be measured.
4	The last span, if not equal to that setting on the dividers, must be separately measured. To do this, step the dividers once more; closing them to fit the distance.
5	Measure this distance on the scale and add it to the sum of the other measurements.
6	The latitude scale nearest the middle of the line to be measured should be used.

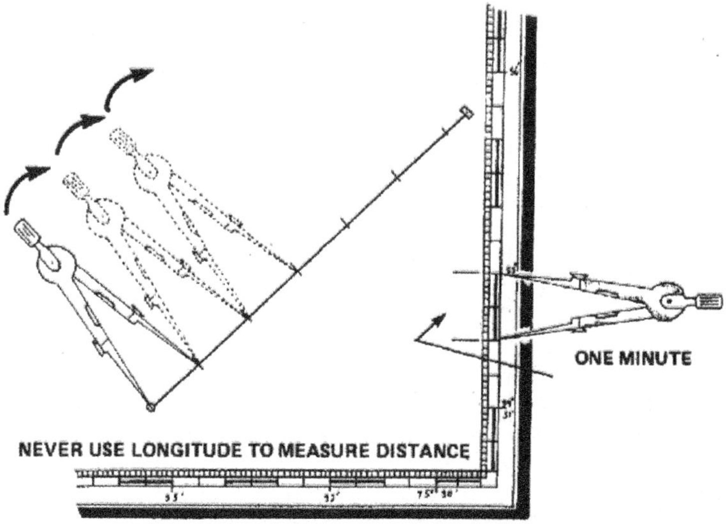
ONE MINUTE
NEVER USE LONGITUDE TO MEASURE DISTANCE

Figure 14-28
Measuring Distance, Latitude

To measure short distances on a chart, the dividers can be opened to a span of a given distance, then compared to the NM or yard scale on the chart. (see **Figure 14-29**)

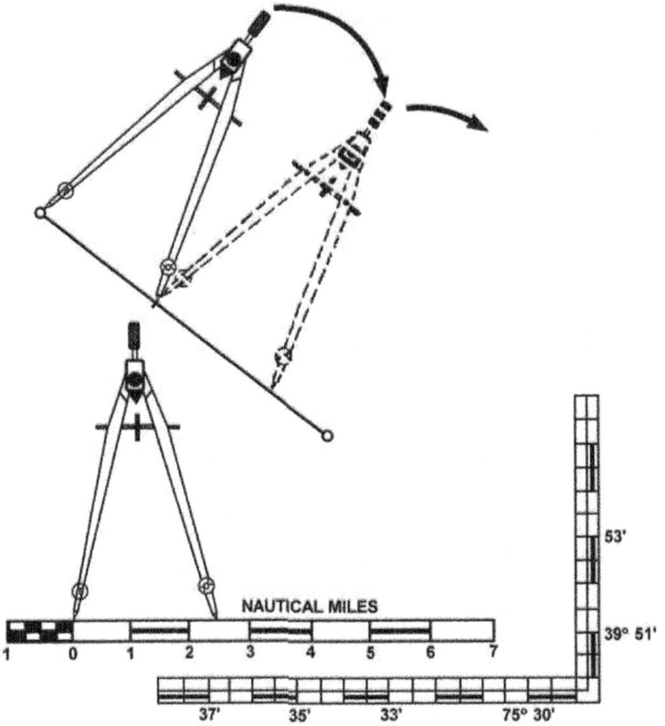

Figure 14-29
Measuring Distance, Nautical Miles

D.39. Time

Time is the third basic element in piloting. Time, distance, and speed are related. Therefore, if any two of the three quantities are known, the third can be found. The basic equations for distance, speed, and time; the speed curve; and nautical slide rule and their use have been discussed earlier.

Plotting Bearings

D.40. Description

A bearing or series of bearings can be observed as compass (C), magnetic (M), true (T), or as a relative bearing (visual or radar). The compass bearing reading usually needs to be converted for plotting and then drawn on the chart as a line of position (LOP).

D.41. Parallel

One common method of plotting bearings on a chart is using parallel rulers or a course plotter. Follow the example below for plotting the bearing onto the chart.

D.41.a. Example

The boat is on a heading of 192° compass. At 1015, a bearing of 040° relative on a water tower is obtained. Deviation (from the boat's deviation table) on the boat's heading is 3° W.

Step	Procedure
1	Correct the compass heading of 192° to the magnetic heading. Write down the correction formula in a vertical line. C = 192° D = 3° W (+E, -W when correcting) M = 189° V = not applicable to this problem T = not applicable to this problem
2	Compute the information opposite the appropriate letter in step 1. Subtract the westerly error, 3° W deviation from the compass heading (192°) to obtain magnetic heading (189°).
3	Add the relative bearing (040°) to the magnetic heading (189°) to obtain the magnetic bearing (229°). 189° (M) + 040° 229° magnetic bearing
4	Place the parallel rulers with their edge passing through the crossed lines at the center of the compass rose and the 229° mark on the inner ring (magnetic) of the compass rose. (see **Figure 14-30**)
5	Walk the parallel rulers to the dot marking the exact position of the water tower.
6	Draw a broken line and intersect the course line (C 189° M).
7	Label a segment of line with the time of the bearing along the top. The segment is drawn near the course line, not the entire length from the water tower.
8	Below the line, label the magnetic bearing 229° M.

At 1015, the boat was somewhere along the LOP. A single line of bearing gives an LOP but the boat's location cannot be accurately fixed by a single LOP.

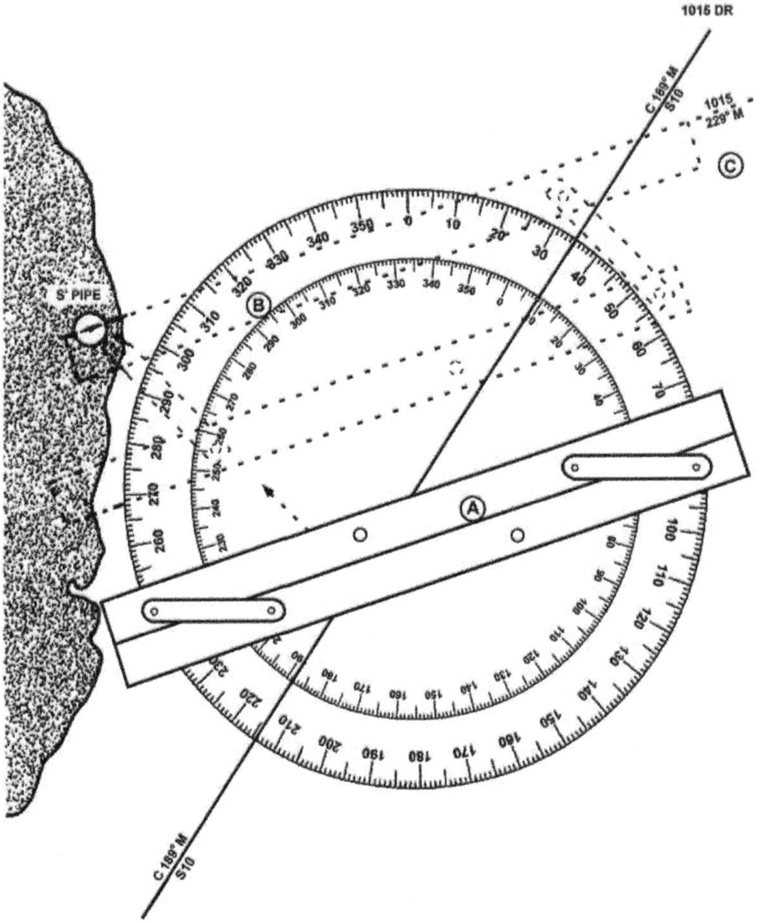

Figure 14-30
Plotting Bearings

Line of Position (LOP)

D.42. Description

The position of a boat can be determined by many methods of piloting. The LOP is common to all methods of piloting. For example, if a standpipe and a flagstaff in a line are observed, the boat is somewhere on the line drawn from the standpipe through the flagstaff and towards the boat. This line is called a range or a visual range.

If the bearing is taken on a single object, the line drawn is called a bearing LOP. The observed bearing direction must be corrected to magnetic or true direction and plotted. The compass rose can be used to provide the direction.

A single observation gives an LOP, not a position. The boat is located somewhere along that LOP. (see **Figure 14-31**)

NOTE A boat's position is somewhere along the line of position.

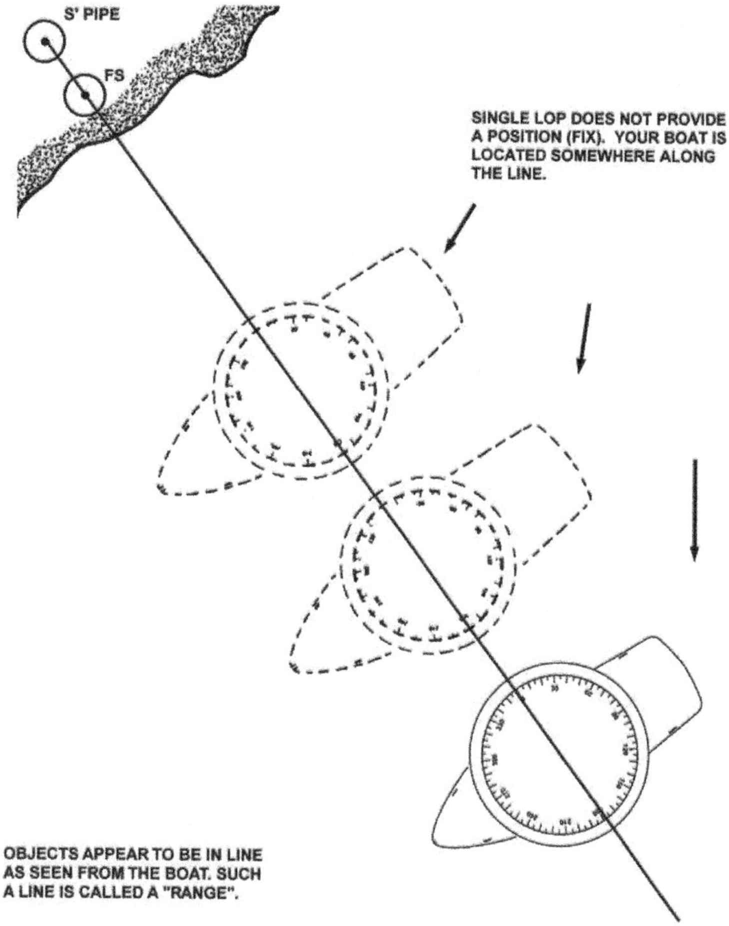

Figure 14-31
Visual Range LOP

D.43. Selecting Objects to Obtain a Fix

The primary consideration in selecting charted objects to obtain a fix is the angle between the bearings. Also, attempts should always be made to take bearings on objects as close as possible to the boat because minor errors in reading are magnified when increasing distance from the object.

NOTE An error of 1 degree at 1 mile will result in an error of 100 feet.

D.43.a. Two Lines of Position

When there are only two LOPs for a fix, the quality of the fix will be best when there is a 90° difference in the lines. Serious error in position could result if a difference of less than 60° or more than 120° between the two lines exist. Therefore, two LOPs should intersect at right angles or near right angles wherever possible.

D.43.b. Three Lines of Position

An ideal fix has three or more LOPs intersecting at a single point and the LOPs have a separation of at least 60°, but not more than 120°.

D.44. Obtaining Fixes

A single line of bearing gives an LOP, and the boat is somewhere along that LOP. Position cannot accurately be fixed by a single LOP. Two or more intersecting LOPs or radar ranges must be plotted to obtain an accurate fix. The greater the number of LOPs or radar ranges intersecting at the same point, the greater the confidence in the fix. For a fix to be accurate, LOPs must be observed at the same time. However, in navigation two or more bearings taken, one after the other, are considered to be observed at the same time (simultaneous).

NOTE

For a fix to be accurate, LOPs must be from simultaneous observation (exact same time). Two or more bearings taken one after the other are considered simultaneous.

D.44.a. Obtaining Bearings

Bearings are obtained by visual sightings across a compass, hand-held bearing compass, relative bearings (dumb compass) or by radar. Then, the direction to the object sighted is recorded, converted to magnetic or true direction, and plotted.

D.44.b. Using Cross Bearings

When using cross bearings, the fix is obtained by taking bearings on two well-defined objects and plotting the observed bearings on the chart. A more accurate fix can be obtained by taking a third bearing on a well-defined object. The three LOPs should form a single point or a small triangle. The boat's position is then considered to be on the point or in the center of the small triangle.

A large triangle is an indication than an inaccurate bearing was taken. Measurements should be double-checked.

CAUTION !

Do not use the hand-held bearing compass on a steel boat. Deviation cannot be determined accurately. Each change in position on deck results in an undetermined amount of deviation.

D.44.b.1. Example

On a compass heading of 330°, a lookout tower and a standpipe are sighted and the crew decides to take a fix. The lookout tower bears 030° (compass) and the standpipe bears 005° (compass). Deviation from the deviation table, on the boat's compass heading (330° C), is 5° E. Plot the fix. (see **Figure 14-32**)

Step	Procedure
1	Correct compass bearing (030°) and (005°) to magnetic bearings. Write down the correction formula in a vertical line. **Lookout Tower** / **Standpipe** C = 030° / C = 005° D = 5° E (+E, - W) / D = 5° E (+E, -W) M = 035° / M = 010° V = not applicable / V = not applicable T = not applicable / T = not applicable
2	Compute information opposite the appropriate letter in step 1. Add the easterly error 5° E deviation to the compass bearings 030° and 005° to obtain magnetic bearings of 035° and 010°.
3	Plot the two magnetic bearings. The prudent sailor will recognize that the accuracy of this fix is doubtful due to the angle between the bearings being considerably less than the desired 60°-120°.

Lookout Tower	Standpipe
C = 030°	C = 005°
D = 5° E (+E, - W)	D = 5° E (+E, -W)
M = 035°	M = 010°
V = not applicable	V = not applicable
T = not applicable	T = not applicable

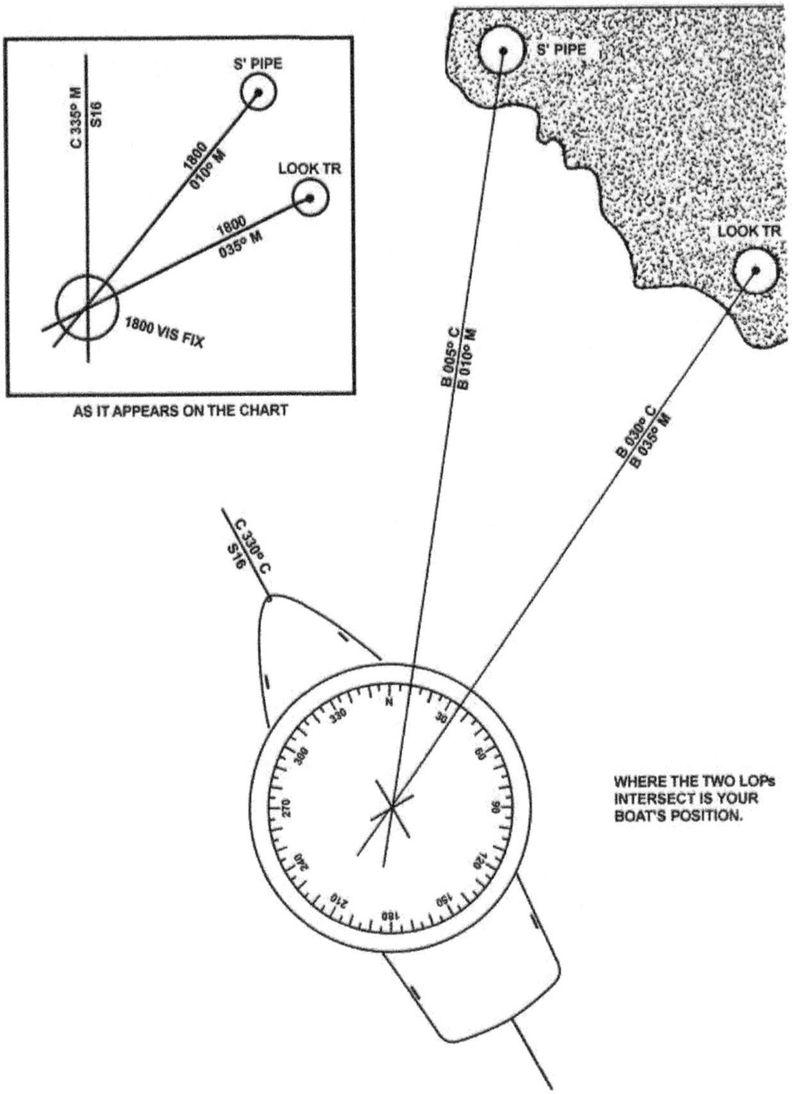

Figure 14-32
Two Ranges

NOTE Compass bearings are not plotted on the chart.

D.44.c. Ranges	When two charted objects are in range, as seen from a boat, the boat is located somewhere on a straight line through these objects. Frequently, a range will mark the center of a channel. The boat is steered so as to keep the range markers in line. Ranges may be established navigational aids or natural ranges such as a church steeple and a water tower. When entering or leaving a harbor, it is often possible to fix the position by means of ranges.
D.44.c.1. Example	While steering on a range (keeping the bow lined up with the two range marks), the time is 0800 when two charted objects (for example, a water tank and smoke stack) line up on the starboard side. The boat's position is at the intersection of the lines drawn through each set of ranges. (see **Figure 14-33**) After having observed two sets of ranges that determined a fix, a magnetic course of 000° M is steered to stay in safe water.

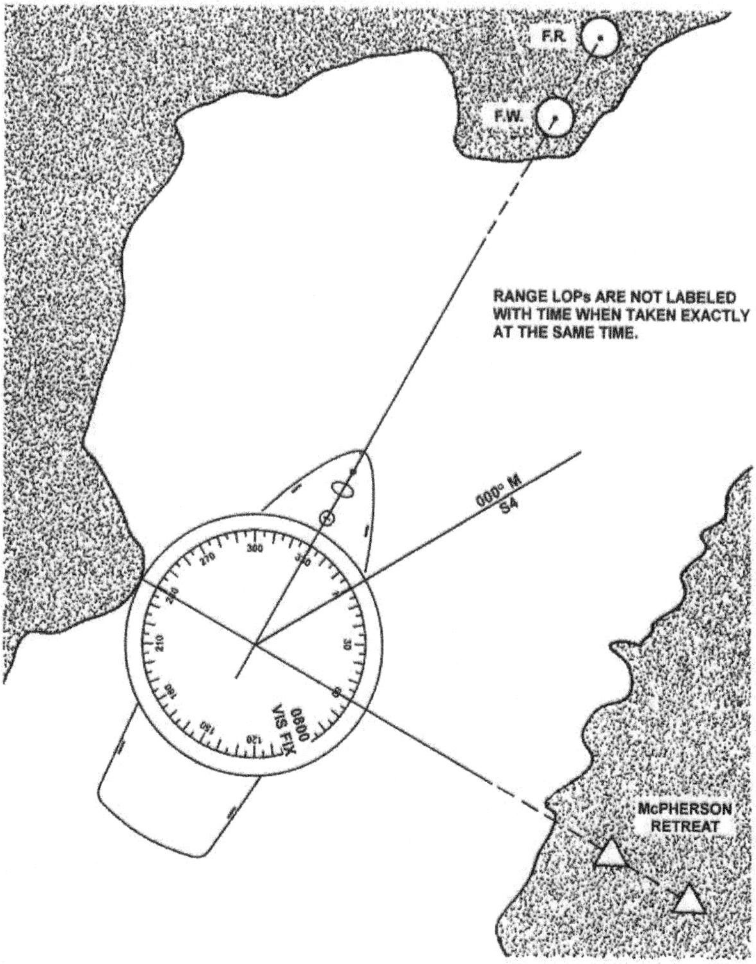

Figure 14-33
Fix by Two Ranges

D.44.d. Running Fix (R FIX)

Often it is impossible to obtain two bearing observations within a close enough interval of time to be considered simultaneous. A running fix (R Fix) can be obtained by using two LOPs acquired at different times. It is determined by advancing an earlier LOP by using dead reckoning calculations of the boats direction and distance traveled during an interval. (see **Figure 14-34**)

Plot a running fix by performing the following procedures:

NOTE The shorter the time interval between LOPs, the more accurate the running fix.

Step	Procedure
1	Plot the first LOP. Plot the second LOP.
2	Advance the first LOP along the DR plot to the time of second LOP. (The first LOP is advanced by moving it parallel to itself, forward along the course line for the distance the boat will have traveled to the time of the second bearing.)
3	Where the two LOPs intersect is the running fix.
4	Avoid advancing an LOP for more than 30 minutes.

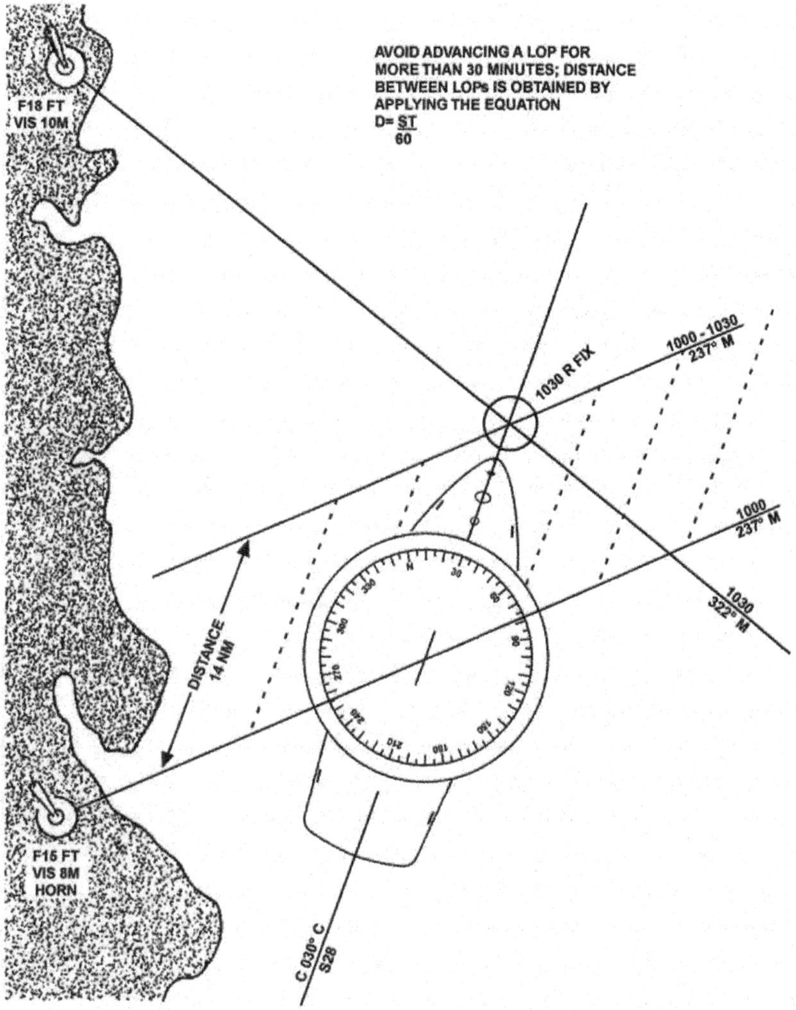

Figure 14-34
Running Fix

D.44.d.1. Example

At 1000, a compass bearing of 240° to a light is observed, which is corrected to 237° M. There were no other well-defined objects from which to obtain a bearing. Since plotting the first LOP the boat has run at 28 knots on a compass course of 030° C.

At 1030, the boat has a second compass bearing of 325° to the light is observed. Plot this as a second LOP and advance the first LOP. The position where they cross is the running fix.

Step	Procedure
1	Obtain the time interval and the distance the boat traveled since the 1000 LOP. (A nautical slide rule may be used) 10 hours 30 minutes <u>-10 hours 00 minutes</u> 30m - time interval Apply the equation for distance (nautical slide rule may be used). D = S x T/60 D= 28 x 30/60 D = 840/60 D = 14 nautical miles
2	Using dividers, measure the distance (14 NM) off of the latitude or nautical mile scale along the course line in the direction traveled.
3	Advance the first LOP, ensuring it is moved parallel to itself, forward along the course line for the distance traveled (14 NM). Draw the LOP labeling the new line (1000-1030) to indicate that it is an advanced LOP.
4	Correct the compass bearing of the second light (325° C) to obtain the magnetic bearing (322° M)
5	Plot the bearing. A running fix has been established by advancing an LOP.

D.44.e. Danger Bearings

Danger bearings are used to keep a boat clear of a hazardous area in the vicinity of the track. Danger bearings are the maximum or minimum bearing of a point used for safe passage. They indicate a charted object whose bearing will place the boat outside that hazardous area. Examples of such dangers are submerged rocks, reefs, wrecks and shoals. A danger area must be established in relation to two fixed objects, one of which is the danger area. The other object must be selected to satisfy three conditions:

- Visible to the eye.
- Indicated on the chart.
- Bearing from the danger area should be in the same general direction as the course of the boat as it proceeded past the area.

Plot a danger bearing by performing the following procedures: (see **Figure 14-35**)

Step	Procedure
1	On a chart, draw a line from the object selected (the leading object) to a point tangent to the danger area closest to the intended passing point. The measured direction of the line from the danger area to the leading object is the danger bearing. **Figure 14-35** indicates that 311° M is a danger bearing.
2	Label the danger bearing with the abbreviation 'DB' followed by the direction (DB 311° M). Frequent visual bearings should be taken. If the bearings are greater than the danger bearing, the boat is in safe water.

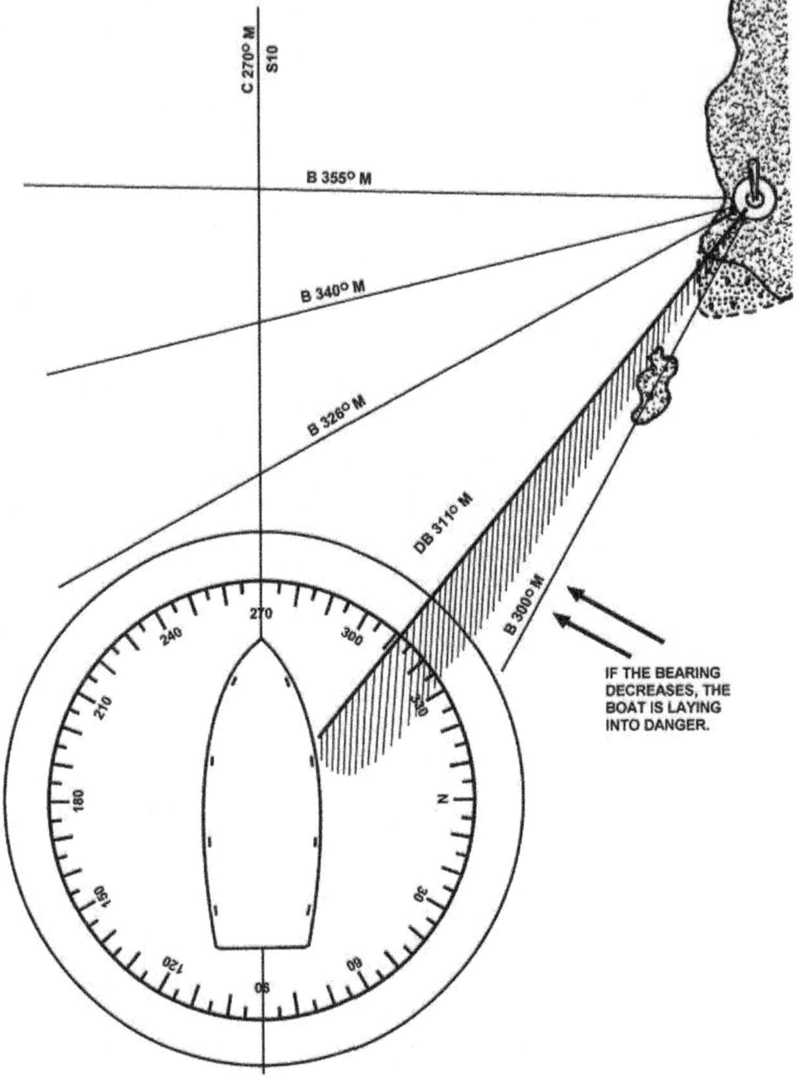

Figure 14-35
Danger Bearings

When a bearing is observed to be less than the danger bearing, such as 300° M, the boat is standing into danger. Danger bearings should have a series of short lines drawn on the danger side for easy identification as shown in **Figure 14-35**.

The label DB may be proceeded by the letters NMT (not more than) or NLT (not less than), as appropriate.

The coxswain should ensure that all crewmembers are aware of where the danger lies. That is, whether the danger includes all degrees less than the danger bearing or all the degrees greater than the danger bearing.

Set and Drift (Current Sailing)

D.45. Description

Current sailing is the method of computing course and speed through the water, considering the effects of current so that, upon arrival at the destination, the intended course (track) and the actual course made good are the same. The difference in position between a DR position and a fix taken at the corresponding time is due to various external forces acting on the boat. These forces are usually accounted for as set and drift.

D.46. Definition

Set is the direction of these forces and includes factors such as wind, current, and sea condition. Set is expressed in degrees. "Set 240° magnetic" means that the boat is being pushed towards 240° magnetic.

Drift is the strength of the set and is expressed in knots. "Drift 1.5 knots" means that the boat is being pushed in a given direction (set) at a speed of 1.5 knots.

D.47. Making Allowances

In working problems involving set and drift, allow for their effect upon the boat. This can be accomplished by comparing actual fix position information with the DR track and determining the difference. However, conditions do not always allow for this. Also, this can only be done after some portion of the voyage has already occurred.

D.48. Tidal Current Charts

Tidal Current Charts are available for certain bodies of water such as Boston Harbor or San Francisco Bay. They graphically indicate the direction and velocity of tidal currents for specific times with respect to the state of the current predictions for major reference Stations. These charts make it possible to visualize how currents act in passages and channels throughout the 12-hour cycle. By referring to the current charts, it is possible to plan a passage that is made quicker by either taking advantage of a favorable current or picking a track that reduces the effect of a head current.

D.49. Tidal Current Tables

Tidal Current Tables are used to predict tidal currents. Examples of how to apply predicted currents are found in the back of the publication. This makes it possible to apply the corrections well in advance so as to avoid the dangers along the way and safely arrive at the destination. This method involves the use of a vector diagram called a current triangle.

NOTE The tidal current directions are shown in degrees true and must be converted to magnetic before plotting the set and drift problem.

D.50. Current

The current triangle is a vector diagram indicating the course and speed the boat will make good when running a given course at a given speed. (see **Figure 14-36**) It can also be used to determine the course to steer and the speed necessary to remain on the intended track. This information may be obtained by using the chart's compass rose for constructing a current triangle to provide a graphic solution.

- The first line (AB) on a current triangle indicates the boat's intended direction and the distance to travel in a given period of time. The length of this line represents the boat's speed in knots.
- The second line, (CB) laid down to the destination end of the intended direction (the first line), shows the set (direction) of the current. The length of this line represents the drift (speed) of the current in knots.
- The third line (AC) provides the resulting corrected course to steer and the speed of advance to arrive safely at the destination. If any two sides of the triangle are known, the third side can be obtained by measurement.

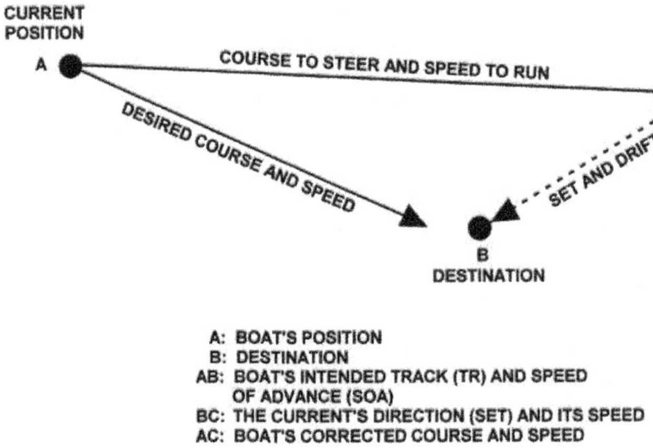

Figure 14-36
Current Triangle

D.50.a. Example

The intended track to the destination is 093° magnetic (093M), the speed is 5 knots, the *Tidal Current Table* for the operating area indicates that the current will be setting the boat 265° true (265T), drift (speed) 3 knots. The local variation is 4° (W). Obtain the corrected course to steer and SOA to allow for set and drift. (see **Figure 14-37**). The nautical miles scale, is provided as an example for measuring "units" of length.)

Step	Procedure
1	Lay out the chart. Think of the center of the compass rose as the departure point. Draw the boat's intended track (093° M) from the center of the compass rose. Make this line 5 units in length to represent 5 nautical miles from the center of the compass rose. Put a small arrowhead at this point. This is the desired course and speed vector.
2	Draw a line for the set and drift of the current from the center of the compass rose towards 261° magnetic (265° T + 4° W (variation) = 269° M).
	Set in the *Tidal Current Tables* is given in degrees true and must be converted to degrees magnetic to be used. Make this line three units long putting an arrowhead at the outer end. This is the set and drift vector.
3	Draw a straight line to connect the arrowheads of the desired course and speed vector and the set and drift vector. This line is the corrected course to steer and speed of advance.
4	Measure the length of this line to obtain the speed (8.7 knots) from the nautical miles scale.
5	Advance the line to the center of the compass rose and read the corrected magnetic course to steer (088° M) from the inner circle of the compass rose.

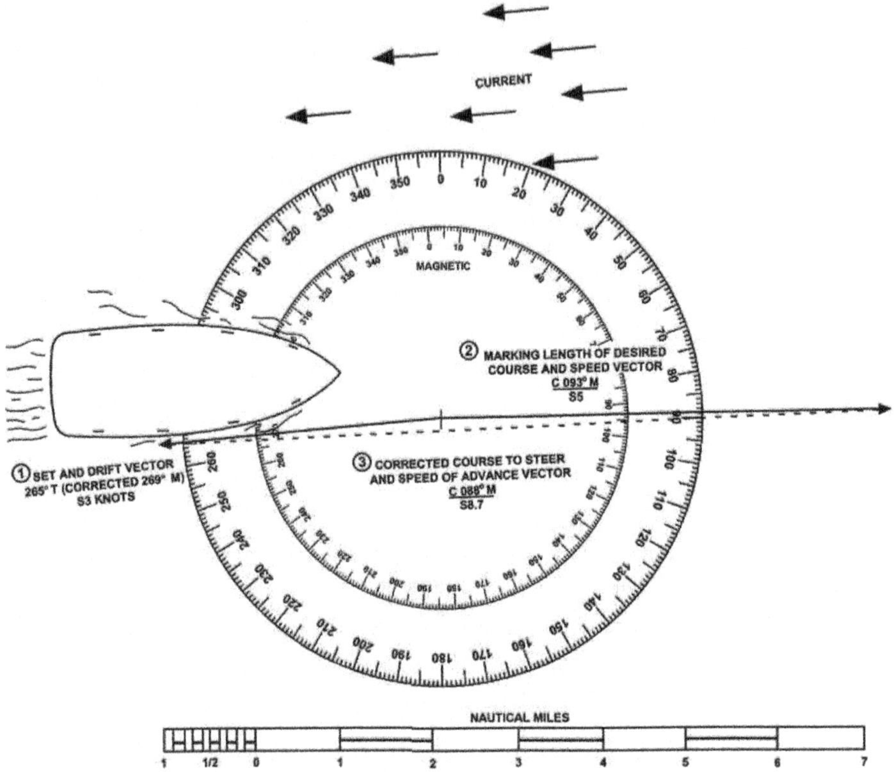

Figure 14-37
Plotting Set and Drift to Set Course to Steer

Using the same figures as shown in the above example, **Figure 14-38** shows what the effect would be if the set and drift is not corrected for by using a current triangle. (see **Figure 14-38**)

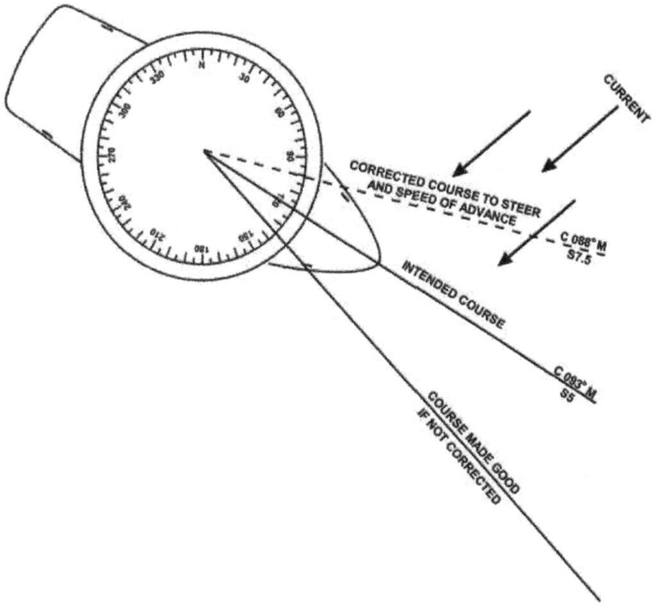

Figure 14-38
Compensating for Set and Drift

Radar

D.51. Description

Radar is an aid in navigation, but it is not the primary means of navigation. Boat navigation using radar in limited visibility depends on the coxswain's experience with radar operation. It also depends on the coxswain's knowledge of the local operating area and is not a substitute for an alert visual lookout.

D.52. Basic Principle

A radar radiates radio waves from its antenna to create an image that can give direction and distance to an object. Nearby objects (contacts) reflect the radio waves back and appear on the radar indicator as images (echoes). On many marine radars, the indicator is called the plan position indicator (PPI).

D.53. Advantages

Advantages of radar include:

- Can be used at night and in low visibility conditions.
- Obtains a fix by distance ranges to two or more charted objects. An estimated position can be obtained from a range and a bearing to a single charted object.
- Enables rapid fixes.
- Fixes may be available at greater distances from land than by visual bearings.
- Assists in preventing collisions.

D.54. Disadvantages

The disadvantages of radar include:

- Mechanical and electrical failure.
- Minimum and maximum range limitations.

D.54.a. Minimum Range

The minimum range is primarily established by the radio wave pulse length and recovery time. It depends on several factors such as excessive sea return, moisture in the air, other obstructions and the limiting features of the equipment itself. The minimum range varies but is usually 20 to 50 yards from the boat.

D.54.b. Maximum Range

Maximum range is determined by transmitter power and receiver sensitivity. However, these radio waves are line of sight (travel in a straight line) and do not follow the curvature of the earth. Therefore, anything below the horizon will usually not be detected.

D.54.c. Operational Range

The useful operational range of a radar on a boat is limited mainly by the height of the antenna above the water.

D.55. Reading the Radar Indicator

Interpreting the information presented on the indicator takes training and practice. The radar indicator should be viewed in total darkness, if possible, for accurate viewing of all echoes. Also, charts do not always give information necessary for identification of radar echoes, and distance ranges require distinct features.

It may be difficult to detect smaller objects (e.g., boats and buoys) in conditions such as:

- Heavy seas.
- Near the shore.
- If the object is made of nonmetallic materials.

D.56. Operating Controls

Different radar sets have different locations of their controls, but they are basically standardized on what function is to be controlled. The boat crew should become familiar with the operation of the radar by studying its operating manual and through the unit training program.

D.57. Reading and Interpolating Radar Images

The PPI is the face or screen of the Cathode Ray Tube (CRT), which displays a bright straight radial line (tracer sweep) extending outward from the center of a radar screen. It represents the radar beam rotating with the antenna. It reflects images on the screen as patches of light (echoes).

In viewing any radar indicator, the direction in which the boat's heading flasher is pointing can be described as up the indicator. The reciprocal of it is a direction opposite to the heading flasher, or down the indicator. A contact moving at right angles to the heading flasher anywhere on the indicator would be across the indicator.

The center of the radar screen represents the position of the boat. The indicator provides relative bearings of a target and presents a map-like representation of the area around the boat. The direction of a target is represented by the direction of its echo from the center, and the target's range is represented by its distance from the center. (see **Figure 14-39**)

The cursor is a movable reference and is controlled by the radar cursor control. The cursor is used to obtain the relative bearings of a target on the indicator.

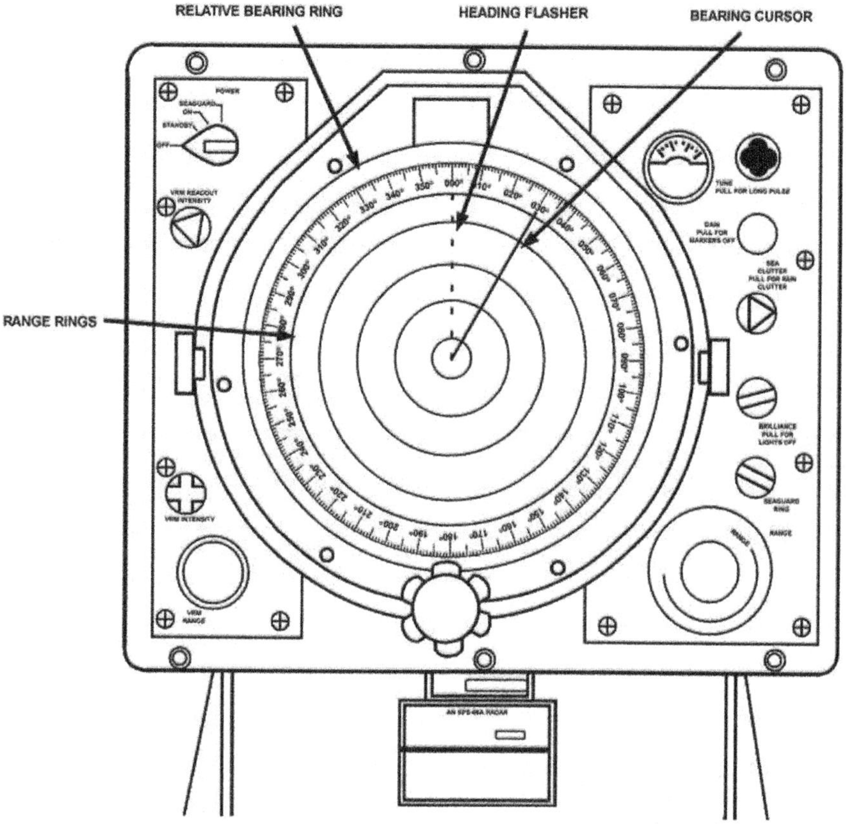

Figure 14-39
Radar Range Rings, Relative Bearing Ring, Heading Flasher, and Bearing Cursor

D.57.a. Radar Bearings

Radar bearings are measured in relative direction the same as visual bearings with 000° relative being dead ahead. (see **Figure 14-39**) In viewing any radar indicator, the dot in the center indicates the boat's position. The line from the center dot to the outer edge of the indicator is called the heading flasher and indicates the direction your boat is heading.

To obtain target relative bearings, the cursor control should be adjusted until the cursor line crosses the target. The radar bearing is read from where the cursor line crosses the bearing ring.

NOTE Like visual observations, relative bearing measurements by radar must be converted to magnetic bearing prior to plotting them on the chart.

D.57.b. Target Range

Many radars have a variable range marker. Crewmembers should dial the marker out to the inner edge of the contact on the screen and read the range directly.

Other radars may have distance rings. If the contact is not on a ring, the distance is estimated (interpolated) by its position between the rings.

D.57.b.1. Example

The radar is on the range scale of 2 nautical miles, and has 4 range rings. Range information is desired for a target appearing halfway between the third and fourth rings.

- Range rings on the two-mile scale are ½ mile or 1000 yards apart (4 rings for 2 miles means each ring equals ¼ of the total range of 2 miles).
- Range is calculated as 1000 + 1000 + 1000 + ½ x 1000 or 3500 yards.

D.58. Radar Contacts

Even with considerable training it may not always be easy to interpret a radar echo properly. Only through frequent use and experience will a crewmember be able to become proficient in the interpretation of images on the radar screen.

Knowledge of the radar picture in the area is obtained by using the radar during good visibility and will eliminate most doubts when radar navigating at night and during adverse weather. Images on a radar screen differ from what is seen visually by the naked eye. This is because some contacts reflect radio waves (radar beams) better than others.

D.58.a. Common Radar Contacts

A list of common radar contacts and reflection quality follows:

Contact	Integrity
Reefs, shoals, and wrecks	May be detected at short to moderate ranges, if breakers are present and are high enough to return echoes. These echoes usually appear as cluttered blips.
Sandy spits, mud flats, and sandy beaches	Return the poorest and weakest echoes. The reflection, in most cases, will come from a higher point of land from the true shoreline such as bluffs or cliffs in back of the low beach. False shorelines may appear because of a pier, several boats in the area, or heavy surf over a shoal.
Isolated rocks or islands off shore	Usually return clear and sharp echoes providing excellent position information.
Large buoys	May be detected at medium range with a strong echo; small buoys sometimes give the appearance of surf echoes. Buoys equipped with radar reflectors will appear out of proportion to their actual size.
Piers, bridges, and jetties	Provide strong echoes at shorter ranges.
Rain showers, hail, and snow	Will also be detected by radar and can warn of foul weather moving into the area. Bad weather appears on the screen as random streaks known as 'clutter'.

D.59. Radar Fixes

Radar navigation provides a means for establishing position during periods of low visibility when other methods may not be available. A single prominent object can provide a radar bearing and range for a fix, or a combination of radar bearings and ranges may be used. Whenever possible, more than one object should be used. Radar fixes are plotted in the same manner as visual fixes.

NOTE If a visual bearing is available it is more reliable than one obtained by radar.

D.59.a. Example

On a compass heading of 300°, a radar contact (image) bearing 150° relative is observed. Deviation, from the deviation table, for the boat's compass heading (300° C) is 3'E.

Obtain the magnetic bearing of the contact by performing the following procedures:

Step	Procedure
1	Correct compass heading of 300° to magnetic heading. Write down the correction formula in a vertical line. C = 300° D = 3° E (+E, -W when correcting) M = 303° M V = not applicable in this problem T = not applicable in this problem
2	Compute information opposite appropriate letter in step 1. Add the easterly error 3° E deviation to the compass heading (300° C) to obtain the magnetic course of 303° M.
3	Add the radar relative bearing (150° relative) to the magnetic heading (303° M) to obtain magnetic bearing of the radar contact (093° M). 303° +150° 453° (greater than 360°) 453° -360° 093° M bearing of contact

D.59.b. Range Rings

Radar range rings show up as circles of light on the screen to assist in estimating distance. Major range scales are indicated in miles and are then subdivided into range rings. Typical range scales for a boat radar are ½, 1, 2, 4, 8, and 16 NM. Typical number of range rings for a particular range scale are shown as follows:

Scale/Miles	Rings	NM Per Ring
½	1	½
1	2	½
2	4	½
4	4	1
8	4	2
16	4	4

D.59.c. LOPs

Radar LOPs may be combined to obtain fixes. Typical combinations include two or more bearings, a bearing with distance range measurement to the same or another object, or two or more distance ranges. Radar LOPs may also be combined with visual LOPs.

Care should be exercised when using radar bearing information only since radar bearings are not as precise as visual bearings. A fix obtained by any radar bearing or by distance measurement is plotted on the chart with a dot enclosed by a triangle to indicate the fix and labeled with time followed by "RAD FIX", such as, 1015 RAD FIX.

D.59.d. Distance Measurement Example

At 0215, the boat is on a course of 300° (303° M). The radar range scale is on 16 miles. Two radar contacts (land or charted landmark) are observed. The first has a bearing of 330° relative at 12 NM. This target is on the third range circle. The second target is bearing 035° relative at 8 NM. This target is on the second range circle. Obtain a distance measurement fix by performing the following procedures: (see **Figure 14-40**)

NOTE Radar ranges are usually measured from prominent land features such as cliffs or rocks. However, landmarks such as lighthouses and towers often show up at a distance when low land features do not.

Step	Procedure
1	Locate the objects on the chart.
2	Spread the span of the drawing compass to a distance of 12 NM (distance of first target), using the latitude or nautical mile scale on the chart.
3	Without changing the span of the drawing compass, place the point on the exact position of the object and strike an arc towards the DR track, plotting the distance.
4	Repeat the above procedures for the second object (distance of 8 NM). Where the arcs intersect is the fix (position). Label the fix with time and 'RAD FIX' (0215 RAD FIX).

NOTE The arcs of two ranges will intersect at two points. In some cases, a third LOP may be needed to determine which intersection represents the fix position.

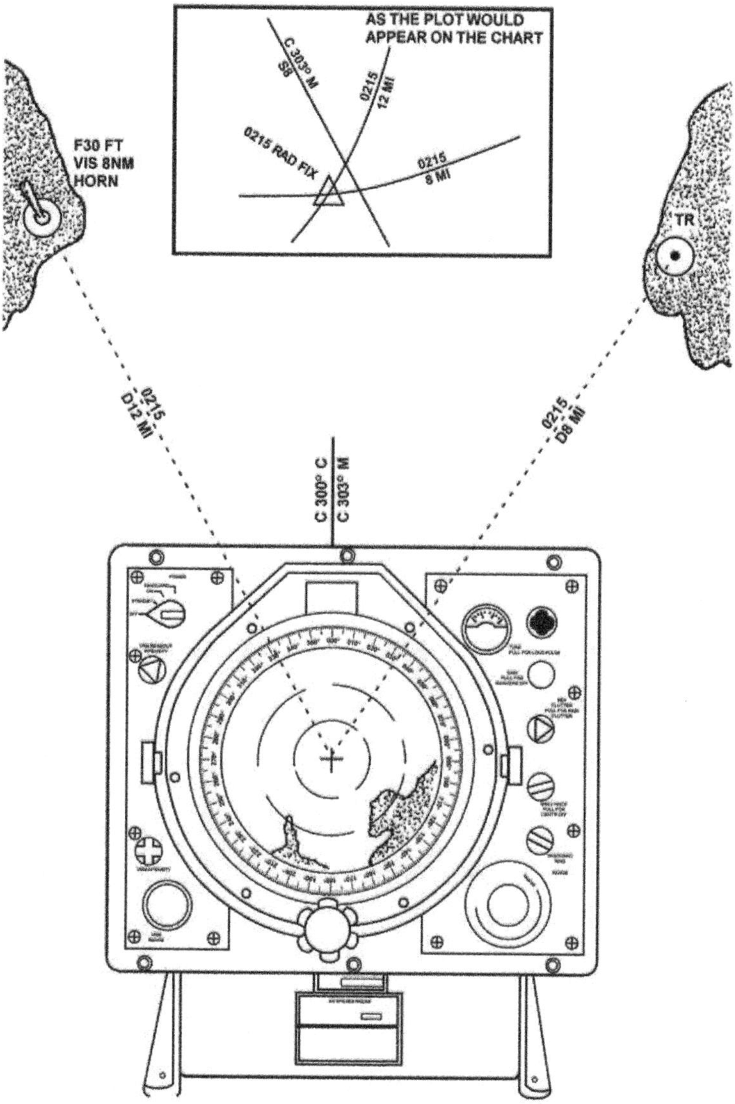

Figure 14-40
Obtaining a Radar Fix Using Two Distance Measurements

D.59.e. Sample DR Plot

A DR plot typically includes many types of LOPs and fixes. **Figure 14-41** is provided as an example of what could appear on a properly maintained DR plot. Some of the fixes within the figure have not been discussed within the text.

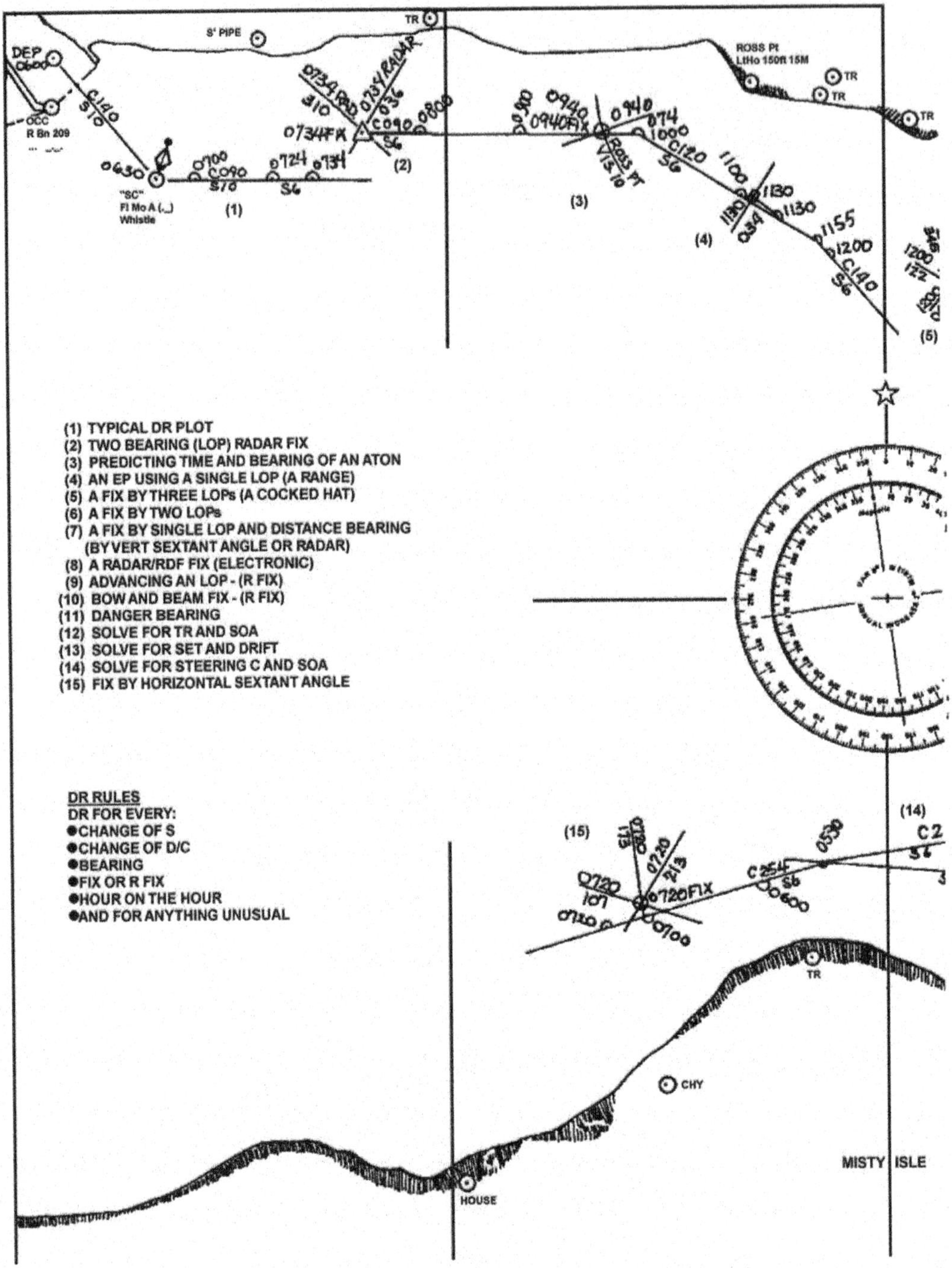
TR
S' PIPE
DEP
0600
OCC
R Bn 209
C140
S10
0630
0700
C090
S10
0724
0734
"SC"
Fl Mo A (._)
Whistle
(1)
0734 FIX
0734 RAD
310
0734 RADAR
036
C090
0800
S6
(2)
0900
0940
0940 FIX
0940
074
1000
C120
S6
ROSS PT
V13:10
(3)
ROSS Pt
LtHo 150ft 15M
TR
TR
TR
1100
1130
1130
1130
034
(4)
1155
1200
C140
S6
(5)
(1) TYPICAL DR PLOT
(2) TWO BEARING (LOP) RADAR FIX
(3) PREDICTING TIME AND BEARING OF AN ATON
(4) AN EP USING A SINGLE LOP (A RANGE)
(5) A FIX BY THREE LOPs (A COCKED HAT)
(6) A FIX BY TWO LOPs
(7) A FIX BY SINGLE LOP AND DISTANCE BEARING (BY VERT SEXTANT ANGLE OR RADAR)
(8) A RADAR/RDF FIX (ELECTRONIC)
(9) ADVANCING AN LOP - (R FIX)
(10) BOW AND BEAM FIX - (R FIX)
(11) DANGER BEARING
(12) SOLVE FOR TR AND SOA
(13) SOLVE FOR SET AND DRIFT
(14) SOLVE FOR STEERING C AND SOA
(15) FIX BY HORIZONTAL SEXTANT ANGLE
DR RULES
DR FOR EVERY:
●CHANGE OF S
●CHANGE OF D/C
●BEARING
●FIX OR R FIX
●HOUR ON THE HOUR
●AND FOR ANYTHING UNUSUAL
(15)
(14)
0720
107
0720
213
0720 FIX
0700
C254
S6
0600
0530
TR
CHY
HOUSE
MISTY ISLE

Figure 14-41
Sample DR Plot

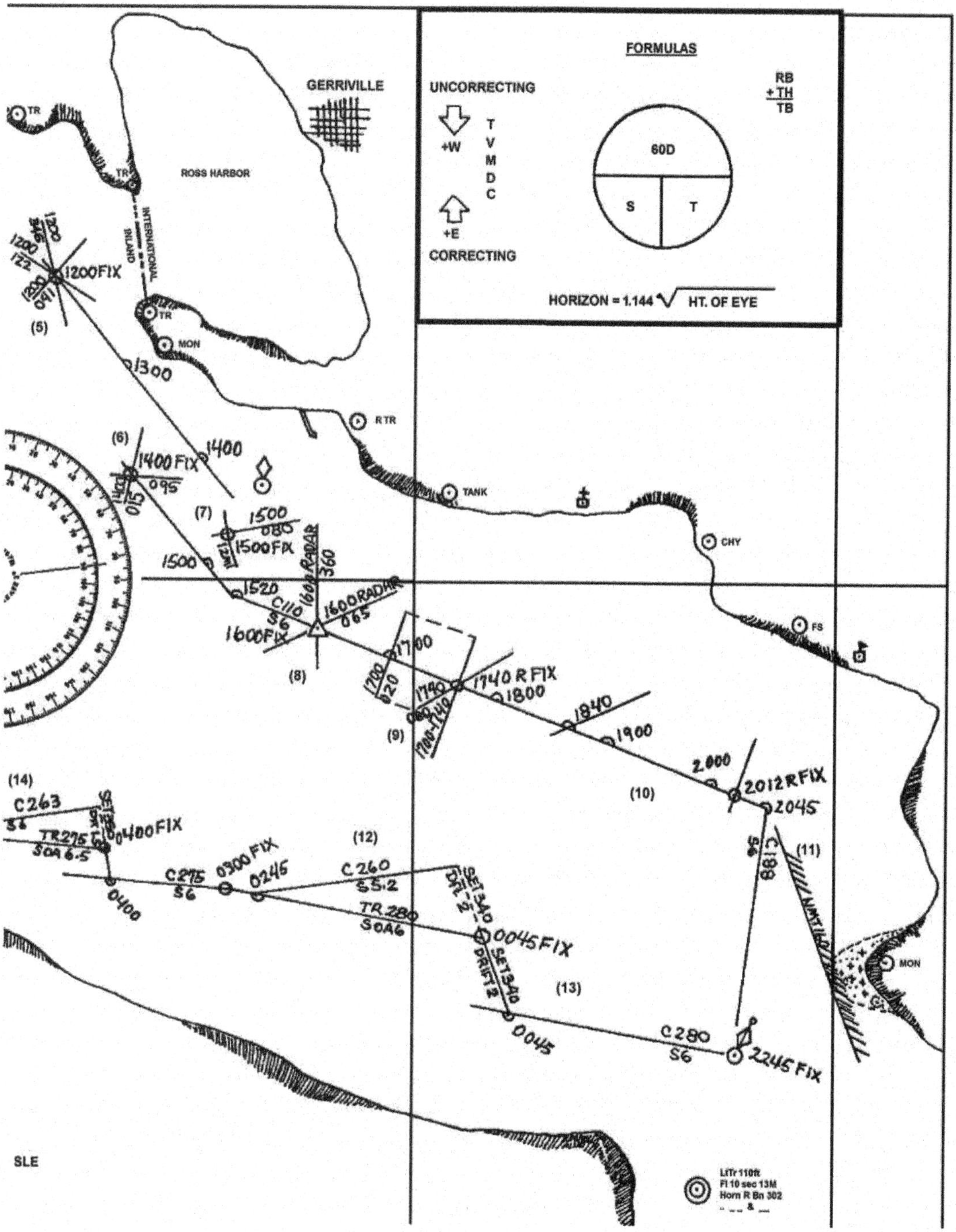

Figure 14-41 (continued)
Sample DR Plot

LORAN-C

D.60. Description

As previously discussed in *Chapter 13, Section D*, LORAN-C is a navigation system network of transmitters consisting of one master station and two or more secondary stations. LORAN-C is a pulsed, hyperbolic (uses curved lines) system. LORAN-C receivers measure the TD between the master transmitter site signal and the secondary transmitter site signal to obtain a single LOP. A second pair of LORAN-C transmitting stations produces a second LOP. Plotting positions using TDs requires charts overprinted with LORAN-C curves. However, most LORAN-C receivers convert LORAN-C signals directly into a readout of latitude and longitude. The mariner then can use a standard nautical chart without LORAN-C curves. It is accurate to better than .25 nautical mile (NM).

D.61. Receiver Characteristics

Different LORAN-C receivers have different locations of their controls, but they are basically standardized on what function is to be controlled. The boat crew should become familiar with the operation of the LORAN-C receiver by studying its operating manual and through the unit training program.

NOTE LORAN-C is not accurate enough for precise navigation, such as staying within a channel.

D.62. Determining Position

Many LORAN-C receivers give a direct readout of latitude and longitude position that can be plotted on the chart. Depending on the receiver, the conversion of LORAN-C signals to latitude and longitude may lose some accuracy. The readout typically goes to two decimal places (hundredths) but plotting normally only goes to the first decimal place (tenths).

Older LORAN-C receivers display only a TD for each pair of stations. By matching these TD numbers to the LORAN-C grid, overprinted on a chart, an LOP can be determined. Intersecting two or more of these LOPs gives a fix.

TDs represent specific intersecting grid lines on a LORAN-C chart. (see **Figure 14-42**) Each line is labeled with a code such as SSO-W and SSO-Y that identifies particular master-secondary signals. Following the code is a number that corresponds to the TDs that would appear on a LORAN receiver on a boat located along the line. Crewmembers should note the TDs and find the two intersecting grid lines; one on the SSO-W axis, the other on the SSO-Y Axis that most nearly match the readings on the boat's receiver.

The first step in plotting a LORAN-C position is to match the numbers on the receiver with the LORAN-C grid on the chart. The point where the two lines meet gives a fix of the position.

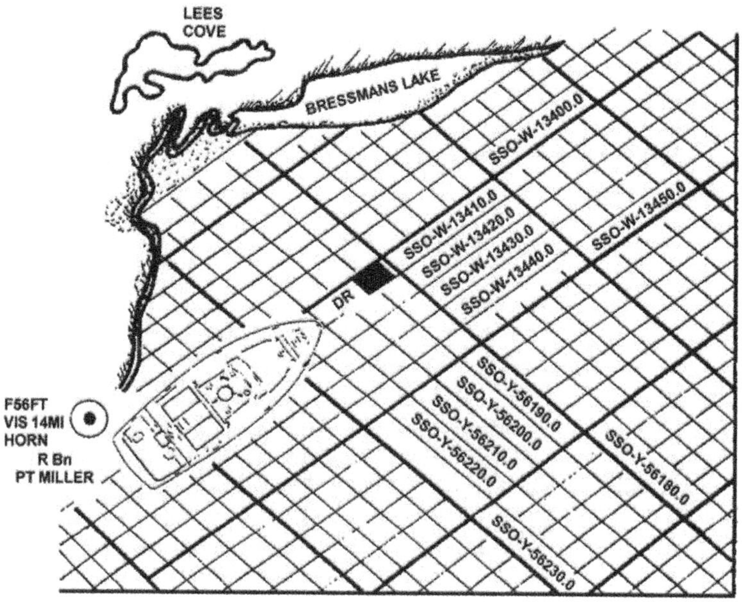

... THE FIRST TD SSO-W-13405.0 LIES BETWEEN SSO-W-13400.0 AND SSO-W-13410.0

... THE SECOND TD SS0-Y-56187.5 LIES BETWEEN SS0-Y-56180.0 AND SSO-Y-56190.0. THESE TWO TD'S PROVIDE A DR OR ROUGH FIX' THE FOUR LINES INTERSECT FORMING A GRID SQUARE.

Figure 14-42
Matching LORAN-C TDs with LORAN-C Grids on a Chart

D.63. Refining a LORAN-C Line of Position

Two LORAN-C readings are given as: SSO-W-13405.0 and SSO-Y-56187.5. The first axis lies between SSO-W-13400.0 and SSO-W-13410.0 and the second axis lies between SSO-Y-56180.0 and SSO-Y-56190.0.

Refine the LORAN-C fix by performing the following procedures: (see **Figure 14-43**)

Step	Procedure
1	Use dividers and measure the exact distance between the LORAN-C LOPs SSO-W-13400.0 and SSO-W-13410.0 on the chart. (see **Figure 14-43**)
2	Without changing the span of the dividers, find the points where the distance between the base of the wedge-shaped interpolator scale on the chart and the topmost sloping edge of the interpolator matches the span of the dividers. Connect these two points with a vertical line. (see **Figure 14-43**)
3	Along the vertical edge of the interpolator are the numbers 0, 1, 2, 3, 4, 5, 6, 7, 8, 9, 10. Beginning at the base, read UP. Each number makes an immediate sloping line on the interpolator. The difference between SSO-W-1 3405.0 and SSO-W-18410.0 is five. Select line five of the interpolator and follow it to the vertical line drawn in step 2.
4	Take the dividers and measure the distance between line five and the base of the interpolator. Without changing the span of the dividers, measure the same distance, away and perpendicular to the line SSO-W-13400.0 on the chart nearest the DR. Measure the direction toward the line SSO-W-13410.0. Take parallel rulers and draw a line parallel to SSO-W- 1 8400.0 at this point. The SSO-W- 1 3405.0 TD is now plotted.
5	Plot the SSO-Y-56187.5 between SSO-Y-56180.0 and SSO-Y-56190.0 using the above procedures.

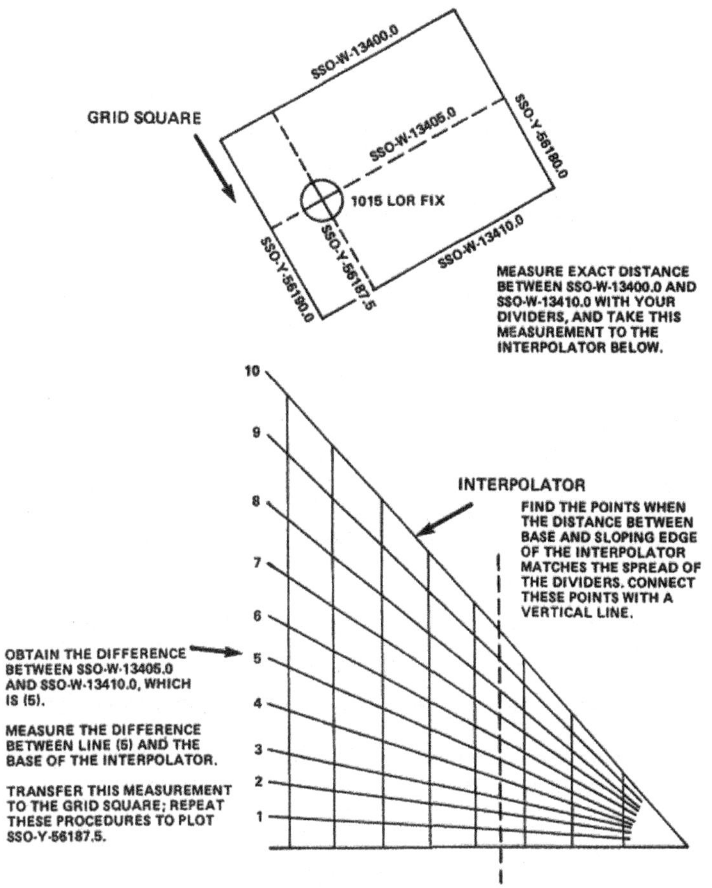

Figure 14-43
Obtaining a LORAN-C Fix on a Grid Square

Global Positioning System (GPS)

D.64. Description

As previously discussed in *Chapter 13, Section D,* the GPS is a radionavigation system of 24 satellites operated by the DoD. It is available 24 hours per day, worldwide, in all weather conditions. Each GPS satellite transmits its precise location, meaning position and elevation. In a process called "ranging," a GPS receiver on the boat uses the signal to determine the distance between it and the satellite. Once the receiver has computed the range for at least four satellites, it processes a three-dimensional position that is accurate to about 33 meters. GPS provides two levels of service - SPS for civilian users, and PPS for military users.

D.65. Standard Positioning Service

The civilian SPS is available on a continuous basis to any user worldwide. It is accurate to a radius within 33 meters of the position shown on the receiver about 99% of the time.

D.66. Precise Positioning Service

PPS provides position fixes accurate to within 10 meters. This service is limited to approved U.S. Federal Government, allied military, and civil users.

D.67. Equipment Features

GPS receivers are small, have small antennas, and need little electrical power. Hand-held units are available. Positional information is shown on a liquid crystal display (LCD) screen as geographical coordinates (latitude and longitude readings). These receivers are designed to be interfaced with other devices such as autopilots, EPIRBs and other distress alerting devices, to automatically provide positional information. Navigational features available in the typical GPS receiver include:

- Entry of waypoints and routes in advance.
- Display of course and speed made good.
- Display of cross-track error.
- Availability of highly accurate time information.

Differential Global Positioning System (DGPS)

D.68. Description

As previously discussed in *Chapter 13, Section D,* the Coast Guard developed the DGPS to improve upon SPS signals of GPS. It uses a local reference receiver to correct errors in the standard GPS signals. These corrections are then broadcast and can be received by any user with a DGPS receiver. The corrections are applied within the user's receiver, providing mariners with a position that is accurate within 10 meters, with 99.7% probability. While DGPS is accurate to within 10 meters, improvements to receivers will make DGPS accurate to within a centimeter, noise-free and able to provide real-time updates.

The Coast Guard uses selected marine radiobeacons to send DGPS corrections to users. DGPS provides accurate and reliable navigational information to maritime users in HEA, along U.S. coastal waters, the Great Lakes, navigable portions of the western rivers, Puerto Rico, Hawaii, and Alaska.

Section E. River Sailing

Introduction

The section provides general information for operating on rivers, with emphasis on the western rivers. The western rivers (Mississippi River system) pose navigational concerns that often are not seen in harbor, coastal, or high seas sailing. Local knowledge is very important. Navigational techniques and the language both have differences that must be learned to become a competent river sailor.

E.1. Major Piloting Differences

Some of the special considerations for river navigation include:

- Charts.
- Mile marks.
- Fixed aids.
- Buoyage.
- Compass.
- DR plot.

E.1.a. Charts

Charts are simple, line drawn "maps" that show the main geographical features of the waterway, the channel or sailing line, prominent man-made objects, and the various aids. River charts do not show landmarks such as stacks, water towers, or antennas. These charts do not always show the geographical names for areas along the bank. River charts only show structures immediately on the banks by symbol and footnote. **Figure 14-44** provides a good example.

NOTE A road map of the operating area is a good supplement for identifiable geographical names.

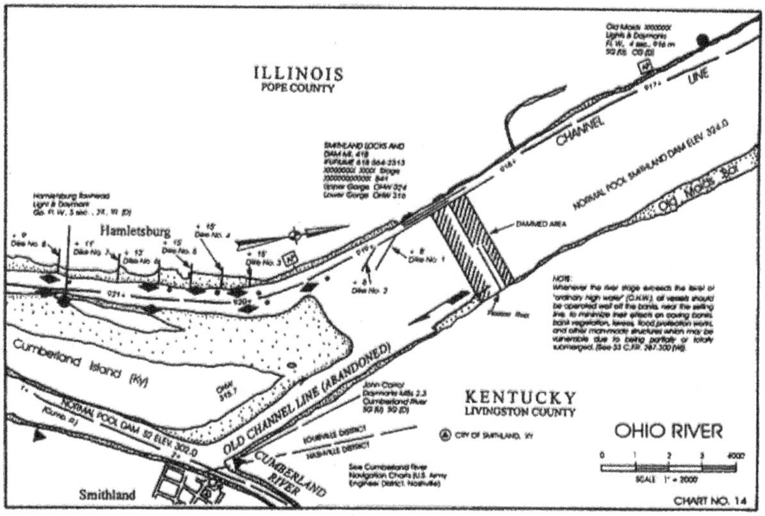

Figure 14-44
Sample River Chart

E.1.b. Mile Marks

The Western Rivers have mile marks (beginning at the mouth or at the headwaters of the stream).

E.1.c. Fixed Aids

Fixed aids (daymarks and lights) display the mile, usually as statute miles, on a "mile" board for that point of the river. Where no aid exists, landmarks such as bridges, creeks, islands, and overhead power lines provide the mile-mark reference.

E.1.d. Buoyage

The U.S. lateral system of buoyage has differences when used on these rivers.

E.1.e. Compass

Compasses are not normally very useful on western rivers because there are no plotting references on the chart and that many rivers meander. However, boat-mounted compasses must be installed. There will be situations where the use of a compass can help determine a position. For example, on a meandering river with no prominent landmarks, comparing the compass heading with the north arrow on the chart will help identify the bend or reach where the boat is operating.

E.1 f. DR Plot

As in coastal sailing, a boat's approximate position is determined by dead reckoning, applying its speed, time, and course from its last known position. However, because many rivers have numerous bends, it often is not possible to maintain a complete DR plot with precise course changes.

E.2. Conditions and Effects

Surface and bottom conditions of a river are unpredictable and can change quickly. Some of the unique situations to deal with include:

- Silting and shoaling.
- Drift.
- Flood or drought.

E.2.a. Silting and Shoaling

Silt is a mass of soil particle carried in water. It can clog boat cooling water intakes and wear out strut bearings and shafts. Silt settles on the bottom as shoaling, either adding to or creating sand bars or mud banks.

E.2.b. Drift

Drift, or driftwood, is floating debris carried by the river flow and washed or lifted from the banks. Running drift can damage a boat.

E.2.c. Flood or Drought

Tides affect rivers near the coast, but a flood or a drought will greatly affect the vertical level (depth) of the entire river.

E.2.c.1. Flood

A flood is created by runoff or drainage from heavy rains or melting snow. Navigating outside the riverbanks requires caution and local knowledge. During a flood condition, some dangers may include:

- Currents are much stronger.
- Channels can shift.
- Obstructions can be hidden under the water.
- Drift hazards (trees and other debris) increase.
- AtoN can be broken.
- Bridge clearances are reduced.

E.2.c.2. Drought

A drought is low water level. This can result in the closing of channels. Snags and obstructions that once were cleared easily become hazards to navigation. Also, sandbars and mud flats will appear where it was once safe to operate.

NOTE

Refer to *Chapter 10, Boat Handling* for information on operating boats in narrow channels.

E.3. Locks and Dams

Locks and dams provide a navigable channel for river traffic. Navigation dams release water, as necessary, to maintain a navigable channel during the navigation season. Locks release water as a part of their normal operation. Both of these can be a safety problem for boats. Knowledge of locks and dams, including location, use and associated hazards, is essential for safe boat operations.

E.3.a. Construction and Operation

The navigation dams on the Mississippi, Illinois, and Ohio rivers can be of different construction. Two types of dam construction are the Tainter gate and the Roller gate. Also, some dam releases are controlled remotely. This is the kind of local knowledge that the boat crew needs to check before operating in that area.

Most people know that water released from a dam can create a powerful, turbulent current going downstream. However, an upstream water current can exist close to the lower or downstream side of a dam. Operating too close to the downstream side of a dam can result in the boat being drawn into the dam.

A strong suction is created by the rush of water underneath the upper side of a roller-gate dam. (see **Figure 14-45**) A boat drifting into the dam on the upper side may not be in immediate danger on the surface but it is possible for boats to be drawn into the gates. These areas are usually marked by danger buoys upstream of the dam and should be avoided as much as possible. If entering this area is a must, the lockmaster should be contacted before entering. If the boat enters this area, crewmembers should not go into the water.

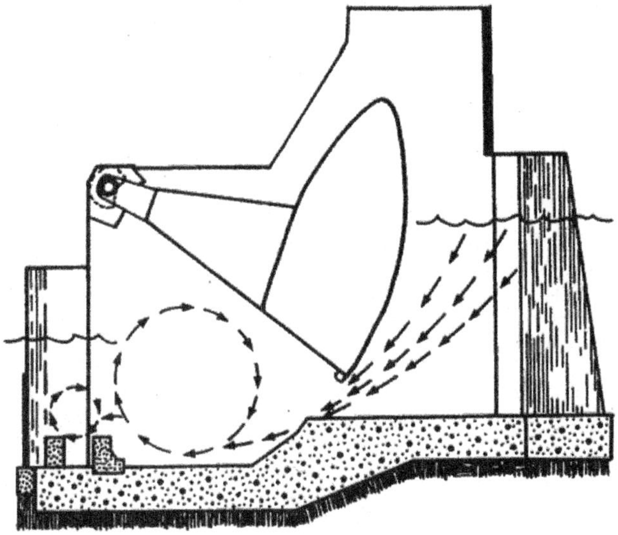

Figure 14-45
Roller Gate Dam

E.3.b. Navigation Displays

When locks at fixed dams and moveable dams have their dams up, they will show navigation lights during hours of darkness. These lights are green, red, or amber and in groups of one, two or three. A circular disc may also be shown. The significance of these displays is explained in local guidance.

E.3.c. Lock Operations

The purpose of a lock is to raise or lower the boat to the level of the channel that it wants to continue to navigate. Locks come in all shapes and sizes, but they all operate on the principle that water seeks its own level. A lock is an enclosure with accommodations at both ends (generally called gates) to allow boats to enter and exit. The boat enters, the gates are closed, and by a system of culverts and valves, the water level in the lock aligns with the pool level of the upstream or downstream side of the lock. The gate then opens and the boat can continue on its way.

E.3.d Locking Procedures

There are many common locking procedures but local regulations can vary. The boat crew must check local guidance for correct locking procedures of each lock. Standard locking signals are shown in **Figure 14-46**. Precautions to take in locking include:

- Do not come closer than 400 feet of the lock wall until the lockman signals to enter.
- Moor to the side of the lock wall as directed.
- If using own mooring lines, they should be at least 50 feet long with a 12-inch eye splice.
- Do not tie mooring lines to the boat; tend the lines as the water level changes.
- Be prepared to cast off lines in an emergency; a small hand axe or hatchet should be available.
- Use fenders.
- Do not moor to ladder rungs embedded in the lock walls.
- Wait for the lockman's signal (an air horn) to depart.
- Depart in the same order of entering the lock with other boats.
- Steer for the channel and keep a sharp lookout for craft approaching from the other direction.

At locks with "small craft signals", signal the lockman the desire to pass. After signaling, stand clear and wait for instructions. Many locks are radio-equipped. Consult the appropriate navigation charts for radio-equipped locks, their frequency and call sign.

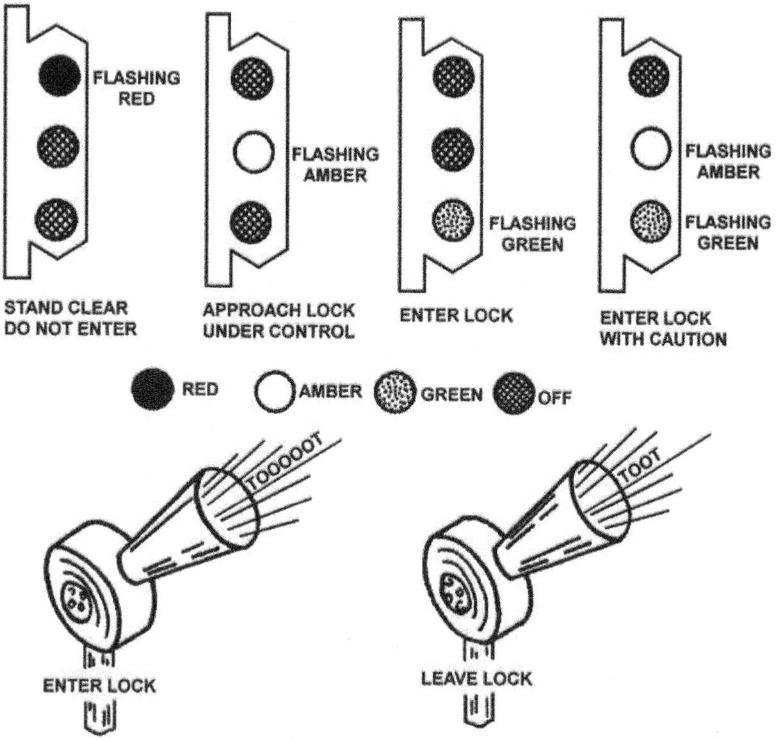

Figure 14-46
Standard Locking Signals

E.3.e. General Considerations

General considerations around locks include:

- The Secretary of the Army sets the priorities for safe and efficient passage of the various types of craft on inland waterways. Priorities, listed in descending order with the highest priority on top, are:
  - U.S. military craft.
  - Vessels carrying U.S. mail.
  - Commercial passenger craft.
  - Commercial tows.
  - Commercial fisherman.
  - Recreational craft.
- Under certain conditions, boats may be locked through with other crafts having a higher priority. This occurs only when there is no delay and neither craft is placed in jeopardy.
- Lockmen have the same authority over a boat in a lock as the traffic police have over a car at an intersection. For safety purposes, obey the lockman's instructions.
- Every boat should carry a copy of, and the crew should be familiar with the regulations governing navigation on the rivers in its AOR.

E.4. Safety Considerations Around Navigation Dams

General safety considerations include:

- Stay clear of danger zones - 600 feet above and 100 feet below dams.
- Approach dams at reduced speed, along the shore at the lock.
- Be "dam" conscious:
  - During the filling process, it is dangerous to approach near the intake ports in the lock walls above the upstream lock gates. The filling process creates a powerful suction as water rushes into the culverts. Boats must stay clear of the locks until signaled to approach.
  - During the emptying process, a strong undercurrent and suction is created in the lock chamber. This suction occurs next to the lock walls and is created by the water rushing into the filling and emptying ports of the lock.
  - Wearing a PFD may not keep a person from being pulled under the water in these circumstances.

E.5. Common River Sailing Terms

Table 14-6 provides terms and their definitions, commonly used in river sailing.

Table 14-6
River Sailing Terms

Term	Description
Auxiliary Lock	A small secondary lock next to the main lock.
Backwater	The water backed up a tributary system.
Bar	A deposit of sand or gravel in or near the channels that, at times, prevents boat traffic from passing.
Bend	A bend of the river, similar to a curve in a highway.
Berm	The sharp definitive edge of a dredged channel, such as in a rock cut.
Bight of a Bend	Sharpest part of a curve in a river or stream.
Bitts, Floating	Part of a lock system for securing a boat waiting in a lock, recessed in lock walls.
Boil	Turbulence in the water resulting from deep holes, ends of dikes, channel changes, or other underwater obstructions.
Caval or Kevel	A steel cleat of special design on barges and towboats for making aft mooring and towing lines.
Chute	Section of river that is narrower than ordinary and through which the river current increases. It is also the passage behind an island that is not the regular channel.
Deadhead	A water soaked wooden pile, tree, or log that floats at the surface of the water (barely awash), usually in a vertical position.
Dike	A structure of pilings or stone that diverts the current of a river.
Down Draft	The natural tendency of a river current to pull the boat downstream when making a river crossing.

Table 14-6 (continued)
River Sailing Terms

Term	Description
Draft	A crosscurrent that is usually designated as an out draft, or as a left- or right-handed draft.
Draw Down	The release of water through one dam before the arrival of a significant increase in water from the upper reaches of the river.
Drift	Debris floating in or lodged along the banks of the river. (Also known as driftwood.)
Flat Pool	The normal stage of water in the area between two dams. It is maintained when little or no water is flowing; therefore the pool flattens out.
Flood Stage	A predetermined level or stage along the main river bank where flooding will occur or may overflow in the particular area.
Foot of _____	The downstream end or lower part of a bend or island.
Gauge	A scale graduated in tenths of a foot that shows the water level or river stage. A lower gauge is one that shows the downstream side of a dam and an upper gauge is one on the upstream side.
Head of _____	The upstream end or beginning of a bend or island.
Left Bank	The left bank of a river when going downstream, properly termed left bank descending.
Levee	An embankment or dike constructed for flood protection.
Lock	A chamber built as part of a river dam to raise or lower boat traffic that wants to pass the dam.
Lock Gate	A moveable barrier that prevents water from entering or leaving a lock chamber.
Mile Board	A 12" x 36" board above a river aid and with the river mileage at that point from a given location.
Open River	Any river having no obstructions such as dams, or when the river stage is high enough to navigate over movable dams.
Pool Stage	The stage of water between two successive dams. It is usually at the minimum depth to maintain the depth in the channel at the shallowest point.
Reach	Usually a long, straight section of a river.
Right Bank	The right bank of a river when going downstream, properly termed as right bank descending.
Slack Water	A location where there is a minimum current.
Snag	Tree or log embedded in the river bottom.
Tow	One or more barges made up to be transported by a boat.
Towboat	A riverboat that pushes barges ahead.

This page intentionally left blank.

Chapter 15
Search and Rescue

Introduction

This chapter provides a general overview of the Search and Rescue (SAR) organization and basic skills and knowledge required to conduct SAR operations as a boat crewmember.

A successful rescue mission depends on correct search planning and execution. The dramatic image of a Coast Guard boat battling wind and sea in the dead of night to save a helpless mariner is only part of the story. The rest of the story involves collecting essential information, planning the correct response, assessing the risk, selecting the proper search and rescue unit, and exercising proper safety precautions.

NOTE

> Specific policies, guidance, and technical information for SAR operations can be found in the *U.S. Coast Guard Addendum to the United States National Search and Rescue Supplement (NSS) to the International Aeronautical and Maritime Search and Rescue Manual*, COMDTINST M16130.2 (series).

In this chapter

This chapter contains the following sections:

Section A. Organization and Responsibility

Introduction

The boat responding to a SAR incident is an operational facility that is one part of the overall SAR system. To enable the boat to effectively perform its operation as a search and rescue unit (SRU), an organization and assignment of responsibilities have been established on a national and international level. This section presents SAR information on the national system.

A.1. Coast Guard Responsibility

SAR coordination responsibility in the United States is divided between the Air Force and the Coast Guard. The Air Force is responsible for inland SAR. The Coast Guard is responsible for maritime SAR which includes:

- Interior river systems.
- Inland waterways.
- Coastal waters.
- Parts of the high seas.

Memorandums of understanding (MOU) with Guam, Alaska and Hawaii state that Coast Guard resources are also responsible for land SAR in these areas (only portions of Alaska).

A.1.a. Coast Guard Application

The Coast Guard promotes safety on, over, and under the high seas and all waters subject to the jurisdiction of the United States. U.S. law states that the Coast Guard shall develop, establish, maintain, and operate SAR facilities and may render aid to distressed persons and protect and save property. It also states that the Coast Guard may utilize its resources to assist other federal and state entities.

A.1.b. Areas of Responsibility

Maritime SAR is divided into two major AORs:

- Atlantic maritime region.
- Pacific maritime region.

The two regions are further subdivided into smaller geographical AORs for better distribution and management of personnel and facilities.

A.1.c. Objectives

Two SAR program objectives are of direct importance to boat crews:

- To minimize loss of life or personal injury and property loss or damage in the maritime environment.
- To minimize search duration and crew risk during SAR missions.

A.1.d. SAR Facts

The majority of SAR cases occur within 20 miles of shore. Coast Guard helicopters and boats, primary quick response assets, handle most of these cases. About 90% of all cases do not require searching. A small percentage of cases involve minor searches (less than 24 hours) and an even smaller percent of these cases involve major searches lasting more than 24 hours. Despite being a small percentage of SAR operations overall, the annual cost for searches is millions of dollars. Boats may conduct operations with helicopters, especially searches or medical evacuations (MEDEVACs). *Chapter 19, Air Operations*, provides more information on operating with aircraft.

A.2. Search and Rescue Coordination

The boat is part of a unit; the unit is part of a Group; the Group is part of a District; and the District is part of an Area. Each link going up this chain of command controls more SAR resources and has wider geographic responsibility than the link below it. The SAR system has three levels of coordination:

- SAR coordinator (SC).
- SAR mission coordinator (SMC).
- On-scene coordinator (OSC).

A.2.a. SAR Coordinator (SC)

The Coast Guard is designated SC for the Maritime Area and the Air Force for the Inland Area. Coast Guard Area Commanders are designated SCs for each of the two maritime SAR regions and so are District Commanders for their SAR regions. The SCs are the top level SAR managers. The SC is responsible for:

- Establishing, staffing, equipping, and managing the SAR system.
- Establishing rescue coordination centers (RCCs).
- Providing or arranging for SAR facilities.
- Coordinating SAR training.
- Developing SAR policies.

A.2.b. SAR Mission Coordinator (SMC)

Each SAR operation is carried out under the guidance of an SMC. The SMC is usually the district RCC or the Group (Activity) OPCEN. The SMC has several duties and responsibilities:

- Obtain and evaluate all data on the emergency.
- Dispatch SRUs based on this information.
- Develop search plans that include determining limits for the search area, selecting the search pattern, and designating the OSC.
- Control the SAR communication network for the assigned mission.
- Monitor progress of the SAR mission and request additional SAR resources as necessary.

A.2.c. On-Scene Coordinator (OSC)

The OSC is designated by the SMC to coordinate the activities of all units when two or more SRUs are on scene for the same incident. The first unit on scene usually assumes OSC until the SMC directs that the person be relieved. The OSC should be the most capable unit, considering SAR training, communications capabilities, and the length of time that the unit can stay in the search area. As the subordinate of the SMC, the OSC has several duties and responsibilities. These are:

- Inform the SMC through periodic situation reports (SITREPs).
- Coordinate the efforts of all SRUs on scene.
- Implement the search action plan from the SMC.
- Control all on-scene communications between SRUs.
- Monitor the endurance of all SRUs and call for replacement units as needed.
- Provide initial briefings and search instructions to arriving SRUs.

A.2.d. Search and Rescue Unit (SRU)

An SRU is a unit with trained personnel and provided with equipment for SAR operations. The SRU responsibilities include:

- Efficiently execute assigned SAR duties.
- Establish and maintain communications with the OSC or SMC, as appropriate, prior to arriving on scene and until released from the case.

A.2.e. Reporting

Unless designated as OSC, or are the single SRU on scene, report to the OSC. If designated as OSC or are the single SRU on scene, assume the duties of OSC and report to the SMC.

A.2 f. Communication

Communications and information flow is critical to good SAR planning and conducting of SAR operations. SRUs must continually keep the OSC, or if an OSC is not assigned, the SMC informed of any changes on scene so that proper, timely, and accurate changes can be made to the search plan. (see **Figure 15-1**)

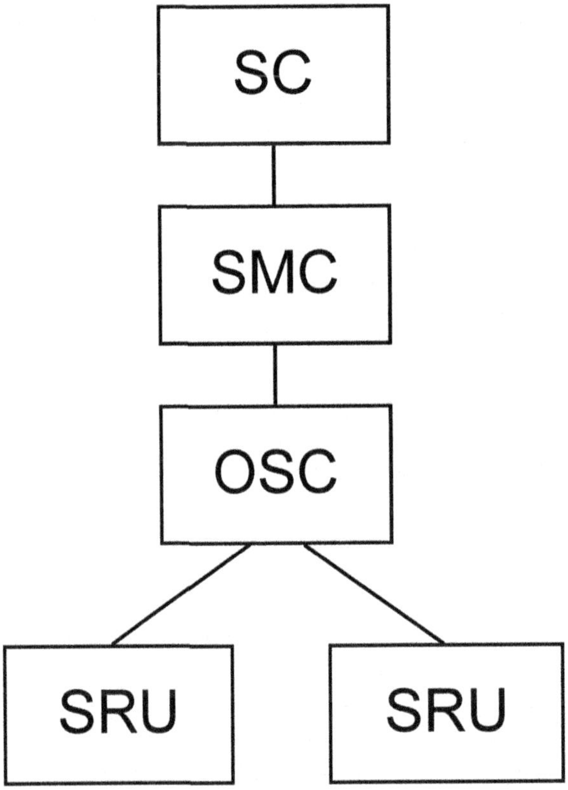

Figure 15-1
SAR Organization

Section B. SAR Emergency Phases

Introduction

Upon receiving an initial report of a distress situation, the SMC should evaluate all available information and, considering the degree of emergency, declare a SAR emergency phase. A boat underway may take these initial steps to respond as the SMC begins work on a search action plan, if needed.

B.1. Emergency Phases

Three emergency phases have been established for classifying incidents and to help in determining the actions to take. These are:

- Uncertainty Phase.
- Alert Phase.
- Distress Phase.

Emergency phases are based on the level of concern for the safety of persons or craft that may be in danger. Each phase requires the collection of data that can assist in determining proper response actions. The emergency phase may be reclassified by the SMC as the situation develops. Also, if sufficient information is received from initial or early reports, one or more phases may be skipped in determining the proper phase for a particular case. The ultimate action could be immediate dispatch of an SRU. Everything possible must be done to make certain that a unit sent on a SAR case is the proper response.

B.2. Uncertainty Phase

An uncertainty phase exists when there is knowledge of a situation that may need to be monitored, or have more information gathered, but does not require dispatching resources. When there is doubt about the safety of an aircraft, ship, or other craft or persons onboard, or it is overdue or failed to make an expected position report, the situation should be investigated and information gathered. The key word is "doubt." A preliminary communications (PRECOM) search is normally conducted during the uncertainty phase. The PRECOM search is conducted by contacting facilities or agencies within a specific area to either locate the vessel or determine if the vessel has been seen.

B.3. Alert Phase

An alert phase is assigned when an aircraft, ship, or other craft or persons onboard are having difficulty and may need assistance, but are not in immediate danger. Apprehension is usually associated with the alert phase, but there is no known threat requiring immediate action. SRUs may be dispatched to provide assistance if it is believed that conditions might get worse. For overdue craft, the alert phase is considered when there is a continued lack of information about its position or condition. The key word is "apprehension." An extended communications (EXCOM) search is normally conducted during the alert phase. The EXCOM search consists of extensive and repeated attempts to communicate with the missing vessel. The SMC may direct SRUs to conduct an EXCOM search with the vessel every four hours for a 24-hour period. Boats may also be deployed to check out any leads.

B.4. Distress Phase

The distress phase is when there is reasonable certainty that an aircraft, ship, or other craft or persons onboard is in danger and requires immediate assistance. This includes a direct report of an emergency or the continued lack of knowledge about a vessel's progress or position. The key word is "danger." SRUs are normally dispatched when this phase is reached.

Section C. Legal Aspects and U.S. Coast Guard Policy

Introduction

Numerous legal issues affect SAR. This section briefly covers general Coast Guard policy guidance relating to SAR. These issues are covered in greater detail in your district operation plan (OPLAN) or standard operating procedures (SOP).

C.1. SAR Agreements

"SAR agreements," formal written documents, are used to resolve coordination problems such as guidance for entering another AOR or providing SRUs to assist another agency or country. These agreements may be at the local level or on an international level. Local regulations should be checked concerning the effect that any treaty or SAR agreement may have within the AOR. Each nation has final right to regulate entry into their territory regardless of treaties that have been signed. Therefore it is important to always be familiar with current policies before conducting SAR outside the normally assigned AOR.

C.2. Distress Beacon Incidents

Distress beacons are one of the most important tools available to people in distress for assisting SAR authorities. The various types of distress beacons, their proper use, additional policy, and general information are described in the *U.S. Coast Guard Addendum to the United States National Search and Rescue Supplement (NSS) to the International Aeronautical and Maritime Search and Rescue Manual*, COMDTINST M16130.2 (series).

C.2.a. General Considerations

Many ships and commercial fishing vessels are required to carry an EPIRB; recreational boats are not required but are strongly encouraged to carry them. The original EPIRB is just like the aeronautical version (the ELT) operated on the frequency 121.5 MHz. However, the 406.025 MHz EPIRB and ELT were developed for satellites to detect these distress alerts. As implied, the receipt of a beacon alert is considered a distress. The response for 406 varies slightly from the 121.5 (see the *U.S. Coast Guard Addendum to the United States National Search and Rescue Supplement (NSS) to the International Aeronautical and Maritime Search and Rescue Manual*, COMDTINST M16130.2 (series)). The increased reliability of the 406 over the 121.5, due to its ability to transmit a data string of identification and contact information, and the sole use of the 406 MHz frequency for distress alerting, permit an immediate response by SAR forces.

C.2.b. Reports of Beacon Alerts

Reports of audible beacon alerts indicate a beacon has been activated. SAR response to an audible beacon signal should be similar to the type of response provided for orange or red flare sightings, discussed later in this chapter. In cases where Coast Guard resources hear the beacon, they normally respond immediately to determine the signal source. Most other audible signal reports come from aircraft.

NOTE

EPIRBs are distress beacons. These beacons shall not be used as datum marker buoys. The beacon's signal may prevent another distress beacon from being properly tracked or reported.

C.3. Flare Incidents

The Coast Guard responds to many flare sightings. Red and orange flares are recognized around the world as marine and aviation emergency signals and must be treated as a distress.

C.3.a. Considerations

The nature of flare distress signaling makes planning and execution of searches difficult due to the wide variation of flare types, possible altitudes, skill and position of the reporting source/observer, weather, and many other factors. For this reason, the accuracy of the information received from the reporting source and/or observer is critical. For example, a hand-held flare in a recreation boat seen on the horizon by a beach observer will be approximately 4 miles away while a parachute flare rising to 1200 feet and seen on the horizon by the same beach observer could be more than 30 miles away. As with all SAR cases, a prompt, thorough, and proper response, including a thorough debrief of the reporting sources(s), yields the best chance for a successful rescue.

C.3.b. Reports of Flare Sighting

It is critical that correct, descriptive, and accurate information be obtained from persons sighting a flare. This requires careful and thorough questioning of the reporting source. The data gathering process requires patience and good interpersonal skills, since reporting sources are rarely familiar with the terms or procedures used by the Coast Guard when investigating flare sightings. A flare reporting checklist must be used to ensure all the proper information is obtained.

Additional information on flare signals and sightings is located in the *U.S. Coast Guard Addendum to the United States National Search and Rescue Supplement (NSS) to the International Aeronautical and Maritime Search and Rescue Manual*, COMDTINST M16130.2 (series).

C.4. Hoaxes and False Alarms

False alarms and hoaxes waste valuable operational resource time and dollars, frustrate both search controllers and those required to respond, and may adversely affect the Coast Guard's ability to respond to real distress calls. It is often very difficult to determine with certainty whether an incident is a false alarm, hoax, or real distress due to sketchy and/or contradictory information.

C.4.a. Hoax

A hoax is a case where information is reported with the intent to deceive.

C.4.b. False Alarm

A false alarm is when someone or something reported to be in distress is confirmed not to be in distress and is not in need of assistance. In a false alarm case, the reporting source either misjudged a situation or accidentally activated a distress signal or beacon resulting in an erroneous request for help, but did not deliberately act to deceive.

C.4.c. Coast Guard Response

Coast Guard units shall respond without delay to any notification of distress, even when a false alarm or hoax is suspected. Until proven differently, these cases should be treated as if they are real distress cases. A distress call that "sounds like a hoax" shall not be merely dismissed without further action. A distress shall be considered to exist until the case is closed, suspended, or downgraded by proper authority.

C.5. Maritime SAR Assistance Policy

The Coast Guard's primary concern in any SAR operation is that proper, timely, and effective assistance be provided. A key issue is that it is always a Coast Guard priority to remove people from danger. When commercial assistance resources are available or may be operating within the AOR, particular guidelines apply depending on the specific situation. These guidelines are published as the Maritime SAR Assistance Policy (MSAP) in the *U.S. Coast Guard Addendum to the United States National Search and Rescue Supplement (NSS) to the International Aeronautical and Maritime Search and Rescue Manual*, COMDTINST M16130.2 (series). More specific guidance is available in the district OPLAN or SOP. The four paragraphs that follow outline some of these guidelines.

C.5.a. Distress

Immediate response will be initiated for any situation when a mariner is known to be in imminent danger. This response may be provided by regular Coast Guard resources, Coast Guard Auxiliary resources, or resources belonging to other federal, private, state, local, or commercial entities; volunteers or good samaritans. The SMC may use all sources of assistance in a distress situation without concern for conflict with private enterprise.

C.5.b. No Conflict Concern - Any Situation

Private organizations (non-commercial), state and local organizations, and good samaritans are acceptable sources of SAR assistance. When volunteered or available, their help can be used without any concern for conflict with commercial providers. However, if their expertise is unknown, the SMC shall more closely monitor the assistance provided. This is especially true in the case of good samaritans.

C.5.c. Non-Distress Cases

When specifically requested assistance, such as a commercial firm, marina, or friend is not available, a MARB may be issued. If a commercial provider is available and can be on scene within a reasonable time (usually one hour or less) or an offer to assist is made by any of the resources listed in the previous paragraph, no further action by the Coast Guard, beyond monitoring the incident, will be taken.

For a non-distress situation where an Auxiliary facility discovers a vessel requesting assistance but which has not contacted the Coast Guard, refer to the *U.S. Coast Guard Addendum to the United States National Search and Rescue Supplement (NSS) to the International Aeronautical and Maritime Search and Rescue Manual*, COMDTINST M16130.2 (series) and the *Auxiliary Operations Policy Manual*, COMDTINST M16798.3 (series) for guidance.

NOTE

> If the commercial provider and the boater in need of assistance do not reach agreement, the Coast Guard must continue to monitor the case.

C.5.d. Non-Distress Use of Coast Guard Resources

Coast Guard resources normally do not provide immediate assistance in non-distress cases where there is alternative assistance available. The Coast Guard both supports efforts of private enterprise and encourages volunteerism in assisting mariners. Coast Guard resources will not unnecessarily interfere with private enterprise. A Coast Guard resource may assist in a non-distress situation when no higher priority missions exist and no other capable resource is reasonably available. (see **Figure 15-2**)

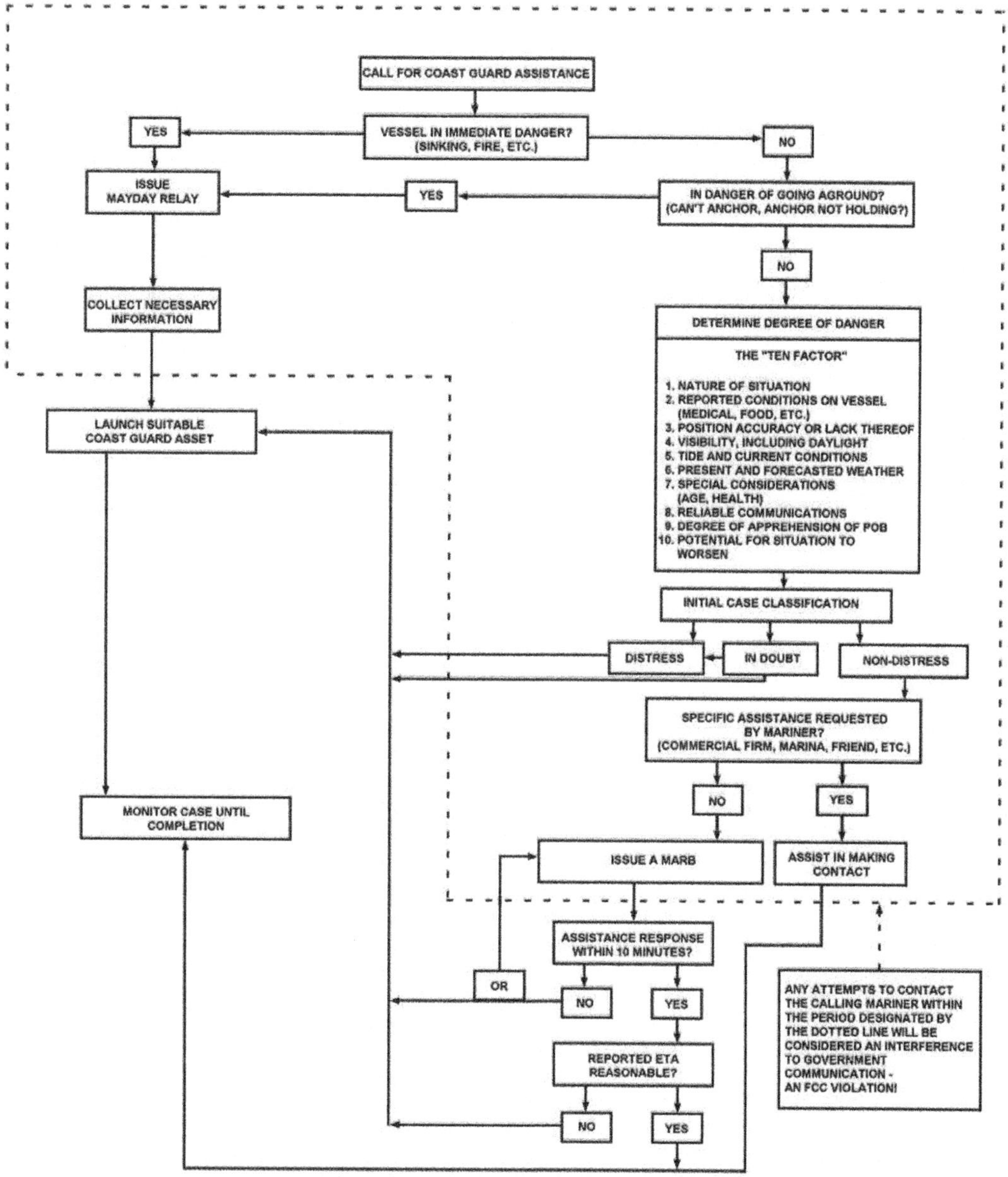

Figure 15-2
SAR Incident Decision Tree

C.6. General Salvage Policy (Other Than Towing)

Coast Guard units and resources are employed for SAR, not for salvage operations. However, if circumstances dictate that salvage operations must be undertaken, the guidance in the *U.S. Coast Guard Addendum to the United States National Search and Rescue Supplement (NSS) to the International Aeronautical and Maritime Search and Rescue Manual*, COMDTINST M16130.2 (series) should be followed. Additional guidance may be found in district and unit SOPs.

C.6.a. General Considerations

During a SAR operation, boat crew and SAR planners should be alert to determine if the situation is changing:

- Has the incident changed from a distress (e.g., people are rescued) to an effort that is now more of a salvage operation?
- Will salvage by the Coast Guard reduce the threat of loss of life or the vessel becoming a hazard to navigation? What can be done to prevent a worsening condition or total loss of vessel?
- Is there a threat of injury to boat crewmembers or damage to the boat that would prevent the SRU from responding to another distress?

C.6.b. Commercial Salvage

When commercial salvers are on scene performing salvage, Coast Guard units may assist them if the salver requests, and the assistance is within the unit's capabilities. However, salvage operations shall be performed only at the discretion of the unit CO/OIC. When no commercial salvage facilities are on scene, Coast Guard units may engage in salvage, other than towing, only when such limited salvage operations (e.g., refloating a grounded vessel, dewatering, damage control measures, etc.) can prevent a worsening situation or complete loss of the vessel. Coast Guard units and personnel shall not unduly hazard themselves at any time by performing salvage operations.

NOTE ✍ Fire fighting policy is discussed in *Chapter 18* of this Manual.

C.6.c. Small Craft

This policy applies to small craft that require salvage other than towing. However, when no commercial salvage companies are available within a reasonable time or distance, the District Commander may modify the policy to provide for refloating a grounded boat which is not in peril of further damage or loss if:

- The Coast Guard units are capable of rendering the assistance.
- The owner requests the assistance and agrees to the specific effort to be made.
- Coast Guard units and personnel are not unduly hazarded by the operation.

C.6.d. Operator Insistence

Occasionally, an operator will insist the Coast Guard take action, such as pulling a vessel from a reef, which the Coast Guard personnel on scene consider unwise. The Coast Guard is under no obligation to agree to any such request or demand. If a decision to comply with such a request is made, it should be made clear to the operator that he is assuming the risk of the operation and the fact that the action is undertaken at his request against Coast Guard advice should be logged.

C.7. General Issues

Other general issues that crewmembers must deal with when performing a SAR mission include the following:

- Public relations.
- Searches for bodies.
- Trespassing.

C.7.a. Public Relations

A SAR operation often creates great interest with the general public and news media. Responsibilities as a boat crewmember do not include providing information to the news media. To avoid wrong information and misunderstandings for the public, all inquires should be directed to the Public Affairs Officer (PAO), Officer of the Day (OOD), OIC, or CO. Relatives of missing persons may also seek information. Coast Guard personnel should show proper concern for their stressful situation but also refer them to the PAO, OOD, OIC, or CO for any information.

C.7.b. Searches for Bodies

United States Coast Guard Regulations 1992, COMDTINST M5000.3 (series), *Chapter 4* states that, "when it has become definitely established, either by time or circumstances, that persons are dead, the Coast Guard is not required to conduct searches for bodies. If, however, requests are received from responsible agencies, such as local police, military commands, etc., Coast Guard units may participate in body searches provided that these searches do not interfere with the primary duties of the units." Since boats are not provided the specific gear or training to conduct searches for bodies, their involvement is usually either as a surface search unit or support platform for other agencies to use their equipment.

C.7.c. Trespassing

SAR personnel should obtain permission from the owner or occupant prior to entering private property. If this is not possible, the Operational Commander must then grant permission before entering private property. Only when saving a person's life, can immediate action be taken.

Section D. SAR Incident Information

Introduction

Once aware of a distress, SAR units attempt to find out as much information about the incident as possible. Standard response procedures and report formats are very important.

Before SAR units are activated, a number of facts about the case must be recorded. These facts fall into two broad categories:

- Initial SAR information.
- Additional SAR information.

Initial SAR information is very important for several reasons. One use of SAR case information by SAR planners is to categorize the case to determine the most appropriate and effective response to provide. SAR planners use every available piece of information to plan the Coast Guard's response, including determining the type of SRU assigned, when it is dispatched, and what type of equipment is taken to the scene.

NOTE

> For guidance and recommended format for standard incident check sheets, refer to the *U.S. Coast Guard Addendum to the United States National Search and Rescue Supplement (NSS) to the International Aeronautical and Maritime Search and Rescue Manual*, COMDTINST M16130.2 (series) and the District SOP.

D.1. Gathering SAR Information

Initial notification that an emergency exists may come from many sources, including:

- Relatives may report that a family member is overdue.
- "MAYDAY" by radio.
- Someone was witness to the distress.

If the caller seems excited, follow the procedures below to help gather information about the case:

Step	Procedure
1	Calm the individual down enough to collect accurate, essential information.
2	Be courteous and show concern for the caller and their situation.
3	Be confident and professional, but not overbearing.
4	Speaking calmly will help ease people's concerns and assure them that the situation is well in hand.
5	Be prepared to write down information (have checklist and pen within reach).

D.1.a. Communication with Reporting Source

It is important to maintain communication with reporting sources, regardless of who they are or how the call was made. Also, keep callers advised of what actions are being taken to resolve the situation they reported.

D.1.a.1. Radio Source

Most distress calls by radio come in on Channel 16, 156.8 MHz. This channel is the maritime VHF-FM international distress and calling frequency. To keep it open for other distresses, the caller is usually asked to move (shift) to a working channel once the initial information (found in D.1.b) is obtained. Since shifting could result in losing communications with the reporting source, the caller is asked to shift back to channel 16 if no reply is heard on the working channel. The transmission may be as follows:

Example: "Vessel in distress, this is Coast Guard Station. Shift and answer channel 21. If no reply is heard on channel 21, shift back to this frequency, channel 16, over."

D.1.a.2. Telephone Source

If calls come in by telephone, the name and number of the person calling should be taken and written down immediately. In the event the call is disconnected, it will be possible to return the call and obtain the needed information. Also, it is important to identify how it may be possible to communicate with the person or vessel that is reported to be in distress. The reporting source should be asked if they know what types of communications equipment are on the vessel. Cellular telephone and pager numbers, types of radio equipment and frequencies monitored might help establish communications with the distressed vessel or person.

D.1.b. Initial Information

Once stable and repeatable communications are established, the most vital information to immediately record is:

- Location of emergency.
- Nature of distress.
- Number of persons onboard (POB).
- Description of the craft.

Response activity can be started once these items are known. Also, realize that this may be the only contact made with the distressed craft or reporting source (e.g., the radio broke, power was lost, or the boat sank).

D.1.c. Location of Emergency

The location of the emergency is the single most important piece of information to obtain. Without a location, it is impossible to send the search and rescue resource. Location can be provided in many different ways and often "local terminology" concerning position can be confusing. The exact location of the disabled vessel should be understood before continuing to gather information from the reporting source. Position can include any or all of the following:

- Position (latitude and longitude) of the incident.
- Bearing and distance from the incident to any points of land or landmarks known or observed.
- Last known position of the incident or distressed vessel.

D.1.d. Nature of Distress

The nature of distress must be clearly understood in order for responding units to be prepared to assist. The emergency may be any one (or combination of more than one) of the following, or it may be some other type of emergency:

- Grounding.
- Sinking.
- Collision.
- Fire.
- Disabled.
- Overdue.
- Medical.

D.1.e. Number of Persons Onboard (POB)

The third most important piece of information to gather from the reporting source is the number of persons onboard. If for some reason the vessel in distress were to sink prior to the SRU's arrival, the number of survivors expected to be in the water would be a vital piece of information to have. Besides the number of POB, other information concerning their condition should be obtained:

- Medical condition of all POB.
- Survival equipment onboard.

D.1 f. Description of the Craft

A good description of the vessel in distress is important so that SAR assets will have an easier time locating the vessel. Information to obtain includes:

- Vessel name.
- Vessel numbers.
- Vessel type.
- Vessel length.
- Vessel color.

When direct communication with the vessel in distress is not available (information about the distressed vessel is being relayed by another source), the initial information about the relaying source should be gathered and recorded.

NOTE In this section, the term "vessel" includes aircraft, person, or any other source of initial SAR case information. In these instances, ALL appropriate identifying information should be obtained.

D.1.g. Additional Location Information

After the nature of the incident has been completely established, additional information about the location should be gathered:

- If the vessel is underway, find out its course, speed and intended destination.
- If the vessel is disabled and drifting freely, ask for the direction they are being set and how fast they are moving.
- If the vessel is anchored or aground, determine if the vessel's position is steady or if they are dragging anchor or being set further aground.
- Always ask for updated position reports until the SRU arrives on scene.

NOTE It is important to have all people onboard ALL vessels don their PFDs as soon as possible.

D.2. Additional SAR Information

Besides recording the SAR information described above, certain additional information is extremely valuable. Information in this category includes:

- Medical data.
- On-scene weather data.
- Overdue data.
- All radio frequencies the vessel can use or monitor, or cellular telephone/pager number if used.

D.2.a. Medical Data

If medical assistance is required, as much of the following additional information should be collected and recorded as possible. Checklists containing complete lists of information to collect can be found in the district OPLAN or SOP and should be used to avoid missing key information. Addition information includes:

- Patient's name, nationality, age, and sex.
- Patient's symptoms and vital signs.
- All medication given to patient.
- All medication available aboard the vessel.

D.2.b. On-Scene Weather

Additional weather information can be useful. The weather on scene may differ from the weather at the dispatcher's location. On-scene weather information is important in determining:

- Type of SRU best suited to respond.
- Datum (the probable location of the distressed vessel).
- Emergency phase.

D.2.c. Overdues

Some reports received will involve people or vessels that are overdue at some location, but no distress will be evident at that time. Information collected at the time of the initial report may prove invaluable later if a search planning effort is begun.

D.2.d. Gathering Data

Gathering the following type of data will avoid possible delays if the person or vessel does not arrive at the destination and further action is required. Sometimes it becomes difficult to reestablish contact with the reporting source to gather additional information when that information is needed. Data collection includes:

- Period of time the vessel has been overdue.
- Vessel's departure point and intended destination.
- Places the vessel planned to stop during transit.
- Navigation equipment aboard the vessel.
- Survival equipment aboard the vessel.
- Number of people aboard the vessel as well as their names, ages, sex, and general health.
- Personal habits of the people aboard the vessel (e.g., dependability, reliability, etc.).
- License plate number and description of the towing vehicle and trailer, if the boat was trailered to the departure point.
- Communications equipment onboard including radio frequencies monitored.
- Additional points of contact.
- Pending commitments (work, appointments, etc.).

Section E. Search Planning

Introduction

Before SRUs are dispatched, careful planning is needed to accurately determine the area where the survivors are or will be located when the boat arrives on scene. Good SAR planning significantly increases the probability of successfully locating and rescuing those in distress. Planning the search involves calculating datum and then outlining the boundaries of the search area. Most search planning is done by the RCC or the Group OPCEN and results in a search action plan. The boat crew then conducts SAR operations based on this search action plan. However, there may be times when the boat crew will have to do basic search planning. Search planning also includes risk management to determine what response, if any, is appropriate and which resources are the right ones to respond.

For more information on search planning, calculation of datum, and the forces that affect datum see the *U.S. Coast Guard Addendum to the United States National Search and Rescue Supplement (NSS) to the International Aeronautical and Maritime Search and Rescue Manual*, COMDTINST M16130.2 (series).

In this section

This section contains the following information:

Datum

E.1. Description

The term "datum" refers to the most probable location of the distressed vessel, corrected for drift over a given period of time. Depending on the information available and its accuracy, datum may be:

- A point.
- A line.
- An area.

As the case develops, datum must be corrected to account for wind and current. Datum is established by the SMC or OSC.

E.2. Datum Point

The datum point is defined as a point at the center of the area where it is estimated that the search object is most likely located.

E.3. Datum Line

If the location of a distressed boat cannot be pinpointed, its intended trackline or a line of bearing may be able to be determined. The datum line is the intended trackline or line of bearing plotted on the chart. Without more information, it is assumed that the distressed vessel may be anywhere along the length of the plot.

The line could also be obtained by using electronic radio direction finding equipment. One direction finder will give one bearing or LOP. If multiple radio direction finders are used, multiple LOPs can be obtained giving a more accurate position.

E.4. Datum Area

When either the exact position of the distress or a datum line cannot be determined, a datum area is developed based on many factors, but including as a minimum:

- Fuel endurance of the vessel in distress.
- Vessel's maximum cruising range.
- Wind and currents which affect the search object.
- Operator's intentions.

E.5. Forces Affecting Datum

As time progresses, datum must be corrected to compensate for the effects of wind, seas, and current. Some of the many natural forces that affect a search object are listed below.

E.5.a. Leeway

Leeway is the movement of a search object through the water. Leeway is caused by local winds blowing against the exposed surface of the vessel.

E.5.b. Local Wind Driven Current

Wind blowing over the water's surface tends to push the water along in the same direction the wind is blowing. This wind current affects the movement of a search object in open waters. Wind-driven current may not be a factor when searching in coastal waters, small lakes, rivers, or harbors because nearby landmasses may block or reduce the effect of wind.

E.5.c. Sea Current

Sea current refers to the movements of water in the open sea.

E.5.d. Tidal Current

The rising and falling of tides cause tidal current.

E.5.e. River Current — The flow of water in a river is called river current. These currents can quickly move a search object over a long distance. This should be considered in rivers or at the mouth of a large river.

NOTE Drift, in search planning, is the movement of a search object caused by all of the environmental forces.

Self Locating Datum Marker Buoy (SLDMB)

E.6. Description — The SLDMB is an oceanographic drifter that provides near real-time surface current data to Coast Guard Search and Rescue (SAR) controllers. The SLDMB System consists of the buoys **(Figure 15-3)** themselves plus the hardware and software to receive, decode, and display buoy positions for Web-based users and database administrators. Although the SLDMB is intended for SAR missions, it may be used to support other missions as well.

NOTE

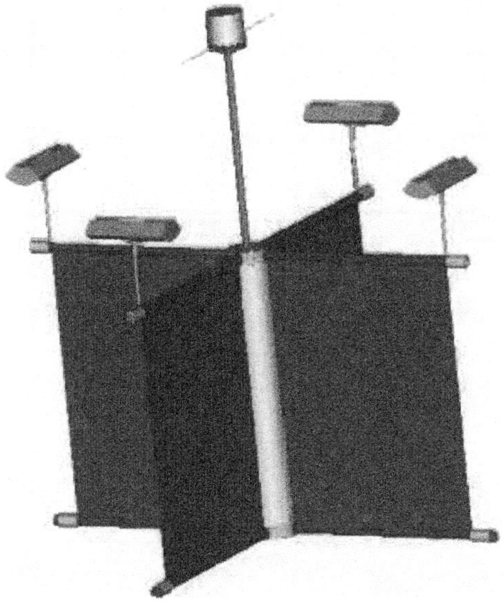

Figure 15-3
Deployed SLDMB (METOCEAN)

E.7 Deployment — SMC is the primary authority for directing the deployment of the SLDMB. They will provide the SRU with the deployment location. The SRU will pass the location, time and Argos ID to SMC immediately after deployment. A step-by-step tutorial can be found at: http://sldmb.osc.uscg mil/DataRequest/TrainingAids.aspx

E.8 Operation — The SLDMB transmits positions to a satellite every 15 minutes for the first two hours and every 30 minutes thereafter. No maintenance is required.

Search Area Description

E.9. Description

The search area is a geographic area determined by the SMC as most likely to contain the search object. The amount of error inherent in drift calculations and navigational capabilities of both the distressed craft and the SRU are used to calculate a search radius.

NOTE

When response times are short, the SMC may use a standard radius, adjusted for physical surroundings. When a search can begin in less than six hours, a six-mile radius around a datum adjusted for drift is usually large enough to include most search objects.

E.10. Methods

Search areas may be described by many methods, including the following:

E.10.a. Corner Point

In the corner point method, the latitude and longitude (or geographic features) of each corner of the search area are given. (see **Figure 15-4**)

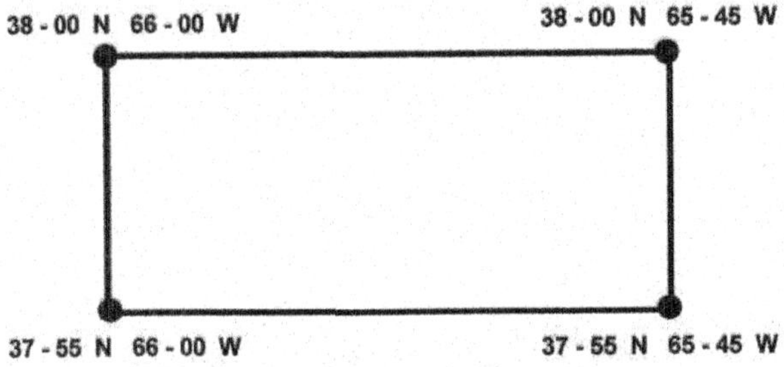

Figure 15-4
Corner Point

E.10.b. Trackline

In the trackline method, the latitude and longitude of the departure point, turn points, and destination point are given with a specific width along the track. (see **Figure 15-5**)

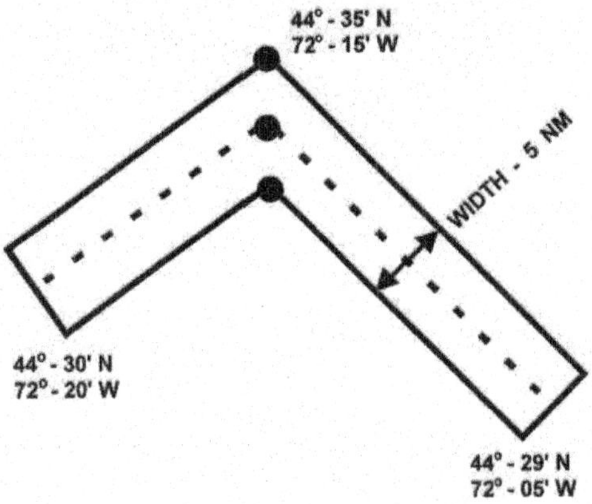

Figure 15-5
Trackline

E.10.c. Center Point (Circle)

In the center point (circle) method, the latitude and longitude of datum are given along with a radius around datum. (see **Figure 15-6**)

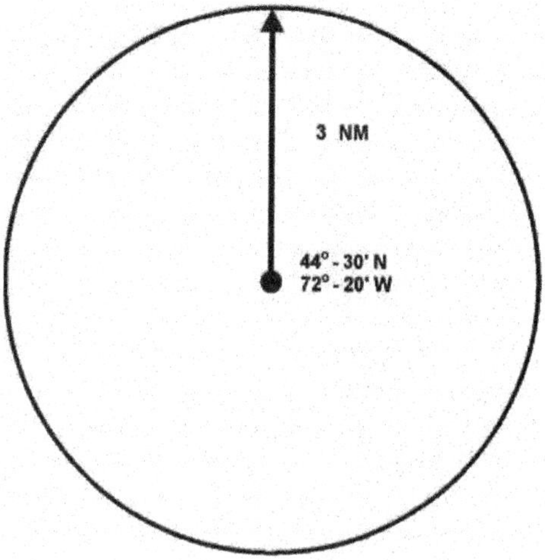

Figure 15-6
Center Point (Circle)

E.10.d. Center Point (Rectangle)

In the center point (rectangle) method, the latitude and longitude of datum are given with the direction of major (longer) axis plus the length and width of the area. (see **Figure 15-7**)

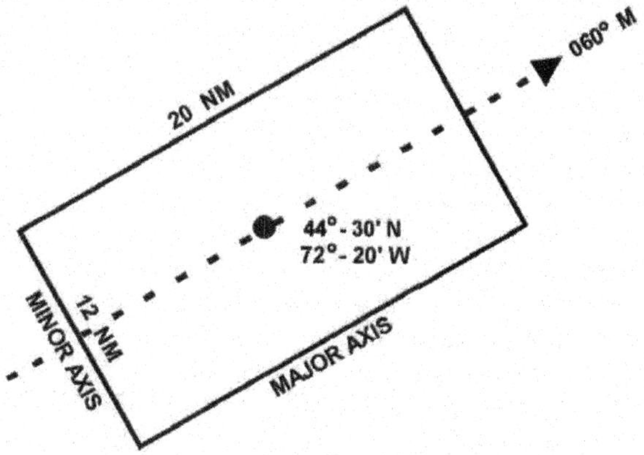

Figure 15-7
Center Point (Rectangle)

E.10.e. Center Point-(Landmark) (Rectangle, Bearing & Distance)

In the center point (landmark) method, the center point, or datum, may also be designated by a bearing and distance from some geographic landmark. (see **Figure 15-8**)

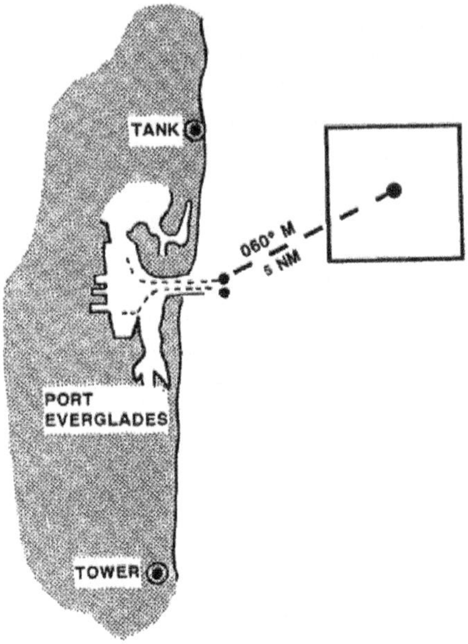

Figure 15-8
Center Point (Landmark) (Rectangle, Bearing & Distance)

E.10 f. Landmark Boundaries	Two or more landmarks are given as boundaries of the search area along a shoreline. (see **Figure 15-9**)

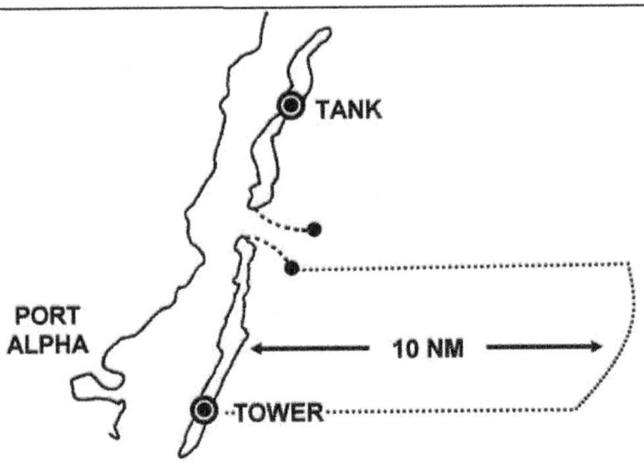

Figure 15-9
Landmark Boundaries

Search Area Coverage

E.11. Description

Search area coverage considers the area to be searched and the SRUs available to search. Once the search area has been determined and the search patterns selected, the next step is to have SRUs conduct the search. Based on the sweep width, an SRU will be assigned its own part of the overall areas to search. Essentially, the boat will start at an assigned commence search point (CSP), steer the track (search leg), and search (sweep down) on both sides of the boat.

E.12. Sweep Width (W)

Sweep width is a distance measured on both sides of an SRU. A sweep width of one mile means ½ mile to starboard and ½ mile to port for a total "width" of one mile. Sweep width is determined by:

- Search object type, size, and construction.
- Environmental conditions.
- Sensor (e.g., visual or radar).

E.13. Track Spacing (S)

Track spacing is the distance between adjacent parallel legs within a search area. These tracks may be the result of successive sweeps conducted by a single SRU or conducted simultaneously by multiple units separated by fixed intervals. Most of the search patterns described in this chapter consist of equally spaced, parallel search legs (tracks). The distance between adjacent search legs is called the track spacing (S). The best track spacing is a distance that permits maximum expectation of search object detection in the shortest period of time.

E.14. Commence Search Point (CSP)

The CSP is a point normally specified by the SMC for an SRU to begin its search pattern.

Search Patterns

E.15. Description

Once a search area has been determined, a systematic search for the object must be planned. Which is the best search pattern to use?

E.16. Considerations

The following should be considered to determine which search pattern to use:

- Weather conditions.
- Size of search area.
- Size of search object.
- Number of search units involved.
- Search area location.
- Time limitations.

E.17. Search Pattern Designation

Search patterns are designated by letters. The first letter indicates the general pattern group:

- T = Trackline
- C = Creeping line
- P = Parallel
- V = Sector
- S = Square

The second letter indicates the number of search units:

- S = Single-unit search
- M = Multi-unit search

The third letter indicates specialized SRU patterns or instructions, for example:

- R = Return
- N = Non-return

E.18. Types of Search Patterns

The most common types of search patterns are discussed below. Detailed descriptions of each pattern are available in the *U.S. Coast Guard Addendum to the United States National Search and Rescue Supplement (NSS) to the International Aeronautical and Maritime Search and Rescue Manual*, COMDTINST M16130.2 (series).

E.18.a. Square (S) Pattern

The Square Search (S) pattern is used when the last known position of a search object has a high degree of accuracy, the search area is small, and a concentrated search is desirable. Square patterns are good for man overboard (MOB) searches.

- Square Single-Unit (SS): In the SS pattern for boats, the first leg is normally in the direction of the search object's drift and all turns are made 90° to starboard. (see **Figure 15-10**)

- Square Multi-Unit (SM): The SM pattern is used when two units are available. The second unit begins on a course 45° to the right of the first unit's course. (see **Figure 15-11**)

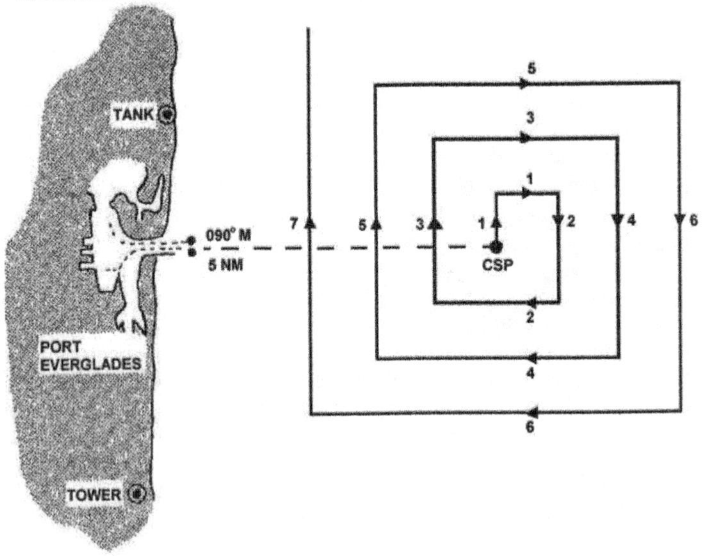

Figure 15-10
Square Single-Unit (SS)

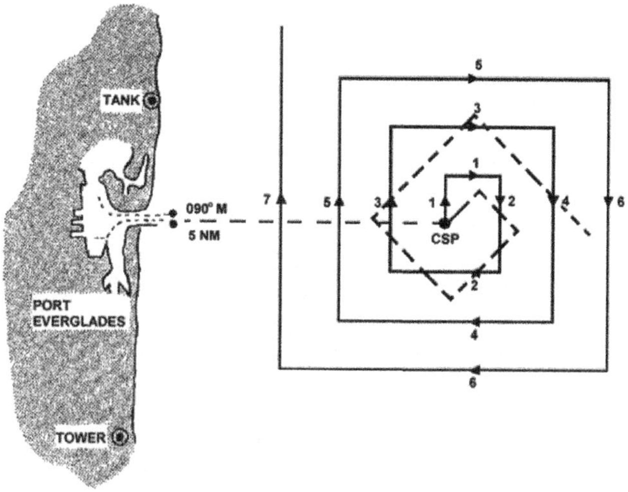

Figure 15-11
Square Multi-Unit (SM)

E.18.b. Sector (V) Patterns

Sector search patterns are used when datum is established with a high degree of confidence but the search object is difficult to detect, such as a person-in-the-water. The search unit passes through datum several times, each time increasing the chances of finding the search object. The pattern resembles the spokes of a wheel with the center of the wheel at datum. Datum should be marked by the first SRU on scene with a Data Marker Buoy (DMB) or other floating object. By marking the center of the search pattern, the coxswain has a navigation check each time the boat passes near the center of the search area (datum). This pattern consists of nine legs. There are two types of sector search patterns.

- Sector Single-Unit (VS): The VS pattern is used by a single boat. The first leg begins in the same direction that the search object is drifting toward. All legs and cross legs of this pattern are of equal length. After running the first leg, the first turn will be 120° to starboard to begin the first cross leg. All subsequent turns will be 120° to starboard to a course determined by adding 120° to the previous course. Every third leg (3rd, 6th, 9th) will start out 120° to the right of your cross leg, but once sighted, you will steer on the DMB. Once you reach the DMB, return to the original course you steered when you started your third leg.

EXAMPLE: Drift is towards the North (000°). A DMB is released at CSP. The vessel then proceeds in the direction of drift (000°). At the end of the first leg, the vessel turns to the starboard 120° and starts the second leg of the search. At the end of the second leg, the vessel again turns to the starboard 120° (now 240°) starting its third leg proceeding back towards the DMB. Once the DMB is sighted, **the vessel will steer for the marker regardless of the course required to intercept** (possibly 245° with the Northern drift). Once the vessel reaches the DMB it returns to the original starting course for the third leg (240°) and starts the fourth leg of the search repeating the same process as the last three legs. (see **Figure 15-12**)

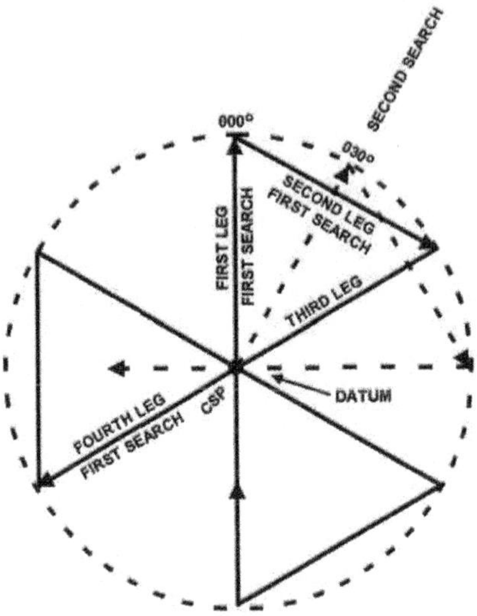

Figure 15-12
Sector Single-Unit (VS)

- Sector Multi-Unit (VM): The VM pattern is used when a second boat is available. The second boat starts at the same datum, but begins the first leg on a course 90° to the left of the first boat. The search is then the same as a VS pattern. The second boat should start the search at a slower speed than the first boat, if both boats start at the same time. When the first boat is one leg ahead of the second boat, the second boat accelerates to search speed. This slow start by the second boat will keep both boats from arriving at the center of the search pattern at the same time. (see **Figure 15-13**)

NOTE

Course and leg identifiers should be carried in each SRU to calculate courses and times for each expanding square and sector search pattern leg. The course and leg identifiers can be easily obtained through the federal stock system, Stock Number SN 7530-01-GF2-9010. (see **Figure 15-14** and **Figure 15-15**)

E.18.c. Parallel (P) Patterns

Parallel track patterns are used when there is an equal probability that the search object could be anywhere in the search area. It is a good pattern to use when the approximate location of the search object is known and uniform coverage is desired. Parallel track patterns are the simplest of the search patterns. Steer straight courses on all legs. Each leg is one-track spacing from the other. The legs are parallel to the long side or major axis of the search area. There are two types of parallel track patterns.

The CSP for parallel patterns is located at a point ½ of the distance selected as the search track spacing inside a corner of the search area. The first and last search legs then run ½-track spacing inside the search area boundaries. This prevents excessive duplicate coverage, eliminates the possibility of leaving an unsearched track at the search area boundary, and gives SRUs in adjacent search areas a margin of safety.

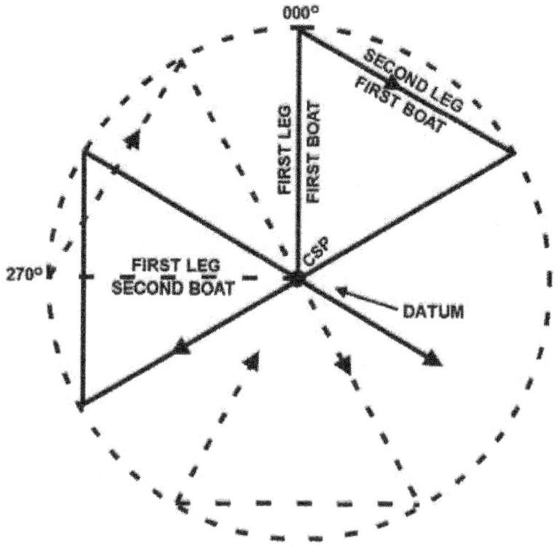

Figure 15-13
Sector Multi-Unit (VM)

E.18.c.1. Parallel Track Single-Unit (PS)	The Parallel Track Single-Unit (PS) pattern is conducted by a single SRU. The legs of the search are run parallel to the long side (major axis) of the search area. (see **Figure 15-16**)
E.18.c.2. Parallel Track Multi-Unit (PM)	The Parallel Track Multi-Unit (PM) pattern is used under the same circumstances as the (PS) but with more than one SRU. (see **Figure 15-17**) The SRUs are separated by a single-track spacing. They search parallel to the long side of the search area. After completing the first search leg, they move over a distance equal to the track spacing times the number of SRUs, and then search back on the reciprocal heading of the first leg.
E.18.d. Creeping Line Single-Unit (CS)	The Creeping Line Single-Unit (CS) pattern is used when the probable location of the search object has been determined to be more likely at one end of the search area than at the other end. Creeping line search patterns are the same as parallel patterns with the exception that the legs are run parallel to the short side (minor axis) of the search area. This pattern's CSP and search legs are also located ½-track spacing inside the search area. (see **Figure 15-18**)
E.18.e. Trackline Single-Unit No Return (TSN) and Trackline Single-Unit Return (TSR)	The Trackline search patterns are used when the only information available on the missing vessel is the intended track. The Trackline Single-Unit No Return (TSN) search follows directly along the intended track of the missing vessel while the Trackline Single-Unit Return (TSR) search course is laid out one-half track space to both sides of the intended track of the missing vessel. (see **Figure 15-19**)
NOTE	In darkness or extremely low visibility, surface search vessels should periodically stop their engines at selected points in the search area and conduct a listening search for a short period of time, then return to covering their assigned search area.

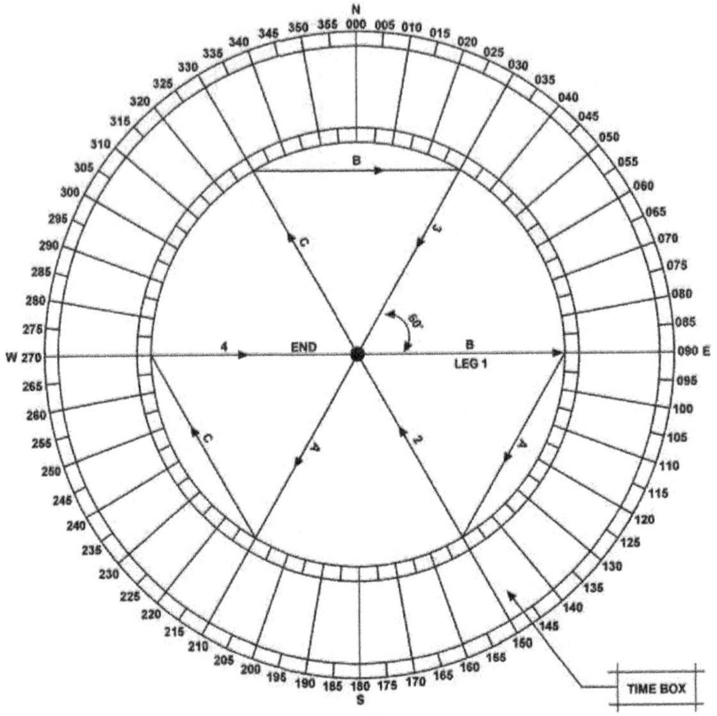

COURSE AND LEG IDENTIFIER FOR SECTOR SEARCH PATTERNS - (VS) - 60° CENTRAL ANGLES

TIME AND DISTANCE TABLE

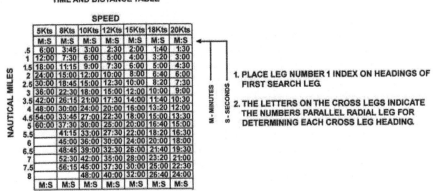

NAUTICAL MILES	SPEED 5Kts	8Kts	10Kts	12Kts	15Kts	18Kts	20Kts
	M:S	M:S	M:S	M:S	M:S	M:S	M:S
.5	6:00	3:45	3:00	2:30	2:00	1:40	1:30
1	12:00	7:30	6:00	5:00	4:00	3:20	3:00
1.5	18:00	11:15	9:00	7:30	6:00	5:00	4:30
2	24:00	15:00	12:00	10:00	8:00	6:40	6:00
2.5	30:00	18:45	15:00	12:30	10:00	8:20	7:30
3	36:00	22:30	18:00	15:00	12:00	10:00	9:00
3.5	42:00	26:15	21:00	17:30	14:00	11:40	10:30
4	48:00	30:00	24:00	20:00	16:00	13:20	12:00
4.5	54:00	33:45	27:00	22:30	18:00	15:00	13:30
5	60:00	37:30	30:00	25:00	20:00	16:40	15:00
5.5		41:15	33:00	27:30	22:00	18:20	16:30
6		45:00	36:00	30:00	24:00	20:00	18:00
6.5		48:45	39:00	32:30	26:00	21:40	19:30
7		52:30	42:00	35:00	28:00	23:20	21:00
7.5		56:15	45:00	37:30	30:00	25:00	22:30
8			48:00	40:00	32:00	26:40	24:00
	M:S	M:S	M:S	M:S	M:S	M:S	M:S

M - MINUTES
S - SECONDS

1. PLACE LEG NUMBER 1 INDEX ON HEADINGS OF FIRST SEARCH LEG.
2. THE LETTERS ON THE CROSS LEGS INDICATE THE NUMBERS PARALLEL RADIAL LEG FOR DETERMINING EACH CROSS LEG HEADING.

Figure 15-14
Course and Leg Identifier for Sector Search Patterns

CH-1

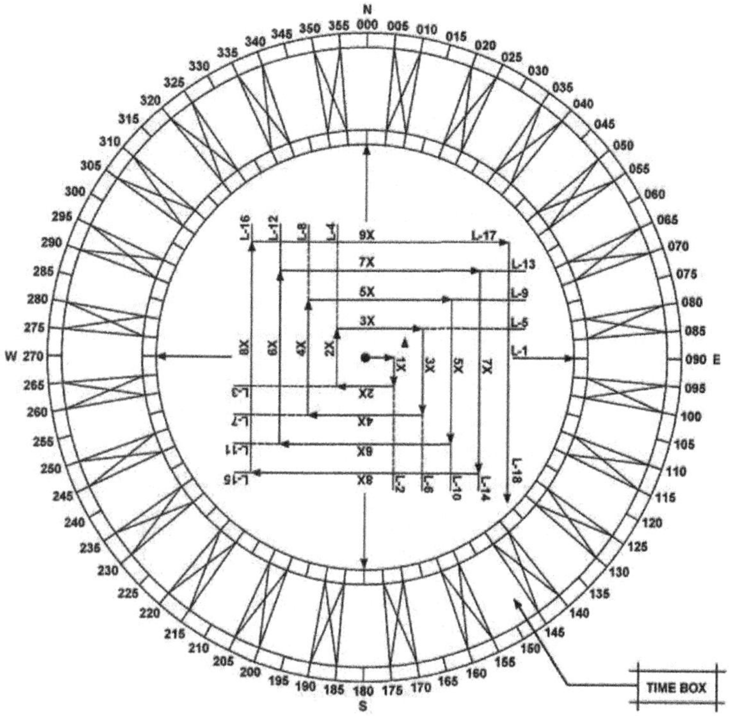

COURSE AND LEG IDENTIFIER FOR EXPANDING SQUARE PATTERN - (SS)

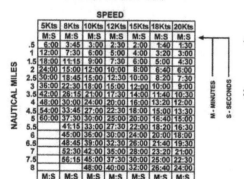

TIME AND DISTANCE TABLE

SPEED

NAUTICAL MILES	5Kts	8Kts	10Kts	12Kts	15Kts	18Kts	20Kts
	M:S	M:S	M:S	M:S	M:S	M:S	M:S
.5	6:00	3:45	3:00	2:30	2:00	1:40	1:30
1	12:00	7:30	6:00	5:00	4:00	3:20	3:00
1.5	18:00	11:15	9:00	7:30	6:00	5:00	4:30
2	24:00	15:00	12:00	10:00	8:00	6:40	6:00
2.5	30:00	18:45	15:00	12:30	10:00	8:20	7:30
3	36:00	22:30	18:00	15:00	12:00	10:00	9:00
3.5	42:00	26:15	21:00	17:30	14:00	11:40	10:30
4	48:00	30:00	24:00	20:00	16:00	13:20	12:00
4.5	54:00	33:45	27:00	22:30	18:00	15:00	13:30
5	60:00	37:30	30:00	25:00	20:00	16:40	15:00
5.5		41:15	33:00	27:30	22:00	18:20	16:30
6		45:00	36:00	30:00	24:00	20:00	18:00
6.5		48:45	39:00	32:30	26:00	21:40	19:30
7		52:30	42:00	35:00	28:00	23:20	21:00
7.5		56:15	45:00	37:30	30:00	25:00	22:30
8			48:00	40:00	32:00	26:40	24:00
	M:S	M:S	M:S	M:S	M:S	M:S	M:S

M - MINUTES

S - SECONDS

1. PLACE INDEX (ARROW NUMBER 1) ON HEADING OF FIRST SEARCH LEG. HEADINGS OF ALL LEGS ARE SHOWN BY THE CORRESPONDING PARALLEL INDEX ARROWS.
2. RECORD TIME TO TURN IN THE TIME BOX FOR EACH LEG. LEG NUMBERS ARE SHOWN ON LEG EXTENSION LINES.

Figure 15-15
Course and Leg Identifier for Expanding Square Pattern

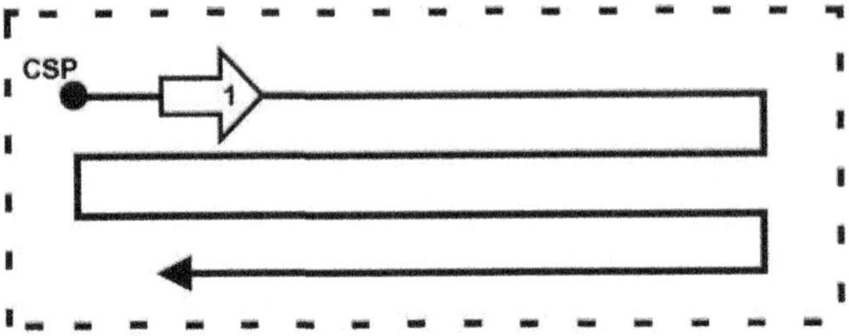

Figure 15-16
Parallel Track Single-Unit (PS)

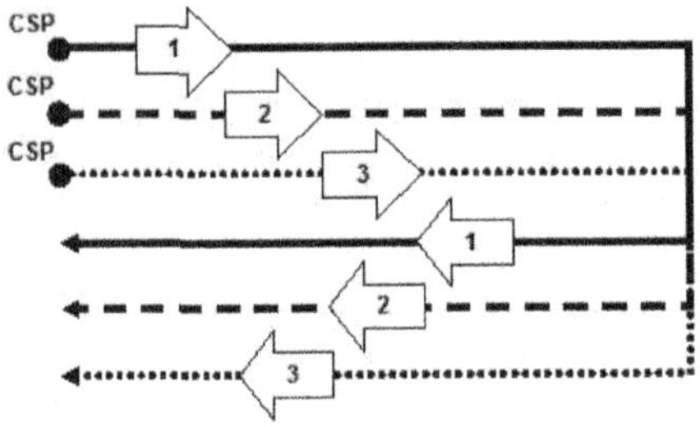

Figure 15-17
Parallel Track Multi-Unit (PM)

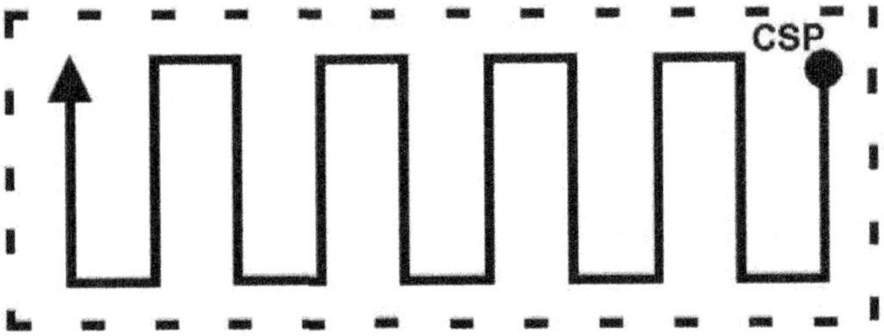

Figure 15-18
Creeping Line Single-Unit (CS)

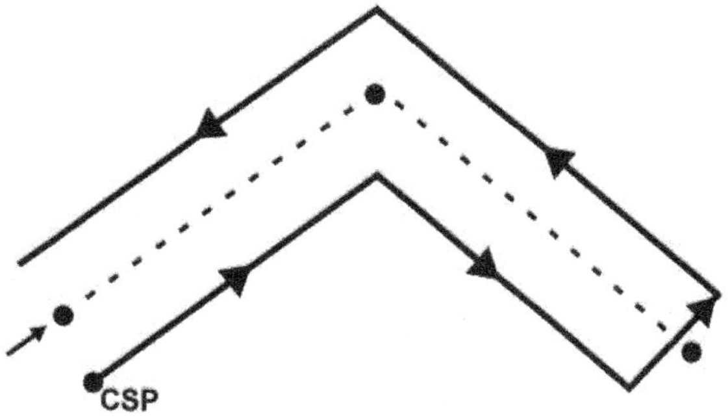

Figure 15-19
Trackline Single-Unit Return (TSR)

E.18 f. Barrier

The barrier pattern is used in areas with strong current, such as a river. The search lies along the path of the current. The boat moves back and forth over the same track. This can be done by steering on an object on each side of the riverbank. The boat moves from one side of the search area to the other while the current carries the water and objects past the search barrier.

Since river currents can vary across the width of a river, a more effective barrier might be established by forming a line abreast. This is done by placing observers on each bank and a boat in the area of swiftest current station keeping between the observers onshore. Additional boats, if available, could be added to the line abreast to reduce the effective track spacing and increase the effective coverage. This technique produces a more effective and predictable barrier.

Initial Response

E.19. Search Patterns and Actions to be Used

The simplified patterns and initial search actions recommended in the coastal search planning section for coastal incidents in the *U.S. Coast Guard Addendum to the United States National Search and Rescue Supplement (NSS) to the International Aeronautical and Maritime Search and Rescue Manual, COMDTINST M16130.2 (series)* are to be used when an SRU arrives on scene and the object of the SAR incident is not initially seen or located. The following patterns and initial search actions are to be used until a complete search plan has been developed by the SMC.

E.20. SRU Actions

Whenever a case occurs which has an SRU on scene and the object of the distress is not immediately seen or located, report the situation to the SMC by the quickest means possible. The SMC will immediately start planning and then develop a search action plan of the SRU. In the meantime, the SRU shall be conducting either an expanding square or sector search using a search radius of 6 NM.

E.21. Initial Response Search Area

If the search object is not located upon arriving on scene, the SRU is to assume it is adrift if the distressed boat did not indicate it was at anchor.

Step	Procedure
1	Draw a circle with a 6 NM radius cantered at the last known position (LKP). If drift is considered to be significant, the SRU should estimate the drift based on local knowledge/on-scene conditions, and center the 6 NM circle on the drifted LKP.
2	Communicate and confirm the new datum with the SMC. Remember that the time of datum must take into consideration the underway transit times for the SRU.
3	Next draw the search pattern within the tangent of the circle. Datum for the search is the CSP. Refer to E.23.c of this section for information regarding track spacing.
4	Orient the search area in the same direction of drift, that is, in the same direction as the total drift vector. (see **Figure 15-20** and **Figure 15-21**)

If the reported position of the distressed craft is in shallow water, it could be at anchor, and a search down the drift line may be appropriate.

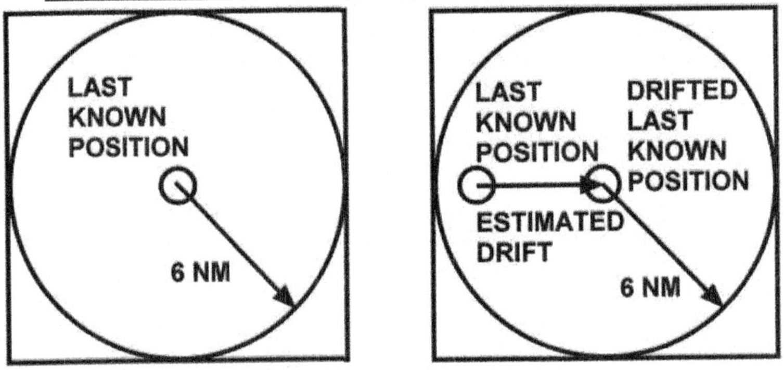

Figure 15-20
Initial Response Search Area

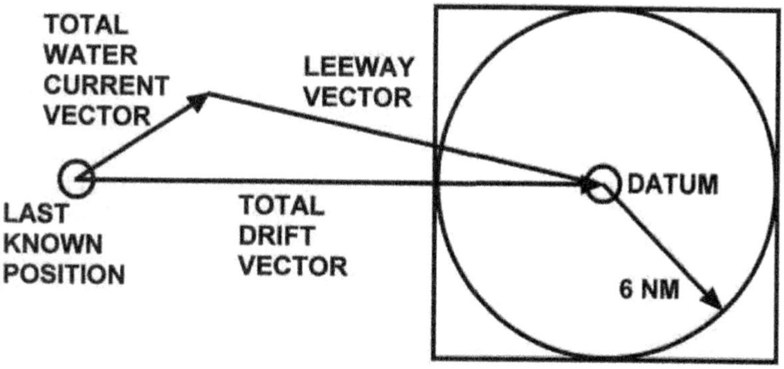

Figure 15-21
Vessel Adrift

E.22. Keeping the SMC Updated

The SRU shall also keep the SMC constantly updated on conditions, findings, and when nearing completion of initial response search. This direction should not preclude an SRU from using an alternate search pattern or area when it is clearly not practical (e.g., narrow waterway or other physical barrier).

E.23 Appropriate Search Pattern

The re-established operations and search procedures for the first SRU on scene should be to immediately report the on-scene conditions and findings to the Station or SMC. Next, the appropriate search pattern should begin.

E.23.a. Surface SRUs

Usually an expanding square (SS) is used. This is because it concentrates the search closer to datum and usually there will only be a short period of time on the initial response before the SMC gives direction and information for conducting and starting a first search. If the search area is confined or there is reason to have a high degree of confidence for the selected datum (e.g., debris found), the surface SRU may use a sector search (VS). Other search patterns may be used as appropriate.

E.23.b. Helicopter SRUs

Helicopters are a suitable platform to execute SS and VS pattern searches. Depending on the proximity to the coast and environmental conditions, a radius larger than 6 NM may be appropriate for a helicopter during the initial search due to a higher search speed.

E.23.c. Initial Track Spacing

Track spacing for the initial response search by surface or helicopter SRUs can be determined by using the following:

Search Object	Good Conditions Wind < 14 kits Seas < 3 ft	Poor Conditions Wind > 15 kits Seas > 3 ft
PIW	0.1*	0.1*
< 15 ft	0.5	0.2
> 15 ft	1.0	1.0

* > 0.1 up to SRUs minimum ability to navigate

CH-1

Section F. Search Preparations

Introduction

Before beginning a search, all available facts about a case must be collected. The SMC should provide most of this information as the search action plan. The checklist below will help determine whether everything needed to begin a mission is available. Once all available facts are collected and the required search planning is performed, the mission is ready to get underway.

NOTE

In an emergency, this information can be passed to the boat crew while en route to a search area.

F.1. Questions

Answers to the following questions will help determine if everything has been accomplished before getting underway:

- What is the object of this search?
- How many people are involved?
- What are the circumstances of their distress?
- What is the assigned search area?
- What search pattern will be used?
- What is the desired search speed?
- What special equipment is required?
- What radio frequencies will be used?
- Are all required charts aboard?
- What are the weather and sea conditions?
- Who is the OSC?
- What unusual circumstances may be encountered? How will they be corrected for?
- What does the vessel in distress have for survival equipment?
- What radio frequencies will they use?
- Are other units assigned? If so:
  - What kind?
  - What are their search areas?
  - What are their search speeds?
  - What search patterns will they employ?

F.2. Briefing Crew

Crewmembers will be briefed before getting underway. Make sure all crewmembers:

- Understand the mission.
- Know what they are looking for.
- Know where the search will be conducted.
- Understand how the search will be conducted.

Section G. Conducting a Search

Introduction

It is critical that an SRU perform all duties assigned in a correct and predictable fashion. In this case, the term SRU includes the vessel, crew, and equipment. Search planners, OSCs, SMCs, and others all make plans based on assumptions they have made. These assumptions are considered when making decisions that could have life and death consequences for someone who may be the object of a major Coast Guard search effort. One assumption made by SAR planners is that the SRU, its crew, and equipment all perform as planned, completing all missions assigned unless advised otherwise.

G.1. Failing a Mission

In some instances, however, SRUs have failed to properly complete their assigned mission. Reasons may include not having proper equipment onboard, or a crewmember not fully prepared, trained, or qualified, or a failure to complete some task. There have been instances when an SRU failed to fully search an assigned area or, due to careless navigation, failed to search in the area assigned. Actual searches and rescues are typically carried out when conditions are at their worst, making even simple and routine tasks extremely difficult. Accurate navigation, observant lookouts, and trained and knowledgeable crewmembers can make the difference between successful cases and disasters.

G.2. Professionalism

All effort expended to carefully gather key information, to plan the most effective search, or to select exactly the right SRU is wasted, if the SRU performing the search or rescue fails to do so in a professional manner to the best of its ability. If not able to complete the search (e.g., equipment failure, poor visibility, or worsening weather), the SMC should be advised of the areas that were searched.

This page intentionally left blank.

Chapter 16
Person-in-the-Water Recovery

Introduction

"MAN OVERBOARD!" is one of the worst alarms to hear while underway. Decisive action is of primary importance when a person falls overboard. Even the best swimmers can become disoriented when unexpectedly falling into the water. Prolonged exposure to rough seas or cold weather can quickly weaken a swimmer. This chapter addresses man overboard (MOB) and person-in-the-water (PIW) recovery procedures, as well as water survival skills. Lives depend on every crewmember performing these procedures competently and effectively.

In this chapter

This chapter contains the following sections:

WARNING

The wearing of jewelry, including rings, wristwatches, necklaces or other items not consisting of organizational clothing, PPE, or uniform articles by boat crew members engaged in hoisting, towing, or other deck evolutions where the potential for snagging exists **is prohibited**. OICs and coxswains will address this during all pre-underway briefs and coxswains shall ensure jewelry is removed prior to beginning all deck evolutions.

Section A. Recovery Methods

Introduction

All crewmembers must be prepared when someone falls overboard. Rehearsing how to react is vital to a successful and safe recovery of the individual. When someone falls overboard, crewmembers should always assume the worst has happened. The person could be suffering from shock, may be unconscious, and possibly injured. Rapid recovery of the person is a must.

The information here is a general guideline. Actual situations will vary and all details pertaining to each are beyond the scope of this publication. A professional understands and rehearses each possibility remembering that the key to a successful rescue is preparation, practice, and alertness.

In this section

This section contains the following information:

General Man Overboard Procedure

A.1. Description

The action taken in the first few seconds after a crewmember falls overboard decides the success of the recovery. An alert crewmember can do much to save the life of someone who might otherwise drown. First actions should be swift and certain.

A.2. Prevention

The first thing every crewmember needs to learn about recovering a person-in-the-water is how to prevent it in the first place. It is every crewmember's responsibility to protect themselves and their fellow crewmembers from falling overboard. Some things to pay particular attention to are:

- Ensure lifelines are up and in good condition.
- Keep decks clear of trip/slip hazards.
- Repair/replace cracked or damaged stanchions.
- Ensure two persons are used when conducting an evolution that might result in falling overboard (anchoring, towing, etc.).
- Ensure safety belts are worn during inclement weather.

Another important piece to the safety of the crew is ensuring that everyone onboard is wearing appropriate PPE. If someone should fall overboard, proper PPE will keep him or her afloat if unconscious, prolong exposure time in the water, and provide signaling devices that will assist rescuers in locating the person.

NOTE More information concerning PPE can be found in *Chapter 6* of this Manual and the *Rescue and Survival Systems Manual*, COMDTINST M10470.10 (series).

A.3. First Sighting

If a person enters the water, the first crewmember to realize that someone has fallen overboard should follow these procedures:

Step	Procedure
1	Spread the alarm in a loud voice by repeatedly calling out, "MAN OVERBOARD!" It is also very important to shout out the location the person fell overboard (port/starboard side, the bow, the stern) For example, if the person fell over the port side, the alarm should be, "MAN OVERBOARD, PORT SIDE!"
2	Maintain sight of, and continuously point (open handed) to the individual in the water while carefully moving to a position in sight of the coxswain or operator. Give clear, loud verbal directions as well as the condition of the PIW (conscious/unconscious, injured, etc.) to the coxswain.
3	If crewmember loses sight of the PIW at anytime, throw a ring buoy with strobe light (or anything that floats) over the side as quickly as possible.

A.4. Coxswain or Operator Actions

Once the alarm has been sounded, the coxswain has several tasks to complete in order to successfully recover the PIW. Though a quick recovery is preferred, at times it is better to slow down, assess the situation, and ensure everything is done properly the first time. Not every MOB/PIW recovery is the same. It is always better to make a correct approach slowly and recover the person on the first attempt rather than an incorrect fast approach resulting in the need for a second try.

There is no single correct order in which the steps below should be executed. Everything depends on the situation at hand. Starting a turn to maneuver back to the PIW is a common first step, but if boat traffic in the area is heavy, turning the vessel might endanger others. Each task is important in its own way and needs to be conducted to ensure a successful recovery.

NOTE Remember…assess the situation before rushing to action!

WARNING

Increasing speed during the recovery turn is not always the best maneuver! A sudden burst of speed or a rougher ride from going faster through the water can make for an unstable platform. Instead of just one person in the water, there could end up being more.

CAUTION !

Always operate at a safe speed!

A.5. Maneuvering Boat to Recover PIW

If someone falls overboard, the boat may have to be maneuvered for a pickup. In most cases, it starts by turning in the same direction the person fell overboard. Turning towards the same side the person fell overboard will "kick" the stern away preventing the propellers from injuring the PIW. If the person falls off the bow, the turn should be in either direction to kick the stern clear. If the person falls off the stern, in some cases, the eddy current located off the transom can hold the PIW tight against the stern. Applying additional power while turning sharply to either port or starboard will push the PIW clear.

In some cases, turning the boat is not possible due to vessel traffic or a narrow channel. In these cases, slowing down and stopping are other options. Once the boat has stopped, the PIW may swim back towards the boat for recovery or after slowing to bare steerageway, spin the boat around and recover the PIW.

An increase in speed is not necessary during the turn. Recovering the PIW as soon as possible is important, but sometimes an increase in speed by the coxswain will catch the remaining crewmembers off guard and possibly eject them from the boat. If operating at high speed when the MOB takes place, it might be best to slow down before starting a maneuver. The coxswain should carry out the turn at a safe speed to ensure a more stable platform for the recovery crew.

A.6. Mark Position

Another important step is to record the boat's position by pressing the appropriate button on the GPS receiver to mark the exact position (datum) of the distress electronically. This will give a position to return to if unable to locate the PIW and the search must be started.

All possible means must be used to identify the position (dead reckoning, visual landmarks, radar, etc.), if the vessel is not equipped with a LORAN-C or GPS receiver.

A.7. Alerting Boats in the General Vicinity

Sounding five or more short blasts on the sound signal, horn, or whistle alerts boats in the area that a danger exists (i.e., a MOB is occurring). Boats in the vicinity may not be aware of what the signal means but at least they will realize something unusual is happening.

A.8. Deploying a Flotation Device

If at anytime the crew loses sight of the PIW, the coxswain should ensure a ring buoy with strobe light (or anything that floats) is thrown over the side (see **Figure 16-1**). This flotation device will serve two purposes. First, the PIW may see the flotation device and be able to get to it increasing their chances of being located and providing additional flotation. Second, the ring buoy or any floating object thrown over the side (if a ring buoy is not available) serves as a reference point (datum) marking the general location of the incident and for maneuvering the boat during the search for the PIW."

CAUTION !

Do not throw the floatable object(s) directly at the PIW. It could cause injury if it hits the individual.

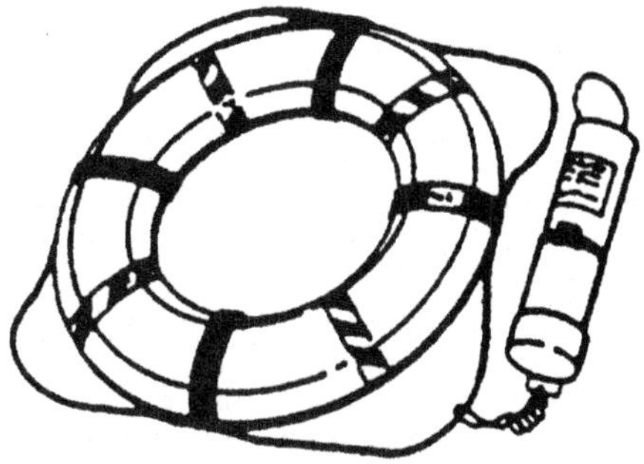

Figure 16-1
Ring Buoy with Strobe

A.9. Assigning Crew Duties

Upon hearing the initial "Man Overboard" alarm, the coxswain will assign duties to each crewmember as follows:

- A pointer will be positioned on or near the bow of the boat (if weather conditions permit). This will normally be the crewmember making the initial report. The pointer will maintain constant sight of the PIW and continually use their hand to indicate the location of the PIW. The pointer will also call out the physical condition of the PIW to affect an appropriate rescue attempt.
- A recovery/pick-up crewmember will be assigned to prepare a heaving line to be used in retrieving the PIW. If the PIW is reported to be unconscious, the recovery/pick-up crewmember will assist in dressing out and tending the surface swimmer. If at anytime the PIW can no longer be seen, the recovery/pick-up crewmember will be instructed to deploy a ring buoy with strobe light (or anything that floats) over the side.
- A surface swimmer will be made ready if needed, as well as another crewmember on the tending line to the surface swimmer's safety harness, whenever the swimmer is in the water.

NOTE

Review section A.33 of this chapter for important information regarding surface swimmers.

A.9.a. The Pointer

The pointer will visually search for the person overboard, and when located, will point to the person overboard at all times. The coxswain will guide on the pointer's hand signals in maneuvering the boat for the recovery approach.

The coxswain should ensure that the pointer is relieved of any other duties that could be distracting.

A.10. Crew Briefing

When the coxswain is ready to commence the recovery approach, he/she must brief the crew on how the recovery will be made and whether it will be accomplished on the port or starboard side. The approach will be influenced by:

- Wind.
- Sea/surf conditions.
- Maneuverability of the boat.
- Maneuvering space restriction.

CH-1

A.11. Informing the Operational Commander

When circumstances and time permit, the coxswain must notify the Operational Commander of the man overboard situation. This should be done as soon as possible after the occurrence.

A.12. PAN-PAN Broadcasts

If the person overboard has not been located and immediately recovered and assistance of other boats is needed, the emergency call signal Pan (pronounced *pahn*) should be transmitted in sets of two for three sets (PAN-PAN…PAN-PAN…PAN-PAN…) on channel 16 or 2182 kHz. This should be followed with the boat's identification, position, and a brief description of the situation. "Mayday" shall not be used. A boat uses a mayday call only when threatened by grave and imminent danger. After returning to datum and completing a quick scan of the area, if the PIW is not found, a datum marker (if one was not dropped initially) should be dropped and a search pattern commenced. The search should be continued until otherwise directed by the Operational Commander. More information concerning search patterns can be found in *Chapter 15, Search and Rescue* of this Manual.

A.13. Requesting Additional Assistance

Requests for additional assistance may be made to the Operational Commander by radio. Also, any craft near the scene may be requested by the coxswain to assist as needed.

A.14. Summary

The general PIW recovery procedures described below apply when an individual falls overboard from any boat. These procedures are in a sequence as it occurs in time:

Step	Procedure
1	Someone falls overboard.
2	The first crewmember to observe the incident calls out "MAN OVERBOARD" and follows this exclamation with the side from which the event occurred or the person was sighted; then maintains sight of and continuously points to the individual in the water.
3	Coxswain will perform the following tasks. The order depends on the situation at hand. Remember - slow down, assess the situation, and take action. • The coxswain turns the boat in the direction indicated in the alarm. Coxswain maintains a safe speed to ensure crew safety while setting up for recovery. • Position is recorded by depressing the LORAN-C or GPS receiver memory/man overboard button (if this equipment is on the boat). • Alert boats in the general vicinity by sounding 5 or more short blasts on whistle or horn. • Ensure a flotation device has been deployed if PIW is no longer visible.
4	The coxswain assigns crewmember duties: • The pointer (or first person to see the member go overboard) moves forward near a pilothouse window (weather permitting), locates the person overboard and points to the location of the person at all times. • The recovery crewmember makes preparation for the pickup.
5	The coxswain makes the recovery approach, briefs the crew on the recovery procedure including which side of the boat the pick-up will occur. Based on existing conditions, the coxswain will select either a leeward or a windward approach.
6	As soon as circumstances permit, coxswain informs Operational Commander of the situation.
7	If additional assistance required, request help from Operational Commander and boats in the vicinity. Issue "PAN-PAN" broadcast.

The Approach

A.15. Description

The coxswain must select an approach that is suitable for the existing conditions. There are two basic approaches:

- A leeward approach (against the wind and current).
- A windward approach (with the wind and current).

WARNING If the PIW does drift aft of the boat, do not back down to effect the recovery. The propeller could injure the person.

A.16. Leeward Approach

The leeward approach is performed with the bow facing into the greatest force of oncoming resistance at the time of pickup using the following procedures: (see **Figure 16-2**) This may be the wind, current, seas, or any combination of the three. There are times when the wind and current are from different directions.

Step	Procedure
1	Select the heading that will best ease the approach, and balance the effect of any swell that might be present.
2	Make the approach rapidly, but as the boat nears the person, reduce wake and slow the boat enough to stop headway with a short backing down burst. The PIW should be next to the recovery area on the boat and the boat should be DIW.
3	Place the engines in *neutral* and, when the person overboard is alongside, have a crewmember make the recovery.
4	For better control during the approach, try to make all pick-ups with your boat heading into the prevailing weather and sea conditions.
5	Take care not to overrun the person overboard or to have so much headway on that the boat drifts beyond the person overboard.
6	If the PIW does drift aft of the boat, do not back down to effect the recovery. The propeller could injure the person. The best course of action should the boat over shoot the PIW is to swing around and make another approach. It is best to make one correct approach slowly than several attempts quickly.

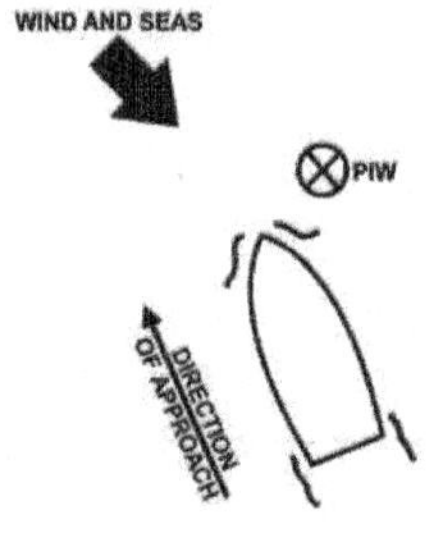

Figure 16-2
Leeward Approach

CH-1

A.17. Windward Approach

The windward approach (see **Figure 16-3**) is performed with the wind coming from behind the boat, when the person overboard is in a confined space, and a leeward approach is impossible. However, a situation where the boat cannot turn into the wind due to superstructure or bow sail area should be avoided. The following procedures should be used for a windward approach:

Step	Procedure
1	The operator must maneuver into a position upwind and up current from the person overboard.
2	Place the engine in neutral.
3	Drift down to the person
4	Ensure that the boat drifts so it places the person overboard along the "recovery" side, but do not allow the boat to drift over the person.

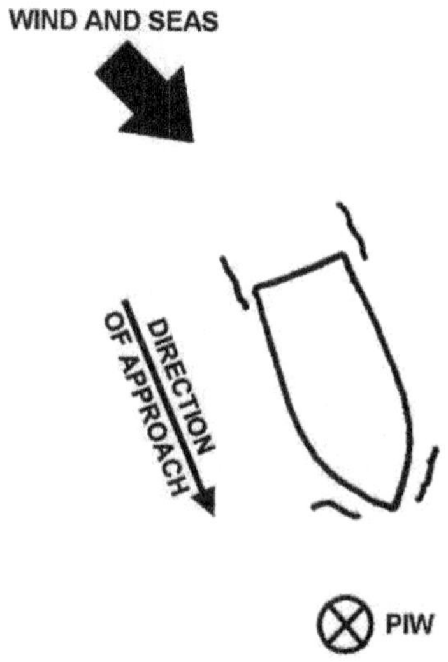

Figure 16-3
Windward Approach

A.18. Windward to Leeward of Multiple PIWs

Depending upon skill and experience, a combination of the windward and leeward approaches may be necessary. One instance may be in the case of recovering multiple PIWs. (see **Figure 16-4**)

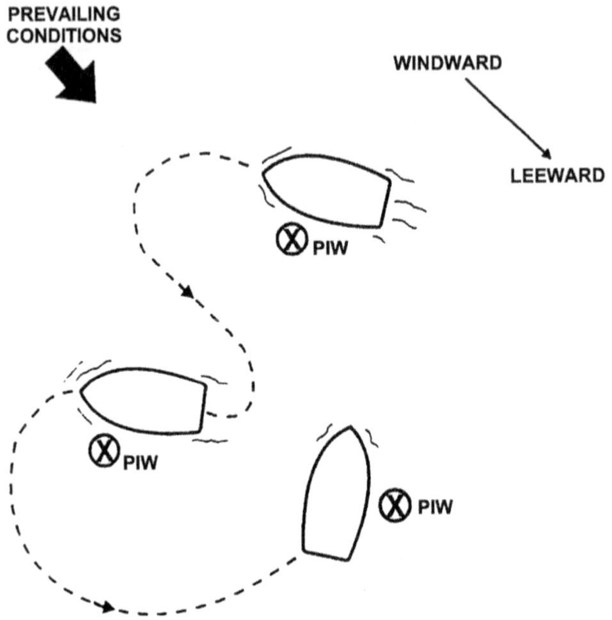

Figure 16-4
Windward to Leeward Approach of Multiple PIWs

A.19. Stopping Immediately

There may be instances when stopping the boat and allowing the person overboard to swim back to the boat, or at least to reach the tethered floating object, is the most appropriate action. This is effective especially if the boat can be stopped quickly after the person falls overboard. The coxswain should always ensure propellers are not engaged anytime someone is in the water near the stern of the vessel.

A.20. Stop, Pivot Return

Another option, particularly in a restricted waterway, is to stop, pivot/back and fill, then return to the PIW. The turning and backing characteristics of the boat and the prevailing wind and sea conditions will dictate how the approach is made. The coxswain will maneuver the boat to the weather side of the PIW so that the boat is set by the wind or seas toward the person rather than away.

A.21. Destroyer Turn

Except in a narrow channel, the coxswain should make the turn to the side that the person fell overboard. This will kick the stern of the boat away from the person preventing injury. This maneuver can be modified for use by twin-propeller boats. Twin-propeller boats are pivoted by putting one engine ahead and the other in reverse. With a single-propeller boat, the rudder should be placed hard over and additional power applied, if conditions permit. (see **Figure 16-5**)

Step	Procedure
1	Make the turn to the side that the person fell overboard.
2	Continue making a complete turn, coming around and approaching the person that fell overboard with the boat's bow directly into the wind/current.
3	Once pointed toward the person, proceed rapidly until close.
4	Then make a slow and deliberate approach to the person, coming to a stop when alongside.

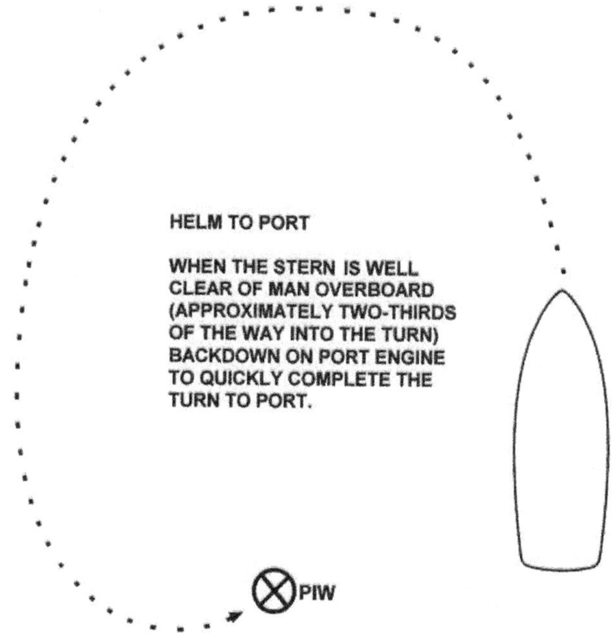

Figure 16-5
Destroyer Turn Man Overboard, Port Side

CAUTION !

Never have the propeller turning when the person overboard is next to the boat. If it is necessary to add power and maneuver with the PIW in close proximity to the boat, turn the bow toward the person, swinging the stern and propeller(s) away and at a safe distance.

A.22. Approaching in Severe Weather Conditions

Severe conditions may dictate that the approach be made from leeward with the bow dead into the seas and/or wind in order to maintain control of the boat. In severe conditions, particularly aboard single propeller boats, this will test the experience and skill of the coxswain. (see *Chapter 20, Heavy Weather Addendum* for more information.)

Approaching in Low Visibility

A.23. Description

During low visibility and night operations, when a crewmember sees another person go over the side, the same general procedures apply. The crewmember seeing the person go overboard shouts, "MAN OVERBOARD!" Coxswain should direct the deployment of a flotation device with strobe (or any other light) attached, if available. They also continue to observe and point to the person overboard as long as possible. The coxswain presses the memory/man overboard button on the LORAN-C or GPS receiver, if so equipped, sounds signals, and goes to the datum using one of the following turns:

- Anderson turn.
- Race track turn.
- Williamson turn.

A.24. Anderson Turn

An advantage of the Anderson turn is that it is the fastest recovery method. A disadvantage is that it is not meant for use by a single propeller boat. The Anderson turn is performed using the following procedures:

Step	Procedure
1	Put the rudder over full in the direction corresponding to the side from which the person fell. Increase power (if conditions permit) on the outboard engine only.
2	When about ⅔ of the way around, back the inboard engine ⅔ or full.
3	Stop engines when the person overboard is within about 15° of the bow.
4	Ease the rudder and back the engines as required to attain the proper final position. (see **Figure 16-6**)

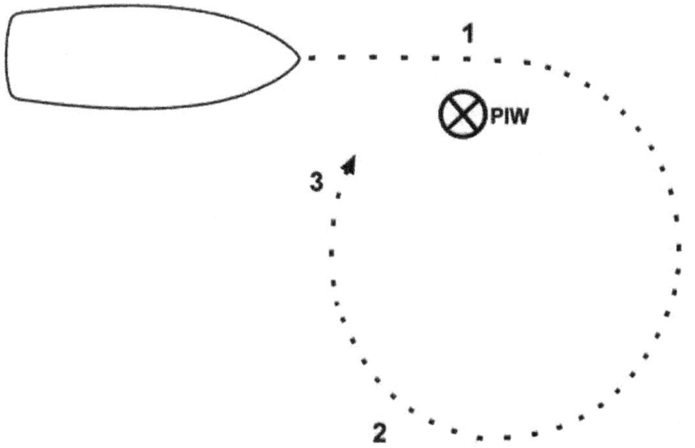

Figure 16-6
Anderson Turn

A.25. Race Track Turn

The final straight leg approach of the race track turn helps for a more calculable approach. The race track turn is performed using the following procedures:

Step	Procedure
1	Put the rudder over full in the direction corresponding to the side from which the person fell and increase speed (if conditions permit).
2	Use full rudder to turn to the reciprocal of the original course.
3	Steady up on this course for a short distance, then use full rudder to turn to the person overboard. (see **Figure 16-7**)

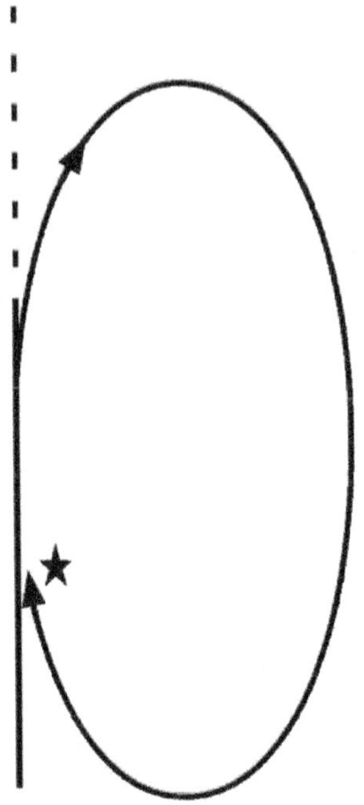

Figure 16-7
Race Track Turn

A.26. Williamson Turn

If an individual falls overboard during periods of darkness or restricted visibility, and the exact time of the incident is unknown, a maneuver known as the Williamson turn should be used to search for the person overboard. The advantage of the Williamson turn, when properly executed, is that it will position the boat on a reciprocal course on its exact original track. This allows the search to commence on the track where the victim fell over, not from a parallel track. Of course, as soon as the alarm is spread the general person overboard procedures will be initiated.

A.26.a. Procedure

The Williamson turn is performed using the following procedures:

Step	Procedure
1	Mark the original course when the alarm was initially spread. Put over a ring buoy strobe or other float to work datum.
2	Alter the course 60° to port or starboard from the original course. It does not matter which direction is chosen. Naturally, if turning to starboard, 60° will have to be added to the original course to know when the correct number of degrees has been transited. If turning to port, the 60° will be subtracted from the initial course.
3	The turn is actually executed while the first two procedures are in progress. In this step, the reciprocal course must be calculated from the original course. That is to say, a new course which runs in the exact opposite direction (180°) from the original course must be figured.
4	Once the correct reciprocal has been calculated and the compass reaches the 60° mark after turning off the initial course, shift the rudder in the opposite direction from the 60° turn and come to the reciprocal course.

A.26.b. Starboard Turn

Figure 16-8 shows how the Williamson turn would look if the 60° turn was to starboard. Point "A" represents the initial course and is illustrated as 000°. At Point B, the compass reads 060°. At this point, the reciprocal course (180°) has been figured. When the compass reaches the 060° mark, the rudder is shifted to the opposite direction (port) of the 60° turn and the boat comes around to the reciprocal. When the 180° course is marked, the boat will continue on this new course and if the person overboard has not been sighted by this time, the boat crew will conduct a search for the victim along this heading. If the individual is not located, the boat should proceed along the track to a point where the member was last known to be aboard. At this point a second datum marker (ring buoy, fender, etc.) is deployed.

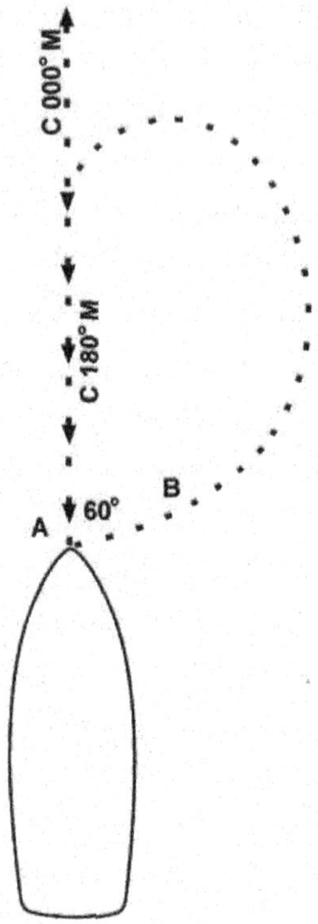

Figure 16-8
Williamson Turn

A.26.c. Maintaining Speed	Speed should not change during a Williamson turn. Any speed adjustments should be made prior to beginning the turn. Speed changes may bring the boat around to the reciprocal course in a different position than the line of the initial course. The danger is that the person overboard may be too far away to locate. The idea behind the Williamson turn is to bring the boat around so that it is on the exact line of the original course, but in the opposite direction.

A.26.d. Calculating the 60° Turn

Once the person overboard alarm is spread, the coxswain turns the boat 60° from the original course to either port or starboard.

If...	Then...
The turn is to starboard,	The 60° must be ADDED to the original course: • Original course marked when alarm was sounded 080° Starboard turn + 060° Shift rudder when compass reads 140°
The turn is to port,	The 60° must be SUBTRACTED from the original course: • Original course marked when alarm was sounded 080° Port turn - 060° Shift rudder when compass reads 020°

A.26.e. Calculating the Reciprocal of a Given Course

Calculating the reciprocal of a given course is done by either adding 180° to the given course or subtracting 180° from the given course. To add or to subtract depends on whether the given course was less than 180° or more than 180°.

A.26 f. Calculating the Reciprocal of a Course Less Than 180°

If the original course is less than 180°, 180° is added to the original course to get the reciprocal.

Example:

Original course	070°
Add 180°	+ 180°
Reciprocal course	250°

A.26.g. Calculating the Reciprocal of a Course More Than 180°

If the original course is more than 180°, 180° is subtracted from the original course to get the reciprocal.

Example

Original course	200°
Subtract 180°	- 180°
Reciprocal course	020°

A.27. While Towing

If, during a towing evolution, an MOB emergency occurs, boat crewmembers should be aware of the severity and danger of the situation. Several problems can occur when dealing with a simultaneous towing and man overboard situation.

WARNING

Never make sharp turns when towing! Turns should be made in slow and small increments. Always try to keep the towed vessel almost directly astern.

A.27.a. Vessel Maneuverability

When boat towing astern:

- A decrease in speed could cause the towed boat to overrun the towing boat. If the towing boat slows and does not tend the towline, the towline could sink and foul the rudder/s and propeller/s.
- If the towing boat turns sharply to either side, tripping can occur. Tripping is when a boat is pulled sideways by an opposing force. If the towline is out of alignment (not in line) and pulls sideways, the towing boat will heel over, often beyond its ability to right itself.

NOTE

Tripping occurs more frequently when the tow is larger than the towing boat.

A.27.b. Weather Conditions

Current, wind, sea, or swell from astern can cause yawing and add to the problem of the tow overrunning the towing boat. Current broadside to the tow creates difficulty in holding the tow due to side slip, causing the tow to yaw.

NOTE

Bar or inlet conditions will compound all these problems.

A.27.c. Pre-Planning

Considering the number of potential problems that can occur, the operator should carefully assess all possible situations and conditions to pre-plan steps to take in case of an MOB emergency.

CAUTION !

Slow calculated moves are better than a "knee jerk" response.

A.27.d. Additional Procedures

If a person falls overboard during a towing evolution, the initial steps discussed earlier in this section (sound alarm, throw ring buoy) should be followed. The following are additional considerations to take which apply to MOB situations specific to towing evolutions.

- If another boat is nearby, get that boat to make the pickup.
- Since tows are made at slow speeds, it may be possible that the towed boat can make the pickup. If the towed boat still has steerage, have them attempt to steer on the PIW and pick them up when alongside. The towing boat should aid in any way possible by slowing down or steering towards the side the PIW is located.
- If towing astern, advise the towed boat of the MOB situation, and have the people on the tow assist in looking for the PIW.
- Be sure to advise the people on the tow that there is a real danger of tripping or broaching if the towed boat shears away violently from alignment.
- Ensure the towline does not sink and become fouled around the rudder/s or propeller/s.
- It might be necessary to drop the tow in order to perform a MOB operation. Consider the environmental factors and water traffic when/if dropping the tow to minimize the possibility of a hazardous situation. Have the tow anchor if possible until the towing vessel can return and continue the tow.
- Never forget that the MOB might be injured if hit by the tow.
- A person who has fallen off the bow or side can be seriously injured or killed by the propellers. Any turns made should move the stern away from the PIW.

A.27.e. Man Overboard from the Towed Vessel

If a person falls overboard from the boat being towed, the initial steps discussed earlier in this section (sound alarm, throw ring buoy) should be followed. If there is no other boat in the area to assist, dropping the tow to recover the PIW is the best choice.

If the MOB takes place in restricted waters, the disabled vessel should be anchored as soon as the tow is released.

NOTE Always ensure everyone onboard the vessel being towed is wearing a PFD.

A.27 f. Towing Alongside

When towing a boat alongside, the initial steps discussed earlier in this section (sound alarm, throw ring buoy) should be followed. Towing alongside allows more freedom to turn. Consider the following points:

- Engines, while useful, will not respond as usual. Remember, the engines were designed to propel one boat, not two.
- When making a turn, turn slowly towards the side with the tow and pivot on the tow. Be careful not to swamp the tow.
- The best approach is to make the pickup on the free side since the operator can better observe the person-in-the-water and the pickup.
- Again, consider dropping the tow.

The procedures will remain the same, whether the person falls from the tow or towing vessel.

A.27.g. Summary

The effect of each action on all of the boats and persons involved should always be considered. People before property. People's safety is the number one priority. People onboard the tow are just as important as the PIW. If the towed boat is not manned, the coxswain should consider dropping the tow! All people and vessels involved should always be informed of every situation.

The best way to handle an MOB emergency is to prevent one from happening. Being aware of the crew; knowing where they are and what they are doing is essential.

Approaching Under Surf Conditions

CAUTION ! The Auxiliary is not authorized to operate in surf conditions.

A.28. Description

Recovering a person overboard in heavy weather requires special precautions beyond the routine described in the section on general person overboard procedure. The general procedure is put into effect as soon as the alarm is sounded. See *Chapter 20, Heavy Weather Addendum, Section D,* for more information.

Recovery

A.29. Description

Recovery techniques for a PIW are the same for any type of distress. Situations could vary from recovering someone from the crew as an MOB, passengers from a ditched aircraft, fisherman from a sinking boat, someone washed off of a jetty, or any other form of emergency where people are in the water.

A.30. Recovery Methods

The condition of the PIW will dictate the type of recovery procedures used. Once the condition of the PIW can be determined, that is, conscious, unconscious, or injured, the coxswain will select one of the procedures below and assign crewmember duties accordingly. Generally, the pickup is completed at the lowest point of freeboard and away from the propellers.

NOTE

"Training boat crews for Person in the Water Recovery requires the use of a life-like dummy (OSCAR). The recommended OSCAR is a stuffed and weighted (approximately 180 lbs dry) Anti-Exposure Coverall secured at the neck and feet."

A.31. Person Overboard is Uninjured and Conscious

Perform the following recovery method when the person is conscious and able to move freely in the water:

Step	Procedure
1	Upon command of the coxswain, a crewmember casts out a heaving line or a float line to the PIW.
2	The person will hold onto the line and be hauled in for recovery by the crewmember tending the line.
3	If the person needs assistance to board the boat: • Two crewmembers could be used to pull the person up out of the water and onto the boat by each placing a hand under the person's armpit (use the other hand to hold onto the boat); or • A recovery strap/piece of line (see **Figure 16-9**) or a boarding ladder may be used if available.

Figure 16-9
Recovering a PIW with a Recovery Strap or Line

A.32. Additional Procedures

The construction of some boats allows the rescue team to reach the victim at the surface of the water.

- The boat crewmembers should physically pick the person straight up out of the water to a sitting position on the gunwale (gunnel). (see **Figure 16-10**)
- Be careful not to drag the person's back across the rail.

Figure 16-10
Recovering the PIW at the Surface of the Water

If only one person is available to lift an uninjured person from the water, perform the following procedures:

Step	Procedure
1	Position the victim facing the boat with both arms reaching upwards.
2	Boat crewmember should reach down with arms crossed and grasp victim's wrists.
3	Boat crewmember should lift the victim straight out of the water while simultaneously uncrossing the arms. This should extract the victim from the water in a corkscrew motion.

If the freeboard of the boat is too high to recover the victim safely, perform the following procedures:

Step	Procedure
1	Use a rescue strap/line under the armpits in a horse collar fashion. (see **Figure 16-9**)
2	The line should cross the chest, pass under each arm, and up behind the head.
3	Use padding for comfort, if available.

A person is light in the water due to buoyancy; however, once free from the water, the person becomes "dead weight." This should be kept in mind and special care should be taken when recovering injured persons.

A.33. PIW is Unconscious or Injured

In the event that the PIW is unconscious or injured, a direct pick up from the boat may be attempted if on scene conditions permit a safe recovery. If conditions are such that a direct pick up would be unsafe, utilizing a surface swimmer to recover the PIW should be considered. The procedures for deploying a surface swimmer are as follows:

CAUTION!

Always use extreme caution when using a boat hook to maneuver an unconscious or injured PIW alongside for pick up.

Step	Procedure
1	The coxswain will designate one of the crewmembers as a surface swimmer.
2	The surface swimmer will don PPE appropriate to the weather conditions as stated in the *Rescue and Survival Systems Manual*, COMDTINST M10470.10 (series), *Chapter 6*. Other pieces of equipment the swimmer could use are, swim fins, a mask and snorkel, and a swimming harness with tending line. (see **Figure 16-11**)
3	For quick deployment, the line should be coiled and attached to the back of the swimmer's harness.
4	When the surface swimmer has reached the unconscious or injured victim and has obtained a secure hold on the person, the crewmember tending the harness line will haul both back to the boat.

A flotation equipped stokes litter is employed to recover a person only if that person is seriously injured and seas are calm. (see **Figure 16-12**)

A.33.a. Surface Swimmer

Surface swimmers are any swimmers not trained as rescue swimmers. Their training is accomplished through Personnel Qualification Standard (PQS). They are deployed from floating units, piers, or the shore. A surface swimmer must wear the appropriate PPE including a swimming harness with a tending line. Another crewmember will tend the harness whenever the swimmer is in the water.

NOTE

Additional information regarding surface swimmers qualification requirements can be found in the *U.S. Coast Guard Boat Operations and Training (BOAT) Manual – Volume I*, COMDTINST M16114.32 (series).

NOTE

The Auxiliary does not have surface swimmers.

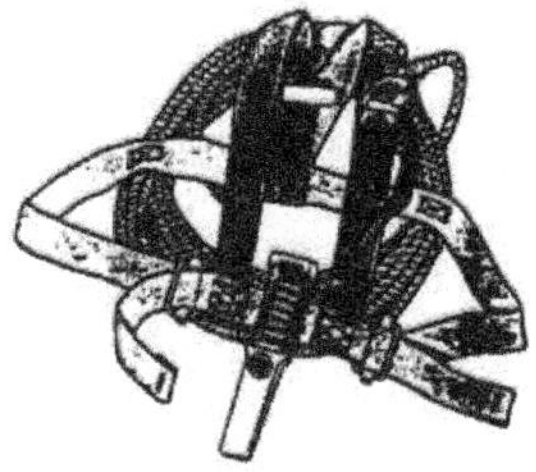

Figure 16-11
Surface Swimmer's Harness

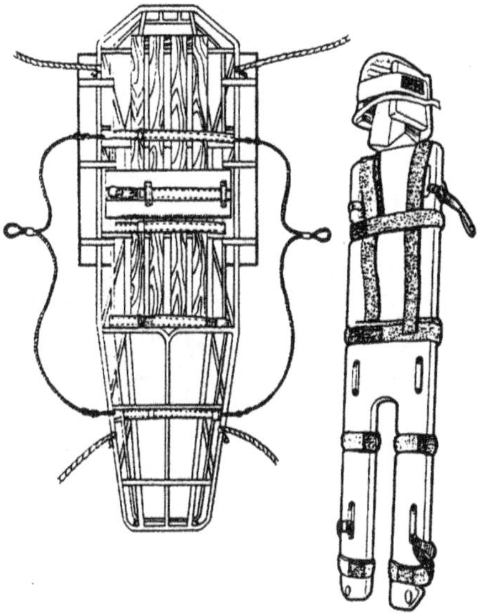

Figure 16-12
Stokes Litter and Miller Board

A.34. Requesting a Rescue Swimmer

The primary mission of the helicopter rescue swimmer is to provide rotary wing stations with the capability of deploying a properly trained and conditioned person to assist persons in distress in the marine environment. The rescue swimmer must have the flexibility, strength, endurance, and equipment to function for 30 minutes in heavy seas, and the skills to provide basic pre-hospital life support for the rescued individual(s). The rescue swimmer's EMT skills may also be used during other SAR cases in which the swimming ability is not required.

If medical assistance is needed, the parent Station shall be advised. The Station may arrange for medical assistance on-scene or at an agreed upon rendezvous point.

A.35. Multiple PIW Recovery

For multiple PIWs, the question becomes which person-in-the-water is recovered first. The answer to this requires the coxswain's best judgment. An accurate assessment once on the scene will dictate the coxswain's response. Consideration should be given to the following:

- Are one or more persons in the water injured?
- Which persons in the water have on PFDs and which do not?
- How close are the persons in the water to the beach or jetty?
- How old are they and what is their physical condition?

A.36. Multiple PIW Recovery (MPR) System

The Multiple Person-in-the-Water Recovery (MPR) System is an inflatable rescue device designed to assist in the retrieval of multiple survivors from the water to the deck of a rescue vessel. (see **Figure 16-13**) The MPR was specifically designed for use on the 41' UTB. When installed and operated correctly, the MPR will inflate in less than 10 seconds and be ready for use. The unique design of this system allows rescuers to descend the ramp to assist in the recovery of multiple PIWs or allows multiple PIWs to easily climb from the water.

Specific instructions will be provided at the Station to 41' UTB crewmembers on use and operation of the MPR system.

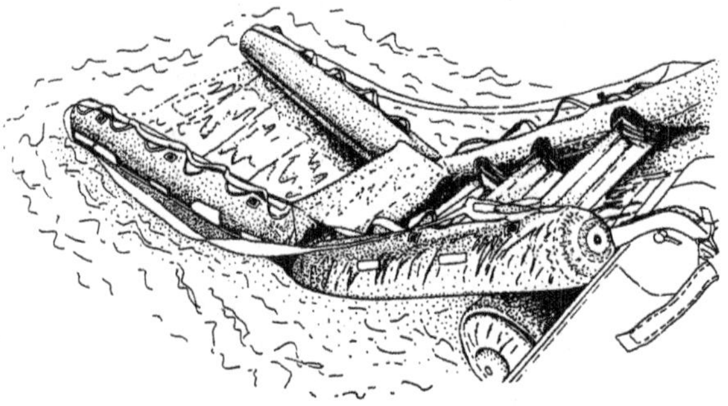

Figure 16-13
Multiple PIW Recovery System

Section B. Water Survival Skills

Introduction

In the event a crewmember enters or ends up in the water due to an emergency, survival procedures should be pre-planned. By doing so, the chances for a successful rescue are increased.

This section addresses the survival techniques that will greatly increase the survival for a PIW. Crewmembers should never forget that wearing all required PPE is the best insurance for survival.

B.1. Cold Water Survivability

The length of time a person can stay alive in cold water depends on the temperature of the water, the physical condition of the survivor, and the action taken by the survivor. **Figure 16-14** and **Table 16-1** illustrate the relationship between an uninjured victim's activity, water temperature, and estimated survival time. Swimming typically reduces a person's chance of survival due to more rapid loss of body heat.

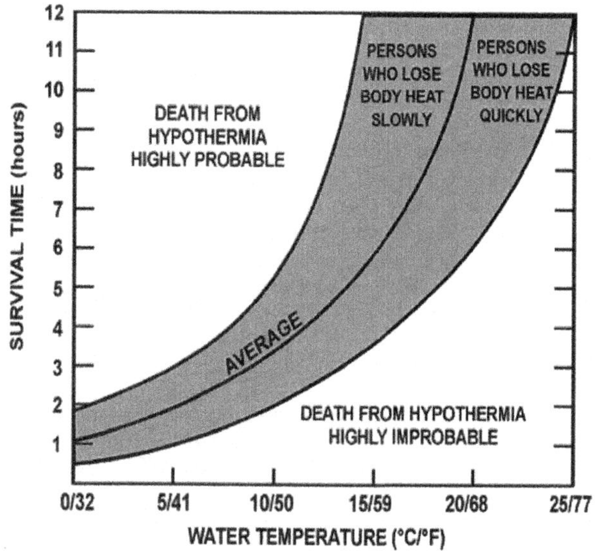

Figure 16-14
Water Chill and Hypothermia

Table 16-1
Survival Times vs. Water Temperatures

How Hypothermia Affects Most Adults		
Water Temperature ° F (°C)	**Exhaustion or Unconsciousness**	**Expected Time of Survival**
Less than 32.5 (0.3)	Under 15 min.	Under 15 to 45 min.
32.5 to 40 (0.3 to 4.4)	15 to 30 min.	30 to 90 min.
40 to 50 (4.4 to 10)	30 to 60 min.	1 to 3 hrs.
50 to 60 (10 to 15.6)	1 to 2 hrs.	1 to 6 hrs.
60 to 70 (15.6 to 21)	2 to 7 hrs.	2 to 40 hrs.
70 to 80 (21 to 26.7)	2 to 12 hrs.	3 hrs. to indefinite
Over 80 (26.7)	Indefinite	Indefinite

B.2. Critical Factors

Time is critical when forced to enter cold water. The loss of body heat is one of the greatest dangers to survival. Critical factors that increase the threat of hypothermia and other cold-water injuries include:

- Prolonged exposure to cold-water temperatures.
- Sea spray.
- Air temperature.
- Wind chill.

B.3. Survival Techniques

Several preventive measures that can be used to increase the chances for successful cold water survival include:

- Put on as much warm clothing as possible, making sure to cover head, neck, hands and feet.
- If the hypothermia protective clothing does not have inherent flotation, put on a PFD.
- Avoid entering the water if possible. If it is necessary to jump into the water, hold elbows close to sides, cover nose and mouth with one hand while holding the wrist or elbow firmly with the other hand.
- Before entering the water, button up clothing, turn on signal lights (only at night), locate your survival whistle and make any other preparations for rescue.

B.4. Water Survival Skills

Water survival skills that should be utilized to increase the chances for surviving cold water immersion include:

- Immediately upon entering the water, become oriented to the surrounding area. Try to locate sinking boat, floating objects, and other survivors.
- Try to board a lifeboat, raft, overturned boat (if floating), or other floating platform as soon as possible to shorten the immersion time. Body heat is lost many times faster in the water than in the air. Since the effectiveness of the insulation worn is seriously reduced by being water soaked, it is important to be shielded from wind to avoid a wind-chill effect. If able to climb aboard a survival craft, use a canvas cover or tarpaulin as a shield from the cold. Huddling close to the other occupants in the craft will also conserve body heat.
- While afloat in the water, do not attempt to swim unless it is necessary to reach a fellow survivor or a floating object which can be grasped or climbed onto.
- Unnecessary swimming will pump out any warm water between the body and the layers of clothing and will increase the rate of body-heat loss. Also, unnecessary movements of arms and legs send warm blood from the inner core to the outer layer of the body resulting in a rapid heat loss.
- The body position assumed in the water is very important in conserving heat. Float as still as possible with legs together, elbows close to your side and arms folded across the front of the PFD. This is called the HELP (Heat Escape Lessening Position) and minimizes exposure of the body surface to the cold water. Try to keep head and neck out of the water (see **Figure 16-15**). However, if wearing a Type III PFD, or if the HELP position turns the body face down, bring legs together tight and arms tight to sides and head back.
- Another heat conserving position is to huddle closely to others in the water making as much body contact as possible. A PFD must be worn to be able to maintain these positions in the water (see **Figure 16-16**).
- Avoid drown-proofing in cold water. Drown-proofing is a technique where the person relaxes in the water and allows their head to submerge between breaths. It is an energy saver in warm water when a PFD is not worn. The head and neck are high heat loss areas and must be kept above the water. That is why it is even more important to wear a PFD in cold water. If a PFD is not worn, tread the water only as much as necessary to keep head out of the water.
- Keep a positive attitude about survival and rescue. This will extend survival time until rescue comes. A will to live does make a difference.

Figure 16-15
Single PIW

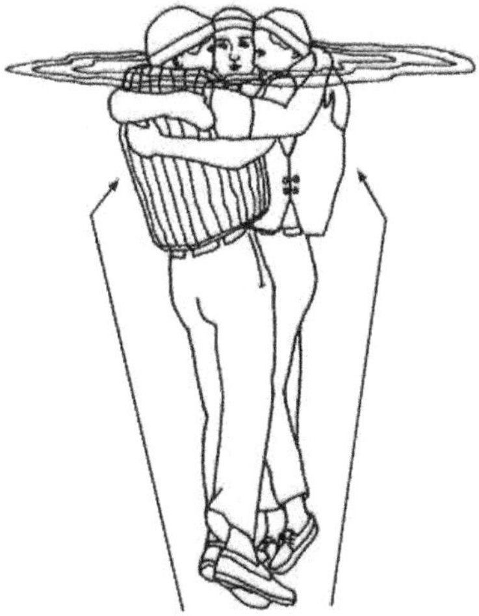

Figure 16-16
Multiple PIWs

CH-1

This page intentionally left blank.

Chapter 17
Towing

Introduction

As a boat crewmember, towing will be one of the missions executed for many types of maritime craft. This chapter covers forces in towing, towing equipment, safety, and procedures. Boat crews need a firm grasp of towing principles to ensure that an evolution does not result in injury, death or further damage to property. No two towing evolutions are exactly the same. Towing should never be considered "routine." Variations in technique and procedures will occur. Knowledge of principles and standard procedures should be applied to account for weather and sea conditions, vessel types, and crew experience. The tow should always be within the crew's and vessel's capabilities.

The *U.S. Coast Guard Addendum to the United States National Search and Rescue Supplement (NSS) to the International Aeronautical and Maritime Search and Rescue Manual*, COMDTINST M16130.2 (series) states policy on vessel-assistance towing. Specific Boat Type Operator's Handbooks, COMDTINST M16114 (series) provide specific procedures for those types of boats. Individual manufacturers' boat owner's guides and product specification sheets provide equipment limitations and safety information. The *U.S. Coast Guard Boat Operations and Training (BOAT) Manual, Volume II*, COMDTINST M16114.33 (series) addresses crew performance requirements. *Chapter 1, Boat Crew Duties and Responsibilities* of this Manual, outlines the towing watch responsibilities. Boat crews should be familiar with and comply with the policies, direction and information in these sources.

In this chapter

This chapter contains the following sections:

WARNING

The wearing of jewelry, including rings, wristwatches, necklaces or other items not consisting of organizational clothing, PPE, or uniform articles by boat crew members engaged in hoisting, towing, or other deck evolutions where the potential for snagging exists **is prohibited**. OICs and coxswains will address this during all pre-underway briefs and coxswains shall ensure jewelry is removed prior to beginning all deck evolutions.

Section A. Towing Safety

Introduction

Safety is always the most important concern when towing. Every towing activity is potentially dangerous. The safety of the crew and the crew of the towed vessel is more important than property, and the primary responsibility in any towing situation is to maintain safety. Towing is a complex evolution. A safe and successful outcome hinges on crew professionalism, ability, and teamwork.

Chapter 4, Team Coordination and Risk Management is dedicated to safety-related items, including risk management and team coordination. Towing-specific applications are covered here.

WARNING

Do not let a perceived need to engage in a towing mission override a complete, honest risk assessment process that emphasizes personnel safety.

A.1. Risk Assessment

Every boat crewmember is responsible for identifying and managing risks. Towing mishaps can be prevented by honestly evaluating risks involved in every step of any towing evolution. Communicating with the towed vessel's crew who may have important information necessary to complete a successful mission is essential.

A.2. Situational Awareness

The dynamics of a towing situation continuously change from the time pre-towing preparations begin until mooring at the conclusion of the mission. All crewmembers must stay fully aware of the constantly changing situation at any given time during a towing evolution. It is important that each crewmember knows what goes on in the surrounding environment and how things change. Crew awareness should be reinforced through communication: commenting on what is believed to be happening, and involving the towed vessel's crew. The "outside" view could provide information on things not visible from the towing vessel.

When clues indicate that situational awareness is being lost, a decision must be made whether or not to continue with the towing evolution. A decision takes the form of action/reaction and communication. Everyone in the crew has a responsibility in the decision-making process.

A.3. Risk Management Planning

Realistic towing training based on standardized techniques, critical analysis, and mission briefing and debriefing will contribute to risk management and the development of a towing risk management plan. All crewmembers must contribute to risk management planning.

Standard precautions in *Section E* of this chapter make up the basis for a towing risk management plan, but each towing evolution is unique, and the plan should be revised according to whatever the situation dictates. Refer to *Chapter 4* for discussion of Risk Assessment and Management.

Section B. Towing Forces

Introduction

Boat crews must understand the forces, or types of resistance, which act on the towed vessel and how to handle the resistance safely. They are the same forces that affect all vessels, but a distressed vessel is limited in how it can overcome them. The towing vessel must provide the means to move the towed vessel. The towline or tow rig transfers all forces between the two vessels. Boat crews must earn to recognize the different forces and each of their effects individually to effectively balance and overcome them when they act together.

In this section

This section contains the following information:

Static Forces

B.1. Description

Static forces cause a towed vessel to resist motion. The displacement or mass of a towed vessel determines the amount of force working against the vessel. The assisting vessel must overcome these forces before the towed vessel moves. Inertia and the moment of inertia are two different properties of static forces that cause resistance in towing vessels.

B.2. Inertia

In this case, inertia is the tendency for a vessel at rest to stay at rest. The more mass a vessel has (the greater its displacement), the harder it is to get it moving.

B.3. Moment of Inertia

The moment of inertia occurs when a towed vessel resists effort to turn about a vertical axis to change heading. The larger the vessel, the more resistance there will be in turning the vessel. Unless necessary in a case of immediate danger, an attempt to tow a distressed vessel ahead and change its heading at the same time should not be used. (see **Figure 17-1**) Both inertia and the moment of inertia will be involved in the resistance of moving the distressed vessel, which can cause potentially dangerous situations and greater resistance for towing. Both vessels, their fittings, and the towing equipment take much less stress and strain when the two forces are conquered individually.

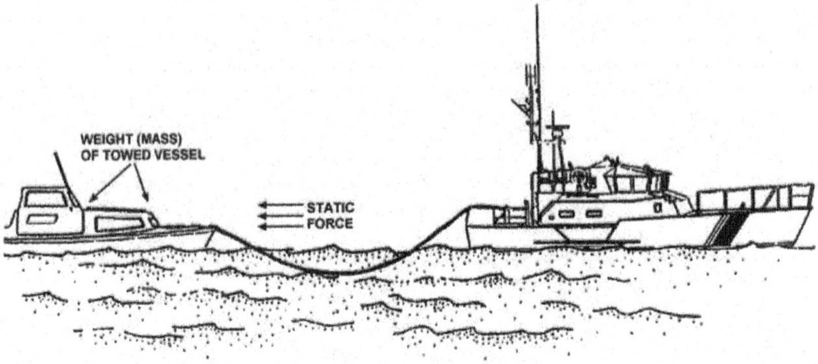

Figure 17-1
Static Forces

Overcome the effects of static forces by starting a tow slowly, both on the initial heading or when changing the towed vessel's heading. A large amount of strain is placed on both vessels, their fittings, and the towing equipment when going from dead-in-the-water to moving in the desired direction and at the desired speed. Extreme caution should be used when towing a vessel of equal or greater mass than the assisting vessel. In such situations, the assisting vessel strains the capacity and capability of its equipment, requiring slow and gradual changes.

B.3.a. Starting the Tow on the Initial Heading

To start the tow on the initial heading, perform the following procedures:

Step	Procedure
1	Apply the towing force on the initial heading to gradually overcome the towed vessel's inertia.
2	As the towed vessel gains momentum, slowly and gradually increase speed.
3	To change the tow direction, make any change slowly and gradually after the towed vessel is moving.

B.3.b. Changing the Towed Vessel's Heading

To change the towed vessel's heading, perform the following procedures:

Step	Procedure
1	Apply the towing force perpendicular to the vessel's heading. Once the towed vessel starts to turn, resistance will develop.
2	Apply turning force slowly and gradually. It is more difficult to change the initial heading of a heavy vessel (one with a high moment of inertia) than a light one.
3	Now, begin to tow in the desired direction and gradually overcome inertia to get the towed vessel moving forward.
4	Once making way, the effects of static forces lessen.
5	Until the tow achieves a steady speed and direction, apply power or turning force to defeat any remaining inertia or to change the towed vessel's momentum gradually.

Dynamic Forces

B.4. Description

Dynamic forces occur once the towed vessel is moving. They are based on the towed vessel's characteristics (shape, displacement, arrangement, rigging), the motion caused by the towing vessel, and the effects of waves and wind. (see **Figure 17-2**)

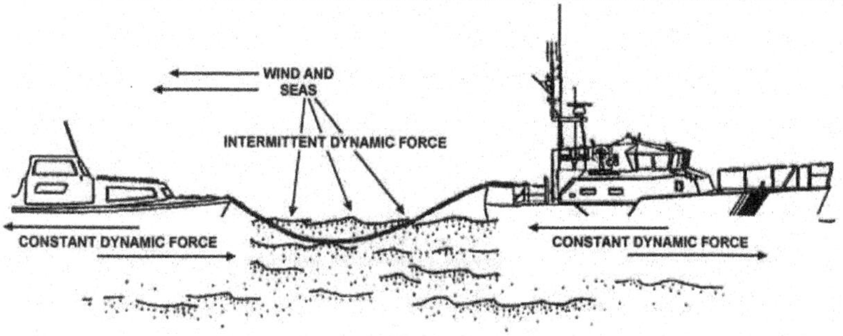

Figure 17-2
Dynamic Forces

B.5. Momentum

Once a vessel moves in a straight line, it wants to keep moving in a straight line. The greater its displacement or the faster it is moving, the harder it is to stop or change the vessel's direction.

B.6. Angular Momentum

Once the vessel's heading begins to change, it wants to keep changing in that same direction. The faster the towed vessel's heading changes, the harder it is to get the tow moving in a straight line.

The towed vessel's momentum will gradually increase with towing speed. Momentum in a straight line will resist effort to change the towed vessel's direction and will tend to keep the towed vessel moving when tension in the towing rig is decreased. If necessary to first change the direction of the tow, the towed vessel will develop angular momentum while the vessel's heading is changing. Towing force opposite the swing may need to be applied before the towed vessel achieves the desired heading. The key to dealing with momentum is to anticipate how momentum will affect the towed vessel's motion and apply an offsetting force early and gradually.

CAUTION !

> Frictional resistance will constantly affect the tow, *normally* keeping some steady tension in the towing rig. Since the shape and wetted surface area of the towed vessel will not change, frictional resistance is managed with towing speed. Higher towing speed causes higher frictional resistance and more strain on the towing rig.

B.7. Frictional Resistance

As a vessel moves, the layer of water in immediate contact with the hull moves. Due to friction between water molecules, the layers of water close to the hull try to drag along. The vessel appears to move "through" the water. This attempt to drag water alongside takes energy. As speed increases, this action becomes "turbulent." This turbulence takes additional energy, and more speed requires even more power.

NOTE

> Frictional resistance also varies with hull shape. Greater underwater (wetted) surface area causes greater frictional resistance. Hull appendages, such as propellers, shafts, skegs, keel, and rudders contribute to wetted surface area and frictional resistance.

B.8. Form Drag

Form drag plays a large role in the ability to control changes in the towed vessel's movement. Different hull shapes react to motion through the water in different ways. The shape and size of the towed vessel's hull can either help or hinder effort to move in a straight line, when changing heading, and motion changes in response to waves due to buoyancy. The less water a hull shape has to push out of its way, the easier it will move through the water. A deep-draft, full-hulled vessel takes more effort to move than one with a fine, shallow hull. A large amount of lateral resistance, spread evenly over the length of the hull, will hinder effort to change a towed vessel's direction, but will help offset angular momentum in steadying up on a desired heading. A towed vessel may be able to help offset form drag by using its rudder.

CAUTION !

It is not always safe to tow a planing hull type of vessel above planing speed. Going from displacement speed to planing speed, or back, can decrease the towed vessel's stability and cause it to capsize. Also, wave drag (even one large wake) could slow the hull down to displacement speed and cause a severe "shock-load" as the towed vessel tries to get back on plane.

B.9. Wave-Making Resistance

A surface wave forms at the bow while the hull moves through the water. The size of the bow wave increases as speed increases, causing the wave to create resistance for the bow to be pulled or propelled through the water.

Boat crews should keep in mind the different hull types of maritime craft, including the towing vessel. In any towing evolution, the boat crew must be able to recognize a vessel's hull type, as well as its critical capabilities and limitations. Dependent on the type of hull, towing vessels must be careful not to tow a vessel faster than the design speed of its hull. Refer to *Chapter 8, Boat Characteristics,* for discussion of different hull types

NOTE

"Shock-load" or "shock-loading" is the rapid, extreme increase in tension on the towline, which transfers through the tow rig and fittings to both vessels.

B.10. Wave Drag, Spray Drag, and Wind Drag

The frictional forces of wave drag, spray drag, and wind drag act on the hull, topsides, superstructure, and rigging. They all have a major effect on the motion of the towed vessel, and the transfer of forces to and through the towing rig. These constantly changing forces all vary with the towed vessel's motion relative to the environmental elements and are directly related to the towed vessel's amount of exposure to them. These forces can add up and cause shock-loading. Wind and wave drag also cause a distressed drifting vessel to make leeway, which is motion in a downwind direction.

B.10.a. Wave Drag

Wave drag depends on the "normal" wetted surface area of the hull and the amount of freeboard exposed to wave action. Wave drag has a large effect on the strain of the tow rig.

- In large seas, be aware of:
  - Combination of wave drag and form drag could overcome the towed vessel's forward momentum and cause the towed vessel to stop and transfer a large amount of strain to the tow rig.
  - Shock-load could damage a vessel's fittings and part the towline endangering both vessels' crews.
- In head seas, be aware of:
  - Towing vessel can only control the effect of wave drag by the speed and angle that the towed vessel encounters the waves.
  - Limiting speed and towing at an angle to the seas to prevent them from breaking over the bow of the towed vessel.
- In following seas, be aware of:
  - Wave drag causing the towed vessel to speed up as the crest approaches, increasing speed to keep tension in the towing rig, and reducing speed as the crest passes.

B.10.b. Spray Drag

Spray drag also provides resistance to the tow. The spray from a wave could slow the towed vessel and increase the amount of shock-loading. Spray drag could also adversely affect the towed vessel's motion by imparting a momentary heel, pooling on deck or in the vessel cockpit, and in cold weather form ice, and thus decrease stability.

B.10.c. Wind Drag

Wind drag can cause shock-loading and have a bad effect on the towed vessel's motions and stability. A steady beam wind can cause list and leeway, while a severe gust can cause a threatening heel. List, heel, and leeway may cause the towed vessel to yaw. A headwind increases tow rig loading in a direct line with the towed vessel while the towed vessel crests a wave, causing shock-loading.

WARNING

> Once making way, a vessel's buoyancy response or the effect of gravity in a seaway may cause severe shock loading.

B.11. Buoyancy Response and Gravity Effects

Boat crews should develop a feel for the towed vessel's initial and reserve buoyancy characteristics, overall stability, sea keeping, response to the prevailing environmental conditions, and the response to being towed. Though a distressed vessel may *seem* stable and sound at rest, its response once in tow could be to capsize. A towed vessel's bow may react to an oncoming wave by pitching skyward, or by "submarining." Buoyancy response to following seas could cause the towed vessel to yaw excessively or gravity may cause it to gain speed and "surf" down the face of a wave.

Combination of Forces and Shock-Load

B.12. Description

During a towing evolution, the boat crew rarely deals with only one force acting upon the tow. The crew usually faces a combination of all the forces, each making the situation more complex. Some individual forces are very large and relatively constant. Crews can usually deal with these safely, provided all towing-force changes are made gradually. When forces are changed in an irregular manner, tension on the tow rig starts to vary instead of remaining steady.

CAUTION !

> Shock-loading may cause severe damage to both towing and towed vessels and overload a tow rig to the point of towline or bridle failure. Shock-loading could also cause momentary loss of directional control by either vessel and could capsize small vessels.

B.13. Example

Even in calm winds and seas, a towing vessel can encounter a large amount of frictional resistance from form and wave drag when towing a large fishing vessel with trawl lines fouled in its propeller and net still in the water. The tow rig and vessel fittings will be under heavy strain, and the tow vessel engine loads will be rather high, but the tow proceeds relatively safely. If suddenly the net tangled and caught on an unseen obstacle, this new "force" acting through the tow rig could immediately increase stress to a dangerous level. This shock-load could part the towline or destroy fittings.

(In the example above, the prudent solution would be to make a "safe" tow by recovering the net or marking it and letting it loose before starting the tow.)

Though this example began as a safe and steady tow, a single unexpected incident could have caused a very dangerous situation. Boat crews should always keep in mind that some degree of shock-loading can occur during any tow evolution.

B.14. Shock-Loading Prevention or Counteraction

Because of the potential dangers, the tow vessel must use various techniques to prevent or counteract shock-loading, or reduce its effect.

Action	Effect
Reduce Towing Speed	Slowing down lowers frictional resistance, form drag, and wave-making resistance. Reducing these forces will lower the total tow-rig tension. In head seas, reducing speed also reduces wave drag, spray drag, and wind drag, lowering the irregular tow rig loads. The total reduction in forces on the tow could be rather substantial. When encountering vessel wake in relatively calm conditions, decrease speed early enough so the towed vessel loses momentum before hitting the wake. A small towed vessel slamming into a large wake will shock-load the tow rig, and may even swamp.
Get the Vessels "In-Step"	Extreme stress is put on the tow rig in heavy weather when the tow vessel and the towing vessel do not climb, crest or descend waves together. Vessels in step will gain and lose momentum at the same time, allowing the towing force to gradually overcome the towed vessel's loss of momentum, minimizing shock-loading. To get the vessels in step, lengthen rather than shorten the towline if possible.

NOTE

> When operating near bars and inlets, getting the vessels in step may be impractical due to rapidly changing water depth and bottom contours.

Action	Effect
Lengthen the Towline	A longer towline reduces the effect of shock-loading in two ways. The weight of the line causes a dip in the line called a catenary. The more line out, the greater the catenary. When tension increases, energy from shock-loading is spent on "flattening out" the catenary before it is transferred through the rest of the rig and fittings. The second benefit of a longer towline is more stretch length. Depending on the type of towline, another 50' of towline length will give 5'-20' more stretch to act as a shock-load absorber. Remember to lengthen the towline enough to keep the vessels in step and minimize the shock-load source.
Set a Course to Lessen the Effect of the Seas	Do not try to tow a vessel either directly into or directly down large seas. Tow on a course to keep the seas 30°-45° either side of dead ahead or dead astern. This may require "tacking" to either side of the actual desired course.
Deploy a Drogue from the Towed Vessel	The drogue (covered in *Section C* of this chapter) may help to prevent the towed vessel from rapidly accelerating down the face of a wave. The drogue does add form drag to the tow, but could prevent shock-load.
CAUTION !	Shock-load can also capsize or swamp the towed vessel. The additional towing force from a shock-loaded towline could cause a smaller vessel to climb its bow wave and become unstable or it could pull the bow through a cresting wave.
Constantly Adjust Towing Vessel Speed to Match that of the Towed Vessel	In large seas, constant "finesse" techniques may reduce shock-loading. This requires the coxswain to constantly observe the towed vessel, and increasing or decreasing towing vessel speed to compensate for the effects of approaching or receding seas on the towed vessel. This takes much practice and experience.
NOTE	Safety demands emphasis on preventing shock-load and reducing its effects. Shock-loading presents a definite possibility of damage to vessel fittings or tow rig failure. One of the more feared possibilities is towline snap-back. Think of this as a greatly magnified version of stretching a rubber band until it breaks. Remember, some nylon cordage can stretch up to an additional 40% of its length before parting.

Section C. Towing Equipment

Introduction

When towing a boat or other maritime craft, always use the proper equipment for the task. Using the proper equipment minimizes accidents and possible injuries. Towing equipment includes:

- Towlines.
- Pendants and bridles.
- Deck fittings.
- Hardware for attaching the towline (skiff hooks, shackles, etc.).
- Fenders.
- Drogues.
- Alongside lines.

This section discusses the design, use, and limits of towing equipment.

In this section

This section contains the following information:

Towlines and Accessories

C.1. Description

Towlines are usually 2-in-1 (double-braided) nylon, two to four inches in circumference. Length can be up to 900 feet. Nylon instead of other synthetic fiber cordage should be used for a good combination of strength and stretch (elongation and elasticity). The Auxiliary is not required to use double-braided nylon for towing and will use a variety of types and sizes of towlines.

NOTE ☞

Refer to *Chapter 7, Marlinespike Seamanship* for a complete table of breaking strength for various circumferences of rope.

CAUTION !

Do not tow beyond the vessel's design limits by simply increasing towline size. If the towline's breaking strength exceeds the limits designed into the vessel's fittings and structure, damage and structural failure may result.

The towing vessel's construction, power, size, and fittings determine towline size (circumference). The proper towline will allow a vessel to tow up to its design limits. The towline will part before damage occurs to a vessel's fittings, structure or hull.

Each Coast Guard boat type has an equipment list that specifies towline length and size. Towlines will usually have an eye spliced into the tow end. Towline length and size will vary on other vessels due to design limits and available space. Offshore or in heavy weather, a towing vessel may need 500 feet or more of towline to keep a towed vessel in step and to minimize the effect of shock-loading.

C.1.a. Towline Storage

Towline is stored on a tow reel with the bitter end secured to the reel with small stuff. The line will lie evenly on the reel. More importantly, to quickly slip (release) the towline in an emergency, the small stuff can be cut with a knife, and the bitter end runs free. When putting new cordage in service as a towline, an eye should be spliced at both ends. This will allow an "end-for-end" switch before part of the towline is beyond useful service.

Many tow reels have mechanical advantage (hand crank, gear train) or electric motors to ease towline retrieval. These devices are only to retrieve a slack towline. Crewmembers should not try to take any tension with these devices. The tow reel should be inspected frequently for easy rotation and adequate lubrication.

NOTE Unless slipping the towline in an emergency, keep at least four turns of towline on the reel. Paying out the entire length can result in loss of both tow and towline.

C.1.b. Towline Condition and Inspection

Safe and efficient towing requires an undamaged, serviceable towline. Whenever any towline damage is found or suspected, crewmembers should remove or repair the damage. If removing damage shortens the towline to less than serviceable length, then the towline should be replaced. Remaining usable sections of a discarded towline can be used for bridles, alongside lines, mooring lines, etc.

Inspect towlines on a regular basis to detect damage from:

- Cuts.
- Chafing.
- Flattening.
- Fusing (caused by overheating or over-stretching).
- Snags.
- Hardening (heavy use will compact and harden a towline and reduce its breaking strength).

If a towline shows any of these characteristics, it should not be used as a towline.

C.2. Towing Pendants and Bridles

It is not always possible, appropriate, or safe to attach a towline from the stern of a towing vessel to a single point on the bow of a distressed vessel. For instance:

- The distressed vessel's deck layout may not have a single direct run through a bull nose.
- There might not be a sampson post or centered bitt.
- The towline might be too large for deck fittings.
- Deck fittings may be improperly mounted, rotted or corroded where they attach to the deck.

In these cases, a pendant or bridle should be rigged. The pendant or bridle forms part of the tow rig, leading from the eye or thimble of a towline to the appropriate location(s) or deck fitting(s) on the towed vessel. Towing pendants and bridles are made of double-braided nylon, Kevlar or wire rope. (Wire rope should be used for large vessels or steel hulls.) The two most common rigs are a pendant and a bridle. Auxiliary facilities will have a variety of pendants and bridles, not necessarily constructed of double-braided nylon or wire rope.

When possible, pendants and bridles should be used with BS equal to or greater than the towline. If the towed vessel's fittings (chocks or cleats) limit bridle or pendant size, "doubling-up" (two bridles or pendants) should be considered. When expected towing force threatens safe working load of the individual bridle legs, if doubling-up, all lengths must be exactly the same so each part shares an equal load.

C.2.a. Pendants

A pendant is used to reduce wear and chafing at the towline end (particularly the eye and its splice). A pendant must be long enough so the towline connection is clear of obstructions on the towed vessel. (see **Figure 17-3**)

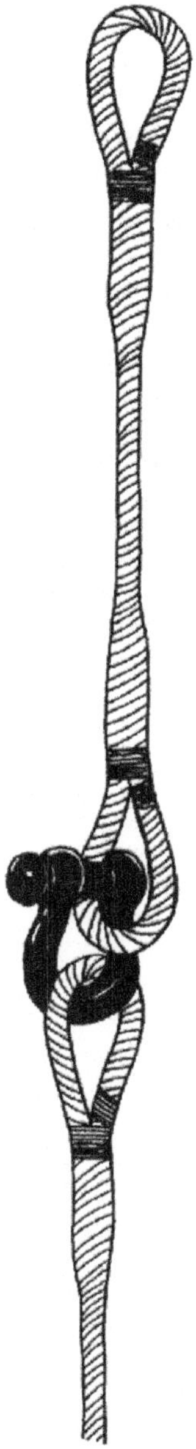

Figure 17-3
Pendant

C.2.b. Bridle

A bridle (a "Y" bridle) is used when both legs can be rigged to exert an equal pull on the hull of a distressed vessel, and is preferred for heavy weather towing. (see **Figure 17-11**) A bridle provides the best results where towed vessel deck fittings (chocks and cleats or bitts) are not right at the towed vessel's bow (as a bullnose), or where obstructions (bulwark or rigging) on the bow prevent a pendant or towline from making a direct lead back to the towing vessel. Use the following list as a guideline for attaching a bridle for towing:

- Use a long bridle when the best attachment points for the towed vessel are well aft to either side of the deck, but maintain a fair lead forward to reduce chafe.
- Remember that the amount of tension on each bridle leg increases with the size of the angle between the bridle legs.
- Keep the legs of the bridle long enough so the angle of the legs stays less than 30°.
- The legs must be long enough to reduce towed vessel yaw.
- Protect bridles with chafing gear when necessary.
- Use thimbles in the bridle leg eyes where they meet.
- When shackled to the towline, remember to mouse the shackle pin.

A bridle is also used by towing vessels without centerline towing capability or with transom obstructions (outboard motors or rigging). The bridle is attached to fittings in a manner to clear the obstructions. Again, bridle leg lengths must be equal to share the strain of the tow.

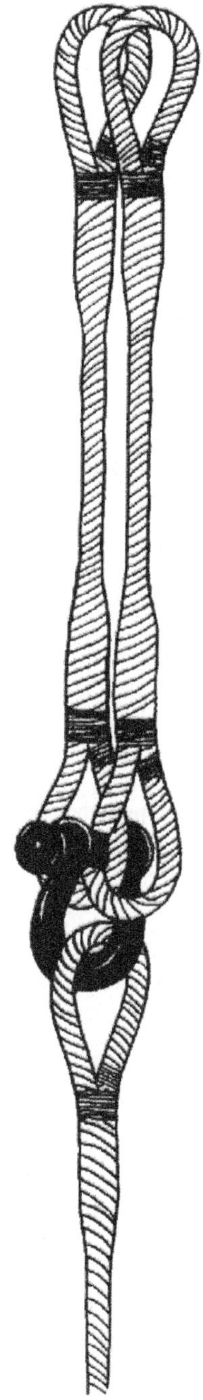

Figure 17-4
Bridle Connection

C.2.c. Pendant and Bridle Condition and Inspection

Safe and efficient towing requires undamaged, serviceable pendants and bridles. Crewmembers should inspect pendants and bridles on a regular basis to detect damage and to ensure bridle leg lengths are equal. For nylon pendants and bridles, the towline condition and inspection list provided in C.1.b should be used.

Wire rope bridles must be inspected for:

- Broken wires.
- Fish hooks (broken ends of wire protruding from the lay).
- Kinks.
- Worn or corroded portions (worn portions of wire rope appear as shiny, flattened surfaces).
- Crushed/flattened sections.

NOTE Inspect towlines, pendants, and bridles after each tow and whenever shock loading has occurred.

Messengers

C.3. Description

A towline is too heavy to cast more than a few feet. In rough weather or when impossible to get close enough to throw a towline to a distressed vessel, a messenger should be used to reach the other vessel. A messenger is a length of light line used to carry a larger line or hawser between vessels.

C.4. Passing a Towline

To pass a towline with a messenger, one end of a small line is attached to the end of the towline and the other end is cast to the other vessel's crew.

The lighter line is used to pull the towline across the distance between the vessels. Sometimes, multiple lines are used as messengers. An intermediate-sized line might be added between a heaving line and towline.

In most cases, a heaving line or float line will be used to make the initial pass to the vessel in need of a tow. If conditions (poor weather, risk of collision) do not permit an approach close enough to use a heaving line (more common in offshore cutter operations), then a bolo or line throwing gun projectile with shot line attached can be used to pass the messenger line to a disabled vessel (if available).

C.4.a. Heaving Line and Heaving Ball

A heaving line is made of light, flexible line with either a rubber ball or a monkey's fist at the throwing end. A heaving line must be in good condition, at least 75 feet long, and free of rot or weathering. (see **Figure 17-5**)

The bitter end of a heaving line is attached to the towline with a clove hitch, bowline, small carbiners, or snap hook. Slip clove hitches may work best in very cold weather because they are easier to untie. The longest heaves are cast downwind, but this may not always be possible. The throw should be targeted above the center of the vessel so the thrown line crosses over the deck and avoids breaking glass or injuring people.

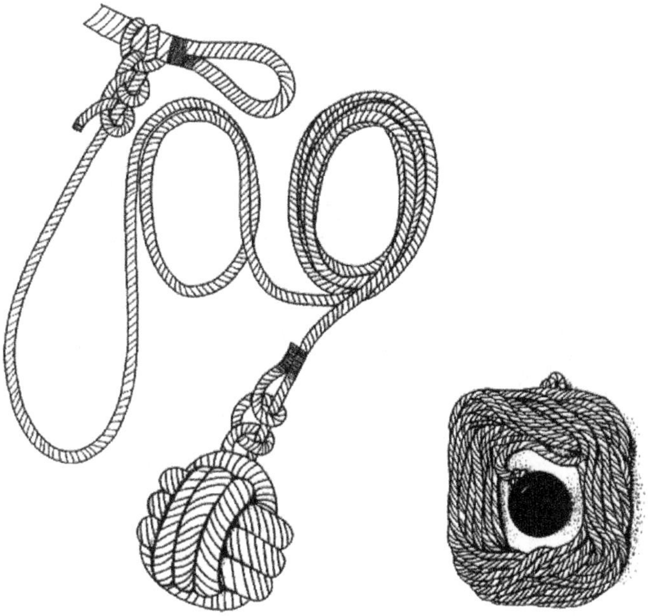

Figure 17-5
Types of Heaving Lines

C.4.b. Float Line

To reach a vessel beyond the range of a heaving line or in an inaccessible position, a buoyant synthetic line may be floated from upstream or upwind. One end is tied to a ring buoy or float, the other end to the towline, and the float line is thrown downstream in the direction of the distressed vessel. The current or wind will carry the float line toward the other vessel. This method is only effective if the wind or current can get the float within range of the other vessel.

Chafing Gear

C.5. Description

Chafing gear protects towlines, bridles, and pendants from wear caused by rubbing against deck edges, gunwales, bulwarks, chocks, taff rail or tow bars.

C.6. Preventing Chafing Damage

Layers of heavy canvas or leather can be tied with small stuff to the towline, bridle, or wire rope at contact points to prevent chafing damage. Sections of old fire hose also work well as chafing gear. Crewmembers must make sure the chafing gear stays in place for the duration of the tow.

C.7. Thimbles

Thimbles are designed to equalize the load on an eye of a line and provide maximum chafing protection to the inner surface of the eye. On double-braided nylon, thimbles made specifically for synthetic lines (see **Figure 17-6**) must be used. Galvanized "teardrop" shaped thimbles are used on wire rope.

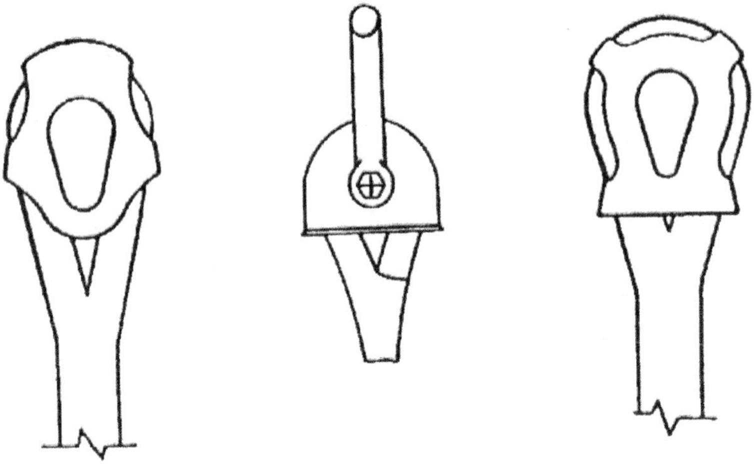

Figure 17-6
Thimbles

Deck Fittings and Other Fittings

C.8. Description

Fittings are attachments or fair lead points on vessels for towlines, anchor lines, and mooring lines. Many fishing and sailing vessels have other attachment points for standing and running rigging that could also provide tow rig attachment points or fair leads. For towing, attachment points and fair leads designed for horizontal loads should only be used.

Common fittings include bitts (mooring and towing), cleats, bollards, and sampson posts. Chocks, tow bars, and taff rails act as fair leads redirecting or supporting the towline. Pad eyes, turning and snatch blocks, winch drums, capstans, and windlasses should also be considered as attachment points or fair leads on a towed vessel. Trailerable boats usually have an eyebolt or eye fitting at the bow for an attachment point.

C.9. Condition and Inspection

The following regular inspections should be conducted of towing vessel fittings:

- Check for cracks, fractures, rust, corrosion, wood rot, fiberglass core softening, or delamination.
- Inspect surfaces that are normally hidden from view, particularly backing plates and under-deck fasteners.
- Tow bars are subject to high vibration and may loosen or cause stress fractures around their foundations.
- Ensure working surfaces are kept free from paint and relieve any surface roughness. A smooth working surface reduces wear, friction and chafing on lines.

C.10. Skiff Hook

The typical skiff hook has a quick-release safety buckle and snap hook clip that can be attached directly to the boathook handle. (see **Figure 17-7**) Skiff hook assemblies are commercially available. Perform the following procedures to use a skiff hook:

WARNING

Do not over stress a skiff hook. Never use one for any operation that might be more of a load than towing small, trailerable boats.

CAUTION !

Use extreme care when removing a skiff hook from a trailer eye fitting. Even at a dock, crewmembers risk injury from vessel movements.

C.7.a. Using a Skiff Hook

Step	Procedure
1	Attach the skiff hook line to a towline with a shackle or double becket bend.
2	Use the skiff hook assembly to reach down and place the hook into a small distressed vessel's trailer eyebolt.
3	Snap the hook into the eye and slip the handle off the round stock and pull back.

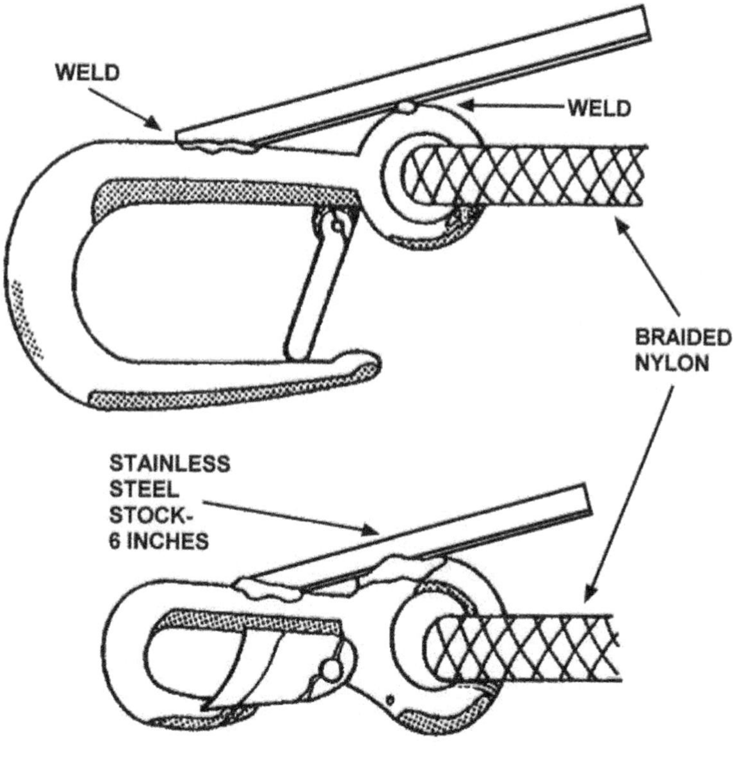

Figure 17-7
Skiff Hook

Drogues

C.11. Description

A drogue is a device that acts in the water somewhat the way a parachute works in the air. The drogue is deployed from the stern of the towed vessel to help control the towed vessel's motions. Coxswains and boat crews must familiarize themselves with the operating characteristics and effectiveness of available drogues, training with and testing drogues under various conditions to learn drogue capabilities. The time to learn about a drogue is before one is needed to deploy.

C.11.a. Towing Conditions

While trailing a drogue from the towed vessel is not common, it may be useful when a distressed vessel has lost rudder control. Normally drogues are not deployed when well offshore but rather inshore where greater control of the towed vessel is required. If necessary to tow a vessel with large swells directly on the stern, it may be more prudent to alter course or lengthen the towline rather than to deploy a drogue. Drogues are typically used when the tow is shortened as in preparing to tow into a bar or inlet. With a short hawser and large swells on the stern, the drogue is deployed to prevent the towed vessel from running up the stern of the towing vessel or "surfing" down the face of a wave. The drogue keeps a steady strain on the towline reducing shock-loading.

C.11.b. Drogue Size

The idea of the drogue is to provide backward pull on the stern of the towed vessel so that the wave will pass under the boat. It is important to match the size of the drogue to the towed boat, its deck fittings, and its overall condition. The larger, well-constructed cone drogues can exert a very large force on a boat's transom so the towed vessel's stern must be carefully examined.

There are numerous types, sizes and styles of drogues, all commercially available. (see **Figure 17-8**) Different-sized drogues are used for different conditions and different vessel sizes. A traditional drogue is a canvas or synthetic cloth cone, with the pointed end open. Drogues of this type have a ring in the base of the cone (the leading edge) to which attaches a four-part bridle. The other ends of the bridle connect to a swivel, which in turn, connects to a line made fast to the stern of the towed vessel. The towed vessel "tows" the drogue. Drogues sometimes have another line attached to the tail end for retrieval.

NOTE

A large drogue can cause stress that will damage a small boat. For a small boat, the larger the drogue used, the slower the towing speed must be. A slight increase in speed causes a tremendous increase in drogue tension.

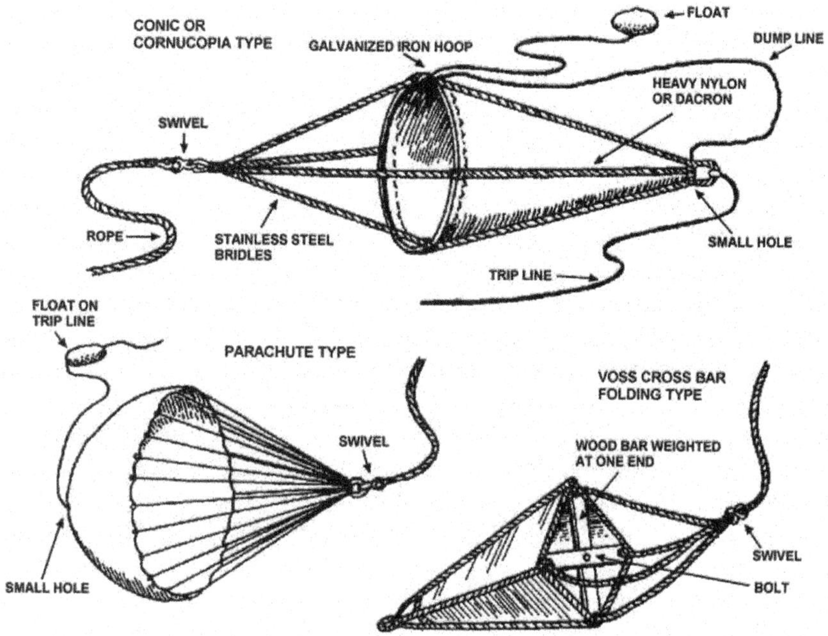

Figure 17-8
Drogue Types

C.12. Preparing the Drogue Gear

To prepare the drogue gear, perform the following procedures:

Step	Procedure
1	For the drogue towline, use 200 feet of 2-inch double-braided nylon.
2	Mark the drogue line every fifty feet.
3	Transfer the drogue rig to a distressed boat before taking it in tow.

The following checklist will help ensure that the drogue rig and related equipment are ready for transfer:

- Visually inspect the drogue rig for worn rusted, or corroded fittings and swivels, correct size shackles, and untangled bridles.
- Ensure that the drogue rig has 200 feet of two-inch, double-braided nylon line properly attached to the bridle swivel using a correctly sized shackle. Make sure it has no sharp fittings or exposed wires, and is stowed in a manner that will keep it intact until it is deployed.
- Provide all necessary equipment with a drogue rig such as extra shackles, bridles, straps, and chafing gear to achieve the best possible connection on the stern of a tow.

NOTE ✍ Auxiliary facilities are not required to carry drogues.

- Place all equipment in a gear bag with laminated written instructions and illustrations on how to rig a drogue, both with and without a bridle. At night attach a chemical light to the bag and include a flashlight inside.
- Attach flotation to the bag (usually a fender) and two lines, each 40 feet in length, to the handles of the gear bag. Bend a heaving line or buoyant rescue line onto one of the lines.

NOTE

> Determine the fittings to which the drogue will connect, how to make the connection, and how much line to deploy before sending it to the tow. Always ask about backing plates, fitting sizes, and strength of materials involved. Be cautious if an attachment point cannot be seen. Rely on experience and judgment.

C.13. Passing the Drogue

Perform the following procedures to pass the drogue:

Step	Procedure
1	Pass the drogue directly from the towing vessel to the towed vessel when in the best position.
2	The drogue and line can be heavy and awkward for the crew of the distressed vessel. If possible, maneuver the rescue vessel to pass the drogue to an area on the distressed vessel where the crew will not have to lift the apparatus a long distance.
3	Instead of immediately taking a boat in tow, stand by and watch the distressed vessel crew ready the drogue rig for deployment.
4	Provide visual inspection, verbal direction, and clarification if necessary.

NOTE

> Unless a crewmember from the towing vessel goes aboard the towed vessel, the towed vessel crew must carry out the following procedures. Provide them guidance and direction as needed.

C.14. Rigging the Drogue for Deployment

Perform the following procedures to rig the drogue for deployment:

Step	Procedure
1	Use attachment fittings as near the centerline as possible.
2	On many vessels, a bridle will be needed to spread the load between two separate fittings to center the drogue towline.
3	Winches, motor mounts, masts, and davit bases are other possible locations for good strong connections.
4	When trying to compensate for a jammed rudder, attach the drogue well off the centerline, close to the quarter, opposite the side where the rudder is jammed.
5	Connect the bridle legs or the drogue lines to the appropriate fittings.

C.15. Deploying the Drogue

Perform the following procedures to begin or resume towing:

Step	Procedure
1	Start the tow moving, and then direct the towed vessel crew to deploy the drogue.
2	Move the tow forward slowly, just enough to control the tow.
3	Direct the towed vessel's crew to recheck connections, put the drogue in the water, and pay out the line slowly from a safe position. Unless circumstances direct otherwise, pay out all 200 feet of drogue line.

WARNING Drogue use does not justify towing through breakers. When in doubt, stay out.

C.15.a. Beginning or Resuming Tow

Perform the following procedures to begin or resume towing:

Step	Procedure
1	Once the drogue sets and starts to pull, slowly increase speed while the distressed vessel's crew observes the rig.
2	Check attachment points and effectiveness of the drogue. If adjustments must be made, slow down and make them.
3	Once the drogue is deployed, pick the most comfortable course and speed. Control of the tow is more important than speed. Towing a drogue at too great a speed may damage the towed vessel or may cause the drogue rig to fail. One of the crew on the towed vessel should monitor the drogue.

C.16. Shortening Up and Recovering Drogue

Because a tripping line is not recommended, several alternate recovery methods are available. If recovery is not properly set up and controlled, a drogue may become fouled on the tow, a buoy, or other object. Perform the following procedures to shorten up and recover the drogue:

Step	Procedure
1	Slow or stop the tow, then haul it in. The primary method for shortening up or recovering a drogue is accomplished by slowing the tow or stopping completely. Have people onboard the tow slowly pull in the drogue. Provide enough maneuvering room to bring the tow around on a course causing little or no tension on the drogue line during recovery.
2	Have another vessel come alongside and transfer the drogue line to it. The second vessel can recover the drogue rig.
3	Attach a color-coded dumping line, a short piece of line run from the bridle shackle to the tail of the drogue, outside the cone.
4	Haul the drogue to the stern and recover and pull the dumping line. When pulled, it inverts the drogue making it easy to recover. A dumping line is only suitable for large drogues that drain slowly.

C.17. Storing Drogue

Perform the following procedures to store the drogue:

Step	Procedure
1	Use a synthetic gear bag to hold the drogue for storage and deployment.
2	Feed the bitter end of the line out through a grommet in the bottom and stuff the remainder of the line inside the bag.
3	Use the drawstring at the top to hold the bag closed.
4	Ensure the line bag can hold 200 feet of 2-inch line.

C.18. Inspecting Drogue Condition

Perform the following procedures to inspect the condition of the drogue:

Step	Procedure
1	Inspect the drogue for tears, cuts and holes.
2	Inspect the drogue towline and bridle using the same guidelines for towlines and bridles as listed in C.1.b.
3	Check for worn, rusted or corroded fittings, swivels and shackles.
4	Ensure there are no sharp edges or points on hardware.

Other Equipment

C.19. Description

Alongside lines, fenders, and general hardware account for other equipment that may be necessary to employ for towing evolutions.

C.20. Alongside Lines

At some point during a tow, the towing vessel most likely will need to tow the distressed vessel alongside in restricted waters or moor to the towed vessel. The towing vessel will usually need a combination of lines to allow for vessels of different size.

C.20.a. Alongside Line Storage

Each Coast Guard standard boat equipment list specifies number, length and size of alongside lines for vessel type. Stowage and weight considerations will guide other vessel types.

C.20.b. Alongside Line Condition and Inspection

Alongside lines must be kept in the same condition as towlines and bridles. (see C.1.b)

C.21. Fenders

Fenders are portable rubber, synthetic, or foam devices that protect a hull when maneuvering in close proximity to other vessels, docks or pilings. Fenders have either eye(s) or a longitudinal hole for attaching lines. They can be spherical, cylindrical, or rectangular prisms. Fender size varies greatly, and the appropriate size should be used depending on the situation. Fenders that will keep space between vessel hulls or rub rails and hulls should be used.

C.21.a. Fender Deployment

Fenders should be used whenever there is the possibility of a hull making contact with another object. They should be strategically placed to account for different hull shapes (maximum beam, tumble-home, flare) or appendages (rub rails, spray rails, trawl rigs, platforms).

WARNING Never use hands or feet to fend off another object (pier, boat, buoy). This could result in serious physical injury. Always use a fender!

C.21.b. Fender Placement

Because vessels are shifted around by water, fenders may need to be moved for best effectiveness, even after strategic placement. Most vessel crews are too small to have a dedicated fender tender; therefore, the need should be minimized beforehand.

C.22. General Hardware

General hardware for use in towing includes shackles, snap hooks, carbiners, swivels, and other items, that should have the following characteristics:

- These items must be made of strong, low-maintenance materials.
- They must be easy to connect and disconnect or open and close by all crewmembers.
- All hardware should resist distortion.
- Shackles need a large enough throat to easily cross an eye or thimble. Captive-pin (safety) shackles should be used wherever possible. The pin should be attached to the shackle with a lanyard to prevent pin loss.

When using general hardware, crewmembers should be sure to:

- Keep all hardware clean and lubricated. Inspect hardware after each use.
- Be particularly cautious of hardware that has been shock-loaded.
- Immediately replace any hardware that is distorted, spreading, excessively worn, or stripped.

Section D. Standard Towing Procedures

Introduction

The procedures listed below are derived from time-tested, experience-based techniques proven to be effective, safe, and efficient. They shall be real actions performed by coxswain and crew. Some of the actions can be executed at the same time to minimize duplication or avoid wasting time. In extreme conditions or emergencies, some actions may not be possible. If actions must be skipped, potential risks should be assessed and managed risk. If a problem occurs at any step in the procedures, it may be safer and easier to "backup" to the last successfully completed step and restart.

In this section

This section contains the following information:

Pre-Towing Procedures

D.1. Description

The amount of effort put into preparing ahead of time will pay off with safer, easier execution of the tow.

NOTE

Throughout the entire towing evolution, open communication between the coxswain and crew and towed vessel is absolutely necessary for safety.

D.2. Receiving Notification and Accepting Task

When notified of a towing mission, the coxswain takes the following procedures as common practice:

Step	Procedure
1	Get as much critical information as necessary.
2	Write down the information.
3	Develop a full understanding of the situation.
4	Make a conscious decision to "accept" the tasking.

The coxswain is ultimately responsible for mission execution, so the tasking should only be confirmed in view of vessel and crew capability. If tasking exceeds vessel or crew capability, particularly if not an actual distress case, the coxswain's concerns should be made clear. Vessel towing limits, maximum range, sea-keeping, crew fatigue, etc. are all essential considerations to assess and manage potential risk.

NOTE

Keep a brief (plastic clipboard and grease pencil) written record of critical information. Include vessel information (length, type, displacement, disability) number of persons on the boat, position, and environmental conditions. A written record allows the crew to concentrate on task completion without having to later rely on memory for needed facts. Repeating information over the radio is frustrating and distracting. As information changes, update your records and notify OPCON.

D.3. Briefing the Crew

The coxswain shall brief the crew as follows:

Step	Procedure
1	Conduct a thorough boat crew briefing.
2	Explain the situation and what might be expected, using the facts.
3	If there is any confusion or uncertainty, clear it right away.
4	The crew must participate and ask relevant questions.
5	Assign personnel to assist with preparations and collect any needed tow rig or assistance items not aboard the towing vessel.
6	Ensure proper safety and personnel protective equipment is donned by the crew.

D.4. Evaluating Conditions

Boat crews shall evaluate conditions for a tow as follows:

Step	Procedure
1	Note how the different environmental conditions will affect the operation.
2	As conditions may likely change during the mission, estimate which phase of the mission will encounter which conditions and whether on-scene conditions will be different from those en route.
3	Keep a record of the present and forecast conditions (do not try to rely on memory) and update as necessary. Necessary condition information includes: • Existing and forecast marine weather (including winds, seas, bar conditions). • Currents and tide (next high/low, slack/maximum). • Daylight/Darkness (sunrise/sunset, twilight).

D.5. Operating and Navigating the Vessel Safely

The only way to perform the tow is get there safely. A sense of urgency should never affect judgment. For safe operation and navigation, the following precautions apply:

Step	Procedure
1	Maintain safe speed for the conditions (seas, visibility, and other traffic).
2	Keep constant awareness of navigational position and navigational hazards.
3	Stay aware of the distressed vessel's position.

D.6. Communicating with Distressed Vessel

Contact should be made with the distressed vessel, if possible. Communication shall be as follows:

Step	Procedure
1	Provide the distressed vessel with ETA.
2	Advise persons on the distressed vessel to put on PFDs (if this has not been done already).
3	Get details of deck layout, fittings and backing plates. Ask about the size of chocks and cleats to determine size of towline, bridle or drogue line and bridle.
4	Ask for information the distressed vessel's crew thinks is important before arriving on scene (lines or gear in the water, nearby vessels, etc.).
5	Determine if anything has changed since the distressed vessel's initial contact with the Operational Commander.
6	Ascertain any sense of heightened urgency.
7	Inform the distressed vessel that once on scene, conditions will be observed and final preparations made before setting up the tow and further instructions will then be provided.
8	Establish and maintain a communications schedule.

D.7. Preparing Equipment

Equipment shall be prepared for the tow as follows:

Step	Procedure
1	With the information known, begin to plan a tow rig.
2	Ready all necessary equipment and re-inspect it (i.e., towline, bridle, shackles, knife, heaving lines, messenger line, chafing gear, etc.) as directed by the coxswain.

D.8. Performing an On-Scene Assessment

Once on-scene, use the following procedures:

Step	Procedure
1	Watch the vessel's movement (pitch, roll) in the seas and determine the effect of wind and current on the distressed vessel's drift rate and lateral movement. Compare it to own vessel's drift. Knowing the different drift rates will help determine the best approach.
2	Evaluate the location and any abnormal condition of deck fittings.
3	Confirm the number of persons onboard and ensure they are wearing PFDs.
4	Note any unusual conditions that may affect towing procedures (i.e., loose gear, rigging, or debris in the water).
5	Communicate any concerns to the distressed vessel.
6	Decide whether to put a crewmember aboard the distressed vessel.
7	Decide if it is best to remove the crew from the distressed vessel.
8	Determine if an equipment transfer (drogue, pump, radio) will be necessary.
9	After evaluating the on-scene situation and making risk assessment, decide whether to tow or not.

NOTE

This period of pre-tow, on-scene analysis is when crew experience and judgment on both vessels must mesh. Discuss concerns before directing action. The distressed vessel's crew may have information that the towing vessel's crew does not. The easiest way to get the big picture may be by circling the distressed vessel, if possible. A method to check drift rate of the distressed vessel is to maneuver the towing vessel onto the same heading as the distressed vessel and stop astern of it. If the distance between the vessels increases, one vessel has a higher drift rate. Note the different angles or aspects the towing vessel and the towed vessel hold towards the winds and seas. The only time the drift rate and aspect will be exactly the same is if the vessels are exactly the same.

D.9. Making-Up the Tow Rig and Preparing for Transfer

Crewmembers should visualize the tow in progress, given all the factors identified in the on-scene assessment. This may help identify any special considerations. Elements of the tow rig should be appropriately sized for the specific distressed vessel (i.e., a 3-inch towline with eye might not fit through a bow chock or around a cleat of a 25-foot boat).

Step	Procedure
1	Set up the tow vessel deck with all equipment staged and ready.
2	Attach 2 heaving lines (one primary, one backup) to the tow rig.
3	Assign crewmembers to each heaving line, and to bitt or line handler duties.

NOTE Pass equipment (pump, drogue, etc.) and transfer personnel before making the approach to transfer the tow rig.

D.10. Determining the Approach

Though optimal to make an approach from down wind and down sea, the drift and aspect of the distressed vessel may determine the approach. A vessel with a large superstructure forward will tend to lay stern-to the wind. (Many outboard-powered vessels exhibit this tendency to "weathervane.") A vessel with deep draft and low superstructure will generally lie broadside to the seas. Of course, there are many positions in between. The approach to a vessel drifting down wind and down sea, "stern to" the wind and seas will be different from the approach to a vessel lying "beam to." The usual approach by a boat to make a tow is with the bow into the seas.

Once the coxswain has determined how to make the approach he/she shall inform the crew, specifically telling them:

- From which side to pass the tow rig (or equipment).
- When (in what relative position of the two vessels) to pass the tow rig.
- Whether to use a heaving line.

D.11. Briefing the Distressed Vessel

Perform the following procedures when briefing the distressed vessel:

Step	Procedure
1	If transferring crew or equipment before the tow, relate when and how.
2	Explain plans and pass safety instructions. Include enough information so the distressed vessel's crew does not have to ask questions once the approach begins.
3	Describe the towing approach.
4	Tell when and how the tow rig will be passed.
5	Give tow rig connection instructions (how to lead, where to attach).
6	Inquire about type and condition of tow connection points.
7	List emergency breakaway procedures.
8	Describe emergency signals.
9	Instruct on general safety during the approach and passing the tow rig.

NOTE Limit the content of this briefing to information the distressed vessel needs to know before the tow begins. Once hooked up and in tow, there will be opportunity to pass additional information.

Towing Astern

D.12. Description

The most common towing technique is to tow the distressed vessel from astern of the rescue vessel.

D.13. Making the Approach

The on-scene assessment gives the knowledge of how conditions affect both vessels. Knowledge and experience with the towing vessel's handling and maneuvering should allow to overcoming conditions and putting the towing vessel in a safe position for the crew to pass the tow rig.

D.14. Establishing a Danger Zone

Before starting the approach, an imaginary danger zone is established around the distressed vessel and the approach is made from the outside. The size of a danger zone depends upon conditions and the arrangement of the distressed vessel. The poorer the conditions, the larger the danger zone. (see **Figure 17-9**).

NOTE

> A boat crew's teamwork, communications, and experience are key to a safe, successful approach.

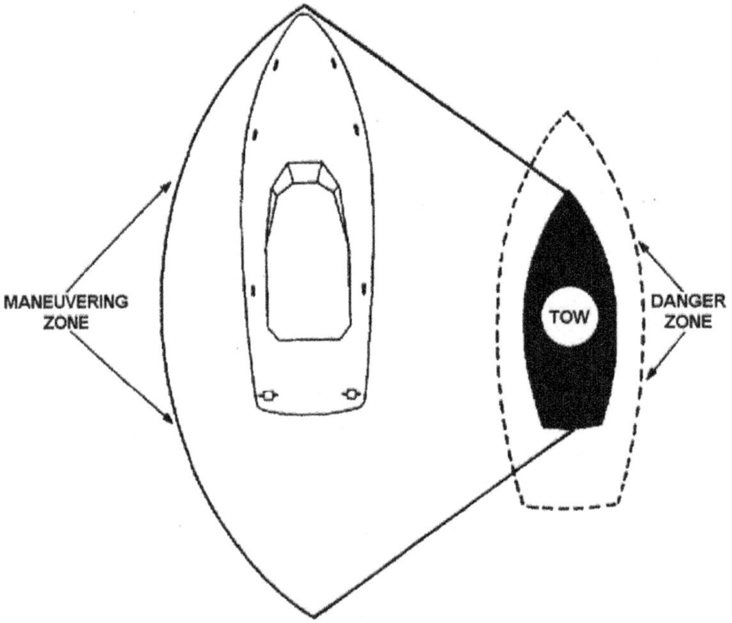

Figure 17-9
Danger Zone

CAUTION !

> The coxswain must let crewmembers know before making correcting maneuvers so that they can tend lines and ready themselves.

D.15. Maneuvering to an Optimum Position

The towing vessel should be maneuvered so that the crew can maximize use of the best deck work area on the vessel for passing and working the tow rig. This will provide the opportunity for better vessel control and visibility for the coxswain, while keeping a safe distance from the distressed vessel, and providing a safe escape route in case of emergency. Perform the following procedures to maneuver to this optimum position:

Step	Procedure
1	In calm conditions, make the approach at an angle that allows the crew the best opportunity to pass the tow rig.
2	In rough conditions, make the approach into the prevailing wind and seas. If the wind is different from the seas, make the approach into the seas. This usually maximizes control for the coxswain and ensures the most stable platform for the crew. A coxswain may split the difference between the wind and seas to hold station.
3	Make the approach at the slowest speed necessary to maintain steerage.
4	Once in the optimum position, station keep on the distressed vessel. Station keeping maintains the position and heading relative to the weather and seas outside the danger zone. This is usually done by use of helm and engine control.
5	To station keep, the coxswain must simultaneously focus on the seas, the bitt and line handlers, and the position with respect to the distressed vessel.
6	Maneuver and apply power early and smoothly as distance and angle to the distressed vessel change.
7	If the towing vessel begins to move towards the danger zone, maneuver to open the distance.
8	If the distressed vessel begins to get away from the towing vessel, close the gap.
9	Use correcting maneuvers (opening and closing) before a problem develops. A small correction early can prevent a large problem later.

NOTE

> Actual maneuvering techniques vary from vessel to vessel and are mastered by practice and experience. Actual station keeping techniques also vary as the specific wind and sea conditions affect the specific distressed vessel.

CAUTION !

Maneuver as required, but it is preferable not to make opening and closing maneuvers when lines are over (except the heaving line). Avoid making correcting maneuvers on the face of a wave.

D.16. Station Keeping

The following procedures apply for station keeping:

Step	Procedure
1	The coxswain now must station keep outside the danger zone and in a maneuvering zone (usually a 90° arc, from 45° off the bow to 45° off the stern, with the distance between vessels no greater than the length of the heaving line) for the crew to pass the tow rig.
2	The coxswain must continue station keeping until the tow rig is connected and the transition to towing astern begins.
3	The crew must make every effort to ensure that passing the tow rig goes smoothly, quickly and safely.
	In calm conditions, station keeping may simply be holding the nearest safe position to take advantage of the best angle for the crew to pass the tow rig. However, even though conditions may be calm, a vessel's wake or a current can suddenly increase the chance of hull-to-hull contact with the distressed vessel. A safe escape route shall be planned for all approaches and while station keeping.

D.17. Passing the Tow Rig

Once optimum position (see **Figure 17-10**) is maintained, the tow rig may be passed as follows:

Step	Procedure
1	All lines, equipment, and connections should already be inspected, made ready, and double-checked.
2	Minimize loose towline on deck by paying out directly from the reel.
3	If the towing vessel is not equipped with a towline reel, fake the towline carefully so that it will not kink or tangle.
4	In heavy weather, use caution to ensure line is not washed over the side and into the screw.

NOTE

While passing and connecting the tow rig, and transitioning to stern tow, use loud and clear communication between crewmembers and coxswain to prevent accidents. Whenever the coxswain directs an action, a crewmember must take that action and reply that the action has been taken. Whenever a crewmember advises the coxswain of status or action, the coxswain must acknowledge same.

D.17.a. Calm Conditions

When passing the rig in calm conditions (no heaving line), the following procedures apply:

Step	Procedure
1	Coxswain directs crew to pass the rig.
2	Line handler hands over or carefully tosses the end of the rig to a person on the distressed vessel. The person receiving the rig must be physically able to haul it to the connecting point and then attach it properly.
3	Line handler advises coxswain that the rig is away.
4	Line handler pays out and takes in towline as required to eliminate any risk of fouling the propellers, rudders, rigging, or other fixtures.
5	Line handler advises the coxswain when the action has been successfully executed, and when the towline is properly secured to the towed vessel.

D.17.b. Using a Heaving Line

When passing a rig using a heaving line the following procedures apply:

Step	Procedure
1	Wet both heaving lines to make them more flexible and minimize risk of them becoming tangled.
2	Take two-thirds of a heaving line coil into the casting hand leaving the remainder in the other hand.
3	Check that the area is clear of people and obstructions.
4	Advise coxswain when ready and await direction before casting.
5	Coxswain direct cast.
6	Call out "HEADS UP" as a warning to people onboard the distressed vessel to take cover and watch out for the toss.

NOTE ✍

It takes practice to cast a heaving line properly. Adapt technique to conditions for a safe and successful result.

D.17.c. Casting

When casting a heaving line, the following procedures apply:

Step	Procedure
1	Cast a heaving line so it falls across the distressed vessel's deck.
2	Tell coxswain when the heaving line has been cast and whether it has been retrieved; fell short, or missed altogether.
3	Advise coxswain whenever a line is in the water, so no maneuvering will be done which could possibly foul the propellers.
4	If the first cast is not retrieved, quickly recover the line and advise coxswain when the second heaving line is ready. When coxswain directs, repeat the procedures.
5	Once line is successfully received on the disabled vessel, untie the unused/unretrieved heaving line from the tow rig (take care to untie the correct line) and advise the coxswain that the rig is ready to be transferred.
6	Coxswain will direct to send the rig; crew replies and begins transferring the rig. Tend the messenger (if used) to reduce the risk of it becoming fouled. Once the rig starts across, maneuvering opportunities become very limited.
7	Advise coxswain of tow rig transfer progress (when bridle is clear or aboard distressed vessel, when towline is going over or aboard, etc.).

D.18. Connecting the Tow Rig

Methods of tow rig connection generally available are: (see **Figure 17-11**)

- Tow rig to fittings.
- Tow rig to trailer eye.

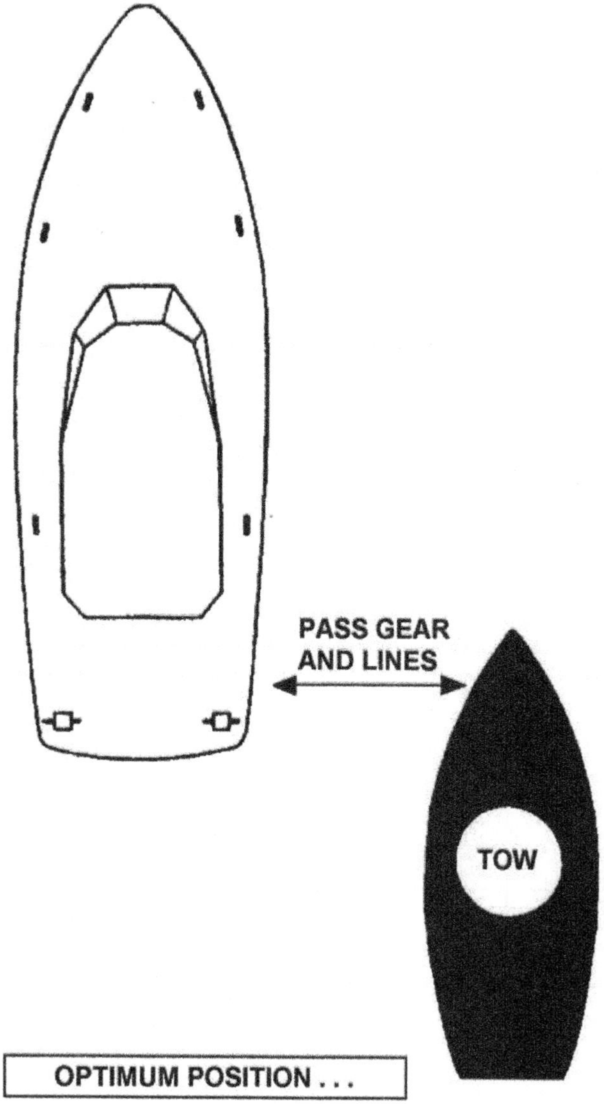

Figure 17-10
Optimum Position for Passing the Tow Rig

Connecting Tow Rig to Fittings

CAUTION ! Though deck fittings should be checked during pre-tow procedures, do not hesitate to stop the connection if something is wrong. If necessary, recover the rig and transfer a crewmember to the distressed vessel to physically inspect the fittings.

CAUTION ! Transfer of people between vessels is not a common practice. Whenever this is considered, it must be conducted with extreme caution for the safety of people on both vessels.

D.19. Description

The attachment point(s) for a tow rig must be sound. Towing places a tremendous strain on deck fittings, especially in rough conditions. On the distressed vessel, bow bitts, forward cleats and Samson posts will usually provide the best attachment points. Fittings secured to a deck with through bolts and backing plates or those secured to the keel or structural framing should always be used. Other fittings, such as pad-eyes or capstans, may also provide solid attachment points.

Unless the towing vessel puts a crewmember aboard the distressed vessel, the towed vessel crew is responsible for these actions. A good brief to the distressed vessel will address each item, but in the rush to get things set up aboard the distressed vessel, the crew may forget important steps. The towing vessel crew must closely watch, and advise when necessary.

CAUTION ! Avoid connecting the towline to an off-centerline fitting on the towed vessel. Use a bridle for an equal amount of strain on both sides of the bow.

D.20. Ensuring a Fair Lead

When ensuring a fair lead, the following procedures apply:

Step	Procedure
1	Lead a single point tow rig (pendant or towline) through or to a fitting as close to the centerline as possible. Once led through a secure chock near centerline, the end of the rig can go to a suitable deck fitting.
2	Lead the parts of a bridle through chocks equally spaced from the centerline.

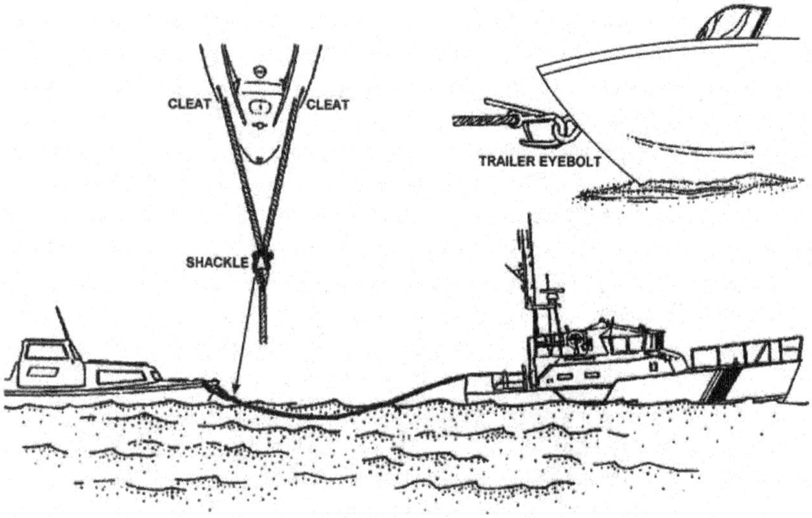

Figure 17-11
Bridle and Trailer Eyebolt Tow Rig Connection

D.21. Making Fast to Fittings

When making fast to fittings, the following procedures apply:

Step	Procedure
1	Connect the eye of a pendant or towline to posts, bitts, or cleats so that it will not come loose when a strain is placed on the rig.
2	Connect the bridle to fittings located at points that allow equal pull to be exerted on them.
3	Check that the center of the bridle is on centerline or the extension of the centerline.
4	Minimize the angle made where the bridle joins the towline by using fittings as far forward as possible. (see **Figure 17-12**)

D.22. Installing Chafing Gear

Where necessary, when installing chafing gear the tow rig should be protected from abrasion or chafing, particularly if the rig takes a sharp turn at chocks or comes close to contact with any obstructions.

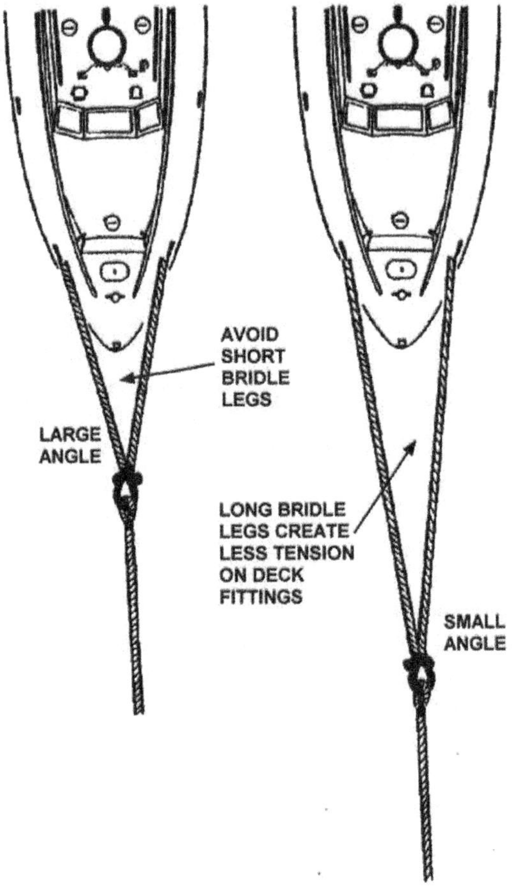
AVOID
SHORT
BRIDLE
LEGS
LARGE
ANGLE
LONG BRIDLE
LEGS CREATE
LESS TENSION
ON DECK
FITTINGS
SMALL
ANGLE

Figure 17-12
Towline Connection Showing Bridle Angle

Connecting Tow Rig to a Trailer Eye

CAUTION !	To reduce risk in connecting the tow rig to the trailer eye, use a skiff hook.

D.23. Description

On smaller, trailerable boats, the trailer eye is frequently the sturdiest fitting available to attach a tow rig. Attaching a towline to the trailer eye is a dangerous technique. It requires the towing vessel to maneuver very close to a distressed boat and requires crewmembers to extend themselves over the side between two vessels, or under the flared bow sections of the distressed boat.

WARNING Do not use a shackle to directly connect a towline to a trailer eye. This requires crewmembers to get too close under the bow of the distressed vessel.

D.24. Attaching the Skiff Hook

A newer style of skiff hook with a quick-release safety buckle and snap hook clip is in common use. Manufacturer instructions should be reviewed for its proper use. The older style skiff hook requires the following procedures:

Step	Procedure
1	Connect the skiff hook pendant to the towline using a double becket bend or shackle.
2	Slide the skiff hook into the boat hook handle.
3	While keeping the pendant taut, extend the boat hook and snap the skiff hook into the trailer eye.

Transitioning to Stern Tow

CAUTION ! Do not put a working turn on the bitt until the rig is securely fastened to a tow and POBs are clear of the bow.

D.25. Moving Away

When moving away, the following procedures apply:

Step	Procedure
1	Once the towline is secured on the distressed vessel, persons on the towed vessel should clear the bow.
2	Slowly move the towing vessel out of optimum position and the maneuvering zone.
3	Give particular attention to the direction the towline tends and the amount of slack in the line.
4	The coxswain instructs the crewmember to take a working turn on the bitt. Different towing bitts require different types of working turns. Use a method to provide enough towline-to-bitt contact surface to ensure control of the towline.
5	Pay out towline gradually in conjunction with the towing vessel's movement.
6	Slowly maneuver to a position in line with the towed vessel's centerline (if maneuvering room permits).
7	Always start the tow by pulling the disabled vessel ahead. Do not try to turn the vessel right away. Pulling on a vessel at a sharp angle increases the initial strain on the towline, could damage equipment, or possibly capsize the boat.

WARNING

> Crews risk injury from a running towline, with the possibilities of injuring their hands and arms in the tow bitt, tow reel, or in bights of line faked on deck. If the towline starts to run, reduce speed immediately. The crewmember working the tow bitt should regain control of the towline after the line stops running.

CAUTION !

> Gradually come to a pay out course. Rapid movements or changes in direction increase the risk of:
> - Fouling the towline in propellers or on deck fittings.
> - Shock-loads.
> - Loss of towline control.

D.26. Maneuvering to Pay-Out Course

Once the distance allows clear movement of a tow the towing vessel can be maneuvered to allow a smooth pay-out of the towline. As tension increases in the towline, static forces will be felt as the tow rig tries to move the towed vessel. Transitioning is the initial test of strength and performance for the tow rig and connections. Each towing vessel will react uniquely to this initial resistance. The pivot-point distance, propulsion and steering, and size difference between towing and towed vessels and weather will determine how the towed vessel will react. Actual maneuvering techniques are mastered through practice and experience. Minimize surge and shock-loading.

The bitt person must have complete control of the towline. Too much towing vessel headway may cause the bitt person to lose control of towline tension, and the towline will start to run.

D.27. Paying-Out the Tow Line

Paying out towline should be continued until the initial amount of towline scope is satisfactory.

WARNING

> Do not attempt to make up the bitt with a strain on a towline. This increases risk of injury by catching hands, fingers, and arms between the bitt and the towline.

D.28. Making Up the Bitt

Once the desired scope of towline is deployed, the coxswain directs the crew to make up the bitt. Forward motion should be stowed enough to slack the towline, and then the proper turns can be applied.

D.29. Setting a Towing Watch

The towing watch has a critical responsibility. In addition to the crewmember assigned, it is a collateral duty for all other crewmembers. The condition of the vessel in tow and the towline must be constantly monitored.

Underway With Stern Tow

D.30. Description

The best course to safe haven is not always the shortest distance. A course that gives the best ride for both vessels should be chosen. At times, the vessels may have to tack (run a zigzag type course) to maintain the best ride. A firm understanding of the dynamic forces in towing help to ensure a safe tow.

D.31. Briefing the Towed Vessel

The following instructions and information that will apply to each step of the tow astern should be shared with the towed vessel:

- General safety (PFDs, staying clear of tow rig, tow rig chafe, location of crew).
- Equipment (pumps, drogues).
- Steering (whether to man helm or lock rudder amidships, whether to steer on towing vessel stern).
- Route to take, expected weather and seas, destination, ETA.
- Lighting, sound signals.
- Communications (primary/secondary radio frequencies, times of status reports).
- Emergencies (breakaways, signals).

D.32. Deploying Drogue

If drogue deployment is necessary, (i.e., to counteract a jammed rudder or other condition), the drogue should be deployed while barely making way before increasing speed to the planned towing speed. (see *Section C, Towing Equipment* for procedures)

D.33. Maintaining a Catenary

Once underway with a tow astern, a proper length of towline should be maintained as discussed in B.12 of this chapter. Gravity causes a "dip" or downward sag (known as catenary) to form in the middle of the towline as it is lengthened. This catenary acts as a natural shock absorber for a tow rig and is a major factor in counteracting shock-loading. (see **Figure 17-13**).

D.34. Staying in Step

The tow should be kept in step at a proper distance behind the towing vessel. When the towing vessel is on a wave crest, the towed vessel should also be on a wave crest several waves astern.

If the towing vessel is riding up a crest while the tow is sliding down a crest, the towline slackens. Control of the tow may be lost. If an adjustment is not made when the towing vessel starts to slide down the crest into the trough, as the towed vessel starts to climb a crest, the towline becomes taut counteract shock-loading the tow rig. To prevent this from occurring, the towline scope should be increased to get the tow on crest at the same time as the towing vessel. Careful increase or decrease of power to vary towing vessel speed may also help.

Other measures that may help to stay in step include:

- Altering course to increase the angle of the tow to the waves (to approximately 45°).
- Deploying a drogue. In really confused seas, drogue deployment could help by preventing the towed vessel from surfing down the face of a wave.

Sometimes conditions make staying in step impossible. In such cases, the techniques above and reduce speed should be used to counteract shock-loading.

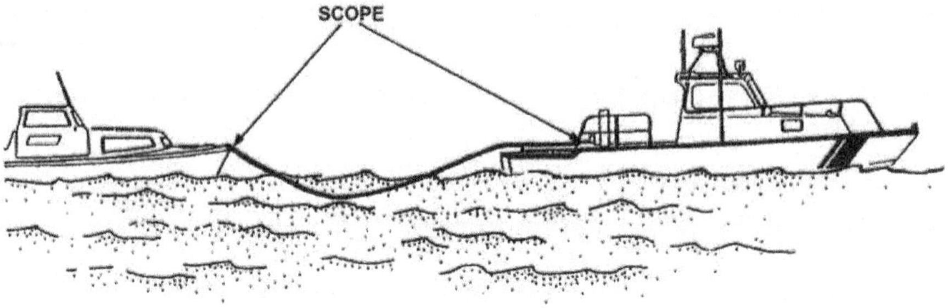

Figure 17-13
Scope of Towline with Catenary

D.35. Minimizing Yaw

The tow is said to yaw when it veers to one side or the other. Yaw can be caused by trim (including list, heeling or rolling, or by a bow-down attitude), rudder problems and wave action. Severe yawing is extremely dangerous and, if not corrected, may cause one or both vessels to capsize. Yawing also places tremendous strain on deck fittings and connections. Ways to reduce or minimize towed vessel yaw include:

- Change towline scope.
- Adjust trim (more easily done on a smaller vessel) to raise the bow or counteract list.
- Decrease speed or alter course to reduce effect of waves and wind.
- Deploy a drogue (particularly to overcome rudder problems).
- Use a bridle.

Crewmembers should keep close watch on the action of the tow and immediately report any unusual movements to the coxswain. If yawing cannot be reduced or controlled, it may be prudent to heave to until sea conditions improve or the source of the yaw is corrected.

NOTE

Currents can cause a relatively constant or gradual offset of the towed vessel from the towing vessel's intended track or heading. Do not mistake this for yaw. (See "Compensating for Current," later in this chapter.)

WARNING

Due to safety concerns, never try to tow a hull faster than the hull design speed. Above hull speed, the vessel will try to ride up on its bow wave, becoming unstable and, in extreme cases, could possibly capsize. Also, wave drag (even one large wake) could slow the hull to displacement speed and cause a severe shock-load in the tow rig as the towing force tries to pull the towed vessel back on plane. In response to this shock-load, the towed vessel could plow its bow into another wave and swamp or capsize.

CAUTION !

Do not overlook the effects of wind and seas on determining safe towing speed. Though conditions can change during a long tow, be particularly careful when transition takes place in relatively protected waters. What may have been a safe speed during transition before could become dangerous for the towed vessel once it gets out of the lee of a headland, wharf, or large vessel.

D.36. Towing at a Safe Speed

A safe and comfortable towing speed maximizes towing efficiency. Damage, sinkings and loss of life have occurred as a direct result of towing too fast. Maximum safe towing speed is based on the vessel's waterline length and hull shape, but wind and sea conditions could dictate a much slower speed. The following formula shows how to calculate maximum safe towing speed:

S = Maximum towing speed (hull design speed)
Ss = Maximum safe towing speed
Lw = Square root of length at waterline
S = 1.34 x Lw
Ss = S - (10% x S) a 10% reduction in the maximum towing speed

For example, to determine a safe towing speed for a boat that has a 36-foot waterline length, the following calculations apply:

S = 1.34 x Lw
S = 1.34 x (square root of 36)
S = 1.34 x 6
S = 8.0 knots
Ss = 8.0 - (.1 x 8.0)
Ss = 8.0 - .8
Ss = 7.2 knots

Figure 17-14 shows calculated safe towing speeds based on waterline length.

If it is possible to tow fast enough to get the vessel up to hull design speed, the strain and stress of the tow can be reduced for both vessels. Often, due to weather, seas, and other conditions, a hull will not be able to be towed fast enough to take advantage of its design. **Figure 17-14** lists the recommended maximum safe speeds for all vessels.

NOTE

Where and to what the tow rig is connected will also have an affect on the towing speed. Example: A small craft can be towed at a greater speed if its trailer eyebolt is used instead of a fitting up on deck. By connecting the towline to the eyebolt, the towline will pull the bow with more upward force compared to pulling the bow down if the tow is connected to a fitting on deck.

MAXIMUM TOWING SPEEDS					
DISPLACEMENT AND PLANING HULL VESSEL TOWING SPEEDS					
VESSEL'S WATERLINE LENGTH	SQUARE ROOT	MAXIMUM TOWING SPEED	VESSEL'S WATERLINE LENGTH	SQUARE ROOT	MAXIMUM TOWING SPEED
20	4 5	6 KNOTS	70	8 4	11 3 KNOTS
25	5 0	6 7	75	8 7	11 7
30	5 5	7 4	80	9 0	12 0
35	6 0	8 0	85	9 2	12 3
40	6 3	8 4	90	9 5	13 0
45	7 0	9 4	95	9 8	13 1
50	7 1	9 5	100	10 0	13 4
55	7 4	9 9	105	10 3	13 8
60	7 8	10 5	110	10 5	14 1
65	8 1	10 8	115	11 0	14 7

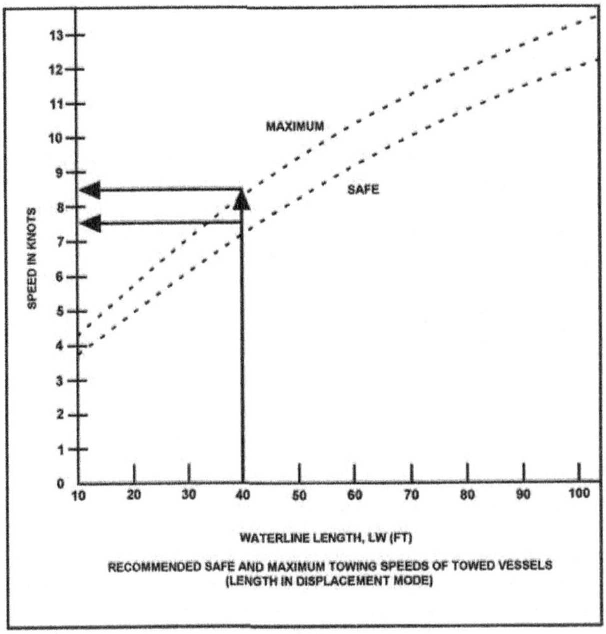

Figure 17-14
Calculated Safe Towing Speeds

Compensating for Current

D.37. Description

Handling a tow becomes more of a challenge when traveling in a river, estuary or other area where tidal currents affect navigation or in areas where major coastal currents or wind-driven currents come into play. This is particularly true near inlets, bars, river mouths, river bends, and areas where currents diverge or converge. Generally, there are four conditions encountered while towing in current:

- Head current.
- Tail current.
- Cross current.
- Combinations of currents.

To effectively deal with any of these, the towing vessel as well as the towed vessel must be navigated. One way to do this is to look at a stern tow as a single long vessel, with the propeller(s) and rudder(s) at the bow, and the pivot point at the stern. Though not a totally accurate picture, it shows that just because the towing vessel (the bow) changes direction, the towed vessel (the stern) will not immediately and automatically follow. Momentum will try to keep the towed vessel going in the original direction. Also, though the crew may frequently "crab" against the current with the towing vessel alone, now they must crab a vessel that becomes longer than the towline.

"Local knowledge" becomes extremely important when dealing with current. The effect of current on vessel navigation at 12-30 knots is far less than the effect while towing at 6-8 knots.

NOTE

> Keep overall tow length in mind. In current, even though the towing vessel may be well clear of obstructions or buoys, the tow rig and towed vessel may be set into them.

CAUTION !

> Regardless of speed over the ground, the tow is still moving through the water. Safe towing speed is based on speed through the water. Avoid towing a vessel above its hull speed or exceed the safe limits imposed by wind and sea conditions. If the current opposes winds and seas, the seas get steeper and break more readily. Increasing the speed through the water places excessive strain on a tow rig and deck fittings. Dynamic forces are still at work.

D.38. Head Current

Head current is a current flowing directly against the steered course. Depending on the velocity of the current and the speed of the tow, speed over the ground may be reduced, stopped, or even reversed. (see **Figure 17-15**).

CAUTION !

> Make sure that both the towing vessel and the tow stay in water deep enough so neither vessel grounds.

D.38.a. Narrow and Straight Waterways

A head current in a "narrow" waterway poses other concerns. In a perfectly straight waterway, shallower water outside a deep channel will provide some relief, provided that the tow remains in deep enough water for safe navigation.

D.38.b. Bends and Turns

When towing in a waterway with bends and turns, the greatest current will be to the outside of the bend or turn. Accordingly, the water will be deepest on the outside. When towing around a bend, the direction of the head current acting on the towing vessel may differ from that on the towed vessel. At a bend, the towed vessel may sheer (or yaw) to the outside of the bend. In these situations, the following procedures apply:

Step	Procedure
1	To deal with a very strong head current, consider waiting for the current to slacken, waiting offshore for tidal conditions to change, or changing destination. Also, if possible, find an area out of the main current flow to make progress.
2	Determine conditions in the river prior to entering. It may be prudent to remain in open water until currents slacken or tidal conditions change.

NOTE Prevent towed vessel sheer by reducing towline length before entering narrower sections of a waterway.

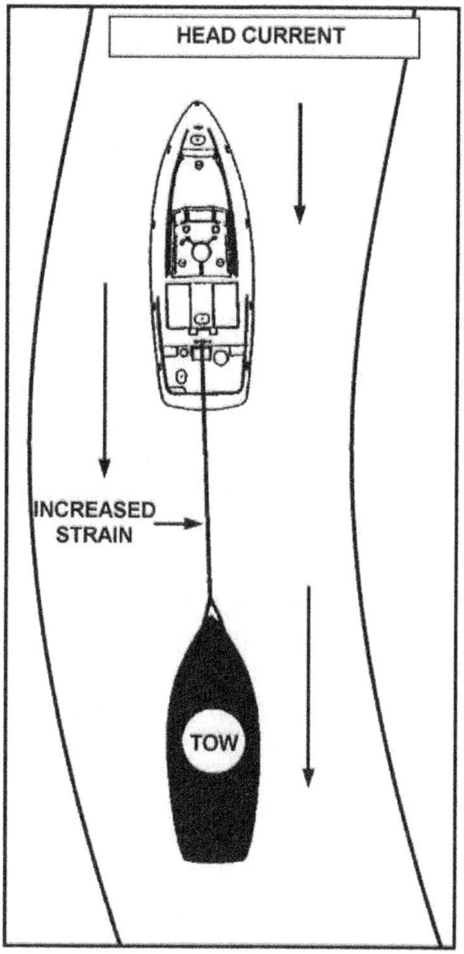

Figure 17-15
Head Current

D.39. Tail Current

Tail current is a current flowing in the same direction as the course steered. Crewmembers should remain aware of how the influence of a tail current affects both vessels. As with the head current, in general, speed through the water indicates appropriate handling procedures, not speed over the ground. (see **Figure 17-16**)

D.39.a. Open Water

In open water, a tail current usually helps the tow along. However, when opposing the wind or seas, the tail current causes steeper waves. The steeper waves may require slowing the towing speed. The tail current should be accounted for when estimating the time of arrival. All course changes or shortening-up of the tow must be done earlier, or the current will carry the tow past the desired point. Then, considerable effort will be needed to go back against the (now) head current.

NOTE

> Compensate for a tail current by taking early action.

D.39.b. Narrow Waterway

As with a head current, a tail current in a narrow waterway also affects how the tow handles. A common situation develops when the towing vessel gets into an area of lesser current than the towed vessel. This often occurs near turns and bends where it appears that the shortest distance is on the inside of the bend. If there is a significant difference in the current, the tow sheers off along the axis of the current. This will possibly cause slack in the tow rig, loss of firm control, and will potentially overrun the towing vessel. To prevent this from occurring, the following procedures apply:

Step	Procedure
1	Minimize the possibility of loss of control in a tail current by staying in the same velocity of current as the tow. As with a head current, one way to do this is by shortening scope of the towline.
2	If a tail current looks as if it will become unmanageable, it may be necessary to change course and steer more into the current.

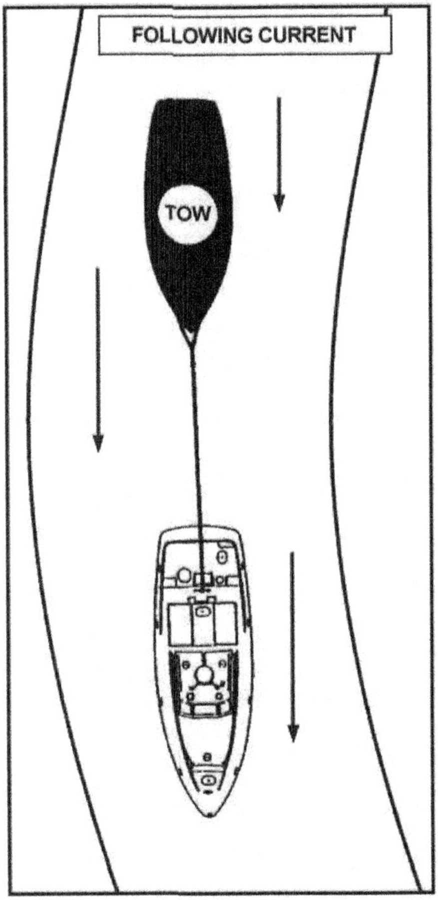

Figure 17-16
Following Current

WARNING

> While towing astern, if there is any crosscurrent in a channel marked by a navigational range, do not steer the towing vessel exactly on the range. Doing so could stand the towed vessel into danger on the down-current side of the channel. If the towed vessel has any problems such as steering or stability, keep the towed vessel in good water (usually the center of the channel, marked by the range). Use the towed vessel's crew to inform the towing vessel when they are the range. Remember, when taking a vessel in tow, the towing vessel becomes responsible for its safety.

D.40. Cross Current

A cross current is a current that is flowing from either side, across the intended track. This current will require the towing vessel to adjust heading for set and drift for both vessels. At a towing speed of 7 knots, a 2-knot cross current will require a heading offset of over 15° in order to follow the intended track. In open water, this may not pose a problem, if the towing vessel adjusts properly throughout the tow. (see **Figure 17-17**).

In restricted waters, suddenly encountering a cross current, such as where a longshore current crosses a harbor entrance channel, could first cause the tow to appear to veer, even though the towing vessel is the one being affected. Then, when the towed vessel encounters the flow, it will appear to veer the other way.

In restricted waters, the towing vessel must adjust accordingly for the amount the cross current offsets the towed vessel from the intended track. The cross current could push the towed vessel into danger. The possibility of a cross current pushing the towed vessel into danger can be minimized through a combination of shortening tow and offsetting the towing vessel's intended track in an up-current direction. Also, if the towed vessel is able, they should be instructed to steer into the current to compensate for the set.

As an example, if a cross-current moving from right to left is present near a channel entrance, the tow should be shortened before entering and the towing vessel should be lined up to the right of the channel centerline. If unable to shorten tow, get well off to the up-current side of the channel centerline.

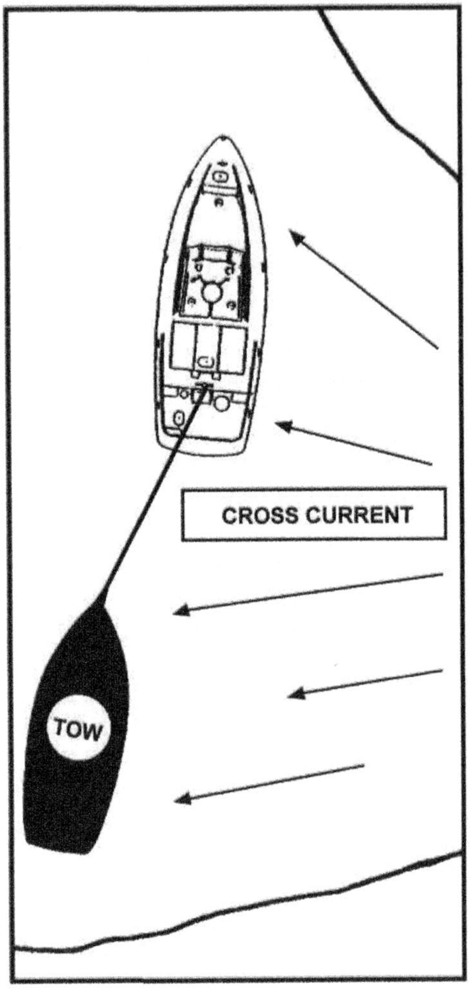

Figure 17-17
Effects of Cross Current

D.41. Combinations of Currents

Seldom will the current be dead on the bow, from directly astern, or exactly on the beam. If it happens to be that way at the moment, it may not be for very long. The marine environment is constantly changing, including the motion of currents. The general principles and specific procedures discussed above should be used to effectively compensate for combinations of currents.

The surface of the water should be closely watched for evidence of current changes. A "tide line" usually appears at the leading edge of a current change or marks the difference between two different flows. A river's color changes because of flow from another river. "Tide-rips" or bar conditions vary with the amount of current. Close attention to how current flows past a fixed object (pier, bridge support, piling) or a buoy will provide a good idea of what direction the current is heading and how fast it is moving.

NOTE There is no substitute for experience and preparation. Learn the area of operations and be alert to hazards as to not be taken by surprise.

Shortening the Tow

D.42. Description

When approaching safe haven, it may be necessary to shorten the towline to safely enter an inlet, cross a bar, tow in a channel, or turn into a basin. The tow should be shortened to increase control in confined areas and in current. The towline must be slack to shorten tow. The coxswain controls the amount of slack and the direction the towline tends while the crew recovers the towline. The crew and coxswain must communicate and coordinate their efforts and actions to make the task as easy as possible without fouling the tow vessel's propellers or rudders. Towline recovery should be kept on the beam or quarter to prevent the slack towline from fouling the propellers.

D.43. Before Shortening a Tow

The following procedures should be performed before shortening a tow:

Step	Procedure
1	Determine a safe area considering wind, depth of water, size of vessel, area to maneuver, current speed and direction, etc.
2	Determine the new desired towline length.
3	Brief the towed vessel's crew.
4	Brief own crew and assign tasks.
5	Reduce speed slowly and gradually to prevent the tow from closing too fast, and risking collision. Due to momentum, a vessel with greater displacement will keep way on longer than a light displacement vessel. A vessel with way on will stop more quickly when turned into the wind and seas.
6	As towline gets slack, direct crew to remove turns from the tow bitt. Crewmember at the bitt pulls slack so as to be ready to take a turn if necessary.

D.44. Learning How to Shorten Tow

The following are procedures describing how to shorten the tow:

CAUTION ! Do not back too quickly and cause a large bight in the towline that increases risk of fouling propellers or rudders. Backing too quickly may also create too much strain for the line handler if the towline bight leads too far forward.

Step	Procedure
1	As pivot begins, the coxswain directs the bitt person to break the bitt and a line handler must begin to pull in the towline. Recover towline and take it up on the tow reel (if equipped). Do not let bights of towline litter the deck or the crew working area.
2	The coxswain backs as necessary to slack the line, which allows the line handler to haul in the line more easily.
3	If the wind is any angle off the bow, ensure the towing vessel is blown away from the towline.
4	If the severity of the weather hampers control of the towing vessel, shorten the tow in segments. If an attempt to shorten must be aborted, the coxswain directs the bitt person to take a working turn and remove any slack. The crew must clear out between the bitt and the towed vessel before there is strain at the bitt. Make up the bitt if needed to hold the strain. The coxswain must then maneuver and restart the procedures.

Once a short tow is set, the "shock absorber" effect of catenary and scope is reduced. Special care should be used to counteract shock-loading.

NOTE In calm conditions, if not much towline was out to begin with, shortening a tow may not be necessary. It may be easier to go directly to an alongside tow.

D.45. Maintaining Control in Rough Conditions

When operating in rough conditions, the following procedures apply:

Step	Procedure
1	Turn into the weather with seas or wind (whichever is greatest influence on tow vessel motion) 30° to 40° off the bow.
2	If a lot of towline must be recovered, put the towing vessel's bow directly into the seas.
3	Whatever angle to the sea is chosen, pivot the towing vessel bow directly into the seas or wind whenever backing down to recover towline.
4	Crew communication and boat handling skills are paramount in this situation to avoid fouling the towline in the towing vessel's propellers.

The greatest control occurs when the wind and seas are off the towing vessel's bow while on the beam of the tow. The wind and seas will drift the tow away from the towline.

Speed should be reduced to lessen the forces on the towed vessel, which in turn are transferred to the towing vessel.

Step	Procedure
1	In heavy weather, constantly adjust towing speed to prevent a tow from surfing on a wave or broaching.
2	If a large wave approaches the stern of a tow, increase tow vessel speed to keep ahead of the tow as it is pushed by the swell.
3	As a tow reaches the crest of a swell, reduce speed. Keep the towline taut. The coxswain must constantly watch the seas astern and the towed vessel until in sheltered waters.
4	Deploy the drogue.

NOTE

This technique is very demanding and must be learned through training and experience. Throttle response (acceleration and deceleration) must be matched to the towed vessel's speed. If this technique is impractical to counteract shock-loading, speed reduction and quartering the seas may be your best options.

D.46. Disconnecting Tow or Towing Alongside

At the safe haven, the towing vessel will either moor the towed vessel or disconnect the tow so the towed vessel can anchor or be assisted by other resources.

NOTE

If disconnecting the tow, determine beforehand whether any other part of the rig will stay aboard the towed vessel. The weight of shackles or a wire-rope bridle will increase the difficulty of towline recovery, and could pose additional risk of fouling in propellers or rudders.

D.47. Disconnecting the Towline

The towline should be shortened up to some extent already. The towed vessel should be turned into the prevailing conditions for better control, making towline recovery easier and safer because there is less towline for the crew to recover and less towline in the water to foul propellers. It also allows the towing vessel to maintain control of a tow a little longer. Once shortened, and with the tow barely moving to allow the towline to slacken, the coxswain signals for the towed vessel crew to disconnect the rig and let it go into the water. The towing vessel crew then hauls it aboard.

Towing Alongside

D.48. Description

When set up properly, an alongside tow allows two vessels to be maneuvered as one. This advantage is necessary when approaching a dock, mooring, or anchorage in sheltered waters, or when maneuvering in congested or restricted waters. Most of the pre-tow procedures used for towing astern described earlier in the chapter remain valid. However, some additional preparations are needed and the make-up of the tow rig and approach will be different. The tow rig configuration and approach will be more like that for mooring. (see **Figure 17-18**).

D.49. Preparation

These following additional preparations apply for an alongside tow.

WARNING

Do not place the towing vessel between a larger towed vessel and a lee shore or obstruction. The towing vessel may not be able to overcome the other vessel's momentum before losing all room to maneuver. As with any towing approach, leave an escape route.

D.49.a. Determining Side of Tow and Approach

Step	Procedure
1	Determine on which side the tow will be rigged.
2	Note the effect of the weather and physical conditions on both vessels and use them to the fullest extent.
3	Although similar to a mooring approach, decide whether it is better to have the wind to set the towed vessel down on the towing vessel, or vice-versa.
4	Assess the other vessel's drift rate and aspect to plan the speed and angle of your approach.
5	If a vessel smaller than the towing vessel is being rapidly set towards a lee shore or obstructions, consider approaching from leeward, if sea room allows.

CAUTION !

Use of a towline as the bowline in an alongside tow puts more line lying on deck and may be a tripping or fouling hazard.

D.49.b. Deciding Use of Towline

If the alongside tow occurs at the completion of a stern tow, the coxswain should decide if the towline will be disconnected from the stern tow, or hauled in while still connected and used as a bow line for the alongside rig. If the stern tow required a bridle, disconnecting part of or all of the rig may be the only option to provide a fair lead for the alongside bow line.

One benefit of using the towline as the bowline for an alongside tow is that should something happen, there is always a line attached to the disabled vessel and returning to a stern tow is possible should the need arise.

D.49.c. Preparing Lines

Crewmembers should ready the proper size and number of lines to rig alongside, determining where the attachment points on the towed vessel will be for each line.

D.49.d. Determining Hull Match

Hull match is determined by assessing how the two hulls will align alongside. In towing alongside, the tow vessel may be angled, slightly bow-in to the towed vessel, with the towing vessel propeller(s) and rudder(s) aft of the towed vessel's transom, rudder, or outdrive(s).

D.49.e. Rigging Fenders

All available fenders should be rigged, except one for hand-tending as the tow approaches, in potential contact points. All fenders should be secured in place, using clove hitches or slip clove hitches, before bringing a tow alongside.

NOTE Keep all lines clear of the water.

D.49 f. Briefing Towed Vessel

The coxswain should brief the towed vessel as follows:

Step	Procedure
1	Advise which side to prepare.
2	If already in stern tow, describe shortening-up and whether towline will be used as bowline or whether (and when, "on signal") to cast off.
3	Describe approach and intended position alongside.
4	Direct the towed vessel to clear as many obstructions from the side as possible (rigging, lines, outriggers, etc.).
5	Direct the towed vessel to place fenders at obvious areas, such as trawler doors or topside vents.
6	Designate attachment points.
7	Direct crew how to assist.

D.50. Making the Approach

When making the approach, two alternatives are possible:

- Use towline as bow line.
- Make free approach.

D.50.a. Using Towline as Bow Line

With towed vessel already in a stern tow, the following procedures apply:

Step	Procedure
1	Use the same methods as shortening the tow to take all headway off the tow before backing down. If the towed vessel has available propulsion, it may be able to assist by briefly backing down. If necessary, use the towline to change the heading of the towed vessel.
2	When the tow has stopped all forward movement, the coxswain directs the crew to "break the bitt". The towing vessel slowly backs and the towline is hauled in.
3	Try to keep some space abeam until the towed vessel is in the proper fore and aft position.
4	As the distance between the vessels decreases and as directed by the coxswain, the crew walks the towline forward to a suitable bow fitting, takes a working turn on the line and takes in slack.
5	The coxswain then moors the towing vessel alongside the towed vessel.

NOTE Show the towed vessel crew where to attach the alongside mooring lines. Perform all line handling at coxswain direction, just as in mooring. Always pass the eye of alongside lines to a towed vessel. Keep the working ends of the lines aboard the towing vessel to adjust or relocate as necessary.

WARNING

Do not fend of boat with your feet or hands.

D.50.b. Making Free Approach

This approach is made as if mooring to a pier, but the first line over will be the bowline. There will not be a spring line to check forward motion with respect to the towed vessel. The coxswain directs the crew to pass the bow line when alongside.

D.51. Rigging Additional Lines Alongside

Once alongside, with the bowline connected, the tow should be positioned so that the towing vessel's propeller(s) and rudder(s) are well aft of the towed vessel's stern. This affords best control for maneuvering in confined areas. Fender placement should be checked and adjustments made so they provide maximum protection at contact points.

D.51.a. Calm Conditions

If there is little or no movement from wind, seas or current, rig lines in the following order:

- Second line: Rig a stern line from the towed vessel's stern to the towing vessel's stern. This line holds the sterns together while setting up the "spring lines".
- Third line: Rig a "tow strap" (forward spring line) from the towing vessel bow or forward mooring fitting to a point aft on the towed vessel.
- Fourth line: Rig a backing line (after spring line) from a quarter location on the towing vessel to a location forward on the towed vessel.

NOTE

For maximum control of a tow, all alongside lines should be as tight as possible. Spring lines are tightened by crewmembers taking up slack obtained when the coxswain throttles *forward* and *reverse* on the inside engine, pulling first against the tow strap then backing down against the backing line.

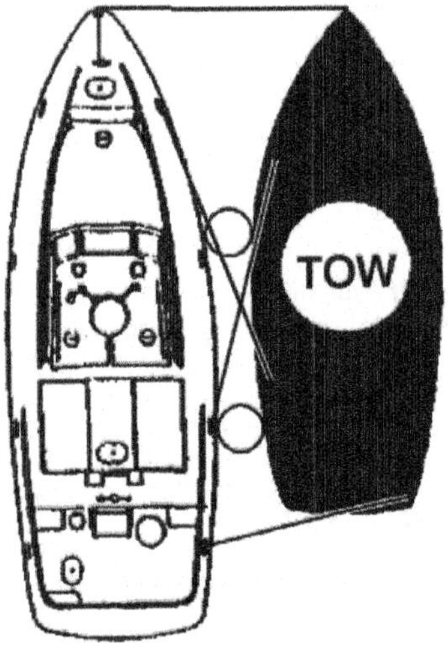

Figure 17-18
Side Tow

D.51.b. Wind, Seas, or Current

If conditions are setting the vessels into danger, (i.e., toward shoals or breakwaters), and time is critical, follow this order to rig the lines:

- Second line: Rig a tow strap so that, once secured, the towing vessel can put headway on and move clear of any dangers.
- Third line: With headway still on, rig a backing line. This will be needed to slow the towed vessel.
- Fourth line: The stern line.

D.52. Maneuvering

Maneuvering with an alongside tow is a challenging boat handling technique. To do it well and to do it safely requires practice and experience. An accomplished coxswain will observe how winds, seas and current affect the combined tow and use these forces to the best advantage, often making the maneuver look easier than it really was.

D.52.a. Approach for Mooring

To moor an alongside tow safely and skillfully, perform the following procedures:

Step	Procedure
1	Anticipate well ahead of time and decrease speed gradually.
2	Place the larger vessel against the dock or mooring.
3	Making an approach into the wind and current if possible.
4	Moor on the protected (leeward) side of a dock or pier.
5	Place a crewmember in a good position as a lookout aboard a towed vessel on approach. This extends a coxswain's vision for clearances and obstructions.
6	Rig fenders and mooring lines from the tow if it is going to be placed against a dock or mooring.
7	The disabled vessel may use rudder control to assist in mooring, if practical.

Sinking Tows

D.53. Description

When it becomes evident that a tow is about to sink, the situation should be very quickly assessed. Quick decisive action to minimize loss of life is the first priority. Once abandon ship procedures are initiated, radio communications will likely be lost. The primary action is to break the tow and rescue the people, either from the deck of the towed vessel or from the water.

A sinking tow can pull the stern of the towing vessel under unless all crewmembers pay close attention to the immediate situation. There might not be enough time to disconnect the towline from the towed vessel once it begins to sink.

If a tow begins to sink, all towing vessel headway is stopped. The force exerted through the towline increases the danger of the towed vessel yawing and capsizing. Every attempt should be made to have the towed vessel's crew disconnect the towline if possible and await rescue.

WARNING

> Do not attempt breaking the bitt if there is a strain on the towline. Instead, cut the towline using a knife. Cut towline directly behind the tow bitt.

CAUTION !

> Be aware that the boat could become fouled in rigging or debris while attempting to rescue survivors.

D.54. Minimizing the Danger

Perform the following procedures to minimize danger in sinking tow:

Step	Procedure
1	When it becomes obvious that sinking cannot be avoided, (e.g., the tow has rolled on one side and is not righting itself or the tow's decks are submerging) and the towed crew was not able to disconnect the tow rig, cut the towline or slip the towline by breaking the bitt.
2	Note the vessel's position by GPS, LORAN or radar fix and request assistance. Once free of the tow, make preparations to rescue people who were onboard.

D.55. Marking the Wreck

If there were no people onboard the tow, the water is shallow (depth less than towline length), and safety permits, the towline should be paid out until the tow reaches bottom. A fender, life jacket, or floatable object should be tied to the remaining towline so it is visible on the surface. The floating object will mark the location of the sunken vessel for salvage later as well as recovery of the towing vessel's towing equipment.

Section E. Towing Precautions

Introduction

The section provides the many towing precautions that shall be taken to ensure successful towing evolutions and prevent potential injury to all persons and vessels involved.

Step	Precaution
1	Maintain communications between coxswain and crew.
2	Have all people onboard a distressed boat don PFDs. If there are not enough PFDs, provide them.
CAUTION !	Do not allow a distressed boat to become endangered while waiting for people to don PFDs. Take immediate action to remove the people or boat from danger.
3	Remove all people from a distressed boat when necessary, safe, or practical.
4	Cast heaving lines well over a boat's center mass so they drop over the deck. Tell people onboard what is going to occur. Call out "HEADS UP" just before casting a heaving line.
5	Establish and maintain clear communications with a towed vessel, including a backup means of communicating. Provide a portable radio if necessary. At a minimum, contact a tow every 30 minutes and more frequently if conditions warrant. Initially, get the following information from the operator of the towed boat: • Condition of towline, chafing gear, towline attachment point, and fair lead hardware. • Level of water onboard/rate of flooding (if taking on water). • Physical condition of people onboard.
6	When underway, keep personnel onboard both boats clear of the tow rig.

Step	Precaution
7	Keep the tow rig attachment point as low and close to the centerline as possible.
8	Do not connect a tow rig to lifelines, stanchions, grab rails, or ladders.
9	Do not connect the tow rig to cleats or bitts that are attached to the distressed boat's deck only with screws. Always check on the condition of deck fitting on the disabled vessel before sending over the towline.
10	Avoid using lines provided by the distressed boat for any part of the tow rig.
11	Avoid using knots to join towlines.
12	Tend a towline by hand until secured to a distressed boat. Then, secure it to a bitt or cleat on the coxswain's command. Use two people, if possible, assigned as line handlers to tend the towline and a crewmember to work the bitt.
13	Do not secure a towline to a bitt or cleat with half hitches. They cause jamming and fusing. Use a round turn with three figure eights to secure the bitt.
14	A crewmember working the bitt or cleat must avoid crossing arms when securing the line to the bitt or cleat. Change hands to avoid becoming fouled in the turns.
15	Ensure the breaking strength of all shackles used in the tow rig is equal to or greater than the breaking strength of the towline.
16	Keep the towline clear of propellers, shafts and rudders.
17	Use chafing gear to minimize damage to a tow rig.
Step	**Precaution**
18	Avoid towing boats that exceed the weight and length limits established for Coast Guard boats.
19	Tow at a safe speed for the prevailing conditions. Prevent shock-loading the tow rig.
20	Do not exceed the hull design speed of the boat.
21	Avoid sudden maneuvers and sharp turns.
22	Use a drogue or bridle to reduce or prevent yawing (as necessary).
23	Have someone at the helm of the towed vessel, if possible. Direct that person to steer the boat directly on the stern of the towing boat. If all people have been removed from a distressed boat, secure the rudder amidships. If a tow has an outboard or inboard/outboard engine, direct the operator to lower the outdrive(s) or motor(s) to normal operating position.
WARNING	Overloading the astern, or along either side of a vessel's centerline, may swamp or capsize a vessel in tow.
24	Keep a towed boat in trim. Consider the following for trim: • Condition of a boat (structural damage, taking on water, etc.). • Structural design of a boat (low transom, low freeboard, etc.). • Cargo (fish holds, gear stowage, etc.) and how free surface effect (dynamics of free moving water in the bilge of a boat) influence ride. • Number and location of people onboard.
25	Maintain a diligent tow watch and frequently account for all people onboard the towed boat either visually or by radio.

Step	Precaution
NOTE	A tow watch has a critical responsibility. In addition to the crewmember assigned, it is a collateral duty for all other members of a crew.
26	Ensure the breaking strengths of bridles in a tow rig are equal to or greater than the breaking strength of a towline or appropriately matched to the requirements of the tow and prevailing conditions.
27	If possible, load GPS positions and do all chart work at the dock. It is very difficult to do all of this while underway and being tossed about.
28	If the possibility exists that a drogue or pump will be required while under tow, pass the equipment before the tow rig is hooked up.
29	After a tow rig is set up, but before it is connected to a tow, a coxswain should inspect the entire tow rig and hookup points.
30	When approaching a distressed boat, a coxswain should establish an imaginary danger zone around the craft based on prevailing conditions.

Chapter 18
Fire Fighting, Rescue, and Assistance

Introduction

As members of the U.S. Coast Guard and the Auxiliary, the boat crews have an important responsibility in maintaining their vessels and assisting those in distress. A primary responsibility of a boat crew is to save lives, not property. However, when and where possible, while managing risks, a boat crew will attempt to save property. Boat crewmembers may be called upon to react to a fire on their own boat, dewater vessels, and right vessels. This chapter discusses:

- Safety and prevention measures to take when on a boat or assisting a distressed vessel.
- How to assess emergency situations.
- How to prevent, identify, and extinguish boat fires.
- How to dewater vessels.
- Several methods on how to right overturned vessels.
- How to control flooding.

It is very important to keep in mind that any vessel can fall victim to tragedy when proper prevention measures or rescue procedures are not followed correctly and precisely.

In this chapter

This chapter contains the following sections:

WARNING

The wearing of jewelry, including rings, wristwatches, necklaces or other items not consisting of organizational clothing, PPE, or uniform articles by boat crew members engaged in hoisting, towing, or other deck evolutions where the potential for snagging exists **is prohibited**. OICs and coxswains will address this during all pre-underway briefs and coxswains shall ensure jewelry is removed prior to beginning all deck evolutions.

Section A. Safety and Damage Control

Introduction

Safety is paramount during all emergency evaluations that a member of a boat crew will be involved in. Mishaps resulting in death or injury have occurred when boat crews responded to vessels in distress. Nearly every mishap that resulted in serious injuries had a common denominator. Serious injuries happen when common sense and a continuing regard for safety give way to reckless urgency.

A boat crewmember's primary responsibility in emergency assistance is saving lives, not property. Boat crews must be aware of their limited roles in emergency assistance, particularly when responding to fire emergencies. Safety begins with assessing primary responsibilities and capabilities for the variety of emergency situations encountered.

A.1. Coast Guard Fire Fighting Activities Policy

Among the provisions of the Ports and Waterways Safety Act of 1972 (PWSA) (33 USC 1221 *et seq.*) is an acknowledgment that increased supervision of port operations is necessary to prevent damage to structures in, on, or adjacent to the navigable waters of the United States, and to reduce the possibility of vessel or cargo loss, damage to life, property, and the marine environment. This statute, along with the traditional functions and powers of the Coast Guard to render aid and save property (14 USC 88(b)), is the basis for Coast Guard fire fighting activities.

The Coast Guard has traditionally provided fire fighting equipment and training to protect the lives of Coast Guard personnel, its vessels, and property. Coast Guard and Auxiliary units are also called upon to assist in fighting major fires onboard other vessels and at waterfront facilities. Although the Coast Guard will help fight fires involving vessels or waterfront facilities, it is not a primary response capability. Local authorities are responsible for maintaining adequate fire fighting capabilities in U.S. ports and harbors. The Coast Guard renders assistance as time and resources are available, based on the level of personnel training and adequacy of equipment available for a specific situation at hand.

A.2. Safety Assessment and Management Guidelines

Emergency situations can cause people to panic or act before thinking despite the best of training and preparation. Therefore, boat crews must work together as a team to minimize any potential or immediate jeopardy for both civilian casualties and themselves. An emergency situation should never be entered without first:

- Assessing the risk involved for the boat crewmembers and civilian victims (risk assessment).
- Being aware of the dynamics of the emergency situation (situational awareness).
- Implementing a control plan that fits each unique emergency (damage control risk management).

A.2.a. Risk Assessment

Risk assessment starts with realizing why mishaps occur. The responsibility for identifying and managing risk lies with every member of a boat crew. Realistic training based on standard techniques, critical analysis, and debriefing missions will help every person in a boat crew to contribute to developing and implementing a risk management plan. A risk management plan identifies and controls risk according to a set of preconceived parameters. Refer to *Chapter 4* of this Manual for a complete discussion of risk assessment and risk management plans.

A.2.b. Situational Awareness

Situational awareness is an important skill to develop as part of learning risk assessment. Situational awareness is the accurate perception of factors and conditions affecting the boat crew at any given time during any evolution. More simply, situational awareness is knowing what is going in the surrounding environment at all times.

Any time there is an indication that situational awareness is about to be lost, a decision must be made as to whether or not to continue with the rescue attempt. Everyone in the crew owns some responsibility for making these important decisions. These decisions take the form of action/reaction and communication.

NOTE Crews who have a high level of situational awareness perform in a safe manner.

A.2.c. Damage Control Risk Management

The precautions listed below include many of the considerations that can form a basis for a general damage control risk management plan. Boat crews should keep in mind that each emergency situation will be unique; therefore the plan must only be used as a general guideline. The experience and knowledge of each boat crew should be merged into a risk management plan and used to fine-tune this list.

- Attempt to account for all persons.
- Ensure all persons onboard the vessel in distress have donned PFDs, if possible.
- Attempt to have all lines (rigging, etc.) removed from the water to avoid fouling the propellers.
- Maintain communications between the coxswain and crewmembers.
- Have all required equipment tested and ready.
- Approach distressed vessel with fenders rigged and lines at the ready.
- Approach a vessel on fire from the windward side.
- Remove survivors first, then back off, and evaluate the fire.
- If the risk of explosion is not known (cannot determine what cargo is onboard), back off and do not attempt to fight the fire.
- Situations may dictate that survivors enter water to be rescued.
- When necessary, dewater the distressed vessel while keeping all equipment aboard the assisting vessel.
- Always keep the Operational Commander or parent unit informed.

NOTE For more information concerning Coast Guard fire fighting policy, see the *U.S. Coast Guard Addendum to the United States National Search and Rescue Supplement (NSS) to the International Aeronautical and Maritime Search and Rescue Manual*, COMDTINST M16130.2 (series).

Section B. Boat Fire Prevention and Susceptible Areas

Introduction

Fire is the greatest single potential for disaster on a boat. The possibility of fire can never be completely eliminated and is always a threat.

Boat crewmembers must be especially alert for fire, its possible causes, and areas on a boat that are very susceptible to fire. There are some causes of fire that are more frequently encountered on boats. Crewmembers should learn to be especially watchful for them.

In this section

This section contains the following information:

Preventive Actions

B.1. Description

In dealing with fire on a boat, the single most important consideration is prevention. During boat and equipment checks, all systems must be inspected including the fuel, oil system, and wiring. Crewmembers should check for abrasions, cracked wiring, loose connections, or pinholes in oil and fuel lines. Any discrepancy must be corrected at the time it is discovered.

B.2. Measures of Practice

The following are also good fire prevention measures for you to practice:

- Keep oil and grease out of bilges.
- Identify and correct any sources of fuel or oil leaks.
- Clean up any spilled fuel or lube oil immediately and properly dispose of it ashore.
- Stow cleaning materials off the boat.
- Keep all areas free of waste material.
- Use proper containers for flammable liquids.
- Be alert for suspicious odors and fumes, and vent all spaces thoroughly before starting engine(s).

Susceptible Areas

B.3. Spontaneous Ignition

This source of fire is often overlooked as a cause of fire aboard a boat. Many common materials are subject to this dangerous chemical reaction. A spontaneous ignition can easily occur aboard a boat when an oil or paint soaked rag is discarded in the corner of a compartment or engine room.

B.3.a. Oxidation

When an area is warm and there is no ventilation, oil on a rag begins to oxidize (to react chemically with the oxygen in the warm air around it). Oxidization is a natural process that produces heat. Heat produced by oxidization causes any remaining oil to oxidize even faster and produce still more heat.

B.3.b. Ventilation

Since heat is not drawn away by ventilation, it builds up around a rag and causes it to get hot enough to burst into flames, after which it can ignite any nearby flammable substances and start a major fire. All of this occurs without any additional or outside source of heat. In this case, fire prevention is a matter of good housekeeping. Cleaning rags and waste should be stored in closed or sealed metal containers and discarded as soon as possible.

B.4. Engine Room Fires

Engine rooms are particularly vulnerable to electrical, fuel, and oil fires. There are several ways that engine room fires can readily start. Water spraying from ruptured seawater lines can cause severe short-circuiting and arcing in electric motors (alternators), electrical panels, and other exposed electrical equipment. This, in turn, can ignite insulation and nearby combustible materials. Even more serious than leaking seawater lines are ruptured fuel and oil lines near electrical equipment. All crewmembers must constantly monitor these lines for leaks.

B.4.a. Electrical System

The electrical system can short and cause a fire. These fires are typically small and easily controlled with either carbon dioxide (CO_2) or dry chemical (PKP) extinguishers.

B.4.b. Fuel Line

If fittings leak, fuel can drip onto a hot manifold and ignite. This situation could continue unnoticed for some time, allowing a major fire to develop when a manifold finally gets hot enough to ignite all leaked fuel.

B.4.c. Lube Oil Line

This line, if leaking or ruptured, will allow lube oil to spill onto a hot engine. As the burning lube oil collects on and around an engine, the engine's fuel supply line would probably be burned through. This would provide a fire with a continuous fuel supply, even after engines have been shut down. Fuel continuing to spill into the bilges, fires can spread and block access to the engine compartment, eventually leading to the development of a major fire.

CAUTION !

> An explosion is a common accident for boats when bilges are not properly ventilated before starting engines. A spark from "turning the key" can instantly ignite the trapped gas creating a potentially deadly explosion.

B.4.d. Bilge Areas

Fire occurs in bilge areas because of fuel or oil accumulation. Most often, oil or gas leaks into bilges from an undetected break in a fuel or lube oil line. The oil vaporizes, and flammable vapors build up in and around bilge areas. Once these vapors are mixed with air in the right proportions, a spark can ignite them and cause a fire or explosion. Bilge fires can move very quickly around machinery and piping and are not easily controlled. They are more difficult to extinguish than most other types of engine room fires. Bilge areas should be watched closely. Oil in a bilge nearly always indicates a leak, and all fuel and lube oil lines should be checked until the leak is found.

B.5. Electrical Circuits and Equipment

With properly insulated and wired equipment, electricity is a safe and convenient source of power. However, when electrical equipment exceeds its useful life, is misused, or is improperly wired, it can convert electrical energy to heat. Equipment then becomes a source of ignition and a "fire hazard." For this reason, electrical equipment must be installed, maintained, tested, and repaired in strict accordance with published regulations.

NOTE

> All work on electrical equipment must be completed by qualified personnel.

B.5.a. Replacement Parts and Equipment

Standard residential or industrial electrical equipment does not last very long at sea. The salt air causes "corrosion," the boat's vibration breaks down the equipment, and a steel hull can cause erratic operation or a shorted circuit. As a result, equipment or its wiring may overheat or arc, causing a fire when flammable materials are located nearby. For this reason, only approved replacement parts and equipment should be installed aboard small boats. Given proper maintenance, these parts and equipment are designed to withstand the strenuous conditions encountered at sea.

WARNING

When a fuse or circuit breaker in a particular circuit is too large, a circuit will not "break" when overloaded. Instead, increased current will continue, a circuit will overheat, and eventually insulation will burn and may ignite other combustible material in the vicinity.

B.5.b. Wiring and Fuses

Insulation on electrical wiring will not last forever. With age and use, it can become brittle and crack. It may be rubbed (chafed) through or broken by abuse or by the vibration of a boat. Once insulation is broken, bare wires may be exposed and are dangerous. A single exposed wire can arc to any metal object. If multiple wires are exposed, they can touch each other and cause a short circuit. Either condition could produce enough heat to ignite insulation on wiring or some other flammable material nearby. Replacing wires that have faulty or worn insulation can prevent this type of fire. Install only fuses and circuit breakers of the proper size for their circuits.

B.5.c. Temporary and Unauthorized Repairs and Patches

"Jury-rigging" of electrical panels to serve additional equipment is a dangerous practice. Wiring in every electrical circuit is designed to carry a specified maximum load. When circuit wiring is overloaded with too many pieces of operating equipment, in addition to possibly damaging the equipment, it can overheat and burn its insulation. Hot wiring can also ignite flammable materials in surrounding areas.

B.5.d. Electric Motors (Alternators)

Faulty electric motors are major causes of fire. Problems may result when a motor is not properly maintained or when it exceeds its useful life. A motor requires regular inspection, testing, lubrication, and cleaning. Sparks and arcing can result if a winding becomes short-circuited or grounded or if the brushes do not operate smoothly. If a spark or an arc is strong enough, it can ignite nearby combustible material. Lack of lubrication may cause the motor bearings to overheat, with the same result.

CAUTION !

Battery gases are highly explosive. Never smoke around a battery and never disconnect, change out, or perform maintenance on a battery until the surrounding space has been thoroughly ventilated.

B.5.e. Charging Batteries

When batteries are charging, they emit hydrogen, a highly flammable gas that is potentially explosive. Hydrogen is lighter than air and will rise as it is produced. If sufficient ventilation is not available at the highest point above where a battery is being charged, hydrogen will collect at the overhead. Then, any source of ignition will cause an explosion and fire.

Section C. Fire Theory, Classifications, and Fuel Sources

Introduction

As a boat crewmember, it is important to understand the theory of fire, the different classifications of fire, and the types of fuels that perpetuate fires. This knowledge will enable boat crewmembers to identify the type of precautions, equipment, and extinguishing agents required to successfully fight fires.

C.1. Fire Theory

Fire is a chemical reaction known as combustion. It is defined as rapid oxidation of combustible material accompanied by a release of energy in the form of heat and light.

C.1.a. Fire Triangle

For years, a 3-sided figure called the fire triangle has been used to describe the combustion and extinguishing theory. This theory states that proper proportions of oxygen, heat, and fuel are required for a fire. If any one of the 3 elements is removed, a fire will cease to exist. (see **Figure 18-1**)

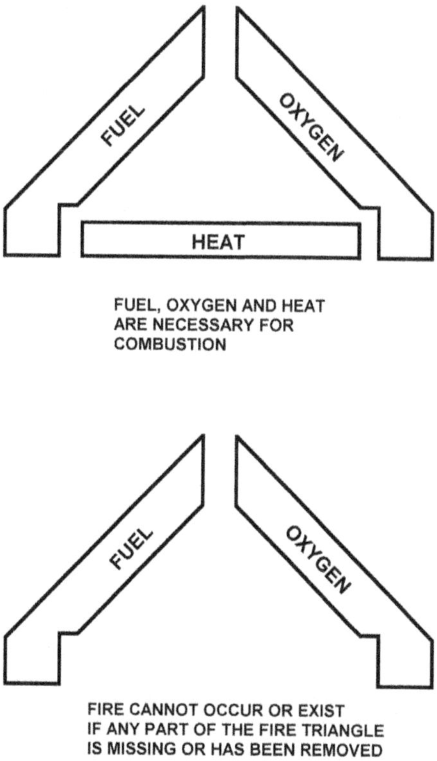
FUEL
OXYGEN
HEAT
FUEL, OXYGEN AND HEAT ARE NECESSARY FOR COMBUSTION
FUEL
OXYGEN
FIRE CANNOT OCCUR OR EXIST IF ANY PART OF THE FIRE TRIANGLE IS MISSING OR HAS BEEN REMOVED

Figure 18-1
Fire Triangle

C.1.b. Fire Tetrahedron

A new theory has been developed to further explain fire combustion and extinguishment. This theory can be represented by a 4-sided geometric figure, a tetrahedron. The base of this figure represents a chemical reaction. The 3 standing sides of the figure represent heat, oxygen, and fuel. Removing one or more of the 4 sides will make a tetrahedron incomplete and cause a fire to be extinguished. (see **Figure 18-2**)

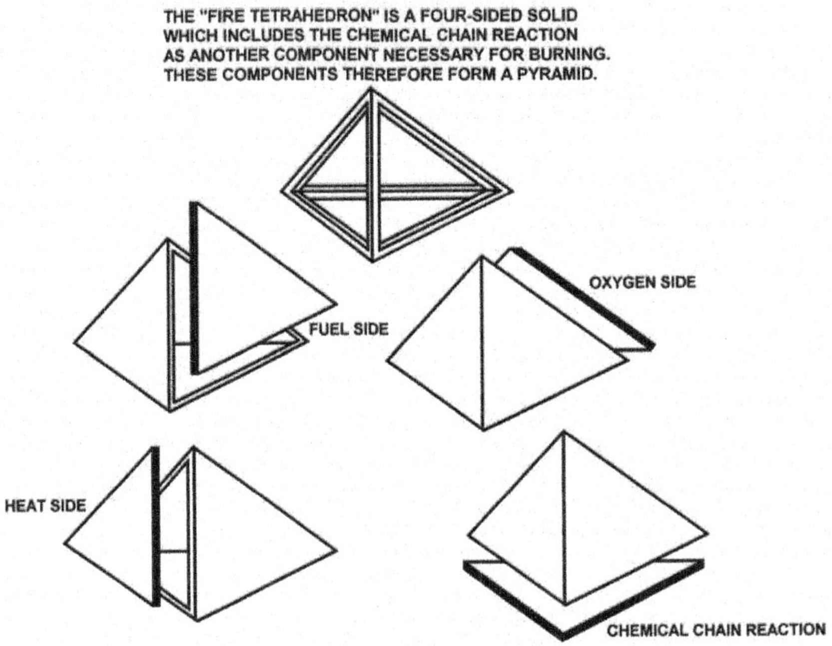
THE "FIRE TETRAHEDRON" IS A FOUR-SIDED SOLID WHICH INCLUDES THE CHEMICAL CHAIN REACTION AS ANOTHER COMPONENT NECESSARY FOR BURNING. THESE COMPONENTS THEREFORE FORM A PYRAMID.
FUEL SIDE
OXYGEN SIDE
HEAT SIDE
CHEMICAL CHAIN REACTION

Figure 18-2
Fire Tetrahedron

C.2. Classification of Fires and Fuel Sources

The following are the four classes of fires:

- Class A.
- Class B.
- Class C.
- Class D.

C.2.a. Class A

A Class A fire involves common combustible materials. Fuel sources within this class include wood and wood-based materials, cloth, paper, rubber, and certain plastics.

C.2.b. Class B

A Class B fire involves flammable or combustible liquids, flammable gases, greases, and similar products. Fuel sources within this class include petroleum products.

C.2.c. Class C

A Class C fire involves energized electrical equipment, conductors, or appliances.

C.2.d. Class D

A Class D fire involves combustible metals. Fuel sources within this class include sodium, potassium, magnesium, and titanium.

Section D. Description and Application of Extinguishing Agents

Introduction

Extinguishing agents are defined as anything that eliminates one or more "sides" of a fire tetrahedron. When any one is removed, fire can no longer exist.

Extinguishing agents can be applied in more than one way. Selecting the most appropriate method for applying extinguishing agents depends on the situation. Below are some general guidelines for applying different agents. Later, the equipment that must be used to apply these extinguishing agents will be addressed.

In this section

This section contains the following information:

How Extinguishing Agents Work

D.1. Description

Extinguishing agents put out fires by breaking one or more of the four elements of a fire tetrahedron. They work by cooling, smothering, chain breaking, or by a process called oxygen dilution.

- Cooling reduces the temperature of a fuel source below the fuel's ignition point.
- Smothering separates a fuel source from its oxygen supply.
- Chain breaking disrupts the chemical process necessary to sustain a fire. The element of a chain that is broken depends upon the class of fire and the type of extinguishing agent used.
- Oxygen dilution is a smothering process that reduces the amount of oxygen available to a level below that required to sustain combustion.

The different fire classes, the fuel source for each class, the type of extinguishing agent for each class, and the primary effect of each agent are described as follows:

Class	Fuel Sources	Primary Extinguishing Agent	Primary Effect
A	Common combustible materials such as wood and wood-based materials, cloth, paper, rubber, and certain plastics.	• Water • PKP (dry chemical)	Removes the heat element.
B	Flammable or combustible liquids, flammable gases, greases, petroleum products, and similar products.	• Foam Aqueous Film Forming Foam (AFFF) • CO_2 • PKP (dry chemical)	Removes the oxygen element.
C	Energized electrical equipment, conductors, or appliances.	• CO2 (Carbon Dioxide) • PKP (dry chemical)	Removes the oxygen element, and temporarily removes elements of oxygen and heat.
D	Combustible metals, such as sodium, potassium, magnesium, and titanium.	• Water (high velocity fog) • Sand (placed underneath the metal)	Removes the heat and oxygen elements.

Applying Water

D.2. Description

Onboard Coast Guard vessels, water for fire fighting comes from a built-in fire pump through the fire main and hose system or from portable fire pumps. Water is applied to a fire using one of three ways:

- Straight (solid) stream.
- High-velocity fog.
- Low-velocity fog.

D.3. Straight (Solid) Stream

A straight solid stream of water is used when long reach and penetrating power are critical.

D.3.a. Class A Fires

On Class A fires, its primary purpose is to break up burning material and to penetrate the base of a flame. Therefore, a solid stream must be directed at the base of flames in a Class A fire.

D.3.b. Class B Fires

A solid stream of water is not effective for extinguishing Class B fires. It can cause a violent fire reaction if a water stream atomizes fuel into the air causing an increased surface area. It could also splash the burning liquids spreading the fire to different areas.

D.3.c. Class C Fires

A straight solid stream of water should not be used on a Class C fire because it is a conductor of electricity. Electric current could travel back through a solid stream of water and be hazardous to a fire fighting team.

D.3.d. Class D Fires

A straight solid stream can also be used on Class D fires for cooling and to wash burning materials over the side.

D.4. High-Velocity Fog

Use of high velocity fog is also an effective method of extinguishing fires.

D.4.a. Class A Fires

High-velocity fog is more useful than a solid stream on Class A fires. One reason is that high-velocity fog can cool a much wider surface than a steady stream and consequently, it can absorb more heat. Additionally, as fog comes into contact with any surface heated by fire, it becomes steam. Steam provides a secondary smothering effect that further aids in extinguishing the fire.

D.4.b. Class B Fires

Because of the cooling qualities of finely divided water particles, high-velocity fog is a successful extinguishing agent on Class B fires. High-velocity fog should be used on flammable liquids only when AFFF (see D.5) is not available.

D.4.c. Class C Fires

When water is broken into small particles (nozzle fog patterns), there is little danger of it carrying electric current making high- or low-velocity fog safe to use on Class C fires. However, the nozzles should be operated at least four feet from a fire source.

D.4.d. Class D Fires

Water is the recommended agent for Class D fires when applied in quantity as fog patterns. When water is applied to burning Class D materials, there may be small explosions. The firefighter should apply water from a safe distance or from behind suitable shelter.

Class D materials will continue burning until the material is completely consumed, but cooling streams of water can control the burn. However, efforts should be directed at jettisoning or washing the materials over the side to avoid accumulating fire-fighting water inside the vessel. Water fog can also be used to protect firefighters from excessive heat.

NOTE

Nozzles can pose an electrical shock hazard to firefighters. If a nozzle or solid stream accidentally contacts electrical equipment or circuits, an electrical charge may be conducted back to the nozzle operator and cause injury.

CAUTION !

Do not wet down the lead attack nozzle man. The combination of moisture and high temperature can cause steam burns.

D.5. Low-Velocity Fog

Low-velocity fog is applied with a vari-nozzle. Low-velocity fog is a pressurized spray less powerful than high-velocity fog. Because low-velocity fog covers more area than high-velocity fog, it may be used most effectively when it is possible to get right up next to the fire.

Low-velocity water fog can also provide a heat shield by forming a screen of water droplets between a firefighter and the fire. When firefighters are properly clothed and hose lines have vari-nozzles, it is not necessary to use low-velocity water for personal protection.

Fog streams used improperly can injure personnel. The fog screen from high-velocity fog can obscure an attack nozzleman's visibility. This is extremely important to remember when no opening exists in the compartment or passageway other than the opening through which the nozzle is being advanced. In spaces with only one opening, heat and smoke can blow back or burst through or around a fog curtain. When circumstances require entering a compartment or passageway that has only one opening, short bursts of solid stream or fog should be directed toward the overhead to knock down the flames.

Using water as an extinguishing agent adds water and weight to a vessel. This can cause the vessel to become unstable. Normally, the water will be removed (dewatered) after the fire has been extinguished. However, to maintain stability and decrease the threat to the crew, the vessel should be dewatered as soon as possible.

D.6. Effectiveness

Water can be effective on all classes of fire, when properly applied for the situation. However, it is most effective for Class A fires. It is recommended for use in Class D (combustible metals) fires for its cooling effect and ability to wash the material away.

Applying Aqueous Film-Forming Foam (AFFF)

D.7. Description

Foam is a blanket of bubbles that extinguishes a fire mainly by smothering. The bubbles are formed by mixing water, air, and a foam-producing agent called foam concentrate. The mixture of water, air, and foam concentrate becomes foam solution.

When using foam, the entire surface of a flame must be covered, otherwise uncovered areas will continue to burn. One gallon of liquid foam concentrate will produce approximately 133 gallons of foam solution. The contents of one 5-gallon can of liquid foam will last about 1½ minutes and will produce about 660 gallons of foam solution.

Foam may be used against Class C fires in an emergency and as a last resort. AFFF concentrate separates at temperatures below 35 °F. This does not affect its usefulness provided the can is shook to re-mix components before use.

D.8. Effectiveness

Foam is effective against Class B fires. Foam solution is lighter than the lightest of flammable liquids. When applied to burning liquids, it floats on the surface and prevents oxygen from reaching the fuel source. In addition, the water content of foam provides a cooling effect on the fire. Once the fire is out, a layer of foam should be maintained over the flammable liquid to ensure the fire stays extinguished.

Applying Chemical Agents

D.9. Description

Chemical agents can be very effective fire fighting tools. However, they can be ineffective and sometimes dangerous if they are not used properly. Learning the proper use of each chemical agent, including its advantages and disadvantages, before using it to fight a fire is essential. Two chemical agents are discussed below:

- Carbon dioxide (CO_2).
- Potassium bicarbonate (PKP) - most likely not found on Auxiliary facilities.

D.10. Carbon Dioxide (CO_2)

CO_2 is a colorless gas about 50 percent heavier than air. When released from its container, the gas expands to 450 times its stored volume and smothers a fire by temporarily removing the oxygen. Because it is a nonconductor of electricity, CO_2 is the primary agent used against electrical fires.

CAUTION !

CO_2 should never be used alone to fight a major fire.

D.10.a. CO_2 Effectiveness

CO_2 is effective on small class A, B, and C fires. It has a very limited cooling capacity and does not permanently remove oxygen from a fuel source. Therefore, CO_2 is only effective in knocking down flames. Unless CO_2 is used continuously until all flames are extinguished, the fire could re-ignite (re-flash). In fact, the likelihood of a re-flash is greater when CO_2 is used against a fire than any other type of agent.

A continuous discharge of CO_2 from a fully charged 10-pound extinguisher will last approximately 40 to 45 seconds. The effective range for the portable CO_2 extinguisher is approximately 5 feet. A distance of more than 5 feet may cause the CO_2 to mix with the air and become ineffective.

WARNING

CO_2 is extremely cold when discharged. The rapid expansion of the gas creates a "snow" that can "burn" or raise blisters if it comes in contact with bare skin. Keep hands on the insulated horn handle when using the CO_2 extinguisher.

D.10.b. Discharging CO_2

CO_2 gas is not a conductor of electricity. However, when discharging the CO_2, static electricity may build up in the horn. This could be quite dangerous when extinguishing a fire where explosive gases are present. The cylinder should always be kept grounded to the deck when discharging to prevent static charge buildup. CO_2 is most effective in closed spaces away from the effects of strong winds. The following are the operating procedures for the CO_2 extinguisher: (see **Figure 18-3**)

Step	Procedure
1	Remove the locking pin from the valve.
2	Carry the extinguisher in an upright position, approaching the fire as close as safety permits.
3	For the smaller 5-pound size, swing the horn up to a horizontal position.
4	For larger CO_2 extinguishers, ensure the CO_2 bottle is in contact with the deck to prevent a static charge from building up within the extinguisher.
5	Grasp the insulated horn handle and squeeze the release lever to start the extinguisher.
6	Direct the flow of CO_2 toward the base of the flame and attack the flame with a sweeping movement of the nozzle.

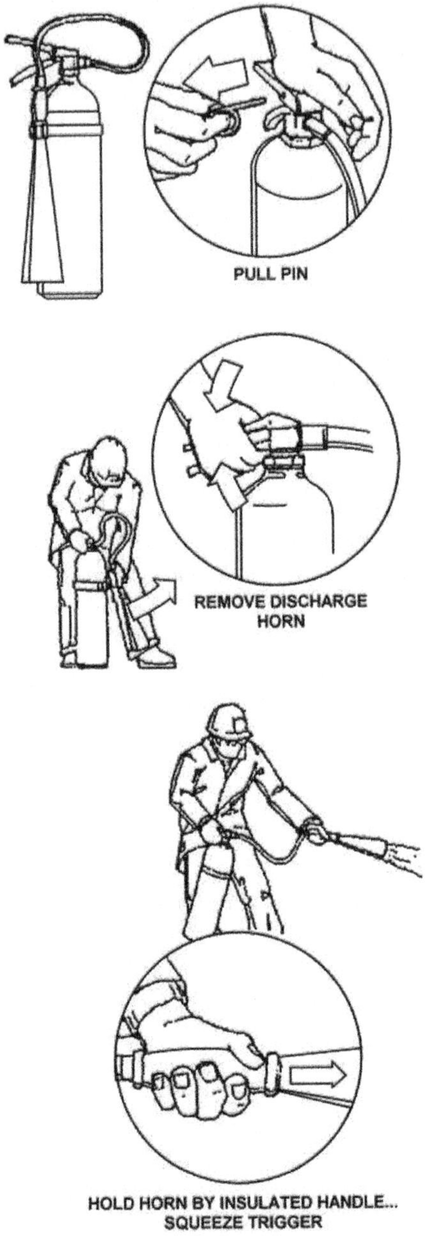
PULL PIN
REMOVE DISCHARGE HORN
HOLD HORN BY INSULATED HANDLE...
SQUEEZE TRIGGER

Figure 18-3
Operating the CO_2 Extinguisher

CAUTION ! PKP, like CO_2, should never be used alone against a major fire for it presents the same hazard of a re-flash as CO_2.

D.11. Potassium Bicarbonate (PKP)

PKP is also known as purple K powder. The ingredients used in PKP are non-toxic. When PKP is applied, a dense cloud is formed in the combustion area that limits the amount of heat that can be radiated back to the heart of the fire. Fewer fuel vapors are produced due to the reduced radiant heat. The dry chemical PKP extinguishes flames by breaking the combustion chain.

D.11.a. PKP Effectiveness

PKP does not have cooling capability. PKP may be effective as a temporary measure for extinguishing a flame, but it dissipates rapidly. Therefore, all hot spots must be cooled to prevent re-ignition. It is effective to some degree on all types of fires, but is particularly effective when used against burning liquids. By first extinguishing a burning liquid with PKP and then laying down a blanket of AFFF to prevent re-flash, dealing with a Class B fire is very effective. Most PKP extinguishers have an effective range of 10-12 feet and will last between 8-20 seconds in continuous use.

D.11.b. Discharging Dry Chemicals

The dry chemical or powder contained in these portable containers is expelled by either a gas cartridge or by stored pressure within the container. The following are the procedures for using this type of extinguisher: (see **Figure 18-4**)

Step	Procedure
1	Operate the dry chemical extinguisher by following the instructions printed on the extinguisher.
2	Control the discharge of the dry chemical by the nozzle shutoff valve for both cartridge-operated and pressurized dry chemical extinguishers.
3	Approach the fire as close as safety will allow.
4	Remove pin.
5	Squeeze trigger.
6	Direct the discharge at the base of the flame and attack with a sweeping movement.

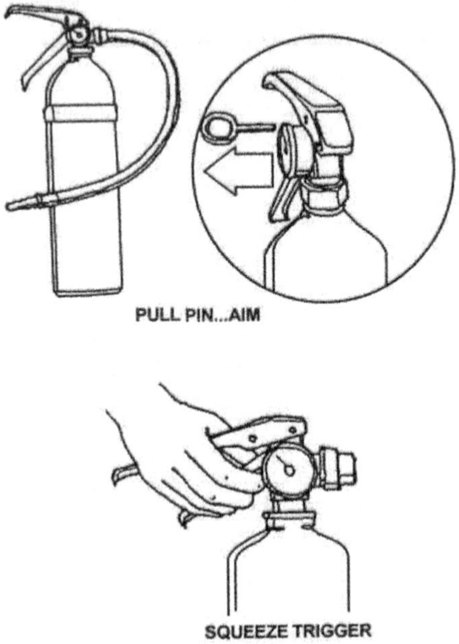
PULL PIN...AIM
SQUEEZE TRIGGER

Figure 18-4
Dry Chemical Extinguisher

Applying Halon

D.12. Description

Halon, a liquefied compressed gas, is odorless, colorless, and electrically nonconductive. Halon differs from the other extinguishing agents in the way it extinguishes fires. It has some of water's cooling effect and some of CO_2's smothering power, but Halon actually reacts chemically with the fire to interrupt the chain reaction that causes fire to spread. This process is known as chain breaking, which was discussed earlier in this section.

Halon flooding systems are typically used to extinguish fires in machinery spaces where Class B and C fires occur.

CAUTION ! Personnel should not remain in a space where Halon has been released unless an oxygen breathing apparatus (OBA) is worn.

D.13. Storage and Safety

All Halon is stored in liquid form in steel storage cylinders. Inside the cylinders, liquid Halon is pressurized using super-pressurized nitrogen. When activated, Halon is expelled as a gas. A Halon flooding system rapidly distributes a 5- to 7-percent concentration evenly throughout any space.

In a space where Halon was released, ventilation must be run on high for a minimum of 15 minutes before personnel re-enter that space without a breathing device. On vessels that have no mechanical ventilation, the space must be thoroughly ventilated using natural ventilation.

D.14. Halon Effectiveness

The mechanism by which Halon extinguishes a fire is not completely understood. Basically, Halon acts by removing active chemicals from spaces involved in a flame chain reaction. Halon complements a total fire fighting system as a final line of defense after other alternatives such as portable extinguishers (if possible) have been used.

Applying FE-241

D.15. Description

Like Halon, FE-241 is a liquefied compressed gas. It is classified as a clean agent, meaning it leaves no residue when used to extinguish fires. Its chemical name is Chlorotetrafluoroethane. Like Halon, it chemically interferes with the combustion process for fire extinguishment. However, FE-241 is an environmentally safe U.S. Coast Guard-approved and EPA-accepted Halon alternate extinguishing agent. This means that FE-241 can be used in place of Halon to extinguish Class C fires.

Section E. Fire Fighting Equipment

Introduction

Specialized equipment is used to apply extinguishing agents. In this section, the basics of how to operate the most common kinds of fire fighting equipment found on Coast Guard boats will be discussed.

In this section

This section contains the following information:

Fire Hose

E.1. Description

A fire hose is a basic fire fighting tool. Although taken for granted, hoses are highly developed tools that must be properly used and maintained.

A standard fire hose is a double-jacketed, cotton or nylon-impregnated, rubber-lined, orange hose. It comes in 2 common diameters, 1½-inch or 2½-inch, and is produced in standard lengths of 50 feet. In some cases, a fire hose on Coast Guard small boats must be shorter than the standard length because of limited space. In addition to the standard lengths, the 1½-inch hoses are available in 25-foot lengths and 2½-inch hoses in 30-foot lengths.

CAUTION ! A charged hose has considerable force. Ensure it is properly manned at all times to prevent it from swinging out of control.

E.2. Safety Precautions

Before using a fire hose, several safety checks must be performed. These checks may seem needlessly time-consuming at a fire scene. Nonetheless, they must be performed to prevent a malfunction in a hose system that could cause even more time to be lost. The following checks should be performed:

- Make certain all hose connections are tight and a hose is free of kinks and twists.
- Ensure the bail on a nozzle is closed before a hose is charged.
- Never lay a hose on an excessively hot deck.
- Be sure there are enough people available to control a fire hose before charging it. Never leave a charged hose unattended.

E.3. Minimum Operators

A minimum of 2 people is recommended to control a 1½-inch hose.

E.4. Coupling

A fire hose has brass or metal fittings, known as male and female couplings at its ends. This allows one hose to be attached to another or to a fitting. A female coupling connects to a boat's fire main or portable pump. A male coupling connects to a nozzle or to a female coupling on another length of hose. To connect lengths of fire hose, crewmembers take half a turn to the left on the female coupling to set the threads, then turn to the right until the connection is tight. Fittings should be hand tight. (see **Figure 18-5**)

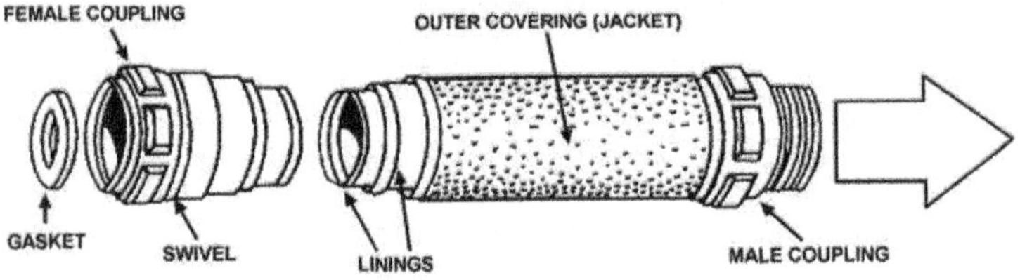

Figure 18-5
Fire Hose Couplings

E.5. Maintenance

Maintenance of fire hoses include the following:

Step	Procedure
1	Remove dirt, grease, abrasives, and other foreign matter from the outer coverings of hoses.
2	Clean fire hoses with a mild soap and water solution (inside and out). Do not use abrasives to clean hoses.
3	After use, properly stow a fire hose as follows: • Check a hose to make sure it is completely drained. • Ensure that a proper gasket is in place inside the female coupling and that it is not cracked or damaged. • Roll hoses so the male coupling is lying between hose layers to prevent damage to a coupling's threads. This also allows the female coupling to be connected, and the hose rolled out without twisting.

Spanner Wrench

E.6. Description

Spanner wrenches are very important when working with fire hoses. As mentioned before, when connecting fire hoses to fittings or another hose, connections should be hand tight allowing for easy disconnect. Sometimes tightening connections only hand tight is not enough. This is where a spanner wrench helps out. Spanner wrenches are also useful if a fire hose is unable to be disconnected from a connection because it has been put on too tight.

A spanner wrench is adjustable so that is can be used with all standard sizes of fire hoses. A range of adjustment is indicated on the handle of a wrench. A curved tip on the working end of a wrench is made to fit all notches in a coupling.

E.7. Safety Precautions

Spanner wrench safety precautions are as follows:

- As with using any wrench, be careful not to get fingers or other objects caught between the wrench and the coupling.
- Ensure the working end of the wrench is in the notch before applying heavy pressure.

E.8. Operation

On properly maintained hoses, connections may be effectively tightened by hand. However, if there is water leakage at a connection, a spanner wrench may be used. Once a wrench is adjusted, the tip of a wrench is inserted into the notch and the wrench handle pulled to the right. (see **Figure 18-6**)

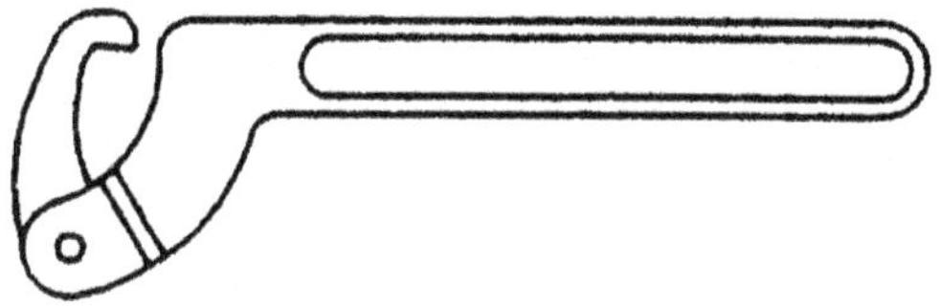

Figure 18-6
Spanner Wrench

E.9. Maintenance

Depending on what they are made of, spanner wrenches may need to be de-rusted, and greased or oiled periodically.

Wye-Gate

E.10. Description

Wye-gates are important fire fighting tools. They allow a single stream of fire fighting water to be divided into 2 streams.

The wye-gate is a Y-shaped fitting used to reduce fire hose line size and allow use of two separate hoses. It has one female 2½-inch inlet opening and two 1½-inch male outlet openings. A female end attaches to a fire main, portable pump, or between fire hose lengths (the 2½-inch being reduced to 1½-inch fire hoses). Male openings receive two 1½-inch fire hoses.

E.11. Safety Precautions

While wye-gates allow additional fire hoses to be directed against a fire, their use may result in a large pressure drop at the nozzle.

E.12. Operation

A wye-gate makes it possible to fight fires with two hoses. A flow of water through each of the 1½-inch openings may be regulated or secured with the valves or gates. The two gates are independent of each other, so one can be closed while the other is open. A gate is opened or closed with a quarter turn. **Figure 18-7** shows a wye-gate with one open and one closed gate. The gate position for each should be noted.

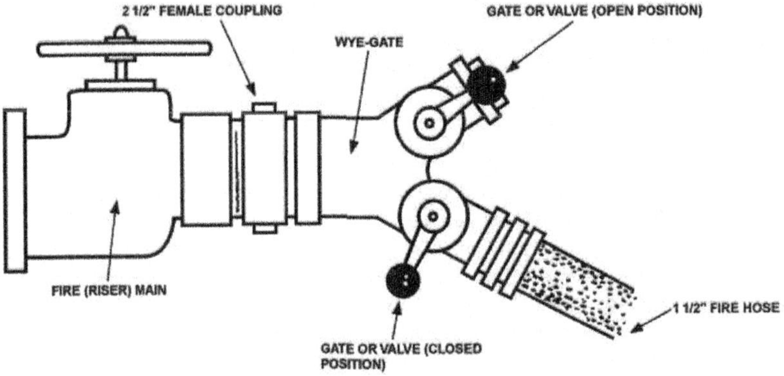

Figure 18-7
Wye-Gate Attached to Fire Main

E.13. Maintenance

Wye-gates must be periodically cleaned of corrosion, and greased or oiled.

Tri-Gate

E.14. Description

Tri-gates, like wye-gates, divide a single stream of fire fighting water. However, they divide a single stream into 3 separate streams instead of only 2 streams.

A tri-gate is another fitting to which fire hoses are frequently connected. A tri-gate has one 2½-inch female fitting to be connected to the water supply and one 2½-inch and two 1½-inch male fittings for discharge openings. A tri-gate, like a wye-gate, is used fighting a fire with multiple fire hoses. (see **Figure 18-8**)

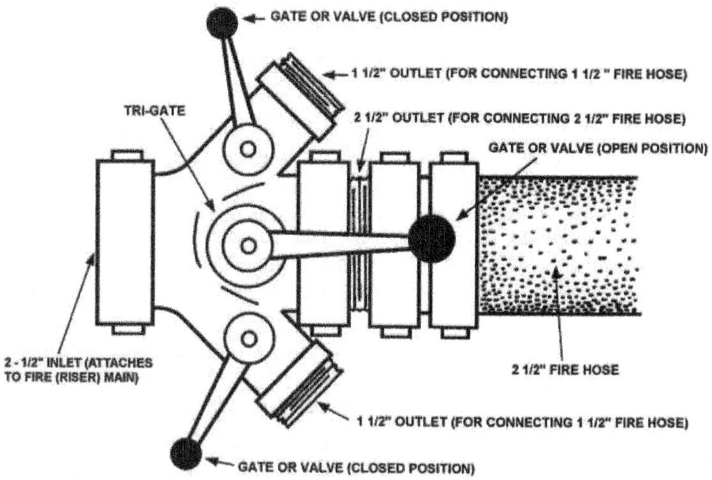

Figure 18-8
Tri-Gate

E.15. Safety Precautions

While tri-gates allow additional fire hoses to be directed against a fire, their use may result in a large water pressure drop at the nozzle.

E.16. Operation

The gates or valves on a tri-gate control the flow of water in the same fashion as regulating gates on a wye-gate. To use the tri-gate, use the following procedures:

Step	Procedure
1	Break out the tri-gate.
2	Connect the tri-gate to the water supply.
3	Connect a length of 2½" fire hose to the tri-gate.
4	Connect a length of 1½" fire hose to the tri-gate.
5	Place the gate regulating handle of the 2½" and 1½" hose outlets of the tri-gate of which the hoses are connect in the *open* position.
6	Ensure the regulating gate of the second 1½" outlet is in the *closed* position.
7	Ensure that whatever the hose leads to (nozzle, monitor) is being tended before charging the fire hoses.
8	Check the tri-gate, valves, and hose connections for water leakage; tighten with a spanner wrench, if necessary.

E.17. Maintenance

Tri-gates must be periodically cleaned of corrosion, and greased or oiled.

Vari-Nozzle

E.18. Description

The vari-nozzle can be used for fighting all classes of fires. In the fog position, it can also be used for personnel protection by creating a shield of water spray.

A Navy vari-nozzle is fitted with a pistol grip handle on the underside of the nozzle and a two-position bail handle on the top that operates the nozzle. The vari-nozzle's spray pattern is adjusted by rotating the variable pattern tip and can range from a 90° wide-angle spray to a narrow straight stream as well as intermediate patterns between these extremes.

E.19. Operation

This nozzle is used with AFFF for extinguishing Class B fires. (see **Figure 18-9**)

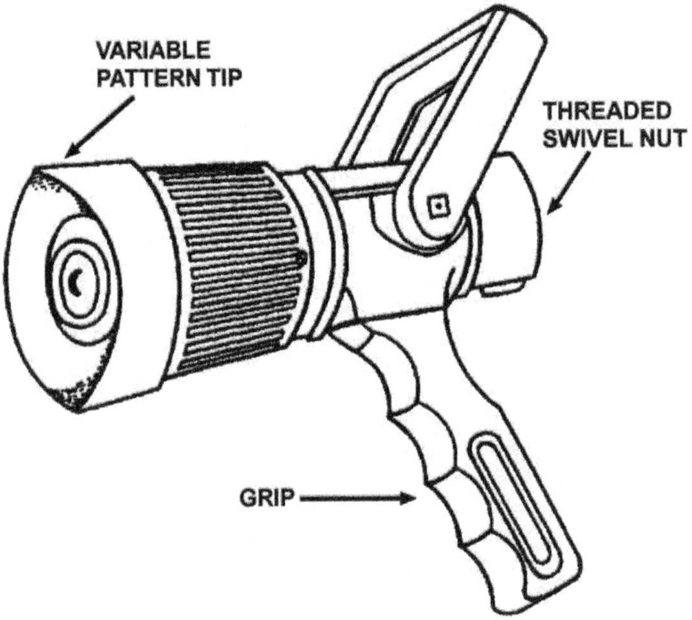

Figure 18-9
Vari-Nozzle

E.20. Maintenance

Maintenance of the vari-nozzle include the following:

Step	Procedure
1	Clean a nozzle with a mild solution of soap and water. Do not use abrasives to clean nozzles.
2	After use, stow the nozzle. Always stow a vari-nozzle with the bail handle in the *closed* position with the nozzle set to a narrow angle (30° pattern) fog.

Drop Pump and AFFF

E.21. Description

Use of a drop pump allows AFFF concentrate to be proportioned with water, adequately agitated, and delivered at a relatively high rate. A drop pump is designed to pump a large volume of water at low pressure.

A drop pump is not intended for fire fighting and therefore is not equipped with fire hose connections. In an emergency situation though, a drop pump can put down a layer of AFFF using its storage container and hoses.

E.22. Safety Precautions

AFFF must be mixed with water. It should not be applied to a fire directly from its container or when it has been mixed with water manually (i.e., without first having it run through the drop pump).

There are drawbacks to using a drop pump in place of the in-line proportioner and vari-nozzle. Once a canister is empty, foam application must be halted so it can be refilled. In addition, the quality and density of foam is not optimum.

E.23. Operation

It is not possible to apply mechanical foam with a drop pump in the conventional way by using an in-line proportioner and vari-nozzle. However, a drop pump can still be used for foam delivery by performing the following procedures:

Step	Procedure
1	Break a pump out from its storage container and set it up to take suction.
2	Fill the storage container with water using the pump discharge hose. It will hold approximately 38 gallons of water.
3	Pour about 2 gallons of AFFF (about one-third of a standard AFFF container) into the pump's storage container.
4	After the storage container is full of water/AFFF mixture, transfer the pump's suction hose from over the side to the storage container (suction is taken from there). A discharge hose is about 15 feet in length. Use it as if it were a vari-nozzle to fight fire in a conventional manner. This method allows a high volume of AFFF to be delivered in a short period of time.

Section F. Fire Fighting Procedures

Introduction

The following paragraphs will explain some safety precautions that must be observed when fighting fire as well as some tactical procedures to follow.

F.1. Coast Guard's Fire Fighting Duty

Boat crewmembers must always remember that boat crews are not fire fighting professionals. According to the Coast Guard Fire Fighting Activities Policy, the boat crews are to support fire fighting professionals if necessary. However, if a boat crew were to be first on the scene of a boat fire or be the victims of a boat fire, their primary responsibility is to save lives, not property. Evacuate all people from a burning vessel, and then follow a risk assessment plan if capable.

Refer to *Section A* of this chapter to view the Coast Guard fire fighting activities policy, and to *Chapter 4* for discussion of a risk management plan.

F.2. Safety Precautions

Fire fighting can be very hazardous to anyone involved. Coast Guard personnel must always be alert and aware of their actions and decisions to avoid being injured or incapacitated performing fire fighting duties that are not their responsibility. Losing the services of any Coast Guard person may keep a boat crew from preventing other injuries, loss of life, or loss of property. Refer to *Chapter 4* of this Manual for a discussion of risk assessment and risk management.

F.2.a. Salvors and Marine Chemists

Shipboard and waterfront fires frequently involve toxic or chemical hazards for firefighters. These hazards may be the source of the fire or produced as a byproduct of fire. Therefore, caution must always be exercised before attempting to fight any type of fire. Requesting trained assistance before becoming involved in fighting a fire of unknown material would be prudent.

Many salvage companies operate over a wide geographic area. Thus, these companies can respond more quickly to these situations. In addition, they employ marine chemists who can obtain temperature readings, check for the presence and concentrations of gases, and can provide information to fire fighting forces about chemical hazards they may encounter during response activities.

F.2.b. Smoke Plumes

Coxswains must always stay well clear of smoke plumes rising from a fire because they greatly reduce visibility and can pose a health hazard. Smoke is a visible product of fire and carries water vapor, acids, and other chemicals produced by fire and can be irritating or toxic when inhaled. A smoke plume is made of suspended particles of carbon and other unburned substances. These products of combustion are released into the atmosphere and travel downwind.

F.2.b.1. Staying Upwind

As a plume expands downwind and outward from a fire, toxic products will be less concentrated. The more toxic a product is, the larger the unsafe area will be, both downwind and to the sides of a plume. The decision to set a perimeter upwind of a toxic smoke or fire plume must be considered and executed when prudent. Individuals who remain a safe distance upwind should not be affected by unseen dangers of a smoke plume.

NOTE Generally speaking, remaining upwind of the fire provides a safe area away from toxic hazards that are released in a fire plume.

F.2.b.2. Maintaining a Safe Distance

Other decisions, such as determining a safe distance from a plume of smoke, should be made and constantly reevaluated as an incident develops. Any change in weather conditions could dictate a need to increase the initial size of a perimeter. A crewmember is considered to be in a danger zone if a smoke plume is visible and radiant heat is felt.

F.2.b.3. Awareness of Gases and Vapors

Smoke plumes also have other factors that must be considered such as the behavior of gases or vapors that extend beyond a perimeter of visible smoke and fire. Burning plastics and rubber products produce gases, heat, flame, and smoke. These byproducts may contain elements of a toxic or lethal nature.

There are many other products of combustion that are dangerous and can be lethal under certain conditions.

F.3. Operations

A boat crew is faced with several responsibilities and decisions when a vessel or waterfront fire occurs. Decisions made may affect lives, millions of dollars in property, and the free flow of maritime commerce. When determining a unit's assistance posture, the following should be considered:

- Level of the threat of fire.
- Jurisdictions involved.
- Capabilities of local fire departments.
- Availability of Coast Guard equipment.
- Level of Coast Guard training.

Generally, Coast Guard personnel shall not engage in independent fire fighting operations except to save a life or in the early stages of a fire, where they may avert a significant threat without undue risk. Coast Guard personnel shall not engage in fire fighting (on other than Coast Guard units) except in support of a regular fire fighting organization and under the supervision of a qualified fire officer.

NOTE

A qualified fire officer is a person who has been trained and certified, under National Fire Protection Association guidelines, to take command of firefighting operations.

F.3.a. Personnel Training

Coast Guard personnel engaged in fire fighting operations must be properly trained and equipped for the task they are assigned. Therefore, the level of Coast Guard involvement is dependent upon available leadership, experience, training, and equipment.

Coast Guard planning and training efforts must be integrated with those of other responsible agencies, particularly local fire departments and port authorities. This is especially important for fires on large vessels and shore structures. COTPs work closely with municipal fire departments, vessel and facility owners and operators, mutual aid groups, and other interested organizations. COTPs have developed a fire fighting contingency plan that addresses fire fighting in each port in the COTP zone.

F.4. Action

When a Coast Guard boat crew becomes involved in fire fighting operations, the situation will typically be one that fosters a great sense of urgency to extinguish a fire as rapidly as possible. All members of a boat crew must remember that haste and lack of a coordinated effort by boat crewmembers can recklessly endanger a boat and all crewmembers.

F.4.a. Crew Brief

A boat coxswain must brief crewmembers before arriving at the scene of a fire. This briefing details each crewmember's assignments and emphasizes safety. Crewmembers are responsible for all duties assigned and must request clarification from the coxswain if they do not clearly understand the tasks assigned. They must break out all necessary gear. All personnel must don battle dress before arriving on scene. Battle dress means that everyone will button their collars, wear gloves, and tuck trouser legs into their socks. The coxswain is responsible for inspecting all other crewmembers and making certain that battle dress has been donned.

F.4.b. Initial Action

The following are procedures initially performed when responding to a fire:

Step	Procedure
1	Approach the boat from upwind.
2	Immediately upon arriving on scene, all crewmembers should check the surrounding vicinity for PIWs.
3	Recover and evacuate all survivors to the Coast Guard vessel.
4	Evaluate their physical conditions and render first aid if necessary.
5	If the extent of injury requires more than minor first aid, immediately transport the injured so they can receive professional medical assistance.
6	Inform operational command and EMS if necessary, of the situation.

These procedures are to be taken before attacking the fire, remembering that life comes before property. If there are no survivors or those recovered are in good physical condition and have been evacuated to a safe place, the next step is to stop and evaluate the fire.

WARNING

If the risk of explosion is not certain, back off a safe distance and establish a safety zone. Do not attempt to fight the fire.

CAUTION !

A crewmember's decision regarding his or her role in the overall situation must be constantly reexamined.

F.4.c. Situation Evaluation

The coxswain and crew must evaluate the following elements of the situation:

- Location and extent of a fire.
- Class of fire.
- Class and extent of all cargo involved.
- Possibility of explosion.
- Possibility of any vessel involved sinking/capsizing within a navigable channel.
- Hazard to the crew.
- Maneuverability of the vessel.
- Weather forecast.
- Risk of a serious pollution incident.

Step	Procedure
1	If a fire can be put out with no danger to the crew or the vessel, proceed.
2	If not, back off and maintain a safety zone so that no other vessel comes too close to the fire scene.
3	After completing the initial evaluation, reevaluate a fire scene/situation frequently. A small fire can rage out of control in minutes and threaten more property and cargo.
4	If a fire must be approached at any time, remember to always approach from windward. (see **Figure 18-10**)
5	If it becomes necessary to tie up alongside a burning vessel to fight a fire or to remove survivors, attach only one line to the vessel and keep a sharp knife accessible for a quick break away.

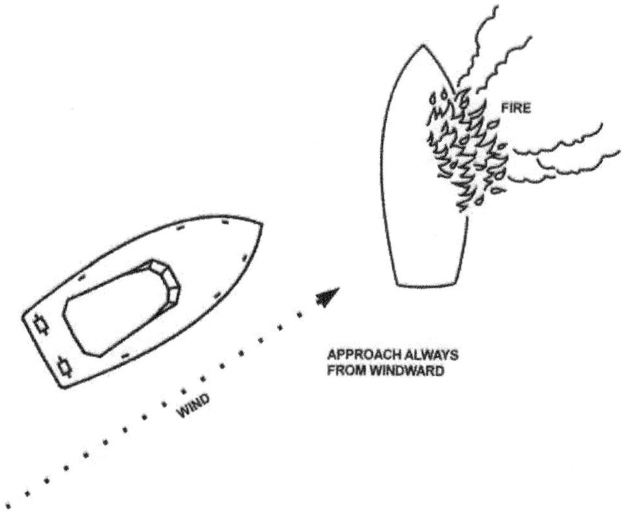

Figure 18-10
Approaching a Boat on Fire

F.4.d. Overhauling

Danger will still exist even after a fire is believed to be extinguished. The process of overhauling the fire is done to avoid fire re-flash as follows:

Step	Procedure
1	When a fire is out, check for hot spots and set a re-flash watch.
2	When danger of re-flash is no longer a concern, dewater the distressed vessel.

Section G. Extinguishing Fires

Introduction

A fire discovered early and quickly fought can usually be extinguished easily. Portable fire extinguishers are used for a fast attack that will knock down flames. However, they contain a limited supply of extinguishing agent. Crewmembers with limited training in using of these extinguishers often waste extinguishing agent by using them improperly. Periodic training, including practice with actual types of extinguishers carried onboard boats, will ensure proficient use of this equipment. Extinguishers that are due to be discharged and inspected should be used for training.

G.1. Safety Rules

The following safety rules should be observed when using portable fire extinguishers:

- Immediately upon discovering a fire, sound an alarm and summon help. Never try to fight a fire alone. Always call for help first.
- Never pass a fire to get to an extinguisher.
- If it is necessary to enter a compartment to combat a fire, keep an escape path open. Never let a fire block a door, hatch, or scuttle. Stay low.
- If extinguishing a fire within a compartment with a portable fire extinguisher fails, get out. Then close the door, hatch, or scuttle to confine the fire.

G.2. Fire Combat

An attack should be started immediately to gain control and to prevent extension of a fire to other areas of a boat. An attack will be either direct or indirect, depending on the fire situation. Both methods are efficient when properly employed.

G.3. Direct Attack

In a direct attack, crewmembers advance to the immediate area of a fire and apply extinguishing agent directly on a fire, if a fire is small and has not gained headway. Once a fire has gained headway, an indirect attack should be used.

G.4. Indirect Attack

An indirect attack is best when it is impossible for crewmembers to reach a fire. Generally, this is in the lower portions of a boat, such as the engine room and bilge areas. The success of an indirect attack depends on completely containing a fire. Every possible avenue a fire may travel must be cut off by closing doors, hatches, and scuttles and by securing all ventilation systems.

G.5. Fire Fighting Procedures on Coast Guard Boats

Every fire will quickly spread to new sources of fuel or oxygen if they are available. However, the path through which a particular fire extends will depend on the location of a fire and the construction of surrounding spaces. These factors must be considered when fighting a fire. In addition, fuel and all products of its combustion will affect fire fighting operations. For these reasons, no fire can be fought routinely, and all fires must be fought systematically. The following procedures should be part of every fire fighting operation:

CAUTION ! Never fight a fire, however small it may seem, until an alarm has been sounded. Once a fire gains intensity, it spreads swiftly.

Step	Procedure
1	Sound an alarm. Any crewmember who discovers a fire or any indication of fire must sound an alarm and give a location (e.g., "FIRE, FIRE, FIRE IN THE BILGES").
2	Evaluate a fire. • Determine the air supply to the fire. • Determine the class of fire (combustible material). • Determine the fuel source to the fire. • Select proper extinguishing agent. • Determine method for fighting a fire (direct or indirect). • Determine how to prevent spread of a fire. • Determine required equipment and crewmember assignments.
3	Determine the need to secure: • Electrical and electronic power panels. • Power to individual electrical and electronic equipment (alternator, radar, inverters). • Engine and fuel supply. • Air intakes (ventilation system, doors, hatches and scuttles).
4	Place all equipment necessary to combat a fire in an open deck area. This includes: • Portable fire extinguishers. • Fire hoses. • AFFF. • Drop pump. • First aid kit.

<table>
<tr><th>Step</th><th>Procedure</th></tr>
<tr><td>CAUTION !</td><td>Water can impair the stability of a boat. Make every effort to limit accumulation of water in compartments. Give preference to fog sprays over solid streams of water. Use only as much water as is absolutely necessary.</td></tr>
<tr><td>5</td><td>Combat a fire with appropriate extinguishing agent(s).</td></tr>
<tr><td>6</td><td>Notify parent unit at the earliest opportunity. Keep them fully advised of the situation.
• Give position.
• Nature of fire.
• Number of POBs.
• Your intentions.
• Keep them advised of changing situation and status of personnel.</td></tr>
<tr><td>7</td><td>Overhauling a fire.
• Once the fire has been extinguished, the spaces involved must be properly ventilated to remove any smoke, explosive, or toxic gases. If there is any doubt as to whether the space might contain harmful fumes, do not enter that compartment. Return to the Station and have the space checked out by trained officials. Be careful when ventilating because the introduction of fresh air into a compartment might cause the fire to re-flash.
• Once in the space, inspect all overhead spaces, decks, and bulkheads.
• Check where wiring and piping penetrates through bulkheads and decks.
• Expose areas that are charred, blistered, or discolored by heat until a clean area is found.
• Pull apart and examine any materials that might have been involved with the fire for hidden fire and hot embers. Jettison (throw overboard) all such material if necessary.
• Set a re-flash watch. One crewmember must be assigned to do nothing but check for re-ignition and to sound an alarm if it occurs.</td></tr>
<tr><td>8</td><td>Restow all fire fighting equipment except those pieces that are being used by the re-flash watch.
• Recharge or replace portable fire extinguishers, even if only partially used, immediately upon arrival back at the unit.
• Swap out used fire hoses with spare dry hoses. Drain, clean, dry, and roll up used hoses for storage.</td></tr>
<tr><td>9</td><td>Conduct a damage control check. Start any necessary dewatering operations. Depending on the severity of the damage, it might be best to tow the damaged vessel back to port where an in depth determination concerning damage to the vessel's systems can be conducted. Utilizing possibly damaged electrical or mechanical equipment might cause further damage or another fire.</td></tr>
</table>

G.6. Fire Fighting Procedures on Auxiliary Boats

Use the following procedures when battling a fire on an Auxiliary boat:

Step	Procedure
1	When a crewmember becomes aware of an engine compartment fire, shut off all engines, generators, and ventilation systems.
2	If boat is equipped with an automatic extinguishing system, ensure it is discharging. If the system is manually operated, energize it and check to ensure it is discharging.
3	Initiate a MAYDAY call to alert boats in the area of the situation.
4	Have all crewmembers don PFDs and everyone move to a smoke-free and flame-free area of the boat.
5	If a life raft or dinghy is available, put it over the side and inflate it, if necessary.
6	• If boat has a built-in CO_2 system, after fire is out, allow time for concentrations of CO_2 to ventilate to the atmosphere before entering the compartment. • On boats fitted with a Halon system, the dangers of toxic gases are not as great when entering the compartment, but always enter with caution. Never enter a compartment after a fire until you are sure it has been properly ventilated.

G.6.a. Opening a Hatch

If someone must open a hatch to discharge a portable extinguisher, expect the possibility of burned hands and/or a singed face can be expected. As the fresh air enters the compartment, it will feed the fire, and cause it to "blow up." The best method of opening a hatch is to stand to the hinged side of the hatch. Then while wearing gloves or using something other than bare hands, the hatch can be pulled open. If the boat has a closed engine compartment and no fixed system, it is a good idea to make a small hole with a pivoted cover into the space. A portable extinguisher may be discharged through this hole. (see **Figure 18-11**)

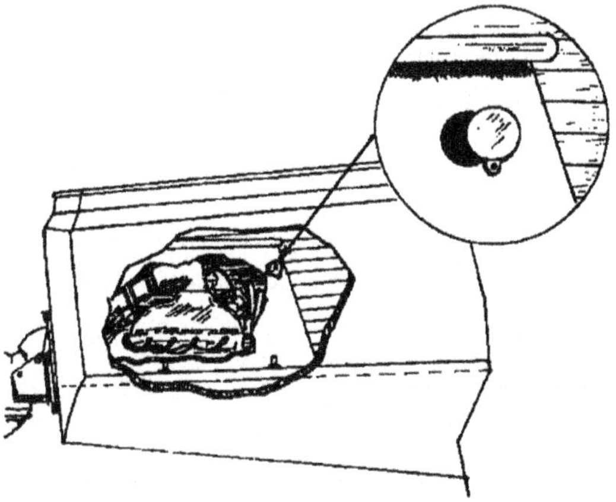

Figure 18-11
Hole for Extinguishing the Engine Compartment

G.7. Fires Aboard Other Boats

Use the following procedures when battling a fire aboard other boats:

Step	Procedure
1	Brief crewmembers on appropriate procedures.
2	Assign each crewmember specific duties.
3	While en route to the scene, establish communications with the distressed boat.
4	Approach the boat from upwind.
5	If no one is onboard, circle the boat (at a safe distance) searching for PIWs.
6	Advise all persons aboard the boat to move to a flame and smoke-free area, topside.
7	Attempt to determine the extent and source of the fire. If it is not obvious, ask the personnel aboard the distressed boat where the fire is located.
8	If the fire is beyond the crewmembers fire fighting capabilities, evacuate the persons from the distressed boat and call for assistance.
9	Check the physical condition of the survivors. If medical treatment is required, proceed to the nearest location where medical help can be administered.
10	If the fire is small and within the crewmember's capabilities, first ensure that the survivors are safe on the boat, another boat, or ashore before attempting to fight the fire.
11	After assessing the situation, fight the fire with the fire fighting equipment available. Avoid placing the crew and transferred survivors in any danger.

G.8. Fire Under Control

Under the following circumstances, a fire may be considered to be under control:

- Extinguishing agent is being applied to a fire and has effectively begun to cool it down.
- The main body of a fire (base) has been darkened. At this point, a fire cannot generate enough heat to involve nearby combustible materials.
- All possible routes of fire extension have been examined and found safe or protected.

G.9. Fire Extinguished

Before a fire can be declared completely out, a coxswain must ensure the following actions have taken place:

- A thorough examination of the immediate fire area has been conducted.
- A complete overhaul of all burned material has been accomplished.
- A re-flash watch has been set.
- All fire fighting equipment has been restowed with the exception of what is being used for the re-flash watch.
- A damage control check has been performed.
- All crewmembers have been accounted for.

G.10. Abandoning a Boat

Crewmembers should not panic and hastily abandon a boat even when a fire is severe. Instead, they should stay calm while using equipment and training to combat the fire. Abandoning the boat should only be considered as a last resort once all available options for extinguishing the fire have been attempted. Aggressive and proficient fire fighting is normally a preferred alternative to abandoning a boat, however, crewmembers should not hesitate to abandon the boat if the following conditions exist:

- Becoming trapped by the flames.
- There is no longer the equipment to fight the fire.
- An explosion is likely (flames by the fuel tanks).
- Similar life threatening situations are apparent.

If able, the coxswain should inform OPCON of location and any other pertinent information. Make sure that:

- Distress call has been initiated.
- All personnel are wearing life jackets.
- Life raft or dinghy is put over, if available.
- Portable radio is taken.
- Extra signaling gear is taken.

Section H. Dewatering

Introduction

Dewatering a vessel is a consideration that is normally secondary to getting a fire put out. That is not to say, however, that dewatering is not important. Indeed, it may be possible to use dewatering equipment to keep the boat from capsizing. Know what equipment is available for dewatering and how to use it.

H.1. Action Before Dewatering

Action taken before beginning to dewater a disabled vessel varies depending upon the nature of flooding. Regardless, a coxswain should always brief crewmembers on what procedures to follow while emphasizing safety. If crewmembers have just put out a fire on a boat, someone must then board the vessel and check for flooding, but only when safety permits. A coxswain will direct crewmembers how to safely accomplish this inspection for flooding.

When responding to a distress call of a disabled vessel taking on water, the initial action on the scene will be as follows:

Step	Procedure
1	Search the immediate area for people in the water.
2	After all survivors are recovered and all persons onboard the sinking craft are accounted for and have been evacuated to a safe place, check the sinking craft for hull damage or other sources of flooding.
3	Before entering any flooded compartment/vessel, every attempt to secure electrical power should be made to reduce the chance of electrical shock.
4	Once a source of flooding is determined, crewmembers may perform procedures to reduce water flow into the boat. Safety of the crew is the first priority. The distressed vessel should not be boarded if it seems unstable and could possibly capsize or sink.
5	Once onboard, the crewmembers should wear PFDs and not go below decks if there is any threat of capsizing or sinking.
6	When flooding has been controlled, or at least reduced to a minimum, dewatering can begin. How a vessel is dewatered depends on the conditions that exist at the scene.

NOTE This Manual does not cover technical information and use of commercial gasoline powered pumps, high capacity, manual, or electrical bailing pumps. See and follow the manufacturing instructions for usage while dewatering.

H.2. Dewatering with an Eductor

Dewatering with an eductor can be performed only when weather conditions permit your boat to safely come alongside a disabled vessel and remain close to it.

An eductor is used in conjunction with the fire pump on the boat. A 1½-inch fire hose attached to one of the 1½-inch outlets of the fire main is connected to the pressure supply inlet of the eductor. A 2½-inch fire hose is connected to the discharge outlet. Larger eductors with 2½-inch supply hoses and 4-inch discharge hoses can be found onboard cutters. The eductor itself is submerged, either vertically or horizontally, in the flooded area to be dewatered. Suction is obtained in either position because of uneven edges of the suction end of an eductor. All eductors operate in fundamentally the same manner. Water from a boat's fire pump is forced through a fire main and out through the discharge hose. As pressure of this rapidly moving water passes over the suction opening, it creates a vacuum. The vacuum, or suction, pulls water up through a suction hose, out through the discharge hose, and over the side of the boat. A discharge hose must always lead over the side and a suction hose must always be placed in flooded areas of a disabled boat. If they are inadvertently reversed, a disabled vessel will quickly be filled with water pumped aboard through the discharge line instead of dewatering it with a suction line. (see **Figure 18-12**)

CAUTION ! Make certain there are no kinks or obstructions in a discharge line. Their presence will cause an eductor to pump water into a flooded boat through the suction line.

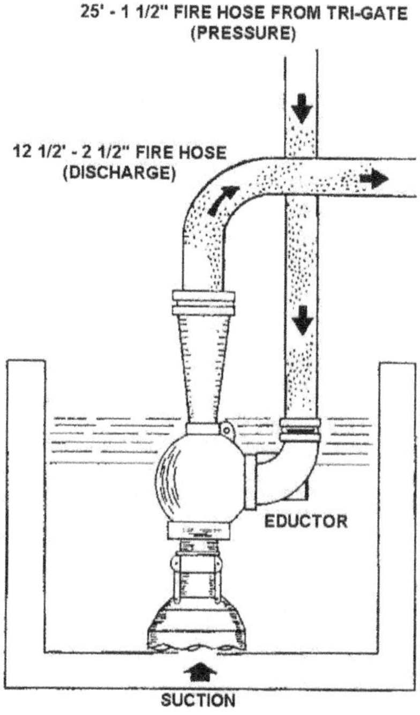

Figure 18-12
Eductor Rigged for Dewatering

WARNING

> Since the drop pump is water cooled, it should not be used to dewater a boat with fuel contamination in its bilges.

H.3. Dewatering Using a Drop Pump

Most Coast Guard boats carry a portable, gasoline-powered drop pump. (see **Figure 18-13**) Dewatering with a drop pump is done with the pump placed on the disabled boat. Depending on the model of drop pump, approximately 100-250 gallons of water per minute (GPM) can be removed from a flooded compartment.

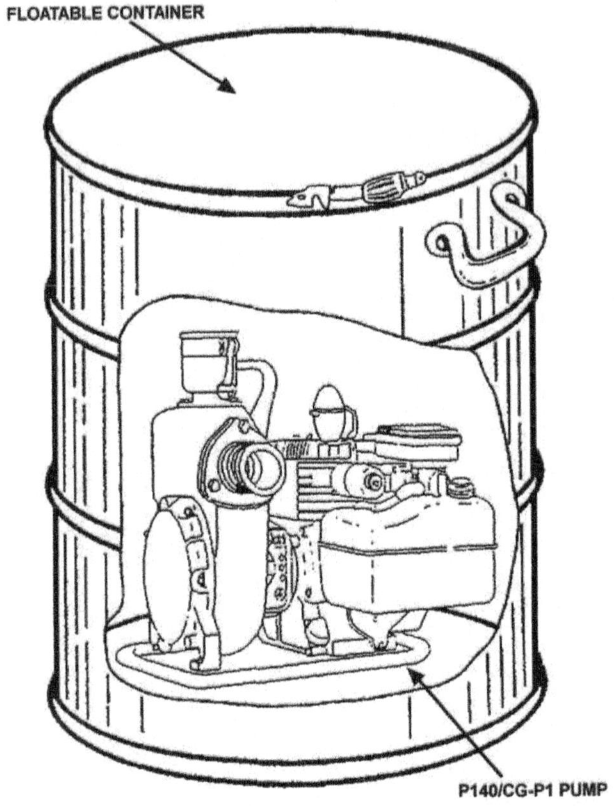

Figure 18-13
Drop Pump

H.3.a. Passing a Drop Pump	When secured in its watertight container, a drop pump can be easily passed from one boat to another. There are two methods for passing a pump.

H.3.a.1. Directly Passing a Drop Pump

The easiest method for transferring a drop pump is to pull alongside the flooding vessel and simply transfer the pump to the other vessel. At least two people are always required to move a pump because it is heavy and awkward to carry.

If coming alongside is not a safe option, use the following procedures to directly pass a drop pump:

Step	Procedure
1	Determine the rate of drift.
2	Secure a 2-inch mooring line to a bridle attached to a pump container or pump container handles. (see **Figure 18-14**)
3	Secure a heaving line to the 2-inch mooring line.
4	Rig a tending line from the pump to the boat to enable controlling the pump's movement once it is in the water and hauling it back in the event of an emergency. (see **Figure 18-15**)
5	Cast the heaving line, and direct people aboard the disabled boat to haul it in.
6	Lower the drop pump overboard and direct people aboard the disabled boat to haul in on the line. Pay out the tending end of the line as it is being hauled in.

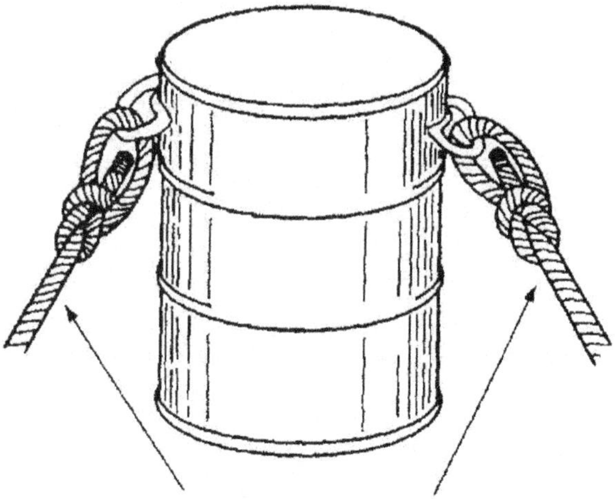
MOORING LINES SECURED TO
CONTAINER HANDLES WITH
BOWLINES

Figure 18-14
Securing Lines to Drop Pump Container

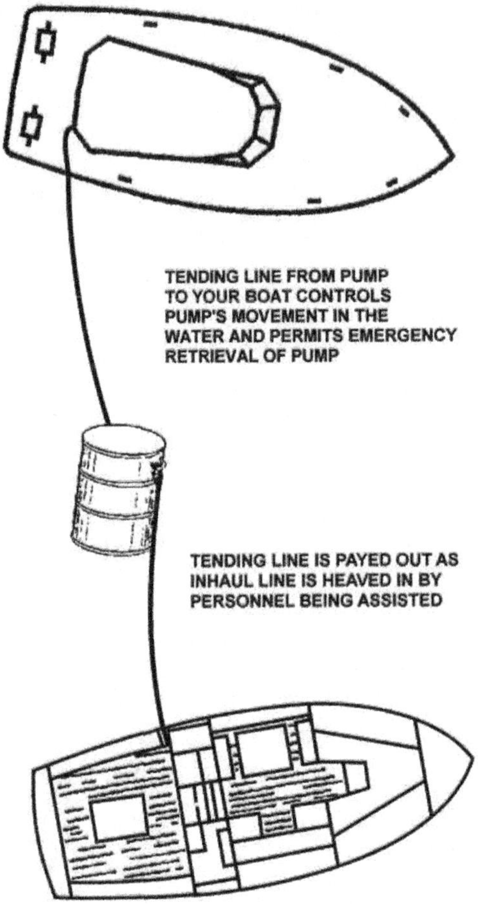
TENDING LINE FROM PUMP
TO YOUR BOAT CONTROLS
PUMP'S MOVEMENT IN THE
WATER AND PERMITS EMERGENCY
RETRIEVAL OF PUMP
TENDING LINE IS PAYED OUT AS
INHAUL LINE IS HEAVED IN BY
PERSONNEL BEING ASSISTED

Figure 18-15
Directly Passing a Drop Pump Using Tending Lines

H.3.a.2. Passing a Drop Pump into a Boat in Tow

As mentioned in *Chapter 17, Towing* , if it becomes necessary to dewater a vessel during a tow, it is easier to transfer the drop pump before placing the vessel in tow. If for some reason the disabled vessel starts taking on water during the tow, use the following procedures to pass the drop pump to the boat in tow astern:

Step	Procedure
1	Rig a bridle to both handles of a pump storage bracket if a permanent bridle has not already been attached.
2	Estimate the distance from the bow of the vessel back to the lowest point along the side of its hull. Make up a length of mooring line approximately equal to this distance. Secure the mooring line to the bridle rigged in step 1 with a shackle.
3	Make a bowline in the other end of the mooring line around the towline. A shackle may be substituted for a bowline. Regardless of the device used, bowline or shackle, the opening must be large enough for the mooring line to run freely down the tow line. (see **Figure 18-16**)
4	Lower the pump over the leeward side and allow it to float back to the boat in tow. (see **Figure 18-17**)
5	Maintain only enough headway for steerage to keep the pump from submerging.
6	Instruct the vessel in tow to turn their rudder so as to head into the wind or current. This allows the pump to drift away from the towed vessel's bow and down its side unobstructed.

NOTE Risk assessment is important should the towed vessel start to take on water. Always consider removing personnel from the vessel.

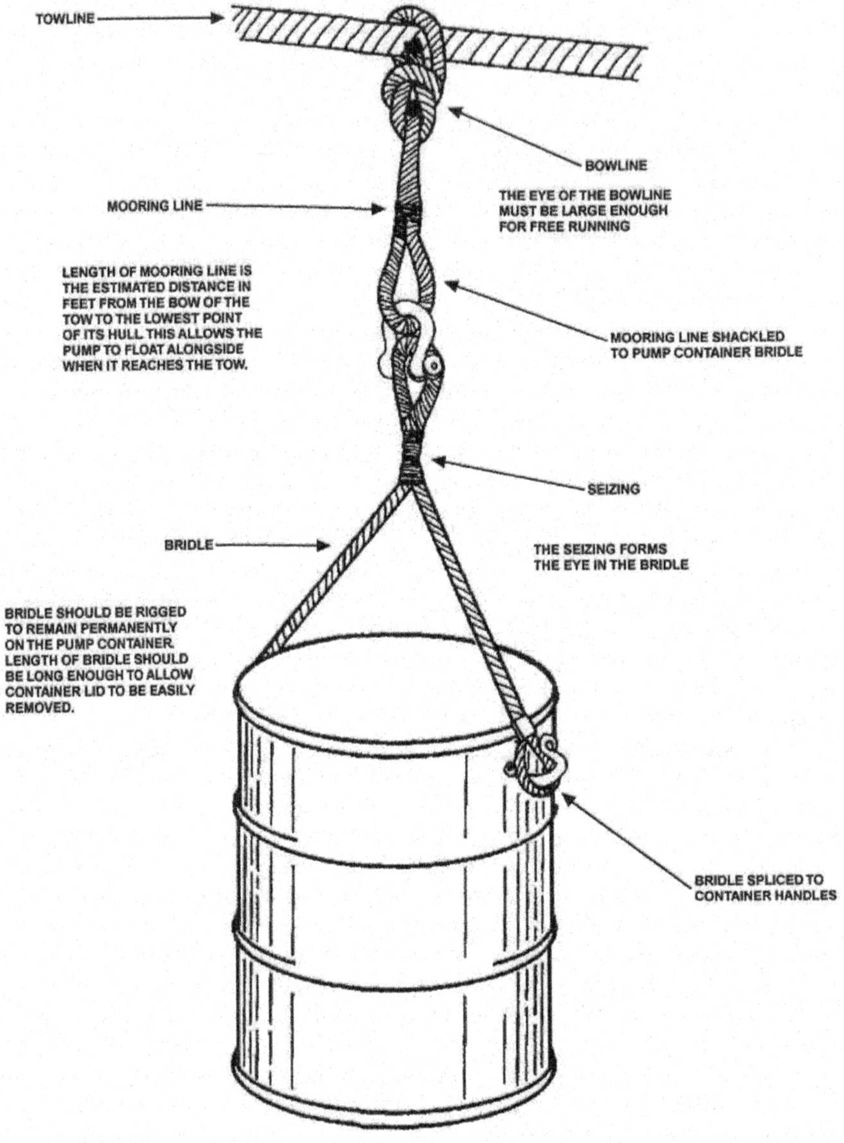
TOWLINE
BOWLINE
THE EYE OF THE BOWLINE MUST BE LARGE ENOUGH FOR FREE RUNNING
MOORING LINE
LENGTH OF MOORING LINE IS THE ESTIMATED DISTANCE IN FEET FROM THE BOW OF THE TOW TO THE LOWEST POINT OF ITS HULL. THIS ALLOWS THE PUMP TO FLOAT ALONGSIDE WHEN IT REACHES THE TOW.
MOORING LINE SHACKLED TO PUMP CONTAINER BRIDLE
SEIZING
THE SEIZING FORMS THE EYE IN THE BRIDLE
BRIDLE
BRIDLE SHOULD BE RIGGED TO REMAIN PERMANENTLY ON THE PUMP CONTAINER. LENGTH OF BRIDLE SHOULD BE LONG ENOUGH TO ALLOW CONTAINER LID TO BE EASILY REMOVED.
BRIDLE SPLICED TO CONTAINER HANDLES

Figure 18-16
Drop Pump on the Towline

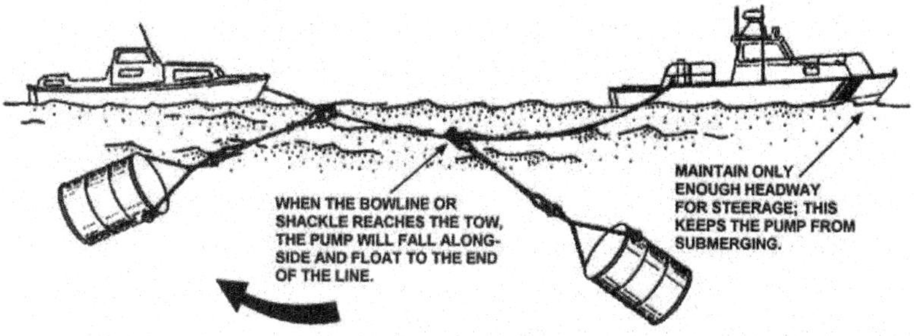
WHEN THE BOWLINE OR SHACKLE REACHES THE TOW, THE PUMP WILL FALL ALONG-SIDE AND FLOAT TO THE END OF THE LINE.
MAINTAIN ONLY ENOUGH HEADWAY FOR STEERAGE; THIS KEEPS THE PUMP FROM SUBMERGING.

Figure 18-17
Passing a Drop Pump on the Towline

H.3.b. Pump Operation

Since the Coast Guard switches out models of drop pumps when newer models become available, every drop pump comes with instructions specifically designed for that model pump. These instructions for operation can be found inside the storage container. These are extremely helpful if the pump is transferred to another vessel to use.

All crewmembers should be familiar with these instructions and practice operating the drop pump often.

The following procedures are the basic steps for setting up and using a drop pump. Again, refer to the instructions that come with the pump for specific operation instructions.

CAUTION !

Breathing exhaust fumes can be dangerous. Do not attempt to start or operate a pump while it is in a container. Once a pump is started, ensure sufficient ventilation is present to allow exhaust gases to dissipate into the atmosphere. Do not operate a drop pump below deck.

Step	Procedure
1	Pull the handle to release the tension ring or undo the locking clips on the storage container.
2	Lift the lid and open the plastic bag. Lift out the drop pump, hoses, and fuel.
3	Check the engine oil level (oil must be visible).
4	Check the fuel tank and connection to the engine. Fill if needed.
5	Mount and connect fuel tank, if applicable.
6	Connect the discharge hose and lay it out on deck so there are no kinks or twists. During operation, the discharge hose should be manned or tied off to prevent flooding into another space.
7	Place the discharge valve on the pump in the *closed* position.

Step	Procedure
8	Attach connection end of suction hose to pump and lower strainer end into compartment to be dewatered.
9	Actuate the hand-priming pump. Grasp the handle, then raise and lower it until the pump is primed. If pump doesn't prime, check suction fitting to ensure it is tight.
10	Place the choke lever on the engine in the "choke" position.
11	Pull the starter cord.
12	Place the engine choke lever in the "run" position and try pulling the starter cord again.
13	After the engine starts, prime the pump again. A pump can run dry for approximately one minute but it was designed to be started only after suction has been taken.
14	Open the discharge valve slowly.
15	Post a watch on the pump. The engine will run approximately 2-3 hours on one tank of fuel. The pump watch must be alert for debris around the strainer and must ensure the strainer remains submerged. Watch for fuel leaks.
16	Stop the pump and check the engine oil level after 5 hours of operation.

H.3.c. Securing a Pump

There are separate procedures for securing a drop pump depending on whether it is being secured because of an emergency or to be stowed.

H.3.c.1. Securing in an Emergency

Perform the following procedures for securing:

Step	Procedure
1	Push the stop lever against the spark plug. This allows a pump to stop for refueling, checking the oil, or standby.

H.3.c.2. Securing for Storage

Perform the following the procedures when securing the pump for storage:

Step	Procedure
1	Disconnect the fuel line. The pump will run for approximately one minute and stop.
2	Remove the suction and discharge hose.
3	Drain both hoses and any water in the pump.
4	Flush pump and hoses with fresh water.
5	Place in a dry, protected area for drying.
6	After drying, restow all gear in a container.

Section I. Righting Powerboats and Sailboats

CAUTION !

Notify the Operational Commander before beginning any type of righting operation. Attempting to right a capsized vessel could cause extensive damage to that vessel. The crew of the disabled vessel is the primary responsibility. Remember, the Coast Guard is not in the salvage business. If available, a salvage company should be contacted for this operation.

Introduction

Any attempt to right a capsized vessel must be carefully thought through before beginning. Boat crews must make absolute certain that all crewmembers from a distressed vessel are accounted for before beginning any procedure to right the vessel. Survivors may be trapped inside the overturned hull.

When an inboard boat capsizes, dewatering cannot begin until the craft has been righted. There are several methods for righting vessels of this type. The best one should be selected after evaluating the conditions on-scene. Regardless of the method used, an accurate count of the persons aboard the capsized boat is always essential. PFDs should be provided to them if necessary, and they should be brought aboard the boat before beginning the righting operation. A disabled craft should be approached cautiously. Watch for debris that may damage the boat or foul its propellers.

I.1. Righting Powerboats

The means selected for attaching lines determines the method of righting. Procedures for each method include:

- Righting by parbuckling.
- Righting using bow and transom eyebolt.
- Righting using towline fore and aft of boat's keel.
- Righting swamped boats astern using trailer eyebolt.

I.1.a. Righting by Parbuckling

Perform the following procedures when righting powerboats by parbuckling: (see **Figure 18-18**)

WARNING

Never have a swimmer attempt to rescue people trapped inside a capsized vessel. Attempt to keep the capsized vessel stable and call for assistance.

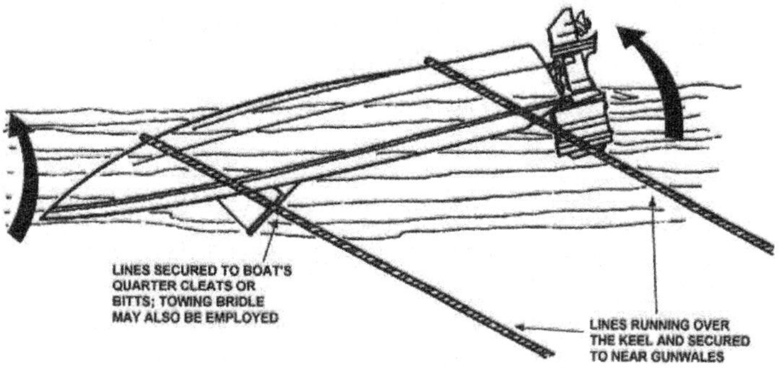

LINES SECURED TO BOAT'S QUARTER CLEATS OR BITTS; TOWING BRIDLE MAY ALSO BE EMPLOYED
LINES RUNNING OVER THE KEEL AND SECURED TO NEAR GUNWALES

Figure 18-18
Righting Powerboats by Parbuckling

CAUTION ! If the weather presents a danger to the person in the water or the boats involved, do not attempt righting.

Step	Procedure
1	Approach a capsized boat cautiously. Keep clear of all lines and debris in the water.
2	Account for all personnel from the capsized boat.
3	Recover all personnel from the water and provide PFDs to them as necessary.
4	Select a crewmember to be the tethered swimmer needed to enter the water to prepare the boat for righting.
5	Direct a crewmember to secure towing bridle or mooring lines to the nearest gunwale of the capsized boat.
6	Then the person-in-the-water leads the bridle lines or mooring lines under the boat and back over the keel. Ensure that these lines are outboard of all handrails, lifelines, and stanchions. Then run the bridle back to the towline, or run the mooring lines to the boat's rear quarter cleats or bitts.
7	Recover the tethered swimmer from the water.
8	Pay out enough on the towline or mooring lines to prevent the boat from hitting the stern during righting and towing. Then, secure the lines.
9	Gradually add power to the boat and increase speed. The boat should right itself.
10	Reduce power so as not to continue to pull the boat over capsizing it again.
11	Bring the righted boat alongside the righting boat and dewater using the most appropriate method.

I.1.b. Righting Using Bow and Transom Eyebolt

Perform the following procedures for righting a vessel using the bow and transom eyebolt:

Step	Procedure
1	Approach a capsized boat cautiously--from downwind, down current, or both, keeping clear of all lines and debris in the water.
2	Account for all personnel from the capsized boat.
3	Recover all personnel from the water and provide them PFDs as necessary.
4	Bring the capsized boat alongside the working area of the boat.
5	Use a shackle to secure your towline to the trailer eyebolt of the capsized boat.
6	Secure a piece of scrap or mooring line to the capsized boat's outboard transom eyebolt (see **Figure 18-19**). It may be necessary to put a tethered swimmer into the water to accomplish this. The line should be strong enough to handle the strain of righting the vessel.
7	Pay out both a towline and a scrap/mooring line and walk the capsized boat to a position astern of and athwartships to (from side to side) the boat.

Step	Procedure
8	Secure the scrap/mooring line to the boat's rear quarter cleat or bitt.
9	Pay out enough towline to permit the boat to remain clear of the stern when righting and towing commences. Secure the towline.
10	Gradually add power and increase speed. When the righting motion begins, cut or slip the scrap/mooring line. The boat should right itself. Tow the righted boat until water is being forced over the transom of the disabled boat.
11	When water ceases to flow over the towed boat's transom, reduce speed gradually, ensuring that enough water has been forced out of the boat during towing to allow it to float on its own.
12	Bring the righted boat alongside the righting boat and dewater it using the most appropriate method.

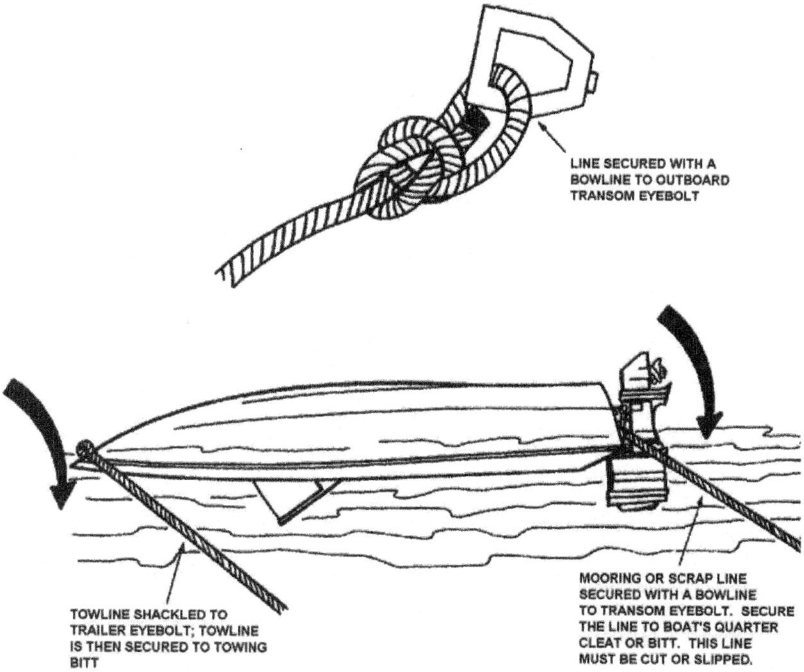

Figure 18-19
Righting Capsized Boats Using Bow and Transom Eyebolts

CH-1

I.1.c. Righting Using Towline Fore and Aft of Boat's Keel

Perform the following procedures for righting a boat using a towline fore and aft of the boat's keel:

Step	Procedure
1	Approach the capsized boat cautiously, from downwind, down current, or both, keeping clear of all lines and debris in the water.
2	Account for all personnel from the capsized boat.
3	Recover all personnel from the water and provide PFDs to them as necessary.
4	Direct a crewmember to act as tethered swimmer and enter the water to prepare the boat for righting.
5	Direct the swimmer to run the towline fore and aft alongside the capsized boat's keel.
6	The swimmer will then secure the towline to the capsized boat's trailer eyebolt with a shackle.
7	Ensure the disabled boat is positioned fore and aft, directly astern of the righting vessel (capsized boat's stern toward the other boat's stern), and that the towline is running fore and aft along the capsized vessel's keel. (see **Figure 18-20**) Recover the swimmer.
8	Pay out enough slack in the towline to permit the boat to clear the stern when righting commences. Secure the towline.
9	Gradually add power and increase speed, pulling on the bow of the capsized boat. This pull will be countered by the aft portion of the disabled boat, which is the heaviest part of the craft. As a result of these two forces, the boat will be righted.
10	Tow the righted boat until water is being forced over the transom of the disabled boat.
11	When water ceases to flow over the towed boat's transom, reduce speed gradually, ensuring that enough water has been forced out of the boat during the towing to allow it to float on its own.
12	Bring the righted boat alongside the righting boat and dewater it using the most appropriate method.

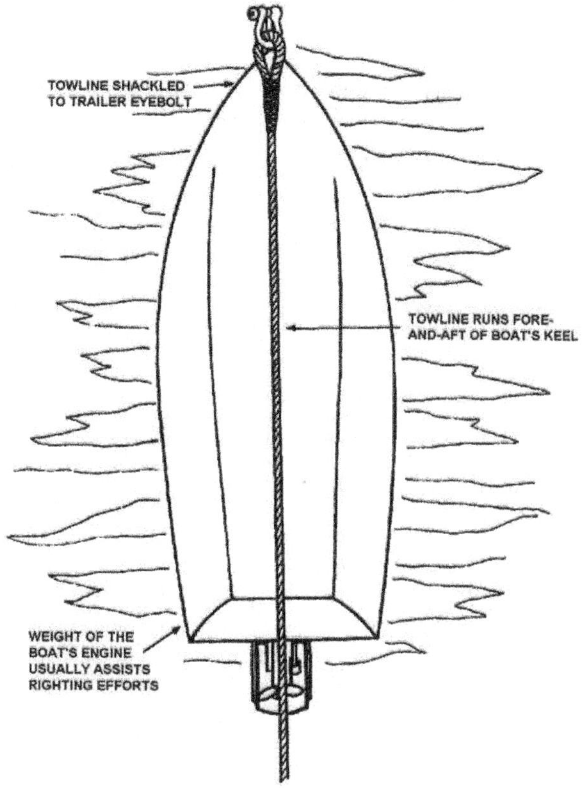

Figure 18-20
Righting Capsized Boats Using Towline Fore and Aft of Boat's Keel

I.1.d. Refloating Swamped Boats Astern Using Trailer Eyebolt

Perform the following procedures for righting a boat that has been swamped from astern: (see **Figure 18-21**)

Step	Procedure
1	Approach a swamped boat cautiously, from downwind, down current, or both, staying clear of all lines and debris in the water.
2	Account for all personnel from the swamped boat.
3	Recover all personnel from the water and provide them PFDs if necessary.
4	Bring the swamped boat alongside the working area of the boat.
5	Secure the towline to the trailer eyebolt of the swamped boat with a shackle.
6	Pay out the towline and walk the swamped boat directly astern of the boat.
7	Pay out enough towline to permit the swamped boat to remain clear of the stern when towing commences. Secure the towline.
8	Gradually add power to the boat and increase speed taking the swamped boat in tow. Tow the boat until water is observed being forced over the transom of the disabled boat.
9	When water ceases to flow over the towed boat's transom, reduce speed gradually, ensuring that enough water has been forced out of the boat during towing to allow it to float on its own.
10	Bring the righted boat alongside the righting boat and dewater it using the most appropriate method.

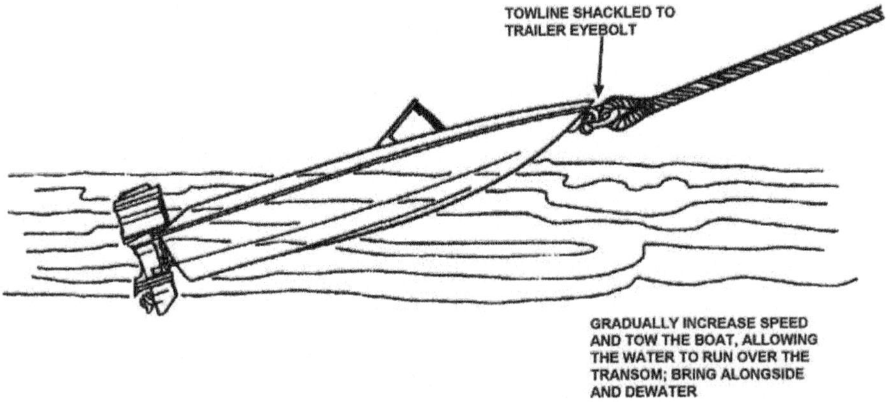
TOWLINE SHACKLED TO TRAILER EYEBOLT
GRADUALLY INCREASE SPEED AND TOW THE BOAT, ALLOWING THE WATER TO RUN OVER THE TRANSOM; BRING ALONGSIDE AND DEWATER

Figure 18-21
Refloating Boats Swamped Astern Using Trailer Eyebolt

I.2. Righting Small Sailboats

The coxswain should approach the capsized sailboat from upwind, up current, or both, remaining clear of lines and debris. All personnel from the sailboat should be accounted for and recovered as necessary. At least one person (tethered swimmer) will be needed in the water to help in righting the boat. Righting should not be attempted if the weather presents a hazard to the rescue boat or personnel.

NOTE

Quite often, sailboat crews are very familiar with righting their vessels should they capsize. If a member of the sailboat's crew wishes to remain in the water and attempt to right the vessel, recover the other people from the water and ensure the remaining crewmember is wearing a PFD before attempting to right the vessel.

Perform the following procedures for righting a small sailboat:

Step	Procedure
1	The person-in-the-water unships or removes the sails.
2	The sails, if removed, should be put aboard the rescue boat or secured to the disabled boat.
3	The person-in-the-water then stands on the keel or centerboard and leans back while holding onto the gunwale. The boat should slowly begin to come back over.
4	Once the sailboat is righted, recover the swimmer and begin dewatering.

NOTE

Sails still hoisted create severe drag and force against righting attempts. They may even cause the boat to capsize again once it is successfully righted.

I.3. Righting Large Sailboats

A procedure called parbuckling may be used to right capsized powerboats or sailboats over 25 feet in length. Also, parbuckling should be used for righting small sailboats that cannot be righted by the method previously described.

A person from the overturned boat or a tethered swimmer from the rescue boat must enter the water to prepare the boat for righting.

WARNING

Do not secure any lines to the masts of sailboats. The force exerted during the righting may cause the mast to fracture.

Perform the following procedures for righting a small sailboat:

Step	Procedure
1	Unship or remove the sails.
2	Have the person-in-the-water run a bridle or towline to the capsized boat.
3	Ensure that the lines rigged for righting, are outboard of all stays, shrouds, lifelines and stanchions.
4	Secure lines to available deck fittings using the same method as with powerboats. (see I.1.a)
5	Connect the other end of the bridle to the towline. Pay out enough line to prevent the distressed boat's mast (if so equipped) from striking the rescue boat should the distressed boat continue to roll in that direction.
6	Recover the person-in-the-water
7	Commence righting by going ahead slowly on the engines.
8	Once a sailboat is righted, crewmembers should board it from the stern (because of the boat's instability) and secure all loose lines.
9	Secure the boom to stop it from swinging and possibly capsizing the boat again.
10	Begin dewatering.

Section J. Flood Control

Introduction

Boats sometimes become damaged in groundings, in collisions, or from striking submerged objects. These mishaps may result in a holed, cracked, or weakened hull. If the hull has been damaged to the extent that water is entering the interior of the boat, it must be plugged or patched to keep the boat afloat.

NOTE

The primary purpose of Coast Guard SAR is to save lives at sea. Conducting damage (flooding) control operations to save property alone should only be done after a complete risk assessment of the situation has been done to ensure the crew will not be subjected to undue risk. If available, salvage services should be considered before conducting this type of operation.

In this section

This section contains the following information:

Plugging Holes

J.1. Plugs

The simplest method of stopping a small hole in wooden or metal hulls is to insert a plug or plugs. Plugs are usually made of a soft wood such as pine or fir. Plugs are used individually if they fit the hole, or in combination with other materials to make a better fit.

J.2. Preparing Plug

Wrapping cloth around each plug before inserting them in the hole will help to keep the plug in place. It also fills the gaps between plugs.

J.3. Inserting Plugs

When plugging holes, it is usually easiest to insert the plugs from the inside. However, sometimes the rough edges protruding inward may make this method impossible. If it is necessary to insert the plugs from the outside, and safe to do so, the inboard end(s) of the plug(s) should be fitted with screw eyes. A line should be attached to each screw eye and fastened to a structure inside the boat. It will hold the plug in place. (see **Figure 18-22**)

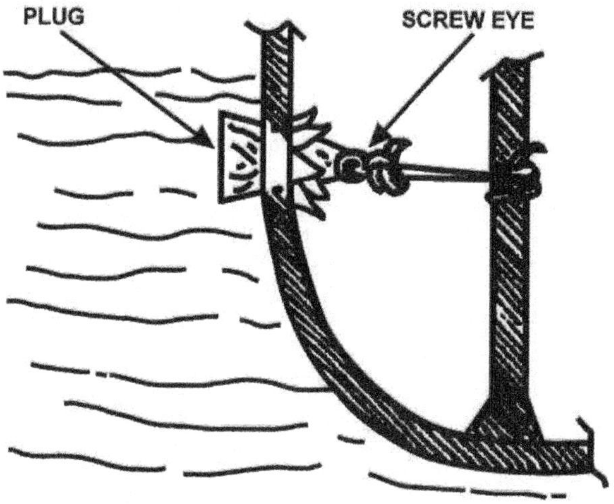

Figure 18-22
Screw Eye

J.4. Large Holes

Large holes are generally too difficult to plug. A patch can be used to reduce the flow of water through a large hole, if an attempt is made.

J.5. Fiberglass Hulls

Fiberglass may the most difficult hull material to plug. Wooden conical plugs driven into the hole may do nothing more than cause further splitting and cracking and add to an already difficult situation. The best method of plugging a hole in fiberglass is to shove some pliable type of material into it such as a rag, shirt, or piece of canvas. A PFD or a blanket may also work well.

Patching Holes

J.6. Holes Below the Waterline

Patching holes below the waterline is usually a difficult task because of the pressure exerted by the water and the inaccessibility to the holed area. Small holes should be patched from the inside. Some type of material should be placed over the hole and hold it in place with another object. For example, if the boat were holed in the bottom, a PFD or seat cushion could be placed over the hole and held in place with a gas can, cooler, or toolbox.

J.7. Large Holes Below the Waterline

Large holes below the waterline are extremely difficult to patch. The pressure of the water flowing through the hole will not usually allow a patch to be installed from the inside.

J.7.a. Collision Mat

If a collision mat (a large piece of canvas or vinyl) is available, it can be used to patch a large hole. Perform the following the procedures while placing the mat over the hole: (see **Figure 18-23**)

Step	Procedure
1	Tie four lines to the corners of the mat (patch).
2	Position the mat by lowering it over the bow.
3	Have someone walk down each side of the boat, two of the lines for each person.
4	Slide the mat along the bottom of the boat.
5	Once the mat covers the hole, secure the four lines topside. The pressure of the water against the patch will also help to hold it in place.

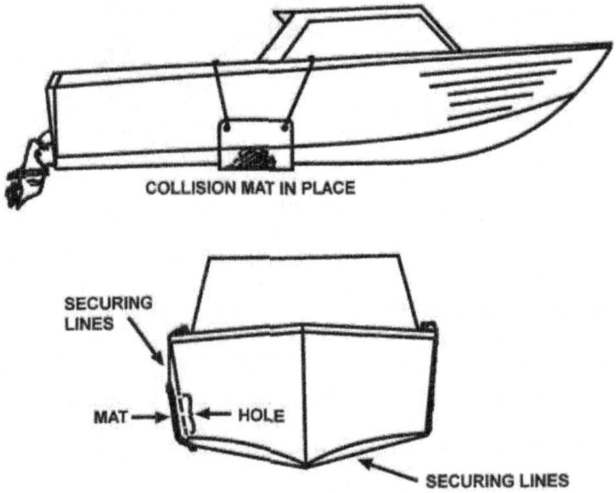

Figure 18-23
Collision Mat

J.7.b. Box Patch

Box patches are effective, even on holes that have jagged edges protruding inward. The box patch is usually a prefabricated box, which is held in place with screws, nails, or it may be wedged in place with anything available. A gasket (anything available) is placed between the box and the hull to make a good seal and to prevent the box from shifting. (see **Figure 18-24**)

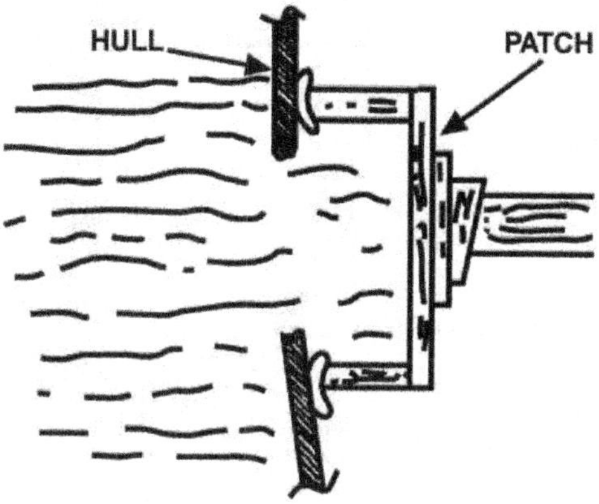

Figure 18-24
Box Patch

J.8. Holes Above the Waterline

Holes above the waterline may be more dangerous than they appear. As the boat rolls, they admit water into the boat above the center of gravity. This water reduces the stability of the boat. Plugs or patches on the inside or outside the hull should be used to cover these types of holes. The following procedures are an effective method for patching holes above the waterline:

Step	Procedure
1	Use a pillow or cushion that has a small hole punched in the center.
2	Place the cushion over the holed area from the outside and back it with a board of the same approximate size. The board should also have a small hole through the center.
3	Pass a line through the board and cushion and knot the end of the line outside the board.
4	Secure the entire patch by attaching the other end of the line to something firm inside the boat. (see **Figure 18-25**)

Figure 18-25
Patching Hole Above Waterline

Patching Cracks

J.9. Cracks in Hulls

To patch a crack in the hull, use the following procedures:

Step	Procedure
1	Stuff the crack with something pliable such as a rag or line.
2	Place a piece of canvas or rubber over the crack to serve as a gasket.
3	Back the patch with a solid object such as a piece of plywood, panel door, or similar material.
4	Use nails, screws, or wedges to hold the patch in place.
5	To prevent the crack from traveling, especially in fiberglass, drill holes at each end of the crack. These holes will relieve the pressure at the ends of the crack, permitting the hull to flex without extending the crack.

Chapter 19
Air Operations

Introduction

Coordinated operation between boats and aircraft creates a valuable team for Coast Guard missions. While an aircraft can generally search an area faster or may arrive on-scene sooner, a vessel can investigate more thoroughly and usually provide more direct assistance. Whether a pollution incident or a SAR case, boats and aircraft may be called upon to work as a team.

Boat operations with aircraft usually involve transfer of a person or equipment between a helicopter (rotary-wing) and a boat. Sometimes, a boat must coordinate with a fixed-wing aircraft. The *U.S. Coast Guard Addendum to the United States National Search and Rescue Supplement (NSS) to the International Aeronautical and Maritime Search and Rescue Manual*, COMDTINST M16130.2 (series) has a list of capabilities and deliverable SAR equipment for each type of Coast Guard aircraft. Auxiliary facilities include fixed-wing general aviation aircraft. Boat crews need to be aware that easily recognized Coast Guard aircraft and some privately owned small aircraft or Auxiliary air facility might try to contact and operate with them.

In this chapter

This chapter contains the following sections:

WARNING

The wearing of jewelry, including rings, wristwatches, necklaces or other items not consisting of organizational clothing, PPE, or uniform articles by boat crew members engaged in hoisting, towing, or other deck evolutions where the potential for snagging exists **is prohibited**. OICs and coxswains will address this during all pre-underway briefs and coxswains shall ensure jewelry is removed prior to beginning all deck evolutions.

Section A. Helicopters and Equipment

Introduction

Excellent multi-mission capabilities are available in the Short-Range Recovery (SRR) helicopter HH-65A and the Medium-Range Recovery (MRR) helicopter HH-60J. Helicopter maneuverability and outstanding crew visible scanning capabilities enable the crew to closely inspect sightings and search shorelines. They are flexible rescue platforms, capable of recovering people from a wide variety of distress situations on land or water. Both helicopters can:

- Hover.
- Deploy rescue swimmers/EMTs or civilian divers.
- Perform hoists using a rescue basket, stokes litter, or rescue strop.
- Deliver equipment (e.g., dewatering pump and fire suppression kits) when available.
- Deploy datum marker buoys.
- Search with radar.
- Provide night illumination.
- Direction find.
- Perform multi-mission patrols.
- Conduct supply/replenishment operations.

NOTE Both aircraft have night vision goggles, and the HH-60J has forward-looking infrared capabilities.

A.1. HH-65A Dolphin

The HH-65A "Dolphin" has two turbine engines that will produce a maximum airspeed of 165 knots. (see **Figure 19-1** and **Figure 19-2**) The HH-65A cannot hover, hoist, or maneuver on just one engine. The normal crew is one or two pilots and a flight mechanic. For rescue missions, a rescue swimmer is normally carried in addition to the three crewmembers. The pilot in command sits in the right seat of the cockpit. Other general information includes:

- Maximum endurance with a crew of two pilots and one crewmember is approximately three hours.
- Maximum of four passengers or survivors (besides the three crew) can be carried.
- Hoist capacity is 600 pounds and the external cargo sling limit is 2,000 pounds.
- It will not land on the water except in an emergency. It will float if it is not badly damaged and the flotation bags are deployed.

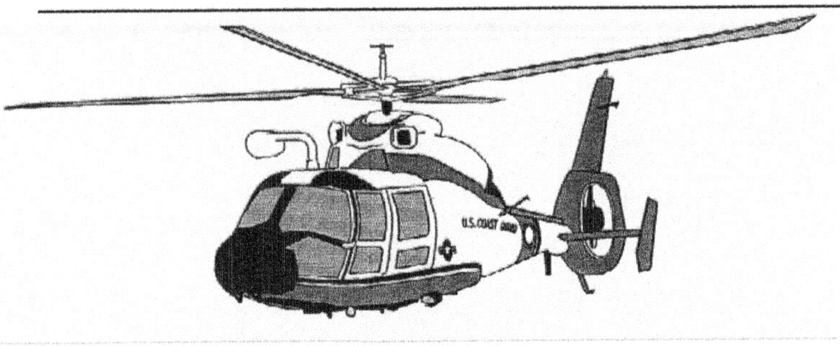

Figure 19-1
HH-65A (Dolphin) Helicopter Left Front View

Figure 19-2 depicts the front, top, and side views of the HH-65A. The fan-in-tail (Fenestron) rotor configuration is evident and is the easy way to visually identify the HH-65A. This Fenestron also gives it a distinct, high-pitched sound.

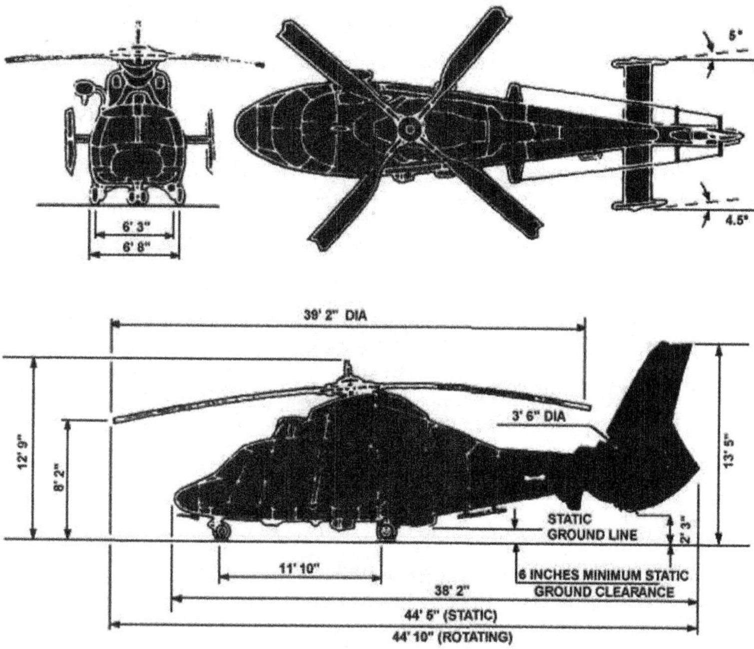

Figure 19-2
Front, Top, and Side Views of the HH-65A Helicopter

A.2. HH-60J Jayhawk

The HH-60J "Jayhawk" has 2 turbine engines that, depending upon the gross weight of the helicopter, will produce a maximum airspeed of 180 knots. (see **Figure 19-3** and **Figure 19-4**) Although equipped with two engines, the HH-60J can normally maintain flight with one engine (the loss of one engine is considered an emergency situation). The normal crew is two pilots and two crewmembers. For rescue missions, a rescue swimmer is normally carried in addition to four crewmembers. Other general information includes:

- Maximum endurance of the aircraft with maximum fuel and crew is approximately six hours.
- Hoist capacity is 600 pounds and the external cargo sling limit is 6,000 pounds.
- It will not land on the water except in an emergency. Even with flotation bags, it will stay afloat only long enough for the crew to exit. The HH-60J is not amphibious.

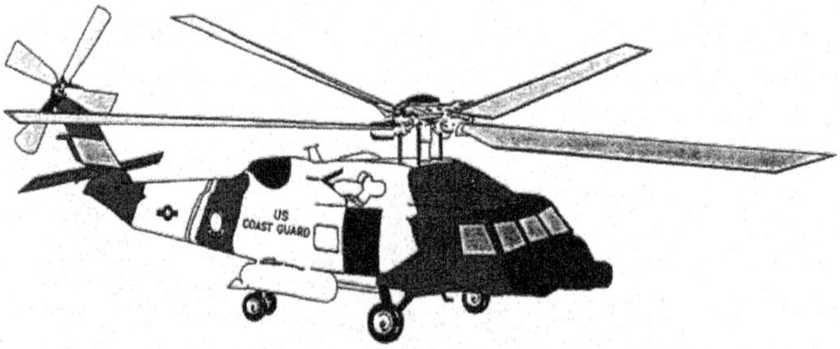

Figure 19-3
HH-60J (Jayhawk) Helicopter

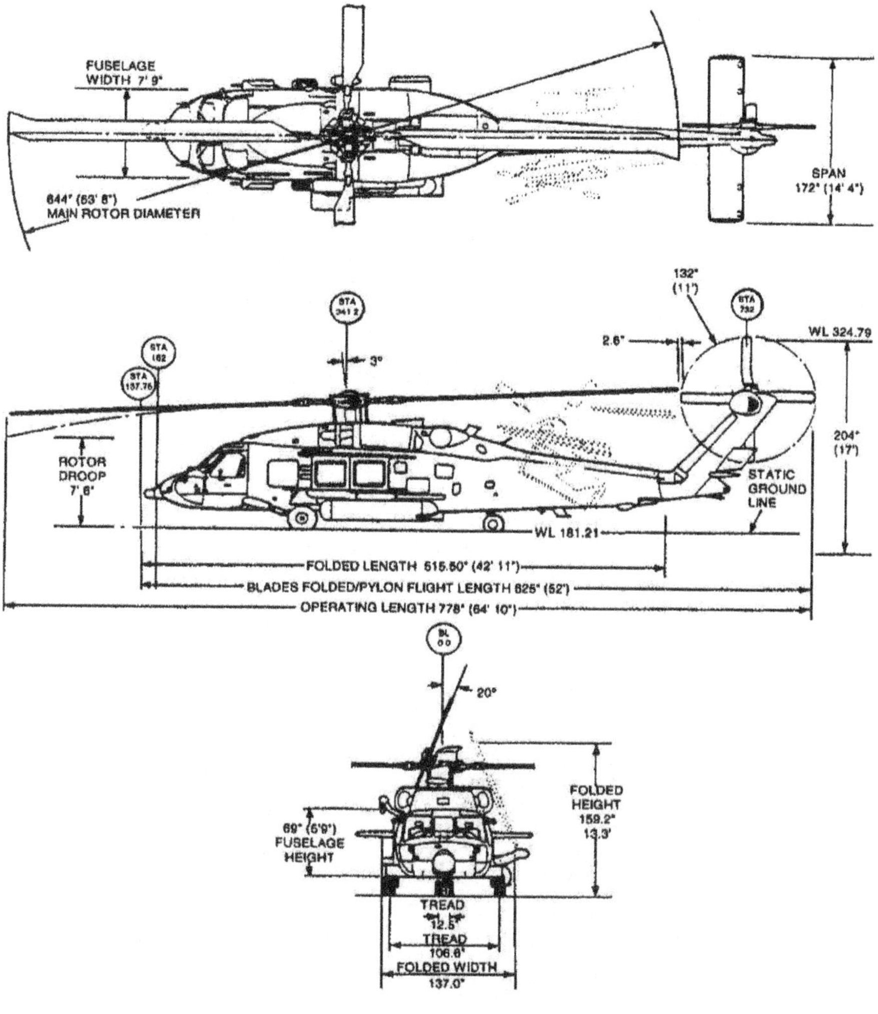

Figure 19-4
Top, Side, and Front Views of the HH-60J Helicopter

A.3. Helicopter Equipment	Hoists by Coast Guard helicopters will normally be done with the following rescue devices and equipment.
A.3.a. Rescue Basket	The multi-jointed (M/J) rescue basket is the primary device for hoisting survivors from land or sea during helicopter rescue operations. It provides protection for the individual being hoisted from dangers, such as striking vessel rigging. It has the capability to float. Hinged at all four corners, it folds inward. (see **Figure 19-5**) The basket is employed for personnel transfer in any weather condition.

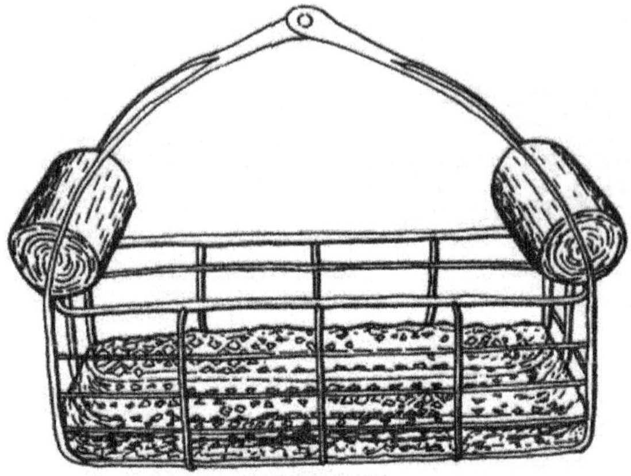

Figure 19-5
M/J Rescue Basket

A.3.b. Stokes Litter

The stokes litter (see **Figure 19-6**) is a stretcher with a flotation collar and chest pad for buoyancy. A 5-pound ballast weight located at the foot end provides stability. A permanently mounted hoisting sling attaches the litter to the helicopter hoist cable. For restraining patients, a minimum of four securing straps, including chest pad, are supplied. Additional information is in the *Rescue and Survival Systems Manual*, COMDTINST M10470.10 (series).

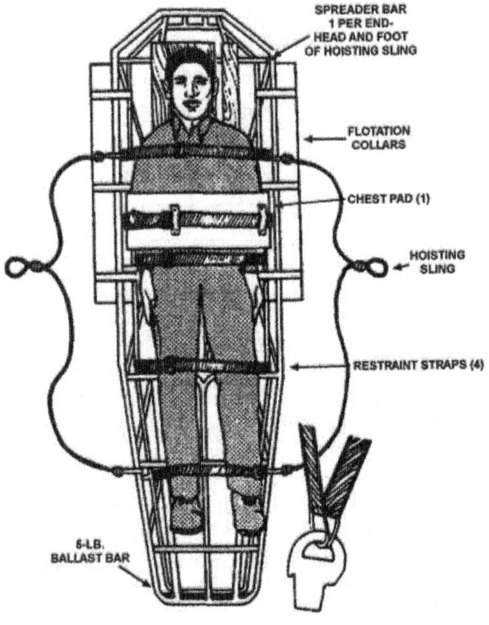

Figure 19-6
Stokes Litter

The stokes litter is used to transfer an injured or unconscious person in any weather condition. It is generally used when the patient's condition prevents use of the basket. When the patient is placed in a litter, a crewmember must tighten all straps to keep the person securely bound to it. There are four straps, as shown in **Figure 19-6**.

A.3.c. Rescue Strop

The rescue strop (see **Figure 19-7**) is used only to rescue persons familiar with its proper use, for example, a military aviator. It can handle one survivor wearing the usual flight gear and PFD.

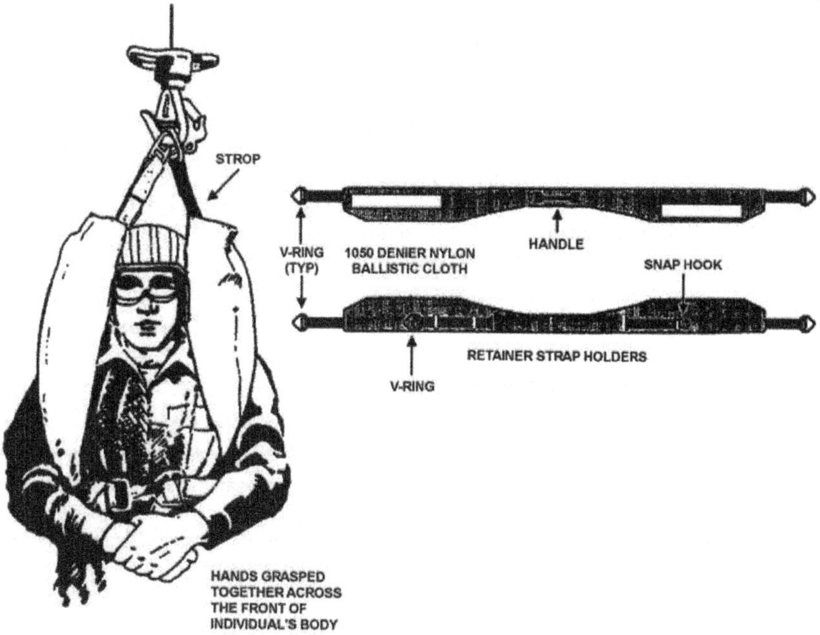

Figure 19-7
Rescue Strop

NOTE

Use of chest retainer strap is mandatory during use of the rescue strop, except when hoisting rescue swimmers.

A.4. Trail Line

Use of a trail line minimizes the time a pilot must maintain a precise stable hover without a reference point. The trail line consists of 105 feet of orange polypropylene line with a weak link and snap link at one end, and a snap hook at the other. The weak link (see **Figure 19-8**) is a safety device between the trail line and hoist hook, which protects the helicopter by not allowing more than 300 pounds of force to be applied to the hoist. If more force is applied, the weak link will part. A 5-pound (or heavier) bag is attached to the trail line snap hook for ease in delivery of the trail line. When used, the trail line will:

- Stabilize a rescue device to prevent sailing, swinging, and possibly becoming fouled.
- Reduce the time a pilot must maintain a precise hover.
- Reduce time on-scene.

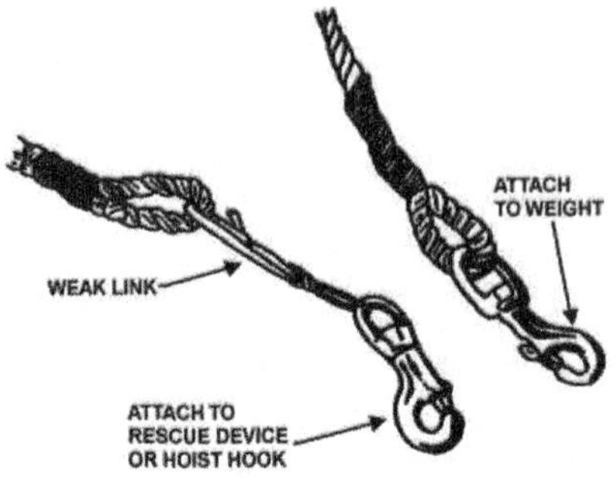

Figure 19-8
Trail Line's Weak Link

A.5. Dewatering Pump Kits

Dewatering pumps provide emergency dewatering for boats in danger of sinking. Under a load, the pump will run 1.5 to 2.5 hours on one gallon of gasoline. The pumps are designed to fit into a standard rectangular plastic container that is droppable.

WARNING

Coast Guard dewatering pumps will not be used to pump flammable liquids.

Section B. Helicopter Rescue Operations

Introduction

This section discusses the procedures and necessary safety precautions involved in a helicopter rescue operation.

In this section

This section contains the following information:

Rescue Swimmer

B.1. Description

The rescue swimmer (RS) is a properly trained and conditioned certified EMT. The RS is trained to deploy from a helicopter to recover an incapacitated victim from the maritime environment, day or night. Since a helicopter has weight and space limitations, a boat may be requested to recover an RS. The RS is equipped with a strobe light and signal flares.

Helicopter Hoisting Operations

WARNING

Safety is always a primary consideration. Anytime the boat coxswain or helicopter pilot feels the operation is unsafe, it should be broken off and, if practical, begun again.

B.2. Description

Helicopter hoisting operations off of a vessel can pose great hazard to the aircrew, boat crew, and to whatever is being hoisted. The safety and efficiency of helicopter hoist operations is greatly improved if the crew of the vessel is briefed in advance on what is required. *Section F* of this chapter has the internationally approved "Sample Briefing to Pass to Vessel Prior to Helicopter Hoisting". This briefing is particularly useful when conducting a boat-helicopter hoist or if asked to brief the distressed vessel as the helicopter is en route. The *U.S. Coast Guard Addendum to the United States National Search and Rescue Supplement (NSS) to the International Aeronautical and Maritime Search and Rescue Manual*, COMDTINST M16130.2 (series) has a similar version.

Boat-helicopter operations require a team effort, alertness, and cooperation among crewmembers aboard both the boat and helicopter. Since the noise level may hinder communications, the coxswain and pilot usually plan the operation before the helicopter is overhead. Once the helicopter is in position, the air crewmember serving as hoist operator gives the pilot maneuvering instructions for guiding the rescue device to the boat deck below. The safety briefing discussed earlier in this section and provided in *Section F* of this chapter provides general guidelines. Specific guidelines for the boat crew are discussed below.

NOTE

The Coast Guard uses the term "hoist" while the international community uses the term "winch". The international version in *Section F* has the term "winch" replaced by "hoist".

B.3. Boat Crew Preparations for Hoisting

Before the helicopter arrives, the coxswain will complete action on the following general categories of preparation:

- Navigation.
- Communications.
- Protective gear.
- Loose gear.
- Rigging.
- Hand signals.
- Briefing crew.

If radio communications are lost and an emergency breakaway is required, the boat's blue emergency light or other emergency signal should be used to signal the breakaway to the helicopter.

B.3.a. Navigation

Charts are checked for hazards that would prevent the boat from maintaining course and speed until the hoist is complete.

B.3.b. Communications

Communications are established with the helicopter as early as possible to exchange information and instructions. This includes:

- Use of primary and secondary working frequencies.
- On-scene weather.
- Exact position.
- Condition of persons, if any, requiring medical attention.
- Any information to aid the pilot in selecting the rescue device.
- Total number of crew and other persons onboard the boat, and total number onboard the helicopter.
- Conduct hoist briefing with the helicopter pilot.

B.3.c. Protective Gear	All protective gear is properly worn, including: • Head (helmet), eye (goggles) and hearing protection shall be worn. • Protection for hands (gloves) is optional. If worn they should be as form fitting to the hand as possible to reduce the possibility of becoming fouled with any of the hoisting equipment. • PFDs, anti-exposure coveralls, and dry suits (depending on weather conditions).
B.3.d. Loose Gear	All loose gear is stowed or secured on deck (e.g., hats, cushions, loose paper, etc.).
B.3.e. Rigging	All antennas, booms, rigging, and flag staff are lowered and secured, if possible.
B.3.f. Hand Signals	One boat crewmember is designated to give hand signals to the hoist operator.
B.3.g. Briefing Crew	The crew and person(s) to be hoisted are briefed regarding the type of hoist to be expected (e.g., basket, litter, or strop).

WARNING A helicopter in flight builds up static electricity that can be transferred to the boat crew through the hoisting cable, rescue device, and trail line. Crews shall ensure that any device lowered from a helicopter is allowed to come in contact (ground) to the boat, water, or a "Deadman's Stick" (static discharge wand), before touching it.

WARNING The downwash of a helicopter is very powerful. It can blow a person overboard. It can also blow loose gear over the side. Loose objects such as articles of clothing can be caught in the air currents produced by the rotor blades and sucked into the engines.

WARNING Never attach, tie, or secure anything to the boat that is also attached to the helicopter.

B.4. Boat Crew Safety Precautions

During the hoisting evolution, safety is paramount. All boat crewmembers will observe the following safety precautions:

- A helicopter in flight builds up static electricity that can be transferred to the boat crew through the hoisting cable, rescue device, and trail line. Crews shall ensure that any device lowered from a helicopter is allowed to come in contact (ground) to the boat, water, or a "Deadman's Stick" (static discharge wand), before touching it.
- Always tend by hand any trail lines, basket slings, or hoisting cable. Do not attach them to the boat
- Always wait for slack in the hoist cable before attempting to hook onto the device to be hoisted. This precaution allows for relative motion between helicopter and boat.
- Always keep the trail line and hoisting cable clear of the boat's rigging.
- Always unhook the rescue device before moving it inside the boat.
- Never stand between the rescue device on deck and the aircraft. If for some reason the hoisting cable went taught the rescue device could be pulled overboard very quickly.
- Always face the aircraft when the rescue device is in the vicinity of the boat.

CH-1

Helicopter-Boat Positioning

B.5. Description

When working with a helicopter at night, crewmembers must never shine a light towards or take flash pictures of the helicopter. The sudden light may temporarily blind or disorient the pilot.

Pyrotechnics or illuminating signals must never be used without contacting the pilot.

B.6. Course and Speed

Hoists from standard boats are normally made from the stern. The pilot normally will direct the coxswain to assume a certain course and speed with a relative wind speed of 15 to 30 knots and 35°-45° off the port bow. (see **Figure 19-9**) Sometimes, sea conditions may require departure from this rule, especially to minimize boat rolling. The boat must maintain a steady course and speed.

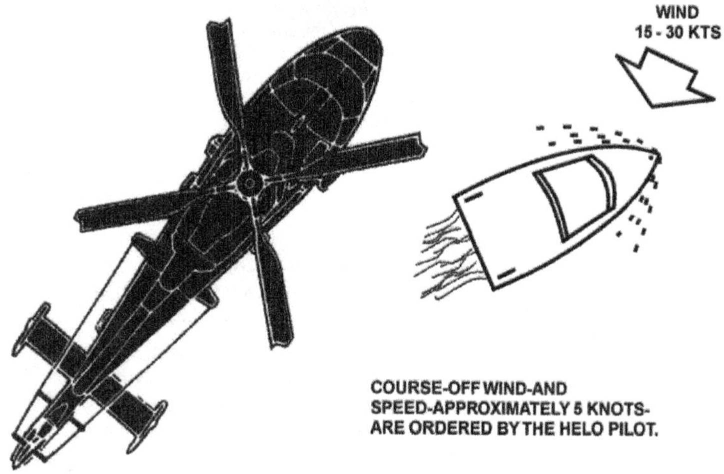
WIND
15 - 30 KTS
COURSE-OFF WIND-AND
SPEED-APPROXIMATELY 5 KNOTS-
ARE ORDERED BY THE HELO PILOT.

Figure 19-9
Helicopter-Boat Positioning

B.7. Nonstandard Boats

Hoists from nonstandard boats (e.g., UTLs, UTMs, or Auxiliary craft) may require a different technique. The helicopter will maintain a steady course and speed while lowering the rescue device to a point below the aircraft near the surface. The boat should approach and maneuver under the hoist for delivery.

B.8. Helicopter-Boat Configuration

The rescue device will be lowered from the right side of the aircraft. The helicopter will approach the boat from astern (downwind) and hover off the port side, aft of amidships. This method of approach allows the pilot and hoist operator (located on the right side of the aircraft) a full view of the boat during the evolution. (see **Figure 19-10**)

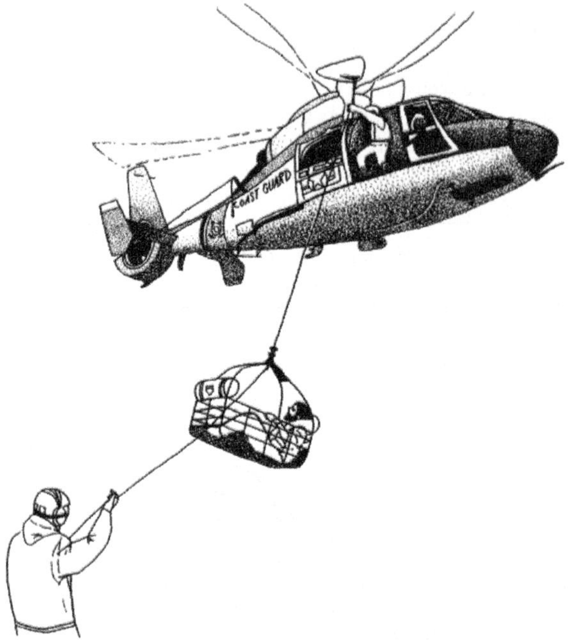

Figure 19-10
Trail Line Delivery of the M/J Rescue Basket

B.9. Dead-in-the-Water

When a boat is dead-in-the-water (DIW), the helicopter may approach the boat's bow on the starboard side. Due to the downwash, the boat will almost always turn clockwise and the aircraft will maintain visual contact by turning in the same direction during the hoist. On smaller platforms, the helicopter will have some control over the vessel by using its rotor wash.

Coast Guard helicopters use different approaches for different styles of vessel if they are DIW. The approach will also vary depending on where the working deck will be. Most Coast Guards boats will work off the stern while some fishing vessels might work off the bow since their stern area contains equipment that could foul the hoist cable. Boat crews must always communicate with the helicopter before a hoisting evolution to ensure both parties know the plan.

Delivery of the Rescue Device

WARNING Never attach the hook to any part of the boat.

B.10. Description

Delivery of a rescue device from the helicopter to a vessel in distress or for training will be accomplished by one of the following three methods:

- Direct delivery.
- Trail-line delivery.
- Indirect delivery.

After the rescue device is delivered (and if previously agreed to in the aircraft brief), a boat crewmember will disconnect the hook before moving away from the delivery/hoisting location. The cable may be re-attached to the device at a time agreed upon with the helicopter pilot.

B.11. Direct Delivery

During direct delivery, the rescue device is lowered directly to the deck of the vessel. The boat crewmember tending the lowered piece of equipment should allow the flight mechanic to keep the hoist cable as plumb as possible to avoid swinging of the rescue device.

B.12. Trail-Line Delivery

During trail-line delivery, a 5-pound or heavier weight bag is attached to the trail line and lowered from the helicopter to the vessel. The helicopter will then back off to a safe hoisting distance while paying out the trail line. The non-weighted end of the trail line is attached to the rescue device (weak link first) (see **Figure 19-10**) and lowered to the vessel (see **Figure 19-11**). Boat crewmembers will tend the trail line by hand-over-hand method, exerting enough strain to guide the rescue device to the delivery point on deck. A second crewmember will assist the crewmember hauling in the trail line by coiling the trail line in a safe place on deck ensuring the line does not get fouled around an object or get blown overboard.

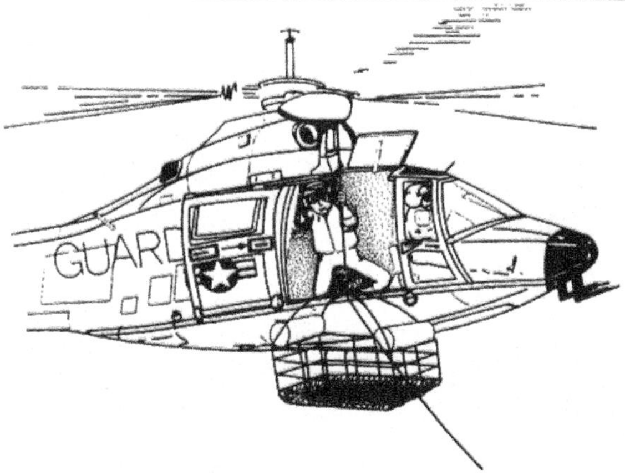

Figure 19-11
M/J Rescue Basket Going Down

B.13. Indirect Delivery

Indirect delivery is designed for delivery of a portable dewatering pump. The trail line, weighted bag attached to the weak link first, is delivered from the helicopter to the vessel. The helicopter will pay out the trail line as the helicopter backs off and establishes a low hover with the rotor blades and downwash clear of all rigging. (see **Figure 19-12**) The hoist operator will then attach the end of the trail line to the pump container and deploy it to the water. (see **Figure 19-13**) The boat crewmember will then pull the pump aboard.

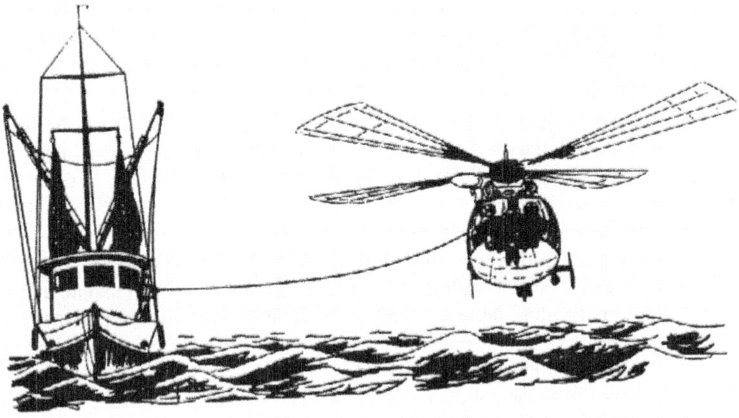

Figure 19-12
Indirect Delivery of Pump

Figure 19-13
Pump in the Water

Hoisting

B.14. Description

Hoisting is the transfer of a person(s) or equipment between a boat and helicopter. Helicopter hoisting operations off a boat can pose a great hazard to the aircrew, boat crew, and the person or equipment being hoisted. A safety brief will be conducted prior to any hoisting operation to discuss the duties and responsibilities of every boat crew member. Close coordination between the boat coxswain and the helicopter pilot are essential for a successful hoisting evolution. Rigging and use of the proper piece of equipment (M/J rescue basket, stokes litter, rescue strop, drop pump, etc.), visual communication (hand signals) between the helicopter rescue hoist operator and boat crew member, and verbal communication between the rescue hoist operator and helicopter pilot will safely guide the equipment to the boat deck during delivery and ensure its safe return to the helicopter as it is retrieved.

CAUTION ! Helicopter rescue baskets are collapsible. When connecting and disconnecting the hoist cable, support both ends of the basket to avoid injury to the person in the basket.

CAUTION ! Do not throw the end.

B.15. Basket Hoist

Every person transferred must wear a PFD and head protection, if available. The person must be positioned in the basket with hands placed palms up under the thighs. This position will keep the arms tucked in close to the body and inside the basket. The crewmember assisting the person into position must ensure that no part of the person's body is outside of the basket and that the basket does not hang up on equipment attached to the boat. When the individual to be hoisted is in the proper position, the boat crewmember will give the "thumbs up" to the hoist operator, who will commence the hoist. (see **Figure 19-14**) If a trail line is used, it should be tended hand-over-hand over the side. When the end is reached, the weighted bag is gently released.

Figure 19-14
M/J Rescue Basket with Person Properly Positioned and Ready for Hoist

B.16. Stokes Litter Hoist

In most cases, the helicopter will provide the litter. When a boat has a hoistable litter (as outlined in the *Rescue and Survival Systems Manual*, COMDTINST M10470.10 (series)), the aircraft commander will determine if it will be used. When the victim is placed in the litter, a boat crewmember must tighten all restraining straps around the person. There are four straps and one chest pad. The crewmember tending the litter must make certain it does not get hung up on boat equipment. When the person is to be hoisted, the boat crewmember will give a "thumbs up" to the hoist operator, who will commence the hoist. If a trail line was used, the crewmember tending the line will keep a steady strain in an attempt to prevent the stokes litter from spinning as it rises to the helicopter.

B.17. Rescue Strop Hoist

The strop will only be used to transfer trained, uninjured military personnel in fair weather. The strop is basically a collar which has one end attached to the hoist cable. When the person to be hoisted positions the collar under the armpits, a boat crewmember must ensure the safety straps are fastened. The end of the collar opposite the hoist cable has a v-ring that attaches to the hook. **Figure 19-7** shows how the strop looks when properly connected. This device is not likely to hang up on attached equipment as easily as the other rescue devices.

B.18. Hoisting of Equipment

All attachment points and the equipment must be secured and monitored to keep it from hanging up.

B.19. Commencing Hoist

When a person or equipment is secured in the rescue device, the designated boat crewmember will give the hoist operator a "thumbs up" hand signal. The hoist operator will then commence lifting the rescue device. During this procedure, the boat crew must ensure the rescue device is not caught on anything attached to the boat.

B.20. Casting Off

When a trail line is employed, a boat crewmember shall tend it until he or she reaches the weighted end. Then the crewmember should gently release the weighted bag over the side of the boat on which the hoist was conducted (normally the port side). The bag should never be thrown upwards towards the rotors.

B.21. Posting Hoist

Once the trail line is cast off, the coxswain will maneuver to starboard and away from the helicopter.

B.22. Emergency Breakaway Procedure

Safety during helicopter operations cannot be overemphasized. Crewmembers must stay alert and report any danger signs. If either the coxswain or pilot feels the operation is unsafe, then a breakaway should be conducted. Procedures for the coxswain to conduct a breakaway are as follows:

Step	Procedure
1	Direct the crew to push the loose cable, rescue device, and trail line over the side (toward the helicopter).
2	Transmit the word "BREAKAWAY" to the pilot.
3	Turn away from the helicopter (most often to the right).
4	Energize the blue emergency light or identification light, if practical or applicable.

B.23. Boat Casualties During Hoisting (Committed)

Boat casualties can and will occur during hoisting operations from a boat. Coxswains must anticipate their immediate actions in response to a casualty during hoist operations in order to prevent fouled or sheared cables, men going overboard, or other injuries.

B.23.a. Engine Casualty

If a boat's engine loses power while the rescue device is on deck, coxswains must maintain course and speed in order to prevent pulling the device off the boat or fouling the cable in the boat's fixed rigging. Generally, the coxswain will have to add power on the good engine and turn toward the good engine in order to maintain course and speed. The helicopter should be notified as soon as possible.

B.23.b. Steering Casualty

A steering casualty should cause the coxswain to signal an emergency breakaway. Every attempt should be made to maintain course and speed by using the engines to steer.

B.23.c. Radio Casualty

A radio casualty may not require an emergency breakaway, but may require the use of an agreed upon hand signal, so that the hoist is aborted safely. If available, the boat should always have backup communication source (second radio, hand-held radio, etc.).

Section C. Helicopter Ditching

Introduction

There is always the possibility a helicopter may have to ditch in the water. Coast Guard air crews receive extensive training in escape procedures for such emergencies. However, they may be disoriented due to personal injuries, aircraft attitude, aircraft damage, and/or environmental factors. For this reason, boat crewmembers must be familiar with emergency exits and entrances. It may be necessary to open emergency exits to pull trapped air crewmembers to safety. The HH-60J has five emergency openings and the HH-65A has four. (see **Figure 19-15** and **Figure 19-16**).

NOTE

Boat Station personnel are encouraged to visit nearby Air Stations or have partner Air Station aircraft visit the Station (if feasible) to receive an emergency exit briefing from qualified air crewmembers.

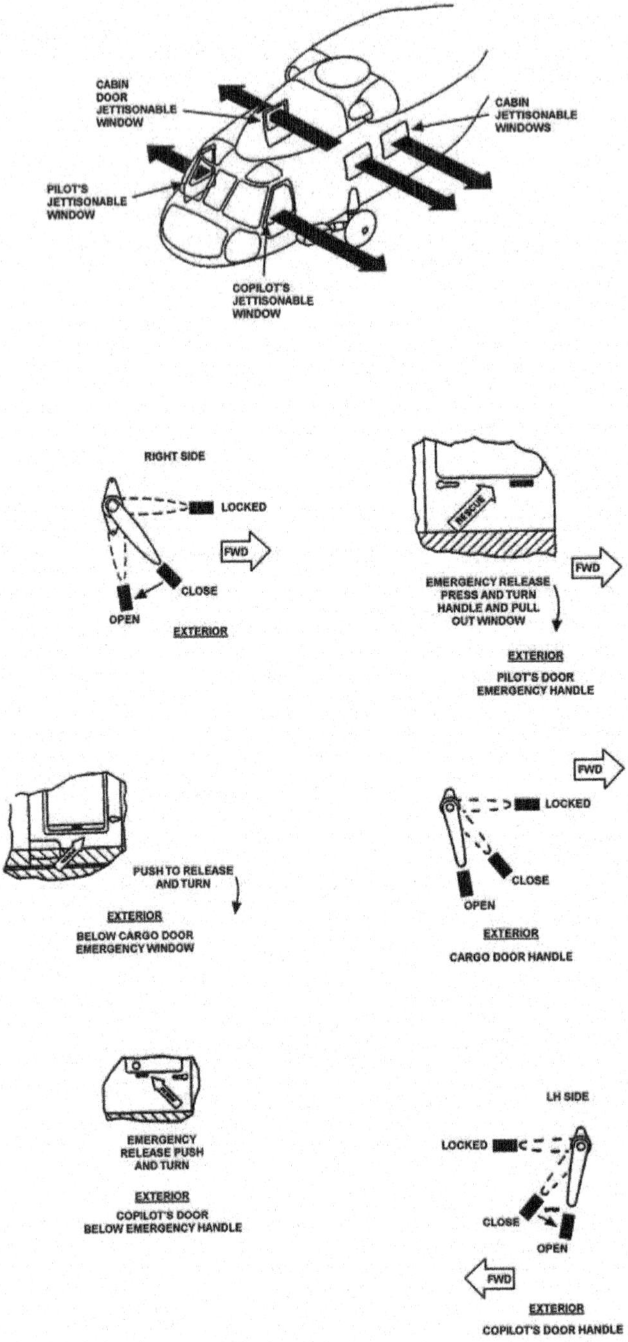

Figure 19-15
HH-60J Emergency Entrances

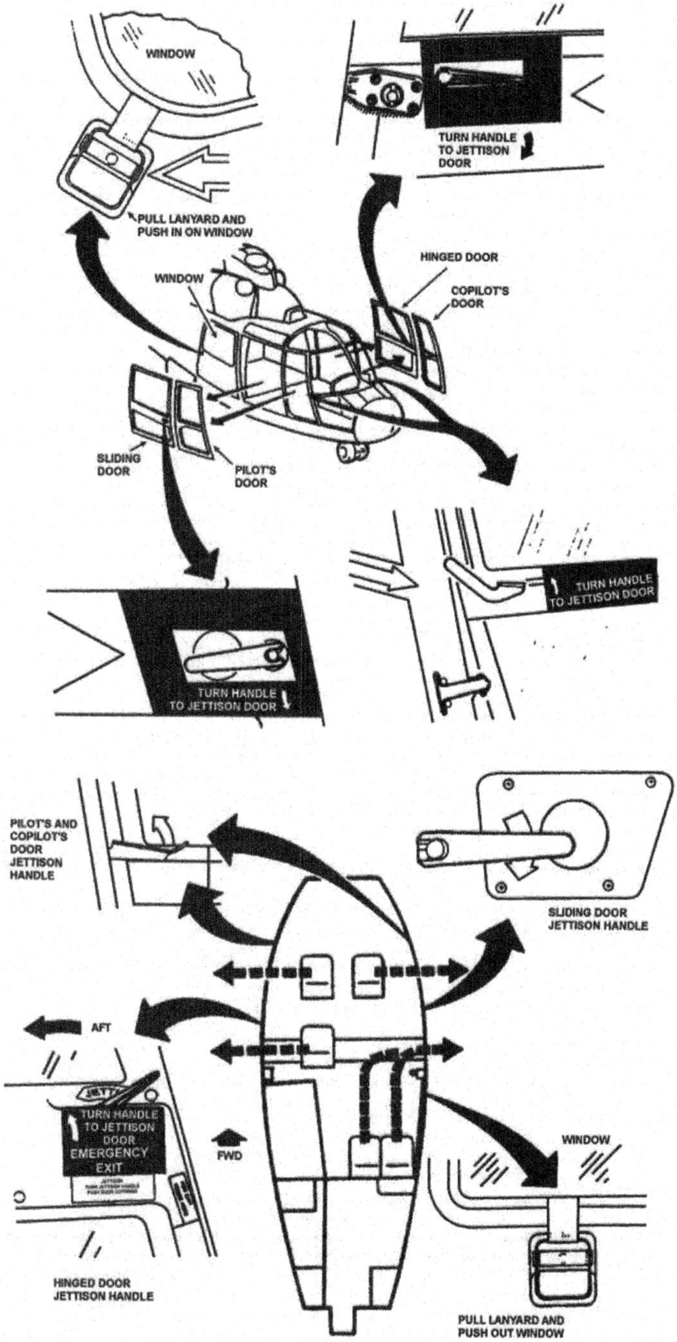

Figure 19-16
HH-65A Emergency Entrances

CAUTION !

Boat crewmembers will not enter an inverted aircraft! Only a qualified diver may enter a helicopter after it has inverted (turned upside-down).

C.1. Assisting a Downed Helicopter

If a helicopter goes down near the boat during a hoist operation or the crew is called to assist a downed helicopter, perform the following procedures:

Step	Procedure
1	Ensure the Operational Commander is advised of the ditching.
2	Approach bow-on from the leeward side of the helicopter.
3	Make minimal wake so the vertical stability is not disrupted (when the helicopter is in an upright position).
4	Be alert to the position of the rotor blades when recovering air crew.
5	If a boat crewmember must enter the water to assist with recovery of the air crew, that crewmember must wear a surface swimmer's harness tended from the boat.

Section D. Helicopter Salvage and Towing

Introduction

After a helicopter ditches and the crew has been rescued, every effort should be made to salvage the airframe before it sinks. A Coast Guard helicopter can survive a ditching in limited wind and sea conditions if its bottom integrity remains intact and flotation bags are deployed. If the helicopter becomes inverted (turned upside-down), it will have more severe damage and a greater risk of sinking.

WARNING

Pyrotechnics become unstable when wet.

D.1. Initial Actions

When a helicopter ditches, the parent air Station will assign a salvage officer and activate their mishap plan. Until the salvage officer arrives on scene, the senior aviator at the scene will act as the salvage officer. Boat handling, maneuvering, and the safety of the boat crew and survivors remain the coxswain's primary responsibility. If the aircraft is upright, the first boat on scene shall:

- Add flotation (e.g., flotation collars, inflatable life rafts, and boat fenders) to the helicopter to keep the helicopter from sinking, if conditions permit. Once positive buoyancy is ensured, the salvage operation can proceed.
- Establish a security watch.

NOTE

The primary concern during salvage is preventing the aircraft from inverting from an upright attitude.

CAUTION !

Do not attempt to tow a helicopter at night, upright or inverted, unless there is no alternative. If towing at night is a must, rig a light on the helicopter when towing between sunset and sunrise, or in restricted visibility.

D.2. General Towing Procedures

Towing a helicopter is not an exact science. On-scene conditions may make it necessary to change from standard procedures. However, safety of people shall never be compromised. When towing a Coast Guard helicopter, use the following general procedures:

Step	Procedure
1	Tow only when the aircraft cannot be hoisted onto a vessel in a timely manner.
2	Have qualified aviation personnel remove the rotor blades (improves stability).
3	Tow only in calm seas.
4	Remove all personnel from the aircraft.
5	Use a drogue, if available, to minimize yawing.
6	Tow at the slowest possible speed (do not exceed 5 knots).
7	Place initial strain on the towing hawser at bare steerageway.
8	Avoid towing the helicopter parallel to the wave trough to minimize risk of capsizing.
9	Make all turns slow and wide to minimize risk of capsizing.
10	Continuously monitor water depth to allow for the greater draft, when towing an inverted helicopter.
11	Tow an inverted helicopter only after additional flotation is attached to it.
12	Establish a tow watch.

D.3. Tow Watch

If any of the following conditions are seen, the tow shall be stopped:

- Change in attitude that would indicate compartment flooding.
- Deflation or loss of any flotation bags or buoyant devices attached to the aircraft.
- Aircraft roll increases to a point where vertical stability may be lost.

D.4. Towing Helicopter Forward

When towing the HH-65A helicopter forward, the towing bridle is attached to both sides of the 14° frame, the vertical frame only on the HH-65A, to which the pilot and co-pilot door is hinged. (see **Figure 19-17**)

NOTE

Tow the helicopter forward whenever possible.

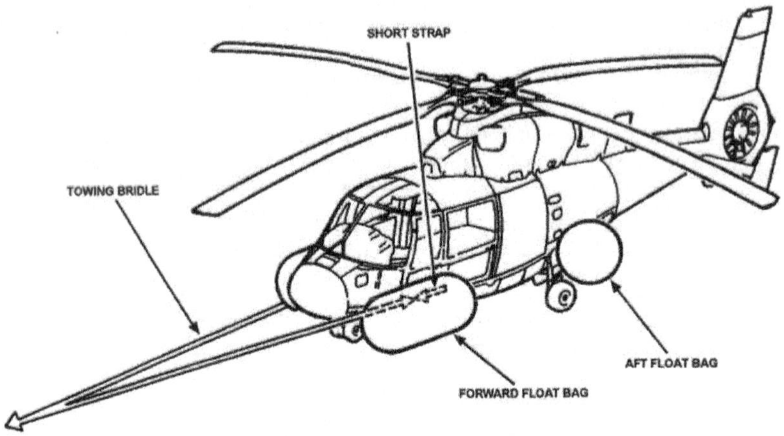

Figure 19-17
Configuration for Towing the HH-65A Helicopter Forward

WARNING

> If the tail cone has flooded, backwards towing will not be possible because the horizontal stabilizer will cause the tail to dive.

D.5. Towing Helicopter Backward

When towing the HH-65A helicopter backward, the towing bridle is attached to the left and right side of the horizontal stabilizer. (see **Figure 19-18**)

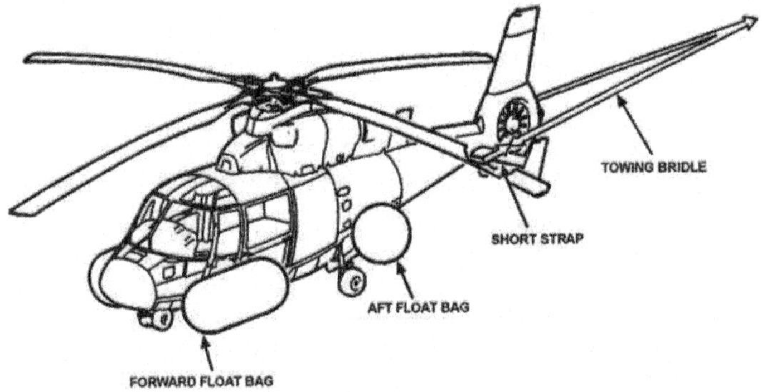

Figure 19-18
Configuration for Towing the HH-65A Helicopter Backward

D.6. HH-60J Helicopter Salvage and Towing

The HH-60J is configured with two flotation bags. When deployed, the bags will provide the air crew with a minimum of two minutes to effectively exit the helicopter. The HH-60J may not remain afloat long enough to be salvaged.

D.7. Multi-Unit (Boat-Helicopter) SAR Operations

As a boat crewmember, there will be many opportunities to work with helicopters on Coast Guard missions. Every opportunity should be taken to become familiar with the operations of the nearest local Coast Guard air Station or other agency (e.g., Navy, Army, Air Force, National Guard, or state). Crewmembers should become acquainted with the different types of aircraft and their capabilities in the local operating area. General information about helicopters includes:

- Helicopters navigate in magnetic direction, similar to boats. They are equipped with superior navigation equipment. Their capabilities often exceed that of the average boat. In coastal operations, they can provide excellent navigation assistance.
- The helicopter's "Night Sun" searchlight is most effective as a search tool only on a clear, dry night. Moisture in the atmosphere refracts/scatters the light, making it less effective.
- When working with a helicopter at night, never launch pyrotechnics/illumination signals (such as the MK-79/80 or M127A1) without first notifying the aircraft.
- When a helicopter hovers over surf or heavy seas, rotor downwash tends to blow the tops off breakers. This spray fills the air and greatly reduces visibility.

Section E. Fixed-Wing Aircraft

Introduction

Boat operations with fixed-wing aircraft are not frequently performed. However, this type of aircraft can provide extended search of an area and increased communication range while the boat does the detailed search and the actual inspection or assistance. Coast Guard aircraft will have their distinctive painting design and carry a VHF-FM radio for contacting maritime vessels. Also, Coast Guard Auxiliary fixed-wing aircraft may be available to assist.

E.1. Auxiliary Aircraft

Auxiliary aircraft are commonly known as general aviation aircraft. They are mostly single-engine land planes, either high wing or low wing. There may be some twin-engine aircraft, seaplanes, or helicopters. Auxiliary aircraft have no special painting design, but all are required to have their Federal Aviation Administration registration numbers on the fuselage or tail. The Coast Guard logo and lettering are not permitted; however, the facility decal is required. The aircraft may also carry the Auxiliary logo decal aft of the wings and/or the word RESCUE on the bottom of the wing or fuselage in 12-inch letters (visible from low altitudes). From the surface, an Auxiliary aircraft looks like any other civilian airplane.

E.2. Communications with Aircraft

Communication between a boat and an aircraft can be done by voice radio or a variety of visual signals. Aircraft are equipped with VHF-AM aeronautical radios. In addition, those performing Coast Guard missions carry VHF-FM radios. The normal method for aircraft-boat contact is by means of the VHF-FM radio, calling on Channel 16 and then shifting over to a working frequency. Air-to-surface and surface-to-air visual signals may be used when a radio is not available.

E.2.a. Air-to-Surface Visual Signals

Figure 19-19 shows air-to-surface signals that an aircraft may send to a boat. An aircraft may use the following signals to direct a boat to a place:

- Circle the vessel at least once.
- Cross the vessel's projected course close ahead at a low altitude while rocking the wings (opening and closing the throttle or changing the propeller pitch may be used instead of rocking the wings).
- Head in the direction in which the vessel is to be directed.

An aircraft may show that assistance of the vessel is no longer required by crossing the vessel's wake close astern at low altitude while rocking the wings (opening and closing the throttle or changing the propeller pitch may be used instead of rocking the wings).

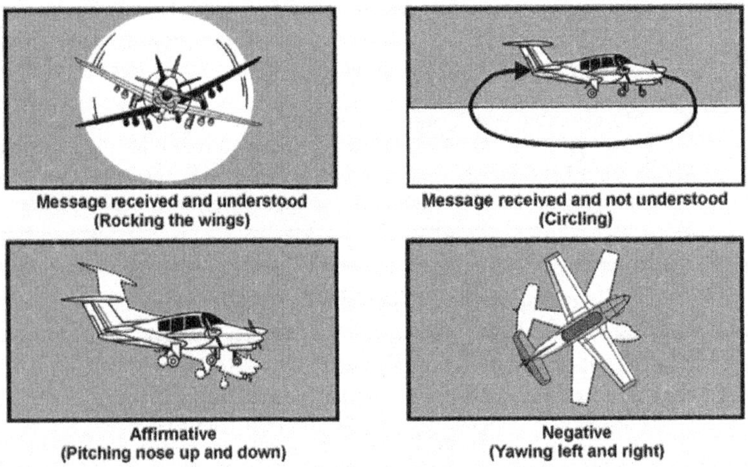
Message received and understood
(Rocking the wings)
Message received and not understood
(Circling)
Affirmative
(Pitching nose up and down)
Negative
(Yawing left and right)

Figure 19-19
Air-to-Surface Visual Signals

E.2.b. Surface-to-Air Visual Signals

Figure 19-20 shows surface-to-air visual signals that a boat crewmember may send to an aircraft. Also, when an aircraft cannot specifically identify the boat it is in contact with, the boat may make a tight turn. This distinctive, circular wake should stand out among the other boats.

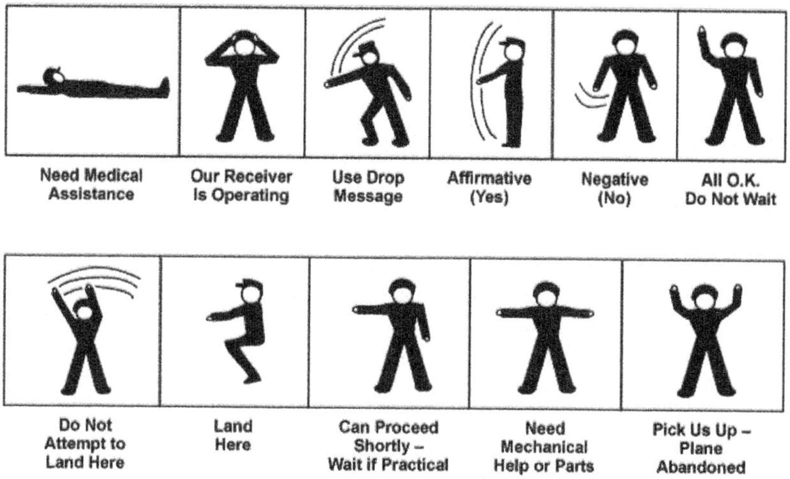

Figure 19-20
Surface-to-Air Visual Signals

E.3. Towing Fixed-Wing Aircraft

Some fixed-wing aircraft are equipped with floats for short periods of travel on the surface of the water. Aircraft are fragile and can be easily damaged by a boat coming into contact. The coxswain should always check with the aircraft crew to determine if a tow is desired and for advice on towing procedures. General guidance includes:

- Approaching the aircraft.
- Picking up the tow.
- Towing the aircraft.

E.3.a. Approaching the Aircraft

When approaching the aircraft, perform the following procedures:

Step	Procedure
1	Ensure the propeller(s) is stopped.
2	Extinguish all open flames and smoking material (aircraft fuel is highly flammable).
3	Approach from upwind (the aircraft will likely have a faster drift rate than the boat).
4	Steer the boat into the wind and back down to the aircraft, but do not come in contact.
5	Use minimum power to maneuver and fend off by hand (do not use a boat hook.).
6	Allow swells from passing boats to subside before getting close.

E.3.b. Picking Up the Tow

When picking up the tow, perform the following procedures:

Step	Procedure
1	Pass the towline to an aircraft crewmember. If such a person is not available, carefully approach and attach the line to the appropriate fitting on the float(s).
2	On single-float aircraft, secure the towline to the towing ring and pass it through the fairlead on the bow of the float, then to the towing boat.
3	On twin-float aircraft, a bridle may be necessary. Connect a tow only to the special fittings provided. Damage could result if any other towing point is used.

E.3.c. Towing the Aircraft

When towing the aircraft, perform the following procedures:

Step	Procedure
1	Tow at low speed.
2	Avoid towing in adverse conditions, if possible.
3	Use a short towline.
4	If directional stability is of concern, consider use of "wing lines" tied to the wing struts or wing tips. Wing lines go from the boat's port quarter to the left wing, and the boat's starboard quarter to the right wing. Do not place any towing strain on the wing lines.
5	The tow watch must watch closely so that the aircraft does not overtake the boat.

Section F. Sample Briefing to Pass to Vessel Prior to Helicopter Hoisting

Introduction

"A helicopter is proceeding to your position and should arrive at approximately ______. Maintain a radio watch on _______ MHz/kHz/Channel ______ VHF-FM. The helicopter will attempt to contact you. Provide a clear area for hoisting, preferably on the port stern. Lower all masts and booms that can be lowered. Secure all loose gear. Keep all unnecessary people clear of the hoisting area. Just before the helicopter arrives, secure the vessel's radar or put it in standby mode. Do not direct lights towards the helicopter, as it will adversely affect the pilot's vision. Direct available lighting to illuminate the hoisting area. When the helicopter arrives, change course to place the wind 30° on the port bow and maintain a steady course and steerageway. As the helicopter approaches, strong winds may be produced by the rotors, making it difficult to steer. The helicopter will provide all the equipment for the hoisting. A line will probably be trailed from the helicopter for your crew to guide the rescue device as it is lowered. Before touching the rescue device, allow it to touch your vessel. This will discharge static electricity. If you have to move the rescue device from the hoisting area to load the patient, unhook the cable from the rescue device and lay the loose hook on the deck so the helicopter can retrieve it. Do not attach the loose hook or the cable to your vessel. The helicopter may move to the side while the patient is being loaded. Have the patient wear a personal flotation device, and attach any important records, along with a record of medications that have been administered. When the patient is securely loaded, signal the helicopter to move into position and lower the hook. After allowing the hook to ground on the vessel, re-attach it to the rescue device. Signal the hoist operator with a "thumbs up" when you are ready for the hoisting to begin. As the rescue device is being retrieved, tend the trail line to prevent the device from swinging. When you reach the end of the trail line, gently release the weight over the side."

NOTE

> The briefing can be used for hoisting operations or it may be requested to pass this guidance on to the distressed vessel as the helicopter is en route to it. Also, some vessels or aircraft may use the term "winch" to mean the same thing as "hoist".

This page intentionally left blank.

Chapter 20
Heavy Weather Addendum

Introduction

Heavy weather conditions can pose many threats to boat crews in their attempts to safely and successfully accomplish mission. It is essential that crewmembers understand the various types of heavy weather operations so that they may plan appropriately and take any necessary precautions to ensure safe operations for all persons and vessels involved.

In this chapter

This chapter contains the following sections:

Section A. Heavy Weather Mission Preparation

Introduction

Any operation executed in heavy weather requires greater crew coordination and communication. Risk is inherently higher due to the environment in which small boat crews operate. A thorough understanding of the risks and benefits for every mission should be the highest priority in mission planning.

In this section

This section contains the following information:

Heavy Weather Risk Management / TCT

A.1. Description

The discomfort that can be experienced when underway on boats in heavy seas is hard to describe to those who have not experienced them before. It can drain a person of all their energy and willpower at the times that they are needed most. It can hamper the capacity for a person to make a rational and prudent decision in tough situations.

In heavy weather, team coordination and risk management decisions are more difficult due to the inherent stress of the environment, mission, and fatigue that the crews will face. Missions in heavy weather are riskier than a mission in calm conditions. The crew must be ready to face unexpected challenges and be prepared to effectively and safely deal with them as they happen. If there are waves of any size, the effects they will have on the boat and crew must be understood.

Chapter 4 of this Manual outlines team coordination and risk management steps that should be taken to reduce the probability of a mishap.

A.2. Risk vs. Gain

As discussed in the *Boat Operations and Training Manual (BOAT) Manual, Volume I*, COMDTINST M16114.32 (series) the following paragraphs establish policy guidelines to be used in making risk versus gain analysis for various boat missions.

A.2.a. Search and Rescue (SAR) and Law Enforcement (LE)

For SAR missions, potential risks to the boat and crew shall be weighed against risks to the personnel and/or property in distress if the mission is not undertaken. Probable loss of the boat crew is not an acceptable risk.

Additionally, the individuals making the decision shall consider the effects of exposing people in distress to the additional risks associated with rescue operations, especially if the physical condition of those persons in distress is already impaired.

In the case of LE, potential risks to the boat shall be weighed against the risk of bodily harm to LE personnel, hostages, and innocent parties if the mission is not undertaken.

A.2.b. Saving Lives

The probability of saving human life warrants a maximum effort. When no suitable alternative exists and the mission has a reasonable chance of success, the risk of damage to or abuse of the boat is acceptable, even though such damage or abuse may render the boat unrecoverable.

The possibility of saving human life or the probability of preventing or relieving intense pain or suffering warrants the risk of damage to or abuse of the boat if recovering the boat can reasonably be expected.

A.2.c. Saving Property

The probability of saving property of the United States or its citizens warrants the risk of damage to the boat if the value of the property to be saved is unquestionably greater than the cost of boat damage and the boat is fully expected to be recoverable.

A.2.d. Federal Law Violations

The possibility of recovering evidence and interdicting or apprehending alleged violators of federal law does not warrant probable damage to or abuse of the boat.

A.3. Decision-Making: Go/No-Go

The decision to go or not to go on a mission in heavy weather is a difficult one to make. Just as the limitations placed on the boats guides decisions, the personal limitations of the crew should be a guiding force. There are many examples of coxswains and surfmen pushing the limitations of themselves, their crew, and the boat to affect a rescue in extreme conditions. There are also examples of coxswains and surfmen who have exceeded their limitations and ended up requiring rescue for their crews. The time to make Go/No-Go decisions does not stop once underway. The crew may find themselves in a situation where they may decide whether or not to continue with a mission. An example of this is after a rollover or knockdown.

Risk assessment is a process that is never ending. Using risk assessment tools such as the GAR Model (found in the *U.S. Coast Guard Addendum to the United States National Search and Rescue Supplement (NSS) to the International Aeronautical and Maritime Search and Rescue Manual*, COMDTINST M16130.2 (series)), open communications between crew and coxswain, and open communications with SAR mission managers and boat crews, are excellent ways to measure the level of risk and to mitigate hazards.

NOTE

The terms "Knockdown" and "Rollover" apply specifically to self-righting boats. A **knockdown** is when a boat has rolled in one direction 90° or greater but does not completely rollover (360°) to right itself. (Example: Boat rolls to port 120° and rights itself by rolling back to starboard.) A **rollover** occurs when a boat rolls in one direction and rights itself by completing a 360° revolution.

Mission Planning for Heavy Weather

A.4. Description

No mission in heavy weather conditions should be a surprise. Thorough understanding of weather forecasting, regional weather patterns, and significant weather systems in the area are required to be able to plan any mission.

The condition of the boat and its equipment, and the experience and capabilities of the crew should be the number one concern in mission planning. No coxswain can help another vessel or person in distress without a capable crew and vessel.

"Life saving vessels fulfill their function under conditions which, for other craft and equipment, are regarded as extreme, to be avoided, if possible. Thus, the concept of "acceptable risk of failure" cannot apply. It is when other vessels have failed that the lifesaving vessel must work," G. Klem, Senior Research Engineer, Norwegian Ship Research Institute.

CH-1

A.5. Boat Readiness

Before leaving the moorings, the operator should ensure that:

- All required equipment is onboard and stowed properly. Loose gear underway in heavy weather creates a hazard for the boat crew and stability of the vessel.
- All systems are operating within required parameters. No restrictive discrepancies that could affect the mission or disabling discrepancies are present.
- There is no question in the mind of the crew that the boat and its equipment are one hundred percent ready for operations.

A.6. Crew Readiness

Crew selection for heavy weather operations should be done with care. Operations in heavy weather or surf are fatiguing and stressful. Some factors to consider are:

- Experience level of coxswain: If a coxswain is uncertain or anxious about the conditions they may encounter, requesting a more experienced heavy weather coxswain or surfman to assist may be the better option.
- Experience level of crew: All operations in heavy weather have an increased level of risk. It may not be appropriate to take inexperienced crewmen without an experienced crewmember as a safety observer. The coxswain/surfman will need assistance to maintain crew control and communication, for safety.
- Physical condition of crew. Operations in heavy weather are extremely fatiguing and challenging physically. Crews should be well rested and in good physical condition before getting underway. Heavy weather operations are no place for a sick crewmember. If there is any doubt about the condition of a crewmember, they should be replaced if personnel allow.
- Mental condition of crew: Operations in heavy weather are extremely fatiguing and challenging mentally as well. Crews should be mentally prepared for the conditions they will encounter. Crewmen that are distracted by family crisis, personal conflict, or extreme apathy for the service should not be the first pick for a heavy weather crew.
- Anticipated length of mission: Missions requiring boats to be underway in heavy weather for long periods are extremely fatiguing. *U.S. Coast Guard Boat Operations and Training (BOAT) Manual, Volume I,* COMDTINST M16114.32 (series) lists fatigue standards for small boats. If personnel permit, taking a second qualified coxswain to act as a relief should be considered. If no relief is available, recommending the use of another Coast Guard resource that is able to operate in heavy weather for longer periods of time should also be considered.

A.7. Survival Equipment

Any crew operating in heavy weather or surf must be properly equipped, as follows:

- Required hypothermia protective clothing.
- Helmet (helmet straps must be secured and adjusted properly).
- Survival vest and equipment.
- Waterproof footwear and gloves should be worn.
- Eye protection may be necessary for visibility, particularly for persons wearing glasses, and will also protect against glass shards should a window be broken.
- Boat crew safety belt must be worn and adjusted correctly.
- Personal seat belt must be worn when in a seat.

The coxswain is responsible for ensuring that all required equipment is worn, and worn correctly.

A.8. Weather

Heavy weather is defined as seas, swell, and wind conditions combining to exceed 8 feet and/or winds exceeding 30 knots. If heavy weather is forecasted, it should be considered when planning a mission. Reliable and up to the minute information is critical for planning. There are many sources of information available to the coxswains, heavy weather coxswains, surfmen, and commands of Stations. Ensuring that the information is found and used is the responsibility of every one involved in the mission.

NOTE

This definition of heavy weather is not intended to define a heavy weather situation for a specific boat type. Heavy weather for each specific boat type may be determined by the coxswain at any time.

A.8.a. Weather Definitions

- Sea state is both the sea swell as well as the significant wave height of the wind waves.
- Significant wave height is the average height of the largest third of the wind waves observed or expected in an area.
- Combined seas is the realistic conditions encountered.
- More definitions are listed in *Chapter 12* and *Appendix A* of this Manual.

A.8.b. Weather Conditions

The weather is the deciding factor that makes heavy weather operations dangerous or impossible. Knowing what conditions the crew will be challenged with is extremely important. Some sources of information are:

- Message traffic from the National Weather Service.
- First-hand observations from shore prior to getting underway.
- The internet - There are many websites available with information ranging from weather buoy and ship observations to satellite photos.
- Other mariners that can be trusted to give accurate weather conditions. Some examples are pilot services and commercial operators.
- The disabled mariner: While most mariners are as accurate as they can be, comparing observations from the mariner with other information available is always prudent. The stress of being in distress in heavy weather can often make large waves appear to be giants.

A.8.c. Specific Area Weather Patterns

This chapter is not the proper place to address all the weather patterns that may be encountered around the country. Some weather patterns can be addressed that affect broad areas. Experience and discussions with local mariners will greatly help the crew know what conditions a particular weather system may do in the area. Nothing will replace the responsibility to know the local area and its weather patterns.

- West Coast: The west coast receives its weather from off shore. A long fetch and often, long duration are a significant influence on the sea conditions likely to be encountered.
- East Coast: The east coast is often in the path of tropical storm systems as well as strong arctic low pressure systems. The gulf stream and a wide, shallow continental shelf are significant influences on the sea conditions encountered.
- Gulf Coast: The gulf coast also has the gulf stream and a wide, shallow continental shelf to influence waves. With relatively little fetch, the major source of heavy weather is tropical storm systems.

Area-specific weather patterns can include, gap winds, dynamic fetch, strong currents, thunderstorms, lightning, freezing spray, steep seas with very short periods, as well as many other phenomenon. Any of these conditions can make operations more difficult and hazardous for the boat and crew.

Waves and Surf

A.9. Description

The ability to recognize wave patterns and characteristics is essential to safe operation in surf and heavy weather. A coxswain operating in these conditions must be able to determine the timing of lulls and series, and estimate wave heights accurately.

A.10. Waves

There are several forces, which create waves at sea, the most significant of which is wind. The factors which determine the characteristics of wind waves are:

- Wind speed.
- Wind duration.
- Fetch (the distance over open water which the wind has blown).

An example of these factors can be seen in the following table:

Fetch (Nautical Miles)	Wind Duration Hours	Wind Speed (Knots)	Sea State (Feet)
5	1	40	4.9
10	3	40	6.5
200	24	40	20

As the wind begins to blow, it creates seas, which are typically steep, choppy, and have little pattern. As the wind continues, the seas begin to become more defined. In heavy weather, observing and measuring waves is important. If the crew can get a general sense of the waves in which they are operating, it will allow the crew to operate accordingly.

Heavy weather waves and seas are generated by weather systems, either local or distant. There are many factors that determine what conditions will be generated by a weather system or series of weather systems. Some factors that will effect wave height include:

- State of the tide: Ebb currents often cause wave speed to decrease and wave height to increase. Conversely, flood currents often cause waves to gain speed and loose height.
- Rainfall: Heavy rainfall can reduce the size of waves, but large runnoffs from rivers may stop the flood current or drastically change the conditions at inlets or bars.
- The width of the body of water: The greater distance the body of water is allows for larger waves to be generated.
- Depth of water: Deeper water allows for larger swells to be generated. As these swells approach shallow water on the coast, they will loose speed and gain height.
- Air temperature: Cold air is denser, causing greater impact on the water and building larger swells than warm air.

See *Chapter 12, Weather and Oceanography* of this Manual for more information.

A.11. Wave Systems

After the deepwater waves are generated far out at sea, they move outward, away from their wind source, in ever-increasing curves, and become what are called swells. The farther the swell moves from its source, the more uniform its characteristics become, as it travels in a series of waves, relatively equidistant, and moving at a more or less constant speed. Because of this, swells generated from storms far out at sea can be distinguished by their smoothness and uniformity from those that are coarser (peaked and irregular) which have recently originated nearby. The usual period of these swells is from 6 to 10 seconds. This corresponds with wave lengths of 184 to 1310 feet and velocities of 18 to 49 knots.

Interference between different swell systems, which are traveling in nearly the same direction, causes groups of waves to travel outward in patches. As these groups of several waves (normally 7 to 12) progress outward, those waves in the forefront disappear and new waves, of the same characteristics, appear at the rear of the patch. This process continues until the waves dissipate their energy at sea, or transfer it to the shore as surf.

The ability to recognize wave patterns and characteristics is essential to safe operation in surf and heavy weather. A coxswain operating in these conditions must be able to determine the timing of lulls and series, and estimate wave heights accurately. Some factors that affect wave patterns are:

- Refraction.
- Reflection.
- Interference.
- Shoaling water.

A.11.a. Refraction

Refraction means bending. Wave refraction occurs when the wave moves into shoaling water, interacts with the bottom and slows down. Naturally, the first part of the waves encountering the shallows slow down first, causing the crests of the waves to bend forward toward the shallower water. (see **Figure 20-1**) The key to the amount to refraction that occurs is the bottom terrain. This can also occur when a wave passes around a point of land, jetty, or an island. (see **Figure 20-2**)

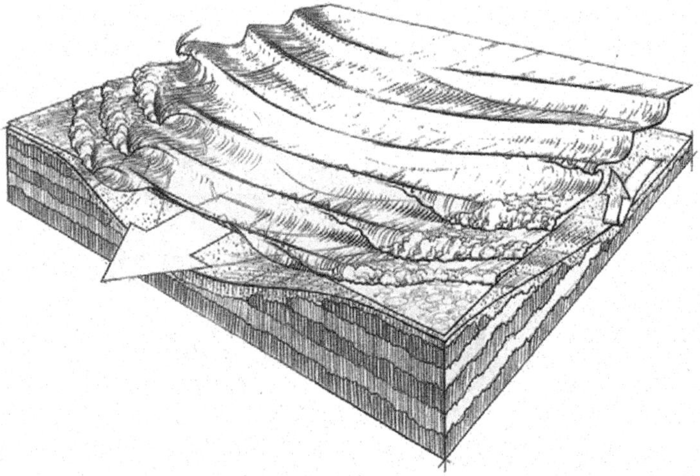

Figure 20-1
Submarine Valley

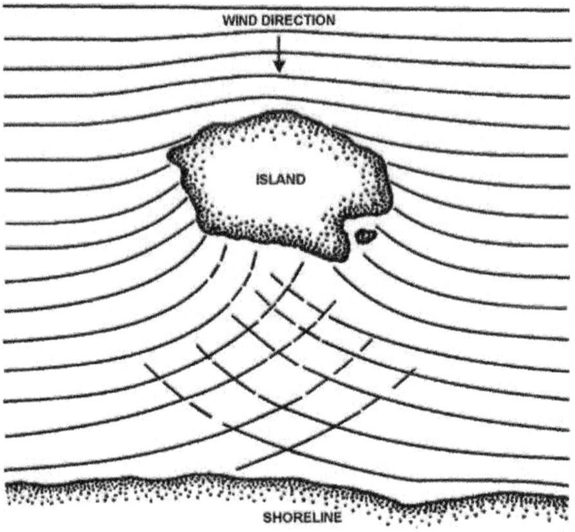

Figure 20-2
Wave Refraction

A.11.b. Reflection

Almost any obstacle can reflect part of a wave, including underwater barriers such as submerged reefs or bars, even though the main waves may seem to pass over them without change. These reflected waves move back towards the incoming waves. When the obstacles are vertical or nearly so, the waves may be reflected in their entirety. (see **Figure 20-3**)

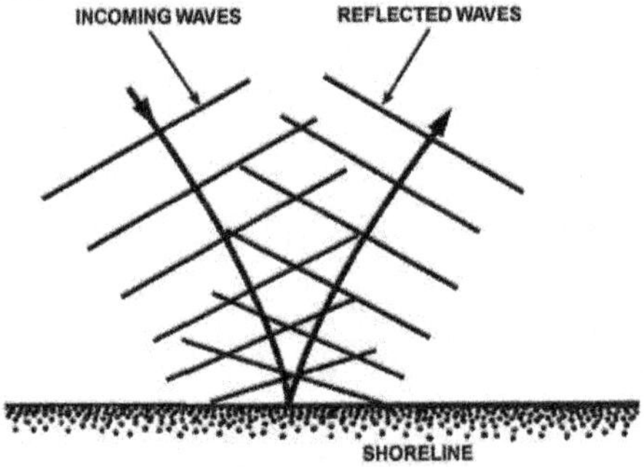

Figure 20-3
Wave Reflection

A.11.c. Interference

Waves which have been refracted or reflected can interact with each other as well as with the incoming waves, and may be additive (or subtractive), resulting in unnaturally high waves. Interference may even result in standing wave patterns (waves that consistently appear to peak in the same spot). Interference can be of particular concern because it may result in a boat being subjected to waves from unexpected directions and of unexpected size. (see **Figure 20-4**)

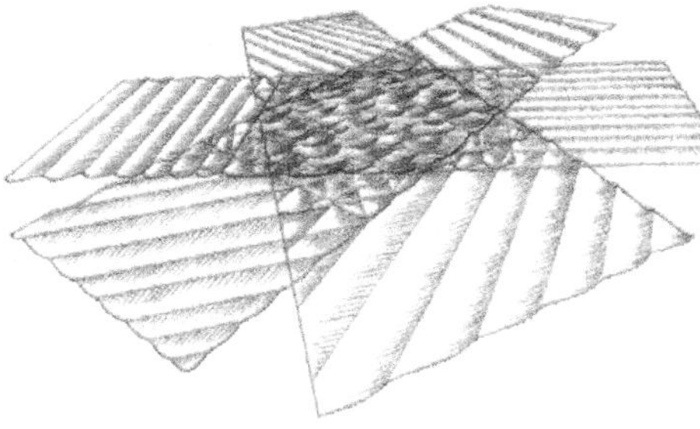

Figure 20-4
Wave Interference

A.11.d. Shoaling Water

Knowledge of the characteristic grouping of waves is useful when operating in shoaling waters such as over bars, in inlets, or working in surf. The wave groups can be observed and their group periods determined. The boat or boats can be best maneuvered during that time when the wave motion is at a minimum, during the space between groups.

When deepwater waves move into shallow waters, the waves are influenced by the bottom, becoming shallow-water waves. In the approach to shore, the interaction with the bottom causes the wave speed to decrease. This decrease causes refractions, and one effect is to shorten the wavelength. As the wavelength decreases, the wave steepness increases and the wave becomes less stable. Also, as the wave moves into water whose depth is about twice the wave's height, the crest peaks up; that is, the rounded crest of a swell becomes a higher more pointed mass of water with steeper sides. This change of waveform becomes more pronounced as the wave moves farther into shallow water. These changes in wavelength and steepness occur before breaking. Finally, at a depth of water roughly equal to 1.3 times the wave height (the actual formula used to determine when the wave will break is when the height is equal to 80% of the depth ratio, H=.8d), the wave becomes unstable. This happens when not enough water is available in the shallow area ahead to complete the crest and the wave's symmetrical form. The top of the onrushing crest is left unsupported and collapses. The wave breaks, resulting in surf. (see **Figure 20-5**)

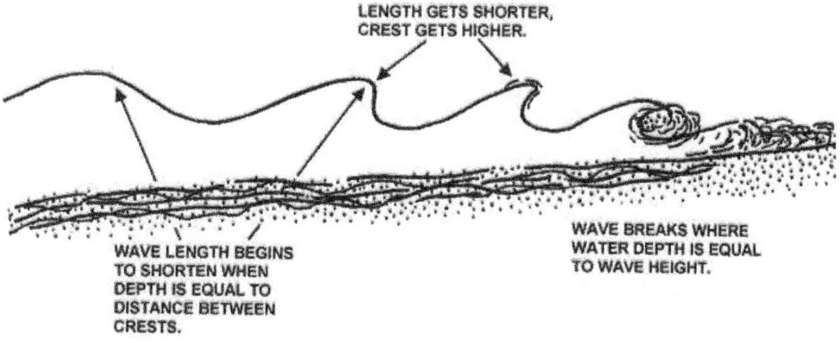

Figure 20-5
Surf

A.12. Timing

The lull period in a wave system is the safest time to transit a bar, inlet, or shoal area in heavy seas/surf. By timing the duration of the lull, a coxswain can be prepared to make a transit while the waves are smaller. They will also have some idea of how much time is available before the next big set comes through. The basic technique is to use a stopwatch. After the last big wave of a series has passed, the time is started. When the first big waves of the next set arrive, the time is stopped. This is the duration of the lull, which may range from less than a minute to several minutes. This pattern should be observed for as long as possible until arriving at a useful consistent time. It may also be useful to time the duration of the series and number of waves in the set.

NOTE | The lull is the time between a series of swells.

A.13. Estimating Wave Height

An accurate estimate of wave height is subjective and sometimes difficult to accomplish, but there are a number of methods that, with practice, will give good results.

A.13.a. Height of Eye or Freeboard

With the boat in the trough and on a level and even keel, any wave that obscures the horizon is greater than the height of a person's eye. The height of eye on a 47' MLB is about 14 feet while seated at the helm or standing on the open bridge. One can also compare a wave to the deck edge or a structure such as the handrail. The wave face is observed while bowing into it and in the trough on an even keel. This is also generally the best method for judging surf.

A.13.b. Comparison with Floating Structures or Vessels

This technique is most useful when observing from land, but may be applied while underway. If the freeboard of a buoy is known to be 13 feet, that information can be used to determine the height of the waves passing it. A buoy can also be used to determine the wave period. One can observe a vessel underway and by estimating the freeboard of the vessel and observing its motions on the water, he or she can gain a fair estimate of the seas in which it is operating.

A.13.c. Comparison with Fixed Structure

Observation of waves as they pass a fixed structure, such as a break-wall, jetty, or pier, can be very accurate and can also provide wave period.

A.13.d. Depth Sounder

Using a digital finder with a fast update speed can be very accurate for determining wave height. By comparing the depth in the trough on even keel with the depth at the crest on even keel, an accurate measurement can be obtained.

All of these methods can be useful and reasonably accurate, but they require practice and experience. By comparing a local Weather Service buoy report with the crew's observations, they can fine tune their sense of wave height. With enough practice, they should be able to judge wave heights simply by looking at the waves themselves.

A.14. Types of Surf

There are three basic types of breaking waves:

- Plunging: see **Figure 20-6**.
- Spilling: see **Figure 20-7**.
- Surging: see **Figure 20-8**.

More information on these three breaking waves can be found in *Chapter 12, Weather and Oceanography*. Each type of breaking waves brings its own hazards, such as suction currents, dropping huge quantities of water, and exerting a great deal of force. It is important to remember that when operating in heavy weather, these hazards are magnified beyond those found during calm water operations.

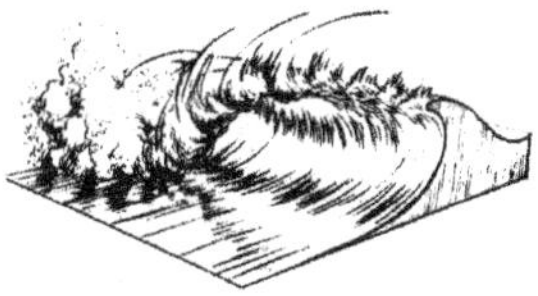

Figure 20-6
Plunging Breaking Wave

Figure 20-7
Spilling Breaking Wave

Figure 20-8
Surging Breaking Wave

A.15. Surf Zone Characteristics

In normal operations and especially in heavy weather, there are a number of conditions created in the surf zone and in individual waves of which the coxswain must be aware. These include:

- Windows.
- High/low side of a wave.
- Wave saddles.
- Closeouts.
- Wave shoulder.
- Rip currents.

A.15.a. Windows

A window is an area where the waves have momentarily stopped breaking, opening up a safer area of operation for your boat. Windows often form in the area of aerated water where a large set of waves has just finished breaking. The window may remain for a long time or may begin breaking again almost immediately. It is preferable to operate the boat in the windows whenever possible.

A.15.b. High/Low Side of a Wave

The "high side" is defined as the section of a wave which carries the most potential energy. It may be the part that is still building towards breaking point, or it may be the part which has already broken. The "low side" is where the least potential energy exists and represents the safest direction to turn when facing the wave/swell. (see **Figure 20-9**) These high and low sides often change rapidly, and the ability to quickly navigate the high and low sides is a critical skill for surf operations.

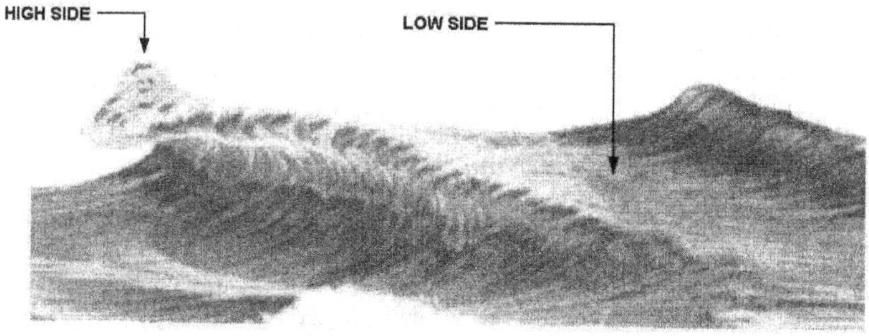

Figure 20-9
High/Low Side of a Wave

A.15.c. Wave Saddles

The "saddle" is the lowest part of a wave, bordered on both sides by higher ones. Often it is a small, unbroken section of a wave that is breaking. It is preferable to drive a boat in the saddles if possible, thus avoiding the white water. While saddles are very useful, they must be watched carefully, because they easily turn into "close-outs."

A.15.d. Closeouts

"Closeouts" occur when a wave breaks from the ends toward the middle, or two waves break towards each other. The middle may look like a good saddle, but can quickly turn into whitewater. Closeouts should be avoided because they can create more energy than a single break.

A.15.e. Wave Shoulder

The "shoulder" is the edge of a wave. It may be the very edge of the whitewater on a breaker, or the edge of a high peaking wave that is about to break. The shoulder is usually lower in height than the middle of the wave. Driving on the shoulders can be particularly useful in a narrow surf zone because it allows driving very close to a break in relative safety.

A.15 f. Rip Currents

Rips are created along a long beach or reef surf zone. The water from waves hitting the beach travels out to the sides and parallel to the shoreline, creating a "long-shore current" that eventually returns to sea. This seaward flow creates deep channels in the sand offshore that can shift from day to day. In the case of a reef, the channels are permanent parts of the reef, but otherwise behave the same. In these channels, the waves or surf are usually smaller because of refraction over the deeper water. Because of this, a rip channel often represents a safer route into or out of a surf zone. A rip current may also carry a person-in-the-water or a disabled vessel clear of the surf zone (see **Figure 20-10**) If using a rip current, great care should be taken to stay in the channel by watching the depth sounder. Boat crews should always be alert for debris, which tends to concentrate in these areas.

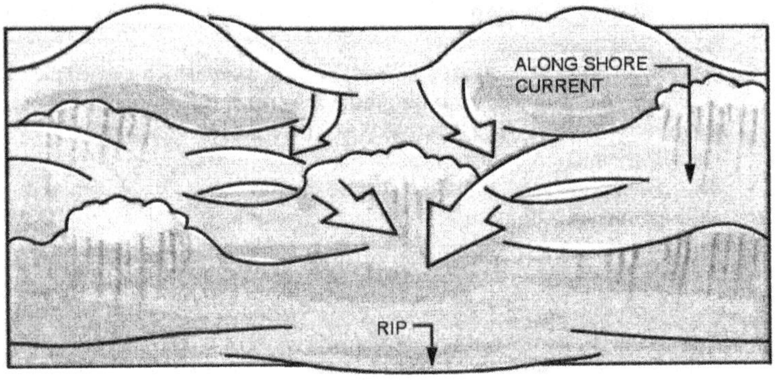

Figure 20-10
Rip Currents

Piloting in Heavy Weather

A.16. Description

The distinction between "piloting" and "navigation" is outlined in many respected publications, including Dutton's *Navigation and Piloting* and Bowditch's *Practical Navigator*. This chapter is designed to offer techniques that are unique to operations in heavy weather situations.

The importance of sound piloting is well-described in Dutton's:

"Piloting requires the greatest experience and nicest judgment of any form of navigation. Constant vigilance, unfailing mental alertness, and a thorough knowledge of the principles involved are essential. In pilot waters there is little or no opportunity to correct errors. Even a slight blunder may result in disaster, perhaps involving the loss of life."

Working in areas close to shore and in shoal waters, the area of operation for small boats, means knowing the location of the boat assumes greater importance in heavy weather. Not knowing the boat's position could result in inadvertent entry into a dangerous surf zone, shoal water or delay assistance to a vessel in distress. Heavy weather brings additional problems to navigation and piloting, which are not found in calm conditions. Not the least of these is the mental approach to the problem. The physical exhaustion found in heavy weather can make it extremely difficult to concentrate, and greatly increase the chance of making a mistake.

A.17. Chart Preparation

A chart is the most important piece of navigational equipment onboard a boat. It can provide a good mental picture of the coastline and bottom contours.

Some thought and preparation should go into the chart before leaving the dock. Crewmembers can make chartlets or laminate charts of a workable size. Laying out clearly readable track lines and courses, out of and into the harbor, with radar ranges, danger ranges, turn ranges, as well as bearings, will make piloting to open water safer. The prepared chart should be checked as well as used in calm conditions before it is used for heavy weather. Making the chart water-resistant using laminates or a chart case will help keep it useable in storm conditions.

Although it may sound trivial, the chart should be folded properly. A chart cannot be prepared for every possible position, and it is very likely that a crewmember will have to plot a position on a chart, layout a track line, and go.

The crewmember will be unable to unfold the chart every time he or she needs the distance scale or compass rose. If possible, datum and ranges to datum should be on the same side of the folded chart. As much of the chart work as possible should be done before leaving the dock. Everyone has felt the urgency of getting underway immediately, but the crew ultimately responsible for the safe navigation of the boat and no level of urgency will be an excuse for running aground or colliding with another vessel.

A.18. Experience

Being prepared is not limited to having the proper or sufficient equipment aboard. Preparation for a heavy weather case involving piloting can begin months before the mission. The primary tool to ensure success in any piloting evolution is local knowledge. The ability to quickly match objects seen visually or on radar with charted objects will increase a coxswain's capabilities. Naturally, calm weather affords the best situation to study the area underway, but observing the AOR during heavy weather from land or sea will enable the coxswain to identify hazardous areas particular to inclement weather. Of course, none of the tools available are useful if the user's not well versed in how to use them. No amount of studying or classroom instruction can substitute for underway training. Every opportunity should be taken to pilot, no matter what the conditions may be. The wise coxswain "over-navigates" the boat during fair weather so that he or she can acquire the skills to navigate in poor weather without fear or nervous strain.

A.19. Electronic Piloting

With a chart, a compass, and a watch onboard, the basic requirements for navigation are available. However, with these basic tools, the crew is limited to dead-reckoning navigation, apart from the use of bearings to check the boats position. Often in heavy weather, visibility is restricted and small boats do not carry hand bearing compasses making the use of visual bearings impossible. It is under these conditions that electronic aids can be most valuable.

A.19.a. Radar Ranges

One of the most under-utilized methods in piloting is radar ranges. Having a beam radar range at the DR positions takes a great deal of the guesswork out of navigation. If there are predetermined ranges laid out, the crew will be able to see at a glance how far left or right of track the boat is, well before reaching the DR position. Having these ranges will also allow making constant minor changes to the course instead of major changes at each DR position. To simplify matters even more, distances should be layed out fore and aft as well. Often it is impossible to have a fixed object directly ahead or astern, but even an object 10° to 30° off the bow or stern will give an approximation of position up the track line. These fore and aft ranges are also critical in computing speed over ground using the three-minute rule and its variations.

A.19.b. Datum

If tasked with piloting to datum, layout ranges from known points of land or from floating aids to navigation to datum. Try to use ranges as close to directly ahead or astern and directly abeam as possible. As the boat approaches the position, it will be easy to determine if it is right or left and too far up or down the track. Then adjust the course as necessary.

A.19.c. GPS

GPS is an extremely accurate navigation tool and it can be a powerful tool to assist in piloting. The waypoint function as well as the Course Deviation Indicator (CDI) can be very useful. However, the tools must not take attention away from the environment and the situation at hand. Situational awareness must be maintained.

A.19.d. Depth Sounder

Using the depth sounder to confirm the position with charted depth of water is often difficult in heavy weather where aerated water can throw off the reading.

NOTE

The three-minute rule is used to determine speed in knots or distance in yards.

Distance traveled in three minutes divided by 100.

Example--

Distance: 1000 yards

Time: 3 minutes

Speed: 10 knots

Section B. Heavy Weather Operations

Introduction

In heavy weather, the safety of the boat depends on the coxswain as much as the boat's design. The coxswain has a job, which requires a high degree of concentration if it is to be done well. Their job is to assess the many factors affecting the boat and take appropriate action on the wheel, throttle, and other controls to ensure its safe transit. A larger than normal wave or one with a breaking crest can arrive with little warning and a critical situation can develop rapidly. At night, the situation is worse due to the very restricted visibility.

Heavy weather is demanding on both the coxswain and the crew and they must do all in their power to remain mentally and physically alert. Proper hypothermia protection and taking every opportunity to rest will reduce the strain on the boat crew.

Operations in heavy weather increases the level of risk, the possibility of causing injury to personnel, and damage to property.

In this section

This section contains the following information:

Forces Affecting Boat Handling

B.1. Description

In heavy weather, the motion of the boat rolling, pitching, and yawing affect handling of the boat. If these motions become excessive or combine, they may become uncomfortable or even dangerous. High winds affect boat handling and may amplify control problems.

B.2. Rolling

Rolling occurs when the boat is running beam to the seas. If the course requires running or turning broadside to heavy seas, the boat will roll heavily, possibly dangerously. In these conditions, it may be best to run in a series of tacks like a sailboat, changing course to take the wind and seas at a 45° angle.

Sea breaks can exert considerable pressure on the side of the boat, which is resisted by the water on the lee side. This can produce a turning moment which if greater than the initial righting moment will result in a knockdown or rollover.

To turn sharply while exposing the boat to a beam sea for the least amount of time, the coxswain should slow down for a few seconds, then turn the helm hard over and apply power. This can be done effectively with a twin-screw boat by using the split-throttle maneuver.

B.3. Pitching

Pitching occurs when the boat is running bow into the waves. The bow of the boat rises over the wave and then drops rapidly into the trough. If the seas become too steep, speed should be decreased. This will allow the bow to rise, meeting the swell, instead of being driven hard into it. Changing course may be the better option to reduce stress on the crew and boat. Again, 45° off the swell may give better control and a better ride.

If conditions become too hazardous, slow until the boat is making bare steerageway and meets the seas on the bow. Again, power should be used to negotiate the wave without sending the boat launching off the back of the seas.

B.4. Yawing

Yawing occurs when the boat is operating in following seas. The boat sheers off to port or starboard due to the action of the waves. The boat surfs down the face of the wave, slowing as the bow digs into the trough. The rudder loses control and the sea takes charge of the stern. At this stage, the boat may yaw so badly as to broach (to be thrown broadside out of control) into the trough. Once the wave clears the stern, it lifts the bow of the boat and the stern begins to slide down the backside of the wave, allowing better rudder control causing the boat to straighten out.

Severe yawing may result in a knockdown, pitch pole, or rollover. Extreme care must be taken when operating in a large following sea, constantly watching behind the boat. Slowing speed or changing course may reduce yawing.

B.5. High Winds

High winds can amplify conditions discussed in the previous sections. It can make routine operations such as towing approaches extremely difficult. Overcoming the affect of wind requires practice and experience on the boat.

Towing in Heavy Weather

B.6. Description

Heavy weather towing is one of the most hazardous missions that may be undertaken. Maneuvering close enough to pass a towline and then controlling that vessel while towing is dangerous for both crews and boats. Towing is covered in *Chapter 17* of this Manual.

B.7. Vessel to be Towed

Before taking any vessel in tow, observe the condition of the vessel. Is it taking on water? How is it riding? A vessel that is in poor condition may be severely damaged by the stresses of heavy weather towing. Some factors to look at are:

- Stability.
- Nature of distress.
- Condition of crew.
- Types and condition of fittings.

NOTE When conditions warrant, pass over emergency equipment, such as pumps or radios, before taking the vessel in tow.

B.8. Before Approaching

Before beginning the approach to the disabled vessel, the coxswain must ensure the crew and boat are prepared as follows:

Step	Procedure
1	Make engine room rounds prior to beginning the approach.
2	Disengage the auto pilot.
3	Ensure control of throttle.
4	Brief the crew and assign duties.
5	Check the towing rig.
6	Determine the danger zone.
7	Observe conditions and see how it affects control of the boat.

In heavy weather, it may be necessary to set up the deck underway at a slow speed to give the crew a safe, comfortable ride.

B.9. Towing Approach

The towing approach requires maneuvering the boat close enough to the disabled boat, maintaining that position, and providing a stable platform long enough for the crew to safely pass the towing rig.

The towing approach in heavy weather is to set up down-swell of the disabled boat with the bow into the seas. When the crew is ready, the coxswain drives the boat into optimum position. (see **Figure 20-11**) It may be necessary to use more power than in calm conditions to get steerageway and make a straight-line approach. Conditions may require stopping below or above optimum position to pass a heaving line.

NOTE

> The optimum position is the position taken by the MLB which allows the crew the maximum amount of time to pass the heaving line and put the tow line over without getting in a hurry. This position gives the coxswain the ability to see the tow rig attachment point and supervise crew while passing the tow rig.

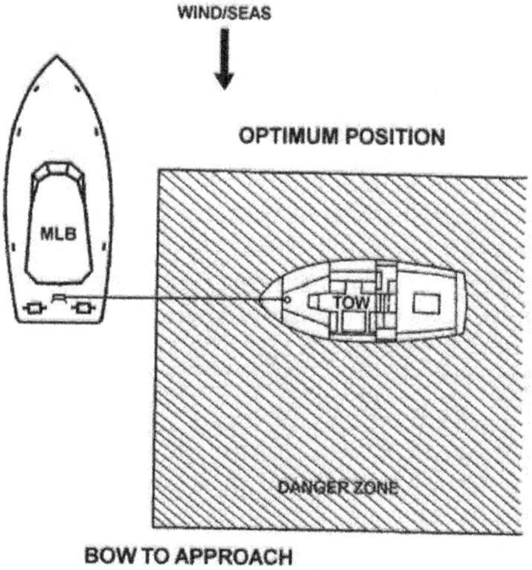

Figure 20-11
Optimum Position

WARNING

> Risk from a running towline is greatly increased in heavy weather conditions. Great care must be taken to reduce surging the towline through the towing bitt as the boats separate and are affected by the seas.

WARNING

> Towing in surf conditions requires specific techniques and should only be attempted when removal of the crew is more dangerous than the potential damages from towing, whether to the disabled vessel or the towing vessel, or injury to personnel.

B.10. Towing Transition

The towing transition occurs once the towline is secured to the disabled vessel and the rescue craft maneuvers to pay out the towline to the desired length to take the vessel into stern tow. In heavy weather it can be one of the most hazardous periods. The coxswain must leave the safety of the maneuvering zone to put the tow behind while the crew is paying out towline.

Some basic rules of transition are:

- Communicate with the crew.
- Begin the transition in optimum position. (see **Figure 20-11**)
- Take the time necessary.
- Get distance between the boat and the disabled vessel.
- Try not to tow the disabled vessel until paying out the desired amount of towline.
- Pay out the towline while in the trough or quartering the swell to reduce surging of the towline.

WARNING

> Constant watch should be kept on the towed vessel and any change in trim or the way the vessel rides should be investigated immediately.

B.11. Towing Astern

In heavy weather conditions, the best course to a safe haven is not always the shortest distance. A course that reduces shock-loading and gives the best ride should be chosen. Information found in *Chapter 17* about combination of forces and shock-load provides direction for towing astern.

WARNING

> Towing during heavy weather conditions is very demanding and must be learned through training and experience. Throttle response (acceleration and deceleration) must be matched to the towed vessel's speed.

B.11.a. Towing in Following Seas

While towing in open waters, it is usually safer to change course to reduce the wave action. This will reduce the yawing and surfing of the towed vessel. Getting both boats in step will also dramatically reduce the forces on the towed vessel. Reducing speed or changing the scope of the towline will also lessen the forces on the towed vessel, which in turn are transferred to the towing vessel.

When approaching the coast, or nearing an inlet or bar, keeping the tow in step as water depth changes becomes very difficult. The coxswain should plan to approach with seas on the quarter to reduce shock-loading. The following techniques should be used to maintain control and reduce the forces affecting tow:

- Constantly adjust towing speed to prevent a tow from surfing on a wave or broaching.
- If a large wave approaches the stern of a tow, increase towing vessel speed to keep ahead of the tow as it is pushed by the swell.
- As a tow reaches the crest of a swell, reduce speed.
- Avoid shock-loading the towline. Keep the towline taut.
- Constantly watch the seas astern and the towed vessel until in sheltered waters or course is changed to reduce influence of the seas.
- Deploy the drogue.

Standing offshore and waiting for better sea conditions may be a safer alternative if controlling the tow or the safety of the tow is in question.

B.11.b. Towing into Seas

Towing into heavy seas creates heavy strain on the towing vessel, the towing equipment, and the towed vessel. One of the most effective techniques to reduce strain is to reduce speed. Lengthening the towline and allowing a greater cantinary will reduce the shock of the seas reducing chafing, stress on the towed vessel, and shockloading.

The placement of the towline on the bow effects the ride of the disabled vessel by pulling it down and often allowing seas to wash over its bow. This can be extremly hazardous to the disabled vessel and affect its stability. Reducing towing speed might help by raising the disabled vessel's bow and reducing the amount of water taken over the bow.

B.11.c. Towing Beam to the Seas

Towing beam to heavy seas will reduce shock-loading and strain on the vessels but it increases the amount both vessels will roll in the seas. Great care should be taken when towing vessels with narrow beams or large liquid storage tanks. Narrow beam boats have less stability and are prone to capsizing. Vessels with large liquid storage tanks such as live wells may experience free surface affect that will greatly effect their stability. Free surface effect is the movement of a liquid (fuel, water) to one side of a partially filled storage tank as the vessel rolls from side to side. This shifting of weight is very dangerous to a vessel's stability.

B.11.d. Shortening Tow

Shortening the tow should be accomplished in open waters where there is plenty of room to manuver. It is most often done prior to approaching an entrance to a harbor or river. By shortening the tow, control of the vessel increases making turning and manuvering in tight quarters easier.

Before beginning, the coxswain takes up a course 10° to 15° off the seas with tow to windward. The wind should set the boat away from ther towline. Speed is reduced until both vessels are stopped. This should set the boat up to put bow into the seas and have the towline off of the quarter. Once the bow is square, then the command is given to break the tow bitt. Keeping the bow square to the seas back and take in the amount of line required. It may be necessary to make more than one attempt to recover the line. Extreme care should be taken to prevent the towline from becoming fouled in the propellers.

Section C. Surf Operations

Introduction

Crews for Coast Guard MLBs and SPCs receive special training for surf operations. All other Coast Guard boats have operating limits that do not allow operations in surf. Safe operation in surf conditions requires excellent boat handling skills, risk assessment, quick reactions, and constant attention from the operator and crew. An understanding of surf behavior and characteristics is also critical. Before entering the surf zone, a coxswain must carefully weigh the capabilities of the boat and crew against the desired outcome.

Because of the substantial differences in handling characteristics found in the various types of lifeboats, much of the information will be of a general nature. Many basic procedures can be applied to all boats but some techniques are type specific. Additional guidance on boat type characteristics can be found in the Specific Boat Type Operator's Handbook, COMDTINST M16114 (series). The reader must also be aware that every area of operation has its own distinctive characteristics and some of the techniques described may not be applicable in these areas. A strong understanding of these characteristics and intimate local knowledge are vital for safe operation.

In this section

This section contains the following information:

Preparations for Surf Operations

C.1. Limitations and Conditions

Maximum operating conditions are set forth in the Specific Boat Type Operator's Handbook, COMDTINST M16114 (series). Maximum training conditions are set forth in the *Boat Operations and Training (BOAT) Manual, Volume I*, COMDTINST M16114.32 (series). These limits have been established based on the capabilities of the boat and a realistic balance of risk versus benefits, and must not be exceeded.

The characteristics of the surf zone in question must also be carefully considered. Conditions such as very short wavelength, extreme reflection, refraction, shallow water or other factors may make an area too hazardous for operations, even though the surf height is within limits.

C.2. Survival Equipment

Any crew operating in the surf must be properly equipped with the following:

- All required hypothermia protective clothing.
- Helmet (helmet straps must be secured and adjusted properly).
- Signaling equipment (normally carried in survival vest).
- Boat crew safety belt worn and adjusted correctly.

Eye protection may be necessary for visibility, particularly for persons wearing glasses, and will also protect against glass shards should a window be broken. Waterproof footwear and gloves should also be worn.

The coxswain is responsible for ensuring that all required equipment is worn, and worn correctly.

NOTE

> All information concerning PPE can be found in the *Rescue and Survival Systems Manual*, COMDTINST M10470.10 (series)

C.3. Crew Procedures

The crew must be placed where they can use the safety belt pad-eyes and be protected from the force of oncoming waves. A large breaker striking the windshield may shatter it, striking the pilothouse may damage it, and striking a crewmember may cause injury.

The motions encountered in the surf can be extreme, and crewmembers must take care to brace properly to reduce body stresses. A shoulder-width stance with the knees flexed will provide the most safety and comfort. Crewmembers should try to anticipate boat motions and work with the motion of the boat, rather than against it.

WARNING

> Do not enter the surf if a vital system is not functioning properly. Surf operations require constant attention from both boat and crew, and any deficiencies can lead to a mishap.

C.4. Pre-Surf Checks

Prior to entering the surf, a complete round must be made of the boat as follows:

Step	Procedure
1	Stow all equipment, particularly large deck items. Unsecured gear becomes dangerous missile hazards in the surf.
2	Make a final check of the engine room and engine parameters, and set watertight integrity.
3	Test run the engines at full power.
4	Check for proper throttle and reduction gear response in both *forward* and *reverse*.

Step	Procedure
5	Check steering for proper effort and full travel, from hard left to hard right and back.
6	Ensure all required survival equipment is donned by all crewmembers.
7	Conduct a proper crew brief.
8	Ensure every crewmember is properly stationed and belted in.

Forces Affecting Boat Handling in Surf

C.5. Aerated Water

Breaking waves cause aerated water in the surf zone. As the wave breaks, it combines with air, creating whitewater on the face of the breaker. As the breaker moves through the surf zone it leaves a trail of pale or white aerated water behind it which takes some time to dissipate. This air-water mix can create changes in a boat's handling, which must be taken into account while maneuvering.

C.5.a. Effect on Propeller

A boat's propeller(s) will not create as much thrust when operating in heavily aerated water. The boat's response may be greatly slowed. This effect can be recognized by:

- Poor acceleration and/or apparently slow throttle response.
- Cavitation and/or excessive engine RPM for a given throttle.
- Poor turning performance, particularly on a twin propeller boat.

C.5.b. Effect on Rudder

A boat's rudder(s) will not direct the propeller force as effectively in aerated water, nor will it have as much steering affect while moving through aerated water. This affect can be recognized by:

- Poor turning response.
- Reduced steering effort, or "light rudders".

C.6. Shallow Water

Operation in very shallow water can be complicated by a serious effect on a boat's maneuverability. This effect, caused by resistance to the bow wave as it contacts the bottom, and drag due to the closeness of the bottom to the boat's hull, propellers, and rudders, can be recognized by:

- Reduced speed over ground.
- Reduced engine RPM for a given throttle position.
- Sluggish response to throttle and steering inputs, leading to poor acceleration and poor turning ability.
- Larger wake then normal.
- Change in trim caused by the bow riding up on its pressure wave, and stern squat caused by propeller suction. This change in trim can lead to grounding of the stern if the water is shallow enough.

NOTE

> The effects of operating in aerated or shallow water are similar to the symptoms of serious engine, reduction gear, or steering problems. Any indication of systems trouble must be investigated as soon as possible once safely clear of the surf zone.

C.7. Changes in Center of Gravity and Trim

Changes in center of gravity or trim can lead to dramatic affects on the stability and handling of a boat in the surf. These changes are caused by either external or internal forces, and can vary widely depending on condition, type of boat, and other factors.

C.8. External Forces

The primary external force for surf operations is the surf itself. A boat's position, speed and heading relative to a wave will dictate the effects on stability and handling. These affects are numerous and will not be covered entirely, but a description of the most significant effects is provided.

C.8.a. Running Stern-To

As an approaching wave reaches the stern, the stern will rise and the center of gravity and the pivot point are shifted forward. As this process develops, the trim of the boat changes and may reach a point where the propellers and rudders are no longer deep enough to be effective. This can cause a severe reduction in maneuverability or complete loss of control as the stern picks up and falls to either side in a broach.

This effect is most common on very steep swells or breakers. It can be greatly amplified if the operator reduces power, which causes an even greater shift in the center of gravity.

C.8.b. Broaching or Running Beam-To

As the approaching wave reaches the boat, it will cause it to heel over and shift the center of gravity to the low side of the boat. This may lead to a reduction in effectiveness of the propeller and rudder on the high side, which will cause reduced maneuverability.

C.8.c. Bow into the Surf

As the approaching wave picks up the bow, the center of gravity and pivot point will shift aft. If the boat does not have enough way on, and the bow is not sufficiently square to the wave, it may cause the bow to fall to one side or the other as the force of the wave pushes it around the new pivot point.

C.9. Internal Forces

There are numerous internal forces that affect the stability and handling of a boat, many of which are permanent aspects of the boat's design. It is the responsibility of the operator to be familiar with the characteristics of the specific boat in question. The following is a description of those factors that are subject to change, or are under the direct control of the operator.

C.9.a. Free Surface Effect

The shifting of fuel or water inside a boat's partially filled tanks can have a great effect on stability and handling.

C.9.b. Unsecured or Impropely Stowed Equipment

Loose equipment can be tossed to one side and affect the boat's stability by placing weight off center. Loose equipment may also result in loss of watertight integrity by breaking windows or damaging watertight fittings.

C.9.c. Changes in Throttle or Helm Input

Generally, a rapid reduction in power will result in a forward shift of the center of gravity, while an increase in power will have the opposite effect. Large steering inputs will cause a boat to heel over, shifting the center of gravity to the low side.

C.10. Knockdown and Rollover Causes

Knockdowns and Rollovers have occurred in a wide variety of situations, and each is somewhat unique. A roll will generally occur when a boat is placed beam-to or broaches in a breaker the same height as the beam of the boat. The operator's actions at this point can determine whether or not the boat is spared. Some knockdowns/rollovers have occurred in lesser conditions and cases of open ocean knockdowns/rollovers have been documented. The steepness of the wave is as dangerous as its height. Any situation that places the center of gravity over the center of buoyancy can result in a knockdown/rollover. A lifeboat operator must be constantly aware of the sea conditions and take action to avoid being caught beam-to or broaching.

NOTE

> The terms "Knockdown" and "Rollover" apply specifically to self-righting boats. A **knockdown** is when a boat has rolled in one direction 90° or greater but does not completely rollover (360°) to right itself. (Example: Boat rolls to port 120° and rights itself by rolling back to starboard.) A **rollover** occurs when a boat rolls in one direction and rights itself by completing a 360° revolution.

C.11. Pitchpole or Bow-On Causes

A pitch pole is when a boat is inverted end-over-end. This can occur when a boat is traveling stern-to a very steep breaker or large wave. As the stern is picked up, the boat begins to surf down the face of the wave. This will cause the center of gravity to shift forward. If the stern rises high enough, the bow will begin to dig deeply into the trough of the wave, and the resistance created will cause the boat to trip over itself, tumbling end-over-end. A reverse pitch pole is also possible if a boat is surfed backwards while bow-to a large breaker.

Pitch poles are rare, but are possible, particularly for a relatively small boat. More often, an impending pitch pole will turn into a broach and knockdown/rollover. The operator must avoid those situations that could lead to a pitch pole since they are violently destructive to the boat and its crew. Broaching and a resulting knockdown/rollover are preferable to pitch poling.

Basic Surf Operations

C.12. Underway Training

The scope of this chapter does not allow a detailed discussion of boat type specific handling characteristics or techniques, but general techniques and procedures can be covered. Because of various local conditions and requirements, there is absolutely no substitute for underway training. Frequent formal training should be conducted by certified personnel in a variety of surf conditions in the local area. Operators should be allowed to acquire the experience necessary to read the waves and get a solid feel for the capabilities and limitations of their boat. Published training limits should not be exceeded for good reason. The majority of surf mishaps have occurred during training rather than actual operations.

WARNING

> Never allow the boat to be caught below a breaking wave. Either allow it to break before it reaches the boat, or get to the top before it falls on the boat. One cubic yard of seawater weighs almost a ton. A 20-foot breaker can drop 1,500 tons of water on the boat, and exert a force of up to 6000 PSI.

C.13. Constant Action

Operations in surf or heavy seas require constant action by the operator. Waves can travel at up to 35 knots, and few boats can outrun a fast wave, or maintain a position on its backside.

Maintaining a 360° watch for approaching waves is critical. The surf zone is a constantly changing, dynamic environment, and the fifth or sixth wave back is often as important as the immediate one. Crewmembers must be alert and familiar with surf characteristics, and a constant high level of communication is vital. The operator must concentrate on positioning the boat to avoid being caught under a breaker, or taking it at the wrong angle. Maneuvering to avoid the breaks is preferable, but if one cannot be avoided, it should be taken bow-on, if possible.

C.14. Techniques

The following description of techniques has been organized to follow the sequences of an actual operational situation, such as entering a beach surf zone to recover persons in the water, or crossing a bar or inlet.

C.15. Entering a Beach Zone or Inbound Transit of Bar/Inlet with Surf on Stern

General procedures for entering a beach zone or transiting inbound a bar or inlet with surf on stern are outlined as follows:

C.15.a. Preparations

Step	Procedure
1	Advise Station and backup resources of intentions.
2	Acquire bar/inlet or surf zone conditions from available sources, such as beach/tower personnel or other vessels in the vicinity. It is very difficult to evaluate actual conditions from seaward.
3	Brief crew and assign duties.
4	Conduct a full pre-surf check of engine room and engine parameters. Check the entire boat for stowage. Set watertight integrity, and check boat crew protective clothing.
5	Test engine and steering system controls.
6	Identify any useful natural ranges and landmarks.
7	Identify safe operating areas and hazards. Evaluate surf conditions and possible safer routes, such as bar/reef openings or rip channels.
8	Stand off and observe wave trains. Attempt to identify any patterns such as lulls or series that may be present.

WARNING

> Reducing speed after the wave has already picked up the boat will likely result in a loss of control and/or broach. Speed must be reduced before the wave arrives.

C.15.b. Execution

It is preferable to transit the surf during any lull period that may exist. The operator should wait until the last big wave in a series has passed and proceed in closely behind it, at maximum safe speed. This reduces the relative speed at which the waves overtake, gives the operator more time to react and gets you through the zone as quickly as possible. It may also provide the best maneuverability for some boats. The operator should attempt to work through the surf zone by driving through windows and wave saddles, thus avoiding the majority of the breakers. Some boats may be fast enough to avoid breakers by maintaining position on the backside of a swell while others will be overtaken by approaching waves.

If operating in an area of limiting maneuverability, such as a narrow inlet or bar, the operator may have to rely strictly on timing the waves and make the transit during lull periods.

To deal with an overtaking breaker or peaking swell, there are a number of techniques, which vary in success and safety based on conditions and type of boat. An operator must understand the effectiveness and safety of a technique for the specific boat, which is gained from training experience.

These techniques are listed in descending order of preference and safety:

- Maneuver left or right (lateral) to avoid the breaker completely, by using windows and saddles.
- Come about in sufficient time to meet the breaker bow-on.
- Reduce speed before a steep, peaking (not breaking) swell reaches the boat, allowing the swell to pass and break ahead, and then immediately increase speed to follow it in.
- As a wave approaches, begin backing square into it. Gain sternway and climb the wave before it breaks. Never allow the boat to be caught under a breaker. If it is necessary to back through the whitewater of a breaker, gain sternway before the whitewater reaches the propellers and rudders. Move smoothly into the wave as it lifts the stem, using only enough power to maintain sternway. The momentum of the boat will break it through the wave. Once the stern breaks through, ease off the throttles and prepare to resume the course ahead.
- If the boat is overtaken by the white water of a breaker, the last resort is to try to get off the wave by applying full throttle, and steering for the "low side" of the wave, hopefully coming out the backside. Do not attempt to ride it out by maintaining course. Something must be done. Never forget to drive the boat.
- A final option may be to back into the surf zone or across the bar, keeping the bow into the seas. This will be very difficult and time consuming. Excellent backing skills are mandatory. Strong opposing currents in the area may make backing impractical. Also, great care must be taken in shallow water, as the propellers and rudders will hit first if the boat strikes bottom.

NOTE

> If there is no discernable lull, it is prudent to remain at sea while waiting for bar conditions to improve (i.e., flood current).

C.16. Transiting with Surf on Beam (Lateral Transit of Surf Zone)

General procedures for transiting with surf on a beam are outlined as follows.

C.16.a. Preparations

Step	Procedure
1	Brief crew and assign duties.
2	Identify safe operating areas and hazards. Evaluate surf conditions and possible safer routes, such as alongshore channels where the surf may be smaller.
3	Advise Station and backup resources.

WARNING Do not get surprised by a breaker on the beam while watching ahead, as there is a good chance of a knockdown/rollover if hit on the beam at slow speed.

WARNING This maneuver is only safe in small conditions and must not be attempted if the operator has any doubts. Wave avoidance is still the preferred technique.

C.16.b. Execution

It is preferable to make a beam transit during a lull, when the seas may be smaller. Wait for the last big series of waves to pass and commence the run. In the absence of lulls, great care and patience must be exercised, because the boat is very vulnerable with the nearly constant beam surf. The operator should use maximum comfortable speed to minimize exposure to beam seas. Speed may be reduced to allow waves to pass ahead of the boat, or increased to avoid a breaker. Good timing, and ability to read several waves back are critical. Any significant waves, which cannot be avoided, must be taken bow-on.

There are several techniques to deal with breaking seas on the beam. The suitability of a technique is dependent on the boat type and present conditions. The operator must have an understanding of the boat's capabilities, as some maneuvers may not be safe or effective in all cases. The following techniques are listed in descending order of preference and safety:

- When it is apparent that the boat is about to be overtaken by a breaker, retain or increase speed and turn to meet it square with the bow. Once square to the wave, the helm must then be returned to amidships and throttles decreased to avoid launching through the crest. Station keep if necessary, and prepare to return to original course.
- If a breaker is approaching from ahead of the boat, decrease speed to allow it to pass ahead. Time the maneuver to reach the back shoulder of the wave just as it passes in front. This timing will allow quickly getting behind the wave and continuing the transit, and hopefully avoid the next wave altogether. The crew must be alert for other waves building off the beam.
- If a wave is some distance off the beam, it may be possible to outrun it by increasing speed. If there is any chance of not beating the wave, turn to meet it or run away from it if space and time permit.
- In some instances, there may be time and room available to find a window by running away from a breaker by placing it on the stern or quarter. This carries all the risks associated with running stern-to, and will also set the boat off the original track line or range, as well as being time consuming. It is not the most efficient means of transiting, but may be a valuable safety maneuver depending on the circumstances.
- When transiting very small surf relative to the size of the boat, it may be possible to maintain or slightly reduce speed and simply turn towards a small breaker at about a 45° angle, resuming course behind it after crossing the crest.

C.17. Station Keeping (Bow into Surf)

Station keeping is maintaining a given position in the surf. Station keeping is necessary to hold position while waiting for a window or lull, or holding position prior to and during recovery of a PIW. Environmental factors such as the surf, wind or currents can make station keeping difficult. Therefore, good backing skills and proper application of power are essential. The following are guidelines for station keeping:

- Use only enough power to maintain position and counteract the force of the oncoming wave. On smaller waves, keeping the bow square with neutral throttles may be all that is needed, while larger waves may require a great deal of power to counteract.
- Using too much power will set the boat out of position and/or launch the boat. Too little power will cause the boat to be set backwards, or broach the boat.
- Keep the bow as square to the seas as possible.
- If the boat is being set towards the seas by current or wind, it may be necessary to back down frequently to hold position, only applying forward power to meet oncoming waves. Wait until a wave crest passes and back down once on the backside. Do not back down on the face of a wave.
- By adjusting power, it may be possible to safely allow a wave to set the boat back to regain position. This technique requires practice, and the operator must maintain control of the maneuver at all times.
- It is possible to move laterally while station keeping by allowing the bow to fall slightly to the desired side and then using the throttles and helm to straighten out as the wave pushes the bow.

For example, to crab sideways to port, allow the bow to fall slightly to port and as the wave pushes the bow, apply power and steer to starboard, finishing the maneuver with the bow once again square to the seas. This maneuver must not be attempted on large waves, and it is important not to allow the bow to falloff so far that the safety and control of the boat are compromised.

WARNING

Do not allow a wave to break over the bow while transiting outbound. If it appears that this may happen, either reach the top before it breaks, or slow down/stop letting it break in front of the boat and then regaining headway in time to meet the whitewater.

C.18. Outbound Transit of Bar/Inlet or Surf Zone (Bow into Surf)

An outbound transit of the surf may be necessary in crossing a bar/inlet or departing a surf zone. The operator should practice wave avoidance by picking a course through the windows and saddles, if available, minimizing risk to the boat and crew. The transit should be made at maximum comfortable speed adjusting to avoid launching over the waves or avoiding them entirely.

The following guidelines apply to an outbound transit:

- Choose a course through windows as much as possible, zigzagging as necessary to avoid breakers. Stay close to the shoulders of the waves to take advantage of any window that may open up behind the wave as it passes.
- If a breaker cannot be avoided, try to go through the wave at the saddle, where it may not be breaking yet, or the force may be less. If both ends of the wave are breaking towards the saddle, the boat may be caught in a closeout. Get through the saddle before

it closes, or slow down to let it closeout well in front of the boat.

- Any breakers that cannot be avoided should be taken bow-on. Slow down and allow momentum to carry the boat through. Do not meet breakers at high speed or the boat may plow into the face, or launch off the back, risking injuries or boat damage.

C.19. Emergency Procedures: Knockdown, Rollover or Involuntary Beaching

A knockdown, rollover or beaching is never routine, but always possible. These unpleasant events must be considered and planned for. Training and experience will give a crewmember the edge, but it can still happen simply because of the severe environment he or she is operating in. The following risk management practices should be followed:

- All crewmembers must be properly outfitted in PPE.
- All crewmembers should be familiar with the causes of a knockdown, rollover or pitch poling, as well as how to recognize an impending event, and what to expect.
- All crewmembers should be well-trained in the procedures to be followed for a knockdown, rollover and involuntary beaching. Crewmembers must be familiar with the procedures for emergency anchoring and drogue deployment as well as the location of necessary equipment. Always brief the crew prior to entering a surf zone.
- Crewmembers should be prepared to take control of the boat should the operator be injured, incapacitated or lost overboard. The crewmember should also have the skills to maneuver the vessel to recover the man overboard.
- A backup surf capable resource or aircraft should be standing by whenever possible, positioned where it can observe the boat working in the surf.
- Backup communications (handheld VHF) should be aboard the boat in case the antennas are lost, or the main radio is damaged.

The risks versus the potential benefits should always be assessed. A sense of urgency must not cloud judgment or cause the loss of situational awareness.

WARNING Do not unfasten safety belt or consider swimming to the surface. It is likely the propellers will still be turning, and the boat is designed to right itself in a few seconds.

C.19.a. Procedures for a Knockdown / Rollover

The following procedures apply in a knockdown/rollover:

Step	Procedure
1	A knockdown/rollover is usually the result of a severe broach. If the lower gunwale is underwater, be prepared to roll. Experience and familiarity with the boat's normal motions may warn of an abnormal situation.
2	If time allows, advise the crew to hold their breath. Hold on firmly to any stable objects. While upside down, the crew will be completely disoriented and unable to see. It is possible to hear the engines.
3	Immediately upon re-righting, assess the situation. The boat is still in the surf and crew must take quick action to meet the next wave correctly or the boat may roll again.
4	Check the crew to ensure that no one is lost overboard or seriously injured.
5	Check the deck and surrounding water for lines or equipment that could disable the boat.
6	If the engines are still running, move to safe water.
7	Once in safe water, the engineer should go below to check for damage. Secure non-vital electrical circuits. The engine room may be coated with water and oil, presenting a fire hazard. If there is no fire, the engineer should dewater the engine room, and check the oil in the engine(s).
8	Check the condition of the boat. Fuel may have spilled from the exterior vents, covering the weather deck and crew. The superstructure may be damaged, windows may be broken, and large fixtures such as the mast, anchor, pump can, towline reel, or helm chairs may be damaged or missing. Installed electronics will likely be inoperative.

C.19.b. Continuing or Returning

After damage and injuries have been assessed, the coxswain must determine whether to continue with the mission or return to the unit. The following factors should be considered:

- Condition of crewmembers.
- Overall material and operating condition of engines and boat structure.
- Condition of electronics, particularly communications.
- Urgency of mission, and availability of backup resources.

Upon returning to the Station, post-knockdown/rollover procedures must be taken in accordance with the Specific Boat Type Operator's Handbook.

WARNING

> Do not expose crewmembers to the likelihood of serious injury or loss overboard by sending them to the bow in heavy surf. It may be safer to sustain a roll while waiting for a lull. This is a judgment call.

C.19.c. Procedures for Involuntary Beaching

If the boat is disabled in or near the surf, it will be driven into the shore. The Station or backup resource must be notified immediately. The chances of a knockdown/rollover or crew injuries can be reduced by taking the following actions:

Step	Procedure
1	Try to set the anchor with as much scope as possible. If more line is needed, bend the towline to the anchor line.
2	If unable to anchor, attempt to set a drogue astern. This will minimize the chance of rolling, and hopefully cause the boat to beach bow first.
3	Stay with the boat and ride it out. The boat may be knocked down and/or rollover several times on your trip to the beach.
4	Once the boat is beached, stay put. The waves will push the boat farther up the beach. Do not be in a hurry to leave the boat.

C.20. Emergency Towing a Disabled Boat from the Surf

Handling towing evolutions in heavy surf is extremely hazardous. The danger involved limits this response to cases involving potential loss of life (see A.2.b. of this chapter). Abandoned boats do not warrant the risk involved to Coast Guard boat crews or boats. Extreme caution must be taken when towing in surf conditions.

WARNING

Towing in surf conditions is an emergency procedure and extremely hazardous. Injury to crewmembers working the deck as well as to personnel on the disabled boat is possible.

C.20.a. Procedures for Emergency Towing in the Surf

Perform the following procedures for emergency towing in the surf:

Step	Procedure
1	Determine if saving the boat is possible. If not, rescue the people onboard. The decision must be made rapidly during your approach.
2	If the boat can be towed, approach from up wind, maneuvering to the inshore side for passing the towline. If the boat's proximity to the beach prevents approaching from the inshore side, it may be necessary to turn the boat and back toward the other boat, but remain ready to meet approaching breakers.
3	Once within working distance of the disabled boat, maintain a bow into the surf position and position crew on the working deck.
4	Pass the heaving line. Extreme care must be taken to maintain control of the lines.
5	Once the disabled boat receives the heaving line, pass the towline. The crewmember tending the towline should be positioned immediately forward of the towing bitt to payout the line.
6	Once the towline is secured to the disabled boat, take a working turn on the tow bitt. More than one figure eight may be needed to control the tow. The towline will surge through the towing bitt as the disabled boat meets breakers. Allow the line to run off the towing reel if needed.
7	With the boat in tow, proceed seaward. Watch the tow at all times but also be aware of the surroundings. If the tow is a small boat, have the passengers move aft and stay low to keep the bow light. If the boat is larger, put it two to three breakers astern. Increase power as the tow meets breakers and decrease power when the tow crests the breakers. Allow plenty of scope in the towline.
8	Once clear of the surf zone, shorten tow and prepare to assist any injured personnel. Dewater the disabled boat if necessary. Make certain the boat is seaworthy for towing.

Section D. Heavy Weather PIW Recovery

Introduction

Recovering a person from the water in heavy weather requires special precautions beyond the routine described in *Chapter 16, Person-In-The-Water Recovery.* It may be considered a given that a MOB/PIW evolution will bring the coxswain and crew to a higher sense of awareness. However, due to the increased risk of operating a boat in heavy weather conditions, special considerations must be given to the level of experience and skill of the boat crew and the capabilities of the boat. It is up to the coxswain, in most cases, to act as he or she sees fit.

NOTE

> Do not attempt a rescue in conditions that exceed the operational limitations of the boat and/or experience/skill level of the crew.

D.1. Man Overboard

The general MOB or PIW procedure is put in effect as soon as the alarm is sounded, but the nature of heavy weather adds complications.

Recovery of a PIW, as in a capsized pleasure craft, is much the same as for a MOB. However, the coxswain may be required to enter the surf/swell by going lateral to it, backing in to a beach, or running stern to the swell using techniques discussed in *Section B* or *Section C* of this chapter. The coxswain will position the boat down swell of the PIW and make the approach as discussed in this section.

D.1.a. Down Swell Run

If needed, the turn to run down swell and approach will be planned differently in heavy weather. The coxswain may not be able to turn the boat immediately after the alarm is given. Doing so may expose the bow of the boat to the swell enough that regaining control and getting the bow back into the seas might be very difficult.

The coxswain will push ahead a safe distance from the man overboard and station keep until the opportunity to turn presents itself. The turn is not made until the coxswain can do so without exposing the beam of the boat to the breaks or excessive swells. This is avoided by timing the turn to correspond with the lull in the breaks. Doing so allows the coxswain to take advantage of any window that may develop. Once the window has been identified, the coxswain turns, either port or starboard, using the techniques described in the *Section B* or *Section C* of this chapter. If the water depth allows, the coxswain continues down swell past the MOB. When passing at a safe distance, an assessment is made as to the condition of the MOB (i.e., conscious and face-up, unconscious and face-down); this will help decide how best to prepare for the final approach.

WARNING — Do not allow any crew to go forward at any time during this evolution. It puts them in great danger and decreases the crew's ability to communicate.

D.1.b. Approach

Once the run down swell is completed, the boat must be turned to make the approach. The turn should be made so as to simultaneously put the bow into the surf/swell and have the PIW directly in front of the boat, keeping in mind the turning radius of the boat and the effect strong winds may have, make adjustments as necessary. This may require some lateral movement down swell of the PIW. The pointer must be able to communicate with the coxswain at all times. Positioning the pointer by the open bridge is recommended.

Once down swell, the coxswain must turn the boat quickly and avoid getting caught broadside to the surf/swell. A break taken on the beam may roll the boat.

After completing the turn into the swell or breaks, forward momentum is stopped and, if practical, station keep is commenced by using references on the beach, jetty, and/or adjacent structures. Doing this will give you time to consider the following:

- Boat position in relationship to the PIW.
- Set and drift of both the boat and the MOB.
- Wind direction.
- Formation of a window/lull near the PIW.
- Reestablishing crew responsibilities (if needed).
- Sending a crewmember to the recovery area.

NOTE — On a CG standard boat, the crew must stay out of the recovery area until the turn is completed, the bow is back into the swell, and the coxswain gives the command.

WARNING — A breaking wave or steep swell can surf a PIW into the side of the boat or move them astern of it!

D.1.c. The Recovery

When making the final approach, the coxswain must adjust the speed to avoid launching the boat off the back side of a wave. He/she should use the bow bitt or other stationary object on the bow as a sight and aim the boat at the PIW. Speed should be reduced to bare steerageway while nearing the PIW. This approach is made so that the PIW is not in danger of being struck by the boat. Timing is essential! If the coxswain is able, he/she should wait for a lull to make the approach.

The crew must keep the coxswain informed of the PIW's relationship to the boat at all times. This can be done by using reference points on the boat and calling distance off the hull.

D.1.c.1. Recovery of a Conscious Person from the Water

Ideally, the boat should be stopped with the PIW at arm's length from the recovery area. This allows the crewmember to simply reach out and pull in the person for recovery. In the event the person is too far away to reach by hand, he or she may be able to swim or be tossed a rescue heaving line and pulled to the recovery area. All options must be considered, keeping in mind that a person suffering from hypothermia and/or exhaustion may not be able to assist when being pulled from the water. Also, using a rescue heaving line in the surf is very risky. The crewmember tending the line must remain alert to keep the line under control at all times, and advise the coxswain when the line is in the water.

CH-1

WARNING

> Backing down must be done before the PIW gets to the recovery area so that the boat has no way on during recovery.

D.1.c.2. Recovery of an Unconscious PIW

Recovery of an unconscious PIW from the surf presents an even greater challenge. Because the PIW is unable to swim or hold on to the rescue heaving line, the coxswain must maneuver the boat so that the PIW is taken alongside. Again, crew communication is critical. The coxswain must steer the boat straight for the PIW and as he or she begins to disappear under the bow flair, turn slightly to port or starboard (depending on which side is most best for recovery), windward of the PIW if possible. At this point, the coxswain will lose sight of the PIW under the bow flair. It is now the pointer's responsibility to inform the coxswain of the location of the PIW, the distance off the hull, and how far the PIW is passing down the hull. When the pointer reports the PIW is approaching the recovery area, the coxswain should begin glancing down at the water, watching for the PIW to appear. When the PIW is in sight, the coxswain may need to make a final speed adjustment. Foam or bubbles passing down the hull can help determine the boat's speed. Having all way-off when the PIW is approaching the recovery area is important for two reasons:

- It is very difficult to maintain a handhold on a person when the boat is still moving ahead.
- Having to back down with the person near the recovery area is dangerous, and the discharge from backing down may push the person farther away from the boat. Again, slow down well before the person is at the recovery area.

To do this, the coxswain may back down on both engines or on the engine opposite the PIW. Backing down on the opposite engine will kick the recovery area toward the PIW. However, the coxswain must not allow the bow to fall off the swell. The use of the boat hook must not be ruled out if the PIW is too far away to retrieve by hand. It is better to use a boat hook and recover on the first approach than to back down or run stern to the surf/swell to make another approach. There may only be one chance to make the rescue – it has to be good!

D.2. Use of a Surface Swimmer

Using a surface swimmer in heavy weather or surf is extremely dangerous and should only be used as a last resort. Having a member of the crew enter the water presents different problems:

- Reducing crew size of an already minimal crew makes it difficult to retrieve the PIW.
- The likelihood of the tending line becoming fouled in the propeller is greatly increased.

D.3. Multiple PIWs

For multiple PIWs, the question becomes "which PIW is recovered first?" This is a hard question to answer and requires the coxswain's best judgment. Once on scene, an accurate assessment will dictate the coxswain's response. Consideration should be given to the following:

- Are one or more PIWs injured?
- Are PIWs wearing PFDs?
- How close are the PIWs to the beach or jetty?
- How old are the PIWs and what is their physical condition?

Using the above criteria may aid the coxswain in making this difficult decision.

Appendix A.
Glossary

Introduction

This appendix contains a list of terms that may be useful when reading this Manual.

In this appendix

This appendix contains the following information:

This page intentionally left blank.

TERM	DEFINITION
Abaft	Behind, toward the stern of a vessel.
Abeam	To one side of a vessel, at a right angle to the fore-and-aft centerline.
Advection Fog	A type of fog that occurs when warm air moves over colder land or water surfaces; the greater the difference between the air temperature and the underlying surface temperature, the denser the fog, which is hardly affected by sunlight.
Aft	Near or toward the stern.
Aground	With the keel or bottom of a vessel fast on the sea floor.
Aids to Navigation (AtoN)	Lighthouses, lights, buoys, sound signals, racon, radiobeacons, electronic aids, and other markers on land or sea established to help navigators determine position or safe course, dangers, or obstructions to navigation.
Allision	The running of one vessel into or against another, as distinguished from a collision, i.e., the running of two vessel against each other. This distinction is not very carefully observed. Also used to refer to a vessel striking a fixed structure (i.e. bridge, pier, moored vessel, etc.) per marine inspection.
Amidships	In or towards center portion of the vessel, sometimes referred to as "midships."
Anchorage Area	A customary, suitable, and generally designated area in which vessels may anchor.
Astern	The direction toward or beyond the back of a vessel.
Athwartships	Crosswise of a ship; bisecting the fore-and-aft line above the keel.
Attitude	A vessel's position relative to the wind, sea, hazard, or other vessel.
Back and Fill	A technique where one relies on the tendency of a vessel to back to port, then uses the rudder to direct thrust when powering ahead. Also known as *casting*.
Backing Plate	A reinforcement plate below a deck or behind a bulkhead used to back a deck fitting. It is usually made of wood or steel and distributes stress on a fitting over a larger area and prevents bolts from pulling through the deck.
Backing Spring (Line)	Line used when towing a vessel alongside which may be secured near the towing vessel's stern and the towed vessel's bow.
Ballast	Weight placed in a vessel to maintain its stability.
Beacon	Any fixed aid to navigation placed ashore or on marine sites. If lighted, they are referred to as minor lights.
Beam	The widest point of a vessel on a line perpendicular to the keel, the fore-and-aft centerline.

TERM	DEFINITION
Beaufort Wind Scale	A scale whose numbers define a particular state of wind and wave, allowing mariners to estimate the wind speed based on the sea state.
Bell Buoy	A floating aid to navigation with a short tower in which there are several clappers that strike the bell as it rocks with the motion of the sea.
Below	The space or spaces that are underneath a vessel's main deck.
Bilge	The lowest point of a vessel's inner hull, which is underwater.
Bilge Alarm System	An alarm for warning of excessive water or liquid in the bilge.
Bilge Drain	A drain used for removing water or liquid from the bilge.
Bilge Pump	A pump used to clear water or liquid from the bilge.
Bitt	A strong post of wood or metal, on deck in the bow or stern, to which anchor, mooring, or towing lines may be fastened.
Boat hook	A hook on a pole with a pushing surface at the end used to retrieve or pick up objects, or for pushing objects away.
Bollard	A single strong vertical fitting, usually iron, on a deck, pier, or wharf, to which mooring lines or a hawser may be fastened.
Bolo Line	A nylon line with a padded or wrapped weight thrown from vessel to vessel or between vessels and shore which is used for passing a larger line (see heaving line).
Boom	A spar used to spread a fore-and-aft sail, especially its foot; without a sail and with a suitable lift attached; it can be used as a lifting device or derrick.
Boundary Layer	A layer of water carried along the hull of a vessel varying in thickness from the bow to stern.
Bow	The forward end of the vessel.
Bow Line	A line secured from the bow of a vessel. In an alongside towing operation, the bow line is secured on both the towing and the towed vessel at or near the bow and may act as breast line of each.
Bowline	A classic knot that forms an eye that will not slip, come loose or jam, and is not difficult to untie after it has been under strain.
Breakaway	Command given by coxswain, conning officer, or pilot when a helicopter hoisting operation, towing, or alongside evolution has to be terminated due to unsafe conditions.
Breaker	A wave cresting with the top breaking down over its face.

TERM	DEFINITION
Breaker Line	The outer limit of the surf.
Breaking Strength (BS)	The force needed to break or part a line. BS is measured in pounds. More specifically, it is the number of pounds of stress a line can hold before it parts.
Breast Line	Mooring or dock line extended laterally from a vessel to a pier or float as distinguished from a spring line.
Bridge Markings	Lights or signs which provide mariners information for safely passing a bridge over a waterway.
Bridle	A device attached to a vessel or aircraft (in the water) in order for another vessel to tow it. Its use can reduce the effects of yawing, stress on towed vessel fittings, and generally gives the towing vessel greater control over the tow.
Broach	To be thrown broadside to surf or heavy sea.
Broadcast Notice to Mariners	A radio broadcast that provides important marine information.
Broadside to the Sea	A vessel being positioned so that the sea is hitting either the starboard or port side of the vessel.
Bulkhead	Walls or partitions within a vessel with structural functions such as providing strength or watertightness. Light partitions are sometimes called partition bulkheads.
Bullnose	A round opening at the forwardmost part of the bow through which a towline, mooring line or anchor line passes.
Buoy	A floating aid to navigation anchored to the bottom that conveys information to navigators by their shape or color, by their visible or audible signals, or both.
Buoy Moorings	Chain or synthetic rope used to attach buoys to sinkers.
Buoy Station	Established (charted) location of a buoy.
Buoyage	A system of buoys with assigned shapes, colors, or numbers.
Buoyancy	The tendency or capacity of a vessel to remain afloat.
Can Buoy (Cylindrical)	A cylindrical buoy, generally green, marking the left side of a channel or safe passage as seen entering from seaward, or from the north or east proceeding south or west.
Capsize	To turn a vessel bottom side up.
Cardinal Marks	Indicate the location of navigable waters by reference to the cardinal directions (N,E,S,W) on a compass.
Casting	See back and fill.

TERM	DEFINITION
Catenary	The sag in a length of chain, cable, or line because of its own weight and which provides a spring or elastic effect in towing, anchoring, or securing to a buoy.
Cavitation	The formation of a partial vacuum around the propeller blades of a vessel.
Center of Gravity	Point in a ship where the sum of all moments of weight is zero. With the ship at rest, the center of gravity and the center of buoyancy are always in a direct vertical line. For surface ships, center of buoyancy is usually below center of gravity, and the ship is prevented from capsizing by the additional displacement on the low side during a roll. Thus the point at which the deck edge enters the water is critical because from here onward, increased roll will not produce corresponding increased righting force.
Center Point Method (Circle)	In SAR, one of several methods to define a search area, in which the latitude and longitude of datum are given along with a radius around datum.
Center Point Method (Rectangle)	In SAR, one of several methods to define a search area, in which the latitude and longitude of datum are given with the direction of major (longer) axis plus the length and width of the area.
Center Point Method (Landmark)	In SAR, one of several methods to define a search area, in which the datum may be designated by a bearing and distance from some geographic landmark.
Centerline	An imaginary line down the middle of a vessel from bow to stern.
Chafe	To wear away by friction.
Chafing Gear	Material used to prevent chafing or wearing of a line or other surface.
Characteristic	The audible, visual, or electronic signal displayed by an aid to navigation to assist in the identification of an aid to navigation. Characteristic refers to lights, sound signals, racons, radiobeacons, and daybeacons.
Chart	A printed or electronic geographic representation generally showing depths of water, aids to navigation, dangers, and adjacent land features useful to mariners (See *Nautical Chart*).
Chine	The intersection of the bottom and the sides of a flat bottom or "V" hull boat.
Chock	A metal fitting through which hawsers and lines are passed. May be open or closed. Blocks used to prevent aircraft or vehicles from rolling. Also, blocks used to support a boat under repair.
Chop	Short steep waves usually generated by local winds and/or tidal changes. Change of operational control. The date and time at which the responsibility for operational control of a ship or convoy passes from one operational control authority to another.
Cleat	An anvil-shaped deck fitting for securing or belaying lines. Wedge cleats are used in yachting to hold sheets ready for instant release.

TERM	DEFINITION
Closeout	The result of a wave breaking, from the ends toward the middle, or two waves breaking toward each other; should be avoided because they can create more energy than a single break.
Closing	The act of one vessel reducing the distance between itself and another vessel, structure, or object.
Clove Hitch	A hitch often used for fastening a line to a spar, ring, stanchion, or other larger lines or cables.
Coast Guard-Approved	Label denoting compliance with Coast Guard specifications and regulations relating to performance, construction, and materials.
Coastal	At or near a coast.
Coil Down	To lay out a line in a circle with coils loosely on top on one anther. (see fake down, flemish down)
Comber	A wave at the point of breaking.
Combination Buoy	A buoy that combines the characteristics of both sound and light.
Combustion	Rapid oxidation of combustible material accompanied by a release of energy in the form of heat and light.
Compartment	A room or space onboard ship. Usually lettered and numbered according to location and use.
Compass	An instrument for determining direction: magnetic, depending on the earth's magnetic field for its force; gyroscopic, depending on the tendency of a free-spinning body to seek to align its axis with that of the earth.
Conventional Direction of Buoyage	The general direction taken by the mariner when approaching a harbor, river, estuary, or other waterway from seaward; or proceeding upstream or in the direction of the main stream of flood tide, or in the direction indicated in appropriate nautical documents (normally, following a clockwise direction around land masses).
Corner Method	In SAR, one of several methods to define a search area. Latitude and longitude or geographic features of corners of search area are identified.
Cospas-Sarsat System	A satellite system designed to detect distress beacons transmitting on the frequencies 121.5 MHz and 406 MHz.
Course (C)	The horizontal direction in which a vessel is steered or intended to be steered, expressed as angular distance from north, usually from 000° at north, clockwise through 360°.
Coverage Factor (C)	In SAR, a measure of search effectiveness; ration of sweep width to track spacing: C = W/S.

TERM	DEFINITION
Coxswain	Person in charge of a boat, pronounced "COX-un."
Crab	To move sidewise through the water.
Craft	Any air or sea-surface vehicle, or submersible of any kind or size.
Crash Stop	Immediately going from full speed ahead to full reverse throttle; this is an emergency maneuver. It is extremely harsh on the drive train and may cause engine stall.
Crest	The top of a wave, breaker, or swell.
Crucifix	Type of deck or boat fitting that resembles a cross, used to secure a line to (e.g., sampson post).
Current (Ocean)	Continuous movement of the sea, sometimes caused by prevailing winds, as well as large constant forces, such as the rotation of the earth, or the apparent rotation of the sun and moon. Example is the Gulf Stream.
Damage Control	Measures necessary to preserve and reestablish shipboard watertight integrity, stability, and maneuverability; to control list and trim; to make rapid repairs of material. Inspection of damage caused by fire, flooding, and/or collision and the subsequent control and corrective measures.
Datum	In SAR, refers to the probable location of a distressed vessel, downed aircraft, or PIW, which is corrected for drift at any moment in time. Depending on the information received this may be represented as a point, a line or an area.
Day Mark	The daytime identifier of an aid to navigation (see *Daybeacon, Dayboard*).
Daybeacon	An unlighted fixed structure which is equipped with a highly visible dayboard for daytime identification.
Dayboard	The daytime identifier of an aid to navigation presenting one of several standard shapes (square, triangle, rectangle) and colors (red, green, white, orange, yellow or black).
Dewatering	The act of removing water from inside compartments of a vessel. Water located high in the vessel, or sufficiently off-center should be removed first to restore the vessel's stability. Used to prevent sinking, capsizing or listing.
Dead-in-the-Water (DIW)	A vessel that has no means to maneuver, normally due to engine casualty. A vessel that is adrift or no means of propulsion.
Dead Reckoning (DR)	Determination of estimated position of a craft by adding to the last fix the craft's course and speed for a given time.
Deadman's Stick	See *static discharge wand.*
Deck	The horizontal plating or planking on a ship or boat.

TERM	DEFINITION
Deck Fitting	Permanently installed fittings on the deck of a vessel which can be attached to machinery or equipment.
Deck Scuttle	A small, quick-closing access hole located on the deck of a vessel.
Deep "V" Hull	A hull design generally used for faster seagoing types of boats.
Desmoking	The natural or forced ventilation of a vessel's compartment to remove smoke.
Destroyer Turn	Used during person overboard situations. The boat is turned in the direction the individual fell overboard, to get the stern of the boat (and the screws) away from the person overboard.
Digital Selective Calling (DSC)	A technique using digital codes which enables a radio station to establish contact with, and transfer information to, another Station or group of Stations.
Direction of Current	The direction toward which a current is flowing. See *set*.
Direction of Waves, Swells, or Seas	The direction to which the waves, swells, or seas are moving.
Direction of Wind	The direction from which the wind is blowing.
Displacement Hull	A hull that achieves its buoyancy or flotation capability by displacing a volume of water equal in weight to the hull and its load.
Distress	As used in the Coast Guard, when a craft or person is threatened by grave or imminent danger requiring immediate assistance.
Ditching	The forced landing of an aircraft on water.
Dolphin	A structure consisting of a number of piles driven into the seabed or river bed in a circular pattern and drawn together with wire rope. May be used as part of a dock structure or a minor aid to navigation. Commonly used when a single pile would not provide the desired strength.
Downwash	The resulting force of the movement of air in a downward motion from a helicopter in flight or hovering.
Draft	The point on a vessel's underwater body, measured from the waterline, that reaches the greatest depth.
Drag	Forces opposing direction of motion due to friction, profile and other components. The amount that a ship is down by the stern.
Drift	The rate/speed at which a vessel moves due to the effects of wind, wave, current, or the accumulative effects of each. Usually expressed in knots.

TERM	DEFINITION
Drogue	A device used to slow rate of movement. Commonly rigged off the stern of a boat while under tow to reduce the effects of following seas. May prevent yawing and/or broaching. (see *sea anchor*)
Drop Pump	A portable, gasoline-powered pump that is transported in a water tight container. Used for de-watering a vessel.
Dry Suit	A coverall type garment made of waterproof material having a rubber or neoprene seal around the neck and wrist cuffs. Allows the wearer to work in the water or in a marine environment without getting wet.
Dynamic Forces	Forces associated with the changing environment e.g., the wind, current, weather.
Ebb	A tidal effect caused by the loss of water in a river, bay, or estuary resulting in discharge currents immediately followed by a low tidal condition.
Ebb Current	The horizontal motion away from the land caused by a falling tide.
Ebb Direction	The approximate true direction toward which the ebbing current flows; generally close to the reciprocal of the flood direction.
Eddy	A circular current.
Eductor	A siphon device that contains no moving parts. It moves water from one place to another by forcing the pumped liquid into a rapidly flowing stream. This is known as the venturi effect. Dewatering equipment used to remove fire fighting and flooding water from a compartment in a vessel.
Emergency Locator Transmitter (ELT)	Aeronautical radio distress beacon for alerting and transmitting homing signals.
Emergency Position-Indicating Radio Beacon (EPIRB)	A device, usually carried aboard a maritime craft, that transmits a signal that alerts search and rescue authorities and enables rescue units to locate the scene of the distress.
Emergency Signal Mirror	A mirror used to attract attention of passing aircraft or boats by reflecting light at them. Such reflected light may be seen up to five miles or more from the point of origin.
Environmental Forces	Forces that affect the horizontal motion of a vessel; they include wind, seas and current.
Eye	The permanently fixed loop at the end of a line.
Eye Splice	The splice needed to make a permanently fixed loop at the end of a line.
Fairlead	A point, usually a specialized fitting, such as a block, chock, or roller used to change the direction and increase effectiveness of a line or cable. It will, in most cases, reduce the effects of chafing.

TERM	DEFINITION
Fairways (Mid-Channel)	A channel that is marked by safemarks that indicate that the water is safe to travel around either side of the red and white vertically striped buoy.
Fake Down	To lay out a line in long, flat bights that will pay out freely without bights or kinks. A coiled or flemished line cannot do this unless the coil of the line is able to turn, as on a reel. Otherwise, a twist results in the line which will produce a kink or jam (see *coil down* and *flemish down*).
Fatigue	Physical or mental weariness due to exertion. Exhausting effort or activity. Weakness in material, such as metal or wood, resulting from prolonged stress.
Fender	A device of canvas, wood, line, cork, rubber, wicker, or plastic slung over the side of a boat/ship in position to absorb the shock of contact between vessels or between a vessel and pier.
Fender Board	A board that is hung outboard of the vessel's fenders. Used to protect the side of a vessel.
Ferry	To transport a boat, people or goods across a body of water.
Fetch	The unobstructed distance over which the wind blows across the surface of the water.
Fitting	Generic term for any part or piece of machinery or installed equipment.
Fix	A geographical position determined by visual reference to the surface, referencing to one or more radio navigation aids, celestial plotting, or other navigation device.
Fixed Light	A light showing continuously and steadily, as opposed to a rhythmic light.
Flash	A relatively brief appearance of light, in comparison with the longest interval of darkness in the same character.
Flashing Light	A light in which the total duration of light in each period is clearly shorter than the total duration of darkness and in which the flashes of light are all of equal duration. Commonly used for a single-flashing light which exhibits only single flashes which are repeated at regular intervals.
Flemish down	To coil down a line on deck in a flat, circular, tight arrangement. Useful for appearance only. Since unless the twists in the line are removed, it will kink when taken up or used. (see *fake down* and *coil down*).
Floating Aid to Navigation	A buoy.
Flood	A tidal effect caused by the rise in water level in a river, bay, or estuary immediately followed by a high tidal condition.
Flood Current	The horizontal motion of water toward the land caused by a rising tide.

TERM	DEFINITION
Flood Direction	The approximate true direction toward which the flooding current flows; generally close to the reciprocal of the ebb direction.
Foam Crest	The top of the foaming water that speeds toward the beach after the wave has broken; also known as white water.
Fore	Something situated at or near the front. The front part, at, toward, or near the front; as in the forward part of a vessel.
Forward	Towards the bow of a vessel.
Foul	To entangle, confuse, or obstruct. Jammed or entangled; not clear for running. Covered with barnacles, as foul bottom.
Frames	Any of the members of the skeletal structure of a vessel to which the exterior planking or plating is secured.
Free Communication with the Sea	Movement of water in and out of a vessel through an opening in the hull.
Freeboard	Distance from the weather deck to the waterline on a vessel.
Furl	To make up in a bundle, as in furl the sail.
Global Positioning System (GPS)	A satellite-based radio navigation system that provides precise, continuous, worldwide, all-weather three-dimensional navigation for land, sea and air applications.
Gong Buoy	A wave actuated sound signal on buoys which uses a group of saucer-shaped bells to produce different tones. Found inside harbors and on inland waterways. Sound range about one mile.
Grabline	A line hung along a vessel's side near the waterline used for the recovery of persons in the water or to assist in the boarding of the vessel.
Grommet	A round attaching point, of metal or plastic, normally found on fenders, tarps, etc.
Ground Fog	See *radiation fog*.
Group-Flashing Light	A flashing light in which a group of flashes, specified in number, is regularly repeated.
Group-Occulting Light	An occulting light in which a group of eclipses, specified in number, is regularly repeated.
Gunwale	The upper edge of a boat's side. Pronounced "gun-ul."
Half Hitch	A hitch used for securing a line to a post; usually seen as two half hitches.

TERM	DEFINITION
Harbor	Anchorage and protection for ships. A shelter or refuge.
Hatch	The covering, often watertight, placed over an opening on the horizontal surface of a boat/ship.
Hawsepipe	A through deck fitting normally found above a line locker/hold which allows for the removal of line without accessing the compartment from below deck. Normally only slightly larger in diameter than the line itself.
Head Up (Heads Up)	A warning given before throwing a messenger, heaving, or towline to alert people to be ready for receipt of line and to avoid being hit by the object being thrown. Potential danger warning.
Heads Up Display	Setting for radar display to show the vessel's course vice North at the top of the screen.
Heading	The direction in which a ship or aircraft is pointed.
Heaving Line	Light, weighted line thrown across to a ship or pier when coming along side to act as a messenger for a mooring line. The weight is called a monkey fist.
Heavy Weather	Seas, swell, and wind conditions combining to exceed 8 feet and/or winds are exceeding than 30 knots.
	NOTE This definition of heavy weather is not intended to define a heavy weather situation for a specific boat type. Heavy weather for each specific boat type may be determined by the coxswain at any time.
Heel	Temporary leaning of a vessel to port or starboard caused by the wind and sea or by a high speed turn.
Helm	The apparatus by which a vessel is steered; usually a wheel or tiller.
High Seas	That body of water extending seaward of a country's territorial sea to the territorial sea of another country.
Hoist	To lift. Display of signal flags at yardarm. The vertical portion of a flag alongside its staff.
Hoisting Cable	The cable used to perform a boat/helo hoisting evolution.
Holed	A hole or opening in the hull of a damaged vessel.
Hull	The body or shell of a ship or seaplane.
Hull Integrity	The hull's soundness.
Hypothermia	A lowering of the core body temperature due to exposure of cold (water or air) resulting in a subnormal body temperature that can be dangerous or fatal. The word literally means "under heated."

TERM	DEFINITION
Impeller	A propulsion device that draws water in and forces it out through a nozzle.
In Step (Position)	The towing boat keeping the proper position with the towed boat. For example; the proper distance in relation to sea/swell patterns so that both boats ride over the seas in the same relative position wave crest to wave crest.
Inboard	Toward the center of a ship or a group of ships, as opposed to outboard.
Inboard/Outdrive (I/O)	An inboard engine attached through the transom to the outdrive.
Incident Command System (ICS)	A management system for responding to major emergency events involving multiple jurisdictions and agencies. Coast Guard facilities may conduct simultaneous operations along with other types of responders under ICS management.
Information Marks	Aids to navigation that inform the mariner of dangers, restriction, or other information. Also referred to as regulatory marks.
Inlet	A recess, as a bay or cove, along a coastline. A stream or bay leading inland, as from the ocean. A narrow passage of water, as between two islands.
Isolated Danger Mark	A mark erected on, or moored above or very near, an isolated danger which has navigable water all around it.
Junction	The point where a channel divides when proceeding seaward. The place where a branch of a river departs from the main stream.
Junction Aid (Obstruction Aid)	Horizontally striped aids that indicate the preferred channel with the top color on the aid. They may also mark an obstruction.
Kapok	A silky fiber obtained from the fruit of the silk-cotton tree and used for buoyancy, insulation and as padding in seat cushions and life preservers.
Keel	The central, longitudinal beam or timber of a ship from which the frames and hull plating rise.
Kicker Hook	See *skiff hook.*
Knockdown	When a boat has rolled in one direction 90° or greater but does not completely rollover (360°) to right itself. (Example: Boat rolls to port 120° and rights itself by rolling back to starboard.)
Knot (kn or kt)	A unit of speed equivalent to one nautical mile (6,080 feet) per hour. A measurement of a ship's speed through water. A collective term for hitches and bends.
Landmark Boundaries Method	In SAR, one of several methods to define a search area, in which datum may be assigned by a bearing and distance from some geographic landmark.

TERM	DEFINITION
Lateral Marks	Buoys or beacons that indicate port and starboard sides of a route and are used in conjunction with a "Conventional direction of buoyage."
Lateral System	A system of aids to navigation in which characteristics of buoys and beacons indicate the sides of the channel or route relative to a conventional direction of buoyage (usually upstream).
Lateral System of Buoyage	See *lateral system.*
Latitude	The measure of angular distance in degrees, minutes, and seconds of arc from 0° to 90° north or south of the equator.
Lazarette	A compartment in the extreme after part of the boat generally used for storage.
Leeward	The side or direction away from the wind, the lee side.
Leeway	The drift of an object with the wind, on the surface of the sea. The sideward motion of a ship because of wind and current, the difference between her heading (course steered) and her track (course made good). Sometimes called drift. In SAR, movement of search object through water caused by local winds blowing against that object.
Life Jacket	See *personal flotation device.*
Life Ring (Ring Buoy)	A buoyant device, usually fitted with a light and smoke marker, for throwing to a person-in-the-water.
Lifeline	Line secured along the deck to lay hold of in heavy weather; any line used to assist personnel; knotted line secured to the span of lifeboat davits(manropes or monkey lines) for the use of the crew when hoisting and lowering. The lines between stanchions along the outboard edges of a ship's weather decks are all loosely referred to as lifelines, but specifically the top line is the lifeline, middle is the housing line, and bottom is the footline. Any line attached to a lifeboat or life raft to assist people in the water. Also called a grab rope.
Light	The signal emitted by a lighted aid to navigation. The illuminating apparatus used to emit the light signal. A lighted aid to navigation on a fixed structure.
Light Buoy	A floating framework aid to navigation, supporting a light, usually powered by battery.
Light List	A United States Coast Guard publication (multiple volumes) that gives detailed information on aids to navigation.
Light Rhythms	Different patterns of lights, and flashing combinations that indicate to the mariner the purpose of the aid to navigation on which it is installed.
Light Sector	The arc over which a light is visible, described in degrees true, as observed from seaward towards the light. May be used to define distinctive color difference of two adjoining sectors, or an obscured sector.

TERM	DEFINITION
Lighthouse	A lighted beacon of major importance. Fixed structures ranging in size from the typical major seacoast lighthouse to much smaller, single pile structures. Placed onshore or on marine sites and most often do not show lateral aid to navigation markings. They assist the mariner in determining his position or safe course, or warn of obstructions or dangers to navigation. Lighthouses with no lateral significance usually exhibit a white light, but can use sectored lights to mark shoals or warn mariners of other dangers.
List	The static, fixed inclination or leaning of a ship to port or starboard due to an unbalance of weight.
Local Notice to Mariners	A written document issued by each U.S. Coast Guard District to disseminate important information affecting aids to navigation, dredging, marine construction, special marine activities, and bridge construction on the waterways with that district.
Log	A device for measuring a ship's speed and distance traveled through the water. To record something is to log it. Short for logbook.
Logbook	Any chronological record of events, as an engineering watch log.
Longitude	A measure of angular distance in degrees, minutes, and seconds east or west of the Prime Meridian at Greenwich.
Longitudinal	A structural member laid parallel to the keel upon which the plating or planking is secured. Longitudinals usually intersect frames to complete the skeletal framework of a vessel.
Longshore Current	A currents that runs parallel to the shore and inside the breakers as a result of the water transported to the beach by the waves.
Lookout	A person stationed as a visual watch.
LORAN-C	An acronym for long-range aid to navigation; an electronic aid to navigation consisting of shore-based radio transmitters
Loudhailer	A loudspeaker; public address system.
Magnetic Compass	A compass using the earth's magnetic field to align the compass card. (see *compass*)
Magnetic Course (M)	Course relative to magnetic north; compass course corrected for deviation.
Maritime	Located on or close to the sea; of or concerned with shipping or navigation.
Mark	A visual aid to navigation. Often called navigation mark, includes floating marks (buoys) and fixed marks (beacons).
Marline	Small stuff usually made of two-strand tarred hemp. Used for lashings, mousing, and seizing.

TERM	DEFINITION
Mast	A spar located above the keel and rising above the main deck to which may be attached sails, navigation lights, and/or various electronic hardware. The mast will vary in height depending on vessel type or use.
Mayday	The spoken international distress signal, repeated three times. Derived from the French *M'aider* (help me).
Medevac	"Medical Evacuation". Evacuation of a person for medical reasons.
Messenger	Light line used to carry across a larger line or hawser. Person who carries messages for OOD or other officers of the watch.
Mid-Channel	Center of a navigable channel. May be marked by safemarks.
Modified U.S. Aid System	Used on the Intracoastal Waterway, these aids are also equipped with special yellow strips, triangles, or squares. When used on the western rivers (Mississippi River System), these aids are not numbered (Mississippi River System above Baton Rouge and Alabama Rivers).
Mooring	A chain or synthetic line that attaches a floating object to a stationary object. (e.g., dock, sinker)
Mooring Buoy	A white buoy with a blue stripe, used for a vessel to tie up to, also designates an anchorage area.
Motor Lifeboat (MLB)	Coast Guard boat designed to perform SAR missions, including surf and bar operations, in adverse weather and sea conditions. They are self-righting and self-bailing.
Mousing	The use of small stuff or wire to hold together components that would otherwise work loose due to friction (i.e., mousing the screw pin of a shackle into place).
N-dura Hose	Double-synthetic jacketed and impregnated rubber-lined hose, orange in color, used in the Coast Guard for fire fighting.
Nautical Chart	Printed or electronic geographic representation of waterways showing positions of aids to navigation and other fixed points and references to guide the mariner.
Nautical Mile (NM)	2000 yards; Length of one minute of arc of the great circle of the earth; 6,076 feet compared to 5,280 feet per a statute (land) mile.
Nautical Slide Rule	An instrument used to solve time, speed, and distance problems.
Navigable Channel	A channel that has sufficient depth to be safely navigated by a vessel.
Navigable Waters	Coastal waters, including bays, sounds, rivers, and lakes, that are navigable from the sea.
Navigation	The art and science of locating the position and plotting the course of a ship or aircraft
Night Sun	A helicopter's light that is an effective search tool at night in a clear atmosphere with no moisture in the air.

TERM	DEFINITION
Noise	The result of the propeller blade at the top of the arc □ ransferring energy to the hull.
Normal Endurance	The average length of time (i.e., the average length of time to expect a boat crew to remain on a mission).
Nun Buoy (Conical)	A buoy that is cylindrical at the waterline, tapering to a blunt point at the top. Lateral mark that is red, even numbered, and usually marks the port hand side proceeding to seaward.
Obstruction Aid	See *junction aid.*
Occulting Light	A light in which the total duration of light in each period is clearly longer than the total duration of darkness and in which the intervals of darkness are all of equal duration. (Commonly used for single-occulting light which exhibits only single occulations that are repeated at regular intervals.)
Officer of the Deck (Day) (OOD)	The direct representative of the Commanding Officer or Officer-in-Charge. Officer of the Deck is a shipboard term, Officer of the Day is used ahore.
Offshore	The region seaward of a specified depth. Opposite is inshore or near-shore.
On Scene	The search area or the actual distress site.
On Scene Commander (OSC)	A person designated to coordinate search and rescue operations within a specified area associated with a distress incident.
Opening	The increasing of distance between two vessels.
Out of Step	The position of two boats (i.e., towing operations) where one boat is on the top of the crest of a wave and the other is in the trough between the waves.
Outboard	In the direction away from the center line of the ship. Opposite is inboard. Also, an engine which is attached to the transom of a vessel.
Outdrive	A transmission and propeller or jet drive attached to the transom of a vessel.
Overdue	When a vessel or person has not arrived at the time and place expected.
Overhauling the Fire	The general procedures performed after a fire has been extinguished. They include breaking up combustible material with a fire axe or a fire rake, and cooling the fire area with water or fog.
Overload	Exceeding the designed load limits of a vessel; exceeding the recommended work load of line or wire rope.
Pacing	Two vessels matching speed and course.
Pad-Eye	A metal ring welded to the deck or bulkhead.

TERM	DEFINITION
Painter Line (Painter)	A line at the bow or stern of a boat which is used for making fast; a single line used to take a vessel in tow alongside, commonly used with ships and their boats when placing the boat into use over the side.
Parallel Approach	An arc approach used where one vessel is approached parallel to another.
Parallel Track Pattern	In SAR, one of several types of search patterns. There are two parallel track patterns; they are (1) single unit (PS) (2) and multi-unit (PM).
Passenger Space	A space aboard a vessel that is designated for passengers.
Persons Onboard (POB)	The number of people aboard a craft.
Personal Flotation Device (PFD)	A general name for various types of devices designed to keep a person afloat in water (e.g., life preserver, vest, cushion, ring, and other throwable items).
Personnel Marker Light (PML)	A device that uses either a battery or chemical action to provide light for the wearer to be seen during darkness.
Piling	A long, heavy timber driven into the seabed or river bed to serve as a support for an aid to navigation or dock.
Pitch	The vertical motion of a ship's bow or stern in a seaway about the athwartships axis. Of a propeller, the axial advance during one revolution. (see *roll*, *yaw*)
Pitchpole	A vessel going end-over-end, caused by large waves or heavy surf. The bow buries itself in the wave and the stern pitches over the bow, capsizing the vessel.
Planing Hull	A boat design that allows the vessel to ride with the majority of its hull out of the water once its cruising speed is reached (e.g., 8-meter RHI).
Polyethylene Float Line	A line that floats, used with rescue devices, life rings.
Port	The left side of the vessel looking forward toward the bow.
Port Hole	An opening in the hull, door, or superstructure of a boat/ship often covered with a watertight closure made of metal or wood.
Port Light	A port hole closure or covering having a glass lens through which light may pass.
Preferred Channel Mark	A lateral mark indicating a channel junction, or a wreck or other obstruction which, after consulting a chart, may be passed on either side.
Preventer Line (Preventer)	Any line used for additional safety or security or to keep something from falling or running free.

TERM	DEFINITION
Primary Aid to Navigation	An aid to navigation established for the purpose of making landfalls and coastwise passages from headland to headland.
Probability of Detection (POD)	The probability of the search object being detected, assuming it was in the areas searched.
Probability of Success (POS)	The probability of finding the search object with a particular search.
Proceeding From Seaward	Following the Atlantic coast in a southerly direction, northerly and westerly along the Gulf coast and in a northerly direction on the Pacific coast. On the Great Lakes proceeding from seaward means following a generally westerly and northerly direction, except on Lake Michigan where the direction is southerly. On the Mississippi and Ohio Rivers and their tributaries, proceeding from seaward means from the Gulf of Mexico toward the headwaters of the rivers (upstream).
Prop Wash	The result of the propeller blade at the top of the arc transferring energy to the water surface.
Propeller	A device consisting of a central hub with radiating blades forming a helical pattern and when turned in the water, creates a discharge that drives a boat.
Pyrotechnics	Ammunition, flares, or fireworks used for signaling, illuminating, or marking targets.
Quarantine Anchorage Buoy	A yellow special purpose buoy indicating a vessel is under quarantine.
Quarter	One side or the other of the stern of a ship. To be broad on the quarter means to be 45° away from dead astern; starboard or port quarter is used to indicate a specific side.
RACON	See *radar beacon.*
Radar	Radio detecting and ranging . An electronic system designed to transmit radio signals and receive reflected images of those signals from a "target" in order to determine the bearing and distance to the 'target."
Radar Beacon (RACON)	A radar beacon that produces a coded response, or radar paint, when triggered by a radar signal.
Radar Reflector	A special fixture fitted to or incorporated into the design of certain aids to navigation to enhance their ability to reflect radar energy. In general, these fixtures will materially improve the aid to navigation for use by vessels with radar. They help radar equipped vessels to detect buoys and beacons. They do not positively identify a radar target as an aid to navigation. Also used on small craft with low radar profiles.
Radiation Fog	A type of fog that occurs mainly at night with the cooling of the earth's surface and the air, which is then cooled below its dew point as it touches the ground; most common in middle and high latitudes, near the inland lakes and rivers; burns off with sunlight.

TERM	DEFINITION
Radio Watch	The person assigned to stand by and monitor the radios. Responsible for routine communication and logging, as well as properly handling responses to emergency radio communications.
Radiobeacon	An electronic apparatus which transmits a radio signal for use in providing a mariner a line of position. First electronic system of navigation. Provided offshore coverage and became the first all-weather electronic aid to navigation.
Range	A measurement of distance usually given in yards. Also, a line formed by the extension of a line connecting two charted points.
Range Lights	Two lights associated to form a range which often, but not necessarily, indicates a channel centerline. The front range light is the lower of the two, and nearer to the mariner using the range. The rear range light is higher and further from the mariner.
Range Line	The lining up of range lights and markers to determine the safe and correct line of travel, the specific course to steer to remain in the center of the channel.
Range Marker	High visibility markers that have no lights. (see *range lights*)
Re-Flash Watch	A watch established to prevent a possible re-flash or rekindle of a fire after a fire has been put out.
Re-Float	The act of ungrounding a boat.
Red, Right, Returning	A saying to remember which aids a crewmember should be seeing off vessel's starboard side when returning from seaward.
Regulatory Marks	A white and orange aid to navigation with no lateral significance. Used to indicate a special meaning to the mariner, such as danger, restricted operations, or exclusion area.
Rescue Basket	A device for lifting an injured or exhausted person out of the water.
Rescue Swimmer	A specially trained individual that is deployed from a helicopters, boats, or cutters to recover an incapacitated victim from the water, day or night.
Retroreflective Material	Material that reflects light. Can be found on equipment such as PFDs or hypothermia protective clothing.
Rig	To devise, set up, arrange. An arrangement or contrivance. General description of a ship's upper works; to set up spars or to fit out. A distinctive arrangement of sails (rigging), as in a schooner rig. An arrangement of equipment and machinery, as an oil rig.
Rigging	The ropes, lines, wires, turnbuckles, and other gear supporting and attached to stacks, masts and topside structures. Standing rigging more or less permanently fixed. Running rigging is adjustable, (e.g., cargo handling gear).

TERM	DEFINITION
Rip Current	A current created along a long beach or reef surf zone due to water from waves hitting the beach and traveling out to the sides and parallel to the shore line, creating a longshore current that eventually returns to sea.
Riprap	Stone or broken rock thrown together without order to form a protective wall around a navigation aid.
River Current	The flow of water in a river.
Rode	The line to which a small boat rides when anchored. Also called an anchor line.
Roll	Vessel motion caused by a wave lifting up one side of the vessel, rolling under the vessel and dropping that side, then lifting the other side and dropping it in turn.
Roller	A long usually non-breaking wave generated by distant winds and a source of big surf, which is a hazard to boats.
Rollover	When a boat rolls in one direction and rights itself by completing a 360° revolution.
Rooster Tail	A pronounced aerated-water discharge astern of a craft; an indicator of waterjet propulsion.
Rough Bar	Rough bar is determined to exist when breaking seas exceed 8 feet and/or when, in the judgment of the CO/OIC, rough bar/surf conditions exist, and/or whenever there is doubt in the judgment of the coxswain as to the present conditions.
RTV	Silicone rubber used for plugging holes and seams. Sticks to wet surfaces and will set up under water. Used in damage control for temporary repairs.
Rubrail	A permanent fixture, often running the length of a boat, made of rubber that provides protection much as a fender would.
Rudder	A flat surface rigged vertically astern used to steer a ship, boat, or aircraft.
Safe Water Marks (Fairways, Mid-Channels)	Used to mark fairways, mid-channels, and offshore approach points, and have unobstructed water on all sides. They may have a red spherical shape, or a red spherical topmark, are red and white vertically striped, and if lighted, display a white light with Morse code "A" (short-long flash).
Sail Area	On a vessel, the amount of surface upon which the wind acts.
Sampson Post	Vertical timber or metal post on the forward deck of a boat used in towing and securing. Sometimes used as synonym for king post.
SAR Emergency Phases	Three phases of SAR levels and responses. These are: (1) uncertainty (key word: "doubt"); (2) alert (key word: "apprehension"); and (3) distress (key words: "grave and imminent danger" requiring "immediate assistance").

TERM	DEFINITION
SAR Incident Folder/Form	A form to record essential elements of a case. Information needed is outlined with blanks left to fill in necessary information as case progresses.
SAR Mission Coordinator (SMC)	The official temporarily assigned to coordinate response to an actual or apparent distress situation.
SARSAT	Search and rescue satellite aided tracking. See *Cospas-Sarsat System*.
Scope	The length of anchor line or chain. Number of fathoms of chain out to anchor or mooring buoy. If to anchor, scope is increased in strong winds for more holding power. Also, the length of towline or distance from the stern of the towing vessel to the bow of the tow.
Scouring	A method to refloat a stranded boat using the current from the assisting boat's screw to "scour" or create a channel for the grounded boat, in the sand, mud or gravel bottom when the water depth allows the assisting boat access.
Screw	A vessel's propeller.
Scupper	An opening in the gunwale or deck of a boat which allows water taken over the side to exit. Common to most self-bailing boats.
Scuttle	A small, quick-closing access hole; to sink a ship deliberately.
Sea Anchor	A device, usually of wood and/or canvas, streamed by a vessel in heavy weather to hold the bow up to the sea. Its effect is similar to a drogue in that it slows the vessel's rate of drift. However, it is usually made off to the bow opposed to the stern as in the use of a drogue.
Sea Chest	Intake between ship's side and sea valve or seacock. Sailor's trunk. A through-hull fitting used in the vessels engine cooling systems. It allows the vessel to take on seawater through a closed piping system.
Sea Chest Gate Valve	A gate valve used in between the sea chest and the fire pump or engine cooling system.
Sea Cock	A valve in the ship's hull through which seawater may pass.
Sea Current	Movement of water in the open sea.
Sea Drogue	See *sea anchor*.
Seabed	The ocean floor.
Search and Rescue Unit (SRU)	A unit composed of trained personnel and provided with equipment suitable for the expeditious conduct of search and rescue operations.
Search Pattern	A track line or procedure assigned to an SRU for searching a specified area.

TERM	DEFINITION
Seaward	Toward the main body of water, ocean. On the Intracoastal Waterway, returning from seaward is from north to south on the eastern U.S. coast, east to west across the Gulf of Mexico, and south to north along the western seacoast.
Seaworthy	A vessel capable of putting to sea and meeting any usual sea condition. A seagoing ship may for some reason not be seaworthy, such as when damaged.
Set (of a Current)	The direction toward which the water is flowing. A ship is set by the current. A southerly current and a north wind are going in the same direction. Measured in degrees (usually true).
Shackle	A U-shaped metal fitting, closed at the open end with a pin, used to connect wire, chain, or line.
Shaft	A cylindrical bar that transmits energy from the engine to the propeller.
Ship	Any vessel of considerable size navigating deepwater, especially one powered by engines and larger than a boat. Also, to set up, to secure in place. To take something aboard.
Shock Load	Resistance forces caused by intermittent and varying forces of waves or sea conditions encounter by a towing boat on its towing lines and equipment.
Short-Range Aids to Navigation	Aids to navigation limited in visibility to the mariner (e.g., lighthouses, sector lights, ranges, LNBs, buoys, daymarks, etc.)
Signal Kit/MK-79	A signal kit used to signal aircraft and vessels. Each cartridge flare burns red, has a minimum duration of 4.5 seconds, and reaches a height of 250' to 600'.
Sinkers	Concrete anchors in various sizes and shapes on the seabed that buoy bodies are attached to by chain or synthetic rope moorings.
Siren	A sound signal which uses electricity or compressed air to actuate either a disc or a cup-shaped rotor.
Situation Report (SITREP)	Reports to interested agencies to keep them informed of on-scene conditions and mission progress.
Skeg	The continuation of the keel aft under the propeller; in some cases, supports the rudder post.
Skiff Hook (Kicker Hook)	A ladder hook or a stainless steel safety hook to which a six inch length of stainless steel round stock has been welded. A hook that is used in attaching a tow line to a small trailerable boat, using the trailer eyebolt on the boat.
Slack Water	The period that occurs while the current is changing direction and has no horizontal motion.
Sling	A type of rescue device used by a helicopter to hoist uninjured personnel; a lifting device for hoisting cargo.

TERM	DEFINITION
Slip Clove Hitch	A hitch used when it may be necessary to release a piece of equipment quickly (i.e., fenders or fender board).
Small Stuff	Any line up to 1.5" in circumference.
Smoke and Illumination Signal	A signal used to attract vessels and aircraft. It has a night end and a day end. The night end produces a red flame, the day end has an orange smoke.
Sound Buoys	Buoys that warn of danger; they are distinguished by their tone and phase characteristics.
Sound Signal	A device that transmits sound, intended to provide information to mariners during periods of restricted visibility and foul weather; a signal used to communicate a maneuver between vessels in sight of each other.
Special Purpose Buoys	Also called special marks, they are yellow and are not intended to assist in navigation, but to alert the mariner to a special feature or area.
Spring Line	A mooring line that makes an acute angle with the ship and the pier to which moored, as opposed to a breast line, which is perpendicular, or nearly so, to the pier face; a line used in towing alongside that enables the towing vessel to move the tow forward and/or back the tow (i.e., tow spring and backing spring).
Square Daymarks	Seen entering from seaward or from north or east proceeding south or west on port hand side of channel (lateral system of buoyage). Green, odd numbered.
Stanchion	A vertical metal or wood post aboard a vessel.
Standard Navy Preserver (Vest Type with Collar)	A Navy PFD vest used by the Coast Guard onboard cutters. Allows user to relax, save energy, increase survival time and will keep users head out of water, even if user is unconscious. Not found as part of a boat outfit.
Starboard	The right side of the vessel looking forward toward the bow.
Starboard Hand Mark	A buoy or beacon which is left to the starboard hand when proceeding in the "conventional direction of buoyage." Lateral marks positioned on the right side of the channel returning from seaward. Nun buoys are red, daybeacons are red, bordered with dark red and triangular shaped.
Static Discharge Wand	A pole-like device used to discharge the static electricity during helicopter hoisting/rescue operations. Also known as a deadman's stick.
Static Electricity	A quantity of electricity that builds up in an object and does not discharge until provided a path of flow.
Static Forces	Constant or internal forces.
Station Buoy	An unlighted buoy set near a large navigation buoy or an important buoy as a reference point should the primary aid to navigation be moved from its assigned position.

TERM	DEFINITION
Station Keeping	The art of keeping a boat in position, relative to another boat, aid, or object with regard to current, sea, and/or weather conditions.
Steerage	The act or practice of steering. A ship's steering mechanism.
Steerageway	The lowest speed at which a vessel can be steered.
Stem	The principal timber at the bow of a wooden ship, to which the bow planks are rabbeted. Its lower end is scarfed to the keel, and the bowsprit rests on the upper end. The cutwater, or false stem (analogous to false keel), is attached to the fore part of the stem and may be carved or otherwise embellished, especially in the vicinity of the head, which usually rests upon it. In steel ships, the stem is the foremost vertical or near-vertical strength member, around which or to which the plating of the bow is welded or riveted. Compare stern-post.
Stem Pad-Eye (Trailer Eye Bolt)	An attaching point available on most trailerized small boats.
Stem the Forces	To keep the current or wind directly on the bow or stern and hold position by setting boat speed to equally oppose the speed of drift.
Stern	The extreme after end of a vessel.
Stokes Litter	A rescue device generally used to transport non-ambulatory persons or persons who have injuries that might be aggravated by other means of transportation.
Strobe Light	A device that emits a high intensity flashing light visible for great distances. Used to attract the attention of aircraft, ships, or ground parties, it flashes white light at 50 plus or minus 10 times per minute.
Strut	An external support for the propeller shaft integral to the hull/under water body.
Superstructure	Any raised portion of a vessel's hull above a continuous deck (e.g., pilot house).
Surf	In the Coast Guard, surf is determined to exist when breaking seas exceed 8 feet and/or when, in the judgment of the CO/OICS, rough bar/surf conditions exist, and/or whenever there is doubt in the mind of the coxswain as to the present conditions.
Surf Line	The outermost line of waves that break near shore, over a reef, or shoal. Generally refers to the outermost line of consistent surf.
Surf Zone	The area where waves steepen and break upon a reef, bar or beach.
Surface Swimmer	In the Coast Guard, a specially trained individual that is deployed from floating units, piers, or the shore to help people in the water.
Survival Kit	A kit designed to aid a person-in-the-water to survive. Consists of a belt attached around the waist. A personal signal kit is also attached. Boat crews are provided with a vest containing the items found in the signal kit as prescribed in the *Rescue and Survival Systems Manual*, COMDTINST M10470.10 (series).

TERM	DEFINITION
Sweep Width (W)	A measure of the detection capability, or distance on both sides of the SRU, based on target characteristics, weather, and other factors.
Swell	Wind-generated waves which have advanced into a calmer area and are decreased in height and gaining a more rounded form. The heave of the sea. See *roller*.
Swimmer's Harness	A harness used to tether and retrieve surface swimmers during rescue/recovery operations.
Tactical Diameter	The distance made to the right or left of the original course when a turn of 180° has been completed with the rudder at a constant angle.
Taffrail	A rail around a vessel's stern over which a towline is passed. Used to reduce the effects of chafing on the towline.
Tag Line	Line used to steady a load being swung in or out.
Tandem	An arrangement of two or more persons, vessels or objects placed one behind the other.
Thimble	A metal ring grooved to fit inside a grommet or eye splice.
Through Bolt	A bolt that is used to fasten a fitting to the deck. It goes through the deck and backing plate (located below deck).
Thumbs Up	A signal given by the designated crewmember to indicate hoisting operation is to begin.
Tidal Current	The horizontal motion of water caused by the vertical rise and fall of the tide.
Tide	The periodic vertical rise and fall of the water resulting from the gravitational interactions between the sun, moon, and earth.
Tie Down	A fitting that can be used to secure lines on a deck or dock.
Toed ("Toed In")	In a side-by-side towing operation, "toed" refers to the bow of the towed boat slightly angled toward the bow of the towing boat.
Topmarks	One or more relatively small objects of characteristic shape and color placed on an aid to identify its purpose. (i.e., pillar buoys surmounted with colored shapes).
Topside	The area above the main deck on a vessel; weather deck.
Tow Line	A line, cable, or chain used in towing a vessel.
Tow Strap	When towing alongside, the tow strap is secured near the towing vessel's bow and the towed vessel's stern (see *spring line*).
Towing Bridle	See *bridle*.
Towing Hardware	Hardware used in towing (i.e., towing bitt, various cleats, bitts, deck fittings, or trailer eyebolts).

TERM	DEFINITION
Towing Watch	A crewmember who monitors the safety of a towing operation. Responsible to the coxswain.
Track Spacing (S)	The distance between adjacent parallel search tracks (legs).
Trail Line	A weighted line that is lowered from a helo before the rescue device. Its purpose is to allow the personnel below to guide and control the rescue device as it is lowered.
Transom	Planking across the stern of a vessel.
Triage	The process of assessing survivors according to medical condition and assigning them priorities for emergency care, treatment, and evacuation.
Triangular Daymark	Entering from seaward, or from the north or east proceeding south or west on starboard hand side of channel (lateral system of buoyage). Red, even numbered.
Trim	The fore-and-aft inclination of a ship, down by the head or down by the stern. Sometimes used to include list. Also means shipshape, neat.
Trim Control	A control that adjusts the propeller axis angle with horizontal.
Tripping Line	Small line attached to the small end of a drogue, so the device can be turned around to be retrieved.
Trough	The valley between waves.
U.S. Aids to Navigation System	A system that encompasses buoys and beacons conforming to (or being converted to) the IALA buoyage guidelines and other short-range aids to navigation not covered by these guidelines. These other aids to navigation are lighthouses, sector lights, ranges, and large navigation buoys (LNBs).
Uniform State Waterway Marking System (USWMS)	Designed for use on lakes and other inland waterways that are not portrayed on nautical charts. Authorized for use on other waters as well. Supplemented the existing federal marking system and is generally compatible with it.
Utility Boat (UTB)	41' UTB, Coast Guard Utility boat is lightweight and possesses a deep "V" planing hull constructed of aluminum. It is fast, powerful, maneuverable and designed to operate in moderate weather and sea conditions. It normally carries a crew of three, a coxswain, boat engineer, and crewmember.
Vari-Nozzle	A fire-fighting nozzle having a fully adjustable spray head that allows the operator to deliver a wide range of spray patterns (from stream to low velocity fog).
Venturi Effect	To move water from one place to another by entraining the pumped liquid in a rapidly flowing stream. It is the principle used by the eductor in dewatering a vessel.
Vessel	By U.S. statutes, includes every description of craft, ship or other contrivance used as a means of transportation on water. "Any vehicle in which man or goods are carried on water." (see *ship*)

TERM	DEFINITION
Waist and/or Tag Line	Lines used to secure the hull or cabin bridles in position for towing.
Wake	The disturbed water astern of a moving vessel.
Watch Circle	The circle in which an anchored buoy or object moves on the surface in relationship to tides, currents and wind.
Watertight Integrity	The closing down of openings to prevent entrance of water into vessel.
Wave	A periodic disturbance of the sea surface, caused by wind (and sometimes by earthquakes).
Wave Frequency	The number of crests passing a fixed point in a given time.
Wave Height	The height from the bottom of a wave's trough to the top of its crest; measured in the vertical, not diagonal.
Wave Interference	Caused by waves, refracted or reflected, interacting with other waves, often increasing or decreasing wave height.
Wave Length	The distance from one wave crest to the next in the same wave group or series.
Wave Period	The time, in seconds, it takes for two successive crests to pass a fixed point.
Wave Reflection	The tendency of a wave to move back towards the incoming waves in response to interaction with any obstacle.
Wave Refraction	The tendency of a wave to bend in response to interaction with the bottom and slows in shoal areas. Refraction also occurs when a wave passes around a point of land, jetty, or an island.
Wave Saddle	The lowest part of a wave, bordered on both sides by higher ones; often small, unbroken section of a wave that is breaking.
Wave Series	A group of waves that seem to travel together, at the same speed.
Wave Shoulder	The edge of a wave. It may be the very edge of the whitewater on a breaker, or the edge of a high peaking wave that is about to break.
Wedge	Used as temporary repair in event of damage aboard vessel. Made of soft wood, they are forced into holes or damaged areas to stop leaking, to plug damaged structures, or to reinforce shoving. Part of a damage control kit.
Well Deck	Part of the weather deck having some sort of superstructure both forward and aft of it. A vertically recessed area in the main deck that allows the crewmember to work low to the water.

TERM	DEFINITION
Wet Suit	A tight-fitting rubber suit worn by a skin diver in order to retain body heat. Designed to protect wearer from exposure to cold, wind, and spray. Constructed of foam neoprene, a durable and elastic material with excellent flotation characteristics. These buoyancy characteristics, which affect the entire body, will cause floating horizontally, either face up or face down.
Whistle	A piece of survival equipment used to produce a shrill sound by blowing on or through it. To summon, signal or direct by whistling. A device for making whistling sounds by means of forced air or steam. A whistling sound used to summon or command. It is attached to some PFDs and is an optional item for the personal signal kit. It has proven very useful in locating survivors in inclement weather and can be heard up to 1,000 yards.
Whistle Buoy	A wave actuated sound signal on buoys which produces sound by emitting compressed air through a circumferential slot into a cylindrical bell chamber. Found outside harbors. Sound range greater than 1 mile.
White Water	See *foam crest.*
Williamson Turn	Used if an individual or object falls overboard during periods of darkness or restricted visibility and the exact time of the incident is unknown. Done by turning 60° to port or starboard from the original course, there shifting rubber until vessel comes about on a reverse course. May be of little value to boats having a small turning radius.
Wind-Chill Factor	An estimated measurement of the cooling effect of a combination of air temperature and wind speed in relation to the loss of body heat from exposed skin.
Wind Direction	The true heading from which the wind blows.
Wind-Driven Current	The effect of wind pushing water in the direction of the wind.
Window	An area where the waves have momentarily stopped breaking, opening up a safer area of operation for a vessel.
Wind Shadow	When an object blocks the wind, creating an area of no wind.
Windward	Towards the wind.
Yaw	Rotary oscillation about a ship's vertical axis in a seaway. Sheering off alternately to port and starboard.

Appendix B.
List of Acronyms

Introduction

This appendix contains a list of acronyms that may be useful when reading this and other Coast Guard manuals.

In this appendix

This appendix contains the following information:

This page intentionally left blank.

ACRONYM	DEFINITION
A/C	Air Conditioning
AAR	After Action Report
ACFT	Aircraft
ACIP	Aviation Incentive Pay
ACMS	Aviation Computerized Maintenance System
ACP	Area Contingency Plan
ACP	Alternate Compliance Program
ACTSUS	Active Suspension
ADF	Automatic Radio Direction Finder
ADSW-AC	Active Duty Special Work in Support of Active Component
ADT	Active Duty for Training
ADT-AT	Active Duty Training for Annual Training
AEO	Assistant Engineering Officer
AEPO	Assistant Engineering Petty Officer
AFC	Allowance Fund Control
AFFF	Aqueous Film – Forming Foam
AIM	Administrative Investigations Manual
AIS	Automatic Identification System
AH	Amplitude Modulation
AMIO	Alien/Migrant Interdiction Operation
AMS	Automated Manifest System
AMVER	Automated Mutual-Assistance Vessel Rescue
ANB	Aids to Navigation Boat
ANS	Aquatic Nuisance Species
ANSI	American National Standards Institute
ANT	Aids to Navigation Team
AOPS	Abstract of Operations
AOR	Area of Responsibility
API	American Petroleum Institute
APPS	Act to Prevent Pollution from Ships
APR	Aid Positioning Report

ACRONYM	DEFINITION
ASB	Arctic Survey Boat
ATB	Aviation Training Boat
AtoN	Aids to Navigation
AtoNIS	Aids to Navigation Information System
ATR	Ammunition Transaction Report
AUXCOM	Auxiliary Boat Commander
AUX DATA	Auxiliary Data
AUXPATCOM	Auxiliary Patrol Commander
AV	Aid Verifier
BA	Bridge Administration
BAC	Blood Alcohol Content
BAS	Basic Allowance for Subsistence
BCEB	Boat Crew Examination Boards
BCM	Boat Crewmember
BCMP	Boat Class Maintenance Plan
BDCM	Buoy Deck Crewmember
BDS	Buoy Deck Supervisor
BECCE	Basic Engineering Casualty Control Exercises
BEQ	Bachelor Enlisted Quarters
BM	Boatswain's Mate
BNTM	Broadcast Notice to Mariners
BO	Boarding Officer
BO/BTM PQS	Boarding Officer / Boarding Team Member Personnel Qualification Standard
BOSN	Boatswain
BS	Breaking Strength
BSC	Boating Safety Circular
BTM	Boarding Team Member
BUSL	Buoy Utility Stern Loading
BWI	Boating While Intoxicated
BWM	Ballast Water Management
C2	Command and Control

ACRONYM	DEFINITION
C2PC	Command/Control Personal Computer
CAC	Crisis Action Center
CASCOR	Casualty Correct
CASREP	Casualty Report
CBL	Commercial Bill of Lading
CB-L	Cutter Boat – Large
CB-M	Cutter Boat – Medium
CB-OTH	Cutter Boat – Over the Horizon
CBRN	Chemical, Biological, Radiological, Nuclear
CB-S	Cutter Boat – Small
CDAR	Collateral Duty Addictions Representative
CDI	Course Deviation Indicator
CDO	Command Duty Officer
CDR	Commander
CDV	Course Deviation Variance
CEM	Crew Endurance Management
CERCLA	Comprehensive Environment Compensation and Liability Act
CEU	Civil Engineering Unit
CF	Comparison Factors
CFC	Combined Federal Campaign
CFR	Code of Federal Regulations
CFVS	Commercial Fishing Vessel Safety
CGADD	Coast Guard Addendum
CGDF	Coast Guard Dining Facility
CGIS	Coast Guard Investigative Service
CGPC	Coast Guard Personnel Command
CIC	Combat Information Center
CIO	Command Intelligence Officer
CISM	Critical Incident Stress Management
CM	Configuration Management
CMAA	Chief Master at Arms

ACRONYM	DEFINITION
CMCO	Classified Material Control Officer
CMG	Course Made Good
CMS	COMSEC (Communication Security) Material System
CO	Commanding Officer
CO/OIC	Commanding Officer/Officer-in-Charge
COCO	Chief of Contracting Officer
COFR	Certificate of Financial Responsibility
COG	Course Over Ground
COI	Certificate of Inspection
COLREG	International Regulations for Preventing Collisions at Sea
COMCEN	Communications Center
COMDTINST	Commandant Instruction
COMINT	Communications Intelligence
COMMS	Communications
CONOPS	Concept of Operations
COR	Certificate of Registry
COTP	Captain-of-the-Port
COTR	Contracting Officer's Technical Representative
CPC	Commandant's Performance Challenge
CPO	Chief Petty Officer
CPR	Cardiopulmonary Resuscitation
CPU	Central Processing Unit
CQA	Commandant's Quality Award
CRT	Cathode Ray Tube
CS	Creeping Line Search
CSIM	Control Station Interface Module
CSMP	Current Ship's Maintenance Project
CSP	Commence Search Point
CSP	Career Sea Pay
CVE	Control Verification Examination
CVS	Commercial Vessel Safety

ACRONYM	DEFINITION
CWO	Chief Warrant Officer
DAMA	Demand Assigned Multiple Access
DAN	Driver's Alert Network
DANTES	Defense Activity for Non-Traditional Education Support
DAPA	Drug and Alcohol Program Administration
DDEC	Detroit Diesel Electronically Controlled
DEER	Defense Enrollment and Eligibility Reporting System
DEMPs	Diesel Engine Maintenance Programs
DF	Direction Finding
DGPS	Differential Global Positioning System
DICP	Drop-In Communications Package
DISREP	Discrepancy Report
DISREPS	Discrepancy Report
DIW	Dead-in-the-Water
DMA	Defense Mapping Agency
DMB	Data Marker Buoy
DMOA	Designated Medical Officer Advisor
DMS	Docket Management System
DO	Defense Operations
DoD	Department of Defense
DONCAF	Department of the Navy Central Adjudication Facility
DOT	Department of Transportation
DPB	Deployable Pursuit Boat
DR	Dead Reckoning
DSC	Digital Selective Calling
DVL	Digital Voice Logger
DWO	Deck Watch Officer
DWONR	Deck Watch Officer Navigation Rules
EAP	Employee Assistance Program
EAPC	Employee Assistance Program Coordinator
EBL	Electronic Bearing Line

ACRONYM	DEFINITION
EC	Electronic Control
EC	Engineering Change
ECM	Electronic Control Module
ECR	Engineering Change Request
ECS	Electronic Chart System
EDF	Enlisted Drug Facilities
EDM	Electronic Display Module
EEZ	Exclusive Economic Zone
EGIM	Electronic Gear Interface Module
ELC	Engineering Logistics Center
ELINT	Electronics Intelligence
ELT	Emergency Locator Transmitter
ELT	Enforcement of Laws and Treaties
EMI	Extra Military Instruction
EMS	Emergency Medical Services
EMT	Emergency Medical Technician
EO	Engineering Officer
EOCT	End-of-Course Test
EP	Estimated Position
EPA	Environmental Protection Agency
EPES	Enlisted Personnel Evaluation System
EPIRB	Emergency Position Indicating Radio Beacon
EPO	Engineering Petty Officer
EPO/EO	Engineering Petty Officer/Engineering Officer
EPS	Environmental Protection Specialist
ERIM	Engine Room Interface Module
ESA	Endangered Species Act
ESD	Electronics Support Detachment
ESU/D	Electronics Support Unit/detachment
ET	Electronics Technician
ETA	Electronic Transportation Acquisition

ACRONYM	DEFINITION
ETA	Estimated Time of Arrival
EXCOM	Extended Communications
FAA	Federal Aviation Agency
FAR	Family Advocacy Representative
FAR	Federal Acquisition Regulations
FBIS	Foreign Broadcast Information Service
FEDEX	Federal Express
FEEF	Federal Energy Efficiency Funding
FFCS	Full Function Crew Station
FID	Field Information Document
FINCEN	Finance Center
FIR	Field Intelligence Report
FL	Fitness Leader
FLOCS	Fast Lubricating Oil Change System
FLS	Fleet Logistics Supply
FM	Frequency Modulation
FMP	Fisheries Management Plan
FOIA	Freedom of Information Act
FOSC	Federal On-Scene Coordinator
FOUO	For Official Use Only
FPCON	Force Protection Conditions
FPM	Feet Per Minute
FRP	Fiberglass Reinforced Plastic
FS	Food Service Specialist
FSC	Federal Supply Classification
FSI	Field Sobriety Test
FSIC	Fiscal, Sanitation, Immigration or Customs
FSO	Food Services Officer
FWPCA	Federal Water Pollution Control Act
FWS	Fish and Wildlife Service
GAR	Green-Amber-Red

ACRONYM	DEFINITION
GDO	Group Duty Officer
GFM	Global Freight Management
GMDSS	Global Maritime Distress and Safety System
G-OCS	Office of Boat Forces
G-OI	Office of Intelligence
GPH	Gallons Per Hour
GPS	Global Positioning System
GRUCOM	Group Commander
GSA	Government Service Administration
GTA	Government Transportation Account
GV	Government Vehicle
HAZCOM	Hazardous Communication
HAZMAT	Hazardous Material
HAZWASTE	Hazardous Waste
HCPV/HIV	High Capacity Passenger Vessel/High Interest Vessel
HDOP	Horizontal Dilution of Precision
HEA	Harbor Entrance and Approach
HELP	Heat Escape Lessening Position
HF	High Frequency
HIN	Hull Identification Number
HS	Homeland Security
HPU	Hydraulic Power Unit
HRSIC	Human Resources Services and Information Center
HSC	Harbor Safety Committee
HUMINT	Human Intelligence
HVAC	Heating, Ventilation, and Air Conditioning
IACS	International Association of Classification Societies
IALA	International Association of Lighthouse Authorities
IAMSAR	International Aeronautical and Maritime Search and Rescue
I-AtoNIS	Integrated Aids to Navigation Information Systems
ICA	Individual Credit Accounts

ACRONYM	DEFINITION
ICAO	International Civil Aviation Organization
ICC	Intelligence Coordination Center
ICLL	International Convention on Load Lines
ICMTS	Interagency Committee of the Marine Transportation System
ICS	Incident Command System
ICV	Intercommunicating Fill Valve
ICW	Intracoastal Waterway
IDT	Inactive Duty for Training
IEC	International Electrotechnical Commission
IIP	International Ice Patrol
IIR	Intelligence Information Report
IIRAIRA	Illegal Immigration Reform and Immigrant Responsibility Act
ILO	International Labor Organization
IMARV	Independent Maritime Response Vessel
IMO	International Maritime Organization
IMPAC	International Merchant Purchase Authorization Card
INA	Immigration and Nationality Act
INS	Immigration and Naturalization Service
IPIECA	International Petroleum Industry Environmental Conservation Association
IPS	International Pipe Standard
IRIS	Incident Reporting Information System
ISC	Integrated Support Command
ISM	International Ship Management
ISO	International Standards Organization
IT	Information Systems Technician
IUU	Illegal, Unreported, and Unregulated
JOOD	Junior Officer of the Day
JQR	Job Qualification Requirement
KO	Contracting Officer
LC	Load Center
LCD	Liquid Crystal Display

ACRONYM	DEFINITION
LCVP	Landing Craft, Vehicle, Personnel
LE	Law Enforcement
LEISII	Law Enforcement Information System II
LEMAN	Law Enforcement Manual
LEO	Law Enforcement Officer
LEQB	Law Enforcement Qualification Board
LEU	Law Enforcement Unit
LHA	Local Housing Authority
LHI	Local Housing Inspector
LIR	Letter Incident Report
LKP	Last Known Position
LLNR	*Light List* Number
LMR	Living Marine Resource
LNB	Large Navigation Buoy
LNG	Liquid Natural Gas
LOA	Length Overall
LOB	Line-of-Bearing
LOC	Letter of Commendation
LOGREQ	Logistics Requirements
LOP	Line of Position
LORAN-C	Long-Range Aid to Navigation
LORSTA	LORAN Station
LOS	Line-of-Sight
LUFS	Large Unit Financial System
LUT	Local User Terminal
LWL	Length on Waterline
MAA	Master at Arms
MARB	Maritime Assistance Request Broadcast
MARPOL	International Convention for the Prevention of Pollution from Ships
MARSEC	Marine Security Conditions
MASINT	Measurement and Signature Intelligence

ACRONYM	DEFINITION
MAW	Maximum Allowable Weight
MBR INT	Member's Initials
MCB	Motor Cargo Boat
MCM	Manual for Courts-Martial
MCS	Master Control Station
MDA	Maritime Domain Awareness
MDV	Marine Dealer Visit
MDZ	Maritime Defense Zone
MEDICO	Medical Advice
MEDEVAC	Medical Evacuation
MEP	Marine Environmental Protection
MEPC	Marine Environment Protection Committee
MER	Marine Environmental Response
MF	Medium Frequency
MHS	Maritime Homeland Security
MI	Marine Information
MI	Maintenance Inspection
MI & R	Maintenance, Improvement and Repair
MIC	Manufacturer Identification Code
MICA	Management Information for Configuration and Allowances
MICA	Machinery Information Catalog Allowance
MIM	Marine Interface Module
MISLE	Marine Information for Safety and Law Enforcement
MJM	Military Justice Manual
MLB	Motor Lifeboat
MLC	Maintenance and Logistics Command
MLCPAC	Maintenance and Logistics Command Pacific
MMD	Merchant Mariner Document
MMPA	Marine Mammal Protection Act
MMS	Minerals Management Services
MMSI	Maritime Mobile Service Identity

ACRONYM	DEFINITION
MOA	Memorandum of Agreement
MOB	Man Overboard
MOU	Memorandum of Understanding
MPR	Multiple Persons-in-the-Water
MPS	Marine Protected Species
MRE	Military Rule of Evidence
MRR	Medium-Range Recovery
MSAP	Maritime SAR Assistance Policy
MSB	Motor Surf Boat
MSC	Marine Safety Center
MSFCMA	Magnuson-Stevens Fisheries Conservation and Management Act
MSO	Maintenance Support Outline
MSO	Marine Safety Office
MSS	Marine Safety and Security
MSST	Maritime Safety and Security Team
MSST	Maritime Shore Security Teams
MTL	Master Training List
MTS	Marine Transportation System
MTSNAC	Marine Transportation System National Advisory Council
MWR	Moral, Welfare and Recreation
NAFA	Non-Appropriated Fund Activity
NAVAIDS	Navigational Aids
NAVRULS	Navigation Rules
NCP	National Contingency Plan
NCW	Naval Coastal Warfare
NDRS	National Distress Response System
NDRSMP	National Distress Response System Modernization Project
NDS	National Distress System
NESU	Naval Engineering Support Unit
NJP	Non-Judicial Punishment
NLB	Nearshore Life Boat

ACRONYM	DEFINITION
NLT	No Later Than
NM	Nautical Miles
NMEA	National Marine Electronics Association
NMFS	National Marine Fisheries Service
NMLBS	National Motor Lifeboat School
NOS	National Ocean Survey
NOAA	National Oceanic and Atmospheric Administration
NRC	National Response Center
NRT	National Response Team
NSARC	National Search and Rescue Committee
NSB	Non-Standard Boat
NSF	National Strike Force
NSFCC	National Strike Force Coordination Center
NSN	National Stock Number
NSP	National Search and Rescue Plan
NSS	National Search and Rescue Supplement
NTP	Naval Training Publication
NVDC	National Vessel Documentation Center
NVIC	Navigation and Vessel Inspection Circular
NWP	Naval Warfare Publication
OBA	Oxygen Breathing Apparatus
O/S WX	On-Scene Weather
OCMI	Officer-in-Charge Marine Inspection
OER	Officer Evaluation Report
OIC	Officer-in-Charge
OIC INT	Officer in Charge's Initials
OJT	On-the-Job Training
OM & S	Operating Materials and Supplies
OMMP	Occupational Medical Monitoring Program
OOD	Officer of the Deck (Day)
OPA	Oil Pollution Act

ACRONYM	DEFINITION
OPAREA	Operational Area
OPCEN	Operations Center
OPCON	Operational Control
OPFAC	Operating Facility
OPLAN	Operations Plan
OPORD	Operations Order
OPORDER	Operations Order
OQB	Operations Qualification Board
ORM	Operational Risk Management
OS	Operations Specialist
OSB	Operations Standards Board
OSC	Operations Systems Center
OSC	On-Scene Commander
OSHA	Occupational Safety and Health Administration
OTC	Officer in Tactical Command
PA	Privacy Act
PAL	Personnel Allowance List
PALMS	Patrol Order Management System
PAO	Public Affairs Officer
PATCOM	Patrol Commander
PAWSS	Ports and Waterways Safety System
PCS	Permanent Change of Station
PDD	Presidential Decision Directive
PDR	Personnel Data Record
PDS	Personnel Data System
PERSRU	Personnel Reporting Unit
PES	Port and Environmental Safety
PFD	Personal Flotation Device
PI	Personnel Inspection
PIAT	Public Information Assistance Team
PIE	Partnership in Education

ACRONYM	DEFINITION
PIW	Person-in-the-Water
PLB	Personal Locator Beacon
PMIS/JUMPS	Personnel Management Information System/Joint Uniform Military Pay System
PMLV	Personnel Marker Light
PMS	Preventative/Planned Maintenance System
PO	Petty Officer
POB	Persons Onboard
POD	Probability of Detection
POP	Planned Obligation Priority
POS	Probability of Success
POPFAC	Parent Operating Facility
POW	Plan of the Week
PPE	Personal Protective Equipment
PPI	Plan Position Indicator
PPS	Precise Positioning Service
PQS	Personnel Qualification Standard
PR	Position Report
PRECOM	Preliminary Communications
PREP	Preparedness for Response Exercise Program
PS	Parallel Search
PSCO	Port State Control Officer
PSU	Port Security Unit
PTO	Power Take-Off
PWB	Port and Waterways Boat
PWSA	Ports and Waterway Safety Act
QAWTD	Quick-Acting Watertight Door
QEB	Qualification Examining Board
QRC	Quick Response Card
RACON	Radar Beacon
RB-HS	Response Boat-Homeland Security
RB-M	Response Boat-Medium

ACRONYM	DEFINITION
RBS	Recreational Boating Safety
RB-S	Response Boat-Small
RCC	Rescue Coordination Center
RDF	Radio Direction Finder
RFMC	Regional Fisheries Management Council
RFMO	Regional Fisheries Management Organization
RFO	Ready for Operations
RIK	Rations-In-Kind
RMS	Readiness Management System
RNAV	Radio Aids to Navigation
ROC/POE	Required Operational Capability/Point of Entry
RP	Responsible Party
RPAL	Reserve Personnel Allowance List
RS	Rescue Swimmer
RSC	Rescue Sub-Center
RT	Receiver/Transmitter
SAFE	Substance Abuse Free Environment
SAI	Small Arms Instructor
SAP	Simplified Acquisition Procedures
SAR	Search and Rescue
SAREX	SAR Exercise
SARMIS	Search and Rescue Mission Information System
SARSAT	Search and Rescue Satellite Aided Tracking
SAT	Subsistence Advisory Team
SATCOM	Satellite Communication
SB	Sailboat
SC	SAR Coordinator
SCUBA	Self-Contained Underwater Breathing Apparatus
SDB	Service Dress Blue
SEAOP	Special and Emergency Operations Procedure
SEPRATS	Separate Rations

ACRONYM	DEFINITION
SF	Safety Factor
SIGINT	Signals Intelligence
SIPRNET	Secret Internet Protocol Routing Network
SITREP	Situation Report
SKF	Skiff
SLDMB	Self Locating Datum Marker Buoy
SMC	SAR Mission Coordinator
SMS	Safety Management System
SMTJ	Special Maritime and Territorial Jurisdiction
SNO	Statement of No Objection
SOA	Speed of Advance
SOG	Speed Over Ground
SOLAS	Safety of Life at Sea
SO-OP	Auxiliary Division Operations Officer
SOP	Standard Operating Procedure
SOPA	Senior Officer Present Afloat
SOPEP	Shipboard Oil Pollution Emergency Plan
SOQ	Sailor of the Quarter
SOS	Save Our Ship
SPC	Special Purpose Craft
SPC (HWX)	Heavy Weather Special Purpose Craft
SPC (LE)	Special Purpose Craft (Law Enforcement)
SPE	Severity-Probability-Exposure
SPF	Sun Protection Factor
SPOC	SAR Point of Contact
SPS	Standard Positioning Service
SRA	Short-Range Aids to Navigation
SROE	Standing Rules of Engagement
SRR	Search and Rescue Region
SRR	Short-Range Recovery
SRS	Synchronous Reference Sensor

ACRONYM	DEFINITION
SRU	Search and Rescue Unit
SS	Square Search
SSB	Single Side Band
SSB-HF	Single Side Band - High Frequency
SSL	Standard Support Level
SSM	Support and Special Mission
SSMR	Shore Station Maintenance Record
SSPO	Station Support Petty Officer
STA OPS	Station Operations
STAN & RFO	Readiness and Standardization Program
STANT	Station Aids to Navigation Team
STAR	Standard Automated Requisitioning
STCW	Standards of Training, Certification and Watchkeeping for Seafarers
STTR	Short Term Resident Training Request
STU III	Secure Telephone Unit
SURPIC	Surface Picture
SWE	Service-wide Exam
SWL	Safe Working Load
TACON	Tactical Control
TAD	Temporary Assigned Duty
TAIT	Temporary Access Inventory Tool
TANB	Trailerable Aids to Navigation Boat
TC	Technical Committee
TCM	Telecommunications Manual
TCOW	Telecommunications Watchstander
TCT	Team Coordination Training
TD	Temporary Duty
TD	Time Difference
TFC	Total Fuel Consumption
THREATCON	Threat Conditions
TMT	Training Management Tool

ACRONYM	DEFINITION
TOI	Target of Interest
TPSB	Transportable Port Security Boat
TQC	Training Quota Management Center
TRACEN	Training Center
TRATEAM	Training Team
TRS	Timing Reference Sensor
TSN	Track Line Non-Return Search
TSR	Track Line Return Search
U/W	Underway
UCMJ	Uniform Code of Military Justice
UEG	Unit Environmental Guide
UEPH	Unaccompanied Enlisted Personnel Housing
UHF	Ultra High Frequency
UMI	Universal Marine Interface
UMIB	Urgent Marine Information Broadcast
UOF	Use of Force
UPF	Unit Performance Factor
UPH	Unaccompanied Personnel Housing
UPS	United Parcel Service
USBP	United States Boarder Patrol
USC	United States Code
USFWS	U.S. Fish and Wildlife Service
USPS	U.S. Power Squadron
USWMS	Uniform State Waterway Marking System
UTB	Utility Boat
UTBSC	Utility Boat Systems Center
UTC	Coordinated Universal Time
UTL	Utility Boat Light
UTM	Utility Boat Medium
UTS	Unit Travel System
VHA	Variable Housing Allowance

ACRONYM	DEFINITION
VHF	Very High Frequency
VRM	Variable Range Marker
VRO	Variable Ratio Oiler
VRP	Vessel Response Plan
VS	Sector Search
VSC	Vessel Safety Check
VTS	Vessel Traffic Services
WP	Working Punt
WAAS	Wide Area Augmentation System
WAMS	Waterways Analysis and Management System
WC	Wellness Coordinator
WLIC	Construction Tender
WLL	Working Load Limit
WPB	Patrol Boat
WR	Wellness Representative
WWM	Waterways Management
XO	Executive Officer
XPO	Executive Petty Officer
XTE	Cross Track Error

Index

A

CPSIA information can be obtained
at www.ICGtesting.com
Printed in the USA
BVOW08s0937120318
510170BV00004B/115/P